IJS STUDIES
Research on Jesuits and t

The Life, Passion, and Death of the Jesuit Rutilio Grande

By Rodolfo Cardenal, S.J.

Afterword by Jon Sobrino, S.J.

Translated by Joseph V. Owens, S.J.

Institute of Jesuit Sources
Boston College

Library of Congress Control Number: 2020941381

ISBN: 978-1-947617-06-3

Copyright 2020 by the Jesuit Conference, Inc., United States.

All rights reserved. No part of this publication may be reproduced, translated, stored in a retrieval system, or transmitted in any form or by any means, electronic, mechanical, photocopying, recording or otherwise, without prior written permission from the publisher.

Authorization to photocopy items for internal or personal use is granted by the Institute of Jesuit Sources provided that the appropriate fees are paid directly to:

>Institute of Jesuit Sources
>at the Institute for Advanced Jesuit Studies
>Boston College
>140 Commonwealth Avenue | Chestnut Hill, MA 02467 | USA

email: iajs@bc.edu
http://jesuitsources.bc.edu

Fees are subject to change

IJS Studies is an imprint of the Institute of Jesuit Sources

The Life, Passion, and Death of the Jesuit Rutilio Grande
Rodolfo Cardenal, S.J.

Contents

Prologue... 1

1. The Origin of His Vocation.. 7
2. A Vocation Built on Fragility... 27
3. San José de la Montaña Seminary.. 45
4. Departure from the Seminary... 81
5. The Pastoral Project... 123
6. The First Stage: The Missions... 157
7. The Second Stage: The Courses and Cursillos................................ 191
8. Parish Life... 221
9. The Parish and the Popular Organizations.................................... 279
10. Persecution of the Church.. 335
11. The Martyrdom... 391
Afterword: The Martyrs and Their Legacy.. 443
Index... 461

Prologue

Archbishop Óscar Arnulfo Romero cannot be fully understood without understanding Rutilio Grande. Not only did both men die as martyrs but their biographies also overlap in a number of surprising ways. Rutilio's ministry came to a violent end on March 12, 1977, just days after Romero began his own ministry as archbishop of San Salvador, on February 22, 1977. The two pastors came from poor families in rural El Salvador. Archbishop Romero was born in 1917 in a small town in the east of the country, while Rutilio was born in 1928 in El Paisnal, a small town in central El Salvador. He was the child of a very unstable family. Both men enrolled at a very tender age in minor seminaries, Óscar in San Miguel and Rutilio in San Salvador. In contrast to Archbishop Romero, Rutilio did not continue with the diocesan clergy and instead entered the Society of Jesus in 1945, after finishing studies at the minor seminary.

Romero and Rutilio both had profound and painful experience of their human frailty, but for different reasons. They both studied abroad, though in different places. The two of them loved the Salvadoran people and the church to the point of giving their lives for them. The guide that both pastors used for their pastoral activity was the universal and continental magisterium of the church, and concretely the Second Vatican Council, the Medellín bishops' conference, and the encyclical *Evangelii nuntiandi*. Both men denounced the injustice that had long kept Salvadorans oppressed, and they proclaimed to the people their liberation. Each in his own sphere, one as a rural priest and the other as archbishop, worked hard to make that liberation a reality. Both had the gift of prophetic preaching, though Rutilio's speech was more Salvadoran and homegrown than Archbishop Romero's. A warm personal friendship united the two men, despite some differences. And both men lived their courageous faith and their obstinate hope to the ultimate consequences.

Shortly after the murder of Rutilio Grande, word spread among the people and in the Salvadoran church—in fact, it became part of the local tradition—that Archbishop Romero had experienced a conversion as a result of Rutilio's death. It was not so much a conversion in the sense of abandoning a life of sin and turning to God as it was a decisive turning toward the people, toward those who were oppressed and repressed by injustice. After the murder of Rutilio, Archbishop Romero began to defend the people's cause with unprecedented vigor and lucidity. But other, isolated voices claimed that Archbishop Romero was a miracle worked by Rutilio himself. This interpretation did not win as much acceptance as the other. In October 2015, however, during a short exchange of impressions I had with Pope Francis, he told me that "the great miracle of Rutilio Grande was Archbishop Romero."

The great influence Rutilio had on the Salvadoran clergy, and on the archdiocese as a whole, helped prepare the path that Romero later traversed during his three years as archbishop. Obviously, Rutilio was not conscious of that influence, which would become clear only later, when some historical perspective became possible. But Rutilio was certainly convinced of the urgent need to preach the Gospel of God's kingdom in order to transform El Salvador's grossly unjust rural society into a social order shaped according to the plan of God. He was also convinced of the need to work diligently to build up the church by drawing on the strength of the people themselves, by forming local Christian communities, and by commissioning laypersons as pastoral agents. The Gospel of Jesus and the universal and continental magisterium of the church marked the path he followed.

The "miracle" of Rutilio can be seen with even greater clarity after his martyrdom. Archbishop Romero took charge of the archdiocese of San Salvador on February 22, 1977, just three weeks before Rutilio's murder. The new archbishop was viewed with great misgivings by most of the clergy, and in some cases even with hostility. Romero did not seem to be the kind of bishop who would continue with the same pastoral approach as his predecessor, Archbishop Luis Chávez, and his auxiliary, Arturo Rivera. Rather, most people had the impression that he had been named precisely to change the pastoral direction of the archdiocese. Knowing Romero well, Rutilio risked his prestige among the clergy by asking them to give the new archbishop a chance. By the end of March, the clergy had put aside their suspicions and had united together around their pastor. The ecclesial unity of the archdiocese was solid.

Romero stressed this unity himself in the homilies he pronounced not only at Rutilio's funeral in the cathedral on March 14 but also at the Mass in Aguilares on June 19 and at the great One Mass celebrated on March 20 (also in the cathedral). From that point on, the archdiocesan church and its pastor, united around the martyrdom of Rutilio, were in close agreement regarding ecclesial mission and identity; they devoted themselves completely to continuing the work of evangelization and preserving the memory of Rutilio and his fellow martyrs. In the years that followed, the archdiocese followed its pastor, Archbishop Romero, with great faith and courage. What had been unthinkable a few weeks earlier became possible in a most unexpected, surprising manner.

These pages relate the life, the passion, and the death of Rutilio Grande. His life was characterized by faithfulness to the Gospel and to the people of God, his two great loves. Rutilio lived the Gospel and preached it with tremendous passion. He trusted completely in the power it had to transform persons and society itself. He was also an ardent defender of the Salvadoran people and, above all, the poor. The church and the formation of its clergy were the great passions that marked his life. Finally, Rutilio was also a Jesuit; he understood and lived his vocation as "the service of faith, of which the promotion of justice is an absolute requirement." He understood well that "reconciliation with God demands the reconciliation of people with one another" (General Congregation 32, decree 4, 2). That is why they killed him.

In his first years of apostolic life, Rutilio formed several generations of seminarians, inculcating in them a vocation of service and urging them to be faithful to the Gospel and to the Salvadoran people. He was among the priests who worked the hardest to ensure that the teachings of Vatican II and Medellín were accepted by the Salvadoran church. The council teachings at first met strong resistance and were accepted only after the 1968 Medellín conference; even then, they were not by accepted by all. The archdiocese of San Salvador accepted the new teachings, but the other dioceses refused to do so. Rutilio was one of those who helped most to overcome the resistance, but not without suffering much misunderstanding, adversity, and rejection, which caused him great suffering. Despite the opposition, he repeatedly urged persons and institutions to change their ways and to respond to the real challenges facing the church and society.

For reasons that will be explained in this book, after working for years in the seminary, Rutilio made a "primary and fundamental option" for the poor, and he dedicated the last four years of his life to proclaiming the Gospel and the justice of the kingdom among the *campesinos* of the parish of Aguilares, which at that time included the town of El Paisnal. He encouraged the formation of local Christian communities and trained laypeople as pastoral agents. In this way, he returned to his roots, to the people he had left three decades before, when he entered the seminary. It was there, among the people, that his murderers found him. They snatched away his life as he was driving with an old man and a young lad, solid symbols of the Salvadoran people. Despite the risks he knew he was running, he did not want to abandon his people. "We must do what God wants" were his last words.

Rutilio lived the option for the poor in an extremely complex social, economic, and political context. The country was undergoing a structural crisis that would culminate in a cruel and bloody civil war twelve years later. His own integrity and faithfulness to the Gospel of Jesus Christ led him to the crossroads of Salvadoran history, to the very place where the life and the death of the majority of the people was being decided. Thus was created a tight and everlasting bond, uniting the history of El Salvador, the people of the parish of Aguilares, and the life of their pastor.

Rutilio's life was marked by a number of highly critical moments. At times, he found himself in ambiguous and complicated situations resulting from serious health issues and his obsession with being faithful to the church, the Society of Jesus, and his own priestly vocation. Often he walked in darkness, unsure of what to do, subject to cruel doubts and worrisome uncertainties. These moments of crisis tested his faith and his trust in God, but no matter how difficult the trial, he always placed himself in the hands of God.

Rutilio Grande was a Jesuit priest who possessed unsuspected human and religious qualities. In his vulnerability, he discovered his greatness. Most of his life passed by in silence. He was not a brilliant student, nor did he stand out as a leader among Jesuits. During the most difficult moments of his life, some of his companions and superiors questioned his suitability to be a Jesuit. Those who knew him well, however, found him to be admirably warm, generous, and helpful. The seminarians and the local clergy he trained knew him to be a humane, affable, and sympathetic companion, though when he had to be, he was also stern and serious. For the inhabitants of El Paisnal and Aguilares and the *campesinos* of the villages, Rutilio was a caring, friendly, and dedicated priest, as he had been also for the Ngäbe Indians of Hato Pilón, Panama, and the *campesinos* of Gaviñay, Ecuador, during the time he spent in those countries. When he became pastor of the parish of Aguilares, his life took on a public aspect that was unusual for him and unexpected. The work he did in the parish had a tremendous influence on the pastoral work of the whole archdiocese of San Salvador, and the influence extended even to the ecclesiastical province of El Salvador.

The present pages have their origin in two biographies I wrote years ago at the request of the then Father Provincial, César Jerez. The first of them, *Rutilio Grande:* Mártir de la evangelización rural en El Salvador (Rutilio Grande: Martyr of rural evangelization in El Salvador) (San Salvador: UCA Editores, 1978), was published anonymously on the first anniversary of his murder, with the due permission of Archbishop Romero, granted in March 1978. This short work was written rapidly so that it could be made available for the first anniversary of the martyrdom of Rutilio and his two *campesino* companions. Because of the intense repression unleashed against the church and the Society of Jesus at that time, it was judged unwise to publish the biography with my name. The prologue simply states that the book was authored by several unidentified Jesuits. For similar reasons of prudence, I suppressed many proper names, especially those of the Jesuits and the informants I interviewed. At that first anniversary and for years afterward, thousands of copies of that biography were circulated. It was finally published with my name in 2015 (San Salvador: UCA Editores).

But the biographical work could not stop there. Rutilio's personal archive merited a more thorough investigation. Thanks to his obsession for documenting his activities, he left to posterity a wealth of documents that deserve to be studied and contextualized. The availability of this information obliged me to write a new, more detailed, and more complete biography. Moreover, the archdiocesan clergy and the archbishop himself, in a homily he dedicated to Rutilio, expressed their desire to have a biography that would preserve the memory of Rutilio and his two companions. Accordingly, in 1978 I dedicated myself to that task, amid others I was working on. The result was the publication of *Historia de una esperanza: Vida de Rutilio Grande* (History of a hope: Life of Rutilio Grande) (San Salvador: UCA Editores, 1985).

The following pages draw on these two earlier works, especially the second, but this third effort includes new features. The perspective is completely new. It is one that was suggested to me by Pope Francis when I met him by chance in the Vatican. At the end of October 2015, I visited the Roman Archive of the Society of Jesus to gather some documentation on Rutilio. In those same days, the archbishop of San Salvador invited me to join a delegation that had arrived from El Salvador to thank Francis for the beatification of Archbishop Romero. When I found myself face to face with Francis, I told him I was the author of the two earlier biographies of Rutilio and was also a member of the commission of experts working on his cause. He told me he was familiar with the first biography. He then looked at me and asked whether we already had a miracle. I told him no. With a big smile, he told me that we *did* have a miracle: "The great miracle of Rutilio Grande was Archbishop Romero!" The serene certainty with which he said this left a profound impression on me. In sharing with me his thoughts about Rutilio, he provided me with the key for understanding and interpreting his life. Accordingly, the aim of this work, *The Life, Passion, and Death of the Jesuit Rutilio Grande*, is to show readers how this "great miracle" came about.

The passage of time has brought to light much new information about the life of Rutilio, and also about the intellectual and material authors of his murder. This new biography includes the names of Jesuits who were close to Rutilio, especially during his time in Aguilares. The testimonies of certain persons, however, still remain anonymous at their express desire. Finally, I have carefully revised the text to make it more lucid and comprehensible, eliminating unnecessary repetitions and explanations and re-ordering some sections to make them more consistent with the course of Rutilio's life.

—Rodolfo Cardenal
San Salvador, June 2016

1. The Origin of His Vocation

Family Roots

Rutilio was born in the small town of El Paisnal (department of San Salvador, El Salvador) on July 5, 1928.[1] He was the youngest child of Salvador Grande and Cristina García. His father was a merchant and an important local political figure. Rutilio was baptized on November 29 by Miguel Villavicencio, pastor of Guazapa, whose jurisdiction included El Paisnal. Although his godfather was Vicente Tejada, the mayor of the town, the man Rutilio always called his "godfather" was Facundo Barrera, who helped him economically during his years as a seminarian and for whom he always felt great affection.

The Grande family had an adobe house with a tile roof, one of the town's better-constructed buildings. It was the center of an intense social life due to his father's commercial and political activity. Not only did Salvador keep the house well stocked with merchandise but he also took his commercial business on the road. Visiting the neighboring towns and villages with an ox-drawn cart, he got to know and be known by many people in the region. The store was a gathering place for customers and others, who passed the time by commenting on the latest happenings among the people. Salvador served as mayor of El Paisnal for many years and at different periods. At that time, El Paisnal was more important than the recently founded town of Aguilares.

The municipality granted considerable power to the mayor. Not only did he have authority over the local police force and the judicial functionaries but he was also the town's principal contact with the civil, military, and ecclesiastical authorities at the national level. Due to the powers granted to the mayor, the Grande family inevitably became involved in one way or another in the struggles among the region's different factions.

The family's good fortune disappeared when Rutilio was three or four years old. The crisis was twofold: economic and familial. According to some reports, his father's business became insolvent when customers failed to pay for merchandise purchased on credit. That explanation is credible, since the economic crisis of 1929 hit the rural zones of El Salvador hard. Wages declined or disappeared completely; unemployment climbed sharply. Like tens of thousands of other Salvadorans, Don Salvador sought work in the banana plantations of northern Honduras, where there was a demand for labor and the wages offered were higher than in the rest of the region. The familial crisis was provoked by the dissolution of the Grande García matrimony, for reasons unknown. Rutilio's

---

1   Central American Archive of the Society of Jesus, henceforth ACSI. Civil Birth Registry 1928. Mayoralty of El Paisnal. The birth record, signed by the mayor, Vicente Tejada, and by Rutilio's father, affirms Rutilio Grande to be a legitimate child of Ladino descent.

mother Cristina remained in El Paisnal and had a daughter, also named Cristina, by José María Ruiz, but she never lived with him. As an elderly woman explained: "They had their romance, [...] as in the old days," that is, in secret.

Flavio, the oldest of the Grande children, became the head of the household. The family leased two *manzanas* (1.4 hectares) in San Antonio El Grande, situated some three leagues (fifteen kilometers) from El Paisnal, where they raised pigs and sowed maize, beans, and rice. They later bought the two *manzanas* with money they had saved, but since the plot could not meet their needs, they leased additional land, which they paid for with firewood and a portion of their crops, equivalent to about one week's labor. The four oldest siblings labored on the farm under the direction of Flavio, whose authority they all recognized. Since Rutilio was still young, he did not accompany them, but each day at noon he conveyed hot food to them. When he arrived at the work site, he would share out the food and prepare coffee, suited to the taste of each. He also helped care for the hogs.[2]

Rutilio was always quite solicitous for his five siblings. During his journeys away from El Salvador, some of which lasted for years, he remained in close contact with them through Flavio. He kept them all informed of his travels, his studies, his health, and his general impressions, and he insisted that Flavio write to him frequently in the name of all, keeping him abreast of all the news in the family and the town. When a letter took too long to arrive, he would irritably protest: "It is true that I am a religious and have renounced many things for love of God. That is quite true. But I have not renounced my love for my land and my family. To the contrary, I love them ardently through God."[3] Rutilio always traveled with a map of El Salvador and another of Central America.[4]

When Rutilio was pastor of Aguilares, he regularly visited Flavio in San Salvador. Sometimes, he would present himself unannounced and invite his brother to take a spin with him in his Volkswagen Safari. The itinerary was invariable: they drove through the towns near San Salvador, but without stopping in any of them. Rutilio disregarded his brother's invitations to stop someplace and have a soft drink. Toward the end of his life, Rutilio paid more frequent visits to his brother Luis, in whose house he frequently took his meals. The main reason for this frequency was that Luis had not married in the church. The two brothers argued about the matter a great deal, sometimes heatedly. Rutilio often good-naturedly asked: "You are going to get married, right?"[5]

Rutilio's brother Alberto took vows as a Salesian brother on December 8, 1947, and he died in San José, Costa Rica, on July 7, 1964. He was known as a

---

2   Author interview with Flavio Grande, San Salvador, December 1979.
3   ACSI. Rutilio Grande to Flavio Grande and family, Córdoba, Spain, n.d.
4   Author interview with Flavio Grande, San Salvador, December 1979.
5   Author interview with Luis Grande, San Salvador, December 1979.

1. The Origin of His Vocation

good religious and a hard worker, but most of all he was a very jovial, happy person. Rutilio and Alberto met in San José in August 1962. "It's hard to describe the tremendous emotion I felt when I found myself face to face with Rutilio," wrote Alberto in a letter to Flavio. "Seeing one another and melting into an embrace were one and the same thing. It was truly a week of great happiness, one that I will never forget."[6]

Joaquín was also a cause of concern for Rutilio. Concretely, he was unhappy with Joaquín's weekend visits to El Paisnal, where he would drink liquor with a neighbor in a public place. His half-sister Cristina caused him even more worries because he saw her as vulnerable and felt unable to help her. When he was pastor of the town, he gave her special attention. He always passed by her house, located at the entrance of El Paisnal, and would stop and talk with her. Even if he was late for an engagement, he always stopped but without getting out of his car. He was especially concerned about the poor relationship between Cristina and her husband, who had obliged her to serve at a beer party in their house. Moreover, the husband was having an affair with the domestic servant and finally ran off with her. Indignant, Rutilio sought him out in San Salvador and rebuked him for his behavior, but he failed to achieve the hoped-for result. Feeling helpless and dejected in the face of Cristina's situation and the public scandal it caused, he limited himself to consoling her.

After his parents separated, Rutilio was placed in the care of his grandmother Francisca, who he claimed "was for me a second mother since I did not know my own mother."[7] According to Rutilio, Francisca was a very religious woman, a "prayer leader" (*rezadora*), in common parlance. Rutilio credited her for setting the foundations of his own spiritual life and his priestly vocation. She taught him to pray after rising in the morning and before going to bed at night. In the evening, the two of them would pray the rosary together. By age seven, Rutilio already knew his grandmother's prayers well. He was familiar with the church services, since Francisca was in charge of cleaning the church and often asked Rutilio to help her with her tasks. Later on, when he was traveling outside El Salvador, Rutilio would always ask Flavio about church life in El Paisnal: who had celebrated Holy Week, how the celebration of the patronal feast had gone, whether there were catechism classes, when the first Communions had been.

From early childhood, Rutilio was characterized by his shyness. He usually stayed in the house, except when his grandmother sent him out on some errand, which he would always carry out quickly and diligently. He did not play much with other children his age, most of whom stayed outside as long as they could, entertaining themselves with their games and their spats. He did not play with

---

6   ACSI. Alberto Grande to Flavio Grande, San José, Costa Rica, October 1, 1962.
7   ACSI. Rutilio Grande to Flavio Grande and the Grande García family, Granada, Nicaragua, Spain, April 3, 1963.

others at school either. During recreation period, he would sit on a bench and watch his companions playing, or he would stay at his desk and review the teacher's lessons. He never bathed naked in the river, as was the custom of other boys in the town. When someone tried to intrude on his privacy, he would at times react strongly, but his displeasure would not last long. He would soon make peace again with those who had upset him, sometimes sending them letters with a few affectionate lines and enclosing a small cross, a piece of fruit, or some candy.

Another characteristic of Rutilio was his extreme sensibility. He would protest vigorously when his desires or fancies were not satisfied, and he would cry when he did not get his way. Flavio remembered him as a delicate boy given to crying, which he thought was due partly to Francisca's pampering but mainly to Rutilio's own nature. Flavio, probably exhausted by the responsibility thrust on him under difficult conditions, had been stern and intolerant with his siblings. Rutilio did not find in him the affection and the support he so badly needed, instead taking refuge in his own inner musings and of course in his grandmother, who provided him the maternal protection he longed for. An elderly woman commented: "Poor child, he never spoke. […] They were poor—things were all over for them."[8]

Rutilio's favorite game was building altars in the corners of the house and the enclosed yard. He would often gather ten or so children his age to make the Stations of the Cross in the yard; he would preside, wrapped in an old piece of cloth. These processions were accompanied by the sound of a bell or a tin can. He also had his playmates pay long visits to the altars he himself set up among the trees in the yard. The children had to follow his instructions to the letter. If they disobeyed, the play could degenerate into a quarrel. Serving as sacristan was Polito, one of Rutilio's inseparable companions in these activities. Later on, Rutilio would organize hikes to the river or neighboring hills, where he would "preach" to his companions, drawing on some of the religious lessons his grandmother had taught him.

The older women in El Paisnal would later recall with admiration the strange and premature vocation of that guileless boy, so innocent and pious, who became Father Tilo. They remembered how Rutilio, as a seminarian, would visit them from time to time. For a long while, he disappeared, but then he finally returned, now as a priest, to say his first Mass in the town. One woman recalled how as a child she had been taught to sing, "Padre Tilo is coming now, so ring the bells, ding, dong, dang." Whenever he visited, the people would receive him with jubilation in the atrium of the church.[9]

---

8   Author interview with Virginia Guzmán, San Salvador, December 1979.
9   Author interview with Antonia Montes, San Salvador, December 1979.

The Vocation

Rutilio's first meeting with Luis Chávez, newly named archbishop of San Salvador, had enormous consequences for his life. Years later, Rutilio wrote to the archbishop: "You came across the path of my life when I was young, you as archbishop and I as a boy of thirteen."[10] "After God, it is to you that I owe my vocation, as a visible instrument of the Lord's grace. The One who had chosen me for this vocation of service to the church wanted to call me explicitly through you."[11] And to another bishop he wrote: "I love and esteem the archbishop as my own father since I have always considered him to be, after God, the father of my vocation."[12]

When the archbishop's visit was announced, the whole town of El Paisnal became mobilized, and Rutilio took part in the general agitation. He never tired of asking his grandmother when the archbishop would arrive—he wanted to see him up close. Before traveling to El Paisnal, Archbishop Chávez stopped in Aguilares, at the house of Facundo Barrera, a generous collaborator in the parish, as was his sister Matilde. "He was like the pastor of La Toma [Aguilares]," recalled Rutilio when Facundo died in 1972. "His house provided hospitality to all good folk, especially priests who were passing through."[13] In Aguilares, Facundo joined the episcopal party as it made its way to El Paisnal, and there, Rutilio, accompanied by his aunt, introduced himself to the archbishop. After the introductions and greetings, Archbishop Chávez asked Rutilio if he knew how to pray. He quickly responded in the affirmative. The archbishop then asked him some questions from the catechism, which Rutilio answered satisfactorily. Pleased and impressed by the twelve-year-old's devotion and knowledge, the prelate invited him to travel with him to the next town, Nueva Concepción. After they had returned to El Paisnal, the archbishop asked if he could take the boy along to the seminary. Rutilio's father, who had by then returned from Honduras, consulted with Flavio, who continued to act as head of the family. Flavio was in favor of the proposal.[14] An elderly woman of El Paisnal understood this development in the context of the crisis the Grande García family was experiencing: "It was out of pity that the archbishop took the boy, and he thought the boy would enjoy it."[15]

On May 8, 1940, Rutilio wrote his first letter to Archbishop Chávez repeating his desire to be a priest. The archbishop responded four days later, on May 12, encouraging him to persevere in his desire and telling him to pray to the Holy

---

10   Here, Rutilio states that he was thirteen years old when he first met the archbishop, but the date recorded for the pastoral visit indicates that he was only twelve.
11   ACSI. Rutilio Grande to Archbishop Luis Chávez, Aguilares, December 17, 1974.
12   ACSI. Rutilio Grande to Bishop Arturo Rivera, Quito, Ecuador, July 27, 1972.
13   ACSI. Rutilio Grande to Matilde Barrera, Quito, Ecuador, March 12, 1972.
14   Author interview with Flavio Grande, San Salvador, December 1979.
15   Author interview with Virginia Guzmán, San Salvador, December 1979.

Spirit so that "his holy desires to be a *priest* will come true, if the Spirit so wishes."[16] He also told Rutilio to continue in school that year and to keep writing to him. The archbishop told Rutilio to ask the school principal for classes, especially in "arithmetic and grammar, which will teach you well the four rules and, if possible, notions about decimals and fraction, as well as the conjugation of verbs."[17] He ended the letter by inviting Rutilio to visit him in San Salvador so that they could talk about his vocation. On the back of the letter, Rutilio wrote: "First letter of the Archbishop: May 1940."[18]

Rutilio's hopes faded, however, when his father became sick and the family finances suffered another blow. On October 19, 1940, Archbishop Chávez wrote another letter, one that Rutilio considered "decisive for my vocation." On the back of it, he wrote, "2nd Letter of the Archbishop, decisive for my voca.: October 1940." In the letter, the archbishop urged Rutilio not to give up and repeated his invitation to visit him in the curia of San Salvador.[19]

On December 9, 1940, at the archbishop's request, the rector of the seminary invited Rutilio to take a test and to discuss a possible solution to the economic difficulty. The seminary was willing to cover the costs of transportation and of room and board at its facilities.[20] On January 16, 1941, the rector informed Rutilio that he had been admitted to the seminary and asked him to arrive by January 29 at the latest.[21] Flavio sold a yoke of oxen in order to buy Rutilio the clothing, shoes, and other personal items required at the seminary. Since the proceeds from the sale were not enough to cover the costs, Facundo Barrera made up for what was lacking. A full scholarship granted by the archbishop resolved the matter of tuition and upkeep, but not Rutilio's personal expenses; these were covered by contributions from the family and from Barrera.[22]

This was not the only occasion on which Barrera provided Rutilio with economic assistance. In his first letter, Archbishop Chávez had suggested that Rutilio ask him for money to pay for particular classes. When Rutilio was accepted in the seminary, Barrera told him that he would help him to buy shoes and some clothing "to the extent that I can." When Facundo died, Rutilio wrote to his sister Matilde:

> I remember with gratitude the assistance he gave me when I was a poor seminary kid. I will never forget it! I would like to have been by his side in

---

16   Emphasis in original. Rutilio used italics and especially capital letters. The emphasis is indicated here only with italics.
17   ACSI. Archbishop Luis Chávez to Rutilio Grande, San Salvador, May 12, 1940.
18   ACSI. Archbishop Luis Chávez to Rutilio Grande, San Salvador, May 12, 1940.
19   ACSI. Archbishop Luis Chávez to Rutilio Grande, San Salvador, October 19, 1940.
20   ACSI. Agustín Bariain to Rutilio Grande, San Salvador, December 9, 1940.
21   ACSI. Agustín Bariain to Rutilio Grande, San Salvador, January 16, 1941.
22   Author interview with Flavio Grande, San Salvador, December 1979.

his final moments and to have presided at the funeral because I always felt personally close to him, as he did to me.

Rutilio was living in Quito at that time.[23]

Rutilio showed great affection for Matilde until she died on July 3, 1974. After her death, he paid off her debts with money he managed with the provincial's permission. He inherited her house, which was located in front of the rectory in Aguilares, and placed it at the service of the parish. After Rutilio's death, the provincial, César Jérez, turned the property over to the archdiocese of San Salvador.[24]

From the time of their first meeting, Archbishop Chávez treated Rutilio as a son, and a profound bond of friendship and loyalty developed between the two men. Rutilio attested that the archbishop fostered his vocation "from the time I was a boy and he made his first pastoral visit to my town, during the five years I was a seminarian, and at various periods of my formation in the Society of Jesus, which I entered with his kind acquiescence."[25] Rutilio considered the archbishop a father to whom he owed his priestly identity. He preserved his correspondence with Archbishop Chávez in a special folder that had the prelate's photo pasted inside the cover. Writing to Arturo Rivera Damas, auxiliary bishop of San Salvador, he confessed: "I have a collection of the letters the archbishop wrote me when I was a boy, which I now keep as a treasure."[26]

On December 29, 1974, Rutilio testified publicly to this close relationship during the celebration in Aguilares of the archbishop's golden anniversary of priesthood. On that occasion, Rutilio said that his first meeting with the archbishop "was an explicit and visible confirmation of my priestly vocation, which I had been sensing for years. He called me in the name of the Lord, and I followed him on the way to the seminary."[27] A few days before, on December 17, the priests of the archdiocese had delivered an official document to the archbishop stating that the president of the republic had sent him a laudatory telegram, the Legislative Assembly had awarded him a diploma of recognition, and many persons and groups had sent their congratulations. After the archbishop had received all these honors, Rutilio wrote that he himself, "this humble priest, approached your office furtively by means of a letter to say how much he esteems you and how grateful he is to you."[28]

---

23 ACSI. Rutilio Grande to Matilde Barrera, Quito, Ecuador, March 12, 1972.
24 ACSI. César Jerez to Archbishop Óscar A. Romero, San Salvador, June 3, 1977.
25 ACSI. Rutilio Grande to Archbishop Luis Chávez. Aguilares, January 11, 1976.
26 ACSI. Rutilio Grande to Bishop Arturo Rivera, Quito, Ecuador, July 27, 1972. Only the two letters cited here are found in this folder and among Rutilio's papers.
27 ACSI. Rutilio Grande. Homage to Archbishop Luis Chávez y González on the fiftieth anniversary of his priesthood. Aguilares, December 29, 1974.
28 ACSI. Rutilio Grande to Archbishop Luis Chávez, Aguilares, December 17, 1974.

On that very special occasion, Rutilio offered to Archbishop Chávez his priesthood and his religious life; together with the church he loved dearly, these were the best possible tribute of love and gratitude he could offer. He concluded the letter by reaffirming his friendship and filial loyalty: "Every day, I commend you earnestly so that the Holy Spirit may give you, as pastor of the church, strength and vigor to confront the serious problems facing our country at the present time."[29]

On another occasion, as Rutilio was reviewing his life while confronting a crisis that called into question his pastoral labors in Aguilares, he wrote to Archbishop Chávez, "You know well the great affection I have had for you since I was a boy."[30] In view of his close relationship with the archbishop, he asked Bishop Rivera to grant him the privilege of delivering the homily at the archbishop's funeral, "unless I be the first to die. Don't forget, and may he be with us for many years to come."[31]

Formation

Rutilio entered the minor seminary of San Salvador on January 31, 1941; he was inscribed as number sixty-four in the register. A week later, he made a three-day retreat directed by Father Santiago Garrido, spiritual director of the minor seminarians. Life in the seminary revolved around devotions, studies,[32] and discipline. Rutilio appears not to have been an outstanding student, to judge from his grades during the first two years, the only ones that have been preserved. One of his seminary companions later testified: "I always noticed his devotion, his very earnest manner, and his dedication to prayerfulness and other virtues."[33] In the school years of 1944 and 1945, he functioned as second warder, with supervisory duties in the dormitory and with the chorus. The handwriting and some of the expressions in the seminary daybook suggest that he kept the journal at least from December 1943 to the middle of 1944.

At some point before concluding his studies at the minor seminary, Rutilio told Archbishop Chávez that he wanted to be "like the fathers at the seminary." The archbishop accordingly referred him to the Jesuits.[34] Thus, when he finished the course at the minor seminary, Rutilio entered the novitiate of the Society of Jesus in Los Chorros, Venezuela; at that time, the vice-province of Central America did not have a novitiate of its own. Rutilio's father signed two authorizations, certified by the mayor of El Paisnal, so that he could travel to any country for the

---

29 ACSI. Rutilio Grande to Archbishop Luis Chávez, Aguilares, December 17, 1974.
30 ACSI. Rutilio Grande to Archbishop Luis Chávez, Aguilares, January 11, 1976.
31 ACSI. Rutilio Grande to Bishop Arturo Rivera, Quito, Ecuador, July 27, 1972.
32 A total of five years: three of grammatical study and two of rhetoric.
33 *Summarium testium*, witness 1, §2. Reference to the *positio*.
34 *Summarium testium*, witness 2, §14.

purpose of continuing his studies. Rutilio arrived in Caracas on September 10, 1945, as a layperson in order to avoid difficulties with the immigration authorities, and he presented himself as a student at the Colegio de San Ignacio in that city. On September 23, 1945, the master of novices, Vicente Pardo, noted Rutilio's name in the admissions register of the novitiate of Los Chorros.[35]

On the back of a photograph of the seminary professors taken during the 1943 school year, Rutilio wrote his personal opinion of each one: Fathers Luis Ciarán and Valentín Arrieta had died that year and were "deeply mourned"; Fathers José Carlucci, Marcelino Redondo, and Victoriano Usubiaga were "also sincerely mourned"; Father Alfonso Bariandarán "abandoned the plow," that is, left the Society of Jesus; and Father Bernardo Aguirre-Ceciaga was a "poor man!" for he was very sick. He expressed high esteem for Brother Félix Barruetabeña, "a religious of true Ignatian stamp," and the rector, Father Agustín Bariain, to whom he was very grateful. The only negative opinion he expressed was about Father Garrido, the spiritual director: "It's time he stopped playing at the game of being a saint."[36]

While in the novitiate, Rutilio gave signs that he had an authentic vocation to the Society of Jesus, thus confirming the opinion of the rector of the minor seminary, who had known him for four years and had informed the Jesuit vice-provincial that Rutilio's vocation was solid. The only fear the rector had was of the reaction of the bishops, since several seminarians had already felt called to the Society of Jesus. The first impression of the novice master was positive. After three months, he informed the vice-provincial of Central America that Rutilio and another novice "were giving a good account of themselves: they were pious, observant, and intelligent."[37] That evaluation persisted during the two years of his novitiate. The novice master was extremely satisfied with Rutilio and the other young Central American. As the end of the novitiate approached, the novice master, with the consensus of his consultors, recommended to the vice-provincial that Rutilio be allowed to make his simple vows since he and the other Central American novice would "with divine fervor, be good and dedicated laborers of the Society."[38] With "genuine joy," Rutilio received the news that he would be allowed to take vows, which he pronounced on September 24, 1947.

One of Rutilio's novitiate companions, a Panamanian named Rosendo Torres, was a cheerful prankster; he remembered Rutilio as being serious and withdrawn, solitary and reticent. Torres used to make fun of his somber manner, and his teasing easily made Rutilio lose his patience.[39] The extreme rigidity and

---

35 ACSI. Vicente Pardo to Álvaro Echarri, Los Chorros, Venezuela, May 13, 1946.
36 ACSI. Photograph of the teachers at San José de la Montaña Seminary, San Salvador, 1943.
37 ACSI. Vicente Pardo to Álvaro Echarri, Villa Pignatelli, Venezuela, December 15, 1945.
38 ACSI. Vicente Pardo to Álvaro Echarri, Villa Pignatelli, Venezuela, June 15, 1947.
39 Personal communication of Father Rosendo Torres with the author, Panama, September 1980.

scrupulosity of the master of novices no doubt helped to reinforce these aspects of Rutilio's temperament.

We do not know what first moved Rutilio to want to be a Jesuit. Later correspondence tells us that at some moment he felt a missionary vocation. A little before making his first vows, he asked the vice-provincial to be sent to the missions in the Far East; this vocation most likely matured during his time in the seminary. "I know what it means, Father. It was one of the things that then moved me to enter the Society: the hope of being one day a missionary among unbelievers."[40] He felt especially attracted to the austere and heroic life of the missionary. "If the Lord grants me this, I will consider myself happy." However, the Jesuits with whom he had talked about this missionary vocation—the spiritual father of the seminary and the master of novices—recommended that he cultivate his indifference and availability. Even so, a "noble heart" could not remain passive. In his letter, Rutilio pressed the point: "I would like to sign these desires with my blood, and in doing so I humbly confess, Father, that I am not yielding to fantasies. I place everything in your hands." The vice-provincial limited himself to encouraging Rutilio to nourish his desire with "holy subordination."[41]

Even though his petition was not granted, Rutilio was so certain of his missionary vocation that he appealed three more times to his superiors: in 1948, 1949, and 1950. "My ideals are none other than: (1) to give my life completely to the Lord, sacrificing all earthly attachments, such as homeland, etc., and (2) to dedicate myself to direct apostolate with the unfortunate."[42] In his petition of January 9, 1950, he expressed his "good desires for holiness, perfection, and indifference before the will of God as manifested through superiors," but he insisted again on his "holy desires to be a missionary."[43] He also shared his sense of a missionary vocation with Archbishop Chávez, who supported him and encouraged him to follow it.[44]

That vocation probably originated in the talks given by the spiritual father of the minor seminary, Father Garrido, who frequently spoke of the great need for missionaries in the Far East and of the difficulties of that style of apostolic life. At that time, the Central American vice-province was a dependency of a Spanish province, which had missions in China. Rutilio naturally felt great apostolic zeal and so decided that he would be a Jesuit missionary. Garrido no doubt had a dramatic and imaginative style that would have roused the enthusiasm of his young audience, and Rutilio was not one to be satisfied with offering prayers and making small sacrifices for the missions.

---

40   ACSI. Rutilio Grande to Álvaro Echarri, Villa Pignatelli, Venezuela, August 15, 1947.
41   ACSI. Álvaro Echarri to Rutilio Grande, Granada, Nicaragua, September 27, 1947.
42   ACSI. Rutilio Grande to the vice-provincial, Cotocollao, Ecuador, June 13, 1948.
43   ACSI. Álvaro Echarri to Rutilio Grande, Granada, Nicaragua, January 23, 1950.
44   ACSI. Letters of June 3, 1947, June 6, 1948, and July 24, 1950.

Rather than being assigned to the missions, however, Rutilio was sent to study classics in Quito, arriving there on October 6, 1947. In reality, he should have been sent straight to philosophy studies because he had already done rhetoric in the minor seminary. When the vice-provincial, Álvaro Echarri, became aware of this, he improvised by telling Rutilio to review his classical studies, but Rutilio had already done that in the novitiate.[45] He was already quite advanced in Latin and had begun studying Greek. He used his time in Quito, therefore, to work on his Greek and improve his Latin by studying the Ciceronian orations. In these efforts, he received assistance from a companion and a professor. He also attended the famous classes of Father Aurelio Espinosa Pólit on the Greek tragedies and took a course on literary criticism and another on sacred eloquence. Besides these formal studies, he read a great deal of literature and worked on Spanish composition.[46]

As 1948 began, since the vice-provincial had still made no decision about his studies, Rutilio finished the course of rhetoric and explored the social sciences. Toward the end of the year, the rector informed the vice-provincial that the two Central Americans, Rutilio being one of them, "are progressing well in their formation and are very edifying. *Laus Deo!*"[47] On March 25, 1950, Rutilio was awarded a diploma in classical humanities, the equivalent of a baccalaureate. He received it as "a sign of the kindness and benevolence" of the "truly magnificent" rector; he wrote that he had earned it "not by any merit of mine, which is scant, for I have, to my chagrin, taken very little advantage of all the wonderful things that are found here."[48] Years later, in June 1962, with this diploma and with a licentiate in philosophy from the Colegio Máximo San Francisco Javier of Oña, Spain, Rutilio attained the title of professor of secondary education, with a specialty in social sciences. After returning to San Salvador, he registered these degrees with the Ministry of Education, thus becoming qualified to teach in San José de la Montaña Seminary.

Rutilio's assignment after finishing college studies in 1950 was also marked by the indecision of the vice-provincial. He was first sent to the Colegio Javier in Panama, where he arrived in mid-April 1950, after making his spiritual exercises in Quito.[49] Later, though, the vice-provincial changed his mind and sent Rutilio to the Colegio Centroamérica in Granada, Nicaragua, to replace a Nicaraguan scholastic who was transferred to Panama. In a further change, Rutilio returned to Panama, where he worked as counselor of students in grades three to six. The counselor's responsibility included supervising recreation periods and the school bus runs. The latter task was particularly onerous because of the heat of

---

45   ACSI. Álvaro Echarri to Vicente Pardo, Granada, Nicaragua, October 28, 1947.
46   ACSI. Carlos Riofrío to Álvaro Echarri, Cotocollao, Ecuador, October 14, 1947.
47   ACSI. Carlos Riofrío to Álvaro Echarri, Cotocollao, Ecuador, December 1, 1948.
48   ACSI. Rutilio Grande to Florentino Idoate, Cotocollao, Ecuador, March 29, 1950.
49   ACSI. Álvaro Echarri to Rutilio Grande, Granada, Nicaragua, January 23, 1950.

the city and the length of the hours: his days began with an hour of meditation at dawn and ended late in the afternoon. The rector of the school, after asking Rutilio about his abilities and inclinations regarding teaching, assigned him to teach Spanish to grades five and six and the first year of secondary.[50]

Rutilio made a good first impression in the school; the rector reported that "he has done quite well."[51] However, soon after the term began, between mid-May and mid-June, Rutilio underwent a very serious crisis of nerves. One day, he apparently lost contact with reality and began to speak unintelligibly. Once the worst of the crisis was past—more will be said of it in the next chapter—he was sent for a rest to the residence of the Church of El Carmen in Santa Tecla, El Salvador.[52] Before long, however, he was assigned to San José de la Montaña Seminary in San Salvador, where he served as sub-prefect of discipline in the minor seminary and taught various courses: sacred history, history of the Americas, Salvadoran history, and penmanship in 1950; history in 1952; and Latin, Spanish, and penmanship in 1953.

In October 1953, Rutilio began his philosophy studies at the Colegio Máximo San Francisco Javier in Oña, a remote Spanish town in the foothills of the Cantabrian Mountains. The first year was very difficult since Rutilio was unable to study with the same intensity and sense of achievement as in earlier years. The high level of abstraction in the subjects he was studying left him perplexed. However he found the second year of philosophy easier and more tolerable; the subjects were less abstract and more interesting. For health reasons, superiors enrolled him in courses that were less academically demanding.

To finalize his philosophy studies, Rutilio wrote a thesis titled "The Conscious and Unconscious Psyche" under the direction of Father José Sagastume and presented it on March 19, 1956. The thesis, of which he wrote only two of the three parts that he originally planned, reviewed the varying definitions of conscious and unconscious, from Scholastic philosophy down to modern times. His treatment was conventional and not very interesting, but the subject undoubtedly had great personal significance for Rutilio. As the final examination in philosophy drew near, he became nervous. "I will do what I can to prepare for the exam," he wrote in a letter. "I will fight off anxiety and accept the result as the will of God."[53] On June 25, 1956, he was awarded the licentiate degree in philosophy.

Rutilio was well known and much loved by the people in the little town of Oña, where he took part in the catechetical activities of the Colegio Máximo. He was the director of the Kostkas Congregation, an association of young people aged twelve to sixteen. He felt more fulfilled when active in apostolic work than

---

50   ACSI. Florentino Idoate to Rutilio Grande, Panama, February 11, 1950.
51   ACSI. Florentino Idoate to Álvaro Echarri, Panama, May 13, 1950.
52   ACSI. Agustín Bariain to Florentino Idoate, Granada, Nicaragua, July 6, 1950.
53   ACSI. Rutilio Grande to Miguel Elizondo, Oña, Spain, April 9, 1956.

1. The Origin of His Vocation

when submerged in books and the abstractions of the classroom. The people of Oña appreciated his kindness and his dedication to the apostolate, and they showed their appreciation at his first Mass.

Rutilio wanted to proceed immediately to theological studies. "I believe I deserve the chance. I have taken care of myself and kept moderation, precisely with a view to my theology studies." Regarding his health, he wrote: "I don't think there is any difficulty, and if there were, I would be the first to make it known."[54] He wanted to study theology in the United States, specifically at the theologate in Kansas, in order to learn English and have a change of scenery. The vice-provincial allowed him to proceed to theology, but he thought that studying in the United States would be too radical a change given Rutilio's fragile health and the difficulty of learning a new language. Some of Rutilio's companions encouraged him to study in the United States precisely because he would find there a healthier and less restrictive ambience than at Oña. Rutilio also imagined that the academic demands would be less rigorous in Kansas and that he could master the language in the course of four years of theology. In the end, though, he left the decision in the hands of the vice-provincial since he had little confidence in his own strength.[55]

In Spain, there were alternatives to Oña. Good theology programs also existed in Granada and in Sant Cugat (Barcelona). The latter reported that they had no space for the 1956–57 school year but that Rutilio could enroll for the following year. The vice-provincial suggested to Rutilio that he could spend the year learning English; if he managed to learn it well, he would send him to Kansas.[56] Rutilio, however, wanted to start his theology studies that year.

The doubts were cleared up by the middle of 1956. If he was to remain in Spain, Rutilio wrote, he preferred Oña, "where I sincerely confess that all has gone well for me in every sense."[57] Rutilio was also interested in the University of Comillas because of the seminary connected to it, for he saw clearly that he would like to dedicate himself to the formation of clergy. But Comillas was out of reach since he lacked the necessary grades. Father Marcelino Zalba, his most important confidant in those years, advised him to stay in Oña, and the rector seconded Zalba's opinion. The provincial recommended that Rutilio interrupt his studies for one year in order to rest, but Rutilio thought a break was unnecessary since he had already found a suitable method of study. Besides, a year of teaching would not provide any rest.[58] Accordingly, Rutilio began his theology studies in the latter part of 1956.

When he finished his third year of theology in 1958–59, Rutilio asked for major orders and was granted them. He took one week of vacation in early

---

54   ACSI. Rutilio Grande to Agustín Bariain, Oña, Spain, December 5, 1955.
55   ACSI. Rutilio Grande to Miguel Elizondo, Oña, Spain, April 9, 1956.
56   ACSI. Miguel Elizondo to Rutilio Grande, Granada, Nicaragua, June 6, 1956.
57   ACSI. Rutilio Grande to Agustín Bariain, Oña, Spain, December 4, 1955.
58   ACSI. Rutilio Grande to Miguel Elizondo, Oña, Spain, June 11, 1956.

1959 to prepare for the "great moment" and made an eight-day retreat after returning to Oña. He sent several invitations to his brother Flavio and asked him to give them to relatives and some friends. He also sent personal invitations to Archbishop Chávez, his godparents in Aguilares, various friends among the Salvadoran clergy, his fellow Jesuits, and his brother Alberto.[59] He also requested a papal benediction, which was granted to him by John XXIII on May 27, 1959.[60]

In responding to Rutilio's invitation, Archbishop Chávez reaffirmed the young Jesuit's vocation:

> I have before me a book you sent me a few months ago, called *We Are Firm*. That is how God our Lord wants you all the days of your priestly life: firm, dedicated, ready to work for his "greater glory." The field that awaits you is spacious, and it is teeming with tremendous needs of all kinds: spiritual, moral, social, economic, etc. There are so many souls waiting for your blessed ministry! There are so many who will be saved by your apostolic labors![61]

Along with thirty-three companions, Rutilio was ordained a priest in Oña on July 30, 1959, by Demetrio Mansilla, auxiliary bishop of Burgos. The sponsors of his ordination were his very close friends Mr. and Mrs. Guerricagoitia. He got to know the Guerricagoitia family though one of their sons, José María, who had been in the seminary with him at the end of his regency. Once, while in Oña, Rutilio had asked his brothers to give José María some assistance in order to return some of the favors that his family had done for Rutilio.[62] When José María left the Society of Jesus in the United States on March 20, 1959, shortly before he was due to be ordained, Rutilio traveled to Bilbao as a "consoling angel" to inform his family, for José María had not written to them since February. Given these circumstances, he told the Guerricagoitias that they need not come to his ordination, but they were present anyway, along with their three children.[63] Mrs. Guerricagoitia even offered to untie hands, which, after being anointed, were bound with a ribbon she herself had brought from Bilbao. The right of unbinding the hands of the newly ordained priest ordinarily corresponded to the priest's mother. Rutilio later sent the ribbon to his family so that they could keep it as a souvenir.

In the first letter he sent to his family after his ordination, Rutilio explained clearly the meaning of his priesthood. Through the bishop, he wrote, he had been granted

---

59   ACSI. Rutilio Grande to Flavio Grande, Oña, Spain, June 19, 1959.
60   ACSI. Rutilio Grande. Memorial card of the ordination.
61   ACSI. Archbishop Luis Chávez to Rutilio Grande, San Salvador, July 18, 1959.
62   ACSI. Rutilio Grande to Flavio Grande, Oña, Spain, July 24, 1953.
63   ACSI. Rutilio Grande to the Grande García family, Oña, Spain, August 7, 1959.

> the great powers of *Jesus Christ*, and I became from that moment *another Christ*, ordained to pardon sins in his name, administer the sacraments of the church, preach the Gospel to the people, and celebrate the Holy Sacrifice, making his *most holy Body* and *Blood* descend miraculously into my hands. [...] You cannot imagine my state of soul in those blessed moments. I felt myself closely embraced by Christ, an intimate embrace that I had craved for so many years. From that sacred summit of *Priesthood*, I had an immediate birds-eye view of all the years that have passed since, as a boy, I first had the desire to be a *Priest*.[64]

Rutilio celebrated his first Mass the next day, the feast of Saint Ignatius. He was granted the privilege of presiding at a solemn high Mass with three ministers. Acting as his sponsors at the Mass were the Salvadoran consul in Burgos, Manuel Villanueva, and his wife. The consul had brought a Salvadoran flag, which was placed beside the altar. Also attending the Mass were residents and summer visitors from the town, members of the Colegio Máximo community, and relatives of the other newly ordained priests who had already celebrated their first Mass. Rutilio wrote that the faculty chorus, reinforced by twelve boy sopranos, was "really something stupendous."[65]

During the Mass, Rutilio reviewed his life and thought especially of his loved ones:

> I offered my first Mass for all of you and for all the deceased of our family. Your beloved names kept passing through my mind. There were moments of quiet weeping, filled with distant memories, filled with names and events, as I looked toward my tiny land, toward my faraway little town.[66]

At the end of Mass, he imparted the papal blessing, especially granted for this occasion. Then he remained in the church for half an hour, seated between the consul and his wife, greeting those attending, who kissed his hands. "Certainly they were blessed moments!"[67]

At the meal following the Mass, seated at Rutilio's table were the Guerricagoitia family, the consul and his family, a Guatemalan Jesuit named Gustavo Oliva, and two other Jesuits who had been with him in the seminary. A special treat was the Salvadoran coffee that someone had brought as a gift to Rutilio. Later on, there was a solemn benediction with the Blessed Sacrament, followed by a musical evening outdoors—"certainly a most pleasant event, bringing to an end that unforgettable day with its tremendous and enduring emotions."[68]

---

64 ACSI. Rutilio Grande to the Grande García family, Oña, Spain, August 7, 1959.
65 ACSI. Rutilio Grande to the Grande García family, Oña, Spain, August 7, 1959.
66 ACSI. Rutilio Grande to the Grande García family, Oña, Spain, August 7, 1959.
67 ACSI. Rutilio Grande to the Grande García family, Oña, Spain, August 7, 1959.
68 ACSI. Rutilio Grande to the Grande García family, Oña, Spain, August 7, 1959.

Meanwhile, Rutilio's godparents in Aguilares had a Mass said on the same day as his first Mass; they both attended it, as did some of their relatives. Rutilio promised them that he would say a solemn Mass in El Paisnal as soon as he returned.[69]

In the inscription on the holy card commemorating his ordination and first Mass, Rutilio asked God to bless "by my consecrated hands the beloved members of my family, my friends and acquaintances, and all those who have helped me ascend to your Altar." In the same letter in which he explained the meaning of his priesthood, he imparted this blessing: "With my hands recently consecrated by the holy anointing, I give to each and every one of you my *priestly* blessing. Kneel down, and it will reach you there, overflowing with affection and delightful memories: *May the blessing of almighty God* [...]."[70]

During those days, Rutilio received many "letters of love and solidarity" from Venezuela, Panama, England, Portugal, Taiwan, United States, Spain, El Salvador, Guatemala, and France. After answering them, he sent them to Flavio. He handed over to the superior the gifts he had received: the electric shaver from the Guerricagoitia family, the alarm clock from the consul, and the clothing from other friends. Among the gifts were several ribbons for binding hands.[71]

Rutilio wrote that these days "have been intensely emotional; they have shaken my whole being, leaving me very tired."[72] The day after his first Mass, he traveled by train to Santelices, a town about sixty kilometers from Oña, to rest for three days at the Guerricagoitia home. He found Santelices "enchanting" and said that the Guerricagoitia family "has really treated me as a son, showing great affection [...] and every sort of kindness, which I will never forget." On August 2, he presided at a solemn Mass in the parish church, assisted by the pastor, "a truly good and beautiful person," with a chorus of fourteen major seminarians. In his homily, Rutilio alluded to his deceased parents, his brothers and sisters, and all his faraway family. The people came forward to kiss his hands, "showing me tremendous affection. [...] They are all truly excellent people, without excluding the children." A photographer took photos during the Mass, and later they ate in a small hotel in the town. The next day, Rutilio presided at a sung Mass in a neighboring town that was celebrating the feast of its patron, Saint Stephen. The pastor offered Rutilio the opportunity to preside and to preach, which he was "delighted" to accept.[73]

On the last day of his vacation, Rutilio went on an excursion with the seminarians but returned to Oña feverish and with chills. He wrote to his brother Flavio, asking him to write to the Guerricagoitias in the name of his family, "without sparing expense or bother." "You cannot imagine," he insisted, "how much they

---

69 ACSI. Rutilio Grande to Flavio Grande, Oña, Spain, July 2, 1959.
70 ACSI. Rutilio Grande to Grande García family, Oña, Spain, August 7, 1959.
71 ACSI. Rutilio Grande to Grande García family, Oña, Spain, August 7, 1959.
72 ACSI. Rutilio Grande to Grande García family, Oña, Spain, August 7, 1959.
73 ACSI. Rutilio Grande to Grande García family, Oña, Spain, August 7, 1959.

went out of their way to take care of me. […] They just love me, as they say in these parts. They have looked after me with exquisite affection despite the painful trial they've had to endure for some months now."[74]

Rutilio devoted the following weeks to rest and relaxation, but without neglecting the children of Oña because "I remembered the times when I was a little seminarian […] I spent my vacations in my town, going on my old horse to Guazapa to hear Holy Mass."[75] He also gave the Spiritual Exercises to a group of students from the schools of the Jesuits and other congregations. The provincial told him to visit other communities and works in Spain since Rutilio had hardly left Oña during his six years there. He put up some resistance but finally agreed to make the trip when they gave him a traveling companion.[76]

Finally, the vice-provincial gave Rutilio permission to do his fourth year of theology in Kansas, but he decided against it: "Poor health made me decline the offer. Living in a country with a foreign language is always a stressful experience."[77]

After finishing his studies in Oña in July 1960, Rutilio rejoined the community of San José de la Montaña Seminary. "For reasons of health, it was advisable that I come here before doing tertianship."[78] He taught classes and was prefect of discipline at the minor seminary, and the rector reported: "He is doing it quite well."[79] In evaluating his work two years later, the rector stated that Rutilio had done his job with "great success and total dedication. I don't know what we'll do without him when he leaves."[80]

In September 1962, Rutilio began his tertianship at the novitiate of Saint Francis Borgia in Córdoba, Spain, under the direction of Father Francisco Cuenca. When he finished tertianship in July 1963, he spent ten days vacationing in Comillas, Santander. He then traveled to Paris and spent the rest of his vacation studying French.[81]

In October 1963, Rutilio enrolled at the Lumen Vitae International Institute of Catechesis and Pastoral Ministry in Brussels and took up residence in the Colegio de San Miguel: "Superiors sent me to Europe again to do tertianship and then to do special studies for a year or two in Belgium or France. I certainly don't see what special merits I had as a person."[82] The seminary rector,

---

74 ACSI. Rutilio Grande to Grande García family, Oña, Spain, August 7, 1959.
75 ACSI. Rutilio Grande to Grande García family, Oña, Spain, August 7, 1959.
76 ACSI. Rutilio Grande to Grande García family, Oña, Spain, August 7, 1959.
77 ACSI. Rutilio Grande to Grande García family, Oña, Spain, August 7, 1959.
78 Archivum Romanum Societatis Iesu (henceforth ARSI). Ladislao Segura to superior general, San Salvador, January 12, 1961. C. América, 1005, XX.
79 ARSI. Ladislao Segura to superior general, San Salvador, January 12, 1961. C. América, 1005, XX.
80 ARSI. Ladislao Segura to superior general, San Salvador, July 14, 1962. C. América, 1005, XXV.
81 ACSI. Rutilio Grande to Flavio Grande, Córdoba, Spain, July 13, 1963.
82 ACSI. Rutilio Grande to Marcelino Zalba, Brussels, February 24, 1964.

however was clear about the reason for Rutilio's further studies: "We need a father who is well prepared in these subjects, which are so necessary in the seminary."[83] Rutilio himself reported: "That's how I came to live in Brussels. I am taking the course at the Lumen Vitae Pastoral Institute. (I am honestly satisfied with it, very satisfied.)"[84] That final phrase in parentheses is found only in the copy of the letter Rutilio kept in his files; he left it out of the letter he sent to Father Zalba.

In Belgium, and especially there at Lumen Vitae, Rutilio was an enthusiastic student of the French style of pastoral ministry. He was profoundly impressed by the biblical and liturgical spirituality of the Benedictines of Saint Andrew's Abbey in Bruges, where he spent Holy Week in 1964. During his time in Brussels, Rutilio acquired many books on pastoral ministry for the seminary library. When he returned to San Salvador, he reproduced and distributed to the seminarians some of the notes he had taken at Lumen Vitae, especially those from the catechesis course of George Decluve. This experience of pastoral work as practiced by the French laid the foundation for Rutilio's later pastoral perspective and activity. He was constantly seeking to create space for the full participation of the people of God, while quashing any kind of clerical authoritarianism. Later in his life, experience moved him gradually to modify some of these views since he considered them too French and not truly Salvadoran.

In order to complete his courses at Lumen Vitae, Rutilio wrote a thesis and took several examinations. While writing the thesis, he served as chaplain to some nuns, who provided him room and board. The academic demands were not easy, he wrote, since "at my age such intellectual efforts take their toll. Thanks be to God, I've come out well, winning a prize for distinguished work." The truth is that Rutilio was very conscious of his age. "We're already getting old. My hair keeps turning white, but that is really nothing, absolutely nothing compared to the cross the Lord has desired to place on the shoulders of our brother Alberto,"[85] who was paralyzed. He therefore changed the itinerary of his return trip. Instead of passing through Mexico, where he would have visited some seminaries, he flew directly from Madrid to San José.

Before returning to Central America, however, Rutilio spent the first days of August in Germany visiting several scholastics from the vice-province and then went to Paris for the rest of the summer. He attended a monthlong course in pastoral ministry at the Abbey of Saint-Denis in Obourg, Belgium. Finally, in December 1964 he visited the Pius XII International Center in Rocca di Papa, Italy, where he became familiar with the Movement for a Better World, founded by Father Ricardo Lombardi.

---

83   ARSI. Ladislao Segura to superior general, San Salvador, January 20, 1963.
84   ACSI. Rutilio Grande to Marcelino Zalba, Brussels, February 24, 1964.
85   ACSI. Rutilio Grande to Flavio Grande, Brussels, July 1, 1964.

1. The Origin of His Vocation

While Rutilio was in Brussels, the superior general granted him profession as a spiritual coadjutor, and he pronounced his final vows on August 15, 1964, in the church of the Saint Michael's College. The vows were received by the rector of the college, Father Joseph Guerdavid. Before pronouncing them, Rutilio relinquished his rights to any family property, passing them over to his brothers Flavio, Joaquín, and Luis.

~

The figure of Rutilio—or Father Tilo, as he was affectionately called—aroused intense sentiments among the neighbors of El Paisnal, who had seen him grow up there and then go away to the seminary in San Salvador and finally overseas. They knew that he was one of them, but at the same time he seemed different because of his studies and his travels. He was "well educated" and "much traveled," besides being a priest. He had lived in countries that were unknown to them, he had acquired manners different from theirs, and he wore a habit or clerical dress. Despite all of these differences, they considered him a son of the town. Even though he had left El Paisnal and ascended in social and sacred rank, they had good reason to feel proud of this priest who had come forth from among the people.

Just as he had promised, Rutilio returned to El Paisnal to say his first Mass. The church was too small for the great crowd that came, which included Archbishop Chávez and several of Rutilio's seminary companions. All spoke well of Rutilio, saying he was "quite gallant," a very Salvadoran expression. That day of his first Mass had all the air of a great feast day. The whole town turned out to give him what they could of the little they had—pastries, corn, coffee, and even mangos—and to show him their affection and their pride. There were poems, fireworks, music, and something of a fashion show. After the Mass, the neighbors were treated with light refreshments, while the special guests enjoyed a meal carefully prepared by Flavio. Flavio did everything possible to make the occasion memorable. He even hired a band to enliven the meal, but Rutilio was not happy with that. He said that if the musicians did not leave he would return to San Salvador immediately. Chagrined, Flavio sent the band away before they even had an opportunity to play. The after-dinner talk lasted well into the afternoon, as the guests shared many memories of his seminary days.[86]

Rutilio always considered himself part of the people. Whenever he visited El Paisnal, he emphatically rejected any special treatment. He wanted to be accepted and treated as the same old Tilo. On one occasion, before he was a priest, he arrived unannounced at the home of a relative who at the time was cleaning the house. When she suddenly saw Tilo in his cassock, she became flustered and

---

86   Author interview with Flavio Grande, San Salvador, December 1979.

protested the unexpected visit. But he affectionately told her, "I am the same Tilo as before, and I will be the same Tilo always. Don't get upset, don't feel regrets. I am the same Tilo, the same Tilo I've always been." According to the testimony of this woman, "he did not like to be called Don Tilo or Father Tilo. No, he was just the Tilo of always." For that reason, he would eat whatever they served him; "he wasn't fussy in the least."[87] He did not like it at all when the country folk went out of their way to give him food that was different from their own. Whenever that happened, he would explain to them that he came only to share what they already had. And he would add, with a certain irony, that he did not want to be like the pastors who grew plump while others went hungry.

It was in this way that the townspeople of El Paisnal and the small farmers of Aguilares parish discovered the kind of priest and pastor Rutilio was. The older women fought among themselves to have him stay in their homes because he did not want to eat or sleep in the rectory; he preferred to ask for a place to stay in some home near the church. When the womenfolk tired of arguing about who would be favored with his visit, they agreed that they would take turns. If any of them failed to respect the agreement, Rutilio would affectionately chide them. Whenever he stayed in their homes, he would share the daily food and sleep in the same conditions as the rest of the family; he was satisfied with any accommodation and would cover himself with whatever was at hand. In his later years, he suffered much because his diabetes restricted his diet and prevented him from working excessively. The country folk learned that he could eat only boiled vegetables and drink plain coffee. He gave his brothers a copy of the diet prescribed by the doctors, but he always made an effort not to cause extra bother or unnecessary expenditure.

Despite his efforts to be close to the people, Rutilio felt that he was not sufficiently identified with them. With his typical solemnity, he addressed a vice-provincial congregation in 1974:

> I still feel myself *to a certain extent dis-identified with the great majority* of the people of our countries, though I recognize that a conversion process began within me some time ago, and I ask God that that process continue so that I can truly be faithful to my vocation as a Christian and a religious in my own element. I declare that I am not a "nationalist" in the pejorative sense of the word—far from it! I lived eight long years in Spain, and practically since age seventeen I have lived among Spaniards in tranquility and peace. But I must confess that I have lived as a *stranger* in my own land, and quite estranged from the great problems around us.[88]

---

87   Author interview with Virginia Guzmán, San Salvador, December 1979.
88   ACSI. Rutilio Grande, "Address to the Vice-provincial Congregation," San Salvador, April 1974.

2. A Vocation Built on Fragility

Rutilio was a weak, even sickly, person. Existing documentation shows that he suffered two serious nervous crises during his years of formation. These crises may have been related to poor nourishment during his childhood, because of his family's poverty, or they may also have resulted from the disintegration of his immediate family, which is only hinted at in the documentation available. Rutilio himself attributed his poor health to malnutrition, austerity of life, and excessive spiritual pressure. He always had a weak constitution, and his body was thin and gaunt. He had initially hoped that he would fill out and gain strength as the years passed, but that did not happen. Toward the end of his life, he suffered from diabetes, a disease that limited his apostolic activity.

The First Episode: A Great Cross

The first nervous crisis happened in Panama between mid-May and mid-June of 1950. When the vice-provincial paid a visit to the college, he found Rutilio in a passive state. After a while, Rutilio began to speak incoherently, and he kept raising his voice until he was silenced by some slaps. After Rutilio was admitted to a clinic, a psychiatrist diagnosed him with catatonic schizophrenia and said that he had a good prospect of recovery. In fact, Rutilio responded well to the treatment.[1] Father Garrido, his former spiritual guide in the minor seminary, attributed the crisis to "his move from studying humanities to teaching in the college in Panama, where he was overwhelmed with work; he became mentally debilitated because of his excessive diligence in helping everybody."[2] Once the worst of the crisis had passed, the vice-provincial sent him to rest at the El Carmen residence in Santa Tecla, El Salvador, where he could enjoy a more benign climate.[3]

But Rutilio was not happy with that restful residence; he felt too confined. Before long, he succeeded in getting himself assigned to the seminary. A year later, in July 1951, he informed the vice-provincial that he felt much better at the minor seminary than he had in Santa Tecla. "I receive great consolation here working with the seminarians, and that is important since this is a marvelous work."[4] He wrote that his responsibilities as prefect, his classes, and his dealings with the seminarians were "good for my health and my somewhat introverted

---

1 ACSI. Agustín Bariain to Cándido Mazón, Granada, Nicaragua, June 30, 1950; Florentino Idoate to Agustín Bariain, Panama, July 5, 1950.
2 ARSI. *Litterae consultoriae* of Santiago Garrido, San Salvador, April 14, 1951. C. América, 1005, XXI, 17.
3 ACSI. Agustín Bariain to Florentino Idoate, Granada, Nicaragua, July 6, 1950.
4 ACSI. Rutilio Grande to Agustín Bariain, San Salvador, July 8, 1950.

character, and besides, I take great natural delight in this work and enjoy doing it." Evidence for this was that he gained weight. In any case, he promised to take care of himself and specifically to take a daily siesta; experience had taught him that he should try to stay calm and to avoid anxiety and "extreme pressure, even with regard to my duties." He was not mistaken, for when he lived in the huge, remote houses of formation, his health suffered notably.

The rector of the seminary, Father Isidro Iriarte, expressed his satisfaction with Rutilio's prefecting work, stating that since his arrival "there seems to be more discipline and seriousness in the minor seminary."[5] The community consultors corroborated this judgment. Early in 1951, Father Ramón Sesma, one of the consultors, observed that Rutilio "had become disoriented in Panama"; he had been hospitalized, but "on leaving the mental hospital he arrived in Santa Tecla seven months ago, and now he is here [in the seminary] working a little. He is a young man with good qualities, but we need to take care of him."[6] The following year, the same consultor wrote that Rutilio, though "mentally disoriented for the two previous years, has happily recovered."[7] When Father Bariain, the vice-provincial, composed the memorial of his canonical visit to the seminary in 1952, he ordered that Rutilio be given an egg for breakfast and that he be allowed free access to the refrigerator between meals.[8] A third report, dated April 1951 and authored by Rutilio's former spiritual father in the minor seminary, Father Garrido, stated that Rutilio "is a young man of the finest qualities [...]. He is now doing his regency admirably here, where he had been a student before entering the Society."[9]

The vice-provincial did not altogether agree with these evaluations, however. Five days before he received Rutilio's letter of July 8, he informed the provincial of Western Castile that "it is quite likely, if not certain, that Grande will leave; he is very sluggish and strange and doesn't do the work assigned to him."[10] Two months later, his negative judgment was even stronger: "Rutilio Grande, now released from the mental hospital, is almost useless. Who knows whether he'll be able to continue?"[11] Despite these negative assessments, Rutilio did not leave the Society of Jesus.

---

5   ACSI. Isidro Iriarte to Agustín Bariain, San Salvador, August 29, 1951.
6   ARSI. *Litterae consultoris* of Ramón Sesma, San Salvador, March 30, 1952. C. América, 1003, XXIV, 7.
7   ARSI. *Litterae consultoris* of Ramón Sesma, San Salvador, March 30, 1952. C. América, 1003, XXIV, 7.
8   ACSI. Memorial of the canonical visit to the San José de la Montaña Seminary, San Salvador, March 1952.
9   ARSI. *Litterae consultoriae* of Santiago Garrido, San Salvador, April 14, 1951. C. América, 1004, XXI, 17.
10 ACSI. Agustín Bariain to Cándido Mazón, Granada, Nicaragua, July 3, 1951.
11 ACSI. Agustín Bariain to Cándido Mazón, Granada, Nicaragua, August 29, 1951.

Rutilio began his studies again in Oña, Spain, in mid-1953. Taking care of his health had again become a priority, and he knew that he could not be negligent. Some of his companions from that time remember him as being serious and withdrawn. Frequent and intense socializing was beyond his capacity. At the end of 1954, a distinguished psychiatrist from Bilbao judged Rutilio to be in good condition, but he needed adequate rest to maintain his equilibrium. Upon rising, he did fifteen minutes of methodical exercises; during the day, he took a forty-five-minute siesta; and at night he got seven mandatory hours of sleep. He did not enjoy sports and did not play them, but on the weekends he would hike in the countryside. He wrote that "these treks through the mountains relax me tremendously and leave me refreshed and ready for the week ahead." The cold weather was good for him: "It has toughened me and marvelously stimulated my appetite."[12] During vacations, he did not touch his books. By taking such steps, Rutilio was able to survive eight long years in the old Benedictine monastery of Oña, a house of formation overflowing with nearly three hundred Jesuits.

Upon finishing his philosophy studies, Rutilio was in good health and good spirits, though he expressed regret that he "could not study as much and as intensely as I wished, since I've always enjoyed studying." He had no difficulty acknowledging this limitation, for in prayer he found the strength he needed to "take things with much peace, method, and order." In fact, during the spiritual exercises he made in 1955, he wrote the following:

> I believe that I have managed to stabilize my method of prayer, and I have found a system for my spiritual life that is unifying, simple, and suited to my way of being. Almost all my attention has been focused on the problem of daily prayer. My reform had to do with that because I am quite convinced that my whole life will proceed by that rhythm.

Nevertheless, Rutilio admitted that he was carrying "a small cross, not to say a large one. [...] This is good ground for cultivating humility and conformity with God's will. Thus has he wanted it, may he be blessed forever."[13]

Early in 1956, Rutilio again reflected on his psychological weakness from the perspective of faith: "It is my cross, I'm sure of that, but I have complete confidence that with the help of God I will overcome every difficulty."[14] Rutilio was surprised by the confidence he felt and by the tranquility it produced in him, despite having to take courses that were academically less demanding:

> I'm amazed by the optimism that God grants me. In the novitiate, I often asked for a strong, heavy cross, but I never imagined that my cross would be like this. For a long time now, I have embraced it with all its consequences. I

---

12   ACSI. Rutilio Grande to Agustín Bariain, Oña, Spain, December 4, 1955.
13   ACSI. Rutilio Grande to Agustín Bariain, Oña, Spain, December 4, 1955.
14   ACSI. Rutilio Grande to Miguel Elizondo, Oña, Spain, April 9, 1956.

enjoy the studies, as I've always enjoyed them. Besides, I'm good at them, but I have to be content with mediocrity in order to be able to get through them. That causes a lot of pain. Moreover, everybody thinks I'm quite well. They see me as outwardly strong and healthy, and I take care not to complain or express my feelings, except with those who guide me.[15] I believe that in this way I please the Lord.[16]

The Second Crisis: Doubts about the Validity of His Orders

As he began his theology studies, Rutilio again received medical treatment. "As long as I'm in studies, these maladies will continue," he wrote.[17] The three years of theology were apparently stressful, as were those preceding his philosophy studies. Despite appearances, Rutilio was in a disturbed state as he was about to receive major orders, as he attested himself:

> The state of my nervous system was deplorable. I would like to have deferred the reception of major orders for some time rather than receive them in those circumstances, for I feared, and with good reason, that I would be left with some disturbance for the rest of my life.[18]

Despite Rutilio's misgivings, the rector of Oña and Father Zalba dissuaded him from postponing ordination since they saw no good reason for his doing so.

The main reason for his troubled state was his uncertainty about the validity of his minor orders. Such doubts, he wrote, "kept me distraught for a long while, especially during the time immediately prior to the reception of major orders. I was terribly tormented by the idea of receiving major orders while I was still in doubt about the validity of the minor orders I had received."[19] He was uncertain about their validity because he had received them "with doubts and internal disturbances, whose cause I explained to you [Zalba] at that time." The assurance of his spiritual guide helped him overcome the uncertainty, but the effort exhausted him.

Rutilio wrote that on the eve of his major orders "I wanted to make sure at all costs that I was serious in my intention to receive them, so that I wouldn't experience the same thing I did when I received minor orders."[20] He tried to avoid a repetition of his earlier qualms by pronouncing a formula that clearly expressed his absolute intention to receive major orders: "I freely and consciously make manifest before God that I wish to receive the major orders of subdiaconate, diaconate, and priesthood, without conditions of any kind and with any

---

15 These were Father José Julio Martínez and especially Father Marcelino Zalba.
16 ACSI. Rutilio Grande to Miguel Elizondo, Oña, Spain, April 9, 1956.
17 ACSI. Rutilio Grande to Miguel Elizondo, Oña, Spain, April 9, 1956.
18 ACSI. Rutilio Grande to Marcelino Zalba, Brussels, February 24, 1964.
19 ACSI. Rutilio Grande to Marcelino Zalba, Brussels, February 24, 1964.
20 ACSI. Rutilio Grande to Marcelino Zalba, Brussels, February 24, 1964.

2. A Vocation Built on Fragility

supposition, even the supposition that by receiving them I was committing some clear sin, *even a formal one*."[21]

Father Zalba told Rutilio not to use the word "formal" but rather the phrase "he might have received them illicitly," because it was more appropriate given his personal situation. Even that advice did not tranquilize him. He wrote that Zalba had given him "a brief and somewhat indecisive response that seemed to me affirmative, but I was frankly left with doubts about it since shortly before that he had told me to suppress that word and replace it with others."[22] Since Rutilio wanted to preserve at all costs the word "formal" in the formula, he continued to explain: "The father has approved the following wording in the formula: '[…] even if by receiving them I were to commit some kind of sin […].' Therefore, […] the idea of formal sin is already implicit in those words approved by the father."[23] But he was immediately assaulted by doubts, thinking it likely that Zalba had not grasped the exact content of the formula "since I had read it to him and he hadn't read it for himself. There was that possibility."

When the day of the subdiaconate ordination arrived, Rutilio was still afflicted by these misgivings. He wondered whether he should consult with Zalba again about the formula or simply proceed on his own, which would mean including the word "formal." That night, during his examination of conscience, he confessed to Zalba but without mentioning his speculations. After his final visit to the Blessed Sacrament and before going to bed, he wrote, "I was tired and tense, but I sat down to write out again the definitive formula, introducing the change that [Zalba] told me to include, without daring for the moment to reinsert the word *formal*."[24] But even that did not leave him tranquil: "No matter how much I turned the matter over in my head, I did not know what to do." Since it was very late, he did not want to seek out Father Zalba. Several times the next day he looked for him in his room but did not find him: "Finally, after many misgivings and doubts, I added the following phrase to the formula: I also declare before God that I wish to receive the major orders, even on the supposition that by receiving them I was committing some kind of sin, even *one that was serious and formal*."[25] That phrase, which he added in order to find peace, became a source of new misgivings.

When the time of the ordination ceremony finally arrived, Rutilio presented himself in the church with the original formula, but he had the added phrase in the breast pocket of his habit. He wrote: "I was experiencing doubts and internal worries. On the one hand, such doubts and worries seemed to me to be scruples that I had to drive way; on the other, they seemed to me to be not scruples but

---

21   ACSI. Rutilio Grande to Marcelino Zalba, Brussels, February 24, 1964.
22   ACSI. Rutilio Grande to Marcelino Zalba, Brussels, February 24, 1964.
23   ACSI. Rutilio Grande to Marcelino Zalba, Brussels, February 24, 1964.
24   ACSI. Rutilio Grande to Marcelino Zalba, Brussels, February 24, 1964.
25   ACSI. Rutilio Grande to Marcelino Zalba, Brussels, February 24, 1964.

reasonable doubts and proddings of my conscience."[26] After mumbling an act of contrition, which left him even more distraught, he muttered another and then a third, but he could find no peace. He felt that he was actually admitting to himself the serious sinfulness of the added phrase:

> With such acts of contrition I was suppressing that phrase in my mind and in my heart, so that in the end my intention to be ordained was no longer absolute. These and other similar thoughts were going and coming within me, and I was besieged by these thoughts and worries even while receiving the subdiaconate.[27]

Still, he did not go to Zalba but rather tried to calm himself with arguments in favor of the phrase. It was in that doubtful and tormented state that he also received the orders of diaconate and priesthood.

Rutilio's doubts about whether he truly had the absolute intention to receive major orders persisted and gave rise to further anxiety and uncertainty. He dissembled and bore with the distress until he decided to speak with Zalba. After listening patiently to Rutilio's prolix exposition, Zalba told him in concise terms that there was no reason for him to be concerned, and he took from him the draft of the formula. However, Rutilio kept the original, the one he had placed in the pocket of his habit, until the end of his tertianship in August 1962, when he finally tore it up. He wrote that "my tearing it up was an incredible feat," but he insisted that he did it because "I was sick and tired of letting it torment me."[28]

Normally, Rutilio would have done his tertianship right after finishing his fourth year of theology, but his superiors considered that his precarious health warranted a break in his formation process. He was consequently assigned again to the seminary in San Salvador, where he arrived quite exhausted.[29] The renewed activity allowed Rutilio to recover his strength, but his superiors remained concerned. The vice-provincial, Father Luis Achaerandio, after consulting with the rector of the seminary, Father Ladislao Segura, informed the superior general that "there are well-founded fears that a regime of recollection and introspection, as in a house of tertianship, would return him to the state he was in during much of his formation, one of dangerous fatigue and even exhaustion."[30] The vice-provincial accordingly asked that an exception be made and that Rutilio be allowed to make his tertianship in one of the houses of the vice-province, specifically in the seminary itself, after making the thirty-day retreat in the novitiate, which at the time was in the residence of the church of El Carmen. The request was denied.

---

26   ACSI. Rutilio Grande to Marcelino Zalba, Brussels, February 24, 1964.
27   ACSI. Rutilio Grande to Marcelino Zalba, Brussels, February 24, 1964.
28   ACSI. Rutilio Grande to Marcelino Zalba, Brussels, February 24, 1964.
29   ACSI. Ladislao Segura to superior general, San Salvador, July 18, 1960.
30   ACSI. Luis Achaerandio to superior general, Rome, July 18, 1960.

That proposal did not come from Rutilio, who the vice-provincial said was a "very good religious and has not asked for this exception, quite the contrary."[31] As the year 1962 began, Rutilio felt concerned that his superiors had not sent him to tertianship: "I arrived at this seminary at the end of July 1960 planning to stay just one year, which is now finished. I don't see that those higher up have any great interest in sending me to tertianship."[32] The probable reason for the caution of "those higher up" was that they felt that tertianship would "compromise the recovery of his weak psychic health. That is why he has still not made his tertianship."[33]

Since the superior general had refused the vice-provincial's request, Rutilio was sent to Europe to do his tertianship. He was able to take advantage of this journey to visit seminaries on the continent and to spend some months at the Lumen Vitae International Institute of Catechesis and Pastoral Ministry. In view of the excellent work Rutilio had done during his regency, the vice-provincial decided to assign him permanently to the seminary of San Salvador. The seminary rector, Segura, assured him that "a great role is awaiting you here," since he had been "a magnificent prefect."[34] The vice-provincial considered that, by studying at Lumen Vitae, Rutilio "could enhance and develop his fine qualities." At the same time, he did not want Rutilio to be subject to a demanding academic regime, which he feared "would be dangerously exhausting" for him.[35]

Meanwhile, Rutilio had already demonstrated that he benefited from being given responsibilities and challenges since they prevented him from becoming isolated:

> Things went quite well for me in my country during the two years I spent in the Interdiocesan Seminary of San Salvador. I got along very well with Father Segura, who was then rector of the seminary. I acted as prefect of discipline and at the same time gave various classes. That type of life, filled with work and responsibility, helped me in every way.[36]

For that reason, he wrote, "I arrived [for the tertianship program] with some fears about the danger that a very recluded, recollected life might mean for me. Even with my ups and my downs, I made my way through the test."[37]

---

31   ACSI. Luis Achaerandio to superior general, Rome, July 18, 1960.
32   ARSI. Rutilio Grande to superior general, San Salvador, February 1, 1962. C. América, 1005, XXVI.
33   ACSI. Ladislao Segura to the vicar general, San Salvador, March 27, 1961.
34   ARSI. Ladislao Segura to superior general, San Salvador, January 20, 1963. C. América, 1006, III.
35   ACSI. Luis Achaerandio to superior general, Rome, July 18, 1960.
36   ACSI. Rutilio Grande to Marcelino Zalba, Brussels, February 24, 1964.
37   ACSI. Rutilio Grande to Marcelino Zalba, Brussels, February 24, 1964.

During the month of spiritual exercises, Rutilio decided to write to Zalba a careful and detailed account of his state of soul. He had tried to do the same in San Salvador, but the intense activity of the seminary had prevented him doing so. He did not do it during tertianship either, but only on February 24, 1964, after moving to Brussels.

Doubts about the Priesthood

Taking precautions, he asked Zalba to be easy on him since "I have decided to tell you […] in writing something about which you already know. Be patient with me."[38] The structure and the tone of the long letter made it plain that doubts were tormenting its author. He consequently made an effort to be thorough and precise. The eight pages were, he confessed, "redacted and retouched several times." He began the letter by giving a brief presentation of his situation and his activity since leaving Oña, so that Zalba would have a clear understanding of the man he was dealing with. In order to have complete certainty about what he had written, Rutilio made a careful comparison of the final copy with the draft, noting in the margins the changes he had made. At the end of the letter, he added fourteen propositions by way of synthesis, to make it easier for Zalba to understand his argument. At the last minute, he also included the formula he recited and the added phrase. Although he did not have the original copies, which he had torn up in a bold moment of courage, he was morally certain that he had reproduced the exact text. Finally, he asked Zalba "very sincerely" to return his letter with his response: "Don't forget (that is, if you don't want to kill me or drive me mad)." We do not know if Zalba returned the letter; most likely he did not because only the draft was found among Rutilio's papers.

The day after he had sent the letter, Rutilio wrote again to Zalba because he had forgotten to mention a miniscule detail. He was anxious "not to have any conflicts afterward, since my spiritual condition with regard to orders is such that almost anything upsets me."[39] The detail in question was that he had forgotten to draw a red arrow on the envelope to insure that Zalba was the active recipient and to avoid "its being opened, even by accident, by the Father Rector of the Gregorian."[40] Since Rutilio did not know Zalba's exact whereabouts, he inserted the envelope containing the first letter into another, larger envelope, which he addressed to the rector of the Gregorian University. He also enclosed a note asking the rector to deliver the sealed envelope to Zalba if he was in Rome or to forward it to his proper address. The problem was not that the rector would read the letter:

---

38   ACSI. Rutilio Grande to Marcelino Zalba, Brussels, February 24, 1964.
39   ACSI. Rutilio Grande to Marcelino Zalba, Brussels, March 12, 1964. Thus, he kept the first letter for more than two weeks before mailing it.
40   ACSI. Rutilio Grande to Marcelino Zalba, Brussels, March 12, 1964.

Rather, I felt true panic at the thought that, were he to open the letter by accident, thinking it was for him, he would then mix the pages up. When he realized the letter was for you, he might fold them up again the wrong way so that they would reach your hands in disarray and be unintelligible.[41]

Rutilio had in fact been very careful in folding the pages of his letter "so that the creases would not prevent you from reading the lines or words that fell precisely on the creases."[42]

Rutilio's peace of soul depended on his being convinced that Zalba had understood clearly the contents of his long letter, so carefully thought out. He wanted there to be no ambiguity in the response as a result of inexact or inadequate comprehension. Rutilio therefore insisted:

When you answer my letter, tell me whether the sealed envelope arrived in your hands with all the pages in order and whether you were able to read the pages well despite the creases. And above all, I ask you again very sincerely that, when you respond, you return to me those eight pages, which I will keep along with your reply. The fact of receiving those pages back, after you have read them, will produce in me the corresponding effects of certainty, etc.[43]

Rutilio was aware that, for Zalba, "all this will appear ridiculous. I beg you to have patience and compassion, and to let me tell you all this" because

you are the only one in whom I have confided regarding this matter. I have not confided and would not dare to confide in any other person. I confide in you despite the good reprimands and rebukes you gave me on many occasions there in Oña. I trust completely in you.[44]

For Rutilio, it was crucial to be able to speak to and to be heard by someone whom he could trust completely because his doubts were calling into question nothing less than the great ideal of his life, his priestly vocation:

Believe me, Father Zalba, I sometimes lose my patience, and I have even asked myself, not without a shudder, whether it would not be better for me to leave the religious life and the exercise of priestly ministry so that I can find the inner peace to which every person has a right. I need to become more integrated psychologically. Doubting about the priesthood is the cruelest torture possible for one who loves his vocation and the priesthood itself as the great ideal of his life. Such doubt disintegrates the very essence of one's innermost self. And naturally, if the doubt is not resolved, the situation

---

41 ACSI. Rutilio Grande to Marcelino Zalba, Brussels, March 12, 1964.
42 ACSI. Rutilio Grande to Marcelino Zalba, Brussels, March 12, 1964.
43 ACSI. Rutilio Grande to Marcelino Zalba, Brussels, March 12, 1964.
44 ACSI. Rutilio Grande to Marcelino Zalba, Brussels, February 24, 1964.

would be unbearable for me in the long run, and it could expose me to dangers of which I now have no inkling.[45]

While awaiting the response that he hoped would restore his peace of mind, he wrote that "I very sincerely entrusted this matter to the Lord this morning, through the intercession of our great saints, Ignatius and Xavier."

The cause of Rutilio's malaise and unhappiness was the same: it was

> the idea that those doubts or disturbances, which were born of the fear of sinning gravely and which I experienced while receiving each of the three major orders, might have diminished, obscured, or simply annulled my intention to be ordained, with the result that those major orders would be invalid or at least doubtful. This has been my problem from the beginning, and it continues to be my problem now.[46]

The months that had passed since the ordination, the assurance that Zalba sought to give him, and Rutilio's subsequent experiences had been of little help: "I must confess that I have not been able to pry out of my soul those doubts and anxieties, which sometimes bother me intensely and cause me tremendous suffering."

The validity of his orders was not Rutilio's only worry. He wrote Zalba that, when speaking to him, "I did not do it with the serenity, exactness, and precision required for such a serious matter. And judging that this is the cause of my present doubts and anxieties, I have decided to put all this *in writing*." He thus emphasized the importance of a correct understanding of his exposition. In his eagerness to attain the exactness and precision desired, Rutilio underlined in red the words that Zalba had previously, before the ordination, proposed that he use instead of the word "formal." He also traced a vertical red line in the margin to designate the unrevised formula, and he underlined in red "the two tremendous words": "grave and formal."[47]

But now Rutilio was not sure whether he had really written "grave" in the added phrase, since he had wavered before the ordination ceremony: "Although I understood well that grave, material, and formal sin was sufficiently expressed in the words 'any class of sin, including formal,' I wanted to make it even more explicit and concrete by adding the word 'grave.'"[48]

By that time, he had no way to overcome his doubts since he had torn up the text. In any case, he wrote,

> I have no doubt that, when writing and adding that phrase to the formula, my intention was to make it clear that I wanted to receive major orders

---

45 ACSI. Rutilio Grande to Marcelino Zalba, Brussels, March 12, 1964.
46 ACSI. Rutilio Grande to Marcelino Zalba, Brussels, February 24, 1964.
47 ACSI. Rutilio Grande to Marcelino Zalba, Brussels, February 24, 1964.
48 ACSI. Rutilio Grande to Marcelino Zalba, Brussels, February 24, 1964.

even under the supposition that by receiving them I would be committing a grave, material, and formal sin.[49]

The word "phrase" also caused him difficulties. By "phrase," he understood the lines added to the formula, but he did not know whether that usage was technically correct:

> The problem consists in knowing whether I, when receiving the three major orders, adhered truly and completely to the spirit and the letter of that phrase added to the formula, or whether, to the contrary, I ended up expressing my intention conditionally under the pressure of the doubts and disturbances aroused by said formula added to the formula.[50]

Rutilio "earnestly begged" Zalba to "respond, taking on complete responsibility and *onerata sua conscientia* [binding himself in conscience]. I will abide by your decision with the help of God." Although Rutilio was well aware that his interlocutor had considered this question already resolved in Oña, the malaise and worry he was experiencing left him no alternative. "Forgive me for being such a nuisance, Father. It is painful and tragic when what one has loved and still loves with the whole of one's life has become a source of torment!"[51]

Zalba's response, dated March 15, 1964, arrived four days later in the hands of Rutilio, who responded promptly:

> When I arrived at Lumen Vitae this morning, I found it [your letter] in my mailbox, and imagine, I didn't open it immediately but waited until I returned to the college to eat. It is true that during the classes […] my imagination went wild. The fact is, we had classes today even though it is the feast of Saint Joseph.[52]

Although Zalba's letter was not found among Rutilio's papers, we can deduce from Rutilio's response that Zalba did not deal with his arguments. His style must have been direct and to the point: "You are careful not to involve yourself in argumentation and reasoning. That is good, I think, because otherwise I would get even more muddled."[53]

Apparently, Zalba reprimanded Rutilio for not having sought him out before the ordination. Rutilio responded to this criticism with a synthesis of his letter of February 24. He cited section 8, where he wrote that "however that may be, the truth is that I am not having a second talk with Father Zalba"; he then

---

49   ACSI. Rutilio Grande to Marcelino Zalba, Brussels, February 24, 1964.
50   ACSI. Rutilio Grande to Marcelino Zalba, Brussels, February 24, 1964.
51   ACSI. Rutilio Grande to Marcelino Zalba, Brussels, February 24, 1964.
52   ACSI. Rutilio Grande to Marcelino Zalba, Brussels, n.d. At the top of the first page is written the word "faithful," meaning that the copy was faithful to the original, which he kept in his files.
53   ACSI. Rutilio Grande to Marcelino Zalba, Brussels, n.d.

immediately explained that the words "however that may be" meant "for one reason or another." He conceded, however, that "it is also true that I could have made a greater effort to look for you in all the places where you might be." In reality, Rutilio appeared to have no good explanation for this oversight: "I certainly cannot state anything definite one way or the other."[54]

In his response, Zalba objected that, either on the day of the priestly ordination or the day after, Rutilio had been evasive when he came to Zalba to ask for a permission (Zalba was prefect of theologians at the time). He asked Rutilio whether things had gone better for him than when he received minor orders. Rutilio tried to explain his evasiveness at that time by saying that he had not answered Zalba's question because it seemed to have been made "in passing or just casually." Now he saw that he should have answered honestly:

> On that occasion, I was walking in with the procession and was certainly very worried, but I gave you a quick, evasive answer, deliberately dissembling and obscuring the reality. As you see, I was reluctant to discuss the problem that certainly was there. In what I wrote on those eight pages I made no mention of that brief talk with you.[55]

Nor did Rutilio make mention of the situation to Father José Antonio Ezcurdia, who had mediated between the two of them "in the laborious matter of the major orders." Moreover, when Zalba took the draft of the formula away from Rutilio, during the final conversation they had in Oña, Rutilio had not told him that he was keeping the original copy.

These indications show, objectively, that Rutilio had not only failed to obey but that he had also concealed facts. But the matter is even more complicated, as Rutilio explained: "I never doubt or question your decisions, but I confess that I often doubt and question the way I explain my problems since what you determine one way or another depends on my explanation. If I recall correctly, I spoke to you about this already on other occasions."[56] Rutilio needed to be completely certain that he had given clear expression to his thoughts and feelings, and he needed to be certain that he had been understood correctly. His lack of certainty, he felt, greatly limited him, and it was, in large measure, the cause of the uncertainties that were tormenting him: "My difficulty is not in blind obedience, but it [the obedience] has to be after I have said everything that I judge it is necessary to say. My difficulty is precisely in explaining my business correctly and clearly in its essence and in its form."[57] Evidence of his predicament is the fact that in this third letter he re-sent the eight pages of February 24, since Zalba had alluded to

---

54 ACSI. Rutilio Grande to Marcelino Zalba, Brussels, n.d.
55 ACSI. Rutilio Grande to Marcelino Zalba, Brussels, n.d.
56 ACSI. Rutilio Grande to Marcelino Zalba, Brussels, n.d.
57 ACSI. Rutilio Grande to Marcelino Zalba, Brussels, n.d.

them; moreover, with a red pen he numbered in the left margin the lines he had cited so that they could be found more easily. He also added the words that might have been hard to read in the original because of the creases. Finally, he asked Zalba to return to him the eleven pages of this third letter:

> And so, Father Zalba, I finish with difficulty, leaving everything in your hands. You will tell me whether, in view of the explanations in this long letter, you have anything new to determine or decide, anything new to declare. Otherwise, I will abide by the declaration you sent me in your letter of March 15.[58]

Among the documents related to this matter, which were carefully filed in a folder marked "Case of Conscience," there was no response from Zalba, perhaps because he did not answer Rutilio's letter.

At the end of December 1964, Rutilio wrote from Italy to a Jesuit in Brussels to tell him, in confidence, that when Rutilio had occasionally confessed to him, the Jesuit had recited the words *Deinde ego te absolvo in nomine Patris et Filii et Spiritus Sancti* (I therefore absolve you in the name of the Father and the Son and the Holy Spirit), omitting from the formula of absolution the words *peccatis tuis* (of your sins). Rutilio thought that it would be good to make him aware of this omission since it might be a common practice.[59]

Learning to Live with Weakness

Rutilio was known for his fragile health, which placed a limit on what he could achieve humanly and apostolically. There are sufficient data to indicate that his personality showed schizoid traits, which were heightened especially when his environment isolated him from the larger world or induced passivity in him. His inordinate desire for excellence and perfection, combined with a compulsive and obsessive scrupulosity, made him pass through periods of distress and anxiety. His desire to please everybody, his extreme concern with appearances, and his fear of looking bad in public, especially in difficult situations, provoked in him uncertainty, nervousness, and anguish; these in turn exhausted him and plunged him into paralyzing crises. When such episodes occurred, Rutilio would physically withdraw, speak little, become unresponsive, and appear worried and fatigued. In some of his darkest moments, he even questioned his priestly vocation.

Rutilio's reserved nature and his difficulty in forming friendships were only accentuated by his personal crises and any external conflict. It was "difficult to be friends with him," stated Father Salvador Carranza, one of the Jesuits who was very close to him and formed part of the missionary team in the parish

---

58   ACSI. Rutilio Grande to Marcelino Zalba, Brussels, n.d.
59   ACSI. Rutilio Grande to Jaime Artajo, Rome, December 22, 1964.

of Aguilares. Carranza described Rutilio as having "an affective nature that was secondary and not too active; he was rather contemplative, very imaginative, and given to colorful expression. He was hesitant in his speech and very circumspect in what he said."[60] Rutilio was generally patient and considerate of others, but at times he showed signs of irritability; they were quite rare, to be sure, but very intense. He overreacted to things that others considered trivial, and the frustrations and frictions of everyday life could sometimes cause him to explode. Sometimes, also, he felt an acute need for the affection of a particular person.

These expressions of emotion were often not true reflections of Rutilio's state of soul, which varied depending on his health and psychological condition. "His personal character," wrote Carranza, " is affected by his health and causes his moods to fluctuate in ways that perplex those around him."[61] Rutilio was well aware of his rapid changes in mood and his contradictory states of soul, and these conditions caused him great suffering and physical exhaustion.

Rutilio's excessive desire for perfection, his need for almost total certainty, and his extreme emotional sensibility made him stubborn, irascible, and indecisive to the point of paralysis—completely contrary to his aspirations. He remained angry for a long time whenever he had serious clashes with the more politicized groups in the parish. It is also true that these incidents were in large measure due to misunderstandings between him and the lay leaders.

Critical matters requiring bold decisions caused Rutilio to vacillate when he was pastor of Aguilares. Novelty, especially when unexpected, provoked in him more uncertainty and fear than he could manage. Thus, while he welcomed the changes in the church and the Society during the 1960s and 1970s, he was troubled by the abandonment of custom and tradition. His unease was due in large measure, it seems, to his inability to reconcile the novelties of those decades with his nearly obsessive fidelity to the church—and concretely to the Salvadoran hierarchy, the nuncio, and the Society of Jesus. His malaise is illustrated in his listing of the irregularities he found in the seminary communities at the beginning of 1962:

> In the year and a half I have been in this house, I have noticed that the scholastics doing their regency here are not accustomed to doing the traditional monthly retreat with its customary practices: a talk by the spiritual father, a practical examination of conscience, and a period of meditation in addition to that of the morning.[62]

In 1968, he also observed, with a certain disquiet, that the major seminarians were no longer putting flowers in the chapel, which was once a common

---

60 ACSI. Salvador Carranza, report *ad gobernandum*, San Salvador, May 23, 1976.
61 ACSI. Salvador Carranza, report *ad gobernandum*, San Salvador, June 19, 1976.
62 ARSI. Rutilio Grande to superior general, San Salvador, February 1, 1962. C. América, 1005, XXVI.

practice whereby the seminarians would collect money among themselves to buy the flowers.[63]

However, whenever Rutilio did make a decision, he proceeded to act, and he did so resolutely and effectively. In other matters, he let people do as they wished, even when he disagreed with them. He never manifested publicly his differences with the other Jesuits on the missionary team or with the lay collaborators of the parish. On the contrary, due to his heightened sense of responsibility, he would defend their activities as much as he would his own.

Occasionally, internal tensions would place Rutilio in awkward situations that were quite disagreeable. One such situation was the 1974 vice-provincial congregation, which caused him some distress. "When he spoke, he was a bit disjointed and irritated," commented Father Segura, his former rector in the seminary; "At the vice-provincial's request, I intervened in a friendly way to calm his impetuousness."[64] In such situations, Rutilio would write freely about his feelings, opinions, and judgments, but he would reach a moment when all his thinking and reflection about the various elements and angles of a conflict left him exhausted. He would then use neither rhetoric nor redundancy in his declarations; the texts he wrote in that state were marked by an almost brutal frankness. For Rutilio, such an exercise was a necessary outlet, and he honestly and humbly recognized it as such. At the same time, he was very conscious of the need to tone down his overly personal statements and assessments, and he did so in friendly, tranquil conversations with his companions and superiors.

Despite his weaknesses and limitations, the Jesuits who knew him well, especially his superiors, agreed that Rutilio had "extraordinary apostolic and pastoral gifts not lessened by [those weakness and limitations]. He knows how to bear his cross interiorly, and it is only by living with him or talking with him personally that the depths of his personality are revealed."[65] Rutilio was undoubtedly a charismatic pastor, and one of his most outstanding pastoral talents was his preaching. His homilies bore witness to his faith in the God of Jesus Christ and to his total commitment to the Salvadoran people. His starting point was always the historical reality of his country, what was actually happening at the moment. From there, he advanced toward Jesus Christ and toward the people. In denouncing injustice, his speech was vibrant, firm, and unyielding; in announcing God's reign, it was brimming with hope and joy. All his preaching was in a language that was very Salvadoran. His homilies were full of picturesque popular expressions that drew especially on the realities of country life.

---

63 ACSI. Rutilio Grande, "Some Experiences and Suggestions," San Salvador, November 3, 1968.
64 ACSI. Ladislao Segura, report *ad gobernandum*, San Salvador, June 19, 1976.
65 ACSI. Salvador Carranza, report *ad gobernandum*, San Salvador, May 23, 1976.

The rector of the seminary, Father Segura, reported that in his work Rutilio was responsible, sociable, and creative although his tendency to be perfectionist sometimes caused problems.[66] In the early 1960s, Segura reported that Rutilio, serving as prefect in both major and minor seminaries, had been "magnificent" and had done his work "extremely well."[67] Discipline in the major seminary was good "thanks to the diligence and good sense of its prefect."[68] Being prefect was not an easy job at all, and it was complicated by the lack of an updated code of conduct and by "the many practical difficulties for discipline due to the coexistence in the same building" of the two seminaries.[69] In fact, during those years the seminary experienced a rapid turnover of prefects, partly for the reasons mentioned and partly because the persons named were not well qualified.

Besides being prefect of the two seminaries, Rutilio worked as seminary secretary and as professor during 1961. Given the number of jobs Rutilio had, the rector feared that "his fragile health might be affected by so much work and responsibility."[70] In 1970, toward the end of his time in the seminary, when Rutilio was prefect of the theology students, the vice-provincial, Father Segundo Azcue, wrote that he had "great intelligence and understood what the seminary should be like."[71] The rector of the seminary similarly asserted that "he knows the students well, he gets along well with the priests and bishops, and he has a good command of the daily routines of the seminary."[72] At the same time, Azcue said, "some feared for his health. In times past, he had to interrupt his studies because of the condition of his nerves, but he has been working many years without any repetition of those crises."[73]

During the 1971 academic year, which he spent at the Colegio Externado San José, Rutilio worked as secretary, technical director, dean of studies, prefect of discipline, and spiritual guide for the older students, and he left the same positive impression: "He accomplished well the tasks assigned to him."[74] According to one Jesuit with much experience, Rutilio stood out at the schools for his balanced judgments when deciding on the expulsion of a student or when dealing with problems with the faculty. He was also much appreciated by many of the students, and this was the case even though that year was a very difficult one for him: he felt like a "bird of passage" at the Colegio Externado since it was not the right place for him. He had gone to the school only reluctantly, and that year was one of disenchantment and discontent.

---

66 ACSI. Ladislao Segura, report *ad gobernandum*, San Salvador, June 19, 1976.
67 ACSI. Ladislao Segura to superior general, San Salvador, January 27, 1962.
68 ACSI. Ladislao Segura to superior general, San Salvador, July 10, 1961.
69 ACSI. Ladislao Segura to superior general, San Salvador, January 27, 1962.
70 ACSI. Ladislao Segura to the vicar general, San Salvador, March 27, 1961.
71 ACSI. Segundo Azcue to superior general, San Salvador, September 15, 1969.
72 ACSI. José Ignacio Scheifler to superior general, San Salvador, July 7, 1970.
73 ACSI. Segundo Azcue to superior general, San Salvador, September 15, 1969.
74 ACSI. Benigno Achaerandio, report *ad gobernandum*, San Salvador, May 22, 1976.

2. A Vocation Built on Fragility

Jesuits who knew Rutilio all agree that at the personal level he was an exquisite human being. He showed concern for those who sought him out and attended to their needs; he listened to people attentively and with sympathy, and he always followed up. He exercised a certain leadership among the diocesan clergy and also among the Jesuit scholastics from Central America. Rutilio knew how to earn the confidence and appreciation of others, "although one always detected in him an enigmatic quality that was difficult to decipher."[75]

For that reason, and despite Rutilio's limitations, superiors placed him in positions of responsibility. He was community consultor of the seminary in 1960–61, community consultor of the Colegio Externado in 1971, auxiliary consultor of the vice-province from April 17, 1967, to June 22, 1970, coordinator of the area of pastoral ministry for the province, secretary of the national council of Jesuits of El Salvador, and secretary of the priests' senate of the archdiocese. His last provincial, Father Jerez, considered him fit to be the superior of either a small community or a residence dedicated to pastoral ministry:

> He is a simple man and a very good religious. He has a special charism for pastoral work and is close to the rural folk. He has the makings of a leader. He has great affection for the church and the Society. He has a tendency to depression, perhaps for reasons of health. Sometimes he has bad moments, and then he is fine. His influence is considerable, and he is able to put together a pioneer team for the work. He is very austere, and he is brave in confronting the powerful of this world. There are moments when he seems to get obsessed for whatever reason.[76]

Rutilio was never made a superior because no new residence or small community was opened in those years. All the same, the *ad gobernandum* reports written by the Jesuits who knew him gave a positive portrayal of Rutilio in the years before his death.

Rutilio learned to accept himself with all his weaknesses and limitations. During the spiritual exercises he made at the end of 1966, he asked for the grace to be able to accept himself as he was because "such is the very clear will of God."[77] He therefore resolved never to give in to pusillanimity or cowardice but to work "like a dog, because my present situation is the best possible, since God wants it so." He realized that he should not fear failure or a life of obscurity. He promised not to be perfectionist but to "learn to swim by swimming." Such resolutions reveal a good degree of self-acceptance, which for him meant not depending on the esteem, the affection, or the appreciation of others. Instead, he felt moved to "quash from the start every purely natural sentiment of delight and satisfaction that the ego might cherish" and to hand himself over without reserve

---

75   ACSI. Salvador Carranza, report *ad gobernandum*, San Salvador, May 23, 1976.
76   ACSI. César Jerez, report *ad gobernandum*, San Salvador, September 17, 1976.
77   ACSI. Rutilio Grande, "Notes on the Spiritual Exercises," San Salvador, November 1966.

to the Father, adopting "an attitude that is willing, even at the human level, to undertake anything without foolish fears." Only then would he be able to achieve "full and constant execution, with saving of time." But to that end, he thought, "how much I need to forget myself!"[78]

Abandoning his fears, his weaknesses, his need to feel secure, Rutilio was left defenseless before Jesus Christ, who was "definitely all that was left to me." Upon reaching this point, the only thing he could do was surrender himself confidently into the hands of the Father of Jesus, even though he might fail and be subject to criticism and reproach:

> For one reason or another, God may want a person to live a hidden life that is a failure at the human level, but it is not necessarily a complete failure for the glory of God. *Always, but especially in these moments of future ??? Confidence in God my Father who guides everything for my good.*[79]

Rutilio had good reasons for placing his confidence in his Father, for

> Christ always waits for us and stays by our side; he always welcomes us with wide open arms and heart; he always understands; he always forgives unhesitatingly (the only difficulty on my part is the lack of sincerity and confidence); he always consoles; for his part he always fulfills, he always encourages, he never fails, he is never in the least bit unfaithful. And all this with the efficacy of God.[80]

---

78 Grande, "Notes on the Spiritual Exercises."
79 Grande, "Notes on the Spiritual Exercises."
80 Grande, "Notes on the Spiritual Exercises."

3. San José de la Montaña Seminary

Rutilio rejoined the staff of the seminary in 1965, once again serving as professor and prefect of discipline. Much influenced by the theology of Vatican II, he introduced new subjects, methods, and activities that were greatly appreciated by the seminarians.

During 1965 and 1966, Rutilio was prefect of the theology students, and in 1967 he was made prefect of both seminaries. In 1966, he began serving as secretary of the seminary and also directed the pastoral experiences of the seminarians. In his final two years at the seminary, 1969 and 1970, he continued as prefect of the two seminaries. He initially resisted remaining in the post but finally acceded because, he explained, "I can see that direct and unified action are important for efficacy and dynamism."[1]

Rutilio initially taught classes of catechesis and liturgy; subsequently he taught Latin, history, religion, and civics in the minor seminary, and in the major seminary pastoral theology and an introduction to the mystery of Christ. Teaching the social sciences especially appealed to him. It was an area in which he felt secure and knowledgeable, so much so that later, when he was asked what he would do if he ever left the Society of Jesus, he answered that he would teach social sciences; after all, he had a degree qualifying him to teach them in secondary schools.[2]

Father Prefect

The prefect of the seminary, according to Rutilio, had to combine discipline with respect for the students; he should promote honesty and integrity rather than hypocrisy, which was a constant danger in a disciplinary system that encouraged obedience. Without neglecting discipline, therefore, Rutilio sought to cultivate personal and collective responsibility. "He taught those of us who were his students," declared Cardinal Gregorio Rosa Chávez in his testimony, "to try to be coherent and clear, without seeking applause."[3] Rutilio constantly strove to create an ambience of less surveillance and more responsibility, especially for those seminarians who proved to be mature and serious. He never put up with mediocrity, however, and so was inclined to expel those who were simply too immature or too stubborn.

The job of prefect was not easy, as was clear from the large number of Jesuits who held the post in both seminaries. What added to the difficulty, especially for

---

1 ACSI. Rutilio Grande, notes, n.d.
2 ACSI. Ministries Commission. Technical Group, survey of Rutilio Grande, San Salvador, 1976.
3 *Summarium testium*, witness 5, §64.

someone like Rutilio, was the lack of a fixed set of rules, as he explained to the superior general:

> A set of rules has in fact been approved, [...] but it has fallen into disuse since the present rector took office. The rules are basically acceptable, and it would be necessary to correct only a few minor things. In other words, at the present moment we are effectively without rules. As prefect of discipline, I am perfectly aware of the disadvantages that ensue.[4]

Despite the difficulties, Rutilio had clear ideas about how to function as prefect. He attempted to balance freedom and authority, kindness and rigor, and he established different levels and modalities for each stage of the formation process, in accord with the maturity of the seminarians. In 1961, some Jesuits in the seminary community expressed the view that Rutilio was very authoritarian in his way of proceeding, but the rector, Father Segura, did not share this opinion. The criticism arose from a few cases of abuse of confidence, something Rutilio did not tolerate.[5]

Without innovating unduly or repressing obsessively, Rutilio used prudence in dealing with tobacco, radio, cinema, and other matters contrary to the rule. Nothing shocked him, and he always strove to be moderate in the measures he took. His views on the wearing of the habit provides a good example. Archbishop José Alfonso Belloso had made the practice obligatory for all seminarians; he did so contrary to canon law, which required it only of clergy. As a result, for years the seminarians had worn the habit all day long: in the classroom, in the dining room, and at community activities. Rutilio and the rector, however, considered the practice problematic because of its costliness, its impracticality, and its tendency to make the seminarians careless about personal hygiene. They agreed that the habit should be worn only on solemn occasions.

As master of ceremonies, Rutilio taught the seminarians how to prepare each liturgical act with great care, down to the most insignificant details. The altar was to be properly arranged and well ornamented. The vestments and the sacred vessels were to be prepared and set in their proper place. The music and the choir were to be well tuned and well rehearsed. Rutilio was also responsible for organizing the solemn feasts in the cathedral—the patronal feast of August 6; the Te Deum of September 15, the national independence day; and the day of the pope—and he rehearsed the liturgies several times with the seminarians to be sure that they came out perfect. All liturgies, especially those in the cathedral, were to be diligently prepared so that their performance was correct and precise. On the solemn feasts, Rutilio made an effort to explain to the faithful each step of the liturgy so that they would better understand its meaning.

---

4   ACSI. Rutilio Grande to superior general, San Salvador, February 1, 1962.
5   ACSI. Ladislao Segura to archbishops and bishops of the ecclesiastical province of El Salvador, San Salvador, June 12, 1961.

Since Rutilio believed that liturgical and choral training should begin in the minor seminary, he wanted the minor seminary to be closely linked to the cathedral and the bishop. In his frequent visits to the cathedrals of other dioceses during the 1960s, he found that the liturgical and choral performance of his minor seminarians was satisfactory: "Indeed, they performed responsibly and efficiently in those areas."[6] The performance of the minor seminarians of the archdiocese seemed to him deficient, however, and he felt obliged to improve it. He thought that in this way he would also bring joy to the heart of Archbishop Chávez. However, in 1969 an excess of work obliged Rutilio to leave the seminary liturgy and the cathedral services in the hands of the fourth-year theology students, whom he supervised.

The prefect of the minor seminary was also responsible for two especially complex tasks. On the one hand, he had to balance discipline with paternal kindness since he was in a way taking the place of the seminarians' parents; on the other, he had to try to inculcate in them good manners and priestly comportment, especially as regards personal hygiene and appearance. Rutilio wanted to avoid the vulgarity and "the plebeian familiarity of slovenly clergy," but without going to the other extreme of stylish elegance and presumption. In a word, he wanted the seminarians to avoid a "worldly spirit."[7]

The prefect's role only accentuated Rutilio's innate concern with order and detail. The notices that he placed on the seminary bulletin boards were famous among the seminarians and drew many comments in the Jesuit community. He made known his disciplinary decisions in the form of a solemn declaration, using a sharp, sarcastic tone. The originality of his style of presentation aroused sympathy and made the seminarians momentarily forget the disciplinary nature of the pronouncement. Rutilio was accustomed to formulate brief but clear codes of conduct, whose enforcement he left in the hands of beadles and sub-beadles, to whom he delegated appropriate authority and autonomy. In this way, he sought to create space for the exercise of initiative and responsibility.

Rutilio believed that the smooth running of the seminary depended not only on discipline but on the rector's ability to coordinate well with the prefects and the spiritual fathers. His regency experience had taught him that when the rector and the prefects were not working in a coordinated manner, difficulties were bound to arise. Responsibility needed to be properly delegated so that the seminarians could see that there was solid and consistent direction. Rutilio disapproved when an individual Jesuit fostered a particular small group of seminarians, allowing them to take liberties that were denied to others. Such conduct was in clear violation of the rector's directives and had negative effects, as Rutilio had seen during regency. Not only did it compromise the

---

6 Grande, "Some Experiences and Suggestions."
7 ACSI. Agustín Bariain, "Memorial of the Canonical Visit," San Salvador, March 1952.

authority of the prefect; it also aroused distrust, hostility, and conflict among the seminarians who were excluded.[8]

Spirituality was another essential dimension of seminary life for Rutilio. During his regency, he had become aware of the importance of good coordination between the prefect and the spiritual father. The spirituality prevailing in the minor seminary at that time left him dissatisfied since it was disengaged from real life. Many seminarians had no plan for spiritual growth, and they went to a variety of spiritual fathers. Rutilio had worked to avoid dispersion while working in the minor seminary in 1953, and now in 1961 he received the strong backing of the rector, Father Segura: "*Spirituality* and *discipline* have improved now that both the major and the minor seminaries have their own prefects and spiritual fathers."[9] One indication of the high level of spirituality was the fact that several major seminarians had made the monthlong Spiritual Exercises the year before. "They make them like perfect novices," wrote the rector.[10] Despite the improvements, the rectory was not totally happy: "I'm always hoping to get another father who is more vibrant, more enthusiastic, more cultivated—someone who has a more open spirit and who is more in tune with the yearnings and the needs of today's seminarians."[11] Two years later, the same rector requested "a pair of priests, spiritual fathers who are truly spiritual," since "spirituality is what most concerns and torments me."[12] The rector and Rutilio were in complete agreement on this point.

Rutilio's personal presence and obvious dedication were immediately felt in the life of the seminary. During his second spell at the seminary, in the early 1960s, an improvement in the discipline of the minor seminary was noted. The rector expressed his satisfaction with the remarkable change experienced during the second half of 1960, in everything from spirituality to courteous behavior to improved grades.[13] While serving as prefect in the major seminary in 1961, Rutilio distinguished himself for his "diligence and good common sense." The discipline in the minor seminary deteriorated noticeably when he left there.[14]

---

8   ACSI. Rutilio Grande, "Assessment of the Progress of the Grammar Division," San Salvador, 1953.
9   ARSI. Ladislao Segura to superior general, San Salvador, January 12, 1961. C. América, 1005, XX.
10 ARSI. Ladislao Segura to superior general, San Salvador, January 12, 1961. C. América, 1005, XX.
11 ARSI. Ladislao Segura to superior general, San Salvador, July 10, 1961. C. América, 1005, XX.
12 ARSI. Ladislao Segura to superior general, San Salvador, January 20, 1963. C. América, 1006, III.
13 ACSI. Ladislao Segura to Enrique Giraldo, visitor, San Salvador, February 20, 1961; Ladislao Segura to superior general, San Salvador, January 12, 1961.
14 ARSI. Ladislao Segura to superior general, San Salvador, January 27, 1962. C. América, 1005, XXV.

3. San José de la Montaña Seminary

Besides being prefect during the 1961 school year, Rutilio taught history to the third-year senior high (baccalaureate) students; Latin, history, and civics to the second-year students; and history and civics to the first-year students. He taught a total of fifteen hours a week.

After working two years (1960–62) in the seminary as a newly ordained priest, Rutilio did his tertianship in Spain (1962–63) and pursued special studies in Belgium (1963–64), returning to the seminary again in 1965. One year later, the rector who had first received Rutilio in the seminary in 1951, Father Bariain, evaluated his work in the following terms:

> We are completely satisfied with him, not only because of his (quite considerable) knowledge of pastoral theory and practice but especially because of his total dedication to the work, his humanity, and his compassionate priestly spirit—qualities that make him pleasing to God and to others. He is largely responsible for the pastoral activity (catechesis, missions, apostolic experiments, etc.) in which the major seminarians are involved these days. [...] He is also in large part responsible for the correct liturgical practice of the seminary, in accordance with the recent norms. The seminarians feel that they are themselves improving and do not cause any disciplinary problems. In the seminary, there is a positive sense of well-being, an apostolic spirit, and great mutual trust. Vocations are strengthened by the well-paced apostolic activities. The seminarians display a good spirit of collaboration with their superiors. The main faults are limited to lateness, neglect of studies, and similar things. There would seem to be no ill-will and notable deviation from the priestly path.[15]

Since the report containing this judgment was written in order to clear up the papal nuncio's doubts about the seminary's management, it is not surprising that it stresses the positive aspects, but the influence of Rutilio is still undeniable. However, Rutilio himself might not have approved of the report, as will be explained below.

At the beginning of the 1960s, the rector was so pleased with Rutilio's work that he was thinking of putting him in charge of the baccalaureate (secondary school) project, which he valued highly. He did not do so since Rutilio was about to leave for tertianship. In 1960, the seminary replaced the traditional plan of studies, which was quite clerical, with the national secondary-school plan. The change was promoted by Father Segura, who considered the baccalaureate course to be "a very effective means for increasing the number of candidates, raising their social level, and improving their perseverance, the sincerity of their vocation, and, even more, the formation itself." He thought that the national curriculum would elevate the academic standard, so that the seminarians could

---

15 ACSI. Report of the seminary rector to the apostolic nuncio, San Salvador, July 1966.

enter better prepared into philosophy studies, being "humanly better-adjusted, more open, and more resolute."[16] Rutilio agreed with the rector's assessment, writing that "the establishment of the baccalaureate program in the seminary has been a great achievement; it gives the seminary some prestige and makes it better known in the nation."[17] The change was not easy, given the poor academic level of the rural schools, the ones attended by most of the minor seminarians. But the results were soon evident, Rutilio reported: "After a long slog, a goodly group ended up very well formed with this plan of studies."[18]

Not all the bishops approved of the change. Some feared that the bachelor's title would increase the number of those leaving the seminary. Some Jesuits also had reservations and were especially concerned about the rector's greater dedication to the minor seminary. Segura did not deny his special interest, but he claimed to have good reasons for it, not least the fact that the minor seminary had more than twice as many students as the major seminary. He also thought that the baccalaureate program should in no way prejudice "the cultivation of Latin," and for this reason, he wrote, "I personally give that class to the little ones, and I closely monitor the development of that important subject in the subsequent years." He further asserted that teaching Latin to the youngest "provides me a great opportunity to foster a cordial and trusting ambience from the start and to acquire better judgment in the selection of the students."[19]

For his part, Rutilio added that "Father Rector is certainly a man dedicated in body and soul to the work of the seminary. He has given himself over to it as his true vocation." Besides introducing the baccalaureate program, Rutilio wrote, "he has achieved many good things during his time as rector," including "bridging the abyss that used to exist between the fathers and the seminary students." Rutilio also had three less positive observations to make about the rector's performance. He mentioned first

> a bit of laxity in matters of discipline. I cite, for example, the ease with which he allows seminarians to go out for more than a day, a practice that unsettles our ambience. The parents themselves are surprised, and some pastors who think poorly of us take advantage of the lax discipline to criticize us.[20]

His second comment was to "recommend that Father Rector be more moderate in his work. He takes too many supplementary and repetition classes with the

---

16 ARSI. Ladislao Segura to superior general, San Salvador, January 27, 1962. C. América, 1005, XXV; and January 12, 1961. C. América, 1005, XX.
17 ARSI. Rutilio Grande to superior general, San Salvador, February 1, 1962.
18 Grande, "Some Experiences and Suggestions."
19 ARSI. Ladislao Segura to superior general, San Salvador, January 27, 1962. C. América, 1005, XX.
20 ARSI. Rutilio Grande to superior general, San Salvador, February 1, 1962. C. América, 1005, XXVI.

baccalaureate students, besides the classes he already has with the students of the major seminary." Rutilio's third and final comment concerned the rector's neglect of the seminary's external relations, an especially sensitive point since "it seems that two of the five bishops […] are not in agreement with the way the seminary is run and would like stricter discipline." Moreover, insufficient attention was being paid to "the benefactors and friends of the seminary": "There is a need for greater contact with them in the form of visits and social events. […] That is why we are becoming isolated. These are impressions I have gathered from outside persons, especially Doña Tula de Meléndez, one of our great benefactors and a faithful friend."[21]

The results of the baccalaureate program were very positive. Of the first class of bachelors, in 1960, Segura wrote: "To judge by the data, we were in first place among all the secondary schools"[22] of the country. The second class also showed outstanding achievement, "a good indication being that all those who presented themselves for the title of bachelor obtained it on the first try."[23] Moreover, the fears of the bishops proved to be unfounded, for there were no mass desertions. So successful was the new plan of studies that in 1968 the Jesuits decided to eliminate the first two years of the minor seminary and to concentrate only on the three years of baccalaureate studies.[24]

Running the minor seminary was always a challenge, and that for several reasons. The admissions process was problematic since the initial selection was not well done. Rutilio believed that, once the students were admitted, a second selection process was needed since many students failed to recognize their obligations as beneficiaries of a free education; they tended to take on a "herd mentality" and feel entitled. The remedy was being stricter with the rebellious boys and more indulgent with those who were poor students but well behaved, as long as they were not "completely dense."[25] In 1969, the rector issued the following warning:

> Something is wrong with the minor seminary. The main problem, in my opinion, is the system for recruiting vocations. Unfortunately, we are not doing it right, and most of the pastors are unconcerned. I believe that of all those who come, only a few have the seed of a vocation.[26]

---

21   ARSI. Rutilio Grande to superior general, San Salvador, February 1, 1962. C. América, 1005, XXVI.
22   ARSI. Ladislao Segura to superior general, San Salvador, January 12, 1961. C. América, 1005, XX.
23   ARSI. Ladislao Segura to superior general, San Salvador, January 20, 1963. C. América, 1006, III.
24   ARSI. José Ignacio Scheifler to superior general, San Salvador, February 23, 1969. C. América, 1007. Consultors. 1969.
25   Grande, "Assessment of the Progress of the Grammar Division."
26   ARSI. José Ignacio Scheifler to superior general, San Salvador, February 23, 1969. C. América, 1007. Consultors. 1969.

The students' familial and social situation presented other difficulties, but in mid-1962 Father Segura had observed a "noticeable improvement"[27] in the performance of the minor seminarians of the archdiocese.

The increase in vocations during the 1960s made the limited physical capacity of the seminary a serious problem. The number of seminarians increased from 134 in 1957 to 235 in 1962, most of them in the minor seminary; the building could accommodate only 220 to 230.[28] There were plans to expand the building, but money was lacking. The rector sought funds from bishops in the United States and Germany. The German bishops donated $60,000, but the needed construction was never carried out. In the late 1960s, the decision was made to separate the major seminary, which was interdiocesan, from the minor seminary, which was archdiocesan, and to turn the latter over to the diocesan clergy. For various reasons, the separation kept getting postponed, but it was finally effected in 1970.[29]

An effort was also made to raise the academic level of the philosophy students. In 1961, Segura asked the humanities faculty of the National University to grant accreditation for the seminary courses, but his request was denied.[30] Subsequently, after he had arranged for the students to receive some courses in pedagogy and education, the Ministry of Education granted them the title of teacher, which allowed them to teach in public schools or to set up new schools and even colleges. Segura wrote that the title of teacher, like that of bachelor, "would bring new prestige to the unappreciated secular clergy and make it easier for those who leave the seminary to readjust to the world."[31] However, he received "a severe admonition" from the Congregation of Seminaries for "having proceeded without authorization." The congregation had been alerted by a Jesuit in the community who accused the rector of wanting to turn the seminary into a teachers' college. The matter caused no further problems, explained Segura, since "they seemed to be satisfied with the explanation I gave them: that it was not the matter of establishing a formal teachers' college but only of offering a few basic courses."[32]

---

27 ARSI. Ladislao Segura to superior general, San Salvador, July 14, 1962. C. América, 1005, XXV.
28 ARSI. Ladislao Segura to superior general, San Salvador, July 10, 1961, January 12, 1962, and January 27, 1962. C. América, 1005, XXV.
29 ARSI. José Ignacio Scheifler to superior general, San Salvador, February 23, 1969. C. América, 1007. Consultors. 1969; and José Ignacio Scheifler to superior general, undated but received in Rome on February 18, 1970. C. América, 1008. Ex officio. 1970.
30 ARSI. Ladislao Segura to superior general, San Salvador, July 10, 1961. C. América, 1005, XX.
31 ARSI. Ladislao Segura to superior general, San Salvador, January 27, 1962. C. América, 1005, XXV.
32 ARSI. Ladislao Segura to superior general, San Salvador, July 14, 1962. C. América, 1005, XXV.

3. San José de la Montaña Seminary

When the Society of Jesus founded the Universidad Centroamericana "José Simeón Cañas" (UCA) in 1965, the rector of the seminary thought that it would be good for the seminarians to do their two years of philosophy at the university's faculty for natural and social sciences, which had more and better professors than the seminary. The plan at first met "very strong opposition" from the bishops, but then, "to our great surprise and after a long meeting, the bishops agreed to the plan *ad experimentum* with five votes in favor and two against."[33] Accordingly, the second- and third-year philosophy students matriculated in the UCA at the beginning of 1968, while the first-year students did a propaedeutic year in the seminary, in accord with the directives of *Optatam totius*.[34] The UCA's academic calendar required the major seminary to shift from a yearlong program to a semester-based schedule. The first two years of the new venture, 1968 and 1969, yielded "very good fruits," and the experience appeared "quite positive."[35] However, two Jesuits in the community expressed negative judgments at the bishops' conference and made an "impression that was quite disagreeable." The rector was later obliged to offer explanations, with the result that both the administration and the community of the seminary experienced an internal crisis that affected Rutilio.

In 1962, the seminary was subjected to an apostolic visitation since some bishops were unhappy with the curriculum and disciplinary changes made by Father Segura. "It so happens," wrote Segura to the general, "that the seminary was in better shape than ever that year."[36] Bishop Mario Casariego of Guatemala, the visitor sent by the Congregation of Seminaries, issued a report that described the life and the running of the seminary in very dark terms. Although the report mentioned some of the difficulties facing the seminary administration during those years, its criticisms were based mostly on impressions, rumors, misunderstandings, and distortions. The rector tried his best to respond to them. Despite the negative report, six years later, in September 1968, the Congregation of Seminaries asked the bishops' conference to leave the Jesuits in charge of the seminary for at least another five years, which would provide sufficient time to prepare a team to replace them. "Not all the bishops were happy with the decision," commented the rector.[37] The bishops' conference subsequently signed a

---

33 ARSI. José Ignacio Scheifler to superior general, San Salvador, February 23, 1969. C. América, 1007. Consultors. 1969.
34 *Optatam totius* is a decree on priestly training, approved by the Vatican in 1965.
35 ARSI. José Ignacio Scheifler to superior general, San Salvador, February 23, 1969. C. América, 1007. Consultors. 1969; and José Ignacio Scheifler to superior general, San Salvador, undated but received in Rome on February 18, 1970. C. América, 1008. *Ex officio*. 1970.
36 ARSI. Ladislao Segura to superior general, San Salvador, July 14, 1962. C. América, 1005, XXV.
37 ARSI. José Ignacio Scheifler to superior general, San Salvador, February 23, 1969. C. América, 1007. Consultors. 1969.

new contract that "required [the Society] to provide professors and commit itself to the work."[38] The statutes and regulations were also approved.[39]

The life of the Jesuits in the seminary was not an easy one, as the rector explained to the superior general: "Almost all of us are overloaded with work and have little hope that the situation will improve."[40] Rutilio also wrote to the general along the same lines: "In general, I can affirm that we are all overburdened in this house. There is a need for at least two more men. [...] [The rector] is sometimes utterly exhausted, despite his great stamina."[41] Not only were the Jesuits too few for the amount of work, but several of those working as prefects in the late 1950s and early 1960s were ill-suited for the job. That resulted, reported Segura, "in a very unstable workforce: five prefects in six years, an equal number of brother secretaries, and a long parade of professors."[42] The rector insistently asked for professors of philosophy and theology, but the vice-province had none available. Nor did requests made of other provinces yield the hoped-for results.[43]

At the end of the 1960s, though the same scarcity of personnel prevailed, the rector reported that "everyone happily accepts this difficult, monotonous life with few human rewards and little affirmation."[44] In the early 1960s, when it was proposed that the Society hand the seminary over to the secular clergy, the rector wrote that "no member of the community wanted us to abandon this work. Without exception, all would very much regret our leaving the seminary."[45] Later in the decade, when the Society again faced this option of turning the seminary over, the vice-provincial judged that the rector at that time, Father José Ignacio Scheifler, "was not well-disposed to the work of the seminary. I believe that not a few in the seminary have thus interpreted his desire to entrust the seminary to the secular clergy."[46]

---

38 ARSI. José Ignacio Scheifler to superior general, San Salvador, February 23, 1969. C. América, 1007. Consultors. 1969.

39 ARSI. José Ignacio Scheifler to superior general, San Salvador, undated but received in Rome on February 18, 1970. C. América, 1008. *Ex officio*. 1970.

40 ARSI. Ladislao Segura to superior general, San Salvador, January 20, 1963. C. América, 1006, III.

41 ARSI. Rutilio Grande to superior general, San Salvador, February 1, 1962. C. América, 1005, XXVI.

42 ARSI. Ladislao Segura to superior general, San Salvador, January 27, 1962. C. América, 1005, XXV.

43 ARSI. Ladislao Segura to superior general, San Salvador, January 27, 1962. C. América, 1005, XXV.

44 ARSI. José Ignacio Scheifler to superior general, San Salvador, February 23, 1969. C. América, 1007. Consultors. 1969.

45 ARSI. Ladislao Segura to superior general, San Salvador, July 14, 1962. C. América, 1005, XXV.

46 ARSI. Segundo Azcue to superior general, San Salvador, September 15, 1969. C. América, 1007. *Elenchi visit*. 1969.

Despite his work as prefect of discipline at the two seminaries, Rutilio left a deep impression on the seminarians. On his birthday and at academic events, the seminarians made public displays of the gratitude and appreciation they had for their "beloved Father Prefect." A great many Christmas cards, addressed to "Dear Fr. Prefect" and dating from his seminary days, are lovingly preserved in Rutilio's personal file. There can be no question that Rutilio dedicated himself without reserve to the seminarians and their priestly formation. He knew how to maintain a careful balance between kindness and friendliness, on the one hand, and the need to demand responsibility and seriousness, on the other. He defended the seminarians when he felt that the rector or the bishops were being unfair to them. When he acted imprudently himself, he knew how to ask forgiveness promptly, with a very personal gesture of humility. He learned that priestly maturity could be achieved only by carefully fostering vocations from the minor seminary on up. Formation was a long, slow task that required patience and perseverance, genuine charisma, and total dedication.

Rutilio was something of a chief priest among the Salvadoran clergy. Not easily forgotten were his "missionary outbursts," which fell like locusts on the towns he visited. Neither were his quaint sayings, his comical announcements, or his original and felicitous metaphors. Wherever the clergy gathered, his idiosyncrasies were affectionately recalled. Several priests credited him with their vocation. Many went to him as their spiritual guide, recognizing his gifts of prudence and wise counsel. He united with them in their vocational crises and in the difficulties they had with their parish ministry.

It is no surprise, then, that Rutilio felt closely identified with the Salvadoran clergy. There can be no doubt that they always acknowledged him as one of their most outstanding representatives. The clerical world gave Rutilio his most life-giving social relations. He was the faithful companion of many priests who were with him in the seminary, and he helped to train many of the younger priests. He confessed that "because of my excessively close bonds with the native clergy of the country (bishops and priests), I feel somewhat restricted in my own [Jesuit] identity."[47] Another time he said that he was not entirely certain whether he was more a Jesuit or more a secular priest. Perhaps, if he had had to decide again, he would have opted for the secular clergy. In fact, some of his fellow Jesuits thought that Rutilio behaved in an excessively clerical manner. He always wore clerical dress: if not a habit, then a black or gray clerical suit.

The Clerical Opening

Though Rutilio excelled in his handling of discipline in the seminary, perhaps his greatest contribution was promoting pastoral ministry among the seminarians.

---

47   Ministries Commission. Technical Group, survey of Rutilio Grande, San Salvador, 1976.

He taught classes in liturgy and catechesis, and he helped organize and direct the solemn liturgical ceremonies, but he also made pastoral practice an essential element in the program of priestly formation.

Like other similar institutions, San José de la Montaña Seminary kept the students isolated from the outer world in order to "protect" their priestly virtue. Such isolation was considered to be the ideal ambience for strengthening the young men's vocation and guaranteeing their perseverance when they returned to society. Most of the Salvadoran bishops defended this type of formation, even after the Second Vatican Council, and it was for that reason that they opposed the seminarians' studying for the baccalaureate in a public school and their studying philosophy at the UCA. They considered such activities to be inappropriate for a seminary; unnecessary contact with the external world was to be avoided.

This conception of priestly formation stressed religious devotion and academic study, so that pastoral practice was kept marginal and reduced to the inevitable minimum. In practice, pastoral ministry depended on the initiative of each seminarian; there was no guidance on the part of the seminary. It was certainly not integrated into the life of the seminary.

Rutilio criticized this marginalization of pastoral practice, claiming that it was tolerated simply as a lesser evil, a sort of "poor relative."[48] He questioned the customary formation plan, contending that the long years of "enclosure" represented a serious danger for the young students, most of whom came from a humble rural background. The traditional seminary removed them from that setting, "processed" them, and then returned them to society as a "finished product." What most worried Rutilio was that the seminarians would develop a type of devotion and an intellectual life that were disconnected from the apostolic dimension of their calling. Given the demanding nature of their ministry, the young priests, once back in the world, would be in danger of falling into pure activism and considering the formation they had received to be useless. When they suddenly found themselves faced with complex pastoral responsibilities for which they were unprepared, they would improvise as best they could, but they would be aware of their deficiencies.[49]

The consequences of that type of formation were evident to Rutilio: since the priests were unable to respond to challenges for which they had not been prepared, their pastoral ministry would not cohere with the lived reality of the people. Their ignorance of the social situation would make their discourse sound "bookish," for they would be unable to speak the simple, direct language of the people. For their part, the laity would reproach the clergy for not understanding the complexity of their lives. Confronted with their limitations, the

---

48 ACSI. Rutilio Grande, "The Challenge of Pastoral Formation in the Seminaries: Part One," San José de la Montaña Seminary, San Salvador.
49 Grande, "Challenge of Pastoral Formation in the Seminaries: Part One."

priests would tend to give into the temptation of demanding blind obedience of the faithful and would fail to foster the close collaboration between clergy and laity that was desirable.

The highly individualistic nature of the formation process was another obstacle to that kind of collaboration. This deficiency, according to Rutilio, not only slighted the lay folk but also caused scandal: even though the priests were all responsible for the same "ecclesial flock," each one worked independently, instead of collaborating together in team ministry. Given these conditions, the clergy were not properly prepared to encourage and confirm their brothers and sisters in the faith.[50]

Despite these problems, the Salvadoran bishops, with the exception of the archbishop of San Salvador, saw no reason whatsoever for altering the seminary's regimen. They felt that several generations of holy priests had been trained under the traditional plan and that they should not give in to the temptation of change for change's sake. Their resistance to change was one of the reasons for their request that the seminary receive an apostolic visitation. Archbishop Chávez, differing from the other bishops, showed great interest in having the seminarians involved in the pastoral reality of the archdiocese from the start of their studies. He felt that the seminary should be closely linked with the church's pastoral ministry.[51]

In the same line of thought, Rutilio held that the seminarians should have a program that balanced spirituality, studies, and pastoral ministry. These three basic dimensions of priestly formation needed to be well integrated in the life of each seminarian. He thought it necessary to avoid "myopic immobility," but that did not mean yielding to "frantic revolution." Training for the priesthood was, in Rutilio's view, a prolonged process of initiation and consolidation. Priestly spirituality was intimately related to service to God and humanity, and so "perfection" could not consist in "splendid isolation." The priesthood had, by its nature, an eminently social dimension. Devotion was to be complemented by studies, especially the study of theology. Moreover, theological training was not to be limited to the time spent in the seminary but should extend through the whole of the priest's life. The job of the seminary was to open new horizons and arouse interest in the intellectual life. Ongoing formation was therefore an important responsibility of all priests. Since seminary studies should correspond to the needs of pastoral ministry, the curriculum should not dwell on obsolete or esoteric questions, but nor should it be simply utilitarian. Finally, seminarians should feel personally responsible for getting a solid formation in order to be effective pastors.[52]

---

50 Grande, "Challenge of Pastoral Formation in the Seminaries: Part One."
51 ACSI. Rutilio Grande, "Meeting of the Major Seminary," San Salvador, February 9, 1968.
52 Grande, "Challenge of Pastoral Formation in the Seminaries: Part One."

Consequently, pastoral ministry for the seminarians was not simply a concession or a relief from studies; it had to be a fundamental dimension of their spirituality and their intellectual formation. The life of the priest was basically an apostolic life, and they would learn to serve only by serving. It followed, Rutilio insisted, that apostolic formation should not be opposed or even juxtaposed to the seminarians' spirituality and studies. Nor was it sufficient for them to engage in intense apostolic activities only on weekends or during vacations, no matter how great the need. Such a pattern would put the pastoral work at odds with the other two dimensions of the seminarians' lives, and it could make them lose interest in their studies because of their artificial nature.[53]

Initiation into the apostolic life should take place through genuine pastoral work. It could not be a question of "playing" at ministry during free moments or of throwing the seminarians indiscriminately into demanding situations; rather, it was a question of giving them limited responsibilities and providing good supervision. The seminarians would not replace the priest in charge, as some were objecting, but would simply collaborate with him as far as they were able. Rutilio was aware of the dangers of his proposal, but he thought that discarding the plan would be detrimental. After all, apostolic activity would constitute the heart of the seminarians' future ministry. Moreover, direct experience of the difficulties of ministry would teach the seminarians helpful lessons and would allow the seminary staff to see the weakness of each seminarian.[54]

In this way, Rutilio introduced novelties into the life of the seminary, with the aim of reconciling the traditional regimentation with greater freedom and personal conviction so that the seminarians could mature in a balanced and responsible fashion. During 1969, he promoted spiritual reading of the Bible in the major seminary, accompanied by introductions and discussions of what was read. He also had the seminarians recite Lauds every morning in place of the traditional midday examination of conscience, and in the evening he had them recite Compline, with a prolonged examination of conscience to conclude the day. He proposed that the spiritual retreats be reformed by eliminating the "talks" and stressing the practice of "review of life" in groups. He had the seminarians of the archdiocese attend Sunday Mass at the cathedral, and he sought to heighten the prominence of the priestly ordinations that year. Finally, as prefect, he supplied the seminarians with more information about what was happening in the church.[55]

In order for good collaboration to exist among the various parts of the seminary, Rutilio thought it vital to set up a formation team, which would include

---

53   Grande, "Challenge of Pastoral Formation in the Seminaries: Part One."
54   Grande, "Challenge of Pastoral Formation in the Seminaries: Part One."
55   Grande, "Some Experiences and Suggestions"; and "Things to Anticipate in the Major Seminary," San Salvador, 1969.

seminarians. The idea was not new; in fact, it went back to the time when he was prefect of discipline in the seminary in the 1950s. He realized then the importance of good coordination among prefect, rector, and spiritual father. "There is no better remedy for our individualism," he wrote, "than teamwork, which reminds us that our priesthood transcends our poor persons and is the instrument by which the whole church exercises its ministry."[56]

This collaboration, as imagined by Rutilio, would bring together three instances: the "review of life" groups, the administrative council, and the Jesuits involved in formation. He proposed that both seminarians and Jesuits should contribute actively to the formation process by means of their ideas and their critiques. Started in 1967 on Rutilio's initiative, the "review of life" groups were considered by his Jesuit colleagues to be perhaps his most important innovation. In fact, Rutilio delegated to this group management of the day-to-day discipline and coordination of the apostolic work. The administrative council was organized in 1968; it included two philosophy and two theology students; they "almost outnumber the fathers," the rector, Father Scheifler, commented with some irony.[57] Finally, during 1970, the philosophy and theology students were organized into different sections, each with its prefect and several advisors, who were appointed after discussion with the seminarians. The prefects and advisors lived with the seminarians and attended their group meetings.[58]

Rutilio wanted the Jesuit staff to participate in pastoral formation since he thought it was the most important aspect of the seminary training. At first, the Jesuits were happy to advise the apostolic groups, but during 1968 many stopped attending the meetings. Expressing his exhaustion and sense of helplessness, Rutilio wrote, "I don't think they understand the enormous importance of such counseling. Some don't even understand the role of an advisor."[59] Despite his discouragement, he hoped that in 1969 the groups and their advisors would function better. The philosophy students had already shown their ineptitude in the religion classes they were giving in various schools of San Salvador, and the weekend apostolates were characterized by dispersion and disorder. Although the ideal was to have a global plan that would encompass the seven years of formation, Rutilio decided that during 1968 it would be advisable to minister only to the parishes without a priest, and to do so in a consistent, planned manner.[60]

True to his ideas about the importance of pastoral work, Rutilio did not confine himself to the seminary. In 1970, he began to visit El Paisnal, which at

---

56   Grande, "Challenge of Pastoral Formation in the Seminaries: Part One."
57   ARSI. José Ignacio Scheifler to superior general, San Salvador, February 23, 1969. C. América, 1007. Consultors. 1969.
58   ARSI. José Ignacio Scheifler to superior general, San Salvador, undated but received in Rome on February 18, 1970. C. América, 1008. *Ex officio*. 1970.
59   Grande, "Some Experiences and Suggestions."
60   Grande, "Meeting of the Major Seminary."

that time had no resident priest. He spent most weekends there in his hometown, accompanied by a group of seminarians. Rare was the weekend when he did not go there, and rare was the Monday when the seminary vehicle did not have problems. The country roads were rough, and Rutilio was not a good driver. He also spent the short August vacation in El Paisnal. During one of his visits, he blessed a school basketball court, built with donations from the people, the town, and the central government; he reported that "even the children work as hard as ants" on the project.[61] These visits were very important for Rutilio since they put him in touch with the harsh reality of the Salvadoran people:

> Traveling to the town from the capital means coming into close contact with all the people's problems, which are of every type: human problems, religious problems, problems of the *minimum vital*,[62] etc. However, there is certainly no need to leave the capital to be in contact with these tremendous problems—there are plenty of them right here.[63]

On August 6, 1970, feast of the Divine Savior of the World, patron of El Salvador, Rutilio delivered a homily in the cathedral that had great consequences for his own life. In the homily, he explained that his visits to the countryside were a way of "identifying with the very being and the very essence of the towns and villages which, across the length and breadth of our land, are home to the majority of the Salvadoran people."[64]

In El Paisnal, Rutilio and the seminarians prepared children for first Communion, promoted the enthronement of the Sacred Heart in the homes, assisted the Knight Adorers of the Blessed Sacrament, organized a women's auxiliary of the Knight Adorers, created a club for adolescents, established a pastoral council including both women and men, attempted to start a cooperative, and worked to improve the church building and the main plaza of the town.[65] Since he was collaborating pastorally with the archdiocese, Rutilio felt obliged to take part in the meetings of the vicariate of Quezaltepeque, to which El Paisnal belonged. He did so even though that region was considered "explosive" by his superiors and was a source of conflict for the archbishop.

Perhaps the most important of all the pastoral ministries in El Paisnal was the accompaniment of the Adorers, whose main activity was spending one night each month doing nocturnal adoration in the church. The organization was made up of adult men, most of them married; before being admitted, they had to have refrained from public quarrels and abstained from alcohol for six months. Any aspirants who were still single had to prepare to get married. Those venerable

---

61 Rutilio Grande, "Regarding a Blessing," *La prensa gráfica*, San Salvador (August 4, 1970).
62 Allusion to the Salvadoran intellectual Alberto Masferrer, who flourished in the 1920s.
63 Grande, "Regarding a Blessing."
64 ACSI. Rutilio Grande, homily. San Salvador, August 6, 1970.
65 ACSI. Rutilio Grande, notebook of activities in El Paisnal.

traditions, however, did not satisfy Rutilio, who wanted to introduce study of the Word of God: "I gradually took away their rosaries and substituted biblical readings with commentaries, in the tradition of preachers," he wrote. What he actually did was introduce the practice of reading the Bible in groups and distribute hundreds of copies of New Testaments for free. He also sold medals.[66]

At this time, the Adorers of El Paisnal numbered four hundred, one hundred from the town and three hundred from the outlying villages. The number of young men requesting admission increased. Rutilio organized committees in various districts—El Jicarón, Las Delicias, Natividad, Tronador, San Antonio Grande, Las Ventanas—as well as a central committee consisting of president, vice-president, secretary, sub-secretary, and treasurer. The monthly adoration took place mainly in the church of El Paisnal, but the practice also spread to the rural districts.[67]

For the feast of Corpus Christi that year (August 30, 1970), the Adorers made a public display of their strength. They set the whole town in motion, inspiring the inhabitants, including the mayor, to collaborate in setting up altars and adorning the streets. After the Mass, a solemn procession set out with "great composure and devotion." There were moments of silence and moments of singing and prayer. In the afternoon, there was a dance at the rectory, enlivened by the seminarians, who played guitars and sang (but did not dance). Rutilio asked those attending to give the seminarians moral support so that they would remain true to their vocation.[68]

Rutilio found in the Adorers "a spontaneous force that can be used for renewing the spirit of the people." He sought to make them into evangelizing agents by establishing a school of catechesis with the help of three religious sisters. He also strove "to make good use of the mystique of these well-disposed farmers, who have such a great spirit of commitment" that they are willing to walk hours from their village to town in order to spend the night in adoration. Gifted with a mystical sense, these small farmers "are having a great impact on their own people, and I want to bring about a complete transformation with their help. Already some candidates are emerging."[69]

Rutilio was thinking of the various ways in which El Paisnal might be transformed. For example, he explored the possibility of founding a Christian-inspired cooperative, centered on the Eucharist:

> Since the beginning of the church, the breaking of the bread has been the starting point of the Christian Revolution: the celebration of the Eucharist gave the people a joyful sense of community. It created a mystique of

---

66 Grande, notebook of activities in El Paisnal.
67 Grande, notebook of activities in El Paisnal.
68 Grande, notebook of activities in El Paisnal.
69 Grande, notebook of activities in El Paisnal.

communal action that prepared the people to practice a sound form of communism: they sold their lands and laid the proceeds at the feet of the apostles. If the apostles had known about cooperatives, they would no doubt have gone about organizing those primitive Christian communities in a more lasting and effective manner. Gathering around and celebrating the Eucharist is something highly explosive: it creates unity and a communal sense of fraternity, which it then converts into vital action with a dynamism which transforms the whole human being and the whole human community.[70]

Rutilio saw the cooperative as a way to recreate in the present the utopian primitive community of New Testament times, but he did not limit himself to imitation. He introduced also the element of community organizing, which he understood to be an essential aspect of the Christian faith. The historical reality could be saved only through a holistic vision free of dualism. This same vision influenced the way Rutilio viewed the formation of the seminarians, especially their apostolic activity in El Paisnal.

Later, when he was pastor of Aguilares, Rutilio lamented the disappearance of the Adorers. "They should not have been suppressed," he wrote, "because it was a good prayer movement." In his homily during the third Festival of Maize, in August 1976, he evoked the example of the "humble adorers" of the Blessed Sacrament:

> They set an example, in their old age, of a changed way of thinking, which I admire. I am willing to kiss their feet because, even though advanced in years, they kept up with the swift advance of the Gospel, and their hearts were well-disposed. They even adapted to the renewal of the parish and abandoned the old forms.[71]

Even though the cooperative was never established, Rutilio continued his efforts and sought other ways to improve El Paisnal. At one point, he planned to organize a group of influential persons in San Salvador for the purpose of applying "discreet" pressure on the government agencies in order to obtain all the things the town needed: classrooms, teachers, books, scholarships to technical institutes, vaccinations, sanitation works, water supply, roads and bridges, nurses, housing, communal works, instruction in farming methods, seeds and fertilizers, and conferences on agricultural topics.[72] Of that long list of desiderata, the only one that materialized was the school in the district of El Jicarón, which he blessed on August 15, 1970. It was built through the efforts of the local people and the collaboration of both the local government and the national program, Community Promotion and Cooperation. Rutilio praised the program, writing

---

70 ACSI. Rutilio Grande to Roberto Maeda, San Salvador, August 25, 1970.
71 ACSI. Rutilio Grande, homily, third Festival of Maize, Aguilares, August 18, 1976.
72 ACSI. Rutilio Grande, "For El Paisnal," San Salvador, September 1, 1970.

3. San José de la Montaña Seminary

that "if the communities themselves collaborated in the work, side by side in solidarity," it would be possible to create the infrastructure the people needed.[73]

Another of Rutilio's initiatives was to convoke the natives of El Paisnal who were living in San Salvador and to ask for their help in improving the situation of their hometown. He invited them to five successive meetings in the seminary. The first invitation he sent out tried to awaken their nostalgia for El Paisnal:

> That little town of yours, and my own as well, located thirty-seven kilometers northwest of our capital, lost among hills like El Gallito and Los Zopes. That little town washed by the Matizate River, in whose waters we as youngsters used to bathe even though our parents beheld us with some distress when we arrived home with bloodshot eyes.[74]

The first meeting he held, on August 28, 1970, was better attended than he expected since he had sent the invitation out only a week before. The ambience was friendly, and those attending greeted one another and talked about their memories of childhood in El Paisnal. Rutilio told them about his visits and activities in the town but also informed them of its lamentable state, due in large part to the "cheap politics" that made it difficult to organize an improvement committee such as existed in other towns.[75]

At the second meeting, on September 11, attendance again exceeded Rutilio's expectations. Those most enthusiastic about the project had begun to make a list of all the former residents of El Paisnal now living in the capital. After greetings and introductions, those attending discussed the possibility of founding a neighborhood association divorced from politics; it would be an organization that included all the "sons and daughters of the town" without distinction, including the Protestant minority. At the following meeting, held on September 25, the board for the neighborhood association was elected. In the meantime, Rutilio created an atmosphere of hope and expectation by convoking twenty-two representatives of the El Paisnal community and informing them about the meetings in San Salvador. They decided they would first hold a meeting in the church and then sponsor a social event in the school. The church would become a sign of unity for the grand family of past and present residents of El Paisnal.[76]

The activity of the group tended to diminish after that, partly because of the crisis that resulted in Rutilio leaving the seminary at the end of 1970; he was, after all, the soul of the group. There were only two other meetings, one at the

---

73 Grande, "Regarding a Blessing."
74 ACSI. Rutilio Grande, circular, San Salvador, August 21, 1970.
75 ACSI. Rutilio Grande, "Meeting of Natives of El Paisnal in the Capital," Friday, August 28, 1970. Notes.
76 ACSI. Rutilio Grande, "Circular [...] to Residents of El Paisnal in San Salvador, September 2, 1970"; and "Circular [...] to Residents of El Paisnal in San Salvador, September 18, 1970."

beginning of 1971 and one at the end.⁷⁷ On January 22, 1971, the group reviewed the activities undertaken in 1970 and made plans for 1971. On November 24, 1971, Rutilio proposed that they plan an excursion by train to the district of San Antonio El Grande, near the Río Lempa. At the same meeting, they decided to entrust the ninety-two *colones* in the treasury to one of the members.⁷⁸ Five years later, when he was pastor of Aguilares, Rutilio requested the money to help with the repairs of the church of El Paisnal.⁷⁹

Before traveling to South America in 1971, Rutilio earnestly begged Archbishop Chávez to appoint a good priest to El Paisnal so that the town would not feel abandoned during his absence. If that was not possible, he asked that a community of religious sisters be sent there, as had already been done in other priestless parishes. As at other times when he was away, Rutilio frequently asked his brother Flavio whether the town was receiving good pastoral care, as the archbishop had promised him it would.⁸⁰

The most important pastoral experiences of the seminary were the three mission camps that Rutilio organized with the seminarians in the parishes of Quezaltepeque (1965), Metapán (1966), and Ciudad Barrios (1967). During the seminary's long vacations, Rutilio, another Jesuit, and about eighty seminarians would move into a parish for two weeks. Each mission was carefully prepared beforehand by Rutilio and the seminarians.⁸¹ Before the mission began, he would give the bishops of the dioceses—San Salvador, Santa Ana, and Santiago de María, respectively—a folder with detailed information about the activities that were planned. These apostolic experiences provided the seminarians with a unique experience of working together intensely as a pastoral team.

The only documentation that has been preserved is that of the first mission, but it can be assumed that the other two were similar. The mission to Quezaltepeque, which took place from January 12 to 24, 1965, had as participants seventy-five major seminarians, seventeen fifth-year minor seminarians, the pastor, and his assistant. During the four days dedicated to preparing for the mission, Rutilio introduced the missionaries to an intense regimen of personal and community prayer, including a holy hour at night. He believed that the success of the experience would be due precisely to such a prayerful approach. During one celebration of the Eucharist, the missionaries contributed money for the poor. Rutilio organized the missionaries into five working groups, each with about twenty seminarians. Every group had a captain, a lieutenant, and

---

77 ACSI. Rutilio Grande, "Circular [...] to Residents of El Paisnal in San Salvador, January 15, 1971."
78 ACSI. Rutilio Grande, "Circular [...] to Residents of El Paisnal in San Salvador, November 16, 1971."
79 ACSI. Rutilio Grande to Daniel Sosa, Aguilares, February 15, 1975.
80 ACSI. Rutilio Grande to Flavio Grande and family, Panama, February 19, 1972.
81 All the Jesuit novices participated in the mission in Ciudad Barrios.

individuals who were responsible for catechesis, liturgy, sports, and other activities. Rutilio divided the parish territory into five zones and assigned a team to each. On January 11, 1965, Archbishop Chávez presided at the Eucharist and sent the missionaries out.[82]

While the traditional parish mission typically emphasized doctrinal, moral, and sacramental themes, this one set out to announce the living, dynamic Christ. It sought to strengthen the church community with infusions of love, understanding, and joy, and it reached out to include even those who did not share the Catholic faith. The mission strove to be a compelling and convincing sign of charity for all. The main aim, therefore, was not to "hunt down cohabiting couples," or hurriedly prepare children for first Communion, or herd people into the confessional, or boldly attack Protestants. The goal of the mission was to offer the people salvation as something marvelous and exciting.[83]

As conceived by Rutilio, the mission was to be a cordial encounter with the people of Quezaltepeque. Accordingly, the missionaries presented themselves in a humble, friendly, and gentle manner. They avoided arguments, even with those who were "on the wrong path"; they did not want to "snuff out the smoldering wick." They also avoided all empty ritual and all appearance of magic. First they would offer religious instruction and then the sacraments. The main objective of the catechesis was to give the people an experience of the living God. Rutilio was concerned not only with the mission activities but with the continuing life of the community, once the missionaries moved on. He therefore asked the missionaries to try to identify the natural leaders and to "set them on fire" because the future would depend on them. After the mission was over, the parish could continue the evangelizing work in collaboration with those leaders.[84]

During the first few days of the mission, all the homes were systematically visited in order to establish solid human contact. Going house to house, the missionaries greeted people, conversed with them, and got to know the situation of the families. In Ciudad Barrios, the seminarians made contact with the people by conducting a census. The visits were supplemented by folkloric performances and by a soccer game between the seminarians and the best team of Quezaltepeque. It was not long before the town folk, especially the soccer players, felt close to the visitors and related to them affably: "We entered into a warm human relationship with the entire city so that the people opened their arms to us and even began to ask us when we would be leaving. The field was ready, well prepared for our missionary activity properly speaking."[85]

---

82 ACSI. Rutilio Grande, "Mission-Camp in Quezaltepeque (January 12–24, 1965)."
83 ACSI. Rutilio Grande, "Various Principles to Reflect on Every Day."
84 Grande, "Various Principles to Reflect on Every Day."
85 Grande, "Mission-Camp in Quezaltepeque (January 12–24, 1965)."

The principal "missionary activity" consisted of catechesis for the children, visits to the homes, formation of small groups for young people and catechists, and Mass with a homily each afternoon; in the evening, there was catechesis for adults, according to age and gender. These activities were developed simultaneously in the five zones into which Rutilio had divided the parish territory.

The main burden of the mission was carried by the teams of seminarians. Every day, they spent a half-hour before breakfast in personal prayer. Each group then divided in two to review the team's activity with the help of the captain and his lieutenant. After breakfast, a plenary meeting was held, during which the five groups shared their reflections and recounted their most interesting experiences. At night, the team captains met together with the priests, who acted as counselors; they worked late into the night to make the mission as fruitful as possible. Rutilio attributed the success of the mission to this careful preparation, which allowed the missionaries to pray, discuss, evaluate, make plans, set norms, foresee difficulties, and decide on the direction the mission should take.[86]

Rutilio planned the mission as a real-life community experience of team ministry whose goal was not to build up just the particular church but the whole Church of Christ. During two weeks of intense pastoral activity, the seminarians saw the need for unity and solidarity, and they learned to work together and yield to others when necessary. In the pastoral activities and the team meetings, they became aware of the importance of certain basic human virtues like a sense of responsibility, a willingness to take the initiative, and congenial collaboration. They also became aware of some vices that were incompatible with the apostolate. During the experience, the seminarians got to know one another better, both as regards their good qualities and their defects.

The first mission camp lived up to Rutilio's expectations:

> It has been a formidable experience! We have fully appreciated the need for prayer, contemplation, and close contact with God in order to be effective in the apostolate. We must thank God for all he has wanted to do through us. [...] To him be honor and glory since without him all our apostolic endeavors, our visits, our words, our actions would have been vacuous, without any meaning at all.[87]

When the experience was over, Rutilio reminded the seminarians that, as apostles, they were called to experience the mystery of Jesus Christ: "This will always be the countenance and the cross of our apostolate, for it was the countenance and the cross of Jesus Christ the Savior. Every day we experience the mystery of Christ in ourselves, in that bittersweet mixture of our qualities and our defects, our temperament and character."[88] He also told them what the people expected of their pastors:

---

86 Grande, "Mission-Camp in Quezaltepeque (January 12–24, 1965)."
87 Grande, "Mission-Camp in Quezaltepeque (January 12–24, 1965)."
88 Grande, "Mission-Camp in Quezaltepeque (January 12–24, 1965)."

3. San José de la Montaña Seminary

We have seen clearly the need for a testimony of life for the people, so that they can see the absolute correlation between what we announce and what we practice: they want to see us as men of God, pure and wholesome, devout and at the same time joyful, happy, and normal. They want to see us united and selfless, free of rancor and foolish pretensions, aspiring only to do what is good for them.[89]

The bishops of the dioceses where the missions took place expressed their satisfaction with what was done. Two days after the end of the mission in Ciudad Barrios (November 29 to December 18, 1967), Bishop Francisco José Castro Ramírez of Santiago de María wrote as follows to the rector of the seminary:

When I attended the closing session in [Ciudad Barrios], I could feel the truly enthusiastic fervor that the fathers and the young missionaries had awakened in those souls, so distant from God many of them. The missionaries even aroused the sympathy of some of our separated brethren. Blessed be God! The sanctifying immersion that those dear faithful received during the mission camp will have lasting effects in the future. The Word of God fell on fertile soil![90]

The mission camp experiences soon came to an end because of the bishops' mistaken pastoral zeal and their lack of vision. The bishops themselves were divided: each one wanted to have his own mission, or at least be able to assign his seminarians as he wished during the vacations. So great was the discord that the vice-provincial told the seminary's rector to cancel the mission camps and leave the seminarians free during the vacation period. The bishops also asked that the seminarians be freed of the obligation of making their retreat in the seminary, with the rest of their companions. Each diocese would organize a retreat for its own seminarians. Paradoxically, the missions were for the benefit of the bishops, and the bishops themselves decided where they would take place. They failed to understand that the experience could be organized only through the seminary, and that the principal beneficiaries were the seminarians. Instead of the missions, they preferred to send their seminarians to attend to the urgent pastoral needs of their dioceses. In the archdiocese, the philosophy students joined with students of Catholic high schools to form apostolic groups that spread out to different parishes during the month of December. The theology students remained at the disposal of the archbishop.[91]

---

89 Grande, "Mission-Camp in Quezaltepeque (January 12–24, 1965)."
90 ACSI. Francisco José Castro Ramírez to José Ignacio Scheifler, Santiago de María, December 20, 1967.
91 ACSI. Rutilio Grande, "Meeting of the Major Seminary," San Salvador, August 14, 1968.

Crisis in the Seminary

In 1968, Rutilio debated whether he should leave the seminary. He felt impotent, discouraged, and even a bit depressed. He asked the vice-provincial for a new assignment at the end of 1968 and then again at the end of 1969, but he remained in the seminary until the end of 1970. These were not the first requests he made to leave the seminary; apparently he had made earlier petitions, during difficult stretches. His Jesuit companions were very familiar with Rutilio's requests to resign, but when they offered to take him at his word, he always backtracked.

Rutilio's first known request was in the early 1960s, shortly after he had begun working in the seminary as an ordained priest. The reason, he claimed, was his inability to get along with the rector, Ladislao Segura. Although the two men had long been good friends, their closeness did not prevent Rutilio from criticizing Segura's "marked individualism" and judging it to be detrimental to the efficient functioning of the seminary. Rutilio thought that the rector's way of proceeding made it difficult to correct errors and make the changes needed. He was even more disturbed that the other Jesuits accepted the rector's questionable decisions in silence. Conflict was inevitable and eventually became more than Rutilio could bear:

> I have suffered to such an extent [...] that I have a deep desire to go someplace else, to some other work. I know that Father Segura appreciates me, and I appreciate him, but my love and esteem for the work of the seminary weigh more heavily. Thus my tragedy.[92]

Despite the reforms that had been made and the dedication of his fellow Jesuits, Rutilio was not happy with the direction of the seminary. Given the importance of the work, the lack of a sufficient number of suitable Jesuits was unacceptable to Rutilio. The vice-provincial was aware of the difficulty, but he did not have enough men to reinforce the seminary. As a result, the seminary community had the impression of being engaged in a fruitless endeavor,[93] and on several occasions they discussed the possibility of turning the seminary over to the bishops.

In Rutilio's opinion, there was no reason for the Society of Jesus to have qualms or fears about training the diocesan clergy since the Society's apostolic mission was open to every possibility. Since Rutilio had great enthusiasm, excellent ideas, and much experience in training clergy, the lack of support and resources made him profoundly unhappy and anxious. He blamed the lack of support on the three universities and the several colleges the province had recently founded. The vice-province consequently found itself "squeezed" by the

---

92   Grande, "Some Experiences and Suggestions."
93   ACSI. *Viceprovincia Centroamericana de la Compañía de Jesús: Survey, XI and XII*, San Salvador: mimeo.

3. San José de la Montaña Seminary

educational sector even though the educational institutions, given their internal dynamics, seemed far removed from the historical challenges of Central American society:

> I believe that if Ignatius were to return, he would abandon a certain type of college in these regions. Following his strategic wisdom, he would take charge of the National Institute because he would surely judge that the lower-class kids there were more capable of influencing people and changing society. They are the ones who are pressured by circumstance; they want change, and they are dynamically poised to bring it about.[94]

The reason for Rutilio's discontent was not only the lack of personnel but also the general orientation of the training process, which seemed to him mistaken. For him, the goal was not to train "generic clergy" but "Salvadoran clergy." The seminary therefore had to open itself fully to Salvadoran reality and become intimately involved with it. He considered the "excessively Spanish emphasis"—observable in the community's customs, opinions, language, and even its diet—to be a nearly insuperable obstacle. The predominance of the Spanish mentality was personally troubling for Rutilio. The Gospel and the Ignatian charism required incarnation: Jesuits were to live in a way similar to the "honest priests of the place" where they resided. During those years, Rutilio was the only active Salvadoran Jesuit in the community, a fact that the bishops noted. The other Jesuits were Spaniards, though some had lived many years in Central America. For Rutilio, the big question was whether Jesuits trained in Europe could help train the future Salvadoran clergy without gaining first a thorough knowledge of the Salvadoran reality. The seminary, including the Jesuit community, needed to be more open as an institution to the social reality within which the clergy would be working:

> I have always been tempted to say the following regarding these matters: let us dedicate some time during our end-of-year vacations to go to the interior of the country, each one with a group of seminarians. Let us put locks on the seminary doors, and let us leave Navarrete [a very elderly and sickly Salvadoran Jesuit] and the watchman, with his dogs and his machete, to take care of the place while we are away. Some other father can take care of the church in any emergency. Let us all go to different regions of the country with the desire to experience firsthand all the immense problems around us, and with the determination to immerse ourselves in the various social situations in which our young men are immersed from the time they are born. All this activity of ours would have the value of a sign, and even if we were aching all over when we returned, we would be returning with existential

---

94 Grande, "Some Experiences and Suggestions."

concerns and with a great desire for a more realistic seminary program. Such a proposal may give the impression of quaint naiveté or simplistic idealism. Indeed, it may be just that, and that is why I speak with humble shyness.[95]

Rutilio believed that the spirit of renewal that would result from such an immersion experience would lead to a complete reformulation of the spiritual, intellectual, and apostolic life of the seminary, for "the theoretical knowledge obtained from census data is not the same as the knowledge gained by personal experience."[96]

The Spaniards' unfamiliarity with Salvadoran reality made it difficult for them to understand the seminarians. Rutilio was able to draw on his own experience in this regard. His background was similar to that of most of the seminarians he had known before entering the Society of Jesus. After entering, however, the training, the travels, the spirituality, and the social relations that had made him a Jesuit had also distanced him from that reality. Thus, he was simultaneously a European-trained Jesuit and a son of the Salvadoran people, and this contradiction had obliged him to forge a synthesis, thanks to which he could now understand both the seminarians and the Jesuits.[97]

Convinced that a more informal atmosphere would help the Jesuits understand the seminarians better, Rutilio proposed that the classification by academic categories be abandoned. His hope was that closer relations between seminarians and Jesuits would allow them to share their successes, their difficulties, and their apostolic ideals with one another.[98] He also advocated changing the dominant theological paradigm since it was excessively European. Even if accompanied by a few "pastoral escapades," that kind of theology would not succeed in forming good pastors during the seven years of seminary training. Rutilio proposed that the European theology be replaced by a theology that started out from the Salvadoran reality and developed theses that truly responded to the challenges presented by that reality. Otherwise, it was unreasonable to ask the new priests to stay up-to-date in a theology that had little relevance to their reality and did little to help them reflect on their pastoral practice.[99]

There was also a need to reconsider the spirituality taught to the seminarians. Rutilio asked for an in-depth study of the spiritual orientation and practices of the major seminary because he felt it was a poor copy of a Jesuit or monastic spirituality, inappropriate for either the present or the future reality of

---

95   Grande, "Some Experiences and Suggestions"; and "Some Data for a Proper Appreciation of the Work Done in the Seminary of San Salvador by the Fathers of the Society of Jesus."
96   Grande, "Some Experiences and Suggestions."
97   Grande, "Some Experiences and Suggestions."
98   Grande, "Some Data for a Proper Appreciation of the Work Done in the Seminary of San Salvador."
99   Grande, "Some Experiences and Suggestions."

the seminarians. Since Rutilio considered the spiritual father at that time to be unsuited for the task, he asked for his removal. Rutilio proposed that there be a better balance between the seclusion of the seminary setting and the apostolic activity proper to the diocesan clergy. Such a balance would require the seminarians' spirituality to be closely related to the liturgy:

> In this regard, unfortunately, we Jesuits certainly do not provide a model. And I believe it must be said that whoever denies this fundamental aspect also denies the priesthood, which is essentially united to the liturgy, since the priest is the man who realizes the work of salvation. We should also mention the liturgical year, which includes the stages of the mystery of salvation from which should emerge the spirituality with its emphases and its dynamism, all according to an organized plan.[100]

The vocational immaturity evident in the major seminary was another problem Rutilio wanted to see corrected. Despite the efforts made to improve the selection of the seminarians who were passing from the minor to the major seminary, Rutilio observed a certain ambivalence regarding the seminarians' behavior, especially that of the philosophy students. This ambivalence was manifested, Rutilio felt, "in a certain area of implicit consent that gives rise to an interior state and, in fact, to certain type of erotic actions allowed *implicite ad experimentum*. Some seminarians are not showing proper reserve in that regard."[101]

Another manifestation of this ambivalence was the "excessively institutional psychology" among the seminarians, which showed itself in a lack of interest in formative reading, a certain lack of priestly concern, an inability to make use of free time and vacations for fruitful activities, and the scant projection toward the larger community. Some young men resented the confinement of the major seminary and wanted to be able to go out more frequently, as they did in the minor seminary. Another problem was the reluctance to do common chores, as if the seminary were not the seminarians' home. Rutilio had to instruct them to sweep the chapel of the major seminary, just as they had done previously with that of the minor seminary. The refusal of some to take on the common chores obliged Rutilio to post lists of those responsible for each job to be done. He also proposed to hand over to the seminarians the administration of a small store, whose earnings would be used to finance general costs and to stimulate the seminarians' sense of initiative, responsibility, and efficiency. They had already demonstrated their prudence and skill in the administration of toilet paper: the initial quota of three *colones* had kept the major seminary well supplied during the whole year.[102]

---

100 Grande, "Some Experiences and Suggestions."
101 Grande, "Some Experiences and Suggestions."
102 Grande, "Some Experiences and Suggestions."

In an effort to overcome the ambivalence in the major seminary, Rutilio wanted to insure that the young men who were passing from the minor to the major seminary were sufficiently mature and well prepared. Some of them might be wonderful lads on the human level but still immature. Rutilio thought that students entering the major seminary should give clear indications of having a well-integrated sexuality and should have made a definite option for celibacy. Such an option was certainly not absolute or irrevocable, but it should have been clearly understood and responsibly accepted.[103]

When the rector objected that Rutilio was asking too much and was failing to consider the psychological development of the young men, Rutilio disagreed. He believed that the rector tended to "psychologize" spiritual direction:

> I don't mean by that that I want in the philosophate only young men who are perfectly balanced in their affectivity, without any of the complications inherent in their age, etc. But I can in no way agree with behavior that is born of an ambivalent stance that is not properly addressed. What is normal is that every young man who is unclear about the matter should ask for *time* to reach sufficient clarity. But let us be honest: if we allow a situation of *experimentum per se* to exist in the philosophate, then we should separate the philosophate from the theologate as soon as possible, and we should implement a specific pedagogy to carry the philosophate forward in those conditions.[104]

The rector's position, according to Rutilio, failed to maintain a proper balance between nature and grace but inclined rather toward the former. That stance explained the ambivalence that reigned in major seminary. While the young men's development needed to be respected, it should not be forgotten that "the priesthood is always an uphill struggle, and it will keep losing ground in the young men's spontaneous appreciation of it. That is a fact." When the rector was proposed as spiritual father for the major seminary in 1969, Rutilio opposed the motion, saying that he lacked clear criteria and a well-defined mystique.[105]

The problem was not the seminarians' lack of psychological development but the inadequacy of the minor seminary's program, which did not allow for a reasonable maturation of the young men's vocation according to the norms of the church. Rutilio identified two chronic problems in the minor seminary. The first was an unsatisfactory admissions process, which allowed individuals of dubious character to enter. He had evidence of the "visits" of girlfriends, the exchange of letters, and the desire to seek out adventures and conversations quite incompatible with a priestly vocation. Many people had the impression that the seminary was a "third-rate school." The other problem was the admission of

---

103 Grande, "Some Experiences and Suggestions."
104 Grande, "Some Experiences and Suggestions."
105 Grande, "Some Experiences and Suggestions."

young men who were interested only in obtaining the baccalaureate degree, an attitude Rutilio could understand, given the difficult economic circumstances of most of the seminarians:

> Our intentions are good, of course, but are sadly conditioned by circumstances that push poor kids and their parents to fight to survive as best they can. The prospect of a college-seminary in the capital is dazzling, and if we have also created a quiet and agreeable environment, that is a lovely honeycomb that is harmful and counterproductive in many ways. We must for the love of God rack our brains and try to find other alternatives. But let us at least be honest and not delude ourselves any more than is necessary. The economic question is a major factor, consciously or unconsciously. There is good reason for that old saying: in order to be a good Christian, one needs decent living conditions, clear-sightedness, sincerity, and freedom from confusion—and all that from the beginning.[106]

The seminary regulations, which had recently been approved by the bishops' conference after several years of elaboration and discussion, were no help. "We jam our fingers with those regulations for lack of knowledge of the reality," complained Rutilio. The problem was not the content of the regulations. "God save me from criticizing their content, which is wonderful and objectively valid and in every way admirable." The problem was in the practice, because they allowed young men to be admitted who were interested only in the baccalaureate degree and who dissemble their true motivation: "In my humble opinion, it would perhaps have been better not to have published those regulations, but rather to have elaborated a basic document to orient all the staff of the minor seminary regarding the constitutive norms of that institution."[107]

Rutilio consequently believed that the bishops were justified in their dissatisfaction with the way the seminary was being run. The vote of confidence the bishops gave the Jesuits was a concession that would insure ongoing mediocrity. In any case, Rutilio thought that there should be constant communication with the bishops. Many prejudices and misunderstandings could have been avoided if the seminary administration had visited the bishops periodically to inform them in detail about the operations of the seminary, and especially about the difficulties. Rutilio was especially critical of the rectors on this point. He also felt that there should be ongoing conversation with the diocesan clergy about the situation of the seminary and the most serious problems. He thought that a good place for such dialogue would be the spiritual exercises that the clergy made each year; that event would also provide the seminary staff an opportunity to get to know the diocesan clergy better.

---

106 Grande, "Some Experiences and Suggestions."
107 Grande, "Some Experiences and Suggestions."

As the 1968 school year ended and plans were being made for 1969, Rutilio advised superiors that he would no longer be prefect and spiritual father of the minor seminary. He also told them that, if they considered it opportune, he was willing to cease being prefect of the major seminary and to dedicate himself solely to teaching. In fact, he said he was ready to leave the seminary completely. His decision was due in part to his growing fatigue and to the malaise he experienced because of the dysfunction in the seminary, but he was also aware that his criticisms were not well received. He said that if he had to remain in the minor seminary, he would be either prefect or spiritual father, but not both, since he did not want to neglect the obligations he already had in the major seminary. For the same reason, he asked to be relieved of the religion class in the minor seminary and the catechesis class in the philosophate:

> In any case, I want it to be known that my disposition is one of total indifference. I am even ready to leave this house if necessary or to remain in it as a simple professor, even if only in the minor seminary. I say this truly giving thanks to God.[108]

In the end, Rutilio accepted the position of prefect in both seminaries, an arrangement that was in accord with his thinking about the need for good coordination and consistent policy. He was also left with the same classes, amounting to eight hours a week, although he received some help with this task. The major difficulty that he and most of the seminary professors had was lack of time to prepare classes. Rutilio was particularly loath to present himself in the classroom without being thoroughly prepared. Despite his qualms, he taught the course on the political constitution to the third and fifth years of the minor seminary; it was a subject in which he was well prepared, and he especially liked to teach it since it provided an opportunity to make the seminarians conscious of the fundamental rights of the Salvadoran people. In later years, when faced with the countless violations of those rights, he used to cry out: "This constitution is now a dead letter!"

In the major seminary, Rutilio taught catechesis to the philosophy students and, with the help of another Jesuit, liturgy to the theology students. He also taught the religion class, but it required considerable effort "since, given the way I conceive this subject, I need great dedication and much time to prepare the *quod disputatur*."[109] He insisted on not teaching any classes during the first month of the school year since he did not want to have to divide his time. His main aim during that month was "to attend only to the good organization and operation" of the seminary.[110]

---

108 Grande, "Some Experiences and Suggestions."
109 Grande, "Some Experiences and Suggestions."
110 Grande, "Some Experiences and Suggestions."

3. San José de la Montaña Seminary

The 1969 school year left Rutilio with an even greater sense of failure, and his frustration was such that on November 30 he asked the vice-provincial to give him a new assignment. Since the formation team had not gelled, there was no dynamism or mystique. The seminary had continued functioning for another year simply out of inertia. The suggestions he had made the previous year had not even been discussed. Rutilio was very disappointed by this negligence, especially given all the changes that were happening in the church.[111]

During the year, the life-review groups had functioned quite well, helping the seminarians to mature and giving them an experience of close collaboration, but the groups were never integrated into the general operation of the seminary, as Rutilio had hoped would happen. This failure left him wondering:[112]

> I always make this rather sad reflection: we have tremendous potential in our communities, which have all kinds of natural, human, and supernatural qualities for group dynamics; nevertheless, we don't realize that potential, or we only half-realize it, even though all of us have good will. Maybe we don't have the proper training. If that's the case, then I will be the first to confess it.[113]

Despite his good will, Rutilio made a mistake in agreeing to be prefect of discipline of both seminaries. What saved the situation a bit was that the spiritual father of the minor seminary dedicated himself to the seminarians with great energy and effectiveness, and that was shown in the results. On the other hand, the spiritual father of the major seminary, who had been recommended by Rutilio, did not live up to his expectations; rather than attend to the needs of the seminarians, he dedicated himself to activities outside the seminary. The consequent neglect had a negative repercussion on the group of twenty-six seminarians who were doing their philosophy studies at the UCA. The spiritual father of the thirty-eight theology students remedied the situation somewhat by helping out with the philosophy students, but the attention given the latter was still inadequate:

> In the midst of this confusion, I find myself, as prefect of discipline, moving on very unreceptive terrain; there is no supernatural motivation or spiritual dynamism on the part of the lads. This year the work has been more arduous and painful than in any previous year in this same job. I have met resistance and a defiant attitude on the part of the lads, especially the university students. As was expected, they entered into crisis, which was salutary in some ways but poorly dealt with—or rather, not dealt with at all.[114]

---

111 ACSI. Rutilio Grande to Father Provincial, San Salvador, November 30, 1969.
112 ACSI. Rutilio Grande to Father Provincial, San Salvador, November 30, 1969.
113 Grande, "Some Experiences and Suggestions."
114 ACSI. Rutilio Grande to Father Provincial, San Salvador, November 30, 1969.

The situation of the seminary was not helped by the fact that the ninety seminarians had to live together in the same building indiscriminately, despite differences in age and activity. "Pedagogically it is completely absurd: one huge amalgamated community, with those recently arrived in the major seminary living alongside those who have been in it seven years, etc. Actually, I'm amazed that worse things have not happened in the major seminary this year!" That "huge amalgamated community" forced Rutilio to be a strict disciplinarian, acting almost as "a cavalry sergeant." This obligation disturbed him profoundly since he was convinced that discipline should be born of the convictions of the seminarians themselves, and not be imposed by external force and intrusive vigilance. He knew that at the best of times the prefect was not viewed kindly by the seminarians, but this year was far from the best: "Compared to past years, I am aware that the turbulence of the 1969 school year has lowered the general esteem and appreciation of the lads for me."[115]

A final factor contributing to Rutilio's sense of failure and frustration was the tension between the Jesuit community and the rector, which increased in the course of 1969. In September, the vice-provincial wrote a letter to Rome describing the problems:

> There has been underlying dissatisfaction in the community, though externally it has been more or less cloaked. This dissatisfaction derives from the distance between the rector and the community, more in the internal, affective order than in external manifestations. It seems to me that the rector is not fully in agreement with the work of the seminary, and I think quite a few in the seminary view him as wanting to hand the work over to the secular clergy. This situation has been aggravated because the attitudes and actions of some members of the community have embittered the rector.[116]

The vice-provincial thought that the conflict was an internal matter, but Rutilio pointed out that it had external repercussions. Concretely, it had kept the formation team from becoming effectively integrated, and it had stymied the emergence of a sense of mystique. For Rutilio, these were essential elements for priestly formation. In a meeting the community had with the bishops' conference, one Jesuit had gone so far as to state that "there was no team in the seminary; there was no mutual understand among us."[117] Rutilio related that in that meeting "we projected an image of how we function: with little community coherence. Some take radical stances while others make open and inconsiderate accusations, and certain persons talk a lot but do nothing and show little enthusiasm for the work,

---

115 ACSI. Rutilio Grande to Father Provincial, San Salvador, November 30, 1969.
116 ARSI. Segundo Azcue to superior general, San Salvador, September 15, 1969. C. América, 1007. *Elenchi visit*. 1969.
117 ARSI. José Ignacio Scheifler to superior general, San Salvador, undated but received in Rome on February 18, 1970. C. América, 1008. *Ex officio*. 1970.

etc."[118] Sadly, the rector had distanced himself not only from the community but from the diocesan clergy, whose criticisms bothered him so much that he prohibited them from staying in the seminary building.[119]

Another consequence of the conflict, according to the vice-provincial's report, was "the almost total suppression of community meetings and sessions with the consultors."[120] Rutilio valued such meetings greatly since he considered them the most effective means for reflecting on the Ignatian charism and analyzing the crisis in the seminary. In his view, the Jesuits were obliged to examine and evaluate their lives and their work, but in the few community meetings that were held there had been no discussion of structural reform of the seminary; talk had been limited to questions of discipline, admission, expulsion, and other marginal matters. To make matters worse, the rector had arbitrarily expelled several seminarians at the end of the 1969 school year.[121]

Rutilio stated that he had made an effort to maintain good personal relations with the rector at that time, just as he had with previous rectors. Despite that effort, he knew that his vision and his way of proceeding in the seminary were not accepted and were the cause of ill-feeling. He had no real desire to interfere in the seminary's administration, but given the responsibilities he had, he found himself constantly needing to do so: "I could not be a mere passive spectator, someone standing on the sidelines. In my judgment, ours is a task of mutual responsibility, shared by individuals closely united by mutual love and by dedication to a work of supreme importance."[122] He had therefore expressed with "simplicity" his reservations about the running of the seminary, "aware of my enormous limitations as guide and educator of the major seminarians and of my need to be helped."[123] As proof of his earnestness, he handed over all his writings to both the rector and the vice-provincial. The rector, however, does not seem to have received well Rutilio's observations, remarking to Rome that "he teaches few classes but he gives plenty of instruction about what the classes of ministry and liturgy should be like."[124]

Rutilio said that he had returned to the seminary in 1965 with "great expectations" since he was "coming with all the inspiration of Lumen Vitae."[125] It was his determination and optimism that inspired the mission camps, introduced

---

118 ACSI. Rutilio Grande to superior provincial, San Salvador, November 30, 1969.
119 ACSI. Rutilio Grande to superior provincial, San Salvador, November 30, 1969.
120 ARSI. Segundo Azcue to superior general, San Salvador, September 15, 1969. C. América, 1007. *Elenchi visit.* 1969.
121 ACSI. Rutilio Grande to Father Provincial, San Salvador, November 30, 1969.
122 ACSI. Rutilio Grande to Father Provincial, San Salvador, November 30, 1969.
123 Grande, "Some Experiences and Suggestions."
124 ARSI. José Ignacio Scheifler to superior general, San Salvador, June 7, 1970. C. América, 1008. *Ex officio.* 1970.
125 ACSI. Rutilio Grande to Father Provincial, San Salvador, November 30, 1969.

the life-review groups, and formulated norms that would help the seminary operate in accord with the Salvadoran reality, the Jesuit *Ratio fundamentalis*, and the documents of Vatican II, especially *Optatam totius* (3, 4; 4, 9; 6, 21). However, his new ideas and ambitious plans aroused little response in the Jesuit community or the seminary administration. In fact, two of the seminary staff "attacked him very harshly" in a meeting they had with the bishops' conference, claiming that "discipline in the seminary was quite deficient."[126] By 1969, Rutilio felt that his five years' work as prefect were more than enough. At that point in his life, he concluded that he had never had a special calling for that kind of responsibility. In reality, the work "did not require brilliance, but simply mutual sympathy and desire," attitudes he had not found.

The tensions Rutilio experienced would not have been beneficial for anybody, and they were much less so for him given his poor health. "I'm amazed," he wrote, "that I have lasted so long a time, especially this year [1969]."[127] The rector of the seminary passed a negative judgment on Rutilio's performance:

> He has separated himself from the others and appears to be out of place. He tends to be taciturn and sullen. Given his psychology and his history—he was sick before—there could be reason to fear for his health and to think that continuing in his job could do him harm, even though his workload has been much reduced this year [1970].[128]

At the end of 1969, Rutilio reached the conclusion that he should leave the seminary: "I am poorly understood by some, and others make me feel nothing less than crucified."[129] He accordingly asked the vice-provincial to give him a new assignment. This decision caused him great pain, but he said he would be leaving the seminary with serenity since he had "complied with the dictates of my conscience. I have a profound love for the Holy Church, of which the Society is a servant."[130] Despite his desire to leave, Rutilio remained in the seminary during 1970, though with less work than in previous years.

The rector also insisted on being relieved of his post, and the vice-provincial agreed that a change should be made

> for the following reasons: (1) he [the rector] himself wants it and asked for it; (2) he lacks aptitude and love for the work of the seminary; (3) in the community there is widespread dissatisfaction with and opposition to the rector; (4) his health is suffering [...]; (5) some bishops and the nuncio

---

126   ACSI. José Ignacio Scheifler to superior general, San Salvador, February 18, 1970.
127   ACSI. Rutilio Grande to Father Provincial, San Salvador, November 30, 1969.
128   ARSI. José Ignacio Scheifler to superior general, San Salvador, June 7, 1970. C. América, 1008. *Ex officio*. 1970.
129   ACSI. Rutilio Grande to Father Provincial. San Salvador, November 30, 1969.
130   ACSI. Rutilio Grande to Father Provincial. San Salvador, November 30, 1969.

himself have at times expressed their desire that the rector of the seminary be a Salvadoran.[131]

Meanwhile, it was proposed that Rutilio be named rector.

---

131 ARSI. Segundo Azcue to superior general, San Salvador, September, 1969. C. América, 1007. *Elenchi visit.* 1969.

4. Departure from the Seminary

The events of 1970 were decisive for Rutilio. The proposal that he be named rector of the seminary came to naught because of two strong interventions he made in the course of the year, both of which involved the magisterium of the universal and the regional church. In his first intervention, he backed proposals advocating the reform of the Salvadoran church in accord with the documents of Vatican II and Medellín. Most of the Salvadoran bishops, however, responded to the proposals for reform with incomprehension and indifference. Undeterred by their negative reaction, Rutilio kept seeking ways to improve the situation. His second intervention arose as an attempt to apply the teachings of the council and the Latin American bishops to the harsh Salvadoran reality, which was crying out for urgent transformation and liberation.

The First Collaborative Pastoral Ministry Week[1]

The Salvadoran church did not accept the teaching of Vatican II until some five years after the council ended. Something similar happened with the teaching of the Medellín conference, which was accepted in El Salvador two years after it ended. The delay in accepting these crucial events in the church's history was due mainly to lack of knowledge and lack of interest on the part of the Salvadoran church. Indeed, the first reaction of most prominent Catholics—bishops, clergy, religious, and lay intellectuals—was obstinate rejection of this teaching of the universal and regional church. The Salvadoran church did not have its first real encounter with Vatican II and Medellín until June 1970, when the first collaborative pastoral ministry week was held. It was convoked by the Salvadoran bishops after a meeting of the Conference of Central American Bishops (Consejo Episcopal de América Central [CEDAC]) in La Antigua, Guatemala.

The reasons for the rejection of the new teaching emerged clearly during the events surrounding that pastoral assembly, events that revealed how basically traditionalist the church was and how closely allied it was with the oligarchy and the military establishment of El Salvador. The sector of the church that was pushing for an eager embrace of Vatican II and Medellín had made a definite option for the poor and for the liberation of the Salvadoran people. This sector included many enthusiastic young priests with good training, who wanted to take action against the oppression and injustice that prevailed in the nation, and among them was Rutilio.

---

1   This section is taken from Rodolfo Cardenal, "La recepción del Vaticano II en la Iglesia salvadoreña," *Revista latinoamericana de teología* 89 (2013): 109–32.

The first collaborative pastoral ministry week brought together eighty-three diocesan priests, thirty religious sisters, two male religious, thirty-two seminarians, and thirty-eight laypeople. Lasting from June 22 to 26, 1970, the week encouraged the participants to use the "See-Judge-Act" method, which was then very popular in Latin America. An earnest effort was made to understand both the human reality and the situation of the church in the light of Vatican II and Medellín. The assembly sought to examine in depth the true nature of the church's mission and then to indicate what practical pastoral lines the church should follow. Those running the event were aware of the dangers of hasty decisions and so refused to present any preconceived plans. They were more interested in having the participants express themselves freely and honestly.[2]

With Arturo Rivera Damas, auxiliary bishop of San Salvador and president of the bishops' conference pastoral commission, presiding over the encounter, the program was directed by Father Edgard Beltrán, executive secretary of the pastoral department of the Bishops' Conference of Latin America (Consejo Episcopal de América Latina [CELAM]), with the assistance of Fathers Freddy Delgado (liturgy), Ricardo Urioste (media), and Juan R. Vega (general secretary). According to the methodology adopted, each session would begin with a keynote address, the content of which would be discussed in fifteen mixed working groups, and then the reflections of the groups would be brought back to the plenary session.[3]

Despite the organizers' efforts to guarantee a high level of participation from all the dioceses, the response was disconcerting. The archdiocese of San Salvador had the most representatives: sixty priests, two male religious, twenty women religious, and twenty-three laypeople. The Santa Ana diocese was represented by ten priests and one woman religious; San Miguel by six priests and one layperson; San Vicente by five priests and nine laypeople; and Santiago de María by two priests. The response of the lay movements was quite low even though their leaders had been invited personally by the conference organizers and the ecclesiastical advisors. The low attendance of religious men and women was partly explained by the fact that most of them worked in education and school was in session that week. The religious organizations and institutes were content to send one or two representatives. The Society of Jesus was no exception. Apart from Rutilio, who participated actively, few other Jesuits attended, and then only intermittently. The most active and enthusiastic groups were the young priests and the young religious, most of whom came from the archdiocese. The seminarians and the university students working in youth ministry stood out in the working groups.[4]

---

2   ACSI. "Acts of the First Collaborative Pastoral Ministry Week in El Salvador, June 22–26, 1970."
3   "Acts of the First Collaborative Pastoral Ministry Week in El Salvador, June 22–26, 1970."
4   "Acts of the First Collaborative Pastoral Ministry Week in El Salvador, June 22–26, 1970"; Javier Llasera, "Crónica de El Salvador: Semana de pastoral de conjunto," *Estudios Centroamericanos (ECA)* 262 (1970): 393ff.

4. Departure from the Seminary

The most notable absence was that of the bishops, which was quite strange since they were the ones who had convoked the conference. Only Archbishop Chávez and his auxiliary, Bishop Rivera, were there for the whole week. Two other bishops, one of whom was Óscar Romero, were present at times, but the other two did not attend at all. On the second day of the conference, the assembly resolved to send a telegram to the absent bishops, telling them that it was the assembly's desire to have them present and to share with them its reflections. Bishop Romero, recently consecrated auxiliary of San Salvador, was present in the plenary session at the time and objected that such a message would be improper since the bishops' conference had convoked the event and Bishop Rivera was already present. Sending the telegram, he warned, might offend the bishops and give rise to misunderstandings. Several persons disagreed with Romero, arguing that the presence of the bishops was important since they were the persons most responsible for pastoral ministry. If they were not present, they would not fully understand the conclusions; they might take them out of context, misinterpret them, and so paralyze the process of *aggiornamento*. And that is precisely what happened. When the assembly voted again, it unanimously resolved to send the following text:

> We are 123 laypeople, religious women, and diocesan and religious priests attending the National Pastoral Ministry Week, and we feel the absence of Your Excellency. Your presence would help us in our efforts to discover and carry out a pastoral ministry suitable for our time. Respectfully, Participants of the National Pastoral Ministry Week.[5]

Bishop Pedro Aparicio of San Vicente responded that he would not attend because he did not want to meet with priests who were not in clerical dress. Bishop Castro Ramírez of Santiago de María replied that he would not attend because he was filling in at the parishes abandoned by the two priests attending the assembly. Bishop José Eduardo Álvarez of San Miguel did not respond. Bishop Benjamín Barrera of Santa Ana attended a few sessions.[6]

The assembly questioned the make-up of the commission charged with formulating the final document—two priests, one woman religious, and two laypeople—because they had been named in an authoritarian manner. Bishop Rivera assumed responsibility for naming them; he explained that he had not used a pastoral or theological criterion but had considered mainly ability and efficiency. The plenary decided not to ask for the commission's resignation; instead, it simply expanded the commission by adding two diocesan priests, one religious priest (Rutilio), one woman religious, and one layperson.

The presentation on the nation's situation was done by Héctor Dada, who was a recognized Christian Democratic intellectual, ex-president of Salvadoran

---

5   "Acts of the First Collaborative Pastoral Ministry Week in El Salvador, June 22–26, 1970."
6   "Acts of the First Collaborative Pastoral Ministry Week in El Salvador, June 22–26, 1970."

University Catholic Action (1959–63), permanent member of the Latin American Secretariat of Pax Romana (1963), co-founder of Pax Romana of El Salvador (1967), deputy of the Christian Democratic Party (1966–70), and member of the municipal council of San Salvador (1970). Dada interpreted the plight of the country using dependency theory, which was very much in vogue at the time.[7] The situation of the church was expounded by Edgard Beltrán, who distinguished two types of mission. One type was quite satisfied with what the church was already doing; it was therefore concerned mainly with increasing the number of persons receiving the sacraments. Those favoring this type of mission were not interested in change and always found ways to avoid renewal efforts. The second type of mission, in contrast, aimed for constant renewal in the church. Those favoring it were constantly searching for improvement and engaging in dialogue; they promoted a continual process of conversion. Complementing Beltrán's exposition was one by Rosendo Manzanares, who was a militant of Salvadoran University Catholic Action, Latin American secretary of Pax Romana-MIEC (1968–70), and a member of the municipal council of San Salvador. He presented a statistical analysis of religious life in the country.[8]

The working groups and the plenary session came to several important conclusions: (1) the church's pastoral ministry had in the past placed more emphasis on individual salvation than on integral personal liberation; (2) catechesis was more intent on teaching doctrine than on cultivating faith; and (3) liturgy had descended into tiresome ritualism. Because of these pastoral deficiencies, the Christian community was being deprived of true formation. Moreover, because of its tacit alliance with the dominant class, the church was not fulfilling its evangelical commitment to justice; it was fearful of losing privileges and suffering persecution.[9]

Beltrán also introduced the second part of the week by explaining the novelty brought about by Vatican II and the need to develop a theology that truly responded to the Salvadoran reality. Drawing on *Gaudium et spes*, he stressed the church's historical responsibility for promoting the kingdom of God, and he explained the various types of consciousness, following Paulo Freire. Father Ignacio Ellacuría continued the exposition by discoursing on the charism and mission of the Latin American church, understanding them in terms of salvation from sin as objectified in social structures. He claimed that private property and the profit motive were the ultimate explanation for the prevailing injustice and institutionalized violence.[10]

---

7   Dependency theory is the notion that resources flow from a "periphery" of poor and underdeveloped states to a "core" of wealthy states, enriching the latter at the expense of the former.
8   "Acts of the First Collaborative Pastoral Ministry Week in El Salvador, June 22–26, 1970."
9   "Acts of the First Collaborative Pastoral Ministry Week in El Salvador, June 22–26, 1970."
10 "Acts of the First Collaborative Pastoral Ministry Week in El Salvador, June 22–26, 1970."

During the final part of the week, the sector commissions and the plenary session elaborated their pastoral conclusions. The assembly organized itself into two major sectors: rural (moderated by Rutilio) and urban. Each sector then subdivided into commissions on faith and evangelization, leadership ministry, youth ministry, social promotion, communications media, education, liturgy, parish life, religious life, and collaborative pastoral ministry. Some of the rural commissions—education, parish life, and religious life—did not function since the participants preferred to place their pastoral emphasis in other areas. Several commissions—communications media, liturgy, ministries, and collaborative pastoral ministry—fused together for practical reasons. Archbishop Chávez joined the commission on urban parish life, Bishop Rivera the commission on collaborative pastoral ministry, Bishop Barrera the commission on faith and evangelization, and the nuncio, Bishop Girolamo Prigione, the commission on ministries. Bishop Romero abstained. The commission charged with producing the final document collected the contributions of the sector commissions and proceeded to elaborate the final document with its conclusions.

The Intervention of Rome and the Bishops' Conference
On July 23, 1970, the bishops' conference declared that several of the conclusions of the National Pastoral Ministry Week were unacceptable since they were contrary to ecclesiastical orthodoxy, discipline, and institutional integrity. The bishops commissioned Bishop Romero (secretary of the conference), Bishop Rivera, and three priests (José López Sandoval, Martín Barraza, and Gregorio Rosa) to redact the final document in accord with their observations. Thus, on October 21, "after listening to the prudent counsel of priests, religious, and laypeople," the bishops' conference published its version of the "Conclusions of the First Collaborative Pastoral Ministry Week in El Salvador. June 16, 1970. Program for Collaborative Pastoral Ministry." Instead of the phrase identifying the author of the original document—"We, the Church of El Salvador"—the new document substituted "The Bishops' Conference," even though not all the bishops had attended the encounter or listened to the opinions of their respective dioceses.[11]

The "Conclusions" presented by the bishops' conference effectively annulled those that had emerged from the pastoral assembly. The new document suppressed the more radical formulations and eliminated the prophetic dimension, as expressed in the solemn declaration with which the assembly document began: "We, the church in El Salvador, laypeople, religious, priests, and bishops, commit ourselves to bringing forth in this country a renewed church that will be a community of love, serving the Salvadoran human community and prefiguring the eternal community." This statement was replaced by the succinct phrase, "In

---

11   ACSI. "Conclusions of the First Collaborative Pastoral Ministry Week in El Salvador," June 26, 1970; and Bishops' Conferences of El Salvador (CEDES), "Plan for Collaborative Pastoral Ministry in El Salvador," San Salvador, October 21, 1970.

the light of the reflection of this First Collaborative Ministry Week." Thus, the assembly's earnest attempt to define the basic mission of the church, as expressed in the original text, was substituted by a simple "reflection" of the bishops. Wherever the assembly raised doubts about the traditional way of doing things, the bishops responded with an ambiguous "maybe."[12]

The assembly had criticized the existing evangelization as incomplete because it failed to seek total human liberation, placed excessive stress on interiority, and was oriented exclusively to transcendence. The bishops eliminated such critique and issued instead a triumphalist statement declaring that evangelization was "complete," even if imperfect despite "the efforts of the bishops." Whereas the assembly had questioned the concentration of catechesis on children, the bishops simply offered an optimistic exhortation, calling for greater vitality and more attention to adults. The bishops also eliminated the assembly's assertions that excessive sacramentalism and magical ritualism were religiously alienating and that they promoted exaggerated individualism and self-confidence. The bishops also refused to recognize the existence of popular religiosity alongside official church practice.[13]

The assembly's condemnation of underdevelopment and dependency was replaced with praise for the country's social, moral, and cultural values. The bishops were willing to acknowledge the existence of foreign domination but not the existence of social contradictions; they eliminated all references to social classes and other social divisions. Where the assembly criticized the notion of private property as an absolute and inalienable value and stated that it was extremely detrimental to the common good, the bishops' version conceded only that an inadequate concept of property could cause grave harm to the common good. The assembly's criticism of the lack of social unity was replaced by criticism of the lack of good planning for coordinated social action. According to the assembly, the church's failure to fight against sin and promote liberation was due in part to inadequate notions about salvation and the church's mission and in part to fear of losing privileges and suffering persecution. The bishops replaced such assertions with an admission that the church, "at once divine and human," was subject to the socioeconomic and cultural conditioning of its environment. They granted that, while the church made "laudable efforts for the social improvement of our peoples, [...] it has not managed to contribute effectively to their liberation and development." Also suppressed by the bishops were the assembly's statements about the hierarchy's connivance with the oppressing classes, its silence in the face of injustice, its refusal to allow the faithful any say in the appointment of bishops and pastors, and the lack of unified criteria for pastoral practices.[14]

---

12   ACSI. Rutilio Grande, "Notes on the CEDES Document."
13   Grande, "Notes on the CEDES Document."
14   Grande, "Notes on the CEDES Document."

Also rejected by the bishops were the assembly's criticisms of priests and consecrated religious for their many faults: lack of concern about the country's social reality, close relations with the dominant class, desire for profits, classist education, division, paternalism, clericalism, marginalization of the laity, substandard preaching, and excessive concentration in urban areas. Even the assembly's criticisms of the laity—spiritual dualism and fear of political compromise—were suppressed. The bishops made an attempt to justify themselves with the argument that some of them had come out in defense of the people. The only real fault they found with themselves was a certain lack of coordination.[15]

The bishops' document then went on the attack, making various accusations against clergy, religious, and laity. The clergy were accused of being paternalistic and authoritarian, of having inadequate priestly formation and spirituality, and of being too few and badly distributed. The religious were criticized for lacking commitment to the Salvadoran reality, a veiled allusion to the fact that most of them were foreigners. Finally, the laity were censured for their passivity with respect to the people and for their lack of responsibility with regard to the church and temporal affairs.[16]

In the second part of their response, the bishops eliminated the section titled "The Church: Sacrament of Salvation for the Whole of Humanity in Its Concrete History" and replaced it with one titled "Theological Reflection," which contained long disquisitions on salvation, evangelization, and the church. All the wording was geared to skirting the assembly's assertion that the church was seen by the people as a force that should be collaborating with them in their struggle for liberation. Such an assertion had serious practical consequences. The assembly had concluded that "the only salvation and liberation promised by the Lord, the one that will be revealed to us in its fullness at the end of time, is already happening" in the organization of the ecclesial base communities, in the active engagement of the poor in the cities and the countryside, in the ecclesial mission, and in the incipient political organization of the people, independently of government and political parties. This nascent reality required "a serious conversion so that we can commit ourselves wholeheartedly to it through effective action."[17]

The document of the bishops' conference was a far cry from the assembly's resolve to move beyond wordy declarations and to undertake pastoral action that would contribute effectively to the liberation of Salvadoran society. The timid hierarchy suppressed everything that seemed radical and adopted instead a triumphalist perspective. The bishops spoke only of correcting capitalism's defects and wanted nothing to do with a total and radical change of its socioeconomic,

---

15 Grande, "Notes on the CEDES Document."
16 Grande, "Notes on the CEDES Document."
17 "Conclusions of the First Collaborative Pastoral Ministry Week in El Salvador."

cultural, religious, and educational structures, along with their ideological justifications. They did not see their task to be raising the consciousness of the poor rural folk, fighting for their liberation, urging all sectors of society to condemn injustice, or supporting the two crucial elements of rural evangelization: the centers for economic development and the itinerant pastoral teams.

In their document, the bishops rejected the assembly's longing for a more liberating liturgy; they refused to condemn ecclesial representatives who defended capitalism in the mass media; they failed to provide the poorer classes better access to church authorities; they played down support for workers' unions by adding that the church would help in that area only "within the limits of its competence"; and they would not allow a competent layperson to be president of the church commission for communications media. In sum, while the bishops refused to commit themselves directly to the liberation of the poor, the radical evangelization and political organization of the poor were already advancing rapidly.[18]

Despite their generally negative stance, the bishops allowed for the creation of lay ministers or delegates, but only as a temporary measure, until there were enough clergy. Their indifference in this matter was shown in their failure to define clearly the identity and the mission of the lay ministers, even though these were themes the assembly had addressed at length. The assembly portrayed lay ministers as persons rooted in the local community and given the mission to preach, baptize, distribute Communion, and preside at matrimonies.

Finally, the bishops asked religious superiors to work together in the collaborative pastoral ministry of the church, but they said nothing about the assembly's proposals recommending that religious congregations evaluate their apostolates in light of the need for collaborative pastoral ministry, take an active part in the life of parishes, and reform their upper-class schools or else close them.[19]

The sharp contrast between the pastoral assembly's conclusions and those of the bishops' conference can be explained by their differing views about the reality of the Salvadoran church. At their meeting of January 12–14, 1970, the conference had made its own diagnosis of that reality, one that was totally opposed to the assembly's diagnosis. According to the bishops, the fundamental problem was to be found in the clergy. The bishop of Santiago de María accused the clergy of laxity for not wearing clerical dress, for being rebellious, for drinking too much, and for taking part in the profane festivities of the people. He felt that the ultimate reason for the church's situation was insubordination and resistance to ecclesiastical discipline. The bishop of Santa Ana thought that the root of the crisis lay in the lack of faith and the predominance of social concerns over religious ones. He therefore proposed a national campaign of spiritualization, modeled

---

18 "Conclusions of the First Collaborative Pastoral Ministry Week in El Salvador"; and CEDES, "Plan for Collaborative Pastoral Ministry in El Salvador."
19 CEDES, "Plan for Collaborative Pastoral Ministry in El Salvador."

after the one organized for the clergy of his diocese; he also wanted more prayer at the sessions of the conference. The bishop of San Vicente wanted more retreat houses for the clergy, and he urged his fellow bishops to stand firm and to coordinate better among themselves.[20]

In a confidential message to the clergy on January 14, 1970, the bishops inveighed against the priests' spiritual laxity, blaming it on their lack of fervent mental prayer and their abandoning of "ecclesiastical clothing" in favor of "peasants' dress, with the result that they are not respected, and they do not respect women." The bishops told the priests that they should not be ashamed of clerical dress because it defended them and kept them safe; it armored them against "certain external assaults," such as liquor, a rebellious spirit, profane festivals and public spectacles, and above all the cinema, which was not just entertainment but a school of violence, pornography, hedonism, and "the brazenness of feminine fashion":

> Nudity, though not in itself obscene, is nonetheless provocative since it stimulates bodily and psychic responses. It is a source of temptation yesterday, today, and tomorrow. There may be some mitigation if *ab assuetis non fit passio*, but the *fomes peccati* [fuels of sin] is always the same, especially in our climate, both for the young and for those at the noonday of life, unless they are misogynist or homosexual and so do not react to the strong attraction of the complementary sex. The danger, then, exists.[21]

The Sacred Congregation for the Clergy praised what it considered the necessary intervention of the bishops' conference in suppressing the affirmations of the pastoral assembly that directly contradicted the universal magisterium and the existing disciplinary norms. However, Rome was still not satisfied because it had found mistaken statements; it therefore required another revision of the document to eliminate any ambiguities. Concretely, the congregation considered too imprecise theological statements such as the following: "Evangelization has not always tried to attain the total liberation of human beings"; "The church's essential mission is to offer human beings integral salvation"; "Evangelization, if authentic and complete, necessarily encompasses the whole sphere of human development"; "The Good News of Salvation brings about the integral liberation of human beings in their concrete situation of oppression"; and "[There is need for] a prophetic voice capable of changing the deficiencies of the dominant system in the country."[22]

The congregation disapproved of the pastoral assembly's statements about the sacraments and church administration, and it judged several pastoral

---

20   ACSI. CEDES, acta 66, January 12–14, 1970.
21   CEDES, "Confidential Message of the Bishops' Conference of El Salvador to the Diocesan and Religious Priests of Their Ecclesiastical Province," San Salvador, January 14, 1970.
22   Sacra Congregatio Pro Clerigis, "Regarding Collaborative Pastoral Ministry in El Salvador," *Acta romana* 11, 2.

proposals to be erroneous. It expressed the fear that, in the name of an ambiguous total liberation, those proposals might reduce the church's mission to the temporal sphere and assign sociopolitical functions to the hierarchy and ordained ministers. Concretely, the congregation rejected the promotion of integral development and unionization as a proper means for developing responsible community leaders committed to liberation; such promotion was considered an intrusion of the ecclesiastical magisterium into politics. The congregation in general condemned all statements that attributed to the hierarchy and ordained ministers social and political commitments with regard to integral liberation. Finally, the congregation considered offensive the assembly's assessments of the social and political reality and the religious situation of the country.[23]

As regards lay participation in ministry, the congregation expressed serious reservations about the role and the functions of the lay delegates and the national commission of collaborative pastoral ministry. It stated that regular delegation of the functions proper to ordained ministers to laypeople was a theological anomaly since it confused hierarchical priesthood with the common priesthood, a confusion that could give rise to invalid and illegitimate juridical acts. The congregation also held that the creation of a national commission of collaborative pastoral ministry—made up of priests, religious, and laypeople—would constitute a clear theological, juridical, and pastoral deviation. Such a commission would have pastoral jurisdiction over priests and religious superiors since its supervisory activity would imply an equivalence of charisms. In practice, it would be directing the pastoral ministry.[24]

The Intervention of Rutilio

Even before the bishops issued their document about the pastoral assembly's conclusions, Rutilio warned them that they would not be able to neutralize the assembly with a simple declaration; such action, he told them, "would be regrettable" because it would provoke a "fateful" confrontation. His letter to the bishops' conference was written out of a desire to avoid such conflict. He was hoping to open a space for dialogue and to moderate the bishops' reactions, which were "bursting forth with a passion."[25] Rutilio's document reached the conference through his personal friend, Bishop Romero.

Before making his plea, Rutilio asked the bishops to be careful in their discernment and to listen to persons who had attended the assembly and were well known for their "good judgment" and "proven prudence." He noted that

---

23 Sacra Congregatio Pro Clerigis, "Regarding Collaborative Pastoral Ministry in El Salvador."

24 Sacra Congregatio Pro Clerigis, "Regarding Collaborative Pastoral Ministry in El Salvador."

25 ACSI. Rutilio Grande, "Representation to the Bishops' Conference of El Salvador," San Salvador, July 23, 1970.

the assembly had certainly had its faults and its final document contained some exaggerations, but

> it would be regrettable to jettison—because of certain expressions deemed rash or because of *certain literary genres*, as I would call them (such as selling one building or another [allusion to the luxurious nunciature], etc.)—totally valid concerns regarding the pressing matter of a pastoral ministry marked with the particular charism of the church of our country.[26]

The basic problem was not trivial because the crisis was the work of God himself. Consequently, Rutilio continued, "it would be wonderful if we could, with a good deal of discernment of spirits, get the car moving again in good form. Let us hope that, with the calm of John XXIII, we can clear the path on which we've collided by force of circumstances."[27]

Rutilio went on to remind the bishops of their enormous responsibility to the Salvadoran people, who were hoping for "something good" from the church since they were still well disposed to religion. The bishops therefore "should not fall sleep at this moment" or withdraw to the "comfortable shade of the institution." The challenges put forth by the pastoral assembly should be taken seriously by everybody, especially the bishops, who should proceed courageously, pronouncing a word of encouragement to keep the hope of the people alive. Falling back on the prevalent "nominal Catholicism" would create a false illusion, as was clear from the rapid urbanization of San Salvador and its surroundings: "Let us not delude ourselves! A large number of these people are entering more rapidly than we think into the great mass of de-Christianized folk. As that mentality advances into the countryside, more of our country folk will be entering the city."[28] Rutilio insisted that there was still time to prevent secularization from reaching the rural areas, where most of the Salvadoran population still lived:

> Let us not be aggrieved if, after we have lost for the church the majority of our people, [we realize that] we gave them a religion which they could not maintain at the first assault of secularity, a religion that did not help them build their world, achieve the integral liberation of their persons (in the acceptable sense of the term), and obtain their inalienable rights.[29]

If the church did not courageously face the challenges of contemporary society, the people would scorn it and condemn it.

---

26   Grande, "Representation to the Bishops' Conference of El Salvador."
27   Grande, "Representation to the Bishops' Conference of El Salvador."
28   ACSI. Rutilio Grande, "Conference of Rev. Father Rutilio Grande, S.J., at the Monthly Meeting of the Archdiocesan Clergy, Tuesday, July 23, 1970."
29   Grande, "Conference of Rev. Father Rutilio Grande, S.J., at the Monthly Meeting of the Archdiocesan Clergy, Tuesday, July 23, 1970."

The assembly's conclusions, Rutilio continued, could not be discarded simply by citing the less than exemplary lives of some priests, or by claiming that the conclusions had been approved under pressure from the university people, because that was false. Rutilio did not justify the clergy's behavior, and he insisted on the need to recognize the validity of the Word of God in itself. As regards the university people, he made it clear that only the leaders of the urban youth ministry groups had attended the assembly and that their contribution had been limited to the working groups.

Rutilio had his own criticisms of the pastoral assembly, but these did not invalidate its most important contributions. He would have liked better preparation, greater representation of the ecclesiastical sector, deeper theological reflection, and more serious study of the country's socioeconomic situation "so that all those tremendous realities might enter the consciousness of many who are asleep and don't know it." He also would have liked to participate in the elaboration of the assembly's conclusions since he had been elected to the commission responsible for the same. Due to carelessness, however, he had contributed to the elaboration of only a page and a half and so had been unable to moderate the tone of the document.[30]

Despite these deficiencies, Rutilio felt that the conclusions contained unquestionable truths, truths that had to be "heeded as much as possible [...] for the good of the church in our country," since it was "not without a certain Providence of God that things happen, even when full of human imperfections." He stated, therefore, that his criticisms should not be misunderstood by the bishops; they were "in no way meant to condemn, but to save as much as possible the proposition of another, as a Saint [Ignatius of Loyola] taught us to do before we pronounce judgments or proceed to actions."[31]

Rutilio made his case with the bishops in private, but he was not taken seriously. Thus, when the bishops published their document, Rutilio felt obliged to challenge their statements, and he did so on November 3, at the monthly meeting of the archdiocesan clergy. "In good conscience," he said of the pastoral assembly's conclusions, "I find nothing contrary to orthodoxy or contrary to ecclesiastical discipline and institutions [...] unless things are taken out of context." He knew that contradicting the bishops' conference in public was "extremely dicey," but

> I do so propelled by my own conscience, and only on condition that I speak here. [...] I do it in this internal forum, not seeking sensationalism and not

---

30 Grande, "Conference of Rev. Father Rutilio Grande, S.J., at the Monthly Meeting of the Archdiocesan Clergy, Tuesday, July 23, 1970."

31 Grande, "Representation to the Bishops' Conference of El Salvador"; and "Conference of Rev. Father Rutilio Grande, S.J., at the Monthly Meeting of the Archdiocesan Clergy, Tuesday, November 3, 1970."

4. Departure from the Seminary

wanting to offend anybody, much less disobey. If I should be in error, I am ready to heed any decision of authority in this matter.[32]

Although Rutilio had tried to understand the bishops' document as "a natural reaction against the radicalization of certain value judgments," the severe condemnation could only be seen as a "regrettable" mistake, because there had been no error. For Rutilio, the ultimate criterion had to be the reality of an oppressed people who were requesting and demanding of the church a word of salvation. The church "can continue to exist, as it has done until now, in a tranquil calm, deficient in critical understanding and spiritual discernment," but it should not forget that it was called to take its place beside the people, "according to the theology of Christ incarnate, in order to redeem the people and bring them to the Resurrection."[33]

Contrary to what the bishops believed, the pastoral assembly had not been a deplorable or unfortunate event; it had been a true reflection of the life of the church, which in fact "is rife with conflicts which have given rise to a crisis in which we are all involved," both the assembly participants for obvious reasons and the bishops themselves for making unfounded value judgments. Nevertheless, Rutilio insisted, no one should lose sight of the fact that God himself was plunging the church into this moment of crisis: it was "an authentic grace of God" and a pressing call to conversion.

The crisis was a sign of the times, that is, an indication that God was asking something more, "because no event escapes this history (of salvation), and God is always walking in our midst even if we have trouble recognizing him." The crisis "is the path of God, which passes through the middle of the human heart. […] Christ thrusts people into a state of crisis, which is a state of salvation":

> The whole of the Bible is a theology of crisis: it is an inspired theological reflection on the radical existential tension in the human person standing before God (vertical dimension) and relating to others (horizontal dimension). God is continually carrying his people toward conversion, from crisis to crisis, from fiasco to fiasco, from faith to faith.[34]

The crisis should therefore be confronted directly without "hiding our heads like an ostrich, in the face of danger and difficulty. A crisis is always there, like a tumor; it needs to be interiorized by faith; it needs to be overcome." Rutilio declared that an institution without tensions was a dead institution. If the church

---

32 "Conference of Rev. Father Rutilio Grande, S.J., at the Monthly Meeting of the Archdiocesan Clergy, Tuesday, November 3, 1970."
33 "Conference of Rev. Father Rutilio Grande, S.J., at the Monthly Meeting of the Archdiocesan Clergy, Tuesday, November 3, 1970."
34 "Conference of Rev. Father Rutilio Grande, S.J., at the Monthly Meeting of the Archdiocesan Clergy, Tuesday, November 3, 1970."

was in crisis, it was because it was full of life and spirit. At this moment, it was good that the assembly's conclusions were awakening the ecclesial conscience: "It is about time that we finally awakened from this painful reality. We have delayed too long" in accepting Vatican II.[35]

One of the most visible consequences of the crisis was the division in the church. "There really are opposed groups in our ranks." The division surprised many, and it made evident the unwillingness of some to dialogue: "We are naked and exposed to all! [...] It seems that we agree that we are not ready for the dialogue we so earnestly propose. At the same time, we are aware that this dialogue among ourselves is necessary and urgent if we want to create ecclesial unity."[36] Rutilio warned that the crisis would not be overcome solely by issuing declarations, as the bishops seemed to believe. Unity could not be imposed by means of "theoretical elucubrations," nor could it be achieved by simply repeating, as some bishops were doing, what was already well known, "without taking into account the many causes for the distress of all of us."

There were already enough documents; in fact, Rutilio claimed, "there are beginning to be too many. They are beautiful, but who knows what use they are. [...] For some time now conclusions such as those of Medellín have been crying to heaven, but they are almost a dead letter!" If the church failed to take action, it would run a grave risk of resembling "a sect of disillusioned sorcerers of heaven," seeking to preserve popular religiosity in order to continue living on earth. Before this desolate panorama, and in the name of fidelity to the Gospel, Rutilio proposed personal and institutional conversion, which required a willingness to forego positions previously taken. For Rutilio, what was most tragic about the events of 1970 was that "there was no bad will on either side—far from it!" Each side had adopted positions and emitted judgments with good intentions, desiring to serve God and church. True conversion would open up space for a sincere and humble dialogue in which participants would respect one another. Only thus could church unity be rebuilt.[37]

The declaration of the bishops' conference was theologically unsustainable, according to Rutilio, because it lacked a solid foundation. Not only did it ignore the teaching of Vatican II and Medellín but it contradicted paragraph 66 of *Gaudium et spes* in affirming the duality of church and world. In a false attempt to save transcendence, the bishops were ignoring the church's commitment to a world in need of salvation (*GS* 66), thereby prescinding from the theology of the people of God (*LG* 9; *GS* 32) and defending an unacceptable individualism. The

---

35 "Conference of Rev. Father Rutilio Grande, S.J., at the Monthly Meeting of the Archdiocesan Clergy, Tuesday, November 3, 1970."

36 "Conference of Rev. Father Rutilio Grande, S.J., at the Monthly Meeting of the Archdiocesan Clergy, Tuesday, November 3, 1970."

37 "Conference of Rev. Father Rutilio Grande, S.J., at the Monthly Meeting of the Archdiocesan Clergy, Tuesday, November 3, 1970."

4. Departure from the Seminary

bishops had forgotten Medellín's prophetic call for the integral liberation of the Latin American peoples. Rutilio considered this oversight surprising "since the most appropriate way to reflect on our own realities is to make use of the theological reflection that has been done at the level of Latin America."[38]

In fact, the bishops' conference did speak about liberation, but not in the same sense as Medellín. Rutilio therefore thought it helpful to remind them that the Latin American bishops had conceived of liberation as the appropriate theological response to the challenges presented by the continental social reality. Influenced perhaps by Ellacuría, Rutilio expressly contradicted the bishops' "developmentalist" perspective. He insisted that the situation of injustice and oppression was not an accidental byproduct of capitalist development but the direct result of unjust social structures, which denied poor people the dignity they deserved as children of God. "In our country," he protested, "these structures, established through the sinful decisions of individuals, are themselves actual situations of sin." They could be maintained only by using oppressive force, which Medellín called "institutionalized violence."[39]

Such a situation of structural sin, which was an objectification of personal and social sin, could be changed only by freeing people from the injustice they were suffering. The lived history of the people was therefore the "theological space" of salvation. The God of Jesus Christ had awakened the people from their lethargy and ushered them into a "situation of exodus." Now the people were waiting for a word of encouragement and hope since they could see on the horizon the liberation they longed for. Even though their liberation would be complete only at the end of time, with the coming of God's kingdom, there was an urgent need to assume responsibility now and to help it come more quickly. It was therefore possible to give the language of oppression and liberation "a solid theological interpretation, with the enormous advantage of its having been worked out in Latin America."[40]

In contesting the position of the bishops' conference, Rutilio made it clear that it was only through the "operative" integration of history and transcendence that the mission of the church and the ministry of priests could be correctly understood:

> We must not consider or imagine the history of salvation as if it were something that subsisted by itself, in absolute independence of human history; as if the realities of human history were unimportant and salvation followed

---

38 Grande, "Notes on the CEDES Document"; and "Conference of Rev. Father Rutilio Grande, S.J., at the Monthly Meeting of the Archdiocesan Clergy, Tuesday, November 3, 1970."

39 "Conference of Rev. Father Rutilio Grande, S.J., at the Monthly Meeting of the Archdiocesan Clergy, Tuesday, November 3, 1970."

40 "Conference of Rev. Father Rutilio Grande, S.J., at the Monthly Meeting of the Archdiocesan Clergy, Tuesday, November 3, 1970."

a different path, one that was simply individual and interior; as if it were to appear only at the very end, at the hour of final judgment.[41]

Since the mission of the church was the very same mission of Jesus, the church was called to save or liberate the ill-fated world. To the extent that liberation advances, human beings will become better, will develop creatively, and will gain ever greater freedom. Since the church is the prolongation of the mission of Jesus, it must be prophetic and have no fear of persecution; it must condemn "economic perversion," the oppression of human beings of every age, and the coveting of wealth and political power, for injustice negates "the fatherhood of God over all humankind, which was definitively sealed in the incarnation."[42]

Perhaps thinking of the bishops' obsession with institutional stability, Rutilio reminded them that Jesus had "proclaimed liberation from the alienation of religious ritual" and had even made the legitimacy of worship dependent on respect for the human person. "Christ thus stressed the provisional, not absolute, nature of every human institution, both in the secular order and in the manifestations of religious organization, judging them by their respect for human beings, the work of God himself." Religion's legitimacy consequently derived from its ability to create free persons. "Precisely because God creates and renews a free humanity, no legitimate religion can allow the enslavement of human beings by anybody, and neither can any humanism that forgets about God."[43]

Throughout his expositions to the bishops and the archdiocesan clergy, Rutilio stressed the urgency of the country's social problems, echoing the passionate pleas of the Latin American bishops who had met in Medellín in 1968, but also applying it to the Salvadoran reality. Rutilio told the bishops and the priests that transformation of the deplorable social reality had to be an "absolute priority" of the ecclesial mission. In fidelity to Jesus Christ, every apostolic endeavor had to be oriented to the salvation of society, which meant the liberation of the people. The incarnation did not allow human beings to encounter God apart from an encounter with one another. Faith was therefore conditioned by social structures: "Liberating action cannot be reduced to a mere ethical appendix in the Christian message and in Christian life. That would degrade human nature, human society, and the world itself, which are realities in which Christ has become incarnate in order to save them and liberate them."[44] Consequently, the Salvadoran church could not evade

---

41 "Conference of Rev. Father Rutilio Grande, S.J., at the Monthly Meeting of the Archdiocesan Clergy, Tuesday, November 3, 1970."

42 "Conference of Rev. Father Rutilio Grande, S.J., at the Monthly Meeting of the Archdiocesan Clergy, Tuesday, November 3, 1970."

43 "Conference of Rev. Father Rutilio Grande, S.J., at the Monthly Meeting of the Archdiocesan Clergy, Tuesday, November 3, 1970."

44 "Conference of Rev. Father Rutilio Grande, S.J., at the Monthly Meeting of the Archdiocesan Clergy, Tuesday, November 3, 1970."

4. Departure from the Seminary

involvement in historical liberation by arguing that it is a task incumbent upon laypeople and not upon clergy. Certainly, said Rutilio, the clergy had to announce the Word of God, call people to conversion, and encourage the community, but they also were called to eradicate the sin of the world. The priestly and apostolic mission was to make Christ present in the world and to lead humankind toward God by helping people to take seriously their obligation to transform the world. But to do that, priests had to make themselves actively present in the concrete reality that needs to be saved.[45]

Due to the influence on him of Vatican II and Medellín, Rutilio's conception of priesthood and ordained ministry was very different from that of the bishops. Rutilio saw the priest as called to "*christify* the world by contributing, to the small extent his ability and grace allowed, to the realization of the plan of God, who wishes to recapitulate all things in Christ." Undoubtedly, the priest was called to follow Jesus, but he should never forget that "while his mission was not that of a politician or a political agitator, his action and his Word had an inevitable impact on public life, with clear resonances in the politics and the institutions of his homeland." Fidelity to Christ and the ecclesial magisterium required abandoning the preconceived, paralyzing conceptions of traditional theology about the church's mission and priesthood. The task ahead was to be open to the newness of liberation, to reconceive priestly life and pastoral ministry from the perspective of liberation, and to act with the freedom of the "unchained word." What was being proposed was not mere humanism, as the bishops feared, but a clear consequence of faith; it was the belief that "the transformation and progress of humanity in history finds its definitive dimension in the fullness of Christ." It was not another "ism" but an awakening of conscience to the demands of the Gospel message.[46]

Rutilio insisted that the priests were not the cause of the crisis, even though the bishops thought so, perhaps in an effort to shift responsibility from themselves. Priests "are rather the victims," Rutilio claimed. At this point, he offered a well-structured critique of the obvious faults of seminary training. Scholastic philosophy was nothing more than "objectifying essentialism" and was therefore "dehumanizing." The theology taught was "polemical, unbiblical, naturalist, and far removed from human and historical reality." The way of life imposed on seminarians instilled in them fear rather than a sense of responsibility. Pastoral ministry tended to consist in administering the greatest number of sacraments possible, out of a belief in their near-magical efficacy. In synthesis, seminary training was not following the teachings of the council and Medellín, which

---

45 "Conference of Rev. Father Rutilio Grande, S.J., at the Monthly Meeting of the Archdiocesan Clergy, Tuesday, November 3, 1970."

46 "Conference of Rev. Father Rutilio Grande, S.J., at the Monthly Meeting of the Archdiocesan Clergy, Tuesday, November 3, 1970."

instructed that priests should be prepared to deal with the serious challenges that the social reality presented to the church. The life of the clergy, which Rutilio knew well, was something that needed to be treated "with sincerity—by humbly accepting and analyzing the facts and by deducing conclusions [...] without pharisaical scandal." He was probably referring to the fact that many priests had a woman companion. The proposal to ordain married men should therefore cause no scandal; it should be considered with serenity since "the facts and reality we see around us require of us a sincere and objective analysis."[47]

In the same vein, Rutilio proceeded to describe with great lucidity the crisis of priestly identity. The traditional, grandiose conception of priesthood was founded on a negation of the common priesthood of the faithful and an exaggerated exaltation of priestly dignity, to the point of making priests feel superior to the angels and, like Christ himself, saviors of souls and representatives of God on earth. This conception had been called into question by Vatican II and by Medellín, but instead of accepting the challenge and seeking to adjust, the clergy had flipped completely, from a triumphalist attitude of feeling superior to a defeatist attitude of feeling inferior:

> Before we were everything. Now we're almost nothing! We are prisoners of outmoded church structures, thought to be rich when most are not, caught between the general indifference of those above and the general distrust of those below. From the hieratic eminence of the priestly class and caste, replete with privileges, titles, and dignities, we begin to descend to the humble valley of reality; we begin to feel like men who are the same as other men, Christians who are the same as other Christians.[48]

The crisis of priestly identity was to be understood as a call for understanding and for conversion. Rutilio urged the priests of San Salvador to seek out ways to overcome their identity crisis, which was causing them great malaise and suffering. The true solution, he told them, was with God, but to find that solution they had to be faithful to grace and live with "hearts permeated by God." There was no reason to fear uncertainty, he told them; complete certainty was foreign to Christianity. Christian life was marked out by periodical crises of purification that paved the way for conversion. All priests were therefore bound to experience "the risk and the adventure of being faithful in movement, in dramatic existential tension, in crisis!"[49]

---

47 "Conference of Rev. Father Rutilio Grande, S.J., at the Monthly Meeting of the Archdiocesan Clergy, Tuesday, November 3, 1970"; and "Representation to the Bishops' Conference of El Salvador."

48 "Conference of Rev. Father Rutilio Grande, S.J., at the Monthly Meeting of the Archdiocesan Clergy, Tuesday, November 3, 1970."

49 "Conference of Rev. Father Rutilio Grande, S.J., at the Monthly Meeting of the Archdiocesan Clergy, Tuesday, November 3, 1970."

4. Departure from the Seminary

Rutilio was asking for the basic proposals of the pastoral assembly to be accepted even though the bishops were opposed to them, but he was not advocating open confrontation. Ecclesial conflict was not an option for Rutilio. He thought it "would be absurd, suicidal, and futile" to waste time in "a constant give-and-take that might never end, wearing ourselves out uselessly in internal fights when the house itself is burning." Moreover, making difficult demands when so many sensibilities were already offended would only make the wounds deeper. "This is not the time to be lamenting or to remain stuck on the beach; there is a truly urgent need to strike out into the deep with sails unfurled." Finally, he felt that it was important to remember that the clergy were quite powerless in the face of episcopal power.[50]

Despite the urgency, Rutilio thought it best not to move too fast in trying to reform the church and transforming the social reality: "Nothing is achieved by great leaps. Simply publishing documents is useless unless people have been made conscious beforehand." That was precisely what had happened with the documents of the council and Medellín. Rutilio saw the danger in pushing too hard with the pastoral assembly's conclusions: "Although the conclusions are good, it is possible that the leaders themselves have not assimilated them or experienced conversion. As a result we might end up just producing more documents." So the paradox persisted:

> I understand and share the just concerns of many who run a high fever as they behold our reality, and with good reason! And the pain only gets worse since we know that we have the channels for effective, decisive, and immediate action in our country, thanks to the recent documents of the church. But we feel stymied because the documents have not been assimilated [...] either by those above or by those below. The fever gets worse when we realize that time and events are moving inexorably forward and that we're under ever greater pressure to give a suitable answer [...] if we don't want to betray Christ and consequently our people. So there is an existential urgency.[51]

Since immobility was inadmissible, an alternative had to be found. Rutilio proposed one that he considered realistic. First, he advised that all useless polemic and divisiveness be avoided because they would only favor the oligarchy and the military regime. It was important to think long term. Then he urged the church "to open a breach in the Wall of Lamentations and [...] dare to live the drama of faith as the history of liberation today," taking advantage of the areas where the pastoral assembly's conclusions and the bishops' document agreed.[52]

---

50 "Conference of Rev. Father Rutilio Grande, S.J., at the Monthly Meeting of the Archdiocesan Clergy, Tuesday, November 3, 1970."
51 "Conference of Rev. Father Rutilio Grande, S.J., at the Monthly Meeting of the Archdiocesan Clergy, Tuesday, November 3, 1970."
52 "Conference of Rev. Father Rutilio Grande, S.J., at the Monthly Meeting of the Archdiocesan Clergy, Tuesday, November 3, 1970."

The Polemics with Traditional Catholics

This polemic within the church was placed on the front pages of the national press by a number of traditional Catholics, who were incensed by the pastoral assembly and its conclusions. Their arguments reflected the conservative thought that prevailed in an influential sector of the Salvadoran church, including most of the hierarchy. The most conspicuous spokesperson for this tendency was the Jesuit-educated Emilio Simán, a militant member of Catholic Action. His first article in the national press discredited the conclusions of the pastoral assembly with the argument that there had not been satisfactory representation of all members of the church. The assembly was therefore unable to speak in the name of the people of God and the church. Simán wrote that the clergy and the religious attending the assembly belonged to the "new wave"; some were heretics, while others were Marxists with "revolutionary tendencies."[53] In subsequent articles, he denounced priests for their many offenses: opposition to the official magisterium, infidelity to their vow of celibacy, blatant disobedience to bishops, profanation of the sacraments, and promotion of hatred and violence.

The laypeople who had participated in the assembly were considered unrepresentative because they were university-trained, unlike most of the laity, or because they were "influenced by Belgian ways"—an allusion to the work of several Belgian priests who were ministering in the inner city of San Salvador and pastoring several youth movements. The true laity were said to be mature Catholics of an older generation, apostolically committed, like Simán himself.[54] These "authentic Catholics," as Simán dubbed them, confessed a Christ who was more divine than human and a faith that was revealed, eternal, and immutable. They conceived the church to be an oasis of peace that provided relief from the trials of life, they demanded fidelity to the magisterium, and they desired to find in the priest a father and a wise counselor. They therefore wanted no politics mixed in with the church's pastoral ministry.

Simán considered many of the pastoral assembly's judgments scandalous, such as the statements that Salvadoran reality was unjust and therefore objectively sinful and that the hierarchy was in league with the oppressing class. He also disagreed with the assembly's criticism of the nunciature for naming bishops without due consultation, perhaps in allusion to the naming of Óscar Romero to be auxiliary bishop of San Salvador. When Romero was consecrated on June 21, Simán came out in his defense: he asked that the new bishop be given respect, devotion, and affection in view of his irreproachable life and his apostolic zeal. His human and supernatural virtues had been recognized by Rome, Simán asserted, and that was why he was "elevated to the dignity of bishop." At

---

53 Emilio Simán, "Diálogo de un laico: Sal sin sabor" [Dialogue of a layman: Salt without flavor], *La prensa gráfica* (July 17, 1970).
54 Simán, "Diálogo de un laico: Sal sin sabor."

4. Departure from the Seminary

that time, Romero and Simán were good friends and close collaborators, but the relationship changed radically when Romero was made archbishop of San Salvador. Simán rejected still other conclusions of the pastoral assembly, such as the discrediting of persons like himself who defended orthodoxy in the press, the criticism of Catholic education for favoring the upper class, and the advocacy of ordination for married persons and especially women.[55]

The traditionalist sector rejected the theology of Vatican II and Medellín as dangerous doctrine, "diffused as good coinage but in reality loaded with doctrinal errors" that confused the faithful. This group especially contested the conciliar definition of the church as the people of God (*Lumen gentium*), claiming that such a definition robbed the church of its identity and secularized it. They argued that, being the body of Christ, the church was a supernatural reality more than it was a people. The traditionalists held that Medellín was the product of the revolutionary younger clergy and had been subject to manipulation by theologians, economists, and sociologists of the left. Pressured by leftist theologians, the assembled bishops had accepted their conclusions too quickly. According to the traditionalists, "it is no exaggeration to state that some [of these theologians] seem to be priests of the political economy rather than priests of the Catholic and apostolic religion," since they prescinded from revelation when speaking of Christ and the church, and they questioned the church's hierarchical structure. Suffering from "delusions of grandeur of a pontifical nature," they substituted unacceptable natural humanism for the customary charity.[56] This traditionalist sector, while rejecting the teaching of Vatican II and Medellín, made no contribution to defining more precisely the church and its mission.

The traditionalist attack was met with a strong response. At the request of Bishop Rivera, apparently, Rutilio came out in defense of the magisterium and the pastoral assembly. While praising Simán's sincerity and valor, Rutilio refuted his opinions, saying that they ignored the true teachings of Vatican II, Medellín, and the pastoral assembly, which Simán had not attended. Rutilio insisted that the assembly's conclusions did not pretend to be the final word but simply material for study, reflection, and further discussion. The final document's concise, bold, and even radical expressions were not to be taken out of the context of the assembly. Rutilio's response avoided the polemical question of ministries but did not backtrack with regard to the role of the laity: "By no means ought it be denied that [women] and other laypeople in particular regions and circumstances can and should provide true ministerial services." On this point, Rutilio called attention to the canonical prescription stipulating that in urgent cases,

---

55   Simán, "Diálogo de un laico: Sal sin sabor"; and Emilio Simán, "Diálogo de un laico: Piedra de escándalo" [Dialogue of a layman: Stumbling block], *La prensa gráfica* (July 22, 1970).

56   Emilio Simán, "Rebeldía y contestación" [Rebellion and response], n.d.; and "Diálogo de un laico: Piedra de escándalo."

such as when a priest is absent for a continuous month, a layperson may baptize, distribute Communion, and preside at a marriage.[57]

The good reception given Rutilio's first incursion into the Salvadoran press encouraged him to publish four more opinion articles[58] in the same paper: "Regarding a Blessing" (August 4), "The Truth Will Make You Free" (August 17), "Religion: Opium of the People?" (August 24), and "Letter to Centeno" (August 29). Many were surprised that the paper gave him space since it had a very narrow ideological orientation. Probably his long friendship with the editor-in-chief of the paper, who also came from El Paisnal, played a part. In any case, the success of his first contribution encouraged him to continue writing, but without putting much stress on social concerns. He accepted the invitation to write but also noted "the tremendous urgency of the social situation."[59]

During this brief period of journalistic activity, which lasted hardly a month, Rutilio continued his debate with the traditionalist Catholic sector, trying to broaden the discussion by providing historical and ecclesiological background. Feeling impelled by both the scandalous social injustices and the majestic teaching of Vatican II and Medellín, he called Salvadorans to contribute to the building of a just society, in conformity with the principles of the kingdom of God. In this way, Rutilio attempted to soften the ideological tone of some of the terms that often aroused suspicion in public discourse—words like "change," "liberation," and "revolution." He attributed the apprehension about such words and their rejection to a poor understanding of their true meaning. Modern ideologies had taken them straight from the Bible, he explained. Christians were therefore not using them illegitimately—quite the contrary. It was true, though, that Christianity had forgotten their true origin, with the result that they had lost their radical evangelical quality.[60]

For Rutilio, Christianity was revolutionary by definition. Christians did not walk about menacingly in the street with machetes or with "hatred in their hearts and blood on their hands, [...] unless it is their own when suffering persecution for their fidelity to the Gospel." The revolutionary character of Christianity could trace its roots back to Jesus Christ, "leader and liberator," whose work had to

---

57 ACSI. Rutilio Grande, "Diálogos con un laico: ¿Sal sin sabor?" [Dialogues with a layman: Salt without flavor?], *La prensa gráfica* (July 25, 1970).
58 In May, *El mundo* published a series of five articles titled "Violence and the Social Situation." They carried the name of Rutilio Grande, but the author was actually the seminary rector, Father José Ignacio Scheifler. Rutilio's name was used since Scheifler was a foreigner and feared deportation if his authorship were known. The practice was common at that time (ARSI, Litt. Annuae, Seminario, C. América, 1501). The series was also published in *ECA* 262 (1970): 369ff.
59 ACSI. Rutilio Grande to Rosalío Hernández, editor-in-chief of *La prensa gráfica*, San Salvador, July 31, 1970.
60 ACSI. Rutilio Grande, "Religión: ¿Opio del pueblo?" [Religion: Opium of the people?], *La prensa gráfica* (August 24, 1970).

4. Departure from the Seminary

continue until all humankind was freed from exploitation and oppression. Theologically, exploitation and oppression were sinful, or more precisely, they were the root and cause of all collective and individual sin. That is why believers were called to eradicate sin from the world, so that the kingdom of God could begin to be built here and now. If Jesus taught his disciples to pray for the coming of the kingdom, it was so that it would somehow take concrete form on the earth. That was why faith was inseparable from the history of humanity. For these reasons, Rutilio asked for those terms be accepted; they were to be used without feelings of guilt or connivance. But one word that he thought should be eliminated from the language was "new-waver":

> All Christians are a valid mixture of all that if they understand the terms correctly and if they identify fully with the Christ of yesterday, today, and forever. They should always be striving hard to be firmly situated in their time and place, but without renouncing the essential and eternal contents of the Gospel, and with their gaze ever searching.[61]

The first article of the series was dedicated to the meaning of benediction. The topic was suggested to him by a benediction he celebrated on August 15, 1970, in the school of El Jicarón, a village in El Paisnal. In the first part of the text, Rutilio explains the Christian meaning of benediction, but he then abandons this perspective and proceeds to make a harsh social critique:

> Through those towns pass the caravans of all the politicians in time of elections, promising many things. They depend on this great silent majority for their triumphs. The landlords use this great majority to work their estates. The intellectuals devise sociological theories and more theories in their laboratories there in the big city. So we all talk and we talk, and meanwhile the great majority of the Salvadoran people, without voice but with vote, […] wait in silence.[62]

The psychological torture suffered by a man condemned to death by firing squad drew from Rutilio another condemnation of the unjust social structures. Such structures, he wrote, force thousands of Salvadorans to roam about "without work, without school, without social security, and without the means to live, vulnerable to any tragedy or mishap. […] It is so difficult to be a human being when caught in these infrastructures of injustice and misery!" The man condemned to death by Salvadoran "justice" made manifest that deeper injustice that cried out to heaven. An orphan since childhood, he had survived on the streets without education and without help from anyone. While the judicial system had found him guilty of a homicide he had committed while

---

61   Grande, "Religión."
62   Grande, "Regarding a Blessing."

intoxicated, Rutilio considered the cause of the crime to have been the man's "unhinged life," which was like that of so many others. The most culpable party, therefore, was the apparently victorious society, well satisfied with the criminal's punishment. Despite its guilt, society had not been punished because justice used different sets of measures: "For some fifty centimeters, for others only forty centimeters, and for a few one hundred centimeters." Although Rutilio believed in a "brilliant Gospel," he had his doubts: "Who knows whether our hearts have been converted to sincere love and a truly human and Christian civilization? The spirit of the scriptures is so different from that of our national reality!" He complained that there was "much hypocrisy, much selfishness, much deception, and little authenticity. We are great friends of the laws and the Gospels written in books, but our hearts are unfeeling when it comes to love, justice, and truth."[63]

Religion was not free of responsibility either. Rutilio accused it of being directly and actively complicit in the prevailing social misery because it justified the exploiters instead of the exploited. Moreover, religion was sedating the people with its preaching, which extolled resignation and so prevented the poor from trying to change the established order. This type of religion was precisely what an unjust society wanted: the job of priests was to dedicate themselves exclusively to worship and the promotion of the ancestral devotions of the faithful. The marginalized masses were told to accept with resignation their poverty and misery as the will of God, meant for their sanctification, while the wealthy few were counseled to accept with humility their privileged position, also as the will of God. Should the consciences of some be bothered by the obvious inequity, they were quieted by the scrupulous observance of ecclesiastical regulations and the practice of charity. Rutilio denounced such religion, saying that it was nothing but a narcotizing drug that masked the rampant injustice and institutionalized violence. Such a conception of religion effectively distorted and discredited the Christian faith, which for him was just the opposite:

> [The faith] obliges us to be totally committed, and it asks us to struggle to put an end to the prevailing disorder, which is now supinely accepted at all levels from the local to the national and the international. Our religion cannot tolerate any injustice. Catholics must name injustice, denounce it, and correct it to the extent that they can.[64]

The church's social teaching was not meant to be opium, even if traditional Catholicism used it as a shield in its attempt to avoid the harsh reality. To the contrary, that social doctrine called for unjust social structures to be replaced by structures that conform to Gospel principles. Believers could not receive the body of Christ without accepting the church's teaching, including its social teaching,

---

63 ACSI. Rutilio Grande, "Letter to Centeno," *La prensa gráfica* (August 29, 1970).
64 Grande, "Religión."

4. Departure from the Seminary

which Pius XII considered obligatory. It was wrong to shirk that responsibility by adducing the complexity of social problems and saying that the people were not prepared for change; such thinking, according to Pius XII, was responsible for erroneous radicalism and progressivism. Rutilio insisted on the urgent need for the church to awaken people's consciences and commit itself to eradicating all sin—which included all injustice, oppression, and marginalization—in order to save individuals and the people of God. It was therefore inevitable that those who felt quite comfortable in their selfish lifestyle would feel indicted and would react with anger.[65]

Rejecting change because it was considered "leftist" was a temptation motivated by fear of the "specter of communism." It was nothing more than a "façade, using individual and collective mechanisms of self-defense, to justify the crudest and purest self-interest; it was an attitude as anti-Christian and atheistic as the most rigid communist philosophical system." Only at the end of time, declared Rutilio, would there be right and left, when the judgment of history makes the definitive separation, according to the truth of God. This truth was to be found in God's Word, and blessed were those who accepted it and lived accordingly.[66]

The Homily of August 6, 1970

This homily was a curious interweaving of traditional motifs with new themes, but the audience that heard it in the cathedral, or at least an important sector of the audience, heard only the novelties, with considerable consequences for Rutilio. August 6 was the feast of the transfiguration of the Lord, the day when the Salvadoran church celebrated the patron of the nation, the Divine Savior of the World. Assembled in the cathedral for the feast were the nation's civil, military, and ecclesiastical authorities and the diplomatic corps of many nations. Rutilio used the occasion to call for the liberation of the Salvadoran people.

The solemn Mass of August 6, during which Rutilio gave the homily, was preceded the day before by vespers and the popular procession—known as the "descent"—of the image of the Divine Savior of the World. Since both activities were by custom organized by the seminarians, Rutilio also took part in them.

Rutilio used the various readings of vespers and the admonitions during the procession to explain to the people the meaning of transfiguration, a theme he took up again the next day in the homily. The people, crowded around the image of the Divine Savior, allowed him to unite faith and homeland:

> That sacred profession of our faith is closely identified with something as distinctive and beloved as is our *Homeland*. That profession of faith can be

---

65   Grande, "Religión."
66   ACSI. Rutilio Grande, "La verdad os hará libres" [The truth will make you free], *La prensa gráfica* (August 17, 1970).

read in our glorious flag, which waves victorious in the wind. If we were to ask every Salvadoran born in this land about this profession of faith, we would hear a loud uproar extending throughout the national territory from one end to the other. That clamor would proclaim: "We believe in God, we love God, and we hope in God."[67]

Rutilio oriented the ceremony of vespers in that direction, transforming it into a celebration of the Word of God. The first reading from *Gaudium et spes*, describing the role of the church in the world, allowed a layperson to place the celebration in its historical context.[68]

Before the start of the procession, the assembled people sang the national anthem, as befitted citizens who were also children of the church. El Salvador, said Rutilio, was an immense temple: "The sacred ground of this temple is our territory with its fourteen departments. [...] The immense roof is the blue sky which stretches over our land and is reflected in our flag. The splendid ornaments of this magnificent temple are our lakes, our volcanoes, our farmlands, our crops."[69] In the course of the procession, Rutilio's commentaries touched on themes related to the confession of faith and fidelity to the homeland. He commented specifically on the motto inscribed on the national flag—"God, Union, Liberty"—and referred to it again in his homily the next day. Rutilio's strong patriotic or nationalist bent can be explained by the reverence all Salvadorans had for their national symbols. People frequently recited with fervor the "prayer to the flag." Rutilio was therefore echoing the general nationalist sentiment and relating it to the Christian faith. In commenting on the motto on the flag, he proclaimed that freedom came only through a transfiguration of the social reality: "We ardently long for the third word imprinted on our banner—that is, *Liberty*—to become a reality for all Salvadorans, through the total *Transfiguration* of our Homeland, according to the proposals of *Christ*, who *Transfigures* the world and all of history with the *Message* of his *Gospel*."[70]

Some of Rutilio's commentaries, amplified through the loudspeakers during the procession, declared in the bold language typical of the epoch how Christ would transfigure El Salvador: "*Jesus Christ* is the number one revolutionary of history. He changed the direction of history. He transformed it into salvation history." And the commentary went on to explain how precisely the revolution of Jesus Christ was to be understood:

---

67   ACSI. Rutilio Grande, "Commentaries for the Procession," San Salvador, August 5, 1970.
68   ACSI. Rutilio Grande, "Celebration of the Word at the Vespers of the Titular Feast of the Republic (August 5) before the Procession," and "Commentaries for the Procession."
69   Grande, "Commentaries for the Procession."
70   Grande, "Celebration of the Word at the Vespers of the Titular Feast of the Republic (August 5) before the Procession."

4. Departure from the Seminary

Christ the Savior is not a revolutionary imbued with hatred and falsehood. He does not sow confusion. He does not build his kingdom on corpses. He does not promote hatred of races or classes. He came to destroy all that. His kingdom is a universal and eternal kingdom, a kingdom of truth and life. We want his kingdom![71]

The archbishop presided at the pontifical Mass on August 6, since the nuncio, who usually presided, was absent; the other bishops concelebrated. As was the custom, Rutilio served as master of ceremonies, and he instructed the seminarians to stay alert and not make mistakes. The seminarians read the admonitions and commentaries that had been prepared by Rutilio.

Ordinarily, the homily on this feast day was a florid piece of oratory that allowed the preacher to demonstrate his rhetorical skills. Rutilio decided to break with that tradition. He began by questioning the motives of his audience, both those in the cathedral and those who were listening on YSAX, the archdiocesan radio station. The point of his questioning was to help everyone "become conscious" so that they could "interiorize the reality in which we are implicated, either by our free choice or by force of circumstances."[72] Rutilio asked his listeners whether their motive in coming to the cathedral or listening on the radio was "mere curiosity." If such was the case, he said, then "something essential is lacking in the layers of our personality, as citizens and as Christians!" He then directly addressed the government officials and the diplomatic corps, questioning their motives. He asked whether they were attending only out of convention, or perhaps out of a desire not to "miss" the spectacle. He voiced the thoughts of the skeptics: "I don't care about the rest. I appear once in a while in church, but I have no clear ideas about what Christianity and the Gospel of Jesus really mean for my life, for my country, or for the whole world. Those things don't concern me!"[73] Rutilio's questioning was not unreasonable since many people were manifestly indifferent. Declaring that the church and the Gospel were a "sacred flame," he then softened his tone by saying that he "would by no means accuse those present of responses" that reflected superficiality and lack of Christian spirit.

Offering a gloss on the questions Jesus asked about John the Baptist, Rutilio declared that Christians were not reeds shaken by the wind, nor were they simply good middle-class folk. Christians should "respond faithfully to all the demands of the Gospel, and they should live in accord with those demands, even to the ultimate consequences!" True Christians recognized Jesus as the Savior and the Christ of God. Their attitude should be one of continual conversion, both personal and social, for they were constantly working for the transformation of humankind. The faith of true Christians should be personal, sincere, and

---

71 Grande, "Commentaries for the Procession."
72 ACSI. Rutilio Grande, homily, San Salvador, August 6, 1970.
73 Grande, homily, San Salvador, August 6, 1970.

profound; it should impel each of them to confess: "I am proud to belong to the Catholic Church by my baptism, because I know what it means for me as a person and for the creation of a better world."[74]

The feast of the transfiguration was the day when Salvadorans consecrated themselves and professed the faith they shared in common:

> Blessed are we if we have on our lips and especially in our hearts this response of true Christians! Even more blessed are we if we not only express it with our lips but also live it fully, to its ultimate consequences. Then we will be, as *Christians* and followers of *Christ*, light for the world, salt for the earth, and transformative leaven for all humanity, in the midst of which the church advances in truly intimate solidarity with the human race and its history.[75]

Having dispelled any doubts about people's motivation and clarified the reasons for the coming together of the Salvadoran people with the political and ecclesiastical authorities, Rutilio could truthfully affirm that the metropolitan cathedral had been constituted the "heart of the Homeland, the center of convergence for all the children of this sacred soil" because "all of us here believe in the Lord and are assembled in his name."[76] He was referring not only to the archbishop—who presided as official witness of the risen Jesus in the midst of the local church, through apostolic succession and Communion with the pope—but also to the other bishops, the circle of priests, the government officials, and, not least, the people of God, who were "crowded around" the others:

> Here we are all united around the altar of *God*, whose name is the first one imprinted on the trilogy of our flag. And we are united precisely beside the altar in the celebration of the Eucharist, forming a *Union* of the Salvadoran family, as the second word on the flag affirms. And we are fraternally united beside the altar of God, crowded around *Someone*, who on the altar and in the Eucharist is precisely our Supreme Mediator before God, the very Word of God made flesh, and our Ultimate Liberator, *Jesus Christ*, Savior of the World.[77]

Rutilio urged the people to follow without "hesitation" this "genuine leader" named Jesus. He was genuine because, unlike most leaders, he plunged into human misery, a misery that "perhaps resembled that of some of our rural folk," and because he became so identified with people that he gave his life for them. Jesus was the "spokesperson of the Father," the messenger who communicated to humankind who God was and what his plans were. Jesus always spoke the truth and lived in accord with it:

---

74   Grande, homily, San Salvador, August 6, 1970.
75   Grande, homily, San Salvador, August 6, 1970.
76   Grande, homily, San Salvador, August 6, 1970.
77   Grande, homily, San Salvador, August 6, 1970.

4. Departure from the Seminary

With his *Message*, the *Supreme Prophet* Jesus entered fully into the life of all human beings. He carried his Word out into the streets and plazas; he preached beside lakes and on high mountains. He stopped to converse with the poor and the rich, with the children and the intellectuals of his time; he even spoke with the bandits and the ladies of the night. As the faithful Prophet of *God*, he announced what was good, and he reinforced it; he bestowed mercy on all, and when this was not enough, he sharpened his words and used them to rebuke the hypocrites who observed the external forms while their hearts were full of cruelty. He denounced them as whitened sepulchers. He rebelled against many things and persons and situations of his time, so we should have no fear in uttering this word "rebel," which we use in its purely evangelical sense.[78]

Rutilio documented the rebellious attitude of Jesus with many citations from the Gospels. While he probably did not read all the citations during his homily, they were published in the text that appeared in *El mundo*:[79]

[Jesus] took a critical stance toward the rich who had no conscience or compassion, saying that they would have difficulty entering into the kingdom of heaven if they persisted in their attitudes (Lk 18,24f.; Mk 10,23ff.; Mt 19,23ff.). […] On the other hand, he gave a warm welcome to the rich people who, like Zacchaeus, acknowledged their errors, their scheming, and their abuse of power. He praised this tax collector who humbly confessed his sins and promised to repair the harm he had done. Jesus was not sparing in his praise when he declared: "Today salvation has come to this house" (Lk 19,9). Jesus cherished his friendship with the wealthy folk who practiced justice, people like Nicodemus, Joseph of Arimathea, and Lazarus (Lk 23,50ff.; Mt 25,57; Jn 3,1ff.).[80]

With Jesus, there could be no possibility of deception or misinterpretation. His words cured "with the harshness proper to God." They are "honey and at the same time bitterness for some consciences. The scriptures pronounce *blessings* on some of their pages, but they also pronounce tremendous curses on other pages that are no less true."[81]

Death was the ultimate challenge: "He was crucified!—we say in the Creed. On expiring, as he bowed his moribund head, he exclaimed in a triumph of *Transfiguration*: 'It is finished' (Jn 19,30), and at that moment the eyes of all human beings of all times were fixed on him."[82]

---

78   Grande, homily, San Salvador, August 6, 1970.
79   "Homily on the Solemnity of the Titular Feast of the Republic," *El mundo* (August 13, 1970), 19.
80   Grande, homily, San Salvador, August 6, 1970.
81   Grande, homily, San Salvador, August 6, 1970.
82   Grande, homily, San Salvador, August 6, 1970.

But "*Christ Jesus* did not remain hanging on a cross, like one defeated. He did not remain forever buried in a tomb!"[83]

The followers of Jesus, the believing community—including those assembled at that moment in the cathedral and around their radios—were called to give continuity to the transfiguration begun by their "Supreme Leader." Rutilio reminded them that that was the commitment they had assumed in baptism:

> We all say that we are baptized and that we are children of this nation. Those baptized include our government officials, ministers of state, intellectuals, professionals, employees, and merchants. Those baptized include our small farmers and their families. And the baptized include as well all of us who are priests, bishops, and religious![84]

"In the ranks of the Church of Christ," Rutilio continued, baptism "should not be just a conventional washing of the head, a customary rite, a purely social act without importance for the individual and society." The baptized should live within the "channels of the Gospel," that is, in a permanent state of conversion with respect to life, the world, and God. "Change your attitude—that was the *slogan* of Jesus."[85]

In El Salvador, "we are accustomed to hear on solemn occasions exuberant praise for the natural beauties of our dear nation. Praise is showered on the enchanting lakes, the flowering coffee groves, the majestic volcanoes," but nothing is said about the real situation experienced by Salvadorans. Not wanting to fall into the same error, Rutilio tried to incorporate that reality into his homily. He again began to question his audience:

> And what do we tell the Salvadoran people? What will we say of all the children of this blessed soil, this place where we all profess to be baptized in the name of *Christ Transfigured*? Are the Salvadoran people transfigured? We repeat the question: Are the Salvadoran people transfigured? Is that immense majority of Salvadorans who live and work in the countryside transfigured? Is that minority that holds in its hands economic clout, decision-making power, and control of all the mass media transfigured?[86]

And to answer his own questions, Rutilio continued:

> We have to make painful confessions. Many baptized persons in our country have still not imbibed the Gospel demands that require of us a transfiguration, and therefore they have not been themselves transfigured in their minds and hearts. They have set up a hedge of selfishness against the

---

83 Grande, homily, San Salvador, August 6, 1970.
84 Grande, homily, San Salvador, August 6, 1970.
85 Grande, homily, San Salvador, August 6, 1970.
86 Grande, Homily, San Salvador, August 6, 1970.

4. Departure from the Seminary

Message of Jesus the Savior and against the challenging voice of the official witnesses of Christ in the church, the pope, and the bishops![87]

Undeniable proof of the rejection of the Gospel was to be found in the deplorable situation of the majority of the Salvadoran people, who were also believers. Rutilio described that reality with great skill, using quotes from *Populorum progressio* (9):

> The keen disquiet that has taken hold of the poor classes in the more industrialized countries is now also taking hold of the poor classes in countries that are almost exclusively agrarian. The subsistence farmers are becoming ever more aware of their *undeserved misery*. In addition, there is the scandal of outrageous disparities, not only in the possession of goods but even more in the exercise of power. While in some regions *a minority* enjoys highly refined living, the rest of the population, poor and dispersed, is deprived of almost all possibilities of personal initiative and responsibility. Often their living and working conditions are unworthy of human beings.[88]

Rutilio took advantage of the opportunity to remind his listeners that the president of the republic, "who honors us with his presence at this solemn act of church and homeland," had promised in his inaugural discourse that his governance would be inspired by that same encyclical. That had no doubt been a "daring and valiant" promise, observed Rutilio, because when the encyclical was published,

> many international centers of power and finance tore their vestments, utterly scandalized, and mounted their well-known mechanisms for defending their deep, dark interests and their highly refined self-regard. The *Wall Street Journal* called the document warmed-over Marxism, and the *Times* of New York took it as an indication that the Catholic Church was lurching to the left. We are not surprised by such reactions from these centers of the most exquisite materialism, which from that point on declared war against the church [...]. Those centers of power have complete control over powerful mass media and certain press agencies, whose output reaches even our own newspapers. [...] These centers of polished materialism, which involve certain minorities in our country that connive with them, would crucify Christ again if he returned to earth and announced his Gospel in this twentieth century of civilization.[89]

But Christians, Rutilio insisted, were obliged to accept the teachings of *Populorum progressio* because they coincided perfectly with "the purest essence of

---

87 Grande, homily, San Salvador, August 6, 1970.
88 Grande, homily, San Salvador, August 6, 1970.
89 Grande, homily, San Salvador, August 6, 1970.

the Gospel of *Jesus, Savior* of all peoples."[90] The salvation offered by Jesus Christ was liberation and transfiguration:

> Christ the Savior came to save the whole human being and every human being in order to transfigure them in every way. He came to make people new and to free them from every situation of sin and misery. He wanted them to take responsibility for themselves and to enjoy all the prerogatives of the children of God that were won for them by the triumph of the resurrection. This transformation of humanity was preached by Christ and won by him, and he requires it of all his followers. It has its starting point in baptism, which is the commitment that every Christian makes with the Risen Christ.[91]

Salvation, therefore, contrary to the dualistic vision characteristic of traditional Catholicism, was not concerned only with the soul of the individual: "If that were so, the individual would cease to be human." The human being was "an integral, inseparable composite of body and soul." Salvation was not something individual and private but had to encompass "the public plaza, the workplace, the world of business, the realm of politics." Salvation was involved "with children, with youth, with adults, and with all social classes without discrimination." It follows, then, that salvation means liberation from all human oppression and, as such, transfiguration.[92]

Rutilio therefore proposed that the church and the government work boldly and efficiently in tandem, seeking the transfiguration of the Salvadoran people,

> the people who live in the valleys, beside the beautiful lakes, along the Lempa River, near the coffee groves and the flowering cane fields, on the slopes of our volcanoes and mountains, in the small towns and villages, in the huge exploding urban concentrations, [...] and alongside the large estates.[93]

This description is no doubt folkloric, but very true to the Salvadoran character. It was the same kind of romantic evocation that Rutilio had previously criticized because it obscured the harsh Salvadoran reality. But now, having already described that reality and asked for its transfiguration, he was free to return to this idyllic imagery so beloved by his people.

Rutilio then assured the president and his government that the church was ready and willing to collaborate with them in this endeavor,

---

90 *Populorum progressio* (The development of peoples) is an encyclical issued by Pope Paul VI in 1967; it affirmed that the world economy should serve all humankind and not just the few.
91 Grande, homily, San Salvador, August 6, 1970.
92 Grande, homily, San Salvador, August 6, 1970.
93 Grande, homily, San Salvador, August 6, 1970.

4. Departure from the Seminary

so that all together, *in solidarity*, we can achieve a complete and authentic transfiguration of each and every one of the inhabitants of this sacred soil on which we were born, which we love, and for whose welfare we must all labor. In this task all our most cherished ideals coincide, since we are baptized Christians and we are citizens as well. The church and the government, showing mutual respect within their distinctive spheres, should collaborate *efficiently, boldly, and urgently* in drafting just, honest, and appropriate laws, as is required by the people's sovereignty, which is affirmed in article 1 of our Constitution.[94]

Rutilio emphasized that the church's collaboration would have to conform to the Gospel and the church's universal teaching. For the commentary that was to be read when the archbishop greeted the president after the Mass, Rutilio wrote: "The children of the church are also the faithful children of the homeland. [...] The church has always been present in the course of our history, through the outstanding deeds of its illustrious children and the heroes of our independence." The singing of the national anthem at the end of the celebration made it clear that the Eucharistic celebration had taken place beside the altar of the homeland.[95]

These statements were not simply concessions made by Rutilio to patriotic sentiment, nor were they spoken to ensure good relations between church and state. The message was different. He wanted it to be known that, just as the clergy had participated actively and resolutely in the founding of the Salvadoran nation, now in this new historical circumstance the clergy, faithful to their tradition, were coming to the defense of the interests of the Salvadoran people. It followed that no one should be surprised by the clergy's commitment to transforming the nation. This theme would appear again in a homily Rutilio gave in Aguilares on September 15, Independence Day.

The clergy's dedication to the cause of the people also had an evangelical basis. Priests, like Jesus, were called to be prophets of the kingdom. Wherever there was poverty and misery, they were to supply the transformative leaven of the Word of God in order to bring about the people's liberation. Wherever there was injustice, they were to cry out for justice to be restored. Poverty and injustice presented the church with what Rutilio called a "revolutionary challenge." Priests were called to cultivate the mystique of "revolutionary" transformation of the world, a mystique that was always ancient and always new. But that did not mean that priests were called to be guerrillas or to arm themselves with machetes; rather, they were to be preachers of the Word of God, which falls "like a seed in our mind, to be fertilized in our heart with the fruits of Christian existence" and which goes forth to meet us "in the furrow of events."[96]

---

94 Grande, homily, San Salvador, August 6, 1970.
95 ACSI. Rutilio Grande, "Commentaries for the Mass of the Titular Feast," San Salvador, August 6, 1970.
96 Grande, homily, San Salvador, August 6, 1970.

Convinced of the transformative power of the Word of God, Rutilio had no hesitation in calling it "revolutionary." Thus, stirred by the revolutionary expectations of the 1960s and 1970s, he boldly proposed a Christian revolution before the country's ecclesiastical, civil, and military authorities assembled there in the cathedral. However, the revolution of which Rutilio spoke was "based on the spirit of the Gospel, whose essence is *Love*, a love which excludes no person who comes into this world, either for skin color, or for social position, or for degree of intelligence, or even for sinfulness, which it seeks to remedy."[97] The Christian nature of this revolution in no way lessens its power to transform society. What is more, Christian revolution was far superior to the leftist revolutions waged in those decades because it purified revolutionary forces of abuses, deviations, and exclusions. Priests therefore had to follow the example of the apostles, who challenged the structures of injustice and misery of their time by means of their example, their word, and their readiness to give their lives. Like Jesus and the apostles, priests would inevitably be misunderstood, but they would also be considered the fathers of all for having set firm foundations for the family of God.[98]

"Christ the Transfigured Savior" would therefore be the true patron of El Salvador only when the Salvadoran people were transfigured. When that happened, all Salvadorans "together, with no one remaining behind," would be able to approach "without regrets" the feet of the Savior of the World. At that great moment,

> we will all reaffirm in good faith once again, as children of this homeland and of the Divine Savior, that third word we proclaim in our *National Anthem* and that waves in the wind on our flag: *Liberty*, full, complete, and definitive liberty for all the *Salvadoran* children of God![99]

Rutilio was awaiting that "not distant" day when

> we can cast a broad blessing on all the territory of our homeland, after it has been transfigured by all its children acting in solidarity according to the will of the Creator. In that day we will all sit at the table of our common Father, safely sheltered, enjoying all the gifts of creation that are made for all human beings.[100]

After the Mass was over, President Fidel Sánchez approached Rutilio to congratulate him on his homily and to ask for a copy. A few days later, Rutilio personally presented a copy to the president, who gave him in return an autographed

---

97 Grande, homily, San Salvador, August 6, 1970.
98 Grande, "Challenge of Pastoral Formation in the Seminaries: Part One."
99 Grande, homily, San Salvador, August 6, 1970.
100 Grande, "Regarding a Blessing."

copy of the Constitution. On solemn occasions in later years, when Rutilio was ministering in Aguilares, he would brandish that copy of the Constitution from the pulpit in order to reaffirm resolutely his faithful compliance.

The Bishops' Veto

Some bishops, however, were unhappy with the homily, which they considered radical and inappropriate. Their discontent only compounded their displeasure with Rutilio's interventions regarding the pastoral assembly. The disgruntled bishops reacted by withdrawing their confidence from Rutilio and vetoing his candidacy for the post of rector of the seminary.

The vice-provincial had in fact already proposed him as a candidate for the post. During his canonical visit to the seminary community in 1969, he concluded that a new rector was needed. The change was made necessary by several factors: the crisis in the community, the situation in the seminary, the rector's own health, and the bishops' and the nuncio's insistence that the post be occupied by a Salvadoran. The nuncio had asked that more Salvadoran Jesuits be assigned to the seminary or at least that "mainly Salvadorans be put in the position of rector" since that "would calm the reverend bishops."[101] This request was confirmed by another channel close to the nunciature and the bishops' conference. "Nationality is not a problem in the college, but it is among the clergy and among the seminarians," commented the rector.[102]

Given those circumstances, the candidacy of Rutilio seemed ideal to the vice-provincial, Father Azcue. "Father Rutilio Grande, a Salvadoran, is already there in the seminary, and he is an ex-student of the seminary to boot. He has very good relations with the reverend bishops and with not a few priests. It is evident that his nomination would be to their liking."[103] A first sounding of the Jesuit community drew a favorable opinion: "On this visitation, I asked several fathers, including one unsympathetic to [Rutilio], and all but one voted in favor of Father Grande. I believe that Father Grande is suitable for running the seminary, although possibly, as time goes by, he will appear less so."[104] Archbishop Chávez also considered Rutilio for the rectorship of the minor seminary of the archdiocese, which had been separated from the major seminary and transferred to the nearby city of Santa Tecla. However, the vice-provincial did not agree to that proposal.[105]

---

101 ARSI. José Ignacio Scheifler to superior general, San Salvador, February 23, 1969. C. América, 1007. Consultors. 1969.
102 ARSI. José Ignacio Scheifler to superior general, San Salvador, February 23, 1969. C. América, 1007. Consultors. 1969.
103 ACSI. Segundo Azcue to superior general, San Salvador, September 15, 1969.
104 ACSI. Segundo Azcue to superior general, San Salvador, September 15, 1969.
105 ACSI. Segundo Azcue to superior general, San Salvador, November 2, 1969.

Since his candidacy was agreeable to the community, Rutilio allowed his name to be proposed to the bishops' conference. He also presented a plan of governance, stating that as rector he would organize a formation team that would attempt to integrate spirituality, apostolate, and studies. His plan proposed to inculcate in the seminarians (1) a more incarnated spirituality, (2) greater understanding and love of the people through the apostolate, (3) better comprehension of the present-day human and social reality, and (4) study of revelation through theological reflection based on real life. To that end, he planned to organize the seminarians into small communities, which, once they were consolidated, would be inserted into the parochial structure of San Salvador and environs. Consequently, the seminary as such would function only as a center of formation. The more formal subjects would be accompanied by complementary studies, according to the needs expressed by the seminarians, so that the seminarians themselves would have an ever greater say in what they studied. This whole process, in Rutilio's conception, would develop in ongoing dialogue with the seminarians and in an ambience of companionship. The members of the formation team would consequently take part in the revision-of-life groups not as directors or simple observers but as participants who would transmit to the groups their spirit of inquiry. Rutilio was hoping that this way of proceeding would help each seminarian develop his own personal synthesis of academic study and lived experience.[106]

In January 1970, the vice-provincial requested *ad gobernandum* reports on Rutilio. The four informants all agreed that Rutilio would be a better rector than the existing one, but they did not consider him the ideal candidate. They agreed that he possessed many of the qualities required for the job. For one thing, he was Salvadoran, an important consideration given the concerns of some bishops and clergy. Moreover, he had shown great religious and priestly spirit; he possessed great charism and demonstrated a sound evangelical freedom; he was known for his kindness, his courage, and his closeness to the people; he was well known in church circles; he had abundant experience in priestly formation; and he was totally dedicated to the seminary. All these qualities made Rutilio the ideal candidate in the eyes of the bishops, the clergy, the seminarians, and the Jesuits.[107]

Despite all these qualities, however, the four informants had reservations, which they expressed quite freely. The greatest difficulty indicated by them was his psychological frailty: "He lacks sufficient psychic resistance," indicated one informant. He is "at the mercy of his nerves, more somber than is good, excessively taciturn," wrote another, who had known Rutilio since he was a child. And a third made note of Rutilio's intense emotion, which he attributed to his temperament and poor health rather than to anything blameworthy. The reports

---

106 ACSI. Rutilio Grande, "Projected Plan for Collaboration with the Seminary," San Salvador, 1970.
107 ACSI. Reports *ad gobernandum* of Rutilio Grande, San Salvador, January 1970.

4. Departure from the Seminary

also coincided in pointing out Rutilio's volatility. Sometimes he behaved as a stern prefect, but at other times he contradicted his own earlier decisions, thus causing confusion and disorder. One of the informants commented that Rutilio would be better as a spiritual guide than as a prefect. Three informants thought that Rutilio was stubborn and domineering; he was intolerant of the views of others. He accepted things he disagreed with out of religious commitment, but his acceptance was contradicted by his strong emotions, sometimes poorly controlled, and by his tendency to become obsessed with unimportant details and minor matters. Two informants indicated that there was a danger that he might be a little inconsiderate in using people for his own ends. The informants feared that these limitations would hinder his ability to manage effectively the business of the rector's office, thus complicating the situation of the seminary. Finally, they warned that "although the decisions are made in community, the rector would have to deal with difficult situations, and he might break down."[108]

In the consultors' meeting of the vice-province, there was apparently insufficient clarity about the wisdom of presenting Rutilio as a candidate for seminary rector. As a result, no decision was made, but the course of events in 1970 made it clear that there was an urgent need to change the rector. Given Scheifler's declining health and the conflict between him the community, which had become known to the seminarians, the decision could be postponed no longer. The vice-provincial, Miguel Francisco Estrada, agreed that a change was needed, but he was unsure what to do:

> I have no clear idea of who can be the seminary rector. The possible solution of naming Father Rutilio Grande as *vice-rector* offers some guarantee of success. He is accepted by the four men who work most immediately with the seminary; he is also accepted by the bishops and the priests [...] and by the seminarians, with whom he is in continual contact. He is also Salvadoran. His health is not robust, but his companions are there to help him and make sure that he does not take on too much work. His main job will be the community and external relations with the bishops and other people.[109]

The question was taken up again in the consultors' meeting of December 1970, where they discussed not only the candidacy of Rutilio but also that of Father Segura. The vice-provincial apparently inclined toward Segura, discounting the opinion of the seminary community, which favored Rutilio. But Segura himself favored Rutilio and even indicated that Rutilio should begin to function as provisional rector, pending the bishops' approval of his nomination. At that point, one of the consultors proposed the following line-up: Segura, Rutilio, and Amando

---

108 ACSI. Reports *ad gobernandum* of Rutilio Grande, San Salvador, January 1970.
109 ARSI. Miguel Francisco Estrada to superior general, San Salvador, September 29, 1970. C. América, 1008. *Praepos. Prov.* 1970.

López, who had just finished his doctoral studies in theology in Strasbourg and was teaching theology at the seminary.[110]

In mid-January 1971, the veto of the bishops' conference put an end to Rutilio's candidacy, which was backed only by the bishops of the archdiocese. The conference also demanded the expulsion of three seminarians, whom Rutilio defended to the point of personally pleading for them. The bishops' first choice for rector was Bishop Romero, but later they changed their opinion and proposed Segura. That candidacy did not prosper either, but this time it was because of the veto of the nuncio, who argued that Segura had been removed from the rectorship by the Holy See. The vice-provincial then proposed López, whom the bishops and the nuncio accepted immediately even though none of them knew him. So great was the bishops' enthusiasm that they announced López's appointment even before securing Rome's approval.

Rutilio wrote to the new rector, explaining his personal situation to him in detail. He decided to communicate with him by means of letter because the failure of his candidacy had provoked in him very strong emotions. Rutilio asked the rector to destroy the letter after reading it, as he had done when he was in crisis about the validity of his major orders. López did as Rutilio requested, and later they had a long conversation. Rutilio understood the bishops' veto to be an expression of their disapproval both of his work and of his simple presence in the seminary. He therefore felt in conscience that he should not continue as prefect, since the prefect had even more responsibility than the rector, nor should he continue as a simple professor. Frustrated and pained, Rutilio asked López to support his decision and not prevent him from leaving. He also asked him not to allow the three seminarians to be expelled, an aim he achieved.

A year and a half later, Rutilio commented to Bishop Rivera that "if that vote had taken place several months earlier, I would have had a near absolute majority in my favor, but I was then still locked into the *status quo*."[111] In hindsight, the reasons for the veto were clear:

> First there was the famous pastoral assembly, with its implications for me. Then came the talk I gave to the archdiocesan clergy, when we were reviewing the conclusions of the same pastoral assembly. Then came my homily on August 6 two years ago. The only thing I remember is that one bishop of my land, after the customary pontifical Mass on that August 6, when I was still tired and sweaty because of the preaching and acting as master of ceremonies, took me by the hand, sequestered me in the room of Modesto López [pastor of the cathedral], and spoke to me in a strange and alienated language, which I still recall with surprise![112]

---

110 ACSI. "Consultors' Meeting of December 11, 1970," Book of Consultors' Meetings of 1970.
111 ACSI. Rutilio Grande to Bishop Arturo Rivera Damas, Quito, Ecuador, July 27, 1972.
112 ACSI. Rutilio Grande to Bishop Arturo Rivera Damas, Quito, Ecuador, July 27, 1972.

4. Departure from the Seminary 119

In fact, the pressures had begun to mount in early May 1970, when Rutilio was helping with the preparations for the episcopal consecration of Bishop Romero. The origin of the pressures seems to have been his work in the seminary, his visits to El Paisnal, and his participation in the meetings of the vicariate of Quezaltepeque. The nuncio and some bishops associated Rutilio with that "explosive group of the vicariate of Quezaltepeque and their accomplices."[113] Rutilio spent two hours talking with the nuncio but failed to get him to understand his situation.

Despite his rejection, Rutilio felt no resentment toward the bishops; he always treated them with respect. When others criticized the stance of some bishop in his presence, even if he thought the bishop's action objectively mistaken, he always urged others to accept the reality and acknowledge the church's weakness. It was no surprise, then, that Rutilio sought to reestablish communication with some of the bishops in June and July 1972, a year and a half after leaving the seminary. From Quito, he wrote to Bishop Romero on the anniversary of his episcopal consecration (June 21), at which Rutilio had been the master of ceremonies.

The occasion had a very particular relevance for Rutilio. According to the testimony of a member of the missionary team of Aguilares, a former companion of Rutilio in the seminary,[114] Archbishop Chávez and Bishop Rivera had charged Rutilio with the tasks not only of telling Romero that they wanted to make him auxiliary bishop of the archdiocese but also of gaining his acceptance. In 1966, Romero had been transferred to San Salvador after more than two decades of pastoral ministry in San Miguel, his diocese of origin. In San Miguel, he had been the bishop's right-hand man, but the clergy did not accept him; they respected him for his priestly integrity, but they feared him. Romero was consequently sent to San Salvador and made secretary of the bishops' conference, with the title of monsignor. He found the ambience of the capital shocking, perhaps even repugnant. Rutilio encouraged him to live in the Jesuit community at the seminary, and it was there that the two of them became close friends.

According to a witness who knew both men, Rutilio "felt great affection for [Romero] because their personal characters and life stories were rather similar."[115] "I know for certain that both of them were good friends," stated a priest who was close to the bishops. Rutilio "had great admiration for Archbishop Romero, and the archbishop also greatly admired Father Grande for his upright life as a priest and for his pastoral work, with which he was in total agreement."[116] A third testimony, given by Cardinal Rosa, states that "they had a great friendship. [...] They enjoyed each other's company, and they talked a lot about their love for the church."[117] Romero himself bore witness to this deep friendship at

---

113 ACSI. Rutilio Grande to Miguel Francisco Estrada, San Salvador, July 5, 1970.
114 *Summarium testium*, witness 2, §28.
115 *Summarium testium*, witness 2, §28.
116 *Summarium testium*, witness 1, §12.
117 *Summarium testium*, witness 5, §72.

the beginning of his homily at the funeral of Rutilio and his two companions in the cathedral of San Salvador.

Contrary to Chávez's and Rivera's hopes, Romero's job as secretary of the bishops' conference did not free him from his "timid, intense, meticulous nature."[118] Besides the labors of his office, he would occasionally attend a meeting of the Cursillo movement,[119] but the rest of the time he spent, as Rutilio would say, "holed up" in the seminary, and more specifically, in his room. The seminarians said that they could hear him typing in his room until late at night. Given this situation, the two bishops and Rutilio considered that promoting him to auxiliary bishop might help him come out of his isolation.

When Rutilio, in compliance with the bishops' request, made the proposal to Romero, he put forth "objections and difficulties that were more material than anything else":

> Rutilio encouraged him, telling him that he, with his seminarians, would take care of everything. [...] He told him to pray over it and consult with some confessor. [...] Romero did consult with some priests; one was a Jesuit and another was Opus Dei. According to Tilo, they all encouraged him, and one of them even offered him material assistance.[120]

The consecration of Romero as bishop was therefore a culminating moment in the life of Rutilio. "Not only was he [Rutilio] close to him [Romero]; he was his factotum" and even administered the finances of the ceremony. Rutilio made Romero's consecration "a great ecclesial event for a church that, two years before Medellín, could not escape from its lethargy." "The photo that ended up as a poster, and that Rutilio kept as a precious jewel, says more than many words":

> They are leaving the great pontifical Mass and the episcopal ordination of Romero. The new bishop goes first, dispensing his first episcopal blessings; behind are the two bishops of the capital, half-serious and half-smiling. A little ahead of them and to their left is Rutilio with his head down, but adeptly performing as a great master of ceremonies. [...] The crozier is a gift of the Jesuits.[121]

In his congratulatory letter, Rutilio assured Romero that he had no doubt about the bishop's good intentions and his great love for the church. Romero responded with a question: "Why should it be necessary, in this sincere love for the church, to have to wound the heart of the persons we most appreciate? Is it a painful part of the passion of the Mystical Body?" He then added: "You have

---

118 *Summarium testium*, witness 2, §28.
119 "Cursillos in Christianity" is an apostolic movement that focuses on showing Christian laypeople how to become effective Christian leaders.
120 *Summarium testium*, witness 2, §28.
121 *Summarium testium*, witness 2, §29.

provided me the greatest priestly contentment on this anniversary you were so kind to remember. [...] Your short but rich thoughts have wrested from me a deep sigh of relief." Romero said that he had just that day visited the Basilica of the Sacred Heart of Jesus, the site of the altar used for his consecration, "and I recalled with renewed sentiments of gratitude and affection all the exquisite work and sacrifice you took on, along with our good lay friends, in order to perform that unforgettable liturgy of which you were the soul."[122]

Upon returning from Quito, Rutilio sought out Bishop Romero and, according to the testimony of Cardinal Rosa, shared with him what he had learned there—"a new form of doing pastoral ministry in the church."[123]

A few days later, at the beginning of July, Rutilio wrote to the bishop of Santa Ana, Benjamín Barrera. The pretext in this case was the patronal feast of the diocese:

> Stealthily, on tiptoes, and with a certain timidity, I want to enter the episcopal residence with this short letter, as I did on those afternoons when I was always kindly received by the reverend bishop, in those good times. [...] He even invited me to have supper with him, with great confidence and with affection I will never forget.[124]

Rutilio insisted that neither the distance nor the very unpleasant events of 1970 had been able to erase those pleasant memories. The events surrounding his leaving the seminary were no more than "curtains of smoke." As he did in his letter to Bishop Romero, Rutilio assured Bishop Barrera that "at no moment did it occur to me to doubt your kind and right intentions":

> I am passionately in love with the church and the Lord whom we all serve! It is possible that in our eagerness we have sometimes hurt persons we love who also love the church with just as much passion. These are the painful implications of the Mystical Body of Christ: the face and cross of the Mystery of the Death and Resurrection—in our own lives![125]

Thus, Rutilio used the same concepts in this letter that appeared in the reply he had received from Bishop Romero.

Bishop Barrera replied very affectionately, telling Rutilio that he should not worry about entering his house timidly or on tiptoes because he also had changed, despite the past "unpleasantness." The "curtains of smoke" would be easily removed, and the old friendship would be restored and strengthened. The bishop then shared with Rutilio his concerns about the seminary, which he

---

122 ACSI. Bishop Óscar A. Romero to Rutilio Grande, San Salvador, June 21, 1972.
123 *Summarium testium*, witness 5, §69.
124 ACSI. Rutilio Grande to Bishop Benjamín Barrera, Quito, Ecuador, July 10, 1972.
125 ACSI. Rutilio Grande to Bishop Benjamín Barrera, Quito, Ecuador, July 10, 1972.

referred to as an "idol" that was moving in "unimaginable directions." He was worried that the seminarians were not receiving proper instruction. Indeed, he wrote, they were presuming to "teach" the bishop "his duties and obligations," when it should be the other way around. "They're always saying it's a 'sign of the times,' but that can neither convince me nor console me. Where are we going to find the solution for such a bitter situation?"[126]

At the beginning of July, Bishop Rivera also wrote to Rutilio to express his regret at what had happened with his candidacy.

> Often the archbishop and I have lamented the fact that your presence in the seminary was not duly appreciated when the question was submitted to a vote. In all truth I have to tell you that López is a great rector. It's a shame that he is not appreciated either.[127]

In his reply, Rutilio tried to console his friend by downplaying the importance of what had happened:

> In the end, dear bishop, all that is in the past. I'm grateful for what you tell me regarding your conversations with the archbishop about that vote to have me remain in the seminary and about your personal judgment on the matter. I am grateful, but I am happy with the Providence of God, which has impelled me along other paths as a result of those events.[128]

Rutilio ended his letter by telling Bishop Rivera that he would commend both him and Archbishop Chávez to the Lord: "I ask the Lord to help you and give you strength so that you do not lose heart in the midst of the inevitable contradictions. It is a question of mentality, a question of joint actions *et reliqua* in the assembly of bishops and in the assembly of priests."[129]

---

126 ACSI. Bishop Benjamín Barrera to Rutilio Grande, Santa Ana, July 16, 1972.
127 ACSI. Bishop Arturo Rivera Damas to Rutilio Grande, San Salvador, July 9, 1972.
128 ACSI. Rutilio Grande to Bishop Arturo Rivera Damas, Quito, Ecuador, July 27, 1972.
129 ACSI. Rutilio Grande to Bishop Arturo Rivera Damas, Quito, Ecuador, July 27, 1972.

5. The Pastoral Project

Rutilio's departure from the seminary left him disoriented. The training of clergy was the work he had always thought to be his true vocation, but now it was not possible. Probably he had never imagined himself being involved in any work other than the seminary. A secondary school like the Externado San José, where they sent him after he left the seminary, was not for him a viable alternative, and he suddenly found himself seeking other possibilities. Though he was unaware of it at the moment, Rutilio's life was passing along paths that were unfamiliar to him but quite congruent with his way of thinking and feeling.

Before the possibility of continuing to work in the seminary was completely closed off to him, Rutilio thought it would be helpful to take a course at the Latin American Pastoral Institute (Instituto Pastoral Latinoamericano [IPLA]), located in Quito, Ecuador. He had already obtained information about the program.

The Encounter with Latin American Pastoral Ministry

Halfway through 1971, when it had already become clear that the Colegio Externado was not the best option for Rutilio, the vice-provincial considered sending him as superior of the Jesuit residence in San José, Costa Rica. The Jesuits in that country served in Our Lady of Lourdes Parish, which had a large and growing population. The vice-province's consultors advised against sending Rutilio there, arguing that in San José he would not have as much influence as he would have in El Salvador. The consultors thought that, given his influence with the Salvadoran clergy and his genius for pastoral ministry, it would not be good for him to be absent from El Salvador for a long period. Rutilio, for his part, did not cherish the idea of being assigned to San José, but he was very eager to attend the IPLA in Ecuador.[1]

Accordingly, Rutilio flew to Nicaragua on December 7, 1971, avoiding farewells: "I found myself all alone at the airport, as I wished, without any fuss or emotion."[2] Stopping first in Managua, he stayed at the Jesuit residence at Santo Domingo Parish in the center of the city, where he felt well received by the community. He traveled around Nicaragua, visiting the works of the Society, and he attended a meeting of the Jesuits of that country on the shores of the Great Lake. Like most Salvadorans who visit Nicaragua for the first time, he was surprised by the sheer extent of its territory, which contrasted sharply with his "sardine-sized" El Salvador. That startling difference made him reflect on the advantages of a

---

1 ACSI. "Consultors' Meeting of August 9, 1971," Book of Consultors' Meeting for 1971.
2 ACSI. Rutilio Grande to Flavio Grande and family, Managua, December 21, 1971.

unified Central America, although he was unable to get his hopes up too high: "It's a shame, but we are so backward in every way with our petty tyrants and primitive ideas! And our masters to the north don't want us to unite either; they want us to continue being their colonies."[3]

On January 3, 1972, Rutilio traveled by land to San José, where he stayed until January 10. Spending the week at the parish residence, he felt somewhat uncomfortable because the community reproached him for having declined the post of superior. Rutilio told them frankly that he had refused the position because he had no clarity about what he would have been able to do there pastorally.[4] During his stay in Costa Rica, he visited the grave of his brother Alberto,[5] who had died there in 1964.

Arriving in Panama City on January 11, 1972, Rutilio stayed with the community of the Colegio Javier. On January 14, he traveled to Toabré and Miraflores (Coclé), where he stood in for the rector at a camp being run by the social service organization of the colegio. He later spent three weeks substituting for the pastor at Las Lajas (Chiriquí). He took advantage of his stay there to study the pastoral ministry of the region and to visit the Ngäbe community in the mountains of Hato Pilón, whom he described as "people completely abandoned by the church and the government." They asked him to baptize their children, but he declined since they were not properly catechized, and he did not have time to instruct them himself. "The days I spent with the Indians were hard," he confessed. On his last day there, they organized a big feast, killing a rooster and serving *chicha* (corn liquor): "They offered me a big cup of *chicha*. Even though I felt my stomach churning and was tremendously afraid of vomiting, I didn't want to offend them in the least, so I downed the big cup with my eyes closed, doing my best to appear calm and collected."[6] Rutilio was so impressed with his visit to the Ngäbe that, if it were up to him, he would have remained "working all my life among those poor Indians in order to lift them up in every sense."[7] On February 18, however, he returned to Panama City and on the twenty-second he flew to Quito.

His trip through Central America provoked amazement and murmurings among the Jesuits, but Rutilio paid them little heed, perhaps because he saw clearly what his objective was: "I am traveling with the hope of refreshing my knowledge." He even thought of writing an account of his experiences for the Salvadoran press. Arriving in Quito, he went to Cotocollao, where he had been a student more than two decades earlier: "I was visiting those places and reliving experiences."[8]

---

3   ACSI. Rutilio Grande to Flavio Grande and family, Managua, December 21, 1971.
4   ACSI. Rutilio Grande to Miguel F. Estrada, Quito, Ecuador, February 26, 1972.
5   ACSI. Rutilio Grande to Miguel F. Estrada, Quito, Ecuador, February 26, 1972.
6   ACSI. Rutilio Grande to Flavio Grande and family, Panama, February 19, 1972.
7   ACSI. Rutilio Grande to Flavio Grande and family, Panama, February 19, 1972.
8   ACSI. Rutilio Grande to Miguel F. Estrada, Quito, Ecuador, February 26, 1972.

5. The Pastoral Project

On March 1, 1972, Rutilio enrolled in the IPLA VII course, which lasted until July 28. There were sixty-nine people matriculated in the course, including two other Salvadoran priests: Higinio Alas and Marcos R. Revelo, who later became auxiliary bishop of San Salvador and then bishop of Santa Ana. Also attending the course were two Augustinian priests who worked in El Salvador.[9] IPLA at that time was one of the most important and creative centers for Latin American pastoral ministry in the decade of the 1970s. By encouraging pastoral and theological thought and creating a space for the exchange of ideas, the institute had made important contributions to the work of the Medellín conference of Latin American bishops in 1968. It was at IPLA that discussion first took place about the need for a specifically Latin American theology. Two exceptional Latin American prelates were linked to this effort: Manuel Larraín, bishop of Talca, Chile; and Leónidas Proaño, bishop of Riobamba, Ecuador. According to Proaño, the threefold mission of IPLA was to facilitate a clear and objective understanding of the Latin American reality, encourage theological reflection on that reality, and promote pastoral planning in accord with that reflection. Its courses were therefore designed to transmit a mystique "that leads us to the audacity and creativity of the Spirit and that fosters originality, dynamism, and community spirit."[10]

The IPLA program consisted of three blocks: (1) Latin American reality and theology of the world, (2) ecclesiology, and (3) Latin American pastoral ministry. Analysis of the Latin American reality from a cultural and socioeconomic perspective was complemented by a theology of the world, which involved studying the "signs of the times," secularization, ideologies, and the relation between church and society as understood by Vatican II. This block emphasized Christian change, revolution, violence, liberation theology, and the sociopolitical implications of pastoral ministry. The ecclesiological block focused on topics such as the church and the kingdom of God, salvation and the visible church, the church as a sacrament of Communion, the theological and pastoral meaning of ministries, the role of the laity, the nature of consecrated life, and the importance of base Christian communities. The third block was dedicated to the social, cultural, and theological dimensions of pastoral ministry and to the practice and structure of collaborative pastoral ministry.

The academic work was supplemented with pastoral experiences, intense community life, close teamwork, and liturgical celebration in which the participants entered fully into the Latin American ecclesial experience. The participants also organized their own seminars and courses in addition to the formal program. At the end of the first stage of the course, the students took part in a field investigation under the direction of sociologists and anthropologists, and in the final stage of the program they were asked to write a pastoral monograph, either

---

9   ACSI. Rutilio Grande to Miguel F. Estrada, Quito, Ecuador, February 26, 1972.
10 Bishop Leónidas Proaño, "Address at the Inauguration of IPLA: Diocesan Institute of Riobamba," in *Leónidas Proaño, 25 años obispo de Riobamba* (Lima: CEP, 1978), 64–65, 246.

individually or as a group. No information is available on Rutilio's monograph. Those who finished the course received a certificate from CELAM attesting to their participation.

At IPLA, Rutilio stood out among his companions by virtue of his leadership qualities, his profound pastoral sense, and his determination to work with the poor. Some joked with him, telling him he would soon be a bishop. Rutilio made some good friends there who tried to stay in touch with him in the years following, but he apparently did not respond to them, perhaps for lack of time or energy to answer their letters. He was not constant either in attending the reunions of IPLA graduates in El Salvador. Parish and archdiocesan responsibilities took up his time and consumed his energy.

Bishop Proaño made a great impact on Rutilio, who found in him "the perfect realization of Paulo Freire and his methodology" and "the incarnation of Gospel values in a prophetic method and philosophy":[11]

> There is no doubt that the reverend bishop of that diocese is a great man, very much in line with the church's current thinking, level-headed, respectful of others, fully involved in the reality of the people, well situated in the historical present, imperturbable in the face of adversities, clear-thinking and decided in his actions, in no way compromised by the establishment.[12]

In the first days of August, after the course was finished, Rutilio accepted Bishop Proaño's invitation to get to know the reality of his diocese. In the company of Alas, he traveled to Riobamba, where he joined one of the missionary evangelization teams. His own team, which included Father Carlos Vera and Sister Sofía Rosero, was sent to the parish of Penique in the province of Chimborazo.

After that, Rutilio spent two weeks in the village of Gaviñay,[13] living in the home of the Carranza Herrera family. The father, Don Mesías, recalls that despite the cold—the village has the lowest temperatures in the parish—Rutilio did not use the family's woolen blankets but only a sleeping bag. The mother, Milita, states that Rutilio liked the aromatic waters, especially *poleo*,[14] which he drank with his *mote* for breakfast.[15] The mission activities took place in the community school, which was reached by crossing a stream. The mud and freezing water were no obstacle for Rutilio, but if the current was too strong, activities were held in the Carranza Herrera household, under a Petromax lamp.[16]

---

11   ACSI. Rutilio Grande, "Notebook with Assorted Notes of IPLA."
12   ACSI. Rutilio Grande to Bishop Arturo Rivera Damas, Quito, Ecuador, July 27, 1972.
13   Personal communication with Father Gilberto Freire, provincial of Ecuador, San Salvador, May 2016.
14   A species belonging to the genus *Mentha*.
15   Generic name for different grains or vegetables cooked with water.
16   Lamp that burns paraffin. ACSI. "Gaviñay and Father Rutilio Grande," testimony of the Carranza Herrera family, Gaviñay, June 6, 2015.

Rutilio was given a warm welcome in all the homes of the community. Everyone who dealt with him agrees that he was a man of God, courteous, kind, unassuming, amiable, and wonderfully approachable. They realized that he was a man dedicated to God and the cause of the poor. One day, as he was eating in the home of Elías Carranza, his host asked him to be the godfather of his recently born son. Rutilio agreed, and the child was baptized with the name Juan Rutilio Carranza Olivo, in honor of his godfather. Many anecdotes and reminiscences about Rutilio remained engraved in the memory of the Gaviñay community. The families not only treasured the stories but transmitted them to the next generation, so that even today many adults think of Rutilio with reverence and affection.[17]

The IPLA experience was a stroke of luck for Rutilio because it taught him how to apply the method of Freire to evangelization, especially in the base ecclesial communities. It also moved him to experience what he called a "second vocation" within his general vocation to the consecrated life.[18] In fact, during those months, he formulated what he called his "primary and fundamental option." He was so enthusiastic about the IPLA experience that he recommended it to Bishop Rivera for the clergy of the archdiocese of San Salvador. Rivera responded that "it would be very painful for us not to be able to send [priests] there, either from here or from the other dioceses."[19]

On his way back from Quito, Rutilio spent three weeks in Panama City in order to learn more about the project in the San Miguelito slum, at that time one of the most original pastoral experiments in Central America. While in Panama, he also investigated the courses given at the Inter-American Cooperative Institute. On his way back home, he wanted to travel to Choluteca, Honduras, to study the pioneering experience of the Canadian priests there, but his Salvadoran nationality made it impossible for him to travel to that country.[20]

His Primary and Fundamental Option

Rutilio's "primary and fundamental option" was a declaration of principles spelling out his commitment to the liberation of the poor and his desire to remain faithful to his vocation as priest and religious. Rutilio apparently began to elaborate these principles during the last two years he spent in the seminary, years that were certainly difficult for him. The document systematizes his long-held hopes regarding the option for the poor and for liberation of the Central American peoples, the same option that the vice-province had made. As a result of

---

17 ACSI. "Gaviñay and Father Rutilio Grande," testimony of the Carranza Herrera family, Gaviñay, June 6, 2015; and "Intervention of Juan Rutilio Carranza Olivo," Gaviñay, June 7, 2015.
18 ACSI. Rutilio Grande to Jesús Bengoechea, Quito, Ecuador, July 23, 1972.
19 ACSI. Bishop Arturo Rivera Damas to Rutilio Grande, San Salvador, July 9, 1972.
20 After the 1969 war, El Salvador and Honduras broke off diplomatic relations.

his search for new horizons after leaving the seminary, Rutilio grew into a more authentically Latin American identity. His search had personal dimensions, but it also had an institutional dimension, for it embodied the challenges clearly enunciated by Medellín and the Thirty-Second General Congregation of the Society of Jesus.

One of Rutilio's basic commitments was "working with a pastoral team in a rural zone or in a marginal urban neighborhood in order to promote integral human development by raising Christian consciousness."[21] For Rutilio, the considerations leading to that option were several: the Central American reality, the Gospel, the teaching of the universal and the regional church (that is, Vatican II and Medellín), the Thirty-Second General Congregation, and the post-1969 declarations of the Central American vice-province.

The constitutive elements of Rutilio's "primary and fundamental option" were a mixed missionary team, pastoral experience in rural zone or a marginal urban neighborhood, close interlocking of evangelization and human advancement, and a methodology for raising Christian consciousness. Drawing on his experience in the seminary, Rutilio stressed the need for working as a team, which meant collaborating as an apostolic community with a shared mission. He believed that such an approach offered the best guarantee of creativity and dynamism. The internal life of the missionary team would be infused with an enfleshed spirituality that would insure good planning, serious reflection, eagerness for study, and a time to rest when needed.[22]

A diocesan priest who was a member of the missionary team pointed out in his testimony that Rutilio was "respectful of the methods and attentive to the physical and spiritual health of all the other priests on the team. He was responsible, reliable, and punctual." On a more personal level, the witness observed, Rutilio

> certainly stood out for his virtues of devotion, integrity, solidarity, and responsibility. He made his meditation and prayed the liturgy of hours. He made his personal prayers very early in the morning, under the calabash tree in the rectory yard. Other times he would pray in his room or before the Blessed Sacrament.[23]

In contrast to the traditional apostolic team, the one proposed by Rutilio would include not only Jesuits but other priests and religious. Besides Rutilio, the team already had another Jesuit, Jesús Bengoechea, who had taught at the seminary during his regency and had previously discussed the project with Rutilio. Also to be included on the team were some women religious and diocesan priests. The combination of Jesuits and women religious on the team was nothing new

---

21 ACSI. Rutilio Grande, "My Primary and Fundamental Option," Quito, Ecuador, 1972.
22 Grande, "My Primary and Fundamental Option."
23 *Summarium testium*, witness 18, §345.

5. The Pastoral Project

since it had been done before in Latin America. What was novel was the inclusion of members of the diocesan clergy. One of Rutilio's dreams was to conduct a pastoral experience that would reintegrate the two clergies, religious and secular, that had become isolated from one another and were sometimes even at odds. He was not unaware of the difficulties of such an endeavor; he was fully conscious of the many suspicions on both sides. Rutilio was opposed to the idea of making the parish a religious fortress; instead, he wanted it to be an open, welcoming space in the center of the diocese. His plan therefore contemplated turning the parish over to the diocesan clergy at the end of five years. The missionary team would then move to another parish.[24]

Another novel aspect of Rutilio's project was the replicable nature of the mission. His hope was that the mission would be attractive enough to inspire imitation in others. If the team was sufficiently original, creative, and dynamic, it would motivate others to undertake similar projects. Therefore, the missionary team could not remain isolated; it had to open itself to the experiences of other similar teams. Its influence would thus be considerably extended, not only to neighboring parishes but to those farther away. When this happened, a more generalized team pastoral ministry could develop.[25]

In Rutilio's vision, a rural zone or a marginal urban neighborhood would be the ideal place to develop such a project, for it was there that the poor were concentrated. From such people, he had come himself, and he wished now to return to them in order to put his knowledge and his experience at their service. Rutilio felt that his travels, his studies, and his previous work had distanced him and even alienated him from his own people, from those to whom he was so indebted. He stated as much dramatically when he spoke at the vice-provincial congregation in April 1974. He told his fellow Jesuits that, even though his weekend visits to El Paisnal had brought him closer to the people, they left him unsatisfied since they seemed to be only a palliative. Those visits, however, had helped him realize the need for drawing on the best of the Salvadoran people in order to transform society; only by developing Christian consciousness among the poor would this be possible.

The more conscious the great majority of the poor became of their situation, Rutilio said, the more they would organize themselves, and the more they would pressure the minorities to make the changes that justice demanded but that those minorities would never undertake on their own. Given the disunity among the people, the dispersion of forces, the disorientation, and the lack of initiative and creativity, Rutilio saw the present moment as decisive. The challenge was formidable, as were the risks. Until then, there had been no adequate pastoral responses to the dire situation of the people. Such responses could

---

24 Grande, "My Primary and Fundamental Option."
25 Grande, "My Primary and Fundamental Option."

emerge only out of the process of the people's own self-transformation. It was therefore necessary for the clergy to become immersed in that process and be open to the urgent appeal of the social reality and the Gospel. The missionary team was to be characterized by radical openness, constant searching, continual conversion, and bold testimony.[26]

While Rutilio was elaborating his pastoral project, the vice-provincial, Father Estrada, was considering where he would assign Rutilio when he returned from the IPLA course. In March 1972, he proposed to Rutilio that he conduct a renewal project in the residences and parishes of the vice-province, with the help of an itinerant team. The idea was to broaden the horizons and "raise the consciousness," as was said in those days, of the Jesuits working in pastoral ministry. The vice-provincial claimed that the men themselves were asking for such renewal. Since the vice-province at that time was reorganizing its apostolic activity in accord with the liberation perspective proposed by Medellín and the Thirty-Second General Congregation, Estrada's proposal fit well within that context.[27]

Another possibility proposed to Rutilio was directing the pastoral experiences of the Jesuit scholastics studying philosophy at the UCA. The experiences would be centered on the parish of Antiguo Cuscatlán, a small municipality bordering on El Salvador and near the university. The residence of the scholastics was located there. The idea was that Rutilio would be the pastor and the students would collaborate with the parish ministry under his direction.[28]

Rutilio declined these various offers. The need to revitalize the vision of the residences and the parishes was real, but he did not agree with the solution proposed by the vice-provincial. The pastoral activity of the vice-province had never been well planned. The residences and the parishes had been set up randomly as Jesuits migrated to them from the schools and other works;[29] they had thus tended to become refuges for individuals who did not fit in anywhere else. Such conditions were not conducive to good pastoral ministry since there were no shared objectives and no teamwork. Rutilio complained that Jesuits "consider [themselves] fit for this quasi-universal ministry" of pastoral work, which in practice is reduced to hearing confessions, saying Masses, baptizing, and attending to the sick.[30] For their part, the Jesuits in the schools thought that pastoral work was something "anybody can do."[31]

The age of the Jesuits living in the residences was another difficulty. Of the forty-seven priests and brothers who, according to the vice-province directory,

---

26   Grande, "My Primary and Fundamental Option."
27   ACSI. Miguel F. Estrada to Rutilio Grande, San Salvador, March 10, 1972.
28   ACSI. Néstor Jaén to Rutilio Grande, San Salvador, July 3, 1972.
29   ACSI. Rutilio Grande to Miguel F. Estrada, Quito, Ecuador, June 27, 1972.
30   ACSI. Rutilio Grande, provincial delegate for pastoral ministry, "Analysis of the Pastoral Ministry of the Province," San Salvador, October 21, 1976.
31   ACSI. Rutilio Grande to Miguel F. Estrada, Quito, Ecuador, June 27, 1972.

5. The Pastoral Project

were assigned to the residences, many were already "well along in years" and naturally resistant to any change. Others were using the residence simply as a place to stay since their activities were outside the pastoral sphere. Of those who were dedicated full time to the work in the residence and the adjoining church, only a few showed any enthusiasm for change. Given these conditions, Rutilio concluded that a renewal project was neither viable nor advisable.[32]

Moreover, Rutilio did not want to present himself to his fellow Jesuits as someone designated to "raise their consciousness." Greater awareness of the social and ecclesial reality needed to be based on experience, and it had to be something desired by the persons involved. Even though the vice-province had decided in September 1970 to commit itself to the liberation of the poor as the best way to implement the decrees of General Congregation 32, many Jesuits were opposed to that decision. Attempting to change their perspective would be very difficult. Another problem was that the residences and parishes of the vice-province generally did not participate in the pastoral projects of their respective dioceses.[33]

While resisting these particular proposals, Rutilio did not reject the idea of getting involved in pastoral work. He thought an attempt could be made to form a permanent team that would be based in one of the residences and dedicated to helping Jesuits involved in pastoral activities. But such an approach would meet up with an enormous obstacle: Jesuits had never proceeded in that manner before, and no attempt had ever been made to "re-educate" older Jesuits. In any case, Rutilio was opposed to the idea of an itinerant renewal team, and he told the vice-provincial so. What he proposed instead, as a perhaps more realistic possibility, was to send Jesuits for renewal programs outside the province. Along the same line, he recommended that the Jesuits in the schools get to know other apostolic experiences; after all, they were the most numerous and also the ones most resistant to change and the option for liberation.[34]

Reality proved Rutilio right. Consequent on a meeting of Jesuits involved in pastoral work—held in San José, Costa Rica, from February 5 to 7, 1974—Rutilio was named the vice-provincial assistant for pastoral ministry. It became clear at that meeting, as each priest explained his style of ministry, that there was no teamwork and little desire to move away from the traditional patterns. Rutilio gave a report of his experience at IPLA, but few showed much interest. Even as vice-provincial assistant for pastoral ministry, he found he could do little to coordinate the area because of the pronounced individualism of the men and their reluctance to change. As a result of the great differences in mentalities and pastoral practices, Rutilio found the job thankless and frustrating. The reality of

---

32 ACSI. Rutilio Grande to Miguel F. Estrada, Quito, Ecuador, June 27, 1972.
33 ACSI. Rutilio Grande to Jesús A. Bengoechea, Quito, Ecuador, July 23, 1972; and Rutilio Grande to Miguel F. Estrada, Quito, Ecuador, June 27, 1972.
34 ACSI. Rutilio Grande to Miguel F. Estrada, Quito, Ecuador, June 27, 1972.

the residences and parishes contrasted sharply with what was happening at Aguilares, which by then had become a model for parish ministry, both for the archdiocese and the vice-province. "For good or for ill, that's the way it is," Rutilio explained to the vice-provincial.[35]

Despite the difficulties, Rutilio distinguished between two types of pastoral activity, and he made recommendations regarding each. First, he recommended that no changes be made with regard to the traditional residences and parishes, which were more oriented to preserving the faith. A second recommendation concerned new pastoral projects; there the assistant for pastoral ministry could play an important role of coordination by helping to identify problems and priorities, organizing meetings and courses, and developing joint processes for planning and evaluation. Rutilio thought that it would also be quite advantageous for the pastoral sector to draw on the resources of UCA's Center for Theological Reflection and the vice-province's Center for Social Research and Action. He was convinced that this type of pastoral activity would grow substantially if more Jesuits were willing to work among the poor masses in the rural zones and the marginal urban areas.[36]

Rutilio's questioning of the traditional way of doing things was a reflection of the crisis running through the whole Salvadoran church. Both the vice-province and the church in general understood that their apostolic activity needed to be reoriented in order to face the social challenges of the region and bring to bear on them the teachings of Vatican II and Medellín. The Jesuits, moreover, had as a vice-province made a firm commitment to the option for liberation. In December 1969, while making their annual spiritual exercises, the Jesuits of Central America evaluated their apostolic activity, and in September 1970 they resolved to make the liberation of the poor a priority of their apostolic work. This reformulation of the identity and the mission of the vice-province provoked a series of personal and institutional crises that were not overcome until the beginning of the 1980s. The harsh reality of Central America forced the Jesuits to decide: Would they preserve obsolete forms and practices, or would they make serious changes in their apostolic work?

When it came to the urgency of changing direction, Rutilio had a certain advantage because he had already experienced the same type of crisis during his last three years in the seminary. He had been able to see at that time how the traditional mentality and the old-style ministry had given way to routine, exhaustion, and lack of apostolic zeal. The Jesuit assembly of 1969 left a powerful impact on Rutilio, for it was his first exposure to the radical perspective of liberation theology. Later, at the IPLA course, he would explore its theoretical and practical implications more deeply. As he himself stated, the insights of

---

35   Grande, "Analysis of the Pastoral Ministry of the Province."
36   Grande, "Analysis of the Pastoral Ministry of the Province."

5. The Pastoral Project

liberation theology motivated him to take the firm stand he did during the conflicts following the pastoral assembly, and it inspired the homily he gave on August 6, 1970. It was in this context that he formulated his "primary and fundamental option."

The questioning of the vice-province's pastoral activity led inevitably to scrutiny of the educational apostolate, especially the secondary schools, where most Jesuits were concentrated. Rutilio's analysis was quite sobering. He claimed that the schools functioned as private businesses, alienated from "the tremendous social, moral, and religious realities" around them. Religion classes and spiritual guidance were imparted in an individualist manner, without any social perspective. The schools' apostolic and spiritual activities were geared more to personal improvement than to social change. The alumni of the schools were "spiritually bourgeois" and failed to engage in apostolic activities or communal efforts. Those Jesuits who possessed a true apostolic spirit, in the strict Ignatian sense, were few, Rutilio judged. Most Jesuits lived secluded in the schools, which were like "little islands" where they languished in their routines. Rutilio expressed surprise that even the fourth-year theologians longed for that sheltered type of life, a sort of "sinecure of the sons of Saint Ignatius." He thought that certain common expressions, such as "the church has asked the Society" or "this is a service of the Society to the church," revealed sentiments that were inimical to the church's well-being.[37]

The Jesuits in the schools had never sat down to discuss seriously the role and purpose of their institutions. The prevailing mindset, in Rutilio's view, was contrary to the bold, resolute, and always innovative vision of Ignatius:

> Given the quasi-business setting in which we more or less move, and the lack of idealism and profound religious understanding of our vocation, it is obvious that prayer does not find the nourishing ground it needs, and there is no palpable experience of the need for prayer to be connected to our daily life.[38]

When answering the survey carried out by the province on this question—a survey originally proposed by the superior general—Rutilio associated apostolic languor with neglect of prayer. He granted that it was difficult to assess a person's fidelity to prayer "since it was a very subjective assessment about something impossible to verify," but he thought that the pronounced individualism and the lack of apostolic spirit of the Jesuits at the seminary were objectively verifiable. Due to individualism, Jesuits living under the same roof and with the same juridical status were effectively working as strangers and were lacking apostolic enthusiasm. As a result, Rutilio wrote, prayer became "something artificial

---

37 ACSI. Rutilio Grande, "Survey on Prayer in the Vice-province," San Salvador, July 14, 1968.
38 Grande, "Survey on Prayer in the Vice-province."

and juxtaposed, an airtight compartment, in no way incarnate or existential, etc. Something ill befitting our life."[39]

Rutilio's solution was to return to the Ignatian ideal. He therefore proposed replacing the outworn community conversations with community-life meetings. In such meetings, there would be a review of life using the see-judge-act process, which was characteristic of the French methodology that had much influenced Rutilio:

> The Society has such wonderful values and such great richness; our only regret would be to fail to make good use of them in these times. The values and essences contained in our Constitutions are so perennial and also so contemporary; we must make a most earnest effort to live them fully and seek ways to make them more effective.[40]

The Option for the Poor

In the vice-provincial congregation of 1974, Rutilio returned to these themes, enriched by his experience of ministry in the parish of Aguilares. Speaking to the Jesuit assembly, he not only reaffirmed his earlier convictions but reformulated them with greater clarity and radicalism, influenced strongly, no doubt, by his experiences in the IPLA course, in the diocese of Riobamba, and in the parish of Aguilares. The 1974 congregation took place in a very tense atmosphere since two opposed tendencies were in open confrontation. One side thought that merely minor adjustments were needed to respond to the challenges being presented by the social reality and the needs of the church. The other side, which included Jesuits like Rutilio, demanded that the vice-province as a body make a decisive option for the poor. The tension deeply affected Rutilio and made him react as he often did in such circumstances: he confessed to speaking "rashly and impulsively, at the risk of appearing simplistic and radical."[41] Some Jesuits in the assembly, particularly his former rector, Father Segura, saw him as "disjointed and intemperate in his speech."[42]

Rutilio's interventions in the assembly hall were likely to be judged not by their intrinsic reasonableness or pertinence but by the political tendency with which he was supposedly identified. Rutilio took precautions in this regard, making it clear that he was speaking for himself alone, not at the request of or in representation of anyone else:

> I recognize that one cannot be neutral: there are paths that are more in accord with the Gospel and more in accord with the historical process of the

---

39 Grande, "Survey on Prayer in the Vice-province."
40 Grande, "Survey on Prayer in the Vice-province."
41 Grande, "Address to the Vice-provincial Congregation."
42 ACSI. Ladislao Segura, report *ad gobernandum*, San Salvador, July 19, 1976.

world and the church itself. Therefore, while respecting a sound pluralism, which may at times be ambiguous, I cannot do less than acknowledge the Ignatian *magis* and embrace *what is most honest, most just, and most appropriate* for our least Society, as an integral part of the church and not a sect, for the service of the world.[43]

Rutilio did not want to present himself as a teacher, a doctor, a technician, or a preacher but simply as a "humble brother" of the assembled companions:

[I am aware of] the danger of being considered simple and not adding anything new to what has already perhaps been repeatedly said in a theoretical way in this hall, but I am very fearful that we will formulate and ratify stances whose contents will only slumber in the depths of many consciences, as has happened with the innumerable documents already published.[44]

Rutilio stressed that he was speaking with "great love" for the Society of Jesus "despite its deficiencies, and likewise for the church, our common mother."

If Rutilio spoke for anyone, it was for the poor masses who lacked any voice. "I want my voice to be the voice of the great majority of the people of my country and of other [Central American countries], as much as possible." He therefore presented himself as one more member of the Salvadoran people: "*Civis Romanus Sum!* [...] by race a blend of *café con leche* and proud of it!" He asked the assembled Jesuits

to be wholly and radically evangelized by taking the side of the smallest, so that they might control their own destiny. [...] Otherwise we will continue to be colonizers if not dominators in one form or another; we will be like the native minorities, taking after the gringos or the Europeans![45]

Rutilio's appeal was directed at Jesuits who, in his mind, were sealed off in a small, elitist circle that was "just as alienated as we are—or even more so—from the global reality of our countries": "We are frankly divorced from our reality, and when I say "reality," I mean not only the human and socioeconomic reality of the whole people but the very first reality, God, the God of Jesus Christ, whom we are bound to proclaim boldly."[46]

Rutilio therefore issued a call for "the greater identification of all of us with the true people of our countries." His summons took on a dramatic tone when he appealed directly to the Spanish priests in the assembly, who were the majority. "I beseech you, dear brother Jesuits from Spain, who are the great majority in this hall, thirty-two of the total of thirty-nine—please hear what I am saying."

---

43   Grande, "Address to the Vice-provincial Congregation."
44   Grande, "Address to the Vice-provincial Congregation."
45   Grande, "Address to the Vice-provincial Congregation."
46   Grande, "Address to the Vice-provincial Congregation."

The predominance of Spanish Jesuits in the vice-province was a thorny and delicate issue that had long been questioned. Rutilio had no doubts about their good intentions, but the problem was the Spanish origin, formation, and culture of those Jesuits, qualities that were accentuated by an epoch that did not encourage contact with the outside world. The Spanish Jesuits had replaced the Mexicans at the end of the 1930s. What bothered Rutilio was not the Jesuits' nationality but their ignorance of the social reality of the people to whom they were ministering. Because of the Spaniards' lack of inculturation, claimed Rutilio, "the Society as such is hardly known, and its transformative influence is scant, or at least it has been among the true people of these countries." Moreover, the "cloistering" of the works, the communities, and the individuals resulted in shortness of vision, half-hearted routines, dissension among the Jesuits, and painful misunderstandings between the Jesuits, on the one hand, and the seminarians, the Salvadoran clergy, and the bishops, on the other.

Rutilio was willing to recognize that some foreign Jesuits had identified themselves closely with the Central American peoples, "more perhaps than some of us who were born here." The action of these Jesuits, however, was provoking "a crisis that was just, salutary, beneficial, necessary, and redemptive, even though some will be crucified for having provoked it and for continuing to provoke it!" These Jesuits, claimed Rutilio, deserved special recognition for showing how the Gospel was to be made incarnate and how the faith was to be made communal, and they deserved unconditional support from the vice-province, which "cannot act like a sect, narcissistically closed in on itself. Such an attitude would be wrong, and it would be heretical to affirm it even of the Universal Church, whose mission is to be a servant."[47]

Underlying Rutilio's intervention in the assembly was a question that arose during his time at the seminary, though he now phrased it more circumspectly: Within a given historical setting, what should distinguish a group of men who were called to leave everything for the kingdom of God and to put their life on the line for the Gospel? Making an option for the liberation of the people raised questions for the Jesuits: they had to ask themselves what was to be done with the schools and with the recently founded universities (except for the one in San Salvador). Rutilio was not opposed to the schools in themselves, but disagreed with the social function they were serving. Despite being the largest sector of the vice-province, the schools refused to open themselves up to the Central American reality:

> I ask myself: What would Ignatius of Loyola do here and now, moved by his special charism, which was not anchored in space and time? What students would he accept? Would it be the plump sons of the ranchers (Cf. James,

---

47 Grande, "Address to the Vice-provincial Congregation."

5. The Pastoral Project

chapter 5, which speaks of those who have fattened their hearts like cattle, and fattening produces plumpness), or would it be the scruffy students of the national institutes, which produce most of the cadets of our military academies and, here in our country, even the presidents of the republic?[48]

Rutilio then moved from the social extraction of the students to the reality of the alumni. He probably had in mind those of the Colegio Externado, where he had worked:

> What have we done with the alumni of our present schools? Have we simply organized a club for them where they can have fun playing ping-pong, or have we tried seriously to give them the various forms of the Spiritual Exercises? Have we helped them grow in their awareness of Gospel values and pointed out to them their great responsibility with regard to the problems of our countries? Who knows if these men who leave our schools are fertile ground for the Gospel![49]

Despite the overall trend, Rutilio could glimpse some hopeful, though insufficient, signs in the Colegio Externado and in the UCA, two institutions that were making an effort to open themselves up to the Salvadoran reality in order to transform it. The college had been unjustly accused of spreading Marxism by exposing its students to the raw reality of the country. An investigation conducted by the Ministry of Education demonstrated that the school program was unobjectionable. At the university, some Jesuits were attempting to turn the curriculum in the direction of liberation, but Rutilio was dissatisfied with the steps that had been taken: "They are still little more than the personal efforts of individuals or small groups of Jesuits."[50]

Despite the resistance and the difficulties, Rutilio declared, it was not a time for the "calamitous laments and woes of the prophets"; what was needed was conversion and fidelity to the Gospel. He urged the assembly to overcome the traditional dualism of faith and politics, which was the principal cause of resistance to change and also of internal division since many Jesuits expressed fears of "being ruled by principles foreign to the faith." Rutilio understood conversion as consisting in a twofold, simultaneous movement. First, it involved turning toward the other person, but such conversion was not easy: "We are not educated for dialogue, even though dialogue is of the purest essence of Christianity because it presupposes mutual love and respect, true communication and understanding, a shared search for the truth, and humility without any self-sufficiency."[51] Rather than for dialogue, "we have been educated for

---

48 Grande, "Address to the Vice-provincial Congregation."
49 Grande, "Address to the Vice-provincial Congregation."
50 Grande, "Address to the Vice-provincial Congregation."
51 Grande, "Address to the Vice-provincial Congregation."

verticality, which leads us in some cases to fierce willfulness and individualism." Such vices have turned Jesuits into "zealots of *orthodoxy* but manifest slackers when it comes to orthopraxis." Only dialogue and respectful openness to others will allow Jesuits to overcome their divisions.[52]

The second movement required by conversion, simultaneously with dialogue, was openness to the impoverished, exploited, oppressed majority of the people, the great "other" that is nothing more than "*Reality* itself":

> First of all [is] the reality of the *Other*, with capital O, that has spoken to us through the radical, incarnate word of Jesus Christ. The second great reality, the *other* with a small O, is humanity itself, whom we serve. But human beings are situated in a concrete *world*, they are inserted into a concrete society, and they are living their own *history*, which is not something in the past even though it is continuous with the past.[53]

Consequently, the desired unity "in truth, in love, and in shared service" will be created through dialogue, which will reveal "the true and objective reality of the *Other*." For Rutilio, it was a question of extrapolating one's own individuality in other persons and in the poor masses.

Finally, Rutilio said that he disagreed with "the language of those who speak of some Jesuits being devoted to strictly pastoral and apostolic activities while others are devoted to activities that are not directly apostolic." For Rutilio, the concept of apostolic mission, both of the Society and the church, did not admit of such duality:

> I humbly believe that, wherever a Jesuit or a group of Jesuits is found, there must be apostolic activity. [...] If someone is an economist and a Jesuit, he will have to shape his specific vocation in ways that will energize the socioeconomic reality of the country, making use of the radical, inquisitive ferment of the Christian faith in the classroom, in study groups, in spiritual and intellectual exercises, etc.[54]

Rutilio did not ignore the risks involved in making an option for the poor. He warned that persecution would be inevitable. The traditional sources of funding would disappear, surveillance would be strict, and detention, deportation, and imprisonment would become regular happenings. One eventuality that Rutilio did not mention was assassination.

Another risk he foresaw was internal division motivated by resistance to conversion. The vice-province was at that moment already experiencing extreme tensions, but as "painful and regrettable" as the divisions might be, they were not

---

52 Grande, "Address to the Vice-provincial Congregation."
53 Grande, "Address to the Vice-provincial Congregation."
54 Grande, "Address to the Vice-provincial Congregation."

to be feared, said Rutilio, because they were rooted in the Gospel, that is, in God himself, not in ideologies:

> The *Sensus Christi*, understood as the very Message of Jesus, has *irremediably* divided the world into two bands, whether we want it or not. This has happened even in the bosom of the church and, I dare say, even in our own order. Everything else will be a matter of prudence or strategic pedagogy, as long as these are compatible with the so-called Third Degree of Humility, the Third Class of Men, and the faithful following of the standard of the true Supreme Captain Jesus, at the hour of the hours.[55]

Rutilio told the assembled priests that they should not forget that the Society of Jesus was called by its vocation to face persecution and division with valor. Worse would be "the danger of not being in step with the changes required by the church and the Society, but that situation in itself would provide an opportunity for conversion and personal evolution."[56]

The Parish of Aguilares

After being assigned to the task of renewing the residences and the parishes, Rutilio reminded the vice-provincial of the pastoral project that he and Bengoechea had already proposed. Rutilio felt that the new project was compatible with the plan of the vice-provincial since it would not prevent him from serving also on the itinerant pastoral team that was planned. He wanted to work on the team, however, only after acquiring some genuine pastoral experience. His reasoning was that "no one gives what he doesn't have."[57] Rutilio finally accepted the position of vice-provincial assistant for pastoral ministry, but he did not want to be a pastor only in theory; he wanted to advise others on the basis of his own experience. He was convinced that the project that he and Bengoechea were proposing could become a truly inspiring alternative for restless Jesuits.

Being assigned the job of renewing the parishes and the residences was not Rutilio's only difficulty. He was proposing to open a new work precisely at a moment when the vice-province was beginning to experience a shortage of personnel. In responding to this legitimate problem, he asserted that the important question was not whether the new work would require additional personnel, but rather what works needed to be closed in order to deal with the historical challenges that the church was then facing. He had clear ideas himself about what works needed to be closed. Schools that were not accomplishing their mission should be closed, he felt, and their personnel assigned to other, more pressing apostolates. The schools should be allowed to continue

---

55   Grande, "Address to the Vice-provincial Congregation."
56   Ministries Commission, Technical Group, survey of Rutilio Grande, San Salvador, 1976.
57   ACSI. Rutilio Grande to Miguel F. Estrada, Quito, Ecuador, June 27, 1972.

only if they renewed their commitment to their true mission, say by becoming a center for youth ministry.[58]

The vice-provincial approved in principle the pastoral project proposed by Rutilio and Bengoechea, but the definitive approval would have to await Rutilio's return to the vice-province from Ecuador. The choice of the parish of Aguilares was not made by Rutilio. Before leaving for the IPLA course, he had talked with Bengoechea, with whom he had been collaborating in the parish of Suchitoto since the beginning of 1971, about his desire to engage in a pastoral experience in a rural area. During that conversation, they apparently agreed that Bengoechea would organize the team while Rutilio was away. Rutilio sent Bengoechea his "primary and fundamental option" from Quito and reaffirmed his desire to take part in a pastoral experience among the poor. While in Suchitoto, Bengoechea established contact with a group of about ten diocesan priests who were meeting periodically under the direction of Father Bernardo Boulang. This influential French priest was visiting different rural and urban parishes for the purpose of promoting the type of pastoral ministry advocated by Vatican II and Medellín. In meetings Boulang held with pastors and their collaborators, they reflected on the work each one was doing and on the situation of the nation and the church. Those outside the group saw it as closed and exclusive.

It was this group that had the idea of situating the pastoral project in the parish of Aguilares. They considered Aguilares ideal because of its geographical location and its socioeconomic characteristics. The parish was located in a zone dominated by large sugarcane plantations and three sugar factories (La Cabaña, San Francisco, and Colima). The city of Aguilares was a very active commercial center with a large work force, but the people were not organized. The planned construction of the Cerrón Grande hydroelectric dam would cause conflict in the zone since the lake created would flood the lands of thousands of small farmers as well as two of the sugar factories. The area had no deep-rooted religious traditions, a circumstance that would make it easier to try new pastoral approaches. The priests' group thought that the church needed to make itself present in the midst of the social conflicts of the zone and that a truly liberating pastoral experience would have vast repercussions. Moreover, the present pastor would soon be leaving the parish, offering a unique opportunity.

The original plan was that the new project in Aguilares would be integrated into the pastoral project that already included the parishes of Quezaltepeque, Suchitoto, and Chalatenango, the pastors of which formed part of Boulang's group. This proposal of integration gave rise to serious internal differences within the missionary team of Aguilares, and the resulting tensions profoundly affected Rutilio. Boulang's group tended to emphasize the political dimension more than the religious one; they therefore gave priority to political formation

---

58   ACSI. Rutilio Grande to Miguel F. Estrada, Quito, Ecuador, June 27, 1972.

5. The Pastoral Project 141

and neglected evangelization. Boulang took a great interest in Aguilares precisely because it offered unique opportunities for political activity, but Rutilio and most of the missionary team preferred to stress evangelization.[59]

Besides belonging to Boulang's group, Bengoechea established close relations with the Jesuit scholastics, some of whom had already visited Aguilares. He also consulted about the project with the vice-provincial and with the seminary rector, Father Amando López. Later on, in August 1972, there was a meeting of the vice-provincial, his assistant for formation, the director of the Center for Social Research and Action, the rector of the seminary, and the superior of the house of formation for the purpose of discussing the appropriateness of taking over the parish of Aguilares. In that ambience of discernment, the parish presented itself as an opportunity for the Jesuits to make an apostolic option for the rural zones.

Consequently, Rutilio was not part of the decision to take on the parish of Aguilares. He certainly accepted the decision, but he had some reservations. Rutilio was a key figure for the project of Boulang and his group since he was Salvadoran, had been born and grew up in the zone, and had demonstrated his aptitude for rural pastoral ministry. Where that group and the Jesuits saw advantages, however, Rutilio saw only difficulties. He had spent his childhood in the region and knew it well, but he was deeply disturbed by the presence in the zone of relatives who were not leading exemplary Christian lives. Rutilio felt that the less than saintly lives of his relatives, no secret in the parish, would not only contradict his own religious and priestly identity but would also reduce his freedom and effectiveness and be a source of bitterness. If the decision had depended on him, he would have chosen another parish. A year later, in early 1975, he told the national council of Jesuits of El Salvador that he had felt pressured by Bengoechea, who had taken advantage of his "disorientation," as well as by Boulang's group and by the group in Chalatenango.[60] Rutilio felt at that moment, as he looked back, that the plans he had discussed with Bengoechea before traveling to Ecuador were "idealistic."[61] A year later, when caught in another crisis, he insisted, "I'm still not convinced that I should do pastoral work near or in the place where I was born. I would be better suited to some other place."[62]

It is worth asking, then, why Rutilio accepted being named pastor of Aguilares. He accepted because others asked him to and because their reasoning convinced him, although his own doubts remained. He agreed to be pastor because the Boulang group, the Chalatenango group, and the Jesuits wanted him in the position. Moreover, when Archbishop Chávez personally asked him to take the

---

59 ACSI. Rutilio Grande, "Presentation to the National Council of El Salvador," San Salvador, March 9, 1975.
60 Grande, "Presentation to the National Council of El Salvador."
61 Grande, "Presentation to the National Council of El Salvador."
62 Ministries Commission, Technical Group, survey of Rutilio Grande, San Salvador, 1976.

post, Rutilio could not bring himself to deny his request. In any case, his arrival in Aguilares was a "forced landing."

Archbishop Chávez named Rutilio pastor of Aguilares *ad nutum episcopi* (at the bishop's nod) on September 22, 1972, and he gave him an allowance of fifty *colones* a month (about twenty dollars at that time), to be financed by the archdiocese. No contract was signed between the archdiocese and the Society of Jesus, and no time limit was placed on the assignment, perhaps because of the confidence the archbishop had in Rutilio and the Society. Two days later, on September 24, Archbishop Chávez officially handed the parish over to Rutilio and his assistants, Fathers Salvador Carranza and Bengoechea. Toward the end of October, a diocesan priest, Octavio Cruz, was added to the team, and in early 1973 another Jesuit, Benigno Fernández.

General View of the Parish

The city of Aguilares began as an agglomeration of huts, illegally erected in a corner of the La Toma hacienda. In 1932, the spontaneous settlement was recognized as the village of La Toma when the landowner ceded land for the construction of streets, a municipal building, a school, a market, and a cemetery. By the time of the Second World War, Aguilares encapsulated the injustices of El Salvador. Rutilio called it "a unique laboratory of the tremendous, macroscopic problems of our tiny republic." Because of Aguilares' key location and its social ferment, whatever happened there had national repercussions. Rutilio and his missionary team took charge of the parish precisely at the moment when the social contradictions were most severe. Their pastoral activity was carried out in that unsettled ambience, which in turn determined in large measure the fate of the pastors.

The Parish of our Lord of Mercies, as it was known, was erected in 1952 when two municipalities (Aguilares and El Paisnal) and three villages of the municipality of Suchitoto (Colima, San Lucas, and Tres Ceibas) were detached from the parish of Guazapa. The archdiocesan decree states that the parish would be the seat of an auxiliary vicariate.[63] In the early 1970s, the parish covered an area of 170 square kilometers and had some thirty thousand inhabitants. The climate was warm and humid, with a notable variation in temperature between day and night.

The parish territory encompassed two distinct regions. One region was the Lempa River valley, dominated by large sugarcane plantations that were in constant expansion until 1976. Some inhabitants of this region lived on or near the plantations while others lived in the city of Aguilares and its environs. The only paved road, known as the Northern Artery, crossed through the plane and

---

63 "Acts of Parish Governance: Book of Minutes." Cf. Napoleón Alvarado and Jesús Octavio Cruz, "Conciencia y cambio social en la hacienda Tres Ceibas (El Salvador): 1955–1976" (Master's thesis, Universidad Nacional de Costa Rica, San José, 1978), 152ff.

Aguilares itself, connecting San Salvador with Chalatenango in the north. The other region was the hill country bordering the valley, where the inhabitants relied mainly on subsistence agriculture; prime among the communities in this region was El Paisnal.

Situated in the middle of the valley, the city of Aguilares was a young urban settlement with about ten thousand inhabitants in 1970, most of them coming from other regions. The city therefore lacked longstanding traditions. Besides commerce, the city's predominant activities were the exercise of professions such as medicine, pharmacy, and teaching and the provision of services such as tailoring, mechanics, carpentry, masonry, barbering, and clerical work. Aguilares had one government school offering three cycles: elementary, middle school, and baccalaureate (high school). The school director was a local politician affiliated to the party in power, but most of the forty-eight teachers belonged to the National Association of Salvadoran Educators, a union allied with an opposition party. The smaller town of El Paisnal had a second government school, with five hundred students and a dozen teachers. The government medical clinic in Aguilares, run by an army captain, had two doctors (one of poor repute), two dentists, and a Red Cross unit. A Lions Club and an AA group were also active in the city. Rutilio noted that both organizations had good people who were concerned about the community's welfare but who tended to be "folks who had cars" and arrogant kids. The Scouts, on the other hand, were more open to the community.

The intense commercial activity of the city took place in small- to medium-sized businesses, in the market posts, and in the streets, where women sold food, drinks, and clothing. The commerce was carried on alongside auto-repair shops, mills for grinding corn, and bus stops. From Monday to Thursday, the bustling markets made the city a convergence point for all types of activities and for people coming from every direction. Since Rutilio remembered the old marketplace from the time he was a boy, he was surprised to see how much the city's commercial movement had grown. While celebrating Mass in one of the markets during the month of June, he reminded the market vendors that June was the month dedicated to the Sacred Heart of Jesus, patron of Salvadoran markets; he told them to keep in mind: "This is your daily life, consecrated to work. Here is your altar, here is your duty."[64]

But the city was also well known for its taverns, where city and country folk spent their meager wages, earned with hard labor, on liquor, gambling, and prostitutes. On the weekends, the clientele of the bars engaged in brawls, most of them violent and bloody, some of them deadly. Ironically, during a novena to the Lord of Mercies, an archdiocesan priest opened a tavern in a property he owned. It quickly became a nuisance and a scandal, with loud music playing at all hours of the night; quarrels erupted when customers refused to pay for their drinks,

---

64 ACSI. Rutilio Grande, "Notes for a Homily: Mass in the Market."

and the neighborhood was invaded by unsavory types. Fed up with the situation, the neighbors wrote to the archbishop asking him to take action in the case.[65]

The widespread practice of prostitution reflected the lack of employment for women. For women, the main option for paid work was serving as domestic help in Aguilares or neighboring cities, or even in San Salvador, where the wages were slightly higher but the mistreatment and humiliation were the same. In sum, wrote Rutilio, Aguilares was "a center of corruption for many people," and the reason was that

> many good people sit with their arms folded, not wanting to get involved in disputes. They say: "So they're opening more houses of prostitution, and they're shooting one another, but that's no reason to defend those who are demanding justice in the estates around here. That's not a concern for religion."[66]

The periphery of the city consisted of informal settlements inhabited by the rural poor expelled from the countryside. Most of these districts lacked basic urban services. The city folk generally ignored the needs of the rural population, who lived in small villages scattered around the countryside. The parish of Aguilares attended to twelve villages located within the bounds of the city,[67] twelve more in El Paisnal,[68] ten in Suchitoto,[69] and one in Quezaltepeque.[70]

In the best of cases, the twenty thousand inhabitants of the rural villages lived in small, insecure, and unhygienic dwellings and possessed a small piece of land for subsistence agriculture. Those who owned no land had to rent a lot from a local landowner. The parish team described the situation of small farmers: "There is plenty of rocky land here, but there's no land for growing corn or beans because the sugarcane empire occupies all the most fertile land in this

---

65 ACSI. Residents of Aguilares to Bishop Chávez, Aguilares, n.d.
66 ACSI. Rutilio Grande to Benigno (Fernández) and Jesús Ángel (Bengoechea), El Jicarón, April 9, 1974.
67 Pichichapa, Las Pampas, Los Piñalitos, Los Mangos, El Llano, El Sapote, El Carmen, San José, Jícaro Grande, Santa Lucía, Las Tunas, and La Florida.
68 San Diego (hacienda San Diego and village San Luis), Potrero Grande (Las Garcitas and haciendas El Tule, La Pita, and San Cayetano), La Cabaña, San Rafael (hacienda San Rafael and El Mirador and villages Valle Nuevo and Huitiupa), El Matazano (haciendas Matazano, Las Araditas, La Aserradera, and El Rancho), San Antonio El Grande (hacienda San Antonio and villages El Pucuyo and Plan del Pino), Los Dos Cerros (hacienda San Francisco and villages Los Dos Cerros and Tecuán), Natividad (hacienda Natividad, village Agua Helada o Bejuco, hacienda Consolación, and village Los Dueñas), El Jicarón (El Escondido, El Tablón, Nance Amarillo), El Tronador (La Ansora, Los Arias, and haciendas El Tronador, Paso Hondo, Joya Grande, San Antonio, La Calzada, and Santa Rita), Las Ventanas (El Tule, El Chagüite, Amayo), and Las Delicias (Las Huertas, El Carmen).
69 Buena Vista, Tres Ceibas, El Líbano, San Lucas, San Francisco, El Chagüitón, El Trapichito, Haciendita (Gramalitos y Gramalones), and Colima.
70 Segura.

jurisdiction." In any case, even if they had land, the rural poor had to work on the plantation during the cane harvest "in order to earn a few cents, while the owners of these huge estates keep depositing their massive fortunes in foreign and local banks."[71]

The village dwellers lacked most basic services. "There is no electric light here in these little villages." The team judged that electricity was "a luxury of the cities and a few towns. I don't think that the Cerrón Grande dam will help these people. They'll be burning their oil lamps for a long time to come."[72] Rutilio found that the villages had "a primitive look." The birth rate was high, but the infant mortality rate was high also, and many people lived in destitution. During Holy Week of 1974, in an effort to touch the conscience of the city dwellers, Rutilio denounced these realities in a "pastoral letter" that was read in the parish church in Aguilares. He said he had written the letter in El Jicarón, while sitting "under a beautiful fig tree, while the hogs were wandering about and the roosters were crowing, but I could see the pale faces of some children with swollen stomachs." He had arrived in the village with a "large caravan of bundles" and a small but heavy electric generator for showing educational and religious films at night. But he could not get the generator to work. "God has given me patience in the midst of that problem with the motor. I am calm and relaxed, thanks be to God!"[73]

Sicknesses that could quickly and easily be treated in the city often meant death in the villages. "If someone's appendix bursts, and he has to be transported down to the hospital in a hand-carried hammock, no sooner will he be going over the first hill than he'll be handing his soul over to the Creator." The physicians in the region provided no services to the inhabitants of the villages:

> No doctors want to come up into these remote and unhealthy places, even though in their university days they were shouting in the plazas a lot of cheap words about serving the people. But once they graduate, neither the doctors nor the lawyers want to visit this region abandoned to the hand of God. Not even the teachers do![74]

While writing his pastoral letter, Rutilio was also listening to the archdiocesan radio station YSAX, the "Pan-American Voice." As the station, full of patriotic sentiment, proudly proclaimed that it was transmitting "from Cuscatlán, this land of

---

71   ACSI. Rutilio Grande to Benigno (Fernández) and Jesús Ángel (Bengoechea), El Jicarón, April 9, 1974.
72   ACSI. Rutilio Grande to Benigno (Fernández) and Jesús Ángel (Bengoechea), El Jicarón, April 9, 1974.
73   ACSI. Rutilio Grande to Benigno (Fernández) and Jesús Ángel (Bengoechea), El Jicarón, April 9, 1974.
74   ACSI. Rutilio Grande to Benigno (Fernández) and Jesús Ángel (Bengoechea), El Jicarón, April 9, 1974.

beautiful cane fields and flowering coffee groves," Rutilio commented caustically: "What could be more ironical!" A little later, he heard some electoral propaganda:

> [We hear the] promises and lies of the pols, who say they speak for the people, but they are interested only in getting votes, winning mayoralties and presidencies, managing public funds to their own advantage, and carrying out some pretty little project every two years at election time (repairing a road, opening a well, etc.). What a sad conception of politics, which is a service for the common good and not a soft job for fattening up pols.[75]

The people had, out of fear, learned to put up with the militarized security forces and the village patrols that backed them up. The patrols, under the command of a commissioner, were made up of local men who had done military service. The commander in Aguilares regularly convoked the patrolmen of the region to give them orientation. The message was always the same. The patrolmen were servants of the nation, defending it against internal and external enemies. Even though the patrols were coordinated by the Ministry of Defense at the municipal, departmental, and national levels, they were in practice at the service of the local boss, who had strong ties with the commander and the municipal authorities. Sometimes, the patrols offered their services to the religious authorities,[76] but for Rutilio the worst aspect of them was that

> these same people of the villages are being betrayed by their own kith and kin, who on the estates act the part of Judas by becoming overseers, foremen, administrators, and civil guards. These so-called Catholics want the Holy Religion to bless their crimes, conceal their manifest sins, and betray the Gospel of Jesus who proclaimed the truth, was imprisoned for speaking it, and in the end killed! I don't know what god those people follow or what Gospel they listen to.[77]

For Rutilio, this was a "very sad" way of interpreting the Good News of Jesus, "whose temple is the entire world, where men and women live their own history and where every person is a living stone of that immense temple of God's creation, both the material creation and the so-called spiritual one." Jesus roundly condemned the exploitation and corruption that enslaved immense multitudes. "That is not human. That is not reasonable. That cannot be tolerated by true religion. That is simply criminal and abusive."[78]

---

75 ACSI. Rutilio Grande to Benigno (Fernández) and Jesús Ángel (Bengoechea), El Jicarón, April 9, 1974.
76 Carlos Rafael Cabarrús, *Génesis de una revolución: Análisis del surgimiento y desarrollo de la organización campesina en El Salvador* (México, DF: Casa Chata, 1983), 168.
77 ACSI. Rutilio Grande to Benigno (Fernández) and Jesús Ángel (Bengoechea), El Jicarón, April 9, 1974.
78 ACSI. Rutilio Grande to Benigno (Fernández) and Jesús Ángel (Bengoechea), El Jicarón, April 9, 1974.

5. The Pastoral Project

The Protestant evangelical groups that were holding missions in the parish were also, according to Rutilio, being paid by the "bosses of these zones" and by "the North Americans." They went about "tiresomely inveighing against smoking and against the poor drunks (the least culpable folk) while they themselves swallowed the beam and the camel of great injustice and wickedness."[79] The church's evangelizing caused great scandal and met much opposition among the powerful precisely because the church made no concession to the prevailing injustice:

> All the local bosses are upset when we preach a Gospel that demands fraternity, equality, and love among all men and women, who are possessors of the entire earth. [...] It is the duty of the government in any nation to make the urgent and necessary changes so that these things get corrected.[80]

The Social Reality

The parish of Aguilares was located in one of the four main sugarcane-producing regions of the country. The land area controlled by the plantations doubled in the decade of the 1960s, in large part because of the US economic embargo against Cuba. Between 1962 and 1973, Salvadoran sugar production experienced a twenty-four percent increase, due mostly to a sharp rise in the price of sugar on the international market. In 1976, however, this trend reversed, in large measure because of a decline in the export price but also because of internal problems.[81]

Around Aguilares, the large estates coexisted with small- and medium-scale production. The region had three factories for processing the cane: La Cabaña, property of the De Sola family; San Francisco, property of the Nottebohn family; and Colima, property of the Orellana Brothers Society. These families resided in San Salvador and had little knowledge of what happened on the estates. Any benign paternalism that might have been shown by the families who owned the plantations got lost as their authority descended to the managers and supervisors who were directly responsible for the enterprise's operation and profitability. The owners of the thirty small- and medium-sized plantations, whose cane was processed in the three large factories, lived in Aguilares, where they also had other businesses.

The high profitability of sugarcane farming until 1976 was due to the low wages and the efficient exploitation of technology and natural resources. The family conglomerates that owned the three factories earned sizable profits, which they promptly invested in other economic activities.

---

79 ACSI. Rutilio Grande to Benigno (Fernández) and Jesús Ángel (Bengoechea), El Jicarón, April 9, 1974.
80 ACSI. Rutilio Grande to Benigno (Fernández) and Jesús Ángel (Bengoechea), El Jicarón, April 9, 1974.
81 Cf. Eduardo Colindres, *Fundamentos económicos de la burguesía salvadoreña* (San Salvador: UCA Editores, 1977).

The rapid expansion of the plantations displaced a majority of the parish's rural residents, some of whom survived by subsistence agriculture while others moved to the outskirts of Aguilares. This process yielded a twofold benefit for capital, since it reduced the costs of labor and the means of subsistence. Moreover, the plantations had available a nearly inexhaustible "reserve army" of workers. The wages paid on the plantations were extremely low, but employers sought to justify them by propagating the idea that the workers wasted their earnings on licentious living. The plantations virtually eliminated the class of small, self-sufficient, relatively independent agricultural producers, whose existence depended on family labor. In their place appeared landless peasants and farmers with tiny parcels of land ill-suited for subsistence. In the early 1970s, nearly half the rural families lacked sufficient land and survived by providing agricultural labor to the estates. They lived in small communities united by ties of blood.[82]

Between 1960 and 1975, the agrarian crisis grew worse, especially in the western and central regions of the country, where forty-one percent of the families had no land and fifty-two percent possessed less than two hectares. By 1975, a mere 1.5 percent of the population controlled half the country's agricultural land, while 92.5 percent had access to less than a half-hectare on average. The small farmers of the cane-producing zones, like Aguilares, had much less land than the coffee-producing zones but slightly more than the cotton-producing zones. In any case, the parcels of land in all regions were so reduced in size and so poorly suited to subsistence crops that they were unable to satisfy the basic needs of the rural poor. Family members were therefore forced to sell their labor to the estates or to the traditional haciendas. The immense majority of the landless peasants formed an idle workforce whose only option was laboring for the large-scale agricultural industries that produced for export.[83]

The subsistence farmers cultivated basic foodstuffs, especially maize, for domestic consumption. When there was excess production, it was sold to the merchants of Aguilares, or it was kept in reserve, to be sold at a better price in months of scarcity. Even the farmers who tried to increase their productivity had relatively meager harvests. A *manzana* (1.75 acres) of maize produced twenty-four hundredweight of grain, even on hilly land, but always with an enormous amount of labor. The diet of rural families generally consisted of some combination of maize, red beans, sorghum, and occasionally rice. The logic of the rural poor had been to obtain the basic means of subsistence through tremendous effort, but by the mid-1970s that logic was wearing thin due to the scarcity of available land and the poor quality of the little that was available.[84]

---

82 Cabarrús, *Génesis de una revolución*, 51.
83 Cabarrús, *Génesis de una revolución*, 51–53, 78.
84 Cabarrús, *Génesis de una revolución*, 81–83, 85, 89.

5. The Pastoral Project 149

The deterioration of the economy of the rural poor was most clearly observable in the increased costs of production. Farmers who had little or no land rented from the plantation, which could thus realize additional profits from its less fertile acreage. The rental prices varied, but they were always high. The small farmers generally paid the rent with wages they earned on the plantations, since paying with the crops produced meant withholding food from the theoretically "cheap" family basket. The farmers who had more land hired workers to farm it so that they themselves could work on the plantations during harvest season without losing their own production. Such hired workers who had no access to land could always seek task work at the plantation as well. Given the scarcity of land, it was not unusual for small farmers to dispute among themselves the parcels that were available. The general situation proved quite advantageous for the plantations: the rural poor were forced to sell their labor, and the greater the pressure on them, the less remuneration they could ask for it.[85]

Besides land, the small farmers needed inputs such as seed, fertilizer, and herbicide to insure good production. Fertilizer was indispensable for cultivating the infertile lands of the plantations. Although the farmers tended to use ever greater quantities of fertilizer, its high price limited its use in places like Aguilares. In fact, the prices of all the inputs tended to increase steadily. Because the small farmers relied heavily on such products, they became increasingly dependent on the merchants who sold agricultural goods and services, as well as on the transnational corporations that produced them. The rise in fertilizer prices, the ever greater need for inputs, and the suspicion that these were being "watered down" caused profound malaise among the farmers and increased their awareness of being exploited. Such a situation might have been avoided if prices had been controlled.[86]

The peasants who lived on the plantations were assigned a dwelling and a very small piece of land for growing vegetables and grains. In return, they were expected to work in the seasons when there was a high demand for labor. By facilitating such settlements, the plantations ensured that they would have a sufficient supply of workers when needed. This resident labor force existed in a state of semi-servitude since they lacked the freedom of the small farmers and were not protected by the government's labor code, so that they were vulnerable to exploitation. When the plantations needed more land and had an excess supply of labor, they dislodged the resident workers. They wanted no unnecessary people on their properties, especially if they could be a potential source of conflict.

The peasant economy depended on the production of the family group, all of whose members contributed their labor and ate from the same parcel of land. The family group could supplement its income with the sale of eggs or an

---

85   Cabarrús, *Génesis de una revolución*, 113.
86   Cabarrús, *Génesis de una revolución*, 99, 111.

occasional hen. A severe economic crisis was met with the sale of a hog, kept in reserve for such a circumstance. A few families would supplement their income with some informal commerce. The small farmers therefore subsisted by their own efforts, though they probably did not cover all their needs; they did not depend on the plantations. The great number of the unemployed kept wages low. Paradoxically, the rural poor did not feel the need to press for higher wages in order to cover the living expenses of their families. Even though the economy would have allowed for better wages, the agricultural workers preferred to take refuge in the subsistence economy. Thus, in 1975 more than half the rural population had to hire out their labor, but they also received help from the peasant community, which eased their economic needs. Such a situation was viable, however, only as long as there was a demand for wage labor on the plantation.[87]

The small farmers sold their labor to the plantations during the harvest in order to earn enough cash to rent land and acquire basic goods in the marketplace. Their earnest desire was to remain close to the land despite the economic forces that were impelling them to become wage laborers. During the sugarcane harvest, Aguilares absorbed workers not only from the immediate region but from Chalatenango as well. The harvest created high expectations since the wages earned there provided the only means for many small farmers to pay off what they owed for land rent and for the purchase of indispensable goods. The meager wages, obtained by great effort during the harvest, were quickly spent in the urban market.[88]

The workers were at the mercy of the caprices of the plantation owners since the labor code applied mainly to permanent urban employees and made no provisions for rural laborers.

With few exceptions, employment in the rural sector was considered temporary. The few laws regulating a minimum wage, task labor, and the length of the work day were constantly flouted with impunity. Worker protest was not only inhibited by fear but neutralized by the excess supply of labor. The periodic inspections by the Ministry of Labor, which could easily be anticipated and prepared for, were ably manipulated by the plantation management. Generally, the inspectors did not speak with the workers, and if by chance they did, the dialogue revealed little; the workers knew that if they complained, they would be defenseless against the reprisals that would inevitably follow and that would make their precarious situation even worse. In sum, the relationship between workers and plantation was one of exploitation and domination.

The post-war agro-export economy erased the differences that had formerly existed among small farmers. The wages were the same for everybody, the lack of social benefits affected all, and the threats to life were similar

---

87 Cabarrús, *Génesis de una revolución*, 97, 117, 118–20.
88 Cabarrús, *Génesis de una revolución*, 73–74.

everywhere. Subsistence agriculture ceased to be the principal activity of the peasant class since an ever greater proportion of their income came from wage labor on the plantations. In the end, small independent producers became farm employees, who supplemented their income with their own individual agricultural efforts. When small farmers all found themselves in the same precarious situation, they felt a certain basic solidarity that opened up the possibility of protest and rebellion.

The agrarian system depended on the balance between population and available land. For a decade, the system gradually modified the diverse economies of both small farmer and capitalist, mainly to the benefit of the latter. But the equilibrium was then disrupted due to the increased number of landless peasants and the intensified exploitation. The poor quality and scarcity of land, the high cost of renting it, and the lack of cash to pay for land and supplies resulted in reduced small-farmer production, both absolutely and with respect to the population as a whole. At the same time, the demand for basic foodstuffs increased; when they were imported, their increased price put them beyond the reach of many. When the rural poor found themselves in such extreme economic distress, a critical point was reached.[89]

The unequal distribution of land demanded a thoroughgoing agrarian reform, a measure highly recommended by international organizations and even by the US-sponsored program Alliance for Progress.[90] The oligarchy, however, was not ready to allow any changes to take place in its principal source of capital accumulation. Resisting all pressure for reform, the oligarchy, backed by the military government, decided to maintain the country's agrarian and economic structure unaltered. Any attempts at agrarian reform or any other kind of reform that would change the established order were denounced as communist, and their proponents were pursued and prosecuted. This situation helps explain the sharp polarization that took place in Salvadoran society during the 1970s.[91]

The systemic crisis placed the rural poor in desperate straits. The implacable logic of capitalism, which left them without land, labor, or income, pushed them toward rebellion. The agitation for change originated not so much in ideology as in the struggle for survival. The agro-export economy, heedless of the level of exploitation and its social consequences, threatened the very existence of the small-farmer economy. The suppression of subsistence agriculture impelled the rural poor to take on wage labor, but without the benefit of a contract. As the rural workforce became progressively proletarianized, it became increasingly more impoverished.[92]

---

[89] Cabarrús, *Génesis de una revolución*, 78, 81, 98, 113.
[90] A US government program aimed at establishing economic cooperation between the United States and Latin America.
[91] Cabarrús, *Génesis de una revolución*.
[92] Cabarrús, *Génesis de una revolución*, 54ff.

In this way, the system itself created the structural conditions that made the rural poor acutely aware of the real reasons for their misery and that drove them to social conflict and rebellion. When the traditional small-farmer economy was destroyed and no reasonable substitutes, such as labor contracts, were offered instead, insurgency became the only real alternative for survival.[93]

Aguilares: A Traditional Parish

The pastors that preceded Rutilio and the missionary team had dedicated themselves to preserving the faith, promoting worship, and building chapels in the villages. They strove to defend Catholicism against the Protestant threat and to organize moralizing campaigns against alcoholism, crime, cohabitation, spiritism, and Protestantism. The principal activity of the priests, however, was worship. Devotion to Mary played a major part in the spirituality of the faithful. Every day, the rosary was prayed in the parish church. On the twelfth of each month, the pastor celebrated Mass in honor of the Virgin of Guadalupe, and a meeting was held afterward. The month of May and the principal Marian feasts were all solemnly celebrated: Fatima on May 13, Carmel on July 16, the Immaculate Conception on December 8, Guadalupe on December 12, and so on. The first Thursdays, Fridays, and Saturdays of each month were also strictly observed. Many feast days included a procession and Eucharistic adoration. The municipal government played an important role in organizing these events.

Activity in the parish diminished between 1959 and 1965, even though Communions increased, a Sunday Mass for children was introduced, and the month of June was dedicated to the Sacred Heart of Jesus. Apparently, the villages were increasingly neglected. Previously, the pastors had carried out two- and three-day popular missions on a regular basis, but such missions are not even mentioned in the minutes of the parish administration during those years. The number of parish organizations was also markedly reduced. Several disappeared altogether, such as the Guard of the Blessed Sacrament, responsible for Eucharistic worship; Catholic Action; the Good Press Apostolate, responsible for publicizing Catholicism; the Adorers; the Nazarenes, responsible for Holy Week; the Adoration of Saint Joseph, dedicated to praying and raising funds for the seminary; and the Apostleship of Prayer. The only active organizations remaining were the catechists, the Guadalupanas, and the Daughters of Mary, who promoted Christian matrimony.[94]

The pastoral ministry of the parish in those years tended toward legalism and austerity. In the early 1960s, the three most important concerns of the pastor were apparently the acquisition of an electronic organ, the construction of the new parish church (begun in July 1960), and the organization of a parish Eucharistic congress, in preparation for the Second National Eucharistic Congress.[95]

---

93 Cabarrús, *Génesis de una revolución*, 54ff.
94 ACSI. "Acts of Parish Governance: Parish of Aguilares."
95 "Acts of Parish Governance: Parish of Aguilares."

5. The Pastoral Project

Parish life was reinvigorated in 1965 with the arrival of a new pastor, but he stayed within the same traditional context. He encouraged the popular devotions and tried to extend their influence to the daily life of the people. He organized religious associations to promote confessions, massive Communions, and fulfilment of the Easter duty. He directed his attention especially toward men, who tended to be resistant. He showed interest in the villages and visited them monthly. He used the tallying of a general census of the population to visit homes and to enthrone the Sacred Heart of Jesus in them. He reorganized the guild of Carmel, the Legion of Mary, the Adorers, and the Youth Social Club. He introduced the celebration of the month of August in honor of the Divine Savior of the World, and he founded a nutritional clinic. During his time in office, the construction of the church was completed, and the parish had an insured income of about a thousand *colones* (about four hundred dollars at the time).

During these years, El Paisnal and its villages received considerable attention thanks to the presence of Rutilio and his seminarians, who visited on the weekends and during some vacation periods. The Adorers became an important religious and social organization even though many were at first scared off by Rutilio's insistence on active apostolate and testimony of life. Those who persevered showed themselves to be seriously committed Christians. During this period, the pastors of the vicariate became more organized among themselves and tried to practice team ministry.[96]

The religious life of the parish of Aguilares was characterized by its zealously observed traditions and its individualism. Most of the population had only a vague awareness of belonging to the church. They had only sporadic contact with the priests but felt a strong desire for the sacraments. Instruction in the faith was reduced to the catechism lessons learned in childhood and the moralizing Sunday sermons of the pastor. Since the content of the catechesis was abstract, dualistic, and authoritarian, the people had created their own religious celebrations independently of the ecclesial institution. These included devotion to the dead—with wakes, prayers, novenas, candles, and memorials—and devotion to the saints (rosaries, May flowers, Holy Week celebrations, palms, sacred cloths, processions, statues and images, incense, floral carpets, etc.). This popular religiosity produced special prayer leaders (*rezadoras*) who conducted the prayers and other devotions. The times of greatest religious intensity were Holy Week, the patronal feasts, and the popular missions, which attracted great crowds.[97]

Much of the people's devotion, especially in the villages, revolved around the *rezadoras*, zealous women who led the celebrations of the important feasts of the liturgical calendar and the significant events of people's lives. These women kept religion alive in the rural world by conducting novenas and leading prayers

---

96 "Acts of Parish Governance: Parish of Aguilares."
97 ACSI. Vicariate of Quezaltepeque, "Initial Project of Collaborative Ministry of the Vicariate of Quezaltepeque," Apopa, May 25, 1975.

whenever people wanted to feel the divine presence. Novenas were an especially popular and widespread practice; they consisted of praying the rosary for nine successive nights for some particular intention. The common denominator of all these religious practices was their fervor.[98] Despite the traditional character of this religiosity, Rutilio considered it to be of great value, and he felt that it should be carefully cultivated.

Given the difficult social circumstances, popular religiosity inculcated resignation and patience. It dealt with the many trials of life as best it could, seeking no rational explanation but attributing them to the inscrutable will of God. Such religiosity possessed no categories by which it could explore an alternative vision, much less motivate serious social change. It did not contemplate any transformation of reality; rather, it feared that change might create dangerous instability.

Since the popular religiosity tended to reinforce the existing social structures,[99] it allowed the pastor to maintain good relations with the plantation and the government. The plantation made regular contributions to parish activities; for example, it might donate a bull to be raffled off to benefit some good work, and it would invite the pastor to administer the sacraments on its compounds during the patronal feast, giving the owners a chance to proudly display their generosity and their Catholicism. Public manifestation of that close relationship helped to legitimize the harsh order imposed by the plantation and the military regime, and to make any attempt to change the order unthinkable. The traditional religiosity consequently became an ideological support of the dominant system.[100]

The catechesis and the preaching stressed that the primary responsibility of the rural poor was practicing virtue in order to save their souls. They were taught to see reality as divided into two opposed realms: on one side were the world, the body, and sin, and on the other were the spirit, the soul, and virtue. All activity in the former sphere was described in negative terms, while activity in the latter was always positive. The primary concern of Christians should not be the historical reality in which they lived but the supernatural realm of the spirit, which was reached by the sacraments, processions, rosaries, and novenas of traditional religiosity. The historical reality was viewed as part of the natural order of creation and so belonged to the untouchable sphere of the divine.[101]

The practices contributing to the salvation of the soul—especially the sacraments—were associated in popular belief with personal and collective sacrifice. The greater the sacrifice—and so the greater the suffering—the more pleasing it was to God. The ability to suffer was therefore irrefutable proof of love for

---

98   Alvarado and Cruz, "Conciencia y cambio social," 155, 229.
99   Napoleón Alvarado, "La organización del proletariado agrícola y el problema de las jornadas de la conciencia religiosa," in *Fe cristiana y revolución sandinista en Nicaragua* (Managua: Instituto Histórico Centroamericano, 1979), 243ff.
100 Alvarado, "La organización del proletariado agrícola."
101 Alvarado and Cruz, "Conciencia y cambio social," 256–57.

5. The Pastoral Project

God, the first commandment. The most common mode of voluntary sacrifice was the economic offering given for the sacraments and other religious activities. The reception of the sacraments ordinarily meant an outlay of money in one form or another. The payments expected were sometimes relatively large, a fact that explains the swollen incomes of some pastors. The cost of a Mass or a baptism was the equivalent of several days' pay for an agricultural laborer. The processions and novenas also involved costs. The missions in the villages often required long and arduous trips, interminable assemblies and rosaries, massive administration of sacraments, and also economic contributions. The Adorers spent Saturday nights praying and singing so that their Sundays were dedicated to catching up on their sleep. Much of the religious and moral leadership of the Adorers derived from this capacity they had for sacrifice.[102]

The traditional religious practices had utilitarian value since the faithful hoped that their sacrifices would be rewarded by God. Certainly, they expected the salvation of their souls, but they also begged for God's help in resolving apparently hopeless situations. The rural poor's precarious existence, resulting from forces beyond their control and comprehension, made divine intercession necessary, for only God could counteract or neutralize those forces. The faithful hoped that their fidelity to ritual would bring them that saving intervention. Whether it did nor not, their hope gave meaning to their constantly threatened lives. Since for them the road to happiness was through suffering and sacrifice, they not only accepted their trials but actively sought them.[103]

The intense ritual activity was correlated with the people's passivity before the historical situation. Their passivity, since it tended to suppress transformative action, was actually a form of "active passivity"; it was essential for preserving the established order. Instead of in transformative human action, the people placed their hope in powerful divine intervention, which was expected to bring salvation both now and at the end of time. The social passivity was so effective that coercion was unnecessary, and the lack of coercion made it all the more difficult for the people to understand their historical reality.[104]

The prevailing morality was based on the seven commandments regulating social relations; it was oriented toward maintaining order and harmony. Since it viewed the commandments from a personal perspective, such morality inclined individuals not to get involved in the affairs of others. Remoteness and isolation were the best ways to avoid sin. In a violence-ridden society, that way of thinking made a certain amount of sense. Offensive words, ruinous rumors, and amorous trysts frequently gave rise to violent confrontations that left people wounded and dead. The moral response to such violence was to avoid conflict by keeping

---

102 Alvarado and Cruz, "Conciencia y cambio social," 251–52, 354–55.
103 Alvarado and Cruz, "Conciencia y cambio social," 253–54.
104 Alvarado and Cruz, "Conciencia y cambio social," 254–55.

one's distance. For that reason, traditional religion and authority figures recommended patience above all. Those who rejected patience as a fundamental virtue were condemned as violent; those who impatiently resisted the demands of capital were committing an unforgivable sin. The commandments played a large part in the morality of the rural poor since they feared that violating them would annul the positive actions they carried out in the realm of the sacred.[105]

As time went by, the interiorization of patience began to fail, and state terror attempted to subdue the rebels. At the urging of the missionary team of Aguilares, the rural poor began to modify their traditionalist worldview. Rejecting passivity and patience, many of them decided to demand their rights and undertake the transformation of their society. At that point, the repression became extremely violent as the powerful attempted to preserve their unjust order.

Perhaps the rural poor had had good reason for seeking their security in the plantation since it was the source of their work, their land, and their income. Moreover, it provided some upward mobility in the hierarchy of jobs to those who showed patience, diligence, and honesty, that is, to those who treated the plantation property as their own. The older family members transmitted these values to the younger. Removing concrete social relations to the sphere of the transcendent, the people tended to view the will of the plantation as the will of God. And ultimately the will of capital took the place of the will of God, for capital was worshiped as an idol.

This traditional religious background represented a great challenge for a missionary team such as the one in Aguilares. According to Rutilio, "the task is thankless and difficult since in a sense it means building the church anew. With the help of the Spirit, we have to try to make the Gospel come alive among these great huddled masses caught up in their popular religiosity."[106]

---

105 Alvarado and Cruz, "Conciencia y cambio social," 255–56.
106 ACSI. Rutilio Grande, "Notes."

6. The First Stage: The Missions

During the last years of his life and after his death, Rutilio was portrayed and maligned as a left-wing politician. Some claimed that his assassination was carried out for political motives. Others were more cautious and only expressed doubts about his parish work. Careful analysis of the pastoral plan of the missionary team and of Rutilio's own activities belies the condemnations and dispels the doubts. Rutilio was a missionary of the Good News. The political consequences of his preaching were a byproduct, not an intended effect.

Leavening the Dough

The missionary team set out to evangelize the parish and build a church made up of vigorous communities. The team understood evangelization as proclaiming the Word of God in its totality, without trimming it, and doing so on the basis of the social situation of the parish. The team's first task, therefore, was to become submerged in the parish in order to become fully aware of its full reality and to acquire a new sensitivity. The team members knew from the start that such openness would force them to question their mental schemes and modify their plans, but there was no other way. Since true evangelization required them to remain open at all times to the reality of the parish, they had to revise and adjust its activities to that reality even when, as will be seen further on, such changes were not easy and occasioned serious crises.[1]

The team had the choice of two possible methods of evangelization. The first method, the one used by the parish of Suchitoto and by Boulang's group, took a sociopolitical approach. The second method based itself on popular religiosity. Influenced by Rutilio, who had profound respect for the people's devotion, the team opted for the second approach. Rutilio refused to force "strange" methods onto the reality of the parish because he thought they would be ineffective. The decision to use the method based on popular religiosity gave rise to tensions within the team because Bengoechea, who remained in close contact with Boulang's group, wanted to follow their more political approach.

Rutilio was firm in rejecting that path, citing the religious character of the people and their radically Christian values. Believing that the political situation in the country required a type of evangelization that was not obviously confrontational, he saw the sociopolitical approach as clearly counterproductive:

---

1 Rutilio Grande, "Aguilares: An Experience of Evangelization in a Rural Parish," *Búsqueda* 8 (1975): 21–48, here 22ff. Published also as Salvador Carranza, "An Experience of Evangelization in a Rural Parish: Aguilares, September 1972–August 1974," *ECA* 348–49 (1977): 838–54, here 832ff.

it would arouse distrust among people unfamiliar with that way of thinking, it would tend to confuse evangelization with politicization, and it would make every church meeting suspicious in the eyes of the military regime. In contrast, evangelization through popular religiosity offered greater space and more flexibility. Moreover, that religiosity was badly in need of evangelization.[2]

Even so, the path taken by Rutilio was not free of ambiguities. The process would be slow, and at some point it would have to deal with the sociopolitical challenges for, as Vatican II and Medellín taught, evangelization demands justice and so must confront the harsh realities faced by the poor. Viewed from an anthropological perspective, moreover, human beings were called to transform their reality and shape their own destiny. Faith, therefore, when properly understood, would inevitably lead to political involvement. At the same time, evangelization and politics were not to be confused; they remained always in a type of dialectical tension. The relationship between them was ambiguous, and the ambiguity could not be resolved by denying either one. Jesus himself had faced the same ambiguity in his own life.[3]

The model was Jesus of Nazareth, whose preaching had strongly impinged on the social reality of his time. In this sense, Jesus "got involved in politics" but without being "a professional politician." Christians, far from shunning political activity, had to become political in order to transform history, but faith could not be used to impose particular policies. Faith included politics, but it also transcended politics. The challenge for evangelization was to avoid "watering down" the Word of God by removing its prophetic dimension. Prophecy was more effective than politics because it transcended the political realm. Even when the Word of God was addressing a concrete reality, it transcended history. It followed, thought Rutilio, that popular religiosity offered the best opportunity for helping people to follow Jesus of Nazareth faithfully and for overcoming the ambiguity that was intrinsic to evangelization.[4]

A member of the missionary team recalled that on one occasion Archbishop Chávez had asked the priests to be prudent in their preaching, but Rutilio, reflecting on the texts for the following Sunday, protested, "How are we going to keep quiet if the Word of God illuminates the reality so clearly? To keep quiet would be to betray the Gospel!"[5] The same witness explained how the missionary team used to prepare the Sunday homilies at their weekly meetings: "There we would share our reflections, and I could see clearly that all Rutilio's motivation came from his faith; he was inspired by his reflection on the Word of God, by his fidelity to the church's teaching, and by the challenges presented to us by the social reality."[6]

---

2   Grande, "Aguilares," 22ff.
3   Grande, "Aguilares," 22ff.
4   Grande, "Aguilares," 22ff.
5   *Summarium testium*, witness 18, §361.
6   *Summarium testium*, witness 18, §361.

6. The First Stage

The priests themselves were somewhat ambivalent: they had to decide what was more important, administering the sacraments or engaging in politics. The missionary team, taking a middle position between these two options, considered its fundamental obligation to be prophetic ministry in which faith and politics, hierarchically ordered, converged. Prophetic ministry, as they understood it, involved condemning the exploiters and raising the awareness of the exploited. The exploiters were to be called to conversion, and the exploited were to be helped to realize their own historical responsibility and their Christian commitment. The team would in this way give people back the voice that had so long been denied them, and they would invite the people to assume responsibility for the transformation of society. The hope was that men and women, feeling renewed and liberated, would rise up in the course of this process of transformation. The missionary team's task was complex: it needed to be creative, critical, and open to dialogue, and it had to take into account many personal and social factors. Using this approach, the team members sought to resolve the crisis of priestly identity that resulted from the Medellín conference.[7]

Rutilio refused to instrumentalize the Word of God or domesticate popular religiosity in order to make them serve a particular political project. He took the more positive approach of evangelizing popular religiosity as a way of creating Christian communities that were dynamic, prophetic, and autonomous. From such communities would emerge pastoral agents and agents of change. "Our intention is not to take the Gospel away from our people and leave them with only the husk, nor is it to lull them in their religiosity under the cover of the same Gospel. As a missionary team we come with the desire to leaven the dough, not just to give out bread!"[8] Rutilio "struggled, and we all struggled hard," recalled one member of the missionary team, "to overcome that sense of fatalism and magic that popular religiosity had implanted" in the people. "In his preaching and in public, [Rutilio] used to insist again and again with the common folk: 'Be careful of putting the blame on God, or thinking that things happen or are the way they are by the will of God.'"[9]

The missionary team's priority was evangelization and conversion, not administering the sacraments and conducting worship, as in the traditional parish. But that did not mean neglecting the sacraments and worship, something Rutilio would never have allowed. "Whenever he was asked, he always went to visit the sick," declared a witness who had been part of the missionary team:

> I accompanied him a couple of times at night. The administration of the sacrament was a liturgy in which we all took part. He would explicitly invite the family to be reconciled with the sick person. We all felt the presence of

---

7 *Summarium testium*, witness 18, §361.
8 *Summarium testium*, witness 18, §361.
9 *Summarium testium*, witness 2, §25.

God healing us. Even during the time of the threats, he kept going out to attend to the sick.[10]

Rutilio also sought to break the link between the sacraments and parish finances. He emphasized the communitarian rather than the individual dimensions of the sacraments, and he sought to give preference to the poor over the powerful. This was a question of emphasis, but it was a very important matter for the missionary team, who saw their main ministry as prophetic service. Evangelization was to be announcement, yes, but also denunciation. It therefore had to take the side of the poor in social conflicts, while evading the enticements of the powerful, whose main interest was deriving legitimacy from the parish.[11]

The team also envisioned a "mobile" church: it was not a question of people coming to the church or of the church going out to the people but of the people themselves becoming the church. As recalled by one missionary team member, the sentiment conveyed to the people was: "We didn't come to bring you to the church or to carry you to the church but to be church with you, here."[12]

According to Rutilio's vision, the missionary team did not arrive in Aguilares to stay there; it was there to evangelize and organize the parish in such a way that it could eventually be run by lay pastoral ministers, assisted by a couple of priests. The priests would concentrate on the tasks reserved to ordained ministers while the laypeople would take charge of all other parochial labors. For this transition to take place, the laypeople would need to be prepared and motivated to take a more active role in the church, and other priests and religious would have to be recruited to collaborate in the work. The missionary team's members, therefore, had no desire to become permanently established in Aguilares, nor did they want to pass through so quickly that their labor was simply a "flash in the pan,"[13] like that of the popular missions. At the same time, no definite period was set for them to remain in Aguilares.[14]

Rutilio's understanding of how best to do pastoral ministry in the parish was correct. It would have been very hard to mobilize society without the popular religiosity that played such a significant role in shaping the identity and forging the unity of the Salvadoran people. It was therefore necessary to take popular religiosity very seriously if the team's goal was motivating people to analyze their social reality for the purpose of freeing themselves from oppression—precisely by transforming that reality.

---

10   *Summarium testium*, witness 18, §350.
11   Grande, "Aguilares," 22ff.
12   *Summarium testium*, witness 2, §18.
13   Rutilio uses the image of the dry husk of a corncob.
14   Grande, "Aguilares."

The Missions

During the missionary team's first months in the parish, from September 1972 until January 15, 1973, the patronal feast, they worked mainly in the city of Aguilares. After that, from the beginning of the dry season until the time of rains in May/June, the team dedicated itself to the villages.[15]

The team's novel pastoral approach made itself felt immediately. On Sunday, October 1, during the morning Mass in the chapel on the La Cabaña estate, the celebrant announced that the regular Sunday Mass there would be suspended so that the priests could attend to the villages on the weekends. This decision was in line with the team's option to give priority to the poor people of the villages rather than to the centers of power. One week later, on October 7, the team began celebrating a weekly Mass in El Paisnal.[16]

A large group of about twenty collaborators, consisting of seminarians, Jesuit scholastics, and university students, supported the team in the first missions it gave. These collaborators played an important role in helping to organize the communities where the missions were held, thus giving the priests freedom to move from one mission center to another. Three other Jesuits—Brother Santana Landaverde and two scholastics studying philosophy at the UCA, Napoleón Alvarado and Juan Ramón Soriano—relocated to Aguilares in order to work more closely with the missionary team. They did not live in the rectory but rented a small room in the city, and they traveled to San Salvador during the week to attend classes. Since their collaboration was temporary due to their status as students, they were not given tasks that the communities could undertake themselves, nor did they become integrated into the missionary team. Later, several local leaders who identified closely with the mission and method of the parish also became part of the group of collaborators.

The first period of intense mission began in Aguilares on November 1, 1972. The city was divided into ten zones, each with a mission center. The team decided to use the term "mission" because of its profound evangelical sense and the appeal it had for popular religiosity, but the mission experience in this case was very different from that of the traditional popular missions. The goal of these missions was to create communities of brothers and sisters dedicated to the creation of a new world free of oppressors and oppressed, according to the plan of God. "God is not up in the clouds lying in a hammock," Rutilio would tirelessly repeat. "God is acting now and wants you to build the Kingdom here on earth."[17] He warned the enthusiasts, however, not to be "rockets," that is, fireworks that fly high into the air and explode with a loud boom but then fall quickly back to earth. The goal of the mission was to produce lasting Christian commitment.[18]

---

15 Grande, "Aguilares."
16 Grande, "Aguilares."
17 Grande, "Notes."
18 Grande, "Aguilares."

The team did not impose the missions but simply offered them, first to the urban zones and then to the rural ones. The response was not long in coming, and there followed seven months of intense activity. The first mission in the Guadalupe neighborhood of Aguilares (November 1–14, 1972) was followed by missions in other neighborhoods: Los Angeles and Romero (November 7–21), Salinas and El Calvario (November 22–December 6), San Antonio and North Central (December 7–21), and finally South Central (December 26–January 5, 1973). The average nightly attendance was sixty adults. A special mission was held for the youth from January 2 to 13, 1973.[19]

The missions in the villages began after the feast of the Lord of Mercies (January 15). The first was in Las Ventanas and La Florida (January 15–28), and it was followed by others:

- Araditas and Huitiupa (January 28–February 11)
- El Líbano and Las Delicias (February 11–25)
- Potrero Grande and Trapichito (February 25–March 11)
- Buena Vista and Jicarón (March 11–25)
- San Antonio El Grande and El Tronador (March 25–April 11)
- El Paisnal (April 8–22)
- Segura-Valle Nuevo and Tres Ceibas (April 29–May).

Participation in the villages greatly exceeded that in the city: an average of 350 adults arrived each night.[20]

The missions were prepared with great care, even in the smallest details. Nothing was left to improvisation. Here, the influence of Rutilio and Bengoechea was unmistakable. Once they accepted an invitation, the missionaries and the local people sought out an appropriate site to set up a mission center. Places linked to the local power structure were automatically excluded. A large mixed commission would then meet in the parish office, where they would be asked to make an official commitment to the mission.[21]

Once the commitment was ratified on both sides, all the relevant information about the urban neighborhood or the village was collected and collated: number of inhabitants, characteristics, needs, conflicts, and so forth. Meetings were held to discuss details and organize commissions for locale, hymns, benches, lighting, clean-up, lodging, food, order, convocation, and so on. The idea was to involve as many neighbors as possible in providing the services that would be needed. During the preliminary meetings, the missionaries explained the requirements for receiving the sacraments. Whereas the traditional popular missions always involved a large sacramental dose, these missions would be

---

19 Grande, "Aguilares."
20 Grande, "Aguilares."
21 Grande, "Aguilares."

6. The First Stage

different. The sacraments would not be administered indiscriminately and carelessly; the goal did not consist in dispensing the largest number possible. Shortly before the missionaries' arrival, a team member would visit the mission center to make sure that everything was in place so that the start of the mission could be officially announced.[22]

The mission proper began with the arrival of the missionaries at the mission center, where they would stay for two weeks. During the two weeks of mission, they would visit people's homes, eating each day with a different family. In this way, they got to know all the neighbors and talked with them about the local situation. Information about the economic, political, social, cultural, and religious characteristics of the place was systematized on cards. These data were "codified"[23] in ways that would generate themes for discussion,[24] and then they were "decoded"[25] by the assembled people in the light of the Gospel. The missionaries dedicated the early afternoon hours to evangelizing the children and the early evening hours to evangelizing the adults.

To create a trusting and lively atmosphere, the evening sessions with the adults would begin with mutual greetings and with a hymn that had a message. Copies of the New Testament were given out to all who wanted them, even if they could not read. An act of community reconciliation was then celebrated, followed by an embrace of peace, a short prayer, and a hymn. A previously chosen scriptural text was then read several times by different readers. After each reading, the people could ask questions, make comments, or offer suggestions. The texts chosen were easy to grasp and also provocative; they contained unsettling or intriguing statements that focused the people's attention on the words and deeds of Jesus and the first Christian communities. The themes progressed in orderly fashion.[26]

---

22 Grande, "Aguilares."
23 Codification, generative theme, and decodification are basic concepts of the pedagogy of Paulo Freire, which was very popular during those years in Latin America. Codification describes the social reality as initially experienced by people. In a second moment, that reality is analyzed from a different perspective, with the codification seen as a mediation between the experienced reality and the theoretical analysis. Cf. Jesus Arroyo, *Paulo Freire: Su ideología y su método* (Zaragoza: Hechos y Dichos, 1973).
24 The generative theme gives rise to other themes, so that knowledge advances and suggests specific actions. Cf. Arroyo, *Paulo Freire*.
25 Decodification involves critical analysis of the codified situation; it is carried out by those directly affected, who begin to perceive the true relation between the codified elements and the constitutive facts of their actual experience. The individuals thus come to recognize themselves in the object and in the real situation in which they live. Decodification moves from the abstract to the concrete. Cf. Arroyo, *Paulo Freire*.
26 Grande, "Aguilares."

Table 1. Texts used in the mission

Objective	Initial text	Complementary texts
Mission: continue the task left to us by Jesus	Mt. 28:16–20	Mt. 10:5–10; Jn., 17:14–24, Acts 1:8–11; Lk. 10:2–12; 10:13–38
Receiving the Word	Mk. 4:3–9	Mk. 4:13–20; Lk. 18:18ff.; Mt. 7:24ff.; Heb. 1:1ff.
Mission of Jesus	Lk. 4:16–21	Mk. 1:14–15; Jn. 17:1ff.; 1:11ff.; 3:16–21; 6:34–40; Mt. 11:1–6
How the first Christians lived	Acts 2:36–47	Acts 4:32–35; Rom. 3:12ff.; 12:1ff.; 1 Cor. 12:12ff.
Making good use of our talents and abilities	Mt. 5:14–20	1 Cor. 12:4–11; Rom. 12:4–8; Eph. 11–16; 1 Cor. 12:12ff.; Mt. 24:45–51; 25:1–13
True religion, words, and deeds	Mt. 7:21–23	Mt. 7:15–20; 5:21–26; 6:1–4; 15:1–11; Jas. 1:19ff.; 2:14ff.; 1 Jn. 3:14ff.; 4:19ff.
Children of God and brothers and sisters to one another	Lk. 5:11–32	I k. 15:1–7; 15:8–10; 16:10–15; Mt. 7:1ff.; 5:43ff.; 6:7–13
Who are we with? Who are the ones being beaten down?	Lk. 10:25–37	Mt. 11:25–30; Lk. 16:19–31; 18:9–14; Jas. 5:1ff.
On what we will be examined at the end of time?	Mt. 25:31–46	1 Cor. 13:1ff.; Lk. 6:2ff.
The honor of serving and the greatness that frees us	Mt. 20:20–26	Jn. 13:1–5; Rom. 13:10–14; 14:13–19
With Jesus or against him	Lk. 12:8–11	Lk. 12:4–6.49–53; 9:57–62.21–26; Acts 4:1ff.; 5:17ff.; 6:8ff.; 8:1ff.
Ferment of the world	Mt. 5:13–16	Jn. 8:12; 1:1–9; Mt. 20:25–28
The commitment to change	Lk. 3:4–20	Acts 9:1ff.; 18:24ff.; 22:1ff.; 26:4–11
Workers of the kingdom, a new society of new men and women	Mt. 13:31–33	Mt. 13:24ff., 36ff.; 13:44–52; 11:12–14

Once the readings were finished, those attending were invited to form small groups of eight or ten persons to converse about the text that had been proclaimed. In the groups, a designated reader slowly read the text once again. A coordinator directed the conversation, and a secretary took notes about what was said so that it could reported back to the assembly. In the plenary session, one of the missionaries or collaborators took notes on what the secretaries reported, respecting their wording as much as possible, and then these notes were systematized. The contributions were read back to the participants, who were invited to probe deeper into the most significant issues through general dialogue. Experience showed the team that the plenary sessions were most beneficial if attendance did not exceed sixty or seventy

6. The First Stage

persons. When that limit was reached, a second assembly was organized and conducted simultaneously. The evening session concluded with communal prayer, announcements, a formal dismissal, and a hymn.[27]

The participants who showed greatest interest in the session were called apart afterward to evaluate it. The missionaries subsequently made their own evaluation and planned the activities of the following day. Every week, usually on Thursdays, the whole parish team met to make a general evaluation.

During each mission, two or three Eucharistic celebrations were held, usually after the celebration of the Word. In proceeding this way, the team made it clear that this was not a traditional mission, which placed great emphasis on the sacraments, but they also avoided having the mission dismissed as "Protestant" for giving a central place to the scriptures. Despite these precautions, there was much murmuring in the more traditional sectors, especially in the villages. People complained that the fathers had changed everything—now they were not even saying Mass! In reality, the most novel aspect of the mission was the emphasis on the sacrament of reconciliation as requiring a change of life and on the sacrament of the Eucharist as a memorial during which individuals and the community committed themselves completely to Christ. Even so, every night the priest made himself available for confessions and personal consultations.[28]

On the next to last night of the mission, the assembly chose the persons whom they wanted to be delegates of the Word, one for every four or five persons attending. The missionary team carefully considered various individuals' attendance, participation, and personal life, but it was the assembly that proposed the candidates, readily and naturally identifying the ones who during the two weeks of mission had shown the greatest ability, dynamism, leadership, and sense of responsibility. After the candidates had expressed their willingness to accept the position, the missionaries warned them that they should not all of a sudden become "preachers"; their position was to be one of service, not a means of domination or self-benefit. They should always be in search of the truth along with the community, which it was their duty to unite and organize. After discussing each candidate's suitability, the assembly then voted. The delegates had to be elected by a majority of votes. Apparently, many delegates, between fifteen and twenty, were chosen in each community, and this suited the missionary team since the large number would keep the community alive. In any case, the measure of the delegates' commitment would be the service they rendered the community, and the numbers could always be revised.[29]

On the last night of the mission, usually a Saturday, the persons chosen as delegates professed their formal commitment before the whole community. The

---

27   Grande, "Aguilares."
28   Grande, "Aguilares."
29   Grande, "Aguilares."

commitment was actually a mutual one, expressed liturgically, between delegates and community. In the same ceremony, the missionaries passed lighted candles to all those preparing for the sacraments: the parents and the godparents of the children being baptized, the children receiving first Communion and their parents, and the couples getting married. The morning of Sunday, the last day of the mission, was the moment for the celebration of the baptisms, the first Communions, and the marriages. Before the mission ended, the missionary team would urge the community to continue in the spirit of the mission, and they would distribute a good number of New Testaments.[30]

The mission was exhausting for the team. Perhaps one of the most difficult aspects for some of the collaborators was living with the local families in very poor conditions. The food was insufficient and of poor quality, generally consisting of beans, tortillas, and eggs. On special days, there might be a little chicken. Sleep was often difficult due to the hard beds, the insects, and the constant noise since the whole family slept in a single room. The odors were also unbearable. To relieve oneself, it was necessary to go off into the woods, and sometimes it was necessary to shoo away the bothersome hogs.

The mission focused on three mutually reinforcing dimensions: evangelization, community creation, and community leadership. The delegates of the Word were responsible for giving continuity to the work of evangelization and to the process of building, organizing, and strengthening the Christian community that arose from the mission. The election of leaders was therefore one of the most important moments of the mission. The constitutive elements of the renewed church of Aguilares were to be the community, the celebration of the Word, and the leadership provided by the delegates.

An introductory course was given to the delegates to familiarize them with their responsibilities, provide them criteria, and instruct them in basic methods for organizing events and running meetings. By the time the missions were finished, ten urban communities and twenty-seven rural ones were meeting weekly to celebrate the Word under the direction of the delegates. At the moment of greatest expansion, there were some three hundred delegates. The missionary team and the collaborators limited themselves to guiding the communities and encouraging their growth in faith and vitality. In the course of time, the delegates with more experience took the place of the collaborators.

Besides organizing and directing the celebration of the Word, the delegates were the main link between the community and the parish. The whole parish was divided into zones, and each had its own center where the delegates from the communities would meet every two weeks. In the alternate weeks, a commission of delegates from each zone would proceed to Aguilares, where, in collaboration with the priest responsible for the zone, they would prepare the next two celebrations

---

30   Grande, "Aguilares."

of the Word. The representatives would then return to the zonal center and share the material for the coming two weeks of celebrations with the other delegates. The delegates in each community met regularly to evaluate the most recent celebration and to prepare for the next one; they planned activities and assigned tasks among themselves. Through these channels, information flowed from the community to the parish and from the parish to the community. Interestingly, the delegates functioned as a sort of collective rather than as a council with officers. In this way, the parish structure was not something imposed from above but rather developed as the result of various experiments, evaluations, and reflections.

Even though the delegates did not form councils, the communities did, and their members were elected every two years. The council meetings, convoked and presided over by the president, began with a reading by the vice-president of the minutes of the previous meeting, after which previous resolutions were reviewed, an agenda was drawn up, and discussion on the various points was held. Rutilio used to recommend that the councils not drag out discussions unnecessarily, that they stick to the topic under discussion, that they respect the person speaking, and that they reach concrete conclusions and commitments. Decisions were made by majority vote. Overall coordination was provided by a general parish council, which consisted of the presidents and vice-presidents of all the community council and met in the parish seat.

To avoid losing direct contact with the communities, the missionary team met with them periodically. One priest was responsible for coordinating the urban communities and another the rural communities. Each priest regularly visited his assigned communities as a "herder."[31] His main role was to attend their meetings, clear up their doubts and confusions, help them evaluate the progress of the community, and meet separately with the delegates. This type of contact insured that neither the priests nor the parish center were displaced by the delegates.

Besides conducting the missions, the parish organized other activities, such as giving pre-baptismal talks on Sundays, preparing animators for the urban communities on Saturdays, and attending to the more than three hundred Adorers. Every March 19 the parish celebrated the feast of Saint Joseph, the patron of Aguilares and El Paisnal. The feast day was preceded by novenas and by nighttime audiovisual sessions in the neighborhoods of both municipalities. In 1973, Holy Week was celebrated in eight mission centers. About seven hundred baptisms were performed, preceded by four sessions of preparation.

The missions mobilized between three and four thousand persons, less than a third of the total population in the parish. Despite this, the missions laid the foundation for a solid parish organization made up of small Christian communities that were led by local leaders, most of them men. During those first months, the parish achieved a clear and strong leadership position among

---

31   Person in charge of caring for livestock.

the people even though its own internal organization was still developing and remained somewhat weak.

The Impact of the Missions

The missions produced great euphoria among the rural poor. Fully aware that they had entered into a new historical stage, the members of the newly formed communities were enthusiastic and profoundly grateful to the missionary team and its collaborators.

A New Religious Vision

The missions provoked, perhaps without intending to do so, a generational change in the religious leadership. The younger generation, quickly and enthusiastically assimilating the new method and the new religious vision, tended to displace the older adults who had formerly been the leaders. This transition was most notable in the Adorers of the Blessed Sacrament, one of the oldest and most prestigious religious organizations. Since the Adorers were already familiar with group methods of prayer and Bible reading, they encouraged many people to join the new communities; in this way, they contributed to the success of the missions, but also to their own displacement.[32]

The Adorers met at 7:00 p.m. on the last Saturday of each month to spend the night in prayer. The vigil began with a Mass, and after an hour of rest they rehearsed the hymns they would sing during the night. At 9:30, there was a penitential celebration, after which they took turns praying until five o'clock Sunday morning. After each hour of prayer, they read some scripture and reflected on it; then they prayed and sang hymns. The vigil ended with the Sunday Mass. Rutilio kept close track of the attendance at each monthly adoration, an old custom of his from the days when he visited El Paisnal with the seminarians. Each village had a small committee that coordinated these activities. An important innovation of the missionary team was to open participation in the association of Adorers to women.[33]

Despite their long history of Eucharistic devotion, the Adorers kept losing members until the association practically disappeared. The older members were reluctant to make further commitments: accustomed as they were to a pleasant night of prayer, they found the changes called for by the missions too radical. The younger Adorers, for their part, discovered other challenges that were more demanding and adventurous. Despite the diminishing numbers, the missionary team supported the Adorers until the association was dissolved. In August 1976, in his homily during the third Festival of Maize, Rutilio expressed his esteem for the "humble Adorers" of the Blessed Sacrament, who

---

32 Alvarado and Cruz, "Conciencia y cambio social," 176, 221–22.
33 Alvarado and Cruz, "Conciencia y cambio social," 176, 185–86.

6. The First Stage

have given an example, in their old age, of a change of mind, which I admire. I am ready to kiss their feet because, despite their years, they have tolerated this advance of the Gospel with a well-disposed heart. Moreover, they have adjusted to the renewal of the parish, and they have put aside those traditions, which perhaps had to give way, though it pained them.[34]

The older Adorers slowly came to understand that the younger members were better able to take on the new challenges. They therefore retired gracefully and contented themselves with providing wise counsel based on their long experience. Despite being displaced, they felt a certain satisfaction as they beheld the younger members "entering into the ways of God."

The missions also helped the people discover the Gospel message and stirred in them a desire to know that message better. The parish distributed thousands of copies of the New Testament to help people learn their way around the scriptures and become more knowledgeable about the Word of God. From that point on, the Word of God became a major factor in their lives, to the point of being excessive at times. For example, they tended to pepper their conversations and arguments with quotes from verses they knew. They also came to realize that not everybody reads the scriptures in the same way. Some found in the Bible a call to fight to be freed from personal and social sin while others were content with the idea of being saved from their personal sins:

> For me, the Bible is a history of the people who walk with God, but some of us understand it in one way, and others in another way. This happens because the Bible commits us to the struggle to free ourselves and others from sin and oppression, but some see it only as freedom from sin, and they think that oppression and injustice exist because God allows them.[35]

The discovery of the Gospel led many parishioners to conversion and a consequent change in conduct, especially in the villages. One neighbor of El Tronador described the conversion as follows:

> Before the mission came, things were terrible. The village was a mess, lots of clandestine liquor. People were getting drunk and doing foolish things. They just spent their time inebriated, drinking booze and ruining their lives. But after the mission all that stopped completely. There were maybe a few beers, but the people were discarding their vices. [...] The village changed in other ways as well. Before, everyone was going his own way. Now people help one another; they may not be organized, but they offer help with

---

34 Grande, homily, third Festival of Maize.
35 ACSI. Luis E. Pellecer, "First Evaluation of Different Aspects of the Literacy Program Developed in Aguilares"; "Some Data Gathered from the Rural Communities (Pastoral Visit)," Aguilares, January 4, 1976.

different activities. Previously there was hostility between hamlets, but all that has changed. Now everything is different. The villagers received the mission with open arms. We ended up with about thirty energetic delegates, and you could see the people's enthusiasm.[36]

The mission transformed the people's traditional image of God. The villagers' testimonies show that the preaching during the mission brought God down from to earth from heaven, presenting him as the God of the Exodus and the God of human history. One farmer expressed this clearly:

> For me God is a spirit who exists in all persons. I believe God is in every human being. They say that God is in heaven, on earth, and in every place, but I believe that he is more here on earth because that is where, history says, Christ comes to preach the Gospel, and that is the mission he has left for us.[37]

Another villager related God to mercy and fraternity and therefore saw him as opposed to injustice:

> For me God is a being who is not seen but is felt. When is he felt? When you sympathize with someone else, when you feel the pain of another [...]. For me God is a spirit who gives strength, force, energy; who is happy when we love and understand one another; when we are neither exploiters nor exploited, when we tell the truth and are lovers of justice. God is happy when we are ready to die for the sake of the truth.[38]

A third testimony is even more radical:

> I believe in a God of justice and love and peace, not in a God who is up in the clouds, or who is in the heart of the exploiters; not in a God of exploitation, not in a God made into money, not in a God made into propaganda, not in a God who is happy with fireworks and the traditional ceremonies.[39]

The people's image of Jesus also changed. Jesus was seen as one sent by God to establish righteousness and justice among human beings. He was therefore seen as a creative, inspiring leader, as the following testimony expresses:

> For me Jesus Christ is our guide. He is a leader who given us a great example with his life. He wanted to transform the world. [...] He was on the side of the poor. He demanded justice, love, understanding, and peace. He told us to love one another, just as he has loved us. He dealt sternly with the

---

36 Pellecer, "First Evaluation of Different Aspects of the Literacy Program Developed in Aguilares"; "Some Data Gathered from the Rural Communities (Pastoral Visit)."
37 "Some Data Gathered from the Rural Communities (Pastoral Visit)."
38 "Some Data Gathered from the Rural Communities (Pastoral Visit)."
39 "Some Data Gathered from the Rural Communities (Pastoral Visit)."

powerful who were exploiting the people. He confronted the hard of heart, he removed the mighty from their thrones, and at every moment he took the side of the poor. He is the first man whom I obey, and I want to follow him to the point of giving my life if necessary.[40]

During the celebration of the Word, the communities delved deeper into the meaning of divine justice. They quickly discovered God's outright opposition to the injustice around them, and they heard God's call to work for another reality, one founded on justice and peace:

> I used to feel that I was a Catholic, but it seemed as though I believed in God and didn't believe. From the time of the mission until now I have felt a change in my being. I have been seeing how we talk about injustice and exploitation. But we have to begin to put what we've learned into practice. Since the mission I have changed, and my ideas have become clearer.[41]

The poor of the villages also discovered that committing themselves to the reign of God and its justice required them to dedicate their lives to others. One of them stated that "in El Paisnal we felt that Rutilio opened up the Gospel and began to explain things to us. With the mission, I began to discover that I was even willing to let them kill me for serving others."[42]

The communities understood Christian commitment as unconditional collaboration with the divine plan to save humanity from every kind of injustice. Those most committed were radicalized by the resistance they encountered. Some favored the use of violent means, which they justified with texts from the Old Testament:

> I am quite ready. Today I am in bad shape, and I feel that following Christ is the way I am going. Right now I have only a few companions. I think about the priests and see them as just interested in money. Where does that lead? I feel enthusiastic when I dialogue with the people who understand me. I am ready to give my life, but fighting.[43]

In the community meetings, the villagers lost their timidity and the inhibitions that had formerly paralyzed them. They realized that they had strong opinions and that they could communicate and defend them. They gained greater confidence in themselves, developed a strong sense of community, became aware of their collective strength, and realized that many of their misfortunes came from their lack of unity. They then began to organize to transform their reality.

---

40 "Some Data Gathered from the Rural Communities (Pastoral Visit)."
41 "Some Data Gathered from the Rural Communities (Pastoral Visit)."
42 "Some Data Gathered from the Rural Communities (Pastoral Visit)."
43 "Some Data Gathered from the Rural Communities (Pastoral Visit)."

The First Labor Conflicts

The new religious consciousness began to make itself felt during the harvest of 1972–73. The cutting of the sugarcane was the most intense period of activity on the planation, especially on the farms that had a factory for processing the harvested cane. It was also the time when the greatest injustices were committed against the workers, especially in the assignment of tasks and in the wages paid. The plantations skillfully concealed many illegal practices by using duplicate payrolls, something very common at the time. Gross violations of the labor code were possible because the Ministry of Labor was in league with the plantation owners. The ministry agents refused to hear the complaints of the workers and consistently rejected their demands.

The 1972–73 harvest, however, saw something different. The workers discovered that the parish was more than willing to hear their complaints and demands. Even when the priests could not remedy the injustice and sanction those responsible, they at least listened attentively, carefully documented the misdeeds, and sometimes even offered practical advice. In a sense, the parish did what the Ministry of Labor should have been doing.

Table 2. Denunciations during the harvest of 1972–73[44]

Production unit	Facts
Hacienda La Galera Owner: Orellana family Overseer: Manuel Tejada Fortnight: December 9–23	Task: eight arm-widths by eight furrows.* Hours: 6 a.m.–6 p.m.** Food: one tortilla and a handful of beans for breakfast and two tortillas and a handful of beans for lunch.
Hacienda San Diego Owner: Hacienda San Francisco Overseer: Encarnación Mata Foreman: Manuel Mata Date: December 10	Task: twelve arm-widths by six furrows.
Hacienda San Diego Date: November 22	Task: fourteen arm-widths by six furrows. Worker fired halfway through the fortnight for denouncing labor violations.
Hacienda Los Mangos Overseer: José M. Hidalgo Fortnight: December 18–31	Hours: 6 a.m.–6 p.m. No payment of bonus or vacations.
Hacienda Los Mangos Foreman: Francisco Aragón Fortnight: January 29–February 10	Task: fourteen arm-widths by six furrows.

---

44   ACSI. Section Rutilio Grande, "Notes on the Parish of Aguilares."

6. The First Stage

Production unit	Facts
Hacienda La Cabaña Owner: De Sola Brothers Overseer: José Jarquín Fortnight: November 4–8	Wages: 2.25 *colones*, without food. Suppression of tenure rights and therefore of indemnification, vacation pay, and bonus. Until 1972, land was granted free to residents.
Hacienda La Cabaña Date: November 20	Thirty workers received 0.50 *colones* instead of the customary 2.25 *colones* for the same labor.
Hacienda La Cabaña Fortnight: December 9–11	Delay in payment of wages and decrease from 0.60 to 0.40 *colones*.
Hacienda San Rafael Owner: Padilla Brothers Date: November 11	Reduction of wages from 3.50 to 2.50 *colones*.
Hacienda El Carao Owner: Hacienda San Francisco Foreman: Juan A. Jiménez Date: December 11	Task: fourteen arm-widths by six furrows.
Hacienda El Carao Date: December 23	Reduction of wages for taking seventh day off.
Hacienda San Francisco Owner: Nottebohn Family Administrator: Eugenio Araujo Date: October 4	Task: twenty arm-widths by six furrows. Hours: 6 a.m.–6 p.m. No food provided, and if they failed to finish the task, they had to continue working the next day for the same wages.
Hacienda San Francisco Date: November 18	The work crew that denounced the abovementioned misdeeds had their wages reduced by one *colon*.
Hacienda San Francisco Fortnight: November 19–26	Task: twenty-two arm-widths by six furrows. The foreman stated that the law did not apply in his cane fields.
Hacienda Santa Rosa Owner: Rolando Castro, leased to David Sandar Foreman: Herminio Estrada Date: November 25–27	Workload was doubled with an increase of 0.05 *colones* instead of 0.30 *colones*. Worker is fired for protesting, despite having resided fifteen years on the property.
Hacienda El Trapiche, leased to Hacienda San Francisco Administrator: Mario López Date: November 23	Task: 18–20 arm-widths by 6 furrows.
Hacienda El Trapiche Date: December 13	Task: twelve arm-widths by six furrows. Hours: 6 a.m.–4 p.m.
Hacienda El Trapiche Date: December 16	Task: eleven arm-widths by seven furrows. Hours: 6 a.m.–3/4 p.m.

Production unit	Facts
Hacienda El Trapichón Owner: Hacienda San Francisco Foreman: Mercedes Deras Date: November 11	Task: twelve arm-widths by six furrows. Hours: 6–7 a.m.–3/4 p.m.
Hacienda Colima Owner: Orellana Brothers Overseer: Manuel Tejada Date: April 22	A resident was denied work and threatened with eviction for saying the pay was bad and workers lived like slaves.
Hacienda El Trapichito Date: April 15–21	Two hundred workers dismissed for cane field fire, allowing employers to avoid paying holiday.
Hacienda El Trapichito Date: April 27	Task: twenty to twenty-five arm-widths by six furrows in a burned cane field.

*Normal daily task: eight arm-widths by six furrows.
**Normal hours: 6 a.m. to 2 p.m.

Perhaps the most important events were the two strikes called during the harvest. The parish had nothing to do with organizing the strikes, but the delegates and other members of the communities were quite involved. The first strike broke out in La Cabaña on May 24, 1973, just as the missions were concluding: the last two missions finished on Sunday, May 27. Previously, there had never been a strike on the plantations, only small-scale skirmishes with some of the work crews. The workers on the plantations were organized into crews that were controlled by foremen. Each foreman chose his workers, and by the second fortnight of the harvest, he knew his workers pretty well. As a result, any worker fired from one crew would have difficulty finding work in another. For their part, the workers avoided working for foremen who imposed excessively arduous tasks.

The protests at La Cabaña revealed a political awareness that was not only unexpected but also quite radical. Most surprised of all was the missionary team. Although they had contemplated some type of political organizing, they were expecting it to happen in three years or so, not in six months. The accelerated politicization of the workers was due not so much to the missions as to other factors: the tremendous injustice that had long characterized the workers' relation to the plantation, the transformation of people's religious worldview, the ancestral confidence of the rural poor in the priests, and the protection provided by the parish. The strike revealed the workers' determination to demand justice, but it also showed the need for some type of organization to achieve justice.

The immediate origin of the strike was the request of the estate overseer that the work crews extend the fortnight, that is, that they work three weeks straight since the harvest was coming to an end. Even though the third week would likely end on Thursday, not Saturday, the overseer promised to pay the full week; the work crews accepted the deal gladly. On Wednesday of the third

6. The First Stage 175

week, most crews decided to work a double shift and finish the harvesting, so that on Thursday they would simply present themselves to be paid. Two rumors, however, began to spread. One was that the plantation would not pay the wages promised, and the other was that the workers would go on strike if that were the case. Meanwhile, the workers were consulting among themselves, saying that "Christians should unite together," as they had been told to do during the mission. To bolster their confidence and valor, they added: "They can't do anything to us if we are united."[45]

Other factors also influenced the workers' decision to declare a strike if they were not paid what had been agreed upon. The large number of strikers, some 1,680, "gave them courage in the face of the guard," the security forces stationed nearby. Moreover, they had machetes and perhaps a pistol or two, according to one witness; among the workers of El Paisnal and Chalatenango, it was common to carry weapons since they often had to spend the night sleeping on the plantations, in the homes of friends, or simply outdoors. Another important factor was that most of the workers would leave the zone immediately after being paid since it was the end of the harvest.[46]

The administrator had originally promised to pay each worker 86.50 *colones*: 52.50 for the May 7–19 fortnight, 26.50 for the third week, and 7.50 for the extra Sunday worked. On payday, a group of armed workers from Chalatenango crowded around the pay window and pressured the first worker in line not to accept the money unless it was complete. These workers were members of the Christian Federation of Salvadoran Farmworkers (Federación Cristiana de Campesinos Salvadoreños [FECCAS]); they had been organized by the pastor of Chalatenango and by Boulang. As it happened, the first worker received only 71.25 *colones*, representing the pay for only three days of the third week, when in fact he had worked four since he had done a double shift. There was no pay at all for the other three days promised by the overseer. The worker was being underpaid by fifteen *colones*. By shortchanging all the workers the same amount, the plantation would be saving about twenty-five thousand *colones* in wages.[47]

The Chalatenango protesters kept threatening the first worker in line: "If you accept that pay, you won't have the pleasure of spending it!" While the worker was vacillating, other workers began to mill around shouting, "Jarquín, son of a whore, pay us what you owe us! Are you not man enough to keep your promise?" The protest began "at Jarquín's place," according to one participant; Jarquín was known as a foreman who "gave out huge tasks." Moreover, "there were about ten men finishing the work from the day before, so a group of us went and told them to stop working and to join the strike."

---

45 ACSI. Documents about the strike at La Cabaña.
46 Documents about the strike at La Cabaña.
47 Documents about the strike at La Cabaña.

Behind the pay window, the administrator, using a loudspeaker, threatened to call the National Guard. He blurted out to the worker standing in front of him, a resident of the plantation, that he still owed money for the maize he had been advanced. He apparently wanted to intimidate the resident with that public reproach, but it had the opposite effect. The resident, feeling humiliated and irate, threw the money at the pay clerk. General mayhem followed, with angry shouts against the administrator and the National Guard, and also applause for the protestors.[48]

The plantation requested additional security forces to reinforce the two units that were already stationed there. In the course of the day, eighteen guards, under the command of a major, arrived from Aguilares, Guazapa, and San Salvador. When an inspector arrived from the Ministry of Labor, he was accosted by a group workers that had been organized by the delegates from Las Ventanas, El Matasano, and Chalatenango. Before the inspector could speak with the administrator and the overseer, the workers gave him their version of events; he limited himself to saying that everything would be straightened out. A group of plantation residents, chosen by the administrator and named by him as representatives of the workers, met with the inspector and four agents of the plantation. Meanwhile, outside it was being rumored that the inspector had been bribed, or that he was not really an inspector since he had arrived on the scene too rapidly. The workers sent a commission to Aguilares to verify his identity, paying the cost of transport among all. In Aguilares, some workers telephoned the Ministry of Labor while others went to the parish to advise the people there about what was happening.[49]

Meanwhile, in La Cabaña the delegates of the Word and the workers from Chalatenango stood in front of the pay window to prevent the workers from collecting their pay. Around noontime, there were several confrontations with the National Guard officers of Aguilares. When reinforcements arrived from Guazapa, the guards pushed the workers back. At that point, the plantation agents had nearly convinced one work crew to accept seventy-five *colones* as their pay, but the Chalatenango group provoked a tumult to keep them from collecting. The guards began beating the workers with the butts of their rifles. After midday, the commission of workers returned from Aguilares with the news that the Ministry of Labor would be sending a delegate. The man who had come earlier was therefore an imposter. A little later, some members of the missionary team arrived on the scene, along with a few collaborators. Their presence encouraged the workers, making them feel supported; it probably also prevented the shedding of blood, since an explosive tension existed between the guards, on the one hand, and the delegates and the men from Chalatenango, on the other. The

---

48 Documents about the strike at La Cabaña; and Cabarrús, *Génesis de una revolución*.
49 Documents about the strike at La Cabaña.

6. The First Stage

workers recognized that the presence of those who specialized in blessings had in fact "blessed" their protest.[50]

At two o'clock in the afternoon, the plantation offered to pay 82.50 *colones*. A little later, a lawyer, summoned from San Salvador by the parish and accompanied by three workers, began negotiations with the plantation. Outside, the major was threatening the workers: "Look, I'm giving you some advice. Don't be stupid. The lawyer can defend himself; he's from the city. But you are poor, and you won't know how to get out of this jam. Don't demand what you haven't earned." The workers responded that their pay was their business and they knew what they were doing. The foremen then succeeded in breaking the strike by offering more money to the resident workers; these were the most vulnerable since their work and their lodging depended on the plantation. The other workers then accepted the final offer of the plantation. They were tired and hungry, it was late, and some of them had to walk long distances to reach their homes. The missionary team left the place around 5:30 p.m. Half an hour later, the guards also withdrew.[51]

Such euphoria took hold of the delegates after the strike that they composed a song: "Now Change Has Come with the Word of God!" They had found their voice and defended their rights in the face of the plantation bosses and the national guards—moreover, they had triumphed. They had discovered the power of unity and planned action: "When had there ever been a protest of all the crews together?" The delegates from Las Ventanas were the ones that stood out most; not only were they more numerous, but they were better known by the other workers, and they brought forward religious reasons to justify the protest. Even though the plantation's reprisals would soon make themselves felt, the community meetings were better attended and more dynamic than ever. In the meetings, they spoke of the need to understand better the demands of Christian commitment and the importance of remaining united in order to avoid defeat.[52]

While it is true that the parish had not organized the strike, the motivation and the impulse had come from the preaching during the missions and from the people's new understanding of the Gospel. The delegates reflected with the people on what happened during the strike, using James 5:2–5 and John 17:21 as texts to guide them. Rutilio, however, drew no consolation from these developments; to the contrary, he experienced a growing malaise because the mobilization was advancing too rapidly. Feeling some concern, he requested through a fellow Jesuit an interview with Francisco H. de Sola, one of the owners of La Cabaña. Rutilio explained in detail to Sola what had happened and the role of the

---

50 Documents about the strike at La Cabaña.
51 Documents about the strike at La Cabaña.
52 Documents about the strike at La Cabaña.

missionary team. Sola accepted his explanations and laid the responsibility for the debacle on the administrator.[53]

The second strike broke out at the end of July on the Hacienda El Matasano. The labor conditions on that plantation were worse than those at La Cabaña. The workers put in more hours than were allowed by the labor code, but they became aware of the violation only when a Jesuit scholastic gave them a copy of the code. After reading the stipulation, they decided that they would work only the hours legally required. The idea originated with the delegates of Las Ventanas, and those of Las Araditas, Aserradera, and El Matasano agreed to put it into practice. On the first Monday of the fortnight, the delegates infiltrated all the crews, attempting to persuade the other workers to abide by the provision in the law code. On Friday, a delegate, who as supervisor was able to circulate among the crews, made it known that a sufficient number of workers were ready to protest. Accordingly, at eleven o'clock on Saturday ten crews declared that their work week was done. At the start of the second week of the fortnight, the delegates repeated the operation, but they widened the circle with the collaboration of the delegates of El Paisnal.[54]

Encouraged by their success, the workers decided not to accept the pay for the fortnight if it was not complete, and they presented three demands: pay for a complete day whenever it was impossible to complete the task assigned; a forty-four-hour work week, as stipulated in the labor code; and reduction of the price of maize sold to residents by the plantation (the price had increased drastically). This final demand did not benefit the workers proposing it, but they included it out of fidelity to the Gospel, hoping to correct an injustice being committed against their companions.[55]

On July 28, the plantation administrator, forewarned by a delegate, presented himself at the pay station, accompanied by an inspector from the Ministry of Labor and four national guards. After a moment's hesitation, the workers decided to maintain the strike. While the crews of workers who did not live on the plantation made ready to receive their pay, the crews of resident workers, who were the most vulnerable, dispersed among those who had no part in organizing the protest. The first worker in line returned the money because the pay was incomplete, and the others shouted their support. The inspector, surrounded by the guards, explained that the pay was correct because the increase in the minimum wage had not yet entered into effect. There followed a heated discussion, in the midst of which the workers presented their demands. Meanwhile, the delegates of El Matasano tried to convince the workers who were anxious to avoid any conflict that they should at least not approach the pay

---

53 Documents about the strike at La Cabaña.
54 ACSI. Rutilio Grande, "Notes about Diverse Strikes and Conflicts."
55 Grande, "Notes about Diverse Strikes and Conflicts."

window. After two hours of protest, the workers won the right to a forty-four-hour week and a small reduction in the price of maize, though not as much as they had requested.[56]

An evangelical pastor and his followers broke the strike at around one o'clock in the afternoon, presenting themselves to receive their wages. This action gave rise to a heated argument with the delegates. The pastor stated that he and his followers were "against spiritual injustice" and insisted that "the delegates should preach the Gospel to everyone and forget about earthly things. They may call themselves Catholics, but it is clear that they are fighting for their own interests."[57]

Later in the day, the workers saw the administrator "having a drink" with the inspector and the national guards in the plantation house. Since those officials had all arrived simultaneously at the pay station, the workers suspected that the inspector had been bribed. The national guards did not intervene in the conflict on this occasion but simply intimidated the crowd by their presence. The protesting delegates were singled out by a foreman and were given no work at the plantation for the next three months.[58]

The two strikes were followed by other labor conflicts of less consequence even though they were caused by the same problems. A dispute arose in La Cabaña two weeks after the strike, and other conflicts took place in San Antonio El Grande and in Gramalitos a month later. At the same time, protests broke out among the crews working at Los Gramales, El Trapichito, Los Mangos, and San Diego. The mobilizations and minor victories increased the workers' euphoria. Previous to that time, the workers had limited themselves to demanding, unsuccessfully, observance of the law, but they had done so without much organization or planning. Interestingly, just as the missions had motivated the workers to engage in social protest, so now the protests were reinforcing the work of evangelization and the Christian communities, especially during those months between May and July 1973. Various communities decided to launch some small projects, such as sowing collective crops and collaborating in the construction of houses, activities they interpreted as following in the footsteps of the earliest Christian communities.[59]

The plantation did not remain passive in the face of worker activism. It adopted a series of coercive measures aimed at checking the labor organizing: it increased the size of work assignments, dismissed malcontents, denied employment to those involved in protests, threatened to evict residents, and refused to rent out its lands. The plantation officials told the workers, "Let the priests give

---

56 Grande, "Notes about Diverse Strikes and Conflicts."
57 Alvarado and Cruz, "Conciencia y cambio social," 196.
58 Grande, "Notes about Diverse Strikes and Conflicts."
59 Grande, "Notes about Diverse Strikes and Conflicts."

you work. Ask them for land to work." La Cabaña drew up a list of the protest leaders and circulated it among the administrators and foremen of other plantations. The largest plantations organized a network of spies with the help of evangelical groups. This maneuver was interpreted by the most astute delegates as a clear manifestation of the influence of US imperialism. Rutilio thought along the same lines:

> For me the Bible is sufficient for our time only in a certain way. There are many people who want to follow it literally, but for me that would be impossible because the ancient times were different from our own. That is why the imperialists make use of these scriptures to create division in Latin American countries. I'm referring to the Protestant sects: they teach the people conformism, telling them that it is wrong to kill and that God forbids them to claim what is not theirs. They say that God came for the poor but wants them to stay poor, that it is wrong to desire what belongs to others. But we understand that claiming the land and our own rights is something we must do. In doing so, we claim what belongs truly to us, not to others.[60]

To make things worse, the plantation increased the number of national guards patrolling their properties in order to intimidate the workers. La Cabaña and El Matasano between them doubled the number of guards to nineteen; the patrols and the plantation officials detained some of the strikers and also issued death threats to the villagers living near El Matasano. Radio announcements and flyers distributed by the plantations attacked the priests wearing "red habits."[61]

Both the military command and the mayor's office of Aguilares alerted the village patrols and ordered them to keep an eye on meetings in the communities and report on what was said there:

> The last time they called us together it was to talk to us about the fathers. They told us to be very careful of them and to spy on their meetings. They said they had heard rumors about what was being discussed, and they didn't understand about that. Then they got tough, saying that the priests are against everybody, against us, against the government, and so we as servers of the government should infiltrate the meetings and inform about what was going on.[62]

These measures did not achieve the expected results in the short run, mainly because the patrols were made up of delegates and members of the communities, who reported nothing to their superiors. The patrol of one village consisted of twenty-two members of the peasant organization FECCAS. Some patrol members went even further and began contradict the commander:

---

60   Cabarrús, *Génesis de una revolución*, 277ff.
61   Alvarado and Cruz, "Conciencia y cambio social," 320.
62   Alvarado and Cruz, "Conciencia y cambio social," 197.

[The patrol's] function used to be grabbing young men and sending them off to be soldiers. We helped the villagers see that we were drafting people from within our own class for the sake of the bourgeoisie, and we were hurting the poor more than anybody. Now the patrols don't do anything to recruit young men of the community. What they do is take them from other communities where there is no consciousness. Otherwise they complain and tell them they're useless.[63]

The Impossible Neutrality

Despite repeated attempts at clarification, the political, military, and economic powers refused to view Rutilio and the missionary team as simple evangelizers. In his "Greeting to the People of God" of April 23, 1973, Rutilio informed the parishioners that he had been sent to faithfully announce the Gospel, but that it was a Gospel that encompassed the whole of human reality. Delivering that message was therefore the only politics he practiced. He also stated that as pastor he was at the service of the whole community, since all its inhabitants had been baptized, and that such service committed him to defending the victims of injustice, whoever they might be, even if they were evangelicals and unbelievers. The missionary team would therefore vigorously denounce every injustice, even when such actions were misconstrued because of the ignorance of some or the malice of others and even if the priests were called "communists" or "politicians." In any case, Rutilio concluded, nobody should be surprised by such maltreatment because the same thing had happened to Jesus.[64]

The extreme social and political polarization forced the missionary team's members to make frequent clarifications about their mission, but the same polarization meant that the clarifications fell on deaf ears. Aware of this situation, Rutilio emphasized, whenever he made a public condemnation, that he was speaking as priest and as pastor. Since any criticism in El Salvador at that time was invariably interpreted as opposition to the military government, Rutilio never tired of repeating that he did not belong to any political party or organization. On one occasion, in a vain attempt to convince his audience, he even swore before God that he was independent of all parties.

The first denunciation of Rutilio came quickly, hardly a month after he was made pastor of the parish. When the mayor ordered several women evicted from the municipal market, Rutilio felt obliged to denounce the action in his homily on Sunday, October 29, 1972. In April and May of that year, the municipality had refused to accept the dues of the market women for twelve consecutive days in order to be able to expel them from their posts for alleged insolvency.

---

63 Cabarrús, *Génesis de una revolución*, 159ff.
64 ACSI. "The Missionary Team of the Parish of Aguilares to All the Faithful Catholic and Other Persons of Good Will," Aguilares, April 23, 1973.

The women appealed to the municipality of San Salvador, run by the Christian Democratic Party; to the Supreme Court of Justice; and to the governor of the department. The mayor admitted to the governor before several witnesses that the reason for the eviction was politics: like most of the other market vendors, these women were Christian Democrats. They were definitively removed from their posts on October 5.

Addressing an overflowing church, Rutilio said that he had personally spoken with the evicted women, who had told him that they had made every effort to pay what they owed; they had committed no grave fault, and they were honest people. There were witnesses who attested that the mayor had acknowledged that the expulsion from the market was due to "politics." Moreover, in previous years the same mayor had ordered the evictions of other vendors because of personal enmity. After giving this background, Rutilio expressed his amazement at how the municipality, governed by honorable persons, could commit acts so contrary to justice, human rights, and the Gospel. He said that he had waited for a while before making a denunciation, hoping that the mayor would rectify the situation, but after reflecting, consulting, and praying about the matter, he realized that he could not remain silent: "In the name of God and of justice, I had to speak out."[65]

The eviction, said Rutilio, violated the "most fundamental law of the republic," and it compromised the democratic character of the country. He informed the congregation that he knew the Constitution well since he had taught it for many years in the seminary. He then read article 24 from the copy of the Constitution that the president had given him after his homily on August 6, 1970. The article in question prohibited government officials from pursuing or harming a citizen for simply belonging to a political grouping. The municipal authority was obliged to procure the good of the whole community, independently of political affiliations. If it failed to do that, it lost its legitimacy. Rutilio recommended in passing that the mayor would do well to study the Constitution in order to avoid any new arbitrary actions. To the objection that the mayor's decision had been backed by a judicial pronouncement, Rutilio responded that justice could be perverted and that it had indeed already been seriously compromised before conscience and before God.[66]

Rutilio concluded that the eviction lacked any foundation in principle and was therefore not only unjust but also a grave sin and a cause of scandal that he as pastor could not ignore. He added that remaining silent or covering the crime up would make him an accomplice of a public sin, and no pastor was allowed to do that. He expressed his hope that the injustice committed would be duly repaired and that such serious violations would not be repeated. In concluding,

---

65   ACSI. Rutilio Grande, homily, Aguilares, October 29, 1972.
66   Grande, homily, Aguilares, October 29, 1972.

6. The First Stage

he said that he knew that his words would be misconstrued, and he had therefore written his homily out that very morning so that there would be no doubt about what he had said. In any case, Christ and his apostles had also been misinterpreted and murdered for announcing the Gospel. There was no alternative, then, than to appeal to the good will of the congregation.[67]

The homily must have bothered the mayor because Rutilio tried to explain to him, in a personal letter written on January 1, 1973, the evangelical nature of the parish's mission. He assured the mayor that the objective was not to contradict the local authorities but to announce Gospel values, which coincided with basic human values. Those were the criteria that guided the parish's action, including its relations with the municipality. It followed that if the authorities governed in accord with those values, they would live in concord with the parish, but if they rejected those values or interfered with them, then denunciation was inevitable. The mayor and the municipal government should keep in mind that as baptized persons they were obliged to respect and promote human and Gospel values. Rutilio then took advantage of the occasion to invite the mayor to the Mass on January 15, the feast of the parish patron.[68] A year later, on the same occasion, Rutilio repeated his personal appreciation of the mayor, while insisting: "In many matters we will disagree with you as long as there is no improvement, and I tell you this clearly because I esteem you and I esteem much more the whole collectivity."[69]

In the middle of 1973, another opportunity presented itself for insisting on the universality of the Gospel in a politically polarized and therefore exclusionary society. The mayors of Aguilares and El Paisnal had invited Rutilio to attend a ceremony to welcome the president of the republic, Colonel Arturo A. Molina, and to take part in a town meeting on June 4. It was all part of the "Fourteenth Tour of Mobile Government."[70] The mayors also asked Rutilio to keep open the main churches in Aguilares and El Paisnal so that they could be visited by the president.[71] Ordinarily, the pastors attended such events and accompanied the president during his brief visit to the church, which would have been carefully adorned for the occasion. But Rutilio wrote to the mayors, informing them that he would not attend the events since his presence would be seen as legitimizing a clearly partisan visit that would definitely influence local politics. Rutilio explained that some people would interpret his presence at the event as favoring one political party over the others. This was inevitable, he wrote, since partisan

---

67 Grande, homily, Aguilares, October 29, 1972.
68 ACSI. Rutilio Grande to José Arnulfo Artiga, Aguilares, January 1, 1973.
69 ACSI. Rutilio Grande to José Arnulfo Artiga, Aguilares, January 9, 1974.
70 The "mobile government" was a practice adopted by Colonel Arturo A. Molina when he was president. It consisted in visits to the municipalities to meet the people and to inaugurate infrastructure projects. He would also visit the parish church.
71 ACSI. José Arnulfo Artiga to the pastor of Aguilares, Aguilares, May 29, 1973.

politics, being poorly understood and crudely practiced, had divided the people. Moreover, the elections of the year before had been denounced as fraudulent and had left many people feeling profoundly disillusioned and resentful.[72]

Rutilio had no desire to take part in the military regime's political games, nor did he side with the opposition. In his letter to the mayor of Aguilares, he reminded him of an unpleasant experience he had previously had with local politics. In the late 1960s, he had agreed to celebrate a Mass in El Paisnal on the day his cousin was being made mayor; his hope was to pacify the discord that had arisen as a result of the election. He agreed to celebrate the Mass on the condition that the outgoing administration also attend, and in his homily he urged the people to promote harmony and peace. Though he insisted that his exhortation had no political motivation, both the losers and the winners of the election misinterpreted his intervention, albeit for different reasons. The discontents protested against Rutilio by placing a sign at the main entrance of the church. What was worse, he wrote to the mayor, "I don't believe the awful consequences have even yet ended because some persons have continued to misconstrue my actions as if they were inspired by party politics. I should never have celebrated that infamous Mass!!" He said that he had not been able to forget those consequences "since I have loved my people, [...] and I have tried to seek what is good as a priest without getting involved in parties unrelated to my mission."[73]

Despite Rutilio's good intentions, his priestly ministry lost credibility in his native town because of the motives imputed to his activities. He was no longer the priest for everyone. It was for that reason that he had originally rejected the idea of taking on the parish of Aguilares. Once he had assumed the position, however, and long before the president's visit, he had decided that he would not contribute to political sectarianism:

> My relatives belong to different political parties, and they are well aware that I have never got involved in affairs of that kind, nor have I collaborated with them in partisan activities. All the well-meaning people of the town will testify to my statements. It is also true that I owe my relatives the respect that they have shown toward me in this regard.[74]

Apart from reasons related to family, Rutilio believed that he could not attend such functions because of the universality of his priestly ministry and the constitutional separation of the church. He had therefore decided, from that point on, not to preside at religious acts or to participate in political acts related to the installation of mayors or other political authorities. He also refused to take part in acts that could be associated partisan politics. The principle of neutrality,

---

72   ACSI. Rutilio Grande to acting mayor Adán Ronquillo, Aguilares, May 24, 1973.
73   ACSI. Rutilio Grande to acting mayor Adán Ronquillo, Aguilares, May 24, 1973.
74   ACSI. Rutilio Grande to Mayor José Arnulfo Artiga, Aguilares, May 30, 1973.

however, did not apply to his preaching. Rutilio warned the mayor of Aguilares that as a priest he was obliged to speak about injustice, poverty, and oppression because they are "topics that I do not consider foreign to my priestly mission, and that is the sense of the church. The religion of Jesus Christ has to do with all the dimensions of human beings both as individuals and as persons in relation with their fellow humans."[75] That was the message the missionary team had declared on April 23, 1973, in its "Greetings to the People of God," and it was what the mayor had already experienced in October 1972.

In any case, the president's visit put Rutilio in a difficult dilemma. If he attended the official acts, the government would be pleased, but he would lose credibility in the eyes of the rural poor. He would be seen as betraying the widespread discontent following the elections by giving religious legitimacy to a government suspected of electoral fraud. On the other hand, if he did not attend the ceremony, the government would consider him a malcontent, as in fact happened. Opting to take the side of the majority of people in his parish and in the nation, Rutilio informed the mayors that he would not attend the official acts, but he added that the churches in Aguilares and El Paisnal would remain open during the president's visit.[76] On prior visits, the president had found the parish church closed.

Probably feeling some malaise, Rutilio wrote the president on the same day of the visit. The letter was a typical one written by a parish priest to a civil or political authority, but it also described the social reality of the countryside and the mission of the parish team. Rutilio explained in detail his reasons for not attending the acts, repeating what he had already told the mayors but omitting the story of the Mass in El Paisnal. He blamed the plantation for the miserable state of his parishioners, most of whom, he said, were forced to live on rugged and rock-strewn marginal lands. Even those residing on the plantation had no security since no law protected their relation to their workplace. Labor relations on the plantation were manifestly unjust. Workers were required to do excessively heavy tasks, and their protests and claims were met with harsh reprisals, in large measure because they were not organized. That same year, the workers living on one plantation had been denied work on two occasions. Rutilio explained to the president about the events at La Cabaña and how the plantation had defrauded the workers by parceling out land to avoid agrarian reform. He stated that access to the land was becoming more and more difficult because the plantations were refusing to lease to small farmers. Meanwhile, the government had established no policies that would enable the rural poor to grow the basic foodstuffs they needed.[77]

---

75   ACSI. Rutilio Grande to Mayor José Arnulfo Artiga, Aguilares, May 30, 1973.
76   ACSI. Rutilio Grande to acting mayor Adán Ronquillo, Aguilares, May 24, 1973; and Rutilio Grande to Mayor José Arnulfo Artiga, Aguilares, May 30, 1973.
77   ACSI. Rutilio Grande to Colonel Arturo Armando Molina, Aguilares, July 4, 1973.

Rutilio closed his letter by denouncing prostitution and alcoholism. While its intense commercial activity made the city of Aguilares a propitious place for prostitution, Rutilio considered it unacceptable that the municipality should receive income from sex workers. Moreover, the authorities at times promoted the sale of alcohol, which flowed freely in the city. One of the councilors of El Paisnal had recently opened a liquor store in the village of Huitiupa. If the government committed itself to solving these basic problems, Rutilio wrote, it would also be eradicating crime, further impoverishment of the people, and the deplorable state of the rural poor. The only thing Rutilio declared to be in good shape was public education.[78]

President Molina, in a brief telegram signed by his private secretary, acknowledged receipt of the letter and added laconically that those were precisely the problems that his government was trying to solve.[79]

Tensions in the Missionary Team

The first stage of the missionary team's work had unquestionably produced excellent results, but the success was accompanied by difficulties and doubts. Rutilio thought that "everything was moving too rapidly." The preaching on the missions, the willingness of the team and its collaborators to live with the poorest neighbors during the mission, their readiness to listen to the complaints and the aspirations of plantation workers, and their presence at La Cabaña during the strike—all these actions produced enthusiasm, confidence, and credibility among a people who were predominantly traditionalist and Catholic. The fruits of these efforts were the Christian base communities, the delegates of the Word, and active lay participation in the structures and activities of the parish. These innovations, however, also polarized the parish community, despite the best intentions of Rutilio and the missionary team. While some parishioners delighted in a church that was close to the poor and defended their interests, others distanced themselves from the parish for the same reason. Crisis broke out in mid-1973, just as the first stage of missions was ending and the team was preparing to begin the second stage.

The crisis developed in two different but related spaces. Externally, the euphoria provoked by the missions motivated the rural poor to organize themselves with surprising speed. Internally, the pastoral method that had been adopted created differences within the missionary team. As already indicated, Rutilio showed some reservations about the mobilizing and organizing activities of those who had attended the missions. He feared that an indiscreet millenarianism, incited by the missions and the early triumphs in the struggle for

---

78   ACSI. Rutilio Grande to Colonel Arturo Armando Molina, Aguilares, July 4, 1973.
79   ACSI. Telegram of Colonel Aníbal Velarde, private secretary. San Salvador, September 17, 1973.

6. The First Stage

workers' rights, would end in a massacre. At the same time, in a situation of such great injustice, it was inevitable that true evangelization would lead people to organize politically in order to defend the rights they had long been denied. The pastor and his team found themselves unexpectedly caught up in a maelstrom of national and regional conflicts. The speed of the process and its possibly dire consequences proved too much for Rutilio, who from that point on experienced considerable anxiety.

Rutilio's fear was justified. After the strike at La Cabaña, the missionary team was accused of being communist and therefore a serious threat to the plantation and the military regime. The label "communist" was used frequently to discredit any type of reform movement, especially if it opposed the government and the established order. Both government spies and plantation agents kept a close watch on the missionary team,[80] but the government did not intervene since it was confident that the local forces could manage the challenge. The regime therefore avoided an open confrontation with the church, which would have been problematic at this point since the regime's legitimacy was being questioned due to the electoral fraud.

Within the team itself, the method of evangelization adopted was giving rise to tension and conflict. Rutilio was firmly opposed to developing any political project as part of the evangelization process. He did not believe that political organization was the job of the parish, and he did not want the parish to be used by other groups with political pretensions. He therefore insisted on drawing a clear line between the parish's work and political organization. Nevertheless, when the moment required, Rutilio was ready to denounce social injustice sternly, and he did not hesitate to defend the right of workers and small farmers to organize in order to demand their rights, even if it meant petitioning the president of the republic.[81]

Boulang apparently offered to coordinate the parish's rural communities, requesting a room in the rectory for that purpose. With the backing of the team, except for Bengoechea, Rutilio refused Boulang's offer and denied his request, asserting that the parish did not need that type of interference. He said that Boulang "moves in a different direction" and warned that "if he takes the finest people from us, we would do best to go elsewhere." Boulang desisted from his attempt to intervene, but he followed the Aguilares experience closely, making his opinions known to the team through Bengoechea. He also financed the purchase of mattresses for the rural villagers who overnighted in the parish. When Boulang left the country at one point, temporarily easing the tension in the team, Rutilio seemed to regain the independence he desired. In September 1975, Rutilio and Boulang met in La Antigua, Guatemala, during a four-week

---

80   Grande, "Notes about Diverse Strikes and Conflicts."
81   Grande, "Notes about Diverse Strikes and Conflicts"; and documents about the strike at La Cabaña.

course sponsored by CELAM. There they had a long, friendly conversation, and Boulang later sent Rutilio a note thanking him for his friendship.[82]

Within the team, Bengoechea continued to insist on abandoning the religious approach and adopting a more political one. The Jesuit scholastics sided with him and resented what they called the authoritarianism of Rutilio, who they said was manipulating the team. As a result, they distanced themselves from Rutilio, preferring to work with Bengoechea. For his part, Rutilio thought that the scholastics had an ambiguous attitude toward authority and were too "critical and impetuous" since they were trying to advance "like a jet in the faith while blithely leveling the culture of the people." Moreover, they showed little appreciation for the Eucharist. Some did not even attend Mass with the people on Sunday. Despite these complaints, Rutilio in his more buoyant moments acknowledged the importance of the scholastics' contributions.

The conflict between Rutilio and Bengoechea became highly personalized. Rutilio was supported by the rest of the team while Bengoechea was favored by the collaborators, the Jesuit scholastics, and the university students. The discrepancy created two spheres of influence with quite divergent dynamics, attitudes, and loyalties. As pastor, Rutilio represented the institutional church and the Jesuit order since he was a member of the vice-province's national council. Bengoechea and the scholastics, for their part, represented the rural communities, into which they had entered rapidly and effectively. The division in the team became manifest in the two types of team meetings that were held: the whole team participated in the first type of meeting, but Rutilio refused to participate in the other type, where "strategies and procedures" were discussed. Bengoechea evaded discussion of the content of those meetings, and when questioned, he would complain of lack of confidence. Rutilio, for his part, lamented Bengoechea's dual loyalty, adducing as evidence several of his activities: (1) soon after arriving in the parish and without knowing the political mood of the region, he had met with local politicians of the opposition; (2) he had brought to the parish UCA students who belonged to the Christians for Socialism Movement; (3) he had invited opposition leaders to speak on political strategy to delegates in a course called "political vaccination"; and finally, he had traveled abroad without giving any explanation.[83]

The activities of Bengoechea and the collaborators in the rural areas were complicating the relations of Rutilio and the rest of the team with the communities and their leaders. Rutilio considered such interference unacceptable; he said he felt reduced "to the role of a wizard, called to officiate here and there." Another serious disagreement arose after the labor protests, when Bengoechea and the collaborators attempted to introduce revolutionary theory and scientific analysis in order to promote worker organization and orient the protests.

---

82 ACSI. Bernardo Boulang to Rutilio Grande, Tegucigalpa, October 29, 1975.
83 ACSI. Rutilio Grande, "Address to the National Council." San Salvador, March 9, 1975.

Such theory and analysis were precisely the focus of Boulang and his group, but Rutilio opposed them on the grounds that they were not the competency of the parish. Rutilio and the team began a dialogue with Bengoechea and the collaborators about the nature of their contributions, which Rutilio attributed to their "great fascination" with Marxist analysis. "They have a very advanced position," he later explained, "without respecting the surrounding milieu"; as a result, they were accelerating a process that Rutilio thought should be allowed to follow its own rhythm.[84]

The final outcome was a missionary team very different from the one imagined and desired by Rutilio. Unity was lacking, and team members did not feel identified with a common project, which Rutilio believed was fundamental. He was surprised by Bengoechea's attitude, especially since they had always maintained good relations when they were together at the seminary and Bengoechea had in the beginning accepted the method agreed on by the team. The experience had begun well: the two men conversed, reflected, and even prayed together, and they concelebrated the Eucharist with the people. But then Bengoechea began to push for a change of methodology and even for a de-emphasis on worship: "He doesn't even say Mass on Sundays, with the excuse of giving courses to delegates," complained Rutilio, who in contrast wanted to integrate the Eucharist into the courses "because the people take great note of these things and would not understand why he was neglecting something so fundamental." The tension made living together very difficult, and Rutilio often exploded.[85] He was finding the complexity of the situation both within the parish and in the region incomprehensible and unmanageable:

> I confess that at certain moments in the process my mind and my conscience have considered various alternatives, experiencing doubts sometimes and trying to keep things in balance, now leaning in one direction, now in another. I see ever more clearly that I must act urgently in order to avoid greater traumas and subsequent complications.[86]

The crisis forced Rutilio to reorganize parish activity in order to give himself more contact with the communities and the delegates. The team members were all assigned specific tasks: Rutilio and Carranza would promote the ministry and formation of pastoral agents in the rural communities and would coordinate the communities; Cruz would coordinate youth activities in both rural and urban areas; and Fernández would look after pastoral ministry in Aguilares and El Paisnal. Bengoechea was left more or less free because he frequently was away, taking part in the activities of the Boulang group. The lay collaborators would

---

84   ACSI. Rutilio Grande, "These Are My Ideas [...]"; and "Address to the National Council."
85   Grande, "Address to the National Council."
86   Grande, "These Are My Ideas [...]."

make whatever contributions they could to the various ministries, but first they would have to pass through a course of initiation, be faithful to the obligations they took on, and attend team meetings. It was to be understood that the ideal candidates for the parish council were the local pastoral agents. The team would ordinarily meet every Monday to review, evaluate, and plan activities; it would also supervise the sectorial meetings. In this way, the team prepared to begin the second phase of parish renewal, which involved both intensive courses and shorter workshops. At that point, Rutilio, much against his will, had to leave the parish because he was diagnosed with diabetes.

The reorganization of parish activity did not resolve the underlying problem. In practice, Bengoechea "took control" of the rural communities and their delegates while Rutilio remained "confined" in the city. Feeling an urgent need to return to the villages, since his origins were there and he had a special charism for rural ministry, Rutilio found the situation intolerable. While making the Spiritual Exercises in Chinandega, Nicaragua, Rutilio discussed his experience in Aguilares with Amando López, the last Jesuit rector of the seminary and one of the martyrs killed at the UCA in 1989. Rutilio decided he should leave the parish in order to put an end to the tensions.

On May 9, 1974, Rutilio asked the vice-provincial for permission to leave Aguilares and go to Panama. He explained to the national council of Jesuits that his differences with Bengoechea were less ideological than temperamental. The council, considering that it would be imprudent for Rutilio to abandon Aguilares in view of the likely negative repercussions for the apostolate, suggested to the vice-provincial that Bengoechea leave the parish for a while since it was time for him to do his tertianship.[87]

---

87   ACSI. National Council, act no. 6, San Salvador, May 9, 1974.

7. The Second Stage: The Courses and Cursillos

The feast of Pentecost 1973 marked the end of the first stage and the beginning of the second, known as the period of the courses and cursillos. This second stage lasted until August 1974. The transition was celebrated with a massive public gathering in Aguilares, during which the people celebrated the coming of the Spirit and asked the Spirit to continue renewing the parish. An unexpectedly large multitude from all the communities crowded into the city and paraded through the streets with joyous festivity. Each community carried posters and banners bearing quotes from the New Testament. The size and the vigor of the demonstration bore witness to the strength of the communities and the credibility of the parish leadership.

Enlivened by several musical groups from the villages, the Eucharistic celebration was exuberant. In his homily, Rutilio encouraged the communities, and he responded to some of the accusations against them that had already begun to circulate. The evangelization process was not Protestantism or crude materialism, he asserted; nor was it politics, and much less was it communism. Rutilio warned that future persecution was inevitable given the deplorable social situation in which people were living. He cautioned that the authorities would spy on parish meetings and deploy national guards throughout the region. Christians would be led away bound and detained in army posts, but there was no reason to fear. Persecution would come to all true Christians since it was the fate of Jesus himself. Rutilio also warned the communities about the dangers of internal conflict and rivalry.

Rutilio went on to explain the principles guiding the work of the missionary team. He stressed, first, that the priests were missionaries and had been sent to announce the Gospel to the whole parish community. They would therefore not provide the sacraments to those who were not truly evangelized. Disregarding this principle would mean acting against the Gospel itself. The second principle was non-involvement in politics. The team had no ties with political parties or political groups of any sort. Their only "politics" was announcing the Gospel and vigorously denouncing injustice in the name of the Gospel. The aim of the team was to create a community of brothers and sisters committed to building a new world according to God's plan, that is, a world that had neither oppressors nor oppressed.

The Eucharist was followed by a lively fiesta on the parish grounds. As they feasted, sang, and laughed, the people from the communities celebrated the coming of the Spirit.

The Courses and the Cursillos

In the second phase of evangelization, the team proposed to deepen the process and so help the communities to grow and mature. During many tedious meetings of reflection and evaluation, three lines of action were decided on: development of the communities, formation of the delegates, and evangelization of popular religiosity.

The missionary team decided not to create more communities since the thirty that already existed were more than the priests and the collaborators could attend to. The priest responsible for the twenty-seven rural communities needed about two months to visit them all, covering three each weekend. Meanwhile, they observed that participation in the celebration of the Word was not what it should have been. Attendance had increased in only four communities, while it had decreased in six and remained level in fourteen. At that time, the celebration of the Word in different places was bringing together 280 men, 450 women, and 165 young people. The delegates had worked hard to increase attendance and improve the manner of celebration, but they had not made sufficient home visits, nor had they visited other communities. When a meeting was held in Aguilares on June 24 to analyze the situation, the representatives of the twenty-seven rural communities complained of being neglected.[1]

Rutilio encouraged the delegates, reminding them that there had been only twelve apostles, and the team sought ways to strengthen the communities by training the delegates and diversifying their functions. Despite the lack of personnel, the team decided not to increase the number of outside collaborators, who at that time numbered about twenty. Since they came from elsewhere, it was feared that their lack of familiarity with the region and their lack of training might create a certain chaos; it was feared that they would interfere in the community processes by failing to take account of the local rhythms and customs.[2]

The consolidation of the communities was accompanied by a second line of action: an intensification of the formation of the delegates of the Word so that they could conduct pastoral activity in the near future. By the middle of 1973, some eighty-eight delegates had ceased to be active for a variety of reasons: lack of will, insufficient faith, unemployment, sickness, vices, and so on. Only nine communities had attempted to hold onto them, while fourteen had done nothing. The team also decided to intensify its work in the city, but without yielding to frenetic activism.[3]

The third line of action had to do with the evangelization of popular religiosity. The team had no intention of suppressing the local traditions, but it wanted to find new forms of liturgical and sacramental expression that would

---

1 Grande, "Aguilares," 22ff.
2 Grande, "Aguilares," 22ff.
3 Grande, "Aguilares," 22ff.

7. The Second Stage

respond to the reality of the communities. The search for those new forms was to be undertaken with the help of the communities so as to avoid the dangers of paternalism and clericalism. In doing this, the team also worked to break the link between sacred worship and economic payments.[4]

Of the three lines of action, the second was the most important because the delegates were meant to constitute the infrastructure on which the life of the parish would rest. Solid formation of the delegates by means of courses and cursillos was therefore meant to respond to the challenges presented by the growth of the communities.

At first, the team sent the delegates to one-week courses that were held outside the parish, but the results were unsatisfactory. Leaving the parish gave the delegates undue distinction, and the courses did little more than drown them in poorly assimilated data that forced them to make impossible leaps. When they returned to their communities, they did not know how to apply the training they had received. In the best of cases, they repeated what they had learned, but they often ended up feeling quite frustrated. Considering these results, the team decided to impart its own courses in Aguilares or in the zonal centers. The delegates attended courses outside the parish only in exceptional cases, such as for cooperative training and a mini-IPLA program of five weeks, and they were always accompanied by one of the priests, who helped them assimilate the experience and see it within the larger pastoral plan of the parish.

The Parish Courses

The parish courses were short and graduated, so as to avoid saturation. After each session, the participants were instructed to do some exercises in their communities, and they were almost immediately able to put the topic of the course into practice since it had been designed to respond to the needs of both the delegates and the communities. The courses involved continuous dialogue in group or plenary sessions, thanks to the interactive method, and they were based on what people had experienced at the personal, community, and national level. Each experience was examined from the perspective of the history of salvation and in the light of faith, and everything was bound together by the Word of God.

In Aguilares, three types of courses were given. The courses for "preparers" trained select delegates to take on the coordination of the various zones into which the parish had been organized. Given their function, the "preparers" were expected to become a key element in the parish structure; they would be the main link between the missionary team and the communities, and as such they would constitute the *ex officio* parish council. The "preparers" were chosen with great care, by surveying opinion at various levels. After doing the surveys, the team would draw up a list of candidates and then discuss with the people in each

---

4   Grande, "Aguilares," 22ff.

zone the criteria for choosing the "preparers." A plenary session of delegates was called to elaborate the definitive list of thirty candidates, and on October 7, 1973, an election was held. The natural leaders of the parish were identified in this process of dialoguing with the most involved delegates and their communities. As it turned out, however, the "preparers" soon became the most important supporters of FECCAS, creating a source of tension with the parish.

Each zone was coordinated by ten "preparers" whose functions included coordination, recordkeeping, finances, information, justice and peace, music, and so forth. The "preparers" played a key role in many aspects of church life: celebration of the Word in the communities, channeling information to and from the parish, developing courses and cursillos, animating community life, promoting consumer cooperatives, analyzing local and national events, and relating to popular organizations that were trying to enter the zone.

The course for preparers lasted thirty-five hours spread over five weekends and beginning on October 14, 1973. In each session, the delegates reflected on biblical themes related to the social situation of the parish and the struggle for justice. They studied the national reality, the structure of sin and violence, the deterioration of social relations, the overcoming of oppression, the restoration of human relations, social liberation, and the plan of God for new men and women united in a new people. After a theme was expounded, the participants, meeting in small groups and plenary sessions, would draw out the message of the biblical text with the help of a song, a game, or reflection on some concrete event. Finally, with the help of group dynamics, graphics, slideshows, games, and dramatic presentations, the message would be related to the concrete situation of the parish and conclusions would be drawn.

During the week, the preparers would do homework on questions such as the following: Why did the people of Israel and the people of El Salvador suffer slavery? What was God's plan for his people and for the parish community? Why was the plantation system radically unjust? What movements in the country were fighting for justice? Which were in the right and why? At the beginning of each weekend session, the participants would reflect on the answers they had arrived at and would discuss them. In this way, they became familiar not only with the Gospel message but also with the value of labor and the great social contradictions of the country. The small groups and the plenary sessions were run by one of the participants, while the plenary sessions were guided by one of the priests, assisted by a collaborator. The method employed stressed that the "preparer" was not a "preacher" but a motivator, someone who broke ground for others and helped them to grow.

Another type of training course had two objectives: preparing new delegates to replace the thirty preparers and creating a uniform method for celebration of the Word, which until then had been highly creative and fluid. This course was given on Sunday mornings and coincided with the course for preparers. After evaluating the ways in which texts were prepared and the Word was celebrated, the participants helped to elaborate a uniform schema that the preparers later took to the communities.

The urban delegates, whose rhythm of life was different from that of the rural delegates, received these training courses in fifteen consecutive afternoons, sometimes in Aguilares and other times in El Paisnal. These courses were given by two delegates, two priests, a preparer, and a collaborator. As was true in all courses, great emphasis was placed on the historical reality, the Bible, and interactive method.

The parish structures took shape as the result of much consultation and reflection during this stage of courses and cursillos. The courses helped define the functions of the delegates and the preparers, and they made the celebration of the Word more unified and systematic. For the celebration in the communities, three elements were important. The first concerned the preparations: locale, benches, light, texts, hymns, and so on. The second element was the most important: the celebration itself. This would begin with a hymn and a greeting. There followed an act of reconciliation, which included an examination of conscience in silence, a hymn, and a kiss of peace. The proclamation of the Word took place in an ambience of personal and community prayer, accompanied by a hymn. The first reading would be taken from a text from the Old Testament, and it was followed by a short commentary. Then a text from the New Testament was read, after which the assembly divided up into groups of six to eight persons, each group with an animator, a lector, and a secretary. After dialoguing about the texts, the groups would come together again, sing another hymn, and then present a summary of their reflections. Doubts were clarified, and further reflection was encouraged. At the end, a general summary was made, with emphasis on the central idea and the conclusions that were drawn. The third element of the celebrations was involving the community in prayer: the people were encouraged to offer petitions, pray the Our Father, make appropriate announcements, and sing a final hymn. Before the people dispersed, they took part in spontaneous activities such as songs, games, collections, and raffles.

The zonal meetings of delegates were also given great formality. Each session was led by a coordinator and a secretary, and it would begin with a hymn and elaboration of the agenda, some of whose points were fixed. The secretary would then read the commitments previously made, and all attending would evaluate their fulfilment; the previous session would also be assessed. After that, the two delegates sent to the zonal meetings would present the scriptural passages for the next celebrations of the Word in the communities, and they would convey any announcements from the parish. The delegates would spend some time studying the texts together, trying to identify the principal themes and looking for points that would enliven their services. The secretary noted down any resolutions made during the session. These meetings were of great importance since they served as the main link between the preparers and the communities, the maintenance and progress of which was highly dependent on the formation given the delegates.

The zonal meetings were run by the preparers. Those attending were divided into two groups, and each group would prepare one of the texts to be used in the next celebration. After the text was read and the principal idea identified, a preparer would then help the group draw out the implications. When the two groups reassembled, each group would read its respective text, comment on it, and present its conclusions. Each delegate was expected to return to his or her community with three things clearly in mind: the text, the central idea, and the parish announcements.

On alternate Saturdays, the preparers met in the parish to prepare for the zonal meetings. The sessions, which were led by a preparer and a priest on the team, used some of the same elements that were used in the zonal meetings, and the group dynamic was also similar. Attendance was taken to verify the presence of all the zones; if any zone was absent, substitutes were named. The session commenced with a hymn, greetings, reconciliation, kiss of peace, and shared prayer. The scriptural texts were then presented, and two groups were formed, each coordinated by a preparer. It was important for the preparers to grasp the central message of the text and the importance it had for community life. These meetings were also sometimes used to give the preparers further training. At the end of the meeting, the preparers reported news from their communities and any requests the people had made, while the parish informed about future activities. Stressing the importance of communication, the missionary team urged the preparers to be diligent in transmitting news and information as faithfully as possible. These meetings were excellent schools for learning responsibility and commitment.

On Fridays, the urban catechists met together with one of the priests to prepare the instruction to be given on Saturday in the ten centers into which the city was divided. The catechetical method used was that of the Providence Center of Santa Ana.

These courses and other parish activities gave parishioners much more familiarity with the Bible than they had before. During the stage of missions, several thousand copies of the New Testament were distributed to those who wanted them, and a complete Bible was given to the preparers and the delegates. The archdiocese donated hundreds of Bibles, some of them for children, to the parish. When evaluating this stage of the parish renewal, one member of the missionary team stated, "We don't really know what is there in the soul of the rural poor, but they certainly give us a great example of what it means to put all your soul into the task."

The Cursillos

The parish courses were followed up in a series of cursillos that treated specific topics and problems that resulted from the pastoral activity as the parish project

7. The Second Stage

developed. Generally given by collaborators, especially the Jesuit scholastics, the cursillos facilitated the integration of reflection groups at the level of the parish, the vicariate, and the nation.

The delegates of the Word were asked periodically to participate in specific cursillos. The delegates preparing people for baptism received formation on the sacrament, which followed the archdiocesan guidelines but interpreted them in the context of the parish; they were also trained to give talks to the parents in their homes. The delegates giving catechesis were taught to use the Providence Center catechism, and those giving pre-matrimonial talks were also shown how to fulfill their mission. The delegates in charge of youth were instructed on how to develop themes and questions of interest to young people. Those acting as coordinators and secretaries were taught how to run effective meetings and how to record important discussions and decisions. The expansion of activities led to the formation of four itinerant teams of delegates who moved around the parish, animating young and old alike.

Other courses were offered to the communities in some zonal centers and a few villages. The course on "the relation of humanity to the earth" was typical of this process of ongoing formation. It began with a parable that was dramatized by a group of local people. After the presentation, the community analyzed the characters in the drama while the collaborators (university students) noted down the phrases used by the people. A third element of the cursillos was the introduction of a Gospel text to throw light on the discussion. Again, the participants' vocabulary and verbal expressions were recorded so that they could be used later to impart literacy lessons to adults.

Starting in 1973, the parish offered literacy courses to adults, both in Aguilares and in some of the villages. The literacy team was made up of collaborators from the Jesuit high school and directed by Luis E. Pellecer, a Jesuit theology student. The method used was that of Paulo Freire, which understood literacy not simply as being able to read and write but as learning to reflect critically about one's social reality. As the students were learning to read and write, they were also becoming aware of their ability to analyze their concrete situation and to work for its transformation. The learning process helped them to be effective communicators of the interests and needs of the people, an essential activity in the parish structure. The literacy program directly benefited the parish's pastoral activity, and later it was also very useful to FECCAS, which was beginning to take shape at that time. Despite difficult circumstances, the learners were highly motivated, and there were few problems in following up on the process.[5]

In the course of two and a half years, 170 rural folk signed up for the literacy courses, and each student attended an average of fifty to sixty hours of class.

---

5   Pellecer, "First Evaluation of Different Aspects of the Literacy Program Developed in Aguilares."

Relatively few dropped out, and they did so mainly for reasons of sickness or excess work; very few left the course because of its method or content. The team estimated a success rate of eighty percent in those who persevered, though the results in the villages were poorer than those in Aguilares. Since the emphasis was on reading more than writing, many still had difficulty writing. "If I write something," one student said, "only I can understand it because I put in too much or too little." Even though all the students could at least write their names, some rural folk wanted more: "If you don't know how to write well, it's like being in the night."[6]

The literacy program came up against several difficulties. Since it was seen as a type of schooling, many people rejected it. School was for young people, not for adults, who were thought to be incapable of book learning due to their age. There were also doubts about the benefits of literacy for subsistence farmers and plantation workers. Schooling was even considered a threat since it was thought to produce idlers and arouse vain desires to pursue further studies. Living conditions presented another obstacle: physical exhaustion and lack of electric light made it difficult to study in the home. Participation of women in the program was especially low since they had no one with whom they could leave their children.[7]

Motivation was probably the most important factor. The rural poor did not see much sense in studying "letters." They questioned the usefulness of learning to read and write—after all, they were already raising their kids, their eyesight was failing, or they had no one to take care of the house:

> They certainly want to learn, and they think it would be great even to learn to sign their names, but what happens is that all the little jobs that need to get done every day in the country leave them no time to spare. After spending the whole day roasting the flesh [under the sun] in those cane fields, one returns home beat and just wants to rest in the hammock.[8]

Sometimes, the most determined students had to put up with the ridicule of others: "I take my reading book out to the cornfield even though many people make fun of me."

Another disincentive to study was fear of reprisals from the plantation, especially loss of work. Some people rejected the literacy program, claiming it was "politically oriented. They refuse to come, saying that it's just politics. Some show little enthusiasm; it's plain they don't want to struggle. They don't know what the struggle is. They're afraid that it will bring them problems. They're up

---

6 Luis E. Pellecer, *Manual del alfabetizador* (Guatemala City: Delgado Impresos, 1978), 18–19.

7 Pellecer, "First Evaluation of Different Aspects of the Literacy Program Developed in Aguilares."

8 Pellecer, *Manual del alfabetizador*, 32.

to their ears in fear" of being denounced or losing their jobs. So great was the fear that some insisted that "unorganized people should not be involved. If they're not in the organization, they have a different ideology." Others with a broader outlook stated that "it is better to involve only people from the same base; we can't deal with just any kind of people; first we have to see how aware they are." Studying while on the plantation was difficult: "You can't take advantage of those little spots for reading while you're resting from work because there are many spies." The workers understood clearly the reason why the plantation was harassing them: "The bosses tremble with fear just at the thought of us uniting."[9]

The obstacles, though many, were overcome both because the people felt a strong need to know how to read and write in order to participate fully in parish activities and because the literacy team worked with tremendous dedication and creativity. "I hadn't finished school," said one man, "but when the community sent me on a cursillos to study medicine, I had to work hard to learn." Many people needed reassurance: "It's not just a matter of learning but of advancing. [...] You have to tell people that it's easy to learn. You have to encourage people a lot and make them see that learning is enjoyable. It's not difficult; they don't ask you questions." And many were happy with the results: "From not knowing anything, from not knowing even the letters of my name, I can now distinguish the letters and advance to reading pieces of words. Even though I can't read them rapidly, it is already a great benefit."[10]

Rutilio considered the literacy courses to be a serious and important work. He thought that the method being used, the same one as in the pastoral work, was quite adequate. Rutilio and Pellecer worked together in the program and became very close, so much so, in fact, that Rutilio gladly allowed Pellecer to do what others were not permitted to do, such as remove the benches from the church or use the church's didactic material.

The missionary team took much interest in courses on cooperatives and even established a consumer cooperative in Aguilares. The first course was offered by the Consumo Salvadoreño Cooperativizado (Salvadoran Consumer Cooperative), and the experience was positive, with several members of both rural and urban communities subsequently being sent to more advanced courses outside the parish; on returning, they gave talks in the villages and in the city. Despite great interest, the consumer cooperative set up in Aguilares ultimately failed because of the steep rise in fertilizer prices during the 1974 crop season, which angered and upset the cooperative members. The tendency of the managing committee to discuss the cooperative's problems in secret also aggravated the

---

9 Pellecer, "First Evaluation of Different Aspects of the Literacy Program Developed in Aguilares."

10 Pellecer, "First Evaluation of Different Aspects of the Literacy Program Developed in Aguilares."

crisis. When Bengoechea, who was in charge of the project, left the parish and the country, the cooperative came to an end.

The Course in "Political Vaccination"

This course, which was called "political vaccination" by Rutilio himself,[11] merits separate treatment because of its importance in shaping the parish and clarifying the parish's stance with regard to partisan politics. The course was given in Aguilares twice, first in mid-September 1973 and then at the end of November 1973, just as the delegates were being asked to choose the "preparers." The objective of the course was to prepare the delegates for the election of mayors and National Assembly deputies, which was to take place in early 1974. The course was called "political vaccination" because the electoral campaigns tended to cause turmoil and division in the communities. These were the first elections to be held after the fraudulent presidential election of 1972. The missionary team proposed to prepare the communities to resist the machinations of the political parties, even before the electoral campaign heated up, and the same time to give them some lessons in good citizenship.

The course was imparted by members of the missionary team in two sessions of three hours each. The first session, for rural delegates, was held on Sunday, September 16, and the second, for urban delegates, was held on Tuesday, September 18. The rural delegates spent the first hour in groups, answering a questionnaire about the nature of politics and how Catholics should relate to politics. They took part in the nine o'clock Mass that Sunday morning, where they heard Rutilio preach on two questions that were posed in the Gospel reading. After Mass, they met together again, discussed the questions from the Gospel, and then added two other questions: What is the aim of the political parties, and what should be the attitude of Catholics toward their proposals? The session finished a little after noon so that the delegates could shop in the market before returning to their communities. The principal conclusion drawn from the sessions was that baptized Christians could not prescind from politics and political action.

The delegates took back to the communities a storybook about the kingdom of God and its justice so that during the week they could reflect with the other delegates of the community about what they had learned. They were asked to take note of how people responded and also to suggest which delegates might be good preparers. In the follow-up session on Sunday, September 30, each participant came with a written report and the names of one or two delegates who might be chosen as preparers.

The storybook contrasted traditional ideas about elections—that Christians should think only of heaven—with the position defended by the delegates and the parish, namely that God's kingdom existed not in the clouds but on earth and

---

11 *Summarium testium*, witness 2, §18.

could be found only by working for justice. This position attempted to respond to those who held that the elections were a political matter and therefore foreign to religion. Such discourse encouraged resignation and a fatalistic attitude:

> You people are looking for land, but the land already has owners. Some of us have more, and others have less, but we must conform to what God has given to each person. Stop talking about agrarian reform! The Gospel doesn't teach us to do that but to be conformed![12]

Some objected to the linking of faith and politics: "We know that you carry about in the same knapsack the Gospel message and the propaganda of the political parties. I think that's dirty politics. A delegate should not be concerned with that!"[13]

The delegates were always to seek the position that was most in accord with justice. The right thing to do, according to the Gospel, was to seek the universal good. It was therefore not just a matter of voting for a particular political party. Christians had a duty to vote for the party that promised the most desirable political reforms. All citizens should vote freely for the party that they judged to be the one most likely to bring about the changes that were necessary. The adoption of this criterion allowed for the coexistence of differing political opinions in the community.

The second session of the course took place on the last Sunday of September. Very early, before the parish Mass, the delegates reviewed in groups how the people reacted in the discussions about the storybook. The groups were then asked to consider several questions: Was it proper to expound political propaganda during the celebration of the Word? Should a delegate who was campaigning for a political party conduct the celebration during the electoral period? Should delegates who assume political leadership put aside for a time their pastoral responsibilities? As in the first session, these questions were complemented by three others: What was the nature of true politics? What were the political parties and what should they be doing? Given the way electoral campaigns were usually run, did delegates do more good by participating in the campaigns or by not getting involved in them?

The basic message of the vaccination course could be expressed in five theses: (1) true politics was pursuit of the common good, and no baptized person, according to the Gospel, could prescind from being committed to that pursuit; (2) the political parties should not seek power at all costs; rather, they should tell the people the truth, fulfill their electoral promises, pursue the general good, and not oppress the rural poor; (3) while the celebration of the Word is open to all, it should not be used to make political propaganda; (4) no delegates involved in an electoral campaign should coordinate the community celebrations because their

---

12   ACSI. "Book of Stories for Delegates' Reflection."
13   "Book of Stories for Delegates' Reflection."

political commitment placed them in grave danger of falling into the same defects as the political parties; and (5) delegates did the most good for the community when they abstained from participating in the electoral campaigns. At the end of the course, the participants were given a copy of the Constitution, in which the articles that guaranteed their political rights and duties were clearly marked.

At the parish Mass on those Sundays, Rutilio explained to the people the missionary team's position on partisan politics. In his homily on Sunday, September 16, Rutilio displayed his pastoral creativity by preaching on the Good Samaritan in an unusual way:

> One day, a man was traveling along the Northern Highway from San Salvador to Aguilares, and he was assaulted by thieves who robbed him of everything, even his clothes. They beat him and left him half-dead. It happened that a soldier was passing along that same stretch of highway, but when he saw the man, he passed by on the other side because he was in a hurry to march in a parade celebrating the independence of the people.[14] A priest also came along, and when he saw the man, he passed on the other side because he was rushing to give a speech on Independence Day. A teacher also passed very close to the place, but she was hastening to take part in the independence parade, so she walked on the other side without stopping. A lawyer and a doctor also passed by at full speed in their cars, but they didn't stop because they had been invited to a party to celebrate the people's independence.
>
> [*Added in the margin*: An "evangelist" also passed by that place but didn't stop because he was on his way to a prayer meeting for Independence Day.]
>
> But a man they called a "communist" in that region happened to drive by that same spot on the Northern Highway, and when he saw the man he felt compassion. He drew near to the man, and he cured and bound his wounds as best he could. Then he lifted him into his car, drove him to a motel, and cared for him there. The next day, when the man they called a "communist" was leaving, he took out some money and gave it to the owner of the motel, telling him: "Take care of this man, and if you spend more than what's here, I will repay you when I return." Well, then, which of these persons do you think was the neighbor of the man who was assaulted by the thieves? The Salvadoran Catholic said, "The one who had compassion on him." Then Jesus told him, "Go and do likewise."[15]

The parable was quite eloquent and needed little explanation, so Rutilio concluded his homily by saying:

> All those persons were speeding along the highway on the day celebrating the people's independence, but who are these people who are supposed to

---

14 The independence of El Salvador and Central America is celebrated on September 15.
15 ACSI. Rutilio Grande, homily, Independence Day, Aguilares, September 16, 1973.

be independent? They are the people who have been left behind, the people stretched out on the road, half-dead and abandoned. Let us not talk so much about "the people," but rather let us show with real deeds that we have love for God and for the people since that is what it means to have faith in God and in his image, the human being.[16]

The course in "political vaccination," then, was designed to inoculate the parish against infection by the political parties. A member of the missionary team testified that the government, the military, and the parties were sending their agents to interrogate Rutilio as to "why his organized villagers had to be shouting 'To the rubbish bin with electioneering!' at their demonstrations":

"Ask them yourselves," Rutilio would tell them. "They're adults. They'll tell you that the word 'democracy' and even the word 'Christian' are poorly used among us. And that they're tired of being used and abused, especially when there are elections. [...] 'We've come this far,' say the villagers, 'and now we have to make changes.'"[17]

The courses and cursillos provided the people with theoretical tools for understanding the national reality and the goals of the parish, and they allowed for the development of a broad network of social relations that included the whole parish territory and even beyond. The Bible courses introduced parishioners to a new world and provided them a new language. Even more importantly, the courses gave the people instruments for analyzing and reflecting on their reality at both a personal and a social level. Bible study helped the rural poor attain greater coherence in their knowledge of the world; they came to understand that they could transform their reality, and they discovered new forms of struggle.

The two biblical figures that appealed most to the people were Moses and Jesus. Moses was an archetype of the great liberator, and the important role he played in Israelite history was stressed by those running the courses. But Jesus, the other archetype, was an even more relevant figure due to his divine condition and his proclamation of the kingdom of God. The image of the rebellious Jesus was especially effective in helping the people overcome their low-esteem, lose their fear of freedom, and reject an attitude of servile submission.[18] As one parishioner explained:

What I like most of all is the explanations they give us in the parish cursillos on Jesus Christ, because from the moment he was born he associated with us, the poor. He was there, and the people followed him, and he was against the powerful. He worried about material things, giving fish and bread to

---

16   Grande, homily, Independence Day, Aguilares, September 16, 1973.
17   *Summarium testium*, witness 2, §22.
18   Alvarado, "La organización del proletariado agrícola," 301ff., 309.

the people, curing the sick, and all that. But the more he did, the more the authorities tried to spy on what he was doing. And he called them sepulchers, hypocrites, and a brood of vipers. Aye! He was preaching equality, and that stung the powerful, and that is why they wanted to kill him. [...] Afterward we talked about all this in our workplace. [...] We had great talks about all that in the work crews. Those who haven't gone yet to the cursillos are now anxious to go so they won't be ignorant of how Jesus Christ is the good news for us poor people.[19]

These two archetypes, Moses and Jesus, each in his own way and according to the circumstances of his time, had obeyed the command of God to free his people and to build up his kingdom. Therefore, according to one delegate, "we have to do the same thing here according to our situation,"[20] persevering in the same mission with unbroken continuity.

The analytical instruments supplied by both the missions and the courses helped people understand the meaning of social sin and the presence of violence in salvation history. In a discussion held in October 1974, the participants accepted violence as a historical necessity, but they understood it as a response to another more basic form of violence, that exercised by the plantations and the local political authorities. The poor could free themselves from that oppressive violence if they remained united and kept up their resistance. The archetype of Moses had a central place in the discussion. "In the Old Testament," argued one of the panelists, "Moses led the people, and he made the very people of God into killers. I see that as something that moves me forward. God himself used violence to destroy evil." Along the same line, another panelist found a justification for violence in the book of Joshua: "In those times, they could not control ambition, and so they formed a great army. They took up weapons and went about destroying the kingdoms that governed unjustly. The Bible is the impulse that moves us toward the violence that is used against other violence."[21]

A third panelist cleverly applied the archetype of Moses to his own situation as a way of stressing the need for unity:

Moses started out like us. We see someone suffering, and we feel a murderous urge, but sometimes it is not worthwhile. For example, Moses killed a man, and what happened? He had to flee. We can't do anything all by ourselves. Perhaps by myself I accomplish nothing, and the same can happen to me as to Moses. He spent years being humbled. That's why we first have to make people conscious, get them all together and plan things out well.[22]

---

19 Alvarado, "La organización del proletariado agrícola," 302.
20 Alvarado, "La organización del proletariado agrícola," 314; and Alvarado and Cruz, "Conciencia y cambio social," 333–34.
21 ACSI. "Discussion on Violence," Aguilares, October 1974.
22 "Discussion on Violence."

The panelists observed that in the book of Maccabees God did not intervene directly: "Instead, what he did was awaken one family from among the people, and they went into combat" to defend human dignity:

> It's not that God is going to liberate the people. There is an awakening. It is the people who have to bring about justice. They [the Maccabees] were a family that formed an army. [...] The Maccabees realized that they could not overcome except by struggling. That is the path that we have to follow. Without violence nothing is gained. They did not observe the commandment, "Thou shalt not kill." The rich are the first to fall.[23]

The espousal of violence reflected in the citations was not motivated directly by the missionary team but rather arose from the people's direct contact with the Bible. The parish had handed out Bibles and instructed the people on how to read and interpret biblical passages correctly. The discoveries the people made and the conclusions they drew cannot be attributed to the missionary team; they flowed from the situation of extreme injustice in which the people were living. The rural poor found that that the history of salvation reflected well their own history. Moses, Joshua, the Maccabees, and Jesus spoke directly to the desperation they were experiencing in their own lives.

The notion of salvation history induced the people to think only in terms of forward advance: triumph was assured; failure was excluded. The rural poor accordingly felt certain that the kingdom of God, which was not to be sought in the great beyond, would arrive in one way or another. Every stage of the struggle would bring triumph to those who were working to build the kingdom of God. That kind of certainty inclined the parishioners toward a type of millenarianism or messianic mentality, but they were not the only ones. Interestingly, this same bold vision was found also among many non-religious poor people in El Salvador who were influenced by Marxism; they had the same certainty of a rapid triumph, but they understood it to be due to the inexorable laws of history. This coincidence of beliefs and attitudes between believers and non-believers revealed the gravity of the economic and political crisis in the Salvadoran countryside. The people's desperation was made evident in their passionate search for security, whether it came from a secular source or a religious one.[24]

In Aguilares, however, millenarianism as such did not prosper, partly because of the influence of the missionary team, which insisted on distinguishing the kingdom of God from any political project. The kingdom transcended all political projects, even the progressive and leftist ones.[25] The failure of millenarianism was also partly due to the influence of the principles of sociological analysis that

---

23 "Discussion on Violence."
24 Alvarado, "La organización del proletariado agrícola," 317, 318.
25 Alvarado, "La organización del proletariado agrícola," 297ff., 316.

had been promoted by Bengoechea and his collaborators. Although the people's understanding of sociological method was not theoretically rigorous, it provided them enough elements to restrain any millenarian tendencies. Even so, there were outbreaks of latent millenarianism. Some villagers, unable to move beyond the archetypal vision, discounted the possibility of reversal. If Moses had liberated the Israelites, if Jesus had done the same, and if Rome had fallen soon after that, then they too could accomplish something similar: before long, both the government and the capitalist system would collapse, just as Pharaoh and Rome had done.[26]

Though it was not the intention of the missionary team, the parish missions and courses became a privileged vehicle for liberating all the latent discontent in the complex, explosive zone of Aguilares. Neither the missionary team nor the outside collaborators had a clear idea of how much the consciousness of the rural poor been transformed. Rutilio was perhaps the most clear-sighted in this regard. Certainly, by the end of 1974 he was quite worried about what he called the "holy impatience" of the people. His suspicions and misgivings had a sound basis, but he was not able to identify the real nature of the challenge.

The Liturgical Celebrations

The second stage of the parish renewal culminated with two important liturgical celebrations that clearly manifested the new ecclesial reality. The first celebration was the Festival of Maize, celebrated on August 18, 1974; it was a novelty introduced into the parish's calendar of feasts. There had already been a Festival of Maize the year before, in August 1973, but the one in 1974 was the first to take place within the new context of parish mobilization.

The Festival of Maize was a community celebration of the crop that most symbolized the reality of the rural poor. Emphasis was placed on community, conviviality, and creativity. In 1974, the festival was organized by the rural communities, whereas the previous year it had been organized by the urban ones. As the communities prepared for the event, the missionary team instructed them about the festival's aims: promoting unity, collaboration, and sharing in the labor and the joy of harvesting the maize. Commissions were organized for all the tasks to be done: shucking the ears, taking the grain to the mill, building the ovens, hauling the firewood, cooking the *atol*,[27] selling the *atol*, preparing and cleaning the calabash cups, selling and collecting tickets, washing the pots and pans, feting the patronesses of the communities, taking care of the entrances, guarding the stage, preserving public order, and so on. Since the expenses of the festival were financed by the sale of *atol*, all the women and men of the communities were able to contribute to the success of the event.[28]

---

26 Alvarado, "La organización del proletariado agrícola," 317.
27 A beverage made from corn flour.
28 ACSI. "Festival of Maize: First Circular," July 14, 1974.

The festival began with a very participatory Eucharist enlivened with hymns and songs. During the offertory, each community presented its finest ears of corn, which were later presented in a competition for the "best ear" of the parish. There were also competitions for the best decoration made from a maize plant and for the best original song in praise of the labor of cultivating and harvesting maize. Those attending the festival enjoyed the inexpensive beverage *atol*, made with fresh ears of maize contributed by the communities. In this way, the parish highlighted the value of the labor of both men and women and joyfully celebrated God's gift of maize, which gave sustenance and hope to the rural poor.

As in every popular celebration, the communities elected patronesses for the festival, but the criteria and the procedures were different in this instance from those normally used. In other festivals, the patronesses were chosen by voting, but often the votes were bought and sold, so that the winner tended to be the candidate with the most economic sway. Moreover, the candidates in other festivals spent a great deal of money on clothing and adornments. The election and the coronation would take place during the festival, and the elegance of the event depended on the prosperity of the village or town. In contrast, the patronesses in the Festival of Maize were chosen, not on the basis of physical beauty or economic influence, but for their readiness to serve and their sense of responsibility for the community:

> That is why they are *Queens*, because they are servants, and they are humble! They are not ashamed to hoist a load of firewood onto their heads and to serve their companion, who also works hard. They are not reluctant or ashamed to get up early in the morning, light their lamp like the woman in the Bible, and make tortillas, so that the sound of the grinding is heard in the village.[29]

The patronesses consequently coordinated the work of the women of their communities during the festival, and they introduced to the public all the members of their communities taking part in the competitions. Each community chose a man and a woman to act as judges of the competitions. Since the missionary team was anxious to avoid excessive rivalry in the competitions, it urged that winners be chosen by popular acclamation. Participation in the competitions was marked by creativity, cooperation, and a general air of festivity. The festival as a whole gave the communities an opportunity to express their vitality and their genius.

Another important event in the parish took place on November 16, 1974, when Archbishop Chávez was celebrating fifty years of priesthood and thirty-six years of episcopacy. The clergy of the archdiocese honored Chávez's years of pastoral ministry publicly and gave him a handsome parchment. President Molina

---

29   ACSI. Rutilio Grande, homily, Aguilares, August 18, 1976.

congratulated him by means of a telegram, and the legislative assembly gave him another parchment of recognition. Countless other persons and groups joined in to congratulate the archbishop and show him their gratitude. A few weeks later, on December 29, Chávez traveled to Aguilares to receive homage from the parish.

Rutilio arranged the celebration of the archbishop's anniversary in such a way as to highlight the role of the delegates of the Word. In fact, he presented the delegates' movement to the archbishop as the best homage the parish could render him. The church was packed for the Eucharist, at the end of which the delegates of forty-six rural and urban communities asked the archbishop to confirm them in their mission. With great emotion, Archbishop Chávez conferred on them the mission of preaching the Gospel and being witnesses of the faith.

In his homily, Rutilio fused his own personal gratitude to the archbishop with the gratitude felt by the whole parish. He united his priestly vocation with that of the archbishop, a relationship that was by no means arbitrary since he had discovered his vocation thanks to his providential encounter with the young archbishop many years before. Two weeks earlier, in a personal letter, Rutilio had thanked the archbishop and had affectionately offered him his priesthood and his consecrated life, two things "that I love as profoundly as I love the *Holy Church*."[30] Although they moved in different orbits, both men had contributed significantly to the renewal of pastoral ministry in the archdiocese, creating new life for the people and providing them new services.

In his homily on December 29, Rutilio portrayed the delegates as the key to the parish's success, affirming that "they surpass me, and I say this with sincere humility, dear brother priests and dear laypeople." The delegates had demonstrated great love for Christ and had dedicated themselves magnificently to forming new communities; they displayed great courage in their apostolic tasks, hiking long distances, spending sleepless nights, and eating poorly—"and all this because of the Gospel!"[31] Their tremendous apostolic zeal, and that of all the people, was a great stimulus to Rutilio's own priesthood, he admitted. The celebration therefore quite fittingly took the form of the Eucharist because "even as they struggle to sow the Gospel, they yearn, along with us, for a more humane and more just world, one in which all Salvadorans can share what we have, seated at the common table of creation as we sit around this Eucharistic table."[32]

Statistically, the two previous years of parish activity represented some two hundred matrimonies, five hundred first Communions, and 1,157 baptisms, fruits of the team of fifty catechists. Compared with the statistics of earlier years, when there were more than four thousand annual baptisms, these results were

---

30 ACSI. Rutilio Grande to Archbishop Luis Chávez. Aguilares, December 17, 1974.
31 ACSI. Rutilio Grande, "Homage to Archbishop Luis Chávez y González on His Fifty Years of Priesthood," Aguilares, December 29, 1974.
32 Grande, "Homage to Archbishop Luis Chávez y González."

very modest. Rutilio explained to Archbishop Chávez that the notable decrease in the administration of the sacraments was due to the greater emphasis on basic Christian formation, in accord with the archdiocesan guidelines. The parish's priority was thorough evangelization of all adults, and this was essential if the sacraments were not to be reduced to meaningless rites divorced from real life.

While reviewing these results, Rutilio expressed his gratitude for the presence and collaboration of the Jesuit scholastics from the start of the experience. He praised their commitment, especially their decision to take up residence in Aguilares in order to be closer to the people. In this way, he explained, their study of philosophy and theology were rooted in the reality of the people. Rutilio made reference to the tensions in the missionary team, but he pitched it as something positive, attributing it to youthful idealism. The enthusiasm of younger team members "has been liberating to those of us who are older from the ever-present temptation to be conformist and stuck in our ways, a temptation into which we often fall." Nor did Rutilio fail to mention Bengoechea as one of the initiators of the experience, though at that moment he was not in El Salvador. Finally, he thanked the archbishop for sending Octavio Cruz, a diocesan priest, to be part of the missionary team.[33]

Rutilio granted that the work had not been easy since many people did not want to see or hear. Despite the resistance, the results of the parish's efforts were there to see: "Front and center [are] the *Delegates of the Word*, who together with us are responsible for this shared undertaking; they are dedicated to building a church rejuvenated by the *Gospel* and to laboring for the 'bold and urgent' changes the world needs."[34] Rutilio ended his homily by asking the archbishop to confirm them all in their mission, "which deserves our lives and even our blood."

This Christian commitment was then expressed through liturgy. A delegate from the rural communities spoke of his ecclesial service, and one from the city explained his dedication to forming a new people and a new community. The liturgy stressed the fact that the delegates had been chosen by their respective communities and had been approved by the missionary team. The delegates were subsequently presented to the archbishop, and the duties of each one were briefly described. They then made a profession of faith and expressed their desire to serve the community in the task that had been assigned to them. Finally, the different lay ministers—delegates, preparers, coordinators, secretaries, community organizers, itinerant teams—passed in turn before the archbishop, who prayed over each group and asked the Lord to confirm them all in their faith and their commitment.

---

33 Grande, "Homage to Archbishop Luis Chávez y González."
34 Grande, "Homage to Archbishop Luis Chávez y González."

Conflict with the Military Authority

The parish suffered a sharp division because of its commitment to justice and its embrace of the Gospel. The opposition between parish and plantation continued, though there was no other incident as serious as the strike in La Cabaña. After the strike, the governing military regime restructured the local division of the Nationalist Democratic Organization (Organización Democrática Nacionalista [ORDEN]), a Cold War-type paramilitary institution that was founded in 1961. The official mission of ORDEN was the spreading of democratic and nationalist ideas in order to prevent the population from being deceived by communist propaganda. Democracy was understood to mean a process of ongoing orderly change that offered the whole population an opportunity for improvement, and nationalism was taken to mean love of country and the development of national identity.[35]

In practice, ORDEN was an anti-communist organization created to control the population. Its principal activities, therefore, were surveillance of the population by means of an elaborate network of spies that reached even the most remote villages and used forceful repression when psychological intimidation did not have the desired effect. To a certain extent, ORDEN replaced the village patrols, which had shown themselves to be untrustworthy. ORDEN was therefore the body that assumed the obligation to contain the popular mobilization being promoted by the parish of Aguilares.

ORDEN also sponsored small local development projects—wells, schools, electrification, sports fields, and so on—as a way of concealing its true aims. It diffused the propaganda of the government and the party in power, and it threatened the rural poor during electoral campaigns so that they would vote for the "right" candidates. A significant portion of the rural population aligned itself with ORDEN for a variety of reasons: the excitement and patriotic sentiment in being associated with it; the backing it had from the army and the presidency; the power and immunity that went with have an ORDEN identity card; the right militants had to bear firearms, an important concession in a macho culture; and the easy access militants had to land, supplies, steady employment, and special health and education benefits.

The commander in Aguilares began spreading rumors among the local commissioners in August 1973, and such rumors, in the sociopolitical culture of that time, were implicit threats. The commander targeted especially the three foreigners on the missionary team—Carranza, Fernández, and Bengoechea—depicting them as communist agitators. In early October, Rutilio and the team met with the commander to try to clarify the matter, but the defamation continued.

---

35 Cabarrús, *Génesis de una revolución*, 168ff.

On Sunday, January 5, 1974, Rutilio denounced the malicious rumors from the pulpit of the parish church, and he named the commander as the person responsible. Aware of the gravity of his denunciation, Rutilio stated at the beginning of his homily that he was not acting rashly but after having reflected, prayed, and consulted with prudent advisors. As he did on other similar occasions, he said that he had his homily in written form so that his words would not later be misconstrued.

Rutilio explained to the congregation that he had tried to correct the rumors in private conversations, following the recommendation of Matthew 18:15, which he read. He spoke of his visit to the commander, whom he called his "brother baptized in the Catholic Church," for the purpose of reporting the murmurings and clarifying the confusion. But three months had passed, and the situation had not improved; in fact, it had gotten worse. Rutilio therefore continued in the solemn tone he used on important occasions:

> Since the matter is serious and involves the good reputation of the fathers here present, and since the common good of the people of our parish requires it, I feel myself obliged as pastor to make plain to our church here assembled all that has happened, just as our Lord teaches us on such occasions. I do so without wishing to offend anyone but seeking only the general good of our people, since it is a matter of justice for persons such as these priests, who have public responsibilities before the entire community. They are not private persons; they hold public positions. My duty therefore is to dispel all doubt regarding accusations in this matter.[36]

In a clear allusion to the commander, Rutilio said that there were persons who called themselves Catholic and wore sheep's wool, "but in their hearts they are rapacious wolves, to judge by what they say and do."

Rutilio then referred to the substance of the rumors attributed to the commander, namely that the people should not listen to the "good fathers" because they were communists and nobody knew where they came from. Moreover, the priests were now agitating the people but "later, without warning, they would leave them in a bind and gaily march off to some other place." Such accusations, Rutilio asserted, were extremely serious because they came from someone who held a public post of great importance: "Certainly these are grave matters, and I would never have spoken in public about such things if there were some other more Christian and amicable way to deal with them." The commander's accusations, he asserted, were false and defamatory and could be attributed only to ignorance or malice. Rutilio declared that if the rumors did not cease, "I will be seriously obliged to have recourse to the supreme authorities or to the tribunals established by justice."[37]

---

36   ACSI. Rutilio Grande, "Admonition in the Church," Aguilares, January 5, 1974.
37   Grande, "Admonition in the Church."

The commander could not claim ignorance to justify his actions because the three priests named in the rumors were well known by the bishops and the archdiocesan clergy. Not only had the archbishop entrusted the parish to them but he remained in close communion with them. In fact, he would be presiding at the Eucharist on January 14, the feast of the Lord of Mercies, patron of the parish, just as he had done the year before. As a way of rebutting one rumor spread by the commander, Rutilio promised: "We will be here for the time necessary, without any limit. Only death will be able to separate us from our parish community."[38]

Rutilio then refuted the commander's assertions about the missionary team. The three priests named in the rumors had a university education, and they were neither reckless nor irresponsible; they were certainly not like "those politicians who roam about looking for lucre." Carranza and Bengoechea had studied at the Gregorian University in Rome, "alongside the pope." Fernández had "done advanced studies in the social sciences at a secular university, the University of Deusto in Bilbao." Given their academic training, the three Jesuits could be teachers in any one of the schools or universities that the Society of Jesus had in Central America. Despite that,

> they wanted to come here, feeling especially called to offer service, along with me, in this parish community; they offered themselves without conditions to the archbishop. They have left their families and their land to give themselves completely to God in the faithful of this church, without any desire to earn money or seek recompense in this life. They have spent long years in our American lands and in our country.[39]

The most ridiculous rumor, Rutilio said, was the claim that he himself was unknown in the parish:

> Regarding poor me, I will only say that I have been widely known in this region since my childhood. Many of you know my relatives with whatever defects and virtues they possess. It is true that I left this region as a child and spent many years abroad for the sake of studies, but despite that, I am one of you, the son of our humble and beloved land.[40]

Although the commander had spoken some deferential words in regard to him, Rutilio said that he totally rejected them because their aim was to denigrate the other three members of the missionary team, "whom I esteem and love in the Lord, as do all the people in the community who truly know them." By way of clarification, Rutilio added that priests, as universal figures, were never

---

38   Grande, "Admonition in the Church."
39   Grande, "Admonition in the Church."
40   Grande, "Admonition in the Church."

"foreigners" in the church: "If we do not admit this, then we do not belong to the Church of Jesus Christ."[41]

Speaking properly as a Salvadoran citizen, a stance in which he delighted, Rutilio denounced the commander's partisan proselytism as a violation of the Constitution:

> The commander should know that both he as a serviceman and we as ministers of the church[42] cannot engage in partisan politics. [...] Despite this, the commander, taking advantage of his post, is doing something strictly prohibited by article 114 of the Political Constitution: in one way or another, he is threatening and pressuring people in different places to make them join or become affiliated with a particular political party. I believe that this is a serious crime; if any of the faithful were to hear of me doing such a thing, they would have the right to denounce me.[43]

Rutilio recommended to the commander that, instead of spreading false rumors, he carry out his duty to protect the population with determination and dedication:

> Would that he were more solicitous and diligent in freeing our beloved city of idlers and drunks and crooks! Would that he mercilessly disarmed all the murderers who wander about! Would that he defended our humble people when they are assaulted with impunity in the haciendas by unscrupulous foremen and petty tyrants![44]

Rutilio did not want his words to be interpreted as derogatory of soldiers generally: "I consider them to be sons of our People. The great majority of them were born among the great masses of our humble people." Priests and soldiers shared the same weighty obligations: "We priests and soldiers must never neglect to defend those who have no voice, those who have too little power and influence to stand on their own, those who need our help and our voice whenever justice has been wounded."[45] Rutilio did not hesitate to situate himself within the nationalist tradition:

> As a priest who attends to humble persons who have no one to speak for them or defend them, I raise my voice in protest, as Father Simeón Cañas[46]

---

41 Grande, "Admonition in the Church."
42 Article 25 of the Salvadoran Constitution prohibits the clergy from engaging in political proselytizing.
43 Grande, "Admonition in the Church."
44 Grande, "Admonition in the Church."
45 Grande, "Admonition in the Church."
46 Priest, academic, and a founding father of the Salvadoran nation in the early nineteenth century. He demanded and obtained the liberation of slaves of African descent in Central America.

did when defending the humblest folk and the perennial slaves, and as Father Delgado and the Aguilar brothers[47] did when they fought for the homeland and for all its inhabitants. I have seen their portraits hanging on the walls of many commanders' officers![48]

Rutilio claimed that he was doing neither more nor less than the founders of the Salvadoran nation, all of them priests, had done in their time. Indeed, politics was "a noble activity that should be pursued not because of financial interests or personal gain but with the sole interest of serving the homeland." And he added: "We would not be fighting our political battles so savagely if there were less ambition and bad will among us, and if all of us were seeking only to serve the common good of the community."

Rutilio apparently was not satisfied with making a public statement because he appealed to President Molina, as he said he would, saying that he wanted to dispel doubts about the nature of his priestly ministry. In a letter dated January 9, 1974, he explained what had happened:

> I tell you with all loyalty that both I personally and my fellow Jesuit priests proclaim throughout this whole wide region Gospel values that coincide completely with the essential values of every human being and with the values enunciated in our Primary Law, the Political Constitution. I sincerely hope that this undertaking of ours does not alarm all your subordinates hereabouts or your fellow party members, if they truly long for a better Homeland.[49]

Rutilio was thus convinced that the coincidence of Gospel values with constitutional ones was sufficient reason for there to be no suspicions about his parish ministry. He believed that if the soldiers, who were from humble stock, could change their mentality, they would make a decisive contribution to the transformation of the Salvadoran people, given the enormous power they had. Otherwise, they would be judged "very severely" by history, as was already the case. Rutilio then suggested to the president that he obtain trustworthy information about the activities of the members of the official party since there was much discontent in the parish, especially among those who were "outstanding" for their honesty and social awareness. It would therefore be wise for the party to propose honest candidates for the municipal council. Rutilio closed his letter with a reference to the commander in Aguilares. He told the president about the malicious rumors, the attempt at dialogue, and the public denunciation he was obliged to make in the interest of justice and the common good.

The president acknowledged receipt of the letter on January 23, but after the elections Rutilio returned to the charge since the commander was not

---

47   Also priests and founders of the Salvadoran nation.
48   Grande, "Admonition in the Church."
49   ACSI. Rutilio Grande to Arturo Armando Molina, Aguilares, January 9, 1974.

removed from his post. Rutilio was received by the president's private secretary concerning an "urgent matter"[50] on March 27, and the conversation dealt with the main arguments of the letter sent to the president. Rutilio introduced himself as the pastor of Aguilares and explained that he and his missionary team were working for the common good of the community, apart from any type of political partisanship. He then informed the secretary about the situation in the zone, mentioning first the irregularities committed by the official party during the recent municipal and legislative elections, irregularities that had caused division in the party's own ranks. On election day, the outgoing mayor had invaded the electoral precinct with thugs and other dubious characters; after they drove away one of the men guarding the voting urns, one urn was moved to a private residence. The result was that the new mayor was imposed by threat of violence. Moreover, several witnesses informed that the urns from El Paisnal had been stolen by unknown persons when they were on their way to San Salvador.[51]

The last point on Rutilio's agenda was the commander, who he claimed had indoctrinated the military patrols and set them against the parish. It is almost certain that Rutilio asked for the commander's dismissal, claiming that since the situation was contrary to the state of law, it was prejudicial not only for the people and the parish but for the government as well. Asserting that a government concerned for its democratic legitimacy should not allow that type of abuse, Rutilio asked simply that the Constitution be respected. The private secretary was evidently impressed by his talk with Rutilio and promised to call him after speaking with the president. Although the call never came, it is likely that this initiative by Rutilio succeeded in halting further repression against the parish community.

In July 1974, Rutilio once again felt the need to explain the nature of his work, this time to the Ministry of the Interior. After introducing himself, Rutilio linked the missionary team to the Jesuits of the UCA and the Colegio Externado. The positions of these institutions were well known to the minister since he had attended a discussion on national problems that President Molina had held with some of the Jesuits. Rutilio told the minister that the best support the Jesuits of Aguilares could offer the government was their service to the people. In the latter part of the interview, he called the minister's attention to the many vices present in Aguilares—prostitution, alcoholism, and firearms—whose eradication was the minister's responsibility.[52]

Prostitution had reached an elevated level in Aguilares due to the tolerance of the local authorities, specifically the last mayor, an alcoholic who had held

---

50   ACSI. Rutilio Grande, telegram, Aguilares, March 15, 1974.
51   ACSI. Rutilio Grande, "Memorandum: Office of the Private Secretary of the Presidency of the Republic," March 27, 1974.
52   ACSI. Rutilio Grande, "Memorandum of the Conversation with the Minister of the Interior," Aguilares, July 31, 1974.

the post for two consecutive periods. Said mayor had authorized the opening of numerous dance halls where prostitutes found employment. Moreover, the constant shootings in the city streets were leaving many wounded and dead. About two and half months previously, a group of citizens had asked the mayor to put an end to these evils, but there had been no response. Subsequently, on July 17, a protest demonstration was organized by members of the parish communities, the neighborhood councils, and the two public schools of the city. Admitting that "the danger existed of opportunistic pols trying to sow division and discontent," Rutilio argued that such protests were the only way to put pressure on the mayor. At the same time, the wide support for the protests made it clear that in Aguilares it was not only the parish that desired social change.

Once Again, "Holy Impatience"

The reorganization of the parish at the end of the second phase did not put an end to the tension between those preferring a more biblical and religious approach and those preferring one that was more sociological and political. All the parishioners were involved in the biblical and religious formation, but the sociological and political formation was reserved for those more advanced. Carranza and Fernández, who identified more with the first tendency, were responsible for the courses given to the delegates. Bengoechea and the Jesuit scholastics, on the other hand, identified more with the second tendency, and they were responsible for the courses given to the preparers, who were the most dynamic element of the parish. Apparently, Rutilio was not involved in giving the courses, but he always conversed with the participants. He also kept in close contact with the communities, the delegates, the preparers, and the catechists. One of his main responsibilities was defending the missionary team and its work against the threats from outside.

Rutilio's leadership was unquestionable and had been strengthened by his public interventions, but he was not the only leader. Each member of the team exercised leadership in the sector in which he worked. Understandably, the communities began to relate with one member of the team more than with others. As the relations among team members became more horizontal, Rutilio began to feel that he was no longer "the pastor" of Aguilares. This change in the team's internal relations produced tensions that culminated in the rupture between Rutilio and Bengoechea, who ended up leaving the parish definitively, as had been recommended by the national council of Jesuits.

For several months, the situation in Aguilares was discussed by the council. Rutilio kept them informed of the ongoing conflicts and constantly asked them for guidance. On October 9, 1974, he wrote to Bishop Proaño to share with him his difficulties and his worries. In his response, the bishop encouraged him to press forward, reminding him that the experience in Aguilares represented a truly novel type of pastoral ministry in Latin America.[53]

Bengoechea's departure brought a more balanced leadership back to the team and terminated the relations with Boulang's group. Bengoechea's space was filled by Cruz, who Rutilio thought would make a fine pastor after the team concluded its mission. Still, Rutilio was not at peace. He was extremely disturbed by doubts since he had ultimate responsibility for the parish and feared that he might betray the trust the archbishop had placed in him. Apprehensive that things were moving too fast, he again complained of excessive activism and short-term responses—what he liked to call "holy impatience"—because they posed a grave danger to the whole parish project. Accelerating the process for the sake of success in the short run could lead to a type of elitism; it could run the risk of developing a few select leaders while neglecting the communities as a whole. Such a way of proceeding would not be walking with the people, as they claimed to be doing, but training an elite group to march in step with the missionary team. Excessive speed and pressure would not permit the assimilation and consolidation of true Christian values.

The distancing of the missionary team from the communities accentuated this danger. Indeed, the work of the preparers had resulted in some weakening of the team's relations with the communities. Moreover, having the delegates attend courses in Aguilares, instead of having the formation team go out to the zones, had diminished the team's contact with the communities. To make matters worse, one group of preparers was tending to separate itself from the parish. Some of the best leaders among the preparers attached themselves to a Jesuit scholastic, and when they found followers in the communities, they put themselves on the same level as the missionary team.

At the end of 1974, the missionary team was reorganized again. Carranza became coordinator of the rural communities, and Fernández of the urban communities. Cruz collaborated with both of them while Rutilio was responsible for general coordination of the whole parish structure.

The Precarious Finances of the Parish

The pastoral approach adopted by the missionary team had negative repercussions on the parish economy. The elimination of stipends for the sacraments reduced parish income considerably. Despite the fact that the missionary team requested no stipends, except in the case of matrimonies, the demand for the sacraments decreased notably, partly because more preparation was required and partly because celebration of the Word became an important form of worship. Most noticeable was the decrease in the number of baptisms due to the stricter

---

53   ACSI. Leónidas Proaño to Rutilio Grande, Riobamba, October 19, 1974.

parish norms. The team also eliminated two other important sources of income, the sung Masses and the prayers for the dead after Mass.

The new policies failed to achieve their objective since in the people's mind the sacraments were closely associated with making an economic contribution; it was this contribution that in a way validated the sacraments since it represented a sacrifice. Eventually, the team proposed a new set of stipends: an ordinary Mass (two dollars); a novena of Masses for a deceased person (twenty dollars); a matrimony of village residents (four dollars); a matrimony of urban residents (six dollars); a matrimony of persons of higher income (ten dollars); a funeral Mass (four dollars); and a Mass with tolling of bells if the deceased died as a practicing Catholic and was free of public scandal (one dollar). Even so, the income received from the stipends did not cover the ordinary expenses of the parish.

Other sources of income included Masses for a special intention and the Sunday collection, which the faithful placed before the altar during the offertory. In Aguilares, there were two Masses on Sunday, at five and at nine o'clock in the morning, and in El Paisnal there was one Mass at seven in the evening. On weekdays, the only Mass was at 6:30 in the evening in Aguilares. According to the account books of the parish, the income from these two sources was modest, not exceeding two hundred dollars a month.

The communities tried to help with parish expenses, but their contribution was small. Except for one community that gave three dollars a month, the contribution of the others was less than one dollar a month. Despite the shortfall, the team was unanimous in not having recourse to the rich in the parish lest their donations endanger evangelical freedom. Fixed fees were also considered inappropriate lest they project the image of a church preoccupied with money. During 1974, the communities ran two fundraising campaigns, but these had modest results. Some communities contributed their surplus maize.

In mid-1973, the parish appealed to Adveniat,[54] requesting $5,000 for the purchase of several items: twenty mattresses for cursillos; sound and video equipment; five hundred hymn books, Bibles, and New Testaments; and a vehicle.[55] The project was approved, and the funds were dispensed partly in 1974 and again in 1975. The parish, for its part, contributed $530. At the end of 1975, the missionary team explored the possibility of presenting another project to Adveniat for 1976–78.[56] Apparently, they also appealed to Misereor.[57] Besides this assistance, the Archdiocesan Pastoral Commission financed half the cost of the mission collaborators who left their ordinary work to help with the task of evangelization.[58]

---

54 The German bishops' agency to finance pastoral programs in Latin America.
55 Rutilio was driving a VW Safari when they killed him.
56 ACSI. "Proyecto *Adveniat*," Aguilares, November 30, 1974.
57 The German bishops' overseas aid and development agency.
58 ACSI. Jesús Bengoechea to Ricardo Urioste, coordinator of the Archdiocesan Pastoral Ministry Commission, Aguilares, April 29, 1973.

The missionary team could also rely on the Society of Jesus for some economic help, but they did not use it except in cases of extreme necessity such as a serious illness or a trip abroad. The reason for this reluctance was that they wanted Aguilares to be a true experience of poverty: "We are involved in an experience that we believe has value for the order itself. The experience would not be valid, or we would render it vain if we depended on the economic means produced by our traditional ministries, which we seek to move beyond."[59]

---

59 "Proyecto *Adveniat*."

8. Parish Life

During the four years and six months that Rutilio was pastor of Aguilares, he worked with the missionary team to develop a highly creative and dynamic pastoral experience, one inspired by Vatican II, Medellín, and *Evangelii nuntiandi*. "In four years," he commented, "we have done what has taken ten years in other places." The experience influenced pastoral practice in other parishes of the vicariate of Quezaltepeque and throughout the archdiocese.

Despite the evident achievements of the missions and the courses, the missionary team still faced enormous challenges. At the beginning of 1976, a majority of the parish's twenty to twenty-five thousand inhabitants had still not been evangelized. The Gospel had taken on real meaning only for about two thousand parishioners. The team therefore felt in no way triumphalist. Much remained to be done. This chapter will tell of what parish life was like after the phase of the courses.

The Challenge of Parish Statistics

Without doubt, almost all the inhabitants in the parish territory were baptized, but Rutilio often called them the "sprinkled" because they were satisfied with just the water of baptism. They wanted their children baptized, and they occasionally attended Mass, but they were not interested in serious Christian commitment.

The missionary team distinguished three sectors in the population. The first lived clearly on the margins of the church. The second were separated from the church by "bad living," such as cohabiting couples who were not married sacramentally. And the third sector, encompassing five to seven thousand persons, was immersed in popular religiosity and therefore participated in processions, patronal feasts, Holy Week celebrations, funeral rites (wakes, prayers, burials), novenas, and Sunday Masses. Of this group some two to four thousand were affiliated with a religious association and participated in its devotions. Their religiosity was characterized by individualism and diligent sacramental practice.[1] Instead of trying to suppress the practices of popular religiosity, the missionary team attempted to evangelize them. It did so by introducing Gospel teachings and values into the Sunday Masses, the choir, the catechesis for sacraments, and the novenas to the Lord of Mercies and to Saint Joseph.

The truly evangelized faithful were a small number in comparison with the total population of the parish. In early 1976, the missionary team calculated that

---

[1] ACSI. "Some Data Gathered from the Rural Communities (Pastoral Visit)," Aguilares, January 4, 1976.

about 1,500 persons had been evangelized, but of these about a thousand still observed the patterns of popular religiosity. No more than three hundred persons could be considered strongly committed Christians, and only half of those participated fully in parish life. The other half had become politicized and so had distanced themselves from the parish.[2]

In January 1976, the roster of the missionary team listed fifty-eight preparers, 326 delegates, thirty-seven imparters of baptismal talks, thirty-six catechists of children, and seventeen missionaries sent out from the parish; the preparers were all male, but the other ministers were both male and female. There were also ninety-six young people organized into seven groups, with eighteen youth leaders. In the rural zone, there were twenty-six communities, but unfortunately no figure is given for urban communities. Twenty-two of the rural communities brought together regularly between 670 and 850 adults for celebration of the Word; they all gave evidence of intense community activity. Most of the communities had at least five meetings of various types a week, and all had at least three. These meetings, led by the delegates, included activities such as celebration of the Word, discussion of common problems, and exhortation to Christian commitment. Among all the communities were to be found twelve musical groups with forty-three instruments.

The consolidation of the communities was not an easy task. Some grew while others entered into crisis and still others saw many departures. An inventory of the state of the communities in late 1975/early 1976 made evident the effects of the activity of FECCAS. Each community had developed its own style of organization, each had a particular rhythm, and each dealt with problems in its own way. There were six communities that had developed a creative internal dynamism that helped them grow: El Trapiche, Tres Ceibas, El Líbano, Araditas, Natividad, and Las Huertas. The delegates of El Trapiche had expanded the community by promoting popular practices such as nativity plays or praying the rosary in people's homes, along with an explanation of a Gospel. They also organized theatrical dramatizations of Gospel passages and, in a second stage, of social problems. The community of Tres Ceibas grew from twenty to forty adults, it had a very active youth group, and it had more meetings than days in the week. Some twenty-seven adults participated in a literacy course, twenty-five children attended catechism classes, and thirty-seven adults had taken part in courses run by the parish. This community prepared the celebration of the Word along with the communities of El Líbano and Buena Vista. Despite all this activity, the community was divided over the meaning of Christian commitment: a year later, toward the end of 1976, sixteen delegates joined ORDEN.[3]

The delegates of El Líbano visited homes regularly and organized the community to repair an access road. The community of Araditas had sixteen new

---

2 "Some Data Gathered from the Rural Communities (Pastoral Visit)."
3 "Some Data Gathered from the Rural Communities (Pastoral Visit)."

delegates as the result of a literacy course, but some of the other delegates, who had been considered solid, ceased to function. The community organized dances and raffles to collect funds for the community hall. The community of Natividad, with thirty adults, was very impulsive, to the point of trying to do away completely with popular religiosity. The community of Las Huertas saw some growth thanks to the theatrical presentations.[4]

Other communities—Buena Vista, El Matasano, and Potrero Grande—were never able to stabilize, nor did they reach higher levels of training and commitment, despite repeated efforts. Buena Vista had only twelve delegates; thirty-six others had quit almost immediately after the mission because they disagreed with the parish's stance. A small group monopolized the community's activities; the village's internal divisions were manifested in the people's erratic participation and the delegates' desertion; meanwhile, the peasant organization FECCAS gained strength among the villagers. The community of El Matasano also showed signs of instability. Participation in activities fluctuated, with people from other communities sometimes attending. The instability was in large measure due to the differences of opinion among the delegates with regard to FECCAS; divisions and debate arose about which had priority, parish activities or politics. An additional difficulty was the chronic indebtedness of the villagers with the nearby haciendas.

The community of Potrero Grande also lost delegates toward the end of 1976. Twelve quit because of discord over FECCAS or reluctance to give up their vices; seven of these were considered very good delegates by the missionary team, but they could not be persuaded to return. Another problem was that women were prevented from attending meetings by their husbands, who objected to their returning late to their homes. Some of the remaining delegates held posts in FECCAS as part of their Christian commitment, but this led to their not assuming responsibilities in the community for lack of time. These delegates also complained about the infrequency of the priests' visits; they wanted the priests to come more often since the only thing that convoked the great majority of the villagers was the Mass. The delegates took advantage of the Mass to recruit new members both for the community and for FECCAS.[5]

Five communities— El Tule, Las Delicias, Huitiupa, El Tablón, and Colima—experienced serious desertions. In El Tule, many people were discouraged and intimidated by rumors, unemployment, fear, and a certain disillusionment with the celebration of the Word; only twenty adults remained firm. The missionary team tried to identify the source of the rumors and the reason for the fear; meanwhile, they used the Eucharistic celebrations to scare away phantasms and insist on more solid evangelization. Because of divisions,

---

[4] "Some Data Gathered from the Rural Communities (Pastoral Visit)."
[5] "Some Data Gathered from the Rural Communities (Pastoral Visit)."

disagreements, and general apathy, the group of delegates in Las Delicias had still not consolidated by October 1975; they held few meetings, and those they held were poorly conducted. The community was very informal; it consisted of between fifteen and twenty adults and ten delegates, most of whom were women. In Huitiupa, which had only two delegates, the community talked about the need for a new mission or the possibility of joining with another community. The community of El Tablón lost half its delegates, and only four of the remaining nine were reliable. The delegates who quit said that they felt personally impugned by all the talk of injustice since they owned small parcels of land.[6]

The community of Colima was formed not at the time of the mission but later on, by delegates from El Tule and Potrero Grande. By October 1975, only twenty adults were attending services there, under the direction of three delegates; coordination was poor, and commitment was deficient. The delegates who ceased functioning said they did so because of fear of public opinion and disagreement with the parish's stance. Some villagers attended the meetings in El Tule, but this community, as indicated earlier, was also in crisis. Apparently, the founders of the El Tule community had decided to dissolve it during the first Holy Week after the mission. Most of the villagers were quite disturbed because the founding delegates were neglecting the traditional religious practices and spoke too much about the Exodus. The situation was complicated by the marital problems of two delegates. The missionary team spoke at length with the villagers and encouraged those who wanted to continue to hold house meetings, rotating from home to home.[7]

When asked about their faith experience, the rural communities responded with a unanimity that surprised the missionary team. Everyone agreed that the Gospel had changed their lives radically, and as proof they cited their reform of life and customs, their move away from sacred images, the formation of strong communities, their greater spirit of equality, their willingness to help one another, their refusal to be conformist, and their desire to organize to fight for their rights. One anonymous person in El Trapiche, probably a literacy student, expressed himself this way:

> The Gospel has helped us transform our lives into a more concrete commitment. By means of study, we have seen that the Gospel is in no way separated from the lives we live. Also, it has awakened us from the ignorant dream that we cave have true religion without being committed to our brothers and sisters.[8]

---

6 "Some Data Gathered from the Rural Communities (Pastoral Visit)."
7 "Some Data Gathered from the Rural Communities (Pastoral Visit)."
8 In the Spanish of this citation and the following one, the spelling of the writer is respected. "Some Data Gathered from the Rural Communities (Pastoral Visit)."

A similar testimony expressed the relation between faith and politics: "We have seen that the evangelized and the organized are committed to motivating the people to fight for what is ours. The commitment of the evangelized and organized is the same, because we are all moving along the same path toward liberation."[9] But others thought very differently: "Christ is not going to feed me, but this organization [ORDEN] is going to feed me." Political factors were the main cause of division in the communities and in the parish itself, but they were not the whole story. The parish agents were trying to win people over with religious discourses that were not altogether dissimilar from those of the regime:

> [A certain delegate] left the meetings of the Word and started promoting ORDEN. Today he is Protestant or Lutheran [...] in the sense that he protests against what he disagrees with. He says he is against us and is going to destroy our chapel and disrupt our meetings. He says they will hold ORDEN meetings there instead. He hasn't said he's Lutheran, but the people have called him that since he uses the Bible to implement ORDEN. He has used the Bible to recruit people. He had to use the Bible just to get the ORDEN committee set up [...] because otherwise nobody would believe him. He acted as we did: he formed groups, he read a text, and he told the people that they had to get organized with ORDEN in order to carry forward the works of the community, because that was what God wanted. He kept feeding them all that bull.[10]

The communities agreed that it was the Gospel that gave rise to FECCAS. The militant members were convinced that peasant organization was the Gospel in action. Most of the organized firmly believed that their political commitment was born of the Gospel. "We come from the Gospel" was the constant refrain of the leaders. The community of El Líbano, for example, had a clear vision of what everyone's mission should be: the rural poor were to be made socially conscious by evangelization, the organized workers and peasants were to unite with the popular forces, and the priests were to visit communities frequently to encourage them. In general, the communities were in favor of participating in the sacraments, the celebration of the Word, and the meetings called by the parish. They thought it important to give moral and economic support to the needy and to defend the interests of the exploited. Six communities saw no problem in collaboration with popular organizations, but others saw the danger of forgetting about the Gospel or creating organizations that were not based on Christian principles. The general assessment of the missionary team was that the parish, at this point, was still at the level of evangelization, except for a few people who had reached a superior understanding of the faith.[11]

---

9   "Some Data Gathered from the Rural Communities (Pastoral Visit)."
10 Cabarrús, *Génesis de una revolución*, 277.
11 "Some Data Gathered from the Rural Communities (Pastoral Visit)."

The communities were struggling to grow and develop under a military regime that was intolerant of any independent organizing in the rural areas. There was always the possibility of repression, and if it came, it could devastate both the communities and the parish, as actually happened shortly after Rutilio's assassination. ORDEN was constantly spreading rumors and threatening the most committed parishioners. Spies kept the communities in a constant state of anxiety. The plantations and the haciendas denied work to the leaders of the communities and evicted tenants if they joined a community. As a result, persevering in a community meant truly abandoning oneself to the hands of God. As we have seen, many people found that too much to ask.[12]

But neither the difficulties nor the threats of repression paralyzed the development of communities or the political organizing. The communities were determined to continue their work, trusting that God would help them since they were striving to extend his reign. When any community suffered repression, the neighboring communities came to its aid and expressed their solidarity. Determined to continue in their undertaking, the communities asked the missionary team not to retreat but to redouble its efforts: "Since you are the ones who have kindled the fire, you have to help keep it burning, and those of us who are committed must continue on, no matter the cost, because that is what God asks of us":

> You have helped to enlighten us by removing our fear so that we became aware of all the injustices we suffer because of just a few persons. We saw that we could begin to liberate all the people who are suffering. Knowing how our ancestors were freed has helped us and will continue to help us. The good we must do is awakening people to the real struggle because we should not be living this way.[13]

The communities considered peasant organizing to be appropriate for Christians since it was aimed at serving others, defending the oppressed, and upholding Gospel values. The community leaders took responsibility for maintaining unity between the Gospel and the organizing, and they were ready to confront the consequences of their commitment. The community members were all aware that they were risking their lives, but they also knew that they were doing so for the sake of truth, justice, and the people.[14]

Especially important for the pastoral plan were the young people. The missionary team wanted them to play a key role in overcoming the problems in the rural areas. Despite the best efforts of the team and the collaborators, however, the attempts to organize the youth failed, mainly for two related reasons: the

---

12 "Some Data Gathered from the Rural Communities (Pastoral Visit)."
13 "Some Data Gathered from the Rural Communities (Pastoral Visit)."
14 "Some Data Gathered from the Rural Communities (Pastoral Visit)."

organizers were unable to overcome the young people's limited vision and their lack of commitment, and they did not how to tune in to the young people's concerns or to discern their deepest needs. The efforts were not a complete loss, though, because many young people unexpectedly became more involved in parish life.[15]

The first attempt to organize the young people was a youth mission in the city of Aguilares in December 1972. The participants in the mission committed themselves to seeking out other young people in the two large schools of the city. In a series of weekly meetings, the young people considered a project that involved introducing Christian principles into the schools, but by mid-1973 the project had failed because most of the participants were studying outside the city. The missionary team made another attempt by holding weekly meetings with eight committed youngsters in the city. In August 1973, after evaluating the earlier experiences, the missionary team decided to try to organize the youth of the villages. With the help of the delegates, they made a careful selection of the young people and offered them a short course in November. The course was followed by meetings in which they discussed educational activities and the celebration of Christmas. The team also made an effort to have the young people take part in the Holy Week celebrations and other parish festivities. The youth groups in the villages started out strong, but in the course of time all but two dissolved. At the end of 1974, no groups had more than eight members, with the exception of Tres Ceibas and El Jicarón, which had twenty-five each. The reasons given for not wanting to get involved included lack of electric light, rain, fatigue, and work. Feeling discouraged, community leaders dedicated themselves to other, more rewarding activities. In a few communities, some young women were taught to sew. The only activities strongly supported by the young people were the dances.[16]

Surprisingly, many young people joined the communities and participated in the activities where they felt welcome. Doing so helped them discover their own creative potential, assimilate principles for living differently, and find effective ways of practicing solidarity. The youth leaders were soon able to attract other young people, but adults were not always eager to have the youth involved in community activities. Whenever there was resistance to the participation of young people, Rutilio would come out in their defense, telling the elders that it was not right to criticize the young:

> It is not enough just to scold. The young people don't see in us the value of true love. Rather, they see selfishness, deceitfulness, lust for lucre, violence, machismo. They see that we climb up on top of other people; they see that we do not love the truth; they see that we change spouses the way we would

---

15 ACSI. "Document on Pastoral Ministry with Young People," Aguilares, n.d.
16 "Some Data Gathered from the Rural Communities (Pastoral Visit)."

change tires on a car. [...] They view politicians as no more than circus clowns, parading, filching, cheating, and the like.[17]

Rutilio told adults that they should set an example for young people and help them develop: "They see what we say and above all what we do." Pleased with the surprisingly positive reaction of young people, the missionary team tried to guide them patiently toward greater integration and participation in the communities. This strategy was in accord with the parish's general principle of not creating ghettos but rather promoting diverse groups that were "convoked and provoked" to be the yeast that leavened the parish dough.[18]

The missionary team did not rest content with the sectors that were enthusiastic and well evangelized; they sought to attend to the whole population in the parish since their mission was to evangelize everybody. The differing levels of penetration, however, raised questions about the rhythm of the process and the symbolic expressions of faith. The magical aspects of popular religiosity made the team think about the possibility of creating a "symbolic vacuum" in order to allow for the emergence of new representations that would express evangelical faith with greater fidelity. For its part, FECCAS raised the question of whether it would be better to use more secular symbols and, if so, how to give them Christian content. Not finding a satisfactory answer to the many questions raised, the team kept searching.

Meanwhile, the team intensified its efforts to evangelize greater numbers by trying to respond to the needs, the doubts, and the aspirations of the people. Every month, the priests visited the city neighborhoods and the country villages, celebrating Mass and administering the sacraments (especially baptism) in a dynamic, participative fashion. They paid special attention to the manifestations of popular religiosity in an effort to deepen their meaning and infuse them with an evangelical quality. They made more frequent visits in Aguilares and El Paisnal; they conducted a census to gain better knowledge of the people; they strove to integrate the destitute into the communities; they abandoned their intransigence with regard to cohabiting couples; and they attended meetings of organizations like the Boy Scouts and Alcoholics Anonymous.

The Pastoral Visit of 1976

The first and only pastoral visit to the parish while the missionary team was there allows us to view its problems from a different perspective. Customarily, the pastoral visit was associated with the sacrament of confirmation and with the money the bishop was given for his ministry. When Rutilio announced the visit

---

17 ACSI. Rutilio Grande, "Schema for the Talk in the El Calvario Neighborhood," Aguilares, n.d.
18 "Document on Pastoral Ministry with Young People."

8. Parish Life

on January 25, however, he warned that the bishop would be confirming only a few adults and the young people who had already made first Communion.

When the pastoral visit took place on March 22–23, 1976, the prelate who came was not Archbishop Chávez, as Rutilio had announced, but his auxiliary, Bishop Rivera. The absence of the archbishop disconcerted the preparers and the delegates, who interpreted it as a criticism of the parish's pastoral approach. The preparers testily informed Bishop Rivera that since the archbishop had visited the neighboring parish of Guazapa, he should also have visited Aguilares. One preparer suggested that the archbishop's absence was due to the fact that he was suspicious of any type of organizing. Another said that he had not wanted to come because he already knew "the things that we were going to tell him." The preparers were confident of Bishop Rivera's support, but they had doubts about the archbishop. Rivera defended the archbishop's decision, saying he was one of the great Latin American bishops. He assured the preparers that the archbishop understood that evangelization would lead to political commitment, but that he had certain reservations about the terminology being used and some of the activities of the more radical labor organizers. When the missionary team met with the bishop, they told him that the delegates' and preparers' interpretation of the archbishop's absence was objectively correct. Evidence of that was that the local authorities had interpreted it as discrediting the parish's work.[19]

In any case, the missionary team organized the pastoral visit so that it included much dialogue between the bishop and the various parish groups. In this sense, the visit was quite innovative compared with traditional visits, which revolved mostly around confirmations and a few Masses in which the homilies moralized about family, sacraments, and popular devotions. Ordinarily, the bishop administered confirmation indiscriminately to large crowds of children, who formed two long lines along the main aisle of the church. Since neither children nor adults understood what was happening, they were easily distracted. Meanwhile, the bishop was soon drained by the heat and the tumult. The traditional pastoral visit left in its wake nothing but the confirmation certificates that had to be turned in to the chancery in San Salvador; the contributions made to the bishop, which he usually donated to the parish; and some devotional books and pious objects that the godparents gave to their godchildren.[20]

During Bishop Rivera's visit to Aguilares there were confirmations, but their administration caused controversy. The preparers and the delegates complained to the bishop because on the first day he had confirmed small children who had not made their first Communion, contrary to what had been agreed upon. As a result, the preparers and the delegates felt discredited. One preparer complained: "The people are now saying that what we're doing is crazy since

---

19   ACSI. "Acts of the Pastoral Visit," Aguilares, March 1976.
20   ACSI. Vicariate of Quezaltepeque, "Suggestions for the Pastoral Visits," June 1976.

the bishop is not as demanding as the parish is," and another stated, "We told the people one thing, but the bishop did something else. Now the people are saying that we are selfish, sneaky villains who don't want to the people to get confirmed." Still another told the bishop that the people in the communities were saying that he was interested only in collecting money, not in evangelization. They also pointed out that many people had gone to Guazapa, where they saw the archbishop confirming small children. Bishop Rivera asked pardon for having acted contrary to the wishes of those responsible for the local pastoral ministry, and he explained that the archbishop had simply confirmed the children who were presented to him. He promised to speak about the matter with the archbishop that same afternoon when he returned to San Salvador, since he did not want to confirm children inappropriately in the remaining two days of his visit.[21]

Apart from these mishaps, the bishop dedicated most of his pastoral visit to conversing with twelve different groups in the parish. He listened to people respectfully and answered their questions concisely, without getting into polemics. In his first dialogue, with representatives of the rural communities, the bishop took the initiative, asking them what changes they had experienced since the missionary team's arrival. Speaking one by one, the representatives stated that they were now living the Gospel in a fresh new way. "We learned to protest," said one, because the missions had helped them understand why they were oppressed; now they were fighting for the poor, just as Jesus their model had done. The wealthy could no longer deceive them so easily, nor could they keep them from following Jesus. The representative from Las Ventanas said that the type of Christianity desired by the rich was now a thing of the past: "We and all the rest of the church feel called to transform reality. We want the church's help so that our flame does not die." The same representative asked for support for FECCAS, which he called "a mother for us."[22]

The representatives also told the bishop about the resistance they had encountered as they tried to spread the Gospel. "When we explain Christianity, most people tell us 'yes,' but when they see how difficult it is, they draw back. Repression has already appeared. Our boss told us that if the priests arrive, he'll drive them away with bullets."[23] Another representative said that "those who have a little land don't get involved in the struggle, and others keep their distance because they love their jobs."[24] Even though the numbers of the truly committed were small, they were determined to continue the struggle so that "our Christianity will help people stay alive, so we can all eat the same food, so we can all clothe

---

21 Vicariate of Quezaltepeque, "Suggestions for the Pastoral Visits."
22 Vicariate of Quezaltepeque, "Suggestions for the Pastoral Visits."
23 ACSI. Representative of Los Mangos, "Acts of the Pastoral Visit," Aguilares, March 1976.
24 ACSI. Representative of Huitiupa, La Cabaña, "Acts of the Pastoral Visit," Aguilares, March 1976.

8. Parish Life

ourselves, so we are all equal. We know that we are acting as God commands us to act."[25]

All the representatives agreed that the changes had unleashed repression. Rumors were circulating in the communities identifying the pastoral agents as communists; harsh criticism and threats were often heard. Our sin, said one representative, has been "enlightening minds." The communities felt that they were being persecuted for the sake of the Gospel: "They spy on meetings and claim that we're talking about communism, not about God. The Gospel is the reason for this persecution."[26] Another representative commented, "As soon as we learned to read the Word of God, we discovered the true Christianity which brings persecution."[27] The representative from Garcita told about his recent imprisonment "for going about preaching the Gospel." The bishop was told that the community leaders were denied work on the plantation or else they were not given their pay; the tenants were evicted from their dwellings and parcels and "had nowhere to stay." The foremen of La Cabaña refused to give work to those who attended community meetings, and they exercised powerful control over their workers with the help of the twenty-four national guards stationed on the plantation.

After expounding their situation, the representatives made several requests of Bishop Rivera: not to abandon his radio program on YSAX,[28] to continue his support of the rural poor and especially FECCAS, to ask President Molina to stop the repression, to use his wisdom to convince the rich not to exploit them, and to ask the owners of La Cabaña to allow the nearby community to use the plantation chapel. The next day, the bishop met with the representatives of the urban communities, and the conversation followed much the same pattern.[29]

On March 21, the bishop had a meeting with the pastoral ministers who prepared people for baptism. The parish's baptismal catechesis at the time was imparted in two three-hour sessions, and its aim, in Rutilio's words, was to "viscerally convulse people with great strokes, in a progressive and varied way."[30] The catechesis combined traditional elements with newer, more evangelical teachings. In each session, the participants reflected in groups on a scriptural text, and then they shared their reflections in a plenary session. In this way, the parents and godparents became more aware of the Christian commitment they were taking on; they realized that it was not just a matter of presenting themselves

---

25 ACSI. Representative of Buena Vista, "Acts of the Pastoral Visit," Aguilares, March 1976.
26 ACSI. Representative of Las Delicias, "Acts of the Pastoral Visit," Aguilares, March 1976.
27 ACSI. Representative of Tres Ceibas, "Acts of the Pastoral Visit," Aguilares, March 1976.
28 Those preparing people for baptism lamented that YSAX was a commercial station, unlike the Protestant stations, which were dedicated only to evangelization. The bishop explained that the reason was lack of financing.
29 ACSI. "Acts of the Pastoral Visit," Aguilares, March 1976.
30 ACSI. Rutilio Grande, "Notes on Pre-baptismal Initiation."

with their donation of two *colones*. Even though the catechesis for baptism was presented well, Rutilio was not satisfied:

> We can hardly give in three or four short talks something that requires long months and years, given the lacunae in our people. Being realistic, let us limit ourselves in that first encounter to give the people a "good shaking" so that they return to their homes with heads bowed and with a harpoon in the depths of their being. [31]

The delegates had the responsibility of continuing the formation of those who had been "sprinkled." Their job was to "keep circling seven times the walls of Jericho" until the people finally converted.

The question of preparing people for the sacraments was raised in these first two meetings with the bishop. The community representatives and those who gave the catechesis informed the bishop of the difficulties caused by the parish's strict observance of the archdiocesan norm laid down in April 1973, which stipulated that the sacraments were to be administered only to persons who were evangelized. The people made fun of the delegates and catechists and said they would go instead to parishes like the cathedral, Tejutla, and Guazapa, which allowed them to "be done with the commitment" by simply paying the stipend. A representative from Guazapa expressed the problem as follows:

> Reverend Bishop, I want to tell you that the priest in Guazapa does not allow freedom of expression. He says that the only malleable matter in the parish is the children and that the adults cannot be changed. That father does not attend the meetings of the vicariate. He traffics with the sacraments. Reverend Bishop, we ask you to assign there a priest who loves the people, not a priest who loves money. [32]

Both the rural and the urban sectors thought that the pastors who did not require catechesis and Christian commitment were simply businessmen who promoted a "bread and tamales" type of Christianity. They said that such pastors were betraying the people and should leave the ministry. Good priests, in contrast, were those "who help to combat the disorder in the land"; they were on the side of the oppressed and came out in their defense. [33]

The pastoral agents, especially the catechists for baptism, asked the bishop to ensure that all parishes observed the conclusions of the recent archdiocesan pastoral encounter. At that meeting, an agreement was reached that the sacraments should be given only to those who had received catechesis and shown Christian commitment. It was very important for the bishops to insist on this point so that

---

31 Grande, "Notes on Pre-baptismal Initiation."
32 ACSI. "Acts of the Pastoral Visit," Aguilares, March 1976.
33 "Acts of the Pastoral Visit," Aguilares, March 1976.

the community leaders would not be ridiculed and lose the respect of the people. Bishop Rivera responded briefly to the most important points.[34]

Shortly after the pastoral visit, the parish of Aguilares publicized the criteria that had been approved by the archdiocese for the administration of baptism. The circular explained the importance of catechesis and Christian commitment, stating that the important thing was not to "throw water on the infants," who had no evil or sinfulness in them. Rather, baptism was an opportunity for the parents and the godparents to "test" whether they were prepared to be responsible before God for the children's Christian upbringing. The children themselves would become personally responsible when they could distinguish between good and evil, that is, when they received first Communion or confirmation. "If you do not want to make the commitment," read the notice, "then there is no sense in baptizing the child. You are trying to deceive God, but God is not deceived when you tell him Yes and then renege and do nothing. It is the parents who are deceived."[35] The circular letter explained that baptism requires changing

> everything that is bad, everything that harms us and our children and all others in the community. To understand the evil that is in us and around us, we have to consider, week after week and day after day, what God is telling us and what we are doing for our brothers and sisters. That is the purpose of the community celebrations. Those who want nothing to do with Christian communities do not want anything to do either with being Christians, and they are not Christians, even if they wash themselves with all the water of the Lempa River.[36]

Finally, the parish made the following disposition with respect to the parents and godparents of children to be baptized:

> Those who do not want to go to talks or anything else are people who are blind and want to leave their children equally blind. If they are unwilling to abandon their vices and bad habits, then they do not want what is good for their children and the families. If the parents live disgracefully, so will the children. It is not enough if the mother wants baptism and the father does not because a wagon makes no progress with just one ox. However, if the mother is separated from the father and takes responsibility, and if she seeks out good godparents, then there can be certainty that the child will be well cared for.[37]

The godparents therefore should be upright persons: "They should not be just social friends; the main thing is that they help the parents care for the child."

---

34 "Acts of the Pastoral Visit," Aguilares, March 1976.
35 ACSI. "Circular Letter on Baptism in Aguilares," Aguilares, April 4, 1976.
36 The Lempa is the biggest river in El Salvador. "Acts of the Pastoral Visit," Aguilares, March 1976.
37 "Acts of the Pastoral Visit," Aguilares, March 1976.

The celebration of the sacrament should be simple and communal. "Baptism is not the time to splurge money or to throw a big party." The circular ended by threatening the curse of God on those who baptized their children unthinkingly or without making a firm commitment.[38]

The third group that dialogued with the bishop consisted of the catechists. They said that their major difficulty was that the parents did not send their children to catechesis: "They say that we teach them nothing and are just filling their heads with strange ideas"[39] like communism.[40] In Buena Vista, the parents criticized as a waste of time the games the catechists organized after class to foster friendship among the children. The parents in Aserradera alleged that their children did not want to attend catechesis, but the children claimed that their parents would not give them permission to go. In Potrero Grande, the catechists won some parents over by means of home visits, but other parents, though they promised to send their children, did not do so out of fear that they would be taught communism. In the Rural Colonization Institute (Instituto de Colonización Rural [ICR]) settlement, the parents treated the catechists poorly. In general, mothers were more receptive than fathers. In some communities, the frequent presence of the national guards frightened the children.[41]

The bishop asked the catechists about the content and the methodology of the catechesis. They explained that they worked at two levels. The basic level involved teaching the children important prayers and some common hymns, and for this they used the Providence Center catechism. For the more advanced children, they discussed texts of the New Testament. They had by that time succeeded in getting the parents in most communities to take care of the first level, while the catechists dedicated themselves to the second level. There were about thirty children in the first Communion groups in the villages, but the catechesis did not end with first Communion; it continued with a view to integrating the youngsters into the community.[42]

The bishop then spoke with the preparers, who briefly explained to him their history and their organization. Bishop Rivera warned them against fostering elitism: "We should not work only with elites, separating them from the community. [...] As leaders we must be interested in all levels of society."[43]

The conversation with the pastoral committee of the city of Aguilares, which took place on March 22, treated the topic of religious celebrations since they were stressed in the report on the committee's activities. The committee members mentioned several points that concerned them: the community aspect

---

38   "Acts of the Pastoral Visit," Aguilares, March 1976.
39   ACSI. Coordinator of Tres Ceibas, "Acts of the Pastoral Visit," Aguilares, March 1976.
40   ACSI. Coordinator Huitiupa, "Acts of the Pastoral Visit," Aguilares, March 1976.
41   "Acts of the Pastoral Visit," Aguilares, March 1976.
42   "Acts of the Pastoral Visit," Aguilares, March 1976.
43   "Acts of the Pastoral Visit," Aguilares, March 1976.

8. Parish Life

of the celebrations; their separation from the mayor's office, which no longer financed them or sent a delegate; and the attempt to control prostitution, which proliferated on such occasions. A teacher also asked the bishop to support his union, which was fighting to maintain pensions for retired teachers. The question of baptisms and the discontent of parents was raised in the conversation, but it was not followed up as it was in other meetings. The committee praised the missionary team for not requesting stipends for their pastoral ministry. When the bishop was asked how long the team would remain in the city, he responded ambiguously: "They are here for a period, but it can be renewed."[44]

Those with whom the bishop spent the most time were the representatives of FECCAS, who explained to him how the Gospel had led them to become organized and politicized. When they asked him his views, Bishop Rivera said that he understood the process: it was important for workers to organize and fight for their rights, which were inalienable. He added that FECCAS was doing good work since it defended the poor, whereas until then most organizations had been founded to defend only the interests of the powerful: "We know that a minority possess much and others have little. We see that those who have money and culture […] get organized. We see that just as the cane growers and cotton growers organize, so also the small farmers organize. Don't let this organization go astray."[45] Bishop Rivera thus agreed that a strong peasant organization was necessary, and he said the same to the parish representatives from the city. He warned, however, about the danger of deviation. If FECCAS was a Christian organization, he insisted, it should maintain its identity as such, even when collaborating with non-Christian groups. He said that organized Christians should be especially careful about Marxist doctrines and strategies since they fueled social polarization. He also explained that it was not the clergy's function to recruit members for unions or peasant organizations, especially since there were so many groups and they were so varied. The clergy's job was to motivate people, not assume leadership. Leadership was a function proper to the laity; the clergy's job was to defend the laity's role, out of a commitment to truth and justice.[46]

At the end of his pastoral visit, the bishop held a meeting with the missionary team, where several critical topics were discussed: (1) the malaise provoked by the archbishop's absence; (2) the existence of two clearly delimited sectors, the 250 to three hundred adults who were "very conscious" and the rest of the parish, who were simply "sprinkled"; (3) the tendency of the former to leave their communities in order to work with FECCAS; and (4) the tendency of FECCAS to become an end unto itself. On this last point, the team drew distinctions, pointing out that some of the more politicized parishioners had become newly aware

---

44 "Acts of the Pastoral Visit," Aguilares, March 1976.
45 "Acts of the Pastoral Visit," Aguilares, March 1976.
46 "Acts of the Pastoral Visit," Aguilares, March 1976.

of the importance of Christian community and had begun working again to foster it. When the bishop asked about the Adorers, with whom he had also met, the missionary team responded that it was the only traditional organization that still existed since the others had been absorbed by the delegates or by FECCAS. The Adorers, however, were only marginally involved in the parish process; they did not have the same prominence as in former years.[47]

When one member of the team asked Bishop Rivera what the other bishops thought about FECCAS, he responded: "Archbishop Chávez sees in politicization the danger of a loss of Christian identity, especially when Marxist language and methods are used. Personally, I think FECCAS is something positive, with its obvious limitations. It creates problems for us, but until now we haven't had much to worry about."[48] He also mentioned that there was opposition to FECCAS in the archdiocese, especially in the parishes near Aguilares. Some pastors had complained that members of FECCAS had come from Aguilares to preach and proselytize in their parishes.

The greatest benefit of the pastoral visit came from the meetings of the different groups with the bishop. The pastoral agents could present to him their achievements and their failures; they could ask him questions and receive explanations; they could make critical observations and do so constructively. The bishop got to know firsthand the concerns, fears, and struggles of that part of the archdiocese. Before leaving, he told the team: "I have never been in a parish with so many people speaking of their experiences with such ease and clarity. It was not as though they had been coached to say something or been given prior preparation." In evaluating the pastoral visit, the team found the bishop to be more radical when speaking privately than when addressing the public.[49]

The Parish Feast Days: "The Parish Is All of Us"

The principal feast days in the parish were the following: Lord of Mercies, patron of the parish (January 15); Saint Joseph, patron of El Paisnal (March 19); Holy Week; Corpus Christi (June); Sacred Heart of Jesus (June); Festival of Maize (August), and first Communions (December). The celebrations observed three principles: preservation of the customs of popular religiosity, emphasis on Christian commitment and community, and catechesis of all the faithful. The parish organized the feast days independently of the mayor's office, which limited itself to sponsoring non-religious activities.

Rutilio prepared the feast-day liturgies well beforehand, out of respect for the people of God; he took great care of the smallest details, especially the readings and the hymns. The lectors were taught how to use the microphone

---

47 "Acts of the Pastoral Visit," Aguilares, March 1976.
48 "Acts of the Pastoral Visit," Aguilares, March 1976.
49 "Acts of the Pastoral Visit," Aguilares, March 1976.

and were instructed to read slowly, loudly, and clearly. The hymns were chosen from the parish hymnbook, and the musicians and chorus were made to rehearse them several times to avoid tonal incongruities. The parish hymnbook, which had been elaborated by the team, was designed to be used in all the diverse moments of parish life. It included traditional religious hymns as well as songs of protest, some well known to the people and some not. The words of the more common hymns were sometimes altered.

The liturgies always began on time, with church and altar fittingly adorned. Rutilio was never seen at the altar with a torn or dirty alb. Persons were appointed to take care of every important aspect of the ceremonies. When Mass was over, Rutilio always went to the door of the church to greet the parishioners and converse with them about what was going on in their lives.

Any problem or accident during the liturgy disturbed Rutilio greatly, as one teacher from El Paisnal recalls. Sometimes, he would even get angry and utter sharp words, but immediately afterward he would ask forgiveness for his harsh remarks. The teacher believes that Rutilio's quick temper did much good since it made people aware of the inconsistency and laxity that often characterized the parish community; his asking forgiveness also taught people that requesting pardon was something quite natural.[50]

Rutilio's passion for good order led him to regulate carefully the use of the parish facilities. Each group had a place assigned for its meetings, which could vary depending on whether it was the rainy or dry season. On weekdays, except Mondays, meetings could take place from seven in the morning until nine at night. (Nobody was allowed to enter on Monday, which was the team's day of rest.) After a meeting was finished, those attending had to leave the place spotless, just as they had found it. The parish office was the place where information could be obtained. Short visits were held in specially designated rooms, and longer visits were held under the calabash tree in the yard, weather permitting. The hall between the parish entrance and the kitchen was not a place to linger; those entering the rectory always needed to be accompanied by a member of the team. There were separate sleeping spaces for men and women attending courses. The men stayed in a house that Rutilio had inherited from the Barrera brothers, and the women in a small house alongside the church. Those using both places were expected to respect the hours for rest: retiring at the hour indicated, not bothering others who were sleeping, and being quiet if they rose early. On Saturdays, when there were often many people overnighting in the parish, special care had to be taken to avoid disorder.

These norms were clearly not observed with all the fidelity that Rutilio would have liked. The purpose of his detailed rules was to maintain strict discipline in the rectory so as to guarantee internal order. Since the groups that

---

50   Author interview with a teacher in El Paisnal, San Salvador, December 1979.

came for courses tended to consider the rectory to be their home, their behavior sometimes contradicted the disciplinary norms, much to Rutilio's displeasure. At times, the resulting disorder caused strong tensions among team members and with other parties.

The team's visits to the communities were announced with anticipation, either from the pulpit or by circulating notices to people's homes. Once a visit was programmed, the delegates met with the designated priest to plan activities. Rutilio would convoke the steering committee of a community by means of a letter that stated the time, the place, and the objectives of the meeting. The parish would distribute more than 2,500 circulars, entrusting the task to adults since children did not do it reliably.

The Patronal Feast

The feast of the Lord of Mercies was prepared by the committees of the communities in the city of Aguilares. Starting in October, the committee presidents would meet with the neighbors to plan the festivities collectively. The main business was collecting funds to finance both the centralized activities and the local ones. The method most used, apart from raffles and other traditional means, was to solicit a contribution by means of an envelope. After drawing up a list of the neighbors who seemed most likely to contribute, the committee made its appeal and kept a detailed record of each donation. The collection was supervised by the general committee, which also apportioned the funds collected to finance the centralized activities. After the feast, a report on total income and expenditure was posted at the entrance to the church, along with a list of the donors and their respective contributions. Rutilio insisted much on this type of procedure in order to avoid any suspicion of misappropriation of funds.[51]

Among the centralized costs for the festivity were the vehicle for the procession of the Lord of Mercies, which took place on January 14; the music for the final novena Mass; the flowers for January 15; the fireworks for the procession and for the Mass on the fifteenth; and the printing of programs and envelopes. Rutilio opposed spending money on flowers; he thought wild flowers were sufficient. The expenditures in the local communities included the fireworks for the entrance of the procession into the community for the novena Mass that corresponded to the community, as well as flowers and other minor expenses. The missionary team got the communities to agree on the joint purchase of items such as flowers.[52]

---

51 ACSI. Feast of the Lord of Mercies, Aguilares.
52 ACSI. Feast of the Lord of Mercies, Aguilares.

Each day of the novena had a special theme, based on a short Gospel text,[53] and each local community was assigned to take charge of the celebration of one day of the novena. The distribution of the days among the communities, as well as the gathering point for the procession to the church, was announced in the program. On the day assigned to it, the community went in procession to the main church, arriving at seven in the evening on the dot, to attend the novena Mass.[54]

Each feast of the Lord of Mercies had a central theme: it was penance in 1975, thanksgiving in 1976, and humble supplication in 1977. On the feast day itself (January 15), the communities entered the temple in procession, each with a poster that identified it and proclaimed a brief message. At nine in the morning, the parish Mass was concelebrated by all the pastors of the vicariate, with the archbishop presiding.

The procession through the city streets took place the evening before the feast, after the seven o'clock Mass. Marking the rhythm of the procession were men and women bearing candles and lined up on either side of the vehicle carrying the image. Preceding the vehicle with the image was a car with a loudspeaker, from which one of the priests directed the hymns and shouted out religious slogans to animate the faithful. If a traditional musical group was present, it marched behind the vehicle with the image. The Adorers were responsible for maintaining order in the procession. After the procession, confessions were heard in the church, and a group of volunteers helped the sacristan clean up.[55]

Rutilio patterned the procession of the Lord of Mercies after the one for the Divine Savior of the World. It was meant to represent a journey of people walking together, "arm in arm," in search of salvation, convinced that "we need to be saved all together, or we will not be saved." In life, as in the procession, Rutilio preached, it was necessary to move forward together, without ever stopping:

> Those who stop will be swept away by the currents of vice and selfishness. […] There is no way you can just sit on a rock. […] You have to join the procession of people who move forward without stopping. […] There are those who will stand and watch from the sidewalks, puzzled, and asking themselves: What's going on in Aguilares? They are the same as ever: sprinkled on the skin but not baptized in the Holy Spirit. Are you also a stranger,

---

53   In 1976, the themes for the novena were the following: "Who Are You Following?" (Mk. 8:27–33), "See What I Do" (Mt. 11:2–6), "Jesus and His Mission" (Lk. 4:16–22), "The Kingdom of God" (Mk. 1:14–19.32–39), "The Beatitudes" (Lk. 6:20ff.), "Who Is the Fallen One?" (Lk. 10:25–36), "Taking Sides with Jesus" (Lk. 12:4–12), "Jesus Suffered Temptations" (Mt. 4:1–11), "What Will We Be Examined On?" (Mt. 25:31–46). ACSI. Patronal feast, Aguilares, January 1976.
54   ACSI. Feast of the Lord of Mercies, Aguilares.
55   ACSI. Feast of the Lord of Mercies, Aguilares.

who does not know what has happened these days in Jerusalem? If there is joy, it is because of the Lord of Mercies!⁵⁶

Passing through the streets of the city, the Lord of Mercies blessed the good people he saw, "urging them to keep struggling and to keep studying his Gospel in the communities, despite the difficulties and contradictions." And he also felt sorry for the evil things he saw:

> There is need for a sewer system to carry away the wicked things that corrupt our community and our young people. [...] The Lord of Mercies will surely view with great pain the abuses that exist throughout our parish: people abusing other people. There are even traffickers of humans! What an abominable sin!⁵⁷

The message of the Lord of Mercies was one of conversion, encouraging the faithful to continue forward on the difficult path of commitment "without being intimidated." Men were urged to use their manhood to promote the Gospel, and women were counseled not to become slaves to men or to allow themselves to be led around like cattle for the pleasure of men. "The holy Patron cannot go out in the city streets to bless neglect and wickedness. Religion is life, not processions and candles."

Jesus Christ was truly alive, "not just in a book or in people's memory." Christians had to "incarnate" him in their personal and community lives. Jesus was like an identity document or a passport⁵⁸ that allows entry into the kingdom of God. "Christ is alive among us. We are not brought together by a dead man. He is the Way, so we have to walk in his footsteps; wherever he put his foot, we must also place ours, step by step, hand in hand." If there were some who could not take part in the procession because "they had to take care of the house," Rutilio urged them to join in by intention. As they progressed, the marchers held candles in their hands, as if to affirm, "We walk with the One who said, 'I am the light of the world.'" They bore the same light of baptism, which had to be kept burning until "the end of the marathon of life"; they had to struggle to keep it from being "blown out by the gusty winds of temptation."⁵⁹

Excluded from the religious events by the parish, the municipality organized civic festivities featuring bands, concerts, beauty contests, dances, sports competitions, games, and so on. Rutilio asked the mayor and the owners of the mechanical rides, which were located in the plaza in front of the church, to keep the noise down and to silence the many loudspeakers during the religious acts.

---

56   ACSI. Rutilio Grande, homily, Aguilares, January 14, 1977.
57   Grande, homily, Aguilares, January 14, 1977.
58   An identity document allowing circulation; it was required at that time.
59   Grande, homily, Aguilares, January 14, 1977.

The Feast of Saint Joseph

The organization of the feast of Saint Joseph, patron of El Paisnal, was similar to that of the patronal feast of Aguilares. In 1973 and 1974, there were two Masses each day of the novena, one in the morning in the church and another in the afternoon in a neighborhood. In 1975, Rutilio eliminated the morning Mass and transferred the afternoon Mass to the church to make it easier for the neighbors. As in Aguilares, the days of the novena were distributed among the community in the neighborhoods, and on their appointed day, the residents of a community would enter the church in procession carrying a small image of Saint Joseph and posters with biblical sayings. The communities would compete with one another in creating elaborate ornaments for the image, which would depend much on the economic resources of the neighborhood. In 1976, after much discussion, it was agreed that, to save unnecessary expense, the same flowers and ornaments would be used three days in a row; thus, the three communities responsible for those days would have to collaborate in preparing the image for the procession. Some neighbors were displeased by this decision and refused to participate.

Ordinarily, a professional altar builder would be paid a hefty fee to construct an altar in honor of Saint Joseph, but since the municipality was no longer involved in the religious events, the altar it ordinarily financed had to be funded otherwise. Along with the mayor, the wealthier residents of Aguilares withdrew their support, feeling displaced since they could no longer monopolize the feast with their money.

The Masses during the novena were celebrated for personal or family intentions. On one day of the novena, Rutilio organized an excursion to the Sucio River with the children. After the children bathed and enjoyed themselves in the river, Rutilio and some of the collaborators used the occasion to teach them some catechism. During the bus trip to and from the river, Rutilio asked the children riddles and rewarded correct answers with a piece of fruit or candy.

On the eve of the feast, March 18, all the villages entered into El Paisnal in procession and were solemnly received in the temple. At seven in the evening, Mass was celebrated, and then a solemn procession set out, the women on one side holding candles and men on the other side bearing torches. On the feast day itself, Rutilio concelebrated the Mass with other pastors of the vicariate. One program for the feast sought to counter Protestant influence in the town with the following explanation:

> The saints are not idols or gods, and neither are their images. We know that the true image of God is our brothers and sisters. Since ancient times we have venerated and remembered the saints as our brothers and sisters, Christians who were faithful to the Word of God. They knew how to follow Jesus Christ and to serve their fellows. We venerate their statues as we venerate those of

our national heroes. The saints and their images remind us how we should serve God and our fellow human beings.[60]

Holy Week

Holy Week offered the opportunity for intense evangelization of the parish. During the many activities and celebrations, the parish emphasized that Holy Week was a time for personal and community renewal, an occasion for deepening one's commitment to following Jesus. It was not to be seen as a celebration disconnected from the rest of people's lives. The whole of life was a continuous "Lent" of death and resurrection. The missionary team took advantage of this time of intense religiosity to try to evangelize the traditional Holy Week customs, which were not altogether Christian. The people would take the saints out in processions, pray to them, and touch them devoutly, but they would pay little heed to what the saints had said or done in their lives. The parish also combated the decidedly non-Christian customs that were constantly gaining ground; for example, many people took the week off to go to the beach and carouse.[61]

The perspective of the evangelized communities regarding Holy Week was very different from that of the traditional faithful: "It is no longer like before, when we thought Holy Week was celebrated with just a procession. We have to struggle to help others and not just have a procession." The delegates preached a living Christ who was being crucified daily anew by social injustice. The communities felt that they were walking along the same road Jesus took; they were taking the same steps, short ones perhaps, but important ones. However, such a perspective did not mean abandoning the processions; they simply needed to be given a proper context and understood differently. Even with the new religious discourse, the processions drew great crowds, but now they were not conducted in silence or in darkness.[62]

During Holy Week, the missionary team, with the help of Jesuit scholastics and university students, spread out to the villages in an effort to reach as many people as possible, but without neglecting the urban centers of Aguilares and El Paisnal, where a priest always remained to preside at the celebrations. In this way, the villagers for the first time could celebrate Holy Week without having to travel to an urban center. Some of the villages even had their own processions. Holy Thursday was the day for first Communions. On Good Friday, there were the Stations of the Cross, during which the delegates read a Gospel text and commented on it. Holy Week ended after the celebration of the Easter vigil on Saturday with a joyous community feast or a trip to the Lempa River, a very popular custom.[63]

---

60   ACSI. "Program: Feast of Saint Joseph," Aguilares, n.d.
61   ACSI. "Evaluation of Holy Week," Aguilares, April 25, 1976.
62   "Evaluation of Holy Week."
63   "Evaluation of Holy Week."

During Holy Week, Rutilio would travel to the villages, visiting homes in the morning, teaching catechism to children in the afternoon, and engaging with adults in the evening. Holy Week was an ideal time to get to know a village. After the religious service on Holy Thursday, people were encouraged to share coffee and cake, and when possible, some food.

The non-evangelized mass of "sprinkled" folk rejected the parish's religious focus as political; some even called it revolutionary and communist. They complained that Holy Week was not being celebrated as it was in former times. At the other extreme, one group of delegates was pressuring to break totally with the old traditions.

The Feast of Corpus Christi

Corpus Christi was traditionally a major feast day in El Salvador, and it was celebrated in Aguilares with great solemnity. After the solemn Mass at nine in the morning, a "demonstration of faith" took place, consisting of a traditional procession in which the Blessed Sacrament, under guard and under canopy, stopped at five altars in different parts of the city. The delegates were in charge of organizing the procession, making sure that the people marched in close ranks, symbolizing their solidarity as the body of Christ. Music was provided by groups from the communities. Flowers, fireworks, and other special arrangements were financed by envelope donations, as was done for the patronal feast.[64]

For the celebration of the feast day in 1975, the design of the altars reveals how the missionary team introduced Gospel themes into traditional liturgical expressions and how it used them to evangelize the people. Each of the five altars was elaborated by several communities and featured a particular text from the Gospels. When the Blessed Sacrament reached an altar, the text was read and commented on by a delegate. At the altar in the neighborhood of El Calvario, where the theme was "the church continuing the mission of Christ," the people were asked to recall the command that Jesus gave to his followers: to go forth announcing salvation to all the world and declaring that those who accept Christ and his message unreservedly and put it into practice would find salvation. "We shouldn't say 'That's the job of the bishops' or 'That's the job of the priests and the pastors.' *No*. It is the task of all of us!" The people were told "not to let their knees tremble, because my *Spirit* will be with you. The task is difficult, but I will be there with you as long as you stay committed and don't grow lax."[65]

At the altar in the Salinas neighborhood, which was dedicated to the primitive Christian community, the emphasis was on how those early Christians had accepted the message of Jesus and put it into practice. Being a Christian, then, "was not just a question of a little water poured on the head or being immersed in a river, but of changing one's way of being," just as those first Christians had

---

[64] ACSI. Rutilio Grande, "Corpus: Outline of Themes," Aguilares, 1975.
[65] Grande, "Corpus: Outline of Themes."

done, for they had recognized that they were "all equal and so they lived that way." The early Christians shared their possessions, they prayed together, and they were always rejoicing. For that reason, "it could be readily seen that they had changed themselves and were changing their community." Those who lived around them were amazed and wanted to imitate them because they saw that their way of life was worthwhile.

At the altar in the Guadalupe neighborhood, dedicated to persecution, the faithful were reminded that Jesus had told his followers that they too would be persecuted by the enemies of truth. The enemies of Jesus had "spied on him and wanted to seize him several times, but he handed himself over to them only when he wanted." Carrying him before the tribunals, they had judged him summarily for revealing "the truth against the lie, the light against the darkness, and love against hate," and they had killed him.[66]

At the altar in the town market, the theme was the need to follow the example of Jesus and continue his mission; the stress was on how Christians were called to be salt of the earth and light of the world. Although these images Jesus used were "quite simple," they "make some people shudder because they feel like salt in their wounds":

> He said things like this, and they are as true as the sun that shines on us. We have a common Father, and so we are all children of God and sisters and brothers with one another. We must experience *Love* so that no *Cain* does harm to his brother under any pretext. [...] "My Father has left the earth and all it contains as an inheritance to all human beings. Don't fight over an inheritance that belongs to all. Live as brothers and sisters. Let no one seek a larger slice than is proper and just. Let those with government posts and greater resources serve others if they want to be saved and to save others."[67]

At the final altar, which was near the parish church, the theme was persecution for the sake of fidelity to the Gospel. The preaching had Jesus telling the people: "When they hear you speaking about my simple message, they will call you 'communists' and say that you want what does not belong to you. They will try to take from you the little you have: the tenant housing, [...] the rocky ground they lent you for your crop," and even your labor. But no one should be surprised at this because "they will fight you and accuse you just as they did me, saying that you go about changing the religion and destroying the temple. They claim to believe in some old things I never taught." The first Christians were persecuted and had to take refuge in the catacombs; meanwhile, their accusers and persecutors thought they were serving God and the homeland.[68]

---

66 Grande, "Corpus: Outline of Themes."
67 Grande, "Corpus: Outline of Themes."
68 Grande, "Corpus: Outline of Themes."

8. Parish Life

The twenty-seven posters elaborated and carried by the communities in the Corpus Christi procession in 1974 reflect the level of evangelization attained by the communities at that time. They all made reference to the feast of Corpus Christi, presenting the Body of Christ as a symbol of the organic unity of their own parish community, whose life depended on the collaboration of all its parts. The body of the community was built up by the mutual responsibility of one and all, and it was broken down by isolation and lack of mutual support. All Christians were children of the same Father and so all were brothers and sisters. When they celebrated the supper of Christ's body and blood, food and drink, they were committing themselves to sharing the same table unselfishly. At the end of life, they would be examined by their deeds, not by their words. Some posters had a biblical message while others combined the Word of God with a message of solidarity.

Table 3. Messages on the posters of the communities

Feast of Corpus Christi, June 30, 1974

Community	Message on the poster
Amayo	Fellow small farmers: let us struggle so that justice is done. That is what Christ asks of us.
Valle Nuevo	Corpus Christi.
El Calvario	In the name of the Lord Jesus Christ, the Christian community asks the mayor for less Corruption and more support for our young people.
Barrios San José and El Paisnal	Be salt for this world.
Buena Vista	Combatting injustice is true Christianity.
Central Norte Aguilares	In the name of Christ: I protest against those who abuse their power simply because they can. I protest against those who are weak because they don't want to do anything.
El Centro, El Paisnal	If we struggle united in love, united we will overcome.
Colonia Romero	God commands that we do justice and that they do us justice.
Colonia Los Ángeles	In the name of Jesus Christ we are in solidarity with the civil, military, cultural, and religious authorities that want to combat every type of Corruption at its roots.
El Líbano	Brothers and sisters, let us struggle for our salvation.

Community	Message on the poster
Las Delicias and El Paisnal	I Paul am a servant of Jesus Christ. God called me and set me apart as his apostle to announce this message of salvation. God delivered this message long ago in the scriptures by means of his prophets.
Colonia San Antonio	Brothers and sisters, we must understand the Word of the Gospel, and that way we will be united in our community. The hunger and misery of our people are caused by the cruel incomprehension of those who profess but do not practice love for our brothers and sisters.
Araditas and Aserradera	We protest against the rich who have taken possession of the lands God left for all of us and not for just a few. About this we cannot remain quiet.
El Tule	We want justice not exploitation.
San Antonio El Grande	The price of rice and beans is as high as the sun. Let us bring it down!
Guadalupe	We ask our delegates to unite with us to preach the Word of God. United in this way we can better serve our community and so bring bread where there is hunger, medicine where there is sickness, and housing where there is destitution. And so we will practice the true Religion that Christ left us, by loving one another.
Jicarón	God made the earth, and just a few people own it while many are dying of hunger.
Las Huertas	Jesus said: I am the bread of life. Whoever comes to me will never hunger. Whoever believes in me will never thirst. John 6:35. As brothers and sisters united in Christ for the Gospel, we will overcome.
Las Tunas	God bless our lands. Help for the school. Long live Corpus Christi!
Potrero Grande	Brothers and sister united, we will overcome. Christ urges us to unite so that, once united, we will rise to new life. We want justice. We need better wages. We want agrarian reform. We want peasant unions.
La Florida	In the name of the Body of Christ, Mr. Mayor, we ask that no more trash be dumped near La Florida.
Las Pampas	United we will overcome.
Los Mangos	United in the name of the Lord we will overcome the injustices of this people.
El Tablón and Escondido	Christ strengthens us. He is our guide. Down with overlords, dictators, and hitmen [...]
Colima	We protests against the high cost of living. We demand agrarian reform.
El Tronador	We suffer exploitation but we seek liberation.

Community	Message on the poster
Tres Ceibas	God said to every living thing that moves on the earth, "I give you food that you may eat," not like today when only a few can eat. Genesis 1:30–31.
Anónima	Long live unity! We want liberation and land to cultivate. No more monopolies in too few hands!

Fuente: ACSI. Slogans on the posters of the communities, Corpus Christi, Aguilares, June 30, 1974.

The feast of Corpus Christ was celebrated in El Paisnal a few weeks after the celebration in Aguilares, and in a similar way. After the Mass, there was a procession that stopped at different stations around the city. The communities of Aguilares and El Paisnal took part in one another's celebration, traveling from one city to the other.

In 1976, the number of people attending the Corpus Christi celebrations declined notably, and there was less collaboration in the preparation of the altars. The missionary team thought that the reduced numbers were caused by fear of repression, especially in the urban communities. The rural communities showed more fortitude, remaining firm despite the risks.

First Communions

First Communions were celebrated with great solemnity within the context of the Eucharist. The sacrament was presented as a lifelong commitment on the part of the children and their parents. Near the end of the catechesis, the parents were summoned and made aware of their responsibility. To show the first communicants the importance of what they were doing, the parents were asked to attend Mass and receive Communion along with their children. The parish asked the parents not to spend a great deal of money on clothes and candles; special dresses and suits were discouraged, and the children's candles were provided by the catechists. Rutilio insisted that first Communion was not a sacrament celebrated for the purpose of making individuals shine or putting a family's wealth on display. The best clothing for the child was good preparation. If a family had the means to buy a new suit or dress for the child, it should be simple clothing suitable for everyday wear. Putting these norms into practice was extremely difficult due to longstanding customs. The catechists had to spend much time trying to convince the parents of the need for simplicity.

The day before the first Communions, the children reviewed the five requirements for making a good confession, using the parable of the prodigal son, and they learned to genuflect on entering or leaving the church. A penitential liturgy was then held, beginning with a hymn related to the parable. Asked whether they wanted to confess their sins before God and the assembly and whether they wanted to be better, the children all responded loudly that they did. The priest then gave them general absolution. Finally, they rehearsed the next day's ceremony.

On the day of the first Communions, there was only one Mass, and all the communities were invited to attend it. The children entered the church in procession and sat in the front pews. At the offertory, they brought their gifts, along with flowers, to the altar. After Mass, the parents and catechists in each neighborhood of the city organized a small community fiesta, complete with tamales, coffee, and piñatas. Excessive expenditures were to be avoided in all such activities since they were meant to be symbols of unity and joy.

The Sacred Heart of Jesus
The month of June was dedicated to the Sacred Heart of Jesus, a devotion much cherished in the marketplaces of El Salvador. The feast therefore had special meaning in a commercial city like Aguilares, whose markets attracted "humble folk, valiant souls who come from the country to this open and welcoming city."[69] The celebration culminated on June 30 with the consecration of the market to the Sacred Heart. Rutilio not only continued this traditional celebration but encouraged the market vendors to participate in it. As mentioned above, the market had a special altar and station for the Corpus Christi procession as well.

A homily Rutilio kept in his files showed that he used one Sacred Heart celebration to inculcate basic ethical principles and to defend the rural poor's right to organize and enjoy the essentials of life. The homily anticipated themes that Rutilio would mention in his final sermon in Apopa on February 13, 1977. The market, he explained, was the place where people obtained the "wherewithal" needed for life; consequently, the commercial transactions there should be just, the scales precise, and the profits honest. He deplored the fact that "the producers are often unjust and abusive, as are those who hoard and speculate with the life of the poor, the poor folk whose wages cannot keep up with the rise in prices."[70] Religion, he asserted, was not something foreign to commerce and the marketplace, nor was it something that mattered only in the month of June.

The main concern of the followers of Jesus in the market should be the multiplication of loaves every day. Jesus became a humble man of the people, the son of a peasant mother and a carpenter father; he learned to ask for bread, the symbol of life:

> Asking for one's daily bread means asking for all the means of sustenance, for bread must be accompanied by all the elements necessary to maintain a human being alive, such as beans and maize and cheese and a little meat—in sum, everything that a healthy, vigorous human organism needs. No one should go about malnourished or weak, subject to any illness that comes

---

69 ACSI. Rutilio Grande, homily in the market, Lk. 9:10–17, Aguilares, n.d.
70 Grande, homily in the market, Lk. 9:10–17, Aguilares, n.d.

along. We have rights to all the good the earth produces, for the only Proprietor is the Creator.[71]

Jesus multiplied loaves and fishes, thereby showing his commitment to the life of humankind. His followers should therefore do the same: multiply bread to provide life for all human beings.

Besides praying, the people had to cultivate the earth, Rutilio insisted, but he protested that the people did not have sufficient land to grow even their basic crops. Calling on the name of God, he demanded that the government enact agrarian reform and allow small farmers to organize to defend their rights as free citizens:

> The cane growers, the coffee growers, and the cotton growers are all allowed to organize! But no organization is permitted for the poor folk who work the land, […] for those who make the cane fields fruitful by their labor, for those who leave the sweat of their brow in the coffee groves and the cotton fields.[72]

The land belonged to everybody, given to us by the only Proprietor so that all peoples might sit at the table together and share bread with one another. "Apart from God there are no owners, no governments, no lords who can dispose of the lives of human beings!" Those who trafficked in slaves and grew fat on the sweat of the poor were accursed; they were the "selfish, unjust rich who think they are gods who own the earth," the very ones Jesus condemned. If by chance Jesus were to pass through Aguilares, "walking these streets and saying the tremendous but simple things that he said, have no doubt about it: he would go straight to jail as a subversive, a communist, a political agitator."[73]

Festival of Maize

The great feast featuring the communities themselves was the Festival of Maize, introduced into the parish calendar in August 1973. The parish team conceived the feast as a way of allowing the communities to celebrate their food and their artistic creations. The festival emerged out of the missionary team's desire to engage in a profound dialogue with the suffering people of the parish. The questionnaires used during the missions and in the first phase of the courses had not achieved their purpose. The team observed that the responses were not completely honest; there was incoherence and distortion in the descriptions of social conditions and the explanation of the causes. The team members therefore felt that they had still not been able to comprehend sufficiently the people's pain.

The Festival of Maize sought to overcome that limitation by giving the people an opportunity to give bold expression to their most intensely felt

---

71 Grande, homily in the market, Lk. 9:10–17, Aguilares, n.d.
72 Grande, homily in the market, Lk. 9:10–17, Aguilares, n.d.
73 Grande, homily in the market, Lk. 9:10–17, Aguilares, n.d.

experiences. The team was convinced that only when the rural poor spoke for themselves could they convey authentically the depth of the deprivation they suffered. Although distortion was still possible, the festival provided sufficient conditions for popular sentiment to be given full and objective expression.

Dedicated to singing the praise of maize, the first three festivals (1973, 1974, 1975) brought to light many real-life situations. The communities sang of the maturation of the cornfields, the injustices suffered when selling their sweat and their blood to the plantations, the increased price of chemical fertilizer, the difficulties parents had in providing tortillas to their children, the change of life brought about by the Gospel, the community efforts to unite Gospel and struggle, the growth of FECCAS and the decision of many to join it, the experience of communal producing for the sake of solidarity, the ever-present fears and the best ways to dispel them, the leadership of the rural poor in their struggle, the need to preserve the gains of FECCAS, and the need to make the voice of the farm workers heard in the city.[74]

In 1975, the boldest artists sang freely about FECCAS, declaring that it was better to die in the struggle than to live exploited in the cane fields. The songs tended to become generic and repetitive, however, so that changes were introduced in 1976 to keep the festival fresh and relevant. The missionary team asked the communities not to repeat songs or overwork themes: "You can do it. God has given you much common sense, and now you have an opportunity to put it into practice." In 1976, it was proposed that the songs take as their main theme not maize, but the work of rural women. Concretely, the people were encouraged to sing of the great need for women to participate actively in the work of building Christian community and promoting agrarian organization. Despite the team's recommendations, the theme of maize did not disappear completely.[75]

The 1976 festival was organized according to the established pattern. On the evening before, the *atol* was prepared, the tents were erected, and the stage was set up in front of the church. Great care was taken to correct some of the errors of the previous year, for in 1975 the invited guests had not been properly attended to, the *atol* had run out too quickly, and there had been some disorder.

As they did every year, despite their limitations, the communities generously contributed their maize and their labor. By fraternally sharing the *atol*, they were tangibly announcing the values of the kingdom of God, even as they denounced the injustice "that leaves not even a branch of the pine tree[76] so that the yellow-bird[77] can continue to sing."[78] During the offertory of the Mass, Rutilio praised the hard work and the dedication of the communities:

---

74   ACSI. "Circular, Festival of Maize," Aguilares, 1976.
75   "Circular, Festival of Maize."
76   Tropical tree of the mimosa family.
77   Type of icterid bird found in El Salvador and Honduras.
78   ACSI. Eucharistic celebration, Festival of Maize, Aguilares, August 16, 1976.

"Ah, Father," some say, "this celebration has cost us a lot!" But that's how it is with the poor and the humble: from the little they have they contribute to the celebration. We saw them coming down from the hills. Even if their crop was spoiled by the rain, even if they have only rocky ground—that matters not! United in community they brought down their maize, and we will savor it as we share it in solidarity.[79]

The tense political atmosphere that year forced the missionary team to take some extraordinary measures. It earnestly asked the communities to stop hurling invectives against the president and the military, to avoid allusions to the ideological conflict between FECCAS and the Front for United Popular Unity (Frente de Acción Popular Unificada [FAPU]), and to abstain from using "naïve Marxist language." The team also warned that it would not allow outsiders to participate in parish activities so that people would be encouraged to speak freely and uncontrollable situations would be avoided. It also asked that the lyrics of songs and the theater scripts be submitted for review beforehand so that any subsequent complaints would be directed against the parish, not the communities. The team also limited the participation of each community to one of the two contests, either song or theater, although additional presentations could still be made outside of the contests.[80]

In his homily at the principal Mass, Rutilio insisted on the need to avoid "literary genres," careless expressions, personal attacks, and invectives that were more fitting for political meetings than for church gatherings.[81] He had two reasons for being so insistent. First, he was personally affected by the pressure being put on the parish and by the political repression in the country as a whole. Second, he feared that attempts would be made to prolong unduly the commemoration of July 30, an important anniversary for the popular organizations since it was on that day that more than a hundred young people had been massacred in San Salvador the year before.

On Sunday, August 16, the Festival of Maize began with the celebration of the Eucharist, dedicated to Mary and peasant women. Amid hymns and acclamations, Rutilio and the concelebrants entered the church accompanied by twelve delegates. The delegates and some of the twenty-four patronesses from the communities were seated in the sanctuary, while those who did not fit remained in the pews:

> So you see, we cannot fit all the patronesses up here. There are about twenty-four in all; some arrived late. Perhaps the poor things are out there

---

79 ACSI. Rutilio Grande, homily during the Festival of Maize, Aguilares, August 16, 1976.
80 ACSI. "Festival of Maize: Something to Anticipate," Aguilares, 1976.
81 ACSI. Rutilio Grande, Eucharistic celebration, Festival of Maize, Aguilares, August 16, 1976.

somewhere, lost, but there is no more room here. Besides, in this country of machismo, it's always the men who want to sing to the women! We ask pardon, for we want to focus on the importance of women in the life of the church in its service to the world.[82]

After the proclamation of the Word, a delegate spoke on behalf of all the communities, laying great stress on the problem of division and inequality. Rutilio then gave an extraordinary homily on Mary, Mother of God and glory of peasant women: "We have wanted to celebrate both peasant women, the quintessence of our mostly rural people, and the women of this city, the destination of many who come from the countryside to transact their business in the stores or the stalls in the market."[83] Rutilio stressed that Mary was also a peasant woman, consecrated to do God's will. Salvadoran society walked in darkness since it was failing to follow Mary's example of faithful obedience to God and service to others:

> So here we are now, celebrating the glorious feast of the Blessed Virgin Mary, who was a simple peasant woman but knew how to win the favor of God. We have to reflect now and realize that we are not doing the will of God completely, as the Blessed Virgin Mary did, because we live disunited. From what I see, some have bread, but others are dying of hunger; some have houses while others have been evicted from theirs. Dear brothers and sisters, that is not the gift of God; that is not the commandment that must be kept. We need to be reconciled with God and put his word completely into practice. It is plain that while some follow the good path, others attack the law of God. Dear brothers and sisters, we are completely overwhelmed in darkness.[84]

Mary was great, Rutilio continued, because she was eager to serve others, and that was why God favored her. The Magnificat (Luke 1:39–56) sings of her greatness with sublime words, but most people were sadly ignorant of that canticle. In fact, Salvadorans were superstitiously "buying Magnificats," the ones sold "as pamphlets, there in the baskets by the cathedral door or in some other great church, [...] but they are not aware of what the Magnificat is":

> Apparently they think that the prayer is for when a cow has gone astray—that's when you pray the Magnificat! [...] Or when I have to put a curse on some women or other who's after my man—then I will pray a Magnificat! [...] "I'm going to buy one in the cathedral. They tell me they sell it there in a pamphlet."[85]

---

82 Grande, Eucharistic celebration, Festival of Maize.
83 Grande, homily during the Festival of Maize.
84 Grande, Eucharistic celebration, Festival of Maize.
85 Grande, homily during the Festival of Maize.

"But no!" Rutilio exclaimed, "The Magnificat is something explosive!" It was the prayer *par excellence*. "That little woman who went up into the mountains let loose her tongue, as has happened also with our brothers and sisters in the countryside." Moreover, it was a most beautiful prayer. "Let us hope that we don't use it to enchant serpents or find lost cows or put curses on anybody! Nor should we go seeking to buy it in some pamphlets." This was the prayer recited by Mary, the most excellent maiden:

> When Elizabeth heard the voice of her cousin as she arrived there at her house, she exclaimed, "How is it possible that the mother of my Lord should come to see me?" She went in search of a platform to parade her around town. [...] "But Mary!" "Ah no, Elizabeth, I am the servant of the Lord."[86]

In this way, Rutilio explained, the maiden who had been chosen as queen showed herself to be a servant. He then distinguished the beauty of Mary from that of the false queens of the big festivals and the beauty contests, such as the "Miss Universe" contest that had just taken place in a luxurious hotel of San Salvador. The example of Mary showed that a queen was "the lovely average woman" who was dedicated to the service of others, "not the model with hornet waist who buys votes at the festivals or there in the Hotel Sheraton." Mary stayed three months with her cousin, "collecting firewood, hauling water, washing clothes for old Zechariah and Elizabeth. There she stayed, instead of being paraded around the region in a procession. Understand well who Mary is."[87]

It was for that reason that the main criterion for electing the patronesses of the local communities was service. That was why the communities had chosen women who

> are not ashamed to hoist a load of firewood onto their heads and to serve their companions, who also work hard. They are not reluctant or ashamed to get up early in the morning, light their lamps like the woman in the Bible, and make tortillas, so that the sound of them grinding meal is heard in the village. It is these little women, then, who are truly queens, because they are patronesses who serve others.[88]

On another occasion, Mother's Day, Rutilio exalted women in similar terms:

> The woman of the early dawns, the woman of the oil lamp, the woman making tortilla, the woman washing clothes in the brook, the woman who earns a few cents selling her goods, the woman who is martyr to the drunk, unfaithful husband, [...] the woman slave, [...] the different woman.[89]

---

86 Grande, homily during the Festival of Maize.
87 Grande, homily during the Festival of Maize.
88 Grande, homily during the Festival of Maize.
89 ACSI. Rutilio Grande, homily on May 12, Mother's Day, Aguilares, n.d.

God had a preferential love for such persons, Rutilio continued, and he showed them his mercy:

> Why? Because there are people around, people with long fangs, who have no fear, not even of God. [...] And who are those who have no fear of God? They are the ones who have denounced our Father and our Brother, those who rise in the morning making the sign of the cross: in the name of coffee, in the name of coffee, and in the name of coffee. In the name of cane, in the name of cane, and in the name of cane. I have said this other times, but it needs to be repeated ad nauseam. God took the mighty down from their thrones; he cast out the self-satisfied because they have their gods right here. He lifted up the lowly and raised them on high. He filled the hungry with good things, and he turned away the mean-hearted rich, those who don't want *atol* for everybody but only for themselves. They want the great goblet for themselves but don't want to share it with their brothers and sisters in this Eucharist of solidarity. And what did he do to those brutes? He stripped them bare and sent them away empty-handed because they are cruel Cains, the ingrates of ANEP![90]

In the last part of his homily, Rutilio offered a general evaluation of the parish's labor, revealing some of the pastoral team's main concerns. The team was especially worried about the preservation of the parish's Christian identity, which had been seriously compromised by the political orientation of FECCAS and the tendency to devalue whatever was not associated with the organization. Rutilio therefore asked the people "not to neglect or minimize or deride in this overall process all that we are doing at different levels."[91]

He then greatly stressed the importance of Christian identity, the starting point for the parish experience in all its dimensions. "We are all Christians," he proclaimed, but "only if we follow the Lord" and only if "our profound motivations are those of Jesus Christ"—including the motivations of those organized with FECCAS:

> When we organize or when we join a rural organization, we should be motivated by what gives life to the movement of our parish and our communities. We should be impelled by the profound motivations of the Gospel. We want a new world! Whatever fruit comes out of the global work of this parish should have the label of "Christian," but not only as a cover. The Gospel must be the deepest root of the validity and the very being of the work of our parish, our community, all the communities of both town and country.

---

90 National Association of Private Enterprise (Asociación Nacional de la Empresa Privada [ANEP]), organization representing the major business interests of El Salvador. Grande, homily during the Festival of Maize.

91 Grande, homily during the Festival of Maize.

8. Parish Life

We are all co-responsible: the one speaking to you, those here in the sanctuary, and all of you! Therefore, the message of Corpus Christi and this great feast is precisely this: Christians, the parish is all of us![92]

Rutilio told the communities that they needed to be congratulated because there were "so many good things" in them. Their faith was not in vain; it had been converted into life. With great emotion, he related how one man had left his job on the plantation in order to serve the Lord, for he could not be a foreman and a servant to his fellows at the same time:

> Congratulations to all of you, brothers and sisters! Congratulations, because the Gospel is intimately united with your lives. You have brought it down to earth. We will hear you sing about it later, and we've already heard about it in the language of our sisters and brothers. […] We will hear it also in the Mass that will follow there on the platform, and in the songs that announce and denounce. So we are receiving good news and commentary.[93]

Despite all the good news, Rutilio stressed the importance of keeping the celebration of the Word at the center of community life: "That is where I want you to put your best effort." The celebration should be the source of Christian dynamism in the villages and the hamlets; it should animate all community activities, including those of FECCAS, which was lacking in Christian values even though it had been born of them. The celebration of the Word had a "primordial importance," and it was open to all those who had a "will to change" and a "humble and sincere desire to be renew" themselves, their communities, and the country. But Rutilio warned: "Be careful! The meetings of the Word of God must be strengthened, and they must never displaced by other meetings, as important as those other meetings may be."[94]

Rutilio therefore urged the people to dedicate themselves to "profound study" of the Bible, reading it as the history of a people's salvation that culminated in Jesus:

> [Read the Bible] not as the Protestants do, taking isolated bits. Those fundamentalists just go about arguing whether the Virgin had eight children or just one son. Of what interest is that to me? Or [they argue about] whether a chicken is to be eaten with its blood or without it. What difference does it make?[95]

The parish promoted the all-important Bible study, which was accompanied by reflection on the national reality. Delegates, coordinators, and preparers were all

---

92 Grande, homily during the Festival of Maize.
93 Grande, homily during the Festival of Maize.
94 Grande, homily during the Festival of Maize.
95 Grande, homily during the Festival of Maize.

asked to take seriously the mandates given them by their communities. In choosing them, the communities had placed their trust in them, and they therefore had a responsibility toward the communities. On them depended "the vitality of the church in each hamlet or village," and "the coherence of all the parish's work."[96]

Toward the end of his homily, Rutilio warned the people of the temptation of letting certain individuals or groups gain too much power; he also advised them to be wary of the fanaticism of delegates who had become sectarian and dogmatic, as some very good ones had. The method of the parish was dialogue, he said, which was completely opposed to the "sad example of some Protestant sects." He therefore asked that the diversity of charisms be respected: "The musicians who sing us their verses, with a message of change and new values, are as important as the humble rural folk who bring benches and arrange them for the celebration, or the humble housewife who claps her tortillas, applauding the works of the parish."[97]

The persons charged with giving the baptismal talks should not become discouraged in the face of the difficulties involved; the talks should continue, "well prepared, well conducted":

> The delegates need to be sharp and stay up with these things, like the new ways of catechizing the children. Take a good look at any society you see thereabouts, and you'll find that they fight over the children because the children "record" everything, young as they are. They have to be oriented according to the models and values of the Gospel, and that is the job of the parents. Don't go looking for Doña Maria to teach catechism to your children. That's your job, Papa![98]

Rutilio closed his homily by declaring that the Eucharist was situated at the center of the parish since it was the celebration of the death and resurrection of the Lord, "the quintessence of our faith dedicated in service to the world":

> Communion is not like eating a cookie. It is a process that comes from life and crosses through these exterior signs and leads to life. It is a process that does not stop here among us. This is Eucharist, but so is the Festival of Maize which we will soon celebrate. This is Eucharist, but so is life in the village, so is life in the field or the shop, so is the struggle for human rights. This is Eucharist, but so is well conducted organizing. In the Eucharist here the values are experienced and made manifest without any shame. The values of the kingdom are proclaimed as we lift the cup and the bread of the One who was crushed because he lived out those values.[99]

---

96 Grande, homily during the Festival of Maize.
97 Grande, homily during the Festival of Maize.
98 Grande, homily during the Festival of Maize.
99 Grande, homily during the Festival of Maize.

Truly committed Christians realized the Eucharist in their lives; they experienced "that profound change that comes with dying to oneself and undergoing the new birth that transforms humanity." It is therefore not enough to pray, "reciting the Magnificat to find an ox"; it is not enough "to come here performing rites lacking in meaning. […] That is detestable; it is a caricature of religion." But neither was it right to let political commitment overshadow the Eucharist and the other sacraments because all of life, including the political dimension, was in need of sacramental expression. "Life is Eucharist."[100]

The offertory of the Mass featured a reading about the origins of maize, taken from the *Popol Vuh*. It was explained that the *Popol Vuh* was the sacred book of the ancient inhabitants of Mesoamerica. After the reading, the patronesses of the communities, as the official queens of the festival, carried maize, tortillas, bread, wine, and the *Popol Vuh* to the altar. Receiving the gifts, Rutilio recited a prayer: "We offer you these gifts, Lord: the humble tortilla, the hosts of our people. We offer you maize, the sweat and lifeblood of our people, from sowing to reaping, from its growing on a small piece of rocky soil to its being carried home on our backs."[101]

The Priests' Senate

The pastoral experience of Aguilares became better known in the archdiocese when Rutilio was elected to the priests' senate in early 1974; he was the only religious priest elected for the senate's 1974–77 term.[102] His election made manifest the prestige and admiration he enjoyed among the diocesan clergy, many of whom had been his students in the seminary. A priest who was a close collaborator of the bishops of the archdiocese testified that Rutilio

> was admired by all of us priests for his virtue and his pastoral work. As pastor of Aguilares he was outstanding. There was much spiritual renewal in the movements of his parish. He was exemplary. He was faithful to the Gospel and to the magisterium. Archbishop Chávez and, later, Archbishop Romero had complete confidence in him; they admired him greatly for his priestly integrity and his pastoral labor.[103]

The testimony of Cardinal Rosa corroborates the "great esteem" the bishops and clergy of the archdiocese had "for [Rutilio's] pastoral knowledge and his gift

---

100 Grande, homily during the Festival of Maize.
101 Grande, Eucharistic celebration, Festival of Maize.
102 The other senators elected at the same time as Rutilio, on February 5, 1974, were Ricardo Urioste, Alfonso Navarro, Ástor Ruiz, Fabián Amaya, Luis Montesinos, and Gregorio Landaverde. Archbishop Chávez had the right to appoint three other priests of his own choosing. ACSI. "Decree Constituting the Priests' Senate of the Archdiocese of San Salvador," San Salvador, February 27, 1974.
103 *Summarium testium*, witness 1, §8.

for coordinating meetings, making syntheses, and issuing reports." Rosa commented further: "He was a discreet man; he was always smiling, but he was quite reserved and kept his head down most of the time. He spoke softly and rarely raised his voice. He didn't look like the typical Jesuit; he was a very pastoral, very spiritual man." Most definitely "he was a man in love with the people; he respected them and fought to defend their rights."[104]

Rutilio faithfully attended the monthly clergy meetings and sometimes gave a talk on the theme of the day. He also frequently took part in the patronal feasts of other parishes and was asked for assistance. The pastor of Chalatenango, for instance, asked Rutilio to do a mission in his parish. In fact, Rutilio was so frequently absent from his own parish that members of the missionary team expressed their concern.

Even though he did not enjoy doing so, Rutilio gave retreats to the clergy on two occasions: November 19–23, 1973, and December 16–20, 1974. The archbishop asked him to give another retreat in 1976, but he declined because of other commitments. "Who am I," he asked aloud on one occasion, "to be giving a retreat to the clergy? Poor me, as stubborn as Jeremiah. I share with you the joys, the desires, the hopes, the pains, the griefs, and the commitments of our priesthood at the present time." Still, when giving the retreat points and talks, he spoke with firm determination, trying not to wound or discourage his fellow priests. "If sometimes I raise my voice," he explained, "I do not exclude myself from condemnation. I want to be the microphone of the One who by his Incarnate Word calls us, reprimands us, and compels us because he loves us." Rutilio's main goal was to restore Christian optimism in an ambience of mutual understanding and acceptance.[105]

The first task undertaken by the newly elected priests' senate was defining its functions with respect to both the city council and the recently created pastoral council. Bishop Rivera stated that the bishops felt the need for the senate's assistance in pastoral more than in jurisdictional matters, although there would be consultation on the latter as well. The senate was expected to be responsive to the concerns of all priests, who rightly wanted church governance to be more agile and representative. The bishops hoped that the senate would maintain close and constant contact with the priests through the vicariates and be creative in undertaking new initiatives.[106]

The senate proceeded to elect officers in accord with its statutes, and Rutilio was elected secretary.[107] As a result, the minutes of the sessions not only record

---

104 *Summarium testium*, witness 5, §58.
105 ACSI. Rutilio Grande, "Considerations on the Incarnation of Jesus Christ and Its Consequences: Exercises for the Clergy," Aguilares, n.d.
106 ACSI. "Act No 1: First Meeting of the Priests' Senate, Term 1974–1977," San Salvador, March 12, 1974.
107 Salvador Colorado was elected president; Alfonso Navarro, pro-secretary; and Ástor Ruiz, temporal coordinator. "Act No 1. First Meeting of the Priests' Senate, Term 1974–1977."

the senate's activities but also reflect to some extent Rutilio's views regarding the activities. The senators agreed to meet on the afternoon of the third Tuesday of each month, as the previous senate had done. Before long, however, they decided to have two monthly sessions, meeting on the second and fourth Tuesday of each month; the average attendance was six or seven members out of a total of ten. Although Rivera, as auxiliary bishop, was an ex officio member of the senate, he rarely attended the sessions, and soon the minutes did not even record his absence.

In its first session, the senate proposed that its main objective be the organization of a pastoral ministry week. The proposal was a daring one considering the problems created by the previous pastoral ministry week, but the bishops' conference, at its January 21–25, 1974, meeting, accepted the idea and even proposed that it be held in the third week of August; it was further agreed that each bishop would name one priest, one religious, and one layperson to the national commission that would organize the pastoral ministry week.[108]

The priests' senate of San Salvador objected to the date proposed by the bishops' conference since it did not allow sufficient time for preparation. They argued that an improvised pastoral would risk being a failure, thus producing unneeded frustration. Expressing its fear of "muddled sessions" and "paper conclusions," the senate thought that there should be a coordinated process that would draw on the grassroots bases of the archdiocese and prepare the week with great care and diligence. The ultimate aim would be to unleash a creative, all-encompassing pastoral dynamic. The San Salvador senate's proposal was agreeable to the episcopal conference; in fact, in January 1975, a year after the decision was first made, the other dioceses had still not named their members for the national commission. There was subsequently no further talk of a national pastoral ministry week, but only of an archdiocesan one.[109]

Since the pastoral council was just being set up, the senate took responsibility for organizing the pastoral ministry week, seeking to include the pastoral council as much as possible. Since, according to the norms of the Sacred Congregation of Clergy, a majority of the members of the pastoral council were to be laypeople,[110] it was proposed that the pastoral agents already working in the parishes be integrated

---

108 ACSI. Freddy Delgado, secretary of CEDES, to Ricardo Urioste, San Salvador, February 22, 1974.
109 ACSI. Freddy Delgado, secretary of CEDES, to Ricardo Urioste, San Salvador, February 22, 1974; and "Act No. 19. Meeting of the Priests' Senate," San Salvador, January 30, 1975.
110 The Second Vatican Council (*Christus Dominus* 25–35) recommended pastoral councils made up mostly of laypersons. Paul VI established the norms for same on August 6, 1969, and the 1971 synod of bishops mandated the establishment of said councils. The Sacred Congregation for the Clergy emphasized the importance and the correctness of the pastoral council on March 15, 1972, stating that its members should represent the whole diocese. Consequently, in whatever way the bishop decided to choose the council members, the majority were to be laypeople. It was the bishop's responsibility to convoke and preside at council meetings, and the opinions of council members were to be taken into account.

into the archdiocesan pastoral bodies. The aim was to extend the experience of Aguilares and other parishes, which were already training their own pastoral agents, to the whole archdiocese. The senate planned to use the pastoral ministry week to create effective pastoral councils at all levels: archdiocesan, vicarial, and parish. It was considered best not to create such councils by episcopal decrees, a procedure that was almost always unsuccessful; rather, they would arise from working with the bases. Making it clear that it wanted always to work with the bases in order to guarantee good results, the senate set up a team for coordination and communication,[111] whose purpose was to open channels of information and consultation with vicariates, parishes, and the clergy in general. The senate members, for their part, offered to help establish personal contacts with the vicariates.[112]

Personally, it was difficult for Rutilio to take part in the organization of the pastoral ministry week: "I agreed to collaborate but not without overcoming profound interior repugnance because of the painful experiences of the first national pastoral ministry week." Once he overcame the repugnance, however, he threw himself into the work and gave thanks to God for it: "Blessed be the Lord. May he keep giving me these loving tests that will help me always to be humble and never self-sufficient, and to strive for better service of the Lord and nothing else."[113]

The preparation for the pastoral ministry week began in March with a survey of priests and religious regarding their major concerns. The response was very poor. Of the three hundred questionnaires sent to the parishes, only fifty were returned, and some of these came from the vicariates. In his report, Rutilio noted that the low level of response called into question the credibility of the senate. In almost half of the returned questionnaires, the formation of pastoral agents was named as a serious problem. At the end of June, the vicariates also became part of the process. Meetings were held with the bishops and were led by Father Beltrán, who knew the archdiocese well from the previous pastoral ministry week. The planning sessions were well attended, although certain people were notably absent. Beltrán also met with groups of religious and laypeople, and at the beginning of August both these sectors joined in vicarial meetings. To some extent, these sessions made up for the poor response to the survey, and they succeeded in mobilizing the bases of the archdiocese.

Rutilio stressed the importance of securing the participation of the military in the process since they were the ones who held real power in the country and

---

111 Bishop Rivera; the priests Ricardo Urioste, Salvador Colorado, Juan León Montoya, Luis Montesinos, and Inocencio Alas; religious sisters Joyce Blum and Lidia Amaya; and religious brother Lucas and Father Márquez.
112 "Act No. 1: First Meeting of the Priests' Senate, Term 1974–1977"; and "Archdiocesan Week of Pastoral Ministry: Report of the Priests' Senate to the Religious and Clergy of the Archdiocese in Connection with the Whole People of God," *Búsqueda* 6 (1974): 66–70.
113 ACSI. Rutilio Grande to Archbishop Luis Chávez, Aguilares, January 11, 1976.

yet knew very little about Christianity and its implications for society. Moreover, if the military remained alienated from the church, it would try to use it for its own ends. It was therefore advantageous to consider how the military might be integrated into the collaborative pastoral ministry of the archdiocese. With the senate's approval, Rutilio referred this matter to the military vicar, José Eduardo Álvarez, bishop of San Miguel, but he rejected the proposal out of hand, arguing that he was not obliged or inclined to recognize the archdiocese's style of collaborative pastoral ministry.[114]

Consultations with the vicariates revealed that they were interested in continuing to hold joint meetings since they were not well integrated at that point. Stressing the importance of the process aspect of the preparation for the pastoral ministry week, the vicariates were not anxious to set a date for its celebration. Responding to the vicariates' concerns, the senate established a team of promotors whose mission was to make sure that the vicarial meetings were held regularly, followed an agenda, kept records, and showed dynamism. The senate named Urioste president of the commission for coordination and communication. In the end, however, preparation for the pastoral ministry week stagnated due to lack of enthusiasm and some ill-conceived appointments that contravened what had been agreed upon. Moreover, the method adopted turned out to be too innovative, especially for the San Salvador metropolitan area.

In May 1974, the senate considered publishing a type of pastoral letter that would have the backing of the bishops. The letter would seek to address the great questions facing the church and to clarify the church's mission in the world; it would describe honestly the social reality of the country and the difficult state of relations with the government. The senate hoped that the letter would be a starting point for further reflection. After a long discussion, however, a sense of frustration came over the senate, which decided not to publish the letter since it lacked realism. The senators were discouraged by the lack of progress in planning the pastoral ministry week and began to wonder about the effectiveness of the senate itself. Interest in the pastoral ministry week diminished as the year progressed, partly as a result of the inertia and inefficacy of the senate, and the idea of a pastoral letter was finally discarded in January 1975.[115]

The senate's problem was twofold. First, the senators expressed themselves so freely and sincerely that their opinions were well known beforehand. The senate was quite representative of the clergy, but the great diversity of the members impeded its effectiveness and made decision-making difficult. Second, the senators were not constant or punctual. They found themselves incapable of acting

---

114 ACSI. "Act No. 18: Meeting of the Priests' Senate," San Salvador, December 11, 1974; and Rutilio Grande to Bishop Eduardo Álvarez, San Salvador, November 19, 1974.
115 ACSI. Rutilio Grande, "Report on the Activities of the Senate, 1974–1977"; and "Act No. 18: Extraordinary Session for Evaluation," San Salvador, December 11, 1974.

with consistency or of working as a team, and their discussions were often taken up with useless points. One senator complained that the senate was not dealing sufficiently with matters affecting the priests themselves. Another grumbled about manipulation but gave no specifics. In an attempt to improve its functioning, the senate's members decided to change some of its procedures: (1) they would meet just once a month, on the third Tuesday, and after each session they would evaluate the meeting; (2) they would do two general evaluations a year; (3) they would invite the archbishop to take part in their discussions and decisions; (4) they would name promotors for the five zones (Cuscatlán, Chalatenango, La Libertad, Quezaltepeque, and San Salvador); and (5) they would inform the rest of the clergy about their activities.[116]

Rutilio's personal evaluation of the first year of activities was more nuanced. Contradicting the majority opinion—that the priests' council and the pastoral council were impractical—he argued they were necessary "in order to get the heavy machinery of the church moving." The archdiocese, he explained, still had much to learn about exercising authority as service; those who had authority found it difficult to govern by humble consensus and sincere consultation with their advisors. "Admitting the truth with humble sincerity means continual conversion and commitment to new and renewed actions within ourselves and within the groups we belong to."[117]

The senate renewed its efforts with the vicariates, meeting with them in mid-February 1975. The senate was happy to learn that, with the exception of Chalatenango, the rural vicariates experienced intense activity during the last months of 1974. Laypeople were playing a more active role in Comasagua and in Quezaltepeque, the vicariate to which Aguilares belonged. The joint meetings of these two vicariates were well attended: seventeen priests, fourteen religious, and forty-four laypeople. After several joint meetings, the vicariates had returned to meeting separately, but they were thinking of meeting jointly again in the future. There was intense activity and much enthusiasm also in the vicariates of Ilopango and Mejicanos, as well as in the northeast sector of San Salvador, where some two hundred persons were being mobilized. During their meetings, they were reflecting on Christology and discussing the national reality. Many were drawn to the meetings more by the opportunity for study and reflection than by anticipation of the pastoral ministry week. Some pastors, however, failed to accompany their lay parishioners, complaining that efforts were being made to impose a predetermined pastoral line. The attitude that prevailed in the vicariates of Cuscatlán and Chalatenango was quite different: in the former, because of the vicar's lack of collaboration, and in the latter, because of the opposition of

---

116 ACSI. Rutilio Grande, "Report on the Activities of the Senate, 1974–1977"; and "Act No. 18: Extraordinary Session for Evaluation," San Salvador, December 11, 1974.
117 ACSI. Rutilio Grande, "Report of the Priests' Senate: Activities of 1974."

the Italian Franciscans, who had charge of the department. The diocesan clergy for the most part were eager to take part in the process. The divergence of attitudes in these vicariates demonstrated that the vicar was a key person for the success of the process. The senate therefore asked the archbishop to exhort the reluctant vicars to collaborate.[118]

The ambience was quite different in the urban vicariates, where distrust, prejudice, and disorientation prevailed. Some vicariates of the capital stayed completely outside the process. The vicariate of La Luz, for example, met only once, and did so for the purpose of questioning the need for a pastoral ministry week; they complained that a clique was trying to impose its pastoral vision on them. Rutilio felt that there was too much "laxity" among the pastors and vicars. The senate concluded that the bishops needed to insist that the faithful be more attentive to the teachings of the Gospel, Vatican II, and Medellín. The criticisms made of the first pastoral ministry week needed to be avoided, namely that it was not representative and that it imposed its views on others.[119] Archbishop Chávez and Bishop Rivera consequently asked all the parishes to submit to them their pastoral plans by June 1975, or at least send a report of their activities. They wanted to know especially about the formation of lay pastoral agents. To assist the parishes, they included with their request a document specifying criteria and offering suggestions about how to elaborate a pastoral plan.

As the parishes and vicariates responded to the bishops' request for information, a commission of the senate, which included Rutilio, analyzed and systematized the information; it then reported its findings at the monthly meeting of clergy in July. Some parishes presented no pastoral plan at all, and some had no experience in the formation of lay pastoral agents, but the overall results of the survey allowed the senate to identify some of the basic characteristics of the pastoral ministry of the archdiocese. They were the preservation of the traditional parish, the formation of lay pastoral agents, and Christian instruction through various courses and through talks in preparation for matrimony and baptism.

Beyond these basic characteristics, the reports from the parishes and vicariates revealed a great variety of pastoral practices. Most of the parishes showed no interest in the social reality of the country, the exceptions being the parishes of the northeast zone of San Salvador and three parishes of the vicariate of Cuscatlán. Also, most of the parishes expressed no need for doing pastoral ministry as a team, the exceptions being the parishes of the northeast zone of the capital and those of the vicariate of Quezaltepeque.

Apart from the vicariates of Zacamil and Ilopango, the metropolitan area was disorganized. One vicariate had elaborated pastoral plans with six parishes

---

118 ACSI. "Act No. 19: Meeting of the Priests' Senate"; and "Act No. 20: Meeting of the Priests' Senate," Apulo, February 18, 1975.
119 ACSI. "Act No. 20: Meeting of the Priests' Senate."

but had an invidious relationship with nearby vicariates. Another vicariate had included in its plan several parishes outside its jurisdiction that were unhappy with their own vicar. In still another vicariate, only two parishes turned in pastoral plans. A noteworthy characteristic of San Salvador, especially the vicariates of San José de la Montaña, La Merced, and Santa Marta, was the strong emphasis on individual morality, doctrinal orthodoxy, and the administration of sacraments without evangelization. Although they spoke about the laity, they said nothing specific about the role the laity had in the life of the church. These parishes also evinced a marked orientation toward charitable works, such as dispensaries, occasional collections for the poor, and first Communions of the poor. In the best of cases, some of the parishes trained social welfare promotors. The evangelizing work and the different groups and associations—Bible study, neo-catechumens, charismatics, cursillos, etc.—showed no clear concern for the social reality of the country, and any talk of the latter tended to arouse fear, suspicion, or an eloquent silence.

The pastoral plan of the vicariate of Quezaltepeque is particularly relevant here because the vicariate included the parish of Aguilares and its plan incorporated some of the most important features of the Aguilares experience. Rutilio and the missionary team attended the vicarial meetings faithfully and participated in them actively. The experience in Aguilares was in harmony with that of other parishes of the vicariate, with the exception of Guazapa. At the end of 1975, the vicariate held a four-day meeting in Apopa to elaborate the pastoral plan requested by the senate, but the pastor of Guazapa left the meeting after a day and a half without offering an explanation.

The vicariate's pastoral plan featured evangelization based on the person of Jesus and his preaching of the kingdom of God, stressing the importance of giving the kingdom a historical dimension: "Only by incorporating the historical life of Jesus Christ into our own practical life here and now will we keep faith with the content of the Creed we profess, the dogmas we hold, and the titles we want to give him." The realization of the kingdom of God obliged the faithful to ask about the identity of those called to the kingdom and about their socioeconomic and religious situation. The vicariate concluded that, in view of that reality, human development was necessary in order for faith to mature. Without human development, evangelization would become abstract, and faith would become individualistic, conformist, and alienating.[120]

The vicariate also attested to the difficulty of evangelizing popular religiosity. Many of the rural poor resisted abandoning their traditional religiosity, while

---

120 ACSI. Vicariate of Quezaltepeque, "An Initial Project of Collaborative Ministry in the Vicariate of Quezaltepeque," Apopa, May 25, 1975; and Vicariate of Quezaltepeque, "Evangelization: Reflection Guide Provided by the Vicariate of Quezaltepeque," Vicariate of Quezaltepeque, October 14, 1975.

at the same time the young were abandoning it because they found no meaning in it. The document noted, however, that young people were restless and were searching for new religious forms. Despite the difficulties intrinsic to evangelization, the vicariate said it was convinced that "there is an urgent need to develop a mature faith that is fully committed to God, to neighbor, and to society." These three commitments reinforced one another mutually, and all were necessary for a truly adult faith. However, these commitments would also give rise to conflicts. "We believe that our preaching will inevitably produce tensions since our social reality negates the life of the kingdom and makes it impossible for people to reach it." The vicariate then asked the question: Is the church ready and willing to accept the consequences of this type of pastoral ministry?[121]

Not everything was negative. The pastors pointed to signs of hope. Many of the rural poor had discovered the personal and communal dimension of their faith. The extraordinary human qualities of some parishioners and the great sincerity of others had created a close bond between faith and sociopolitical commitment. But the pastors also observed that the people's new political consciousness had led some to exaggerate the importance of political action. Organizers were even using people's religiosity for political ends, but then suppressed the religious aspects when they did not serve their ends. Still others had abandoned the faith, though without forgetting their Christian roots.[122]

The vicariate declared that believing in Jesus involved acting as Jesus acted and giving reasons for the hope that generates life. Since Christian truth had to become real in history by means of practice, its validity would be decided in the interval between its being announced and its becoming reality through the commitment of Christians. For the vicariate, this commitment would mean evangelizing people at all levels, renewing the methods and contents of the catechesis and the liturgy, and constant theological updating of the parish teams. Moreover, it would require personalized formation of the members of the Christian communities, not mass indoctrination with a stress on individual salvation; such formation had to be creative and enlivening, helping people to overcome their docile submission to "providence."[123]

Regarding practice, the vicarial plan laid down norms for administering the sacraments, especially baptism and matrimony, and for training pastoral agents. The pastors agreed to emphasize the salvific, communitarian dimension of the sacraments rather than the economic aspect. They decided that there should be no baptism without catechesis and that public sinners—adulterers, alcoholics,

---

121 Vicariate of Quezaltepeque, "Initial Project of Collaborative Ministry in the Vicariate of Quezaltepeque."
122 Vicariate of Quezaltepeque, "Initial Project of Collaborative Ministry in the Vicariate of Quezaltepeque."
123 Vicariate of Quezaltepeque, "Initial Project of Collaborative Ministry in the Vicariate of Quezaltepeque."

unjust employers, sowers of division, etc.—should not be allowed to be godparents; an assessment needed to be made of the motivations and the Christian commitment of parents and godparents. If necessary, a testimony of life would be requested. In the case of matrimony, there would be evaluation and preparation, and care was to be taken that ceremonies avoid manifest social differences in the adornments and music.[124]

Since the primary function of pastoral agents was to serve the community, they should be mature, creative persons with stable marriages and a certain economic security; they should know the local culture well and be able to exercise leadership in the community; they should be able to communicate to others the importance of evangelical conversion, the need to defend the freedom and the rights of all, and the responsibility people had to shape their own history. But even these important qualities were not sufficient: pastoral agents needed to receive basic training and then continue to receive permanent formation in the various courses offered by the vicariate. At the same time, the vicariate warned of the dangers that needed to be avoided. For example, pastoral agents should not take on a clerical identity; to the contrary, they should preserve their lay identity because that was the best way to express their Christian character. Moreover, they should not distance themselves from their communities or consider themselves on a higher social level. The vicariate pronounced against the professionalization or the sacralization of services rendered to the community.[125]

The vicariate favored the strengthening of female leadership and the appointment of women as pastoral agents; it was convinced that women were called to play an all-important role in the church, and this conviction was corroborated by its own experience. Analysis of the new services offered in the parishes of the vicariate demonstrated that the contributions of women had been decisive. The vicariate considered indispensable the clear-sightedness of women, their generous dedication, their readiness to engage in struggle, and their fortitude in the midst of conflict. These were all qualities in which they vastly superseded men. In the view of the vicariate, there was no way that the church, presently dominated by men and consequently suffering from rigidity and insensitivity, could do without women. The vicariate concluded its plan by determining that meetings would be held every three months to evaluate the execution of the plan.[126]

After reviewing the information provided by the parishes and vicariates, the senate identified the two most important themes: (1) the national reality and the church, and (2) popular Catholicism, evangelization, and the church. Each

---

124 Vicariate of Quezaltepeque, "Initial Project of Collaborative Ministry in the Vicariate of Quezaltepeque."
125 Vicariate of Quezaltepeque, "Evangelization: Reflection Guide Provided by the Vicariate of Quezaltepeque."
126 Vicariate of Quezaltepeque, "Evangelization: Reflection Guide Provided by the Vicariate of Quezaltepeque."

vicariate could choose one of the themes for study, and the conclusions reached were to be sent to the senate within three months. The vicariates of Quezaltepeque, Montserrat, and San José de la Montaña chose the second theme, while Ilopango, Zacamil, and Chalatenango chose the first. On the other side of the archdiocese, the vicariates of Cuscatlán, San Francisco, and La Merced chose the first theme, and those of Comasagua and Santa Cruz chose the second. The vicariates took the task seriously, and their discussion of the themes made their meetings more dynamic. The contributions of all the vicariates were shared at the monthly clergy meeting on November 4, 1975. Meanwhile, religious women and men held a separate meeting to prepare for the pastoral ministry week. In view of the considerable progress made with these activities, the senate decided to schedule the pastoral ministry week for early January 1976.

The vicariates remained quite busy with preparations during the months of November and December. Encouraged by a commission of the senate, they made the Spiritual Exercises, during which they reviewed the path they had followed since June 1975 while looking forward to the pastoral ministry week. On September 16, the senate named an organizing commission, with Urioste as executive secretary. As the commission entered into feverish activity, the senate suspended its ordinary sessions.

The other great concern of the senate, apart from the pastoral ministry week, was the general welfare of the clergy. The senate had many responsibilities: it tried to stay informed about the concrete situation of the priests and to facilitate communication between them and the bishops; it spent much time discussing the seminary, which was passing through a serious crisis; it prepared and evaluated the monthly meetings of the clergy, trying to relate them to the dynamics of the pastoral ministry week; it dealt with the personal problems of the priests; it responded to the bishops' inquiries about filling vacancies, taking care to designate priests who would not provoke unsettling ruptures with the pastoral line of the previous pastors; and it urged the bishops to name vicars who were willing to collaborate with the pastoral process of the archdiocese.[127]

In two cases, Rutilio asked the bishops to name good pastors in the vicariate of Quezaltepeque. In March 1974, when vacancies opened up in the parishes of Apopa and Opico, he asked for two priests who were dynamic, open, available, close to the people, ready to respond to the zone's challenges, and willing to collaborate with the vicariate's pastoral style. Although he knew the request was unrealistic, he asked the archbishop to assign two priests to each parish.[128]

At a senate meeting on June 17, 1975, in the presence of the vicar of Quezaltepeque, Rutilio recommended that the pastor of Tacachico remain in his post since he did good work and was well integrated into the vicariate team. He

---

127 ACSI. "Act No. 2: Meeting of the Priests' Senate," San Salvador, March 26, 1974.
128 "Act No. 2: Meeting of the Priests' Senate"; and "Vicarial Meeting," Apopa, May 27, 1974.

complained about the sudden arrival of an itinerant ex-Augustinian missionary in the parish of Guazapa since his activities were not in keeping with the pastoral line of the vicariate and the archdiocese. When a senator warned of the danger of creating "chemically pure" vicariates, other senators responded that the naming of pastors should take into consideration the situation of the parish and the vicariate, as well as the optimal distribution of available resources, as determined by the joint planning process.[129]

The senate also advised the bishops and offered them criticism. Rutilio at times questioned appointments made by the archbishop, and he complained that the bishops never reported to them on matters relating to the bishops' conference: the senate was never consulted about the points of the agenda, and it was never informed about what was discussed.[130] The secrecy surrounding the bishops' conference became a topic of discussion six months later, when the senate observed that the bishops were not abiding by the dispositions of the universal magisterium regarding the consultative function of the presbyterate. The senators repeated their desire to be taken more into account since they were the primary collaborators of the episcopacy.[131]

The plight of the nation always had a place on the senate's agenda. The senators kept the bishops informed about important national developments, and they insisted on the need for the church to examine that national reality in a critical spirit, from the vantage point of the Gospel. They urged the bishops to make the church's mission quite clear to the people, who felt frustrated at having been denied their most basic rights for so long. Since the senators came from different zones and diverse social sectors, they could put together a fairly complete picture of what was happening nationwide. The heightened conflict in the country, Rutilio argued, required the church to remain alert and lucid so as not to be surprised or overwhelmed by events. If caught unprepared, the church would find itself in the rearguard, "being towed along," unable to fulfill its mission of inspiring and illuminating the nation.[132]

The priests' senate of 1974–77 closed its term with an emergency meeting called for January 29, 1977, to deal with the increased persecution of the church. The final minutes were edited by Rutilio a day or two later. During those three years, the senate had held thirty-five sessions, and Rutilio had carefully recorded each of them and had regularly sent out reports on the meetings to all the priests. In his general report, presented on February 1, 1977, Rutilio pointed out that during those three years "we have come across landslides in our path, both normal events and serious setbacks in our history that are *in no way* divorced from

---

129 ACSI. "Act No. 22: Meeting of the Priests' Senate," San Salvador, June 17, 1975.
130 ACSI. "Act No. 27: Meeting of the Priests' Senate," San Salvador, March 16, 1976.
131 ACSI. "Act No. 30: Meeting of the Priests' Senate," San Salvador, June 20, 1976.
132 "Act No. 22: Meeting of the Priests' Senate."

the vital process of the pastoral ministry week, which encompasses the story of a unique history of salvation."[133] After the report was read, the assembled clergy proceeded to elect a new senate.

The Pastoral Ministry Week

With the archbishop presiding, the pastoral ministry week took place from January 5 to 10, 1976; participation was excellent, some 290 persons. Besides the bishops of the archdiocese, participants included 111 priests, five men religious, forty-three women religious, four seminarians, and 125 laypeople. The vicariate of Quezaltepeque was represented by eleven priests, two religious sisters, one seminarian, and sixteen laypeople. Those attending from the parish of Aguilares were Rutilio, two other members of the missionary team, a Jesuit theology student, and seven laypeople.

Archbishop Chávez confirmed the organizing commission named by the senate;[134] the commission was responsible for documenting the activities of the week and handling the motions presented. A commission of synthesis was named to sum up the contributions of each day and prepare the final document. The daily activity of the week consisted in relatively brief talks followed by break-out sessions in which fifteen groups reflected on and discussed the material presented, working from a set of questions.

The first day, dedicated to study of the national reality, included three talks: "Criteria and Principles for Grasping the Reality," by Father Jesús García; "Interpreting the National Reality" by Román Mayorga, rector of the UCA; and "Interpreting Our Continent," also by García. The small groups discussed (1) the social divisions in the archdiocese and their consequences and (2) the influence of the economy and politics on religion. The discussions of the first day made evident the great need that existed to promote and train laypeople as pastoral agents and to create Christian communities committed to seeking "integral salvation."

Rutilio initiated the labors of the second day with a presentation on the nature of popular religiosity and its Christology. In his talk, he defended the importance of starting from the cultural base of popular religiosity even when it tended to favor fatalism, individualism, and divisiveness. These elements were no doubt an obstacle to change, but popular religiosity also had elements that favored change. The correct attitude, therefore, was to struggle against the negative elements and promote the positive ones. In the afternoon session, Rutilio raised some questions about traditional conceptions of God, Christ, the church, and evangelization.

The third day was dedicated to theological reflection on the two themes treated in the previous days, the national reality and popular religiosity, in light

---

133 Grande, "Report on the Activities of the Senate 1974–1977."
134 Bishop Rivera, Ricardo Urioste, Fabián Amaya, and Ástor Ruiz, executive secretary.

of a talk presented by one Brother Gil: "Christology as the Basis of a New Ecclesiology That Is Fundamentally Evangelization." The groups discussed various subjects: the meaning of liberation in Genesis, Exodus, and the prophets; the origins of religious conflicts in the archdiocese; the national reality and the religious reality of the country, viewed according to the criteria of Jesus Christ. In the afternoon, the groups identified what they thought were the major temptations of the archdiocese: triumphalism, return to the past, monopoly of sacramental power, manipulation of the poor, restraint of the clergy out of fear of government repression, preservation of sacramental ministry for economic reasons, splurging of money on patronal feasts, the divisiveness of party politics, and the favoring of those who follow the pastor but not Jesus Christ. The groups also identified clear signs of liberation: people committed to service of the poor, the UCA, the testimony of the pastoral agents, the pastoral letters, the *Justice and Peace* bulletin, the new line adopted by the archdiocesan weekly *Orientación*, the morning prayer on radio station YSAX, and the courses on human development.

The fourth day of the week was dedicated to examining the work of evangelization. Fabián Amaya presented the key aspects of an evangelization that was "liberating," and Juan R. Vega spoke about the "Social and Global Dimensions of Evangelization." The small groups pointed out that the topics most often treated in traditional evangelization were personal conversion, individualistic morality, vertical love for God, the divinity of Christ, eschatology disconnected from history, assistance-type charity, obedience to authority, and ritual. On the other hand, the topics neglected were the social reality, the social problems, and the transformative power of the Gospel. The major deviations pointed out by the groups were assistance-type charity, excessive insistence on heaven, absence of *aggiornamento*,[135] and the church's failure to listen to the faithful, consider their circumstances, or help them in the process of personal maturation. The final recommendation was that pastoral agents should receive an integral formation. In the afternoon session, the groups reflected on three more themes: the relationship between evangelization and social problems, the evangelization of oppressed majorities and privileged minorities, and the role of lay pastoral agents in evangelization.

The final day of the week was dedicated to drawing conclusions. The themes that dominated the discussion were the creation of Christian communities; the selection, formation, and accompaniment of pastoral agents; and the establishment of an archdiocesan pastoral council. The assembly accepted the senate's proposal that a majority of the council be laypeople, as the Holy See had specified. It was thus decided that the pastoral council would be made up of the bishops, twelve priests, and nineteen laypeople. It was also recommended that the

---

135 *Aggiornamento*, meaning "bringing up to date," was a key word used during the Second Vatican Council to indicate the need to relate the church to the modern world.

council coordinate closely with the vicariates and that the priests on the council be recompensed for lost income due to work they did for the council.

The final document of the pastoral ministry week, "Reflections of the Archdiocesan Pastoral Ministry Week,"[136] was edited by Bishop Rivera, Amaya, and Rutilio, who was nominated by the senate. The text included the talks, the contributions of the groups, and a general plan for collaborative pastoral ministry. Doubtlessly influenced by the experience of the previous pastoral ministry week, the commission did not present the reflections as a complete, definitive treatise on evangelization, much less a script with magical solutions. The document was approved by the bishops and given to the senate on February 16, 1976; the senate in turn presented it to the monthly meeting of clergy on February 24. But the pastoral ministry week did not stop there: the vicariates, anxious to continue the reflections begun in 1974, proposed to study carefully the results of the week and delve deeper into certain themes. The pastoral ministry week thus gave rise to an open-ended process during which various pastoral options were suggested and tried.[137]

The value of the document, "Reflections of the Archdiocesan Pastoral Ministry Week," was not that it revealed new and original realities; its great value resided in the fact that its contents resulted from the reflection of some three hundred laypersons, priests, religious, and bishops, most of whom were directly involved in pastoral work. In the course of the week, the parish of Aguilares was especially recognized for its pastoral work, and appreciation was shown for the generous collaboration of the team and above all the laity of the parish in preparing the week. At the meeting called in late December 1975 to prepare the vicariate's participation in the pastoral week, the parish of Aguilares had offered a series of carefully elaborated expositions on the Salvadoran social reality, the religious typologies, and various pastoral tendencies. The parish paradoxically downplayed the various crises provoked by the prophetic impact of the evangelization process. The general impression, both in the vicariate and during the pastoral ministry week, was that "these people are doing extremely well; that's what we want to do too."

The "Reflections" document inverted the order of themes and began with popular religiosity. It reaffirmed Rutilio's thesis that evangelization was not possible without taking popular religiosity into account, since that was the reality of the people. According to Medellín, the type of pastoral ministry associated with that religiosity emphasized preservation of the faith through the sacraments but put little stress on instruction. While appreciating the efforts made by that type of ministry, "Reflections" insisted on the need to discern the various elements

---

136 "First Week of Pastoral Ministry of the Archdiocese of San Salvador, January 5–10, 1976: Reflections on the Archdiocesan Pastoral Ministry Week," San Salvador, 1976.
137 "First Week of Pastoral Ministry of the Archdiocese of San Salvador, January 5–10, 1976," 1–2.

of popular religiosity in order to see which were valid, which could be rescued, and which were anachronistic and unhelpful. Preserving popular religiosity simply because it had at one time been valid and useful would be committing an injustice against both the past and the present. Not all the elements of popular religiosity were equally legitimate; indeed, some of them militated against true evangelization. Ultimately, the criterion for judging the elements of popular religious was their fidelity to the Gospel.[138]

"Reflections" was generally critical of popular religiosity, considering erroneous its concept of a miracle-working God who on the one hand was paternalistic and protective and on the other terrible and punishing. The document discarded this mistaken conception, affirming instead that God was a Father who loved and liberated humankind and was deeply concerned about human suffering. Human beings, created by God in his image and likeness, were called to cooperate with him in transforming the world. The false image of God that prevailed in popular religiosity needed to be corrected so that the people might overcome the temptation to fatalism and their exaggerated tendency to sacralize persons (thus making people submissive and easy to manipulate), to sacralize nature (thus absolutizing the right to private property), and to sacralize times and places (thus fostering superstition and a mythic worldview).[139]

Corresponding to that false idea of God, the document continued, was a false idea of Christ, which varied according to the social background of the believers. The economically privileged thought of Christ as divine more than human, and they imagined him dwelling only in heaven and in churches. For them, raw human reality in its historical concreteness was something foreign to Christ. Their Christ was the Christ of the good death, the Christ of good hope, the consoler and the forgiver; he was a Christ of individualistic morality who healed bad consciences. Such characteristics made him very useful to those who had a monopoly on power. For their part, the poor, dispossessed majority believed in a Christ who was crucified but not risen; a Christ who taught resignation and hope in the hereafter; a Christ before whom they laid down, with exaggerated piety, all their worries and frustrations. They also believed in a kingly Christ, "glorious and majestic," who in no way corresponded to the prophet Zechariah's vision of divine royalty or to the humble gesture of the Jesus who knelt down and washed the feet of his disciples. The document declared that the archdiocese rejected such conceptions since they lent themselves to manipulation, justified unfair social differences, and fostered devotions that diluted Christianity with superstition.[140]

---

138 "First Week of Pastoral Ministry of the Archdiocese of San Salvador, January 5–10, 1976," 4–5.
139 "First Week of Pastoral Ministry of the Archdiocese of San Salvador, January 5–10, 1976," 5–7.
140 "First Week of Pastoral Ministry of the Archdiocese of San Salvador, January 5–10, 1976," 6–8.

To these conceptions of God and Christ there also corresponded a conception of the church. Some progress had been made in overcoming the idea that true worship of God could take place only in churches, but the idea of church as the people of God had still not taken hold: the pyramidal vision of church persisted, one in which the laity existed on the bottom. The priests themselves had in large measure contributed to those misconceptions, presenting themselves as gifted with magical powers. Ecclesiastical power had historically been conceived and exercised as privilege and not service, with the result that the people passively submitted while the power itself was usurped and used by privileged social groups.[141]

Uncritical catechesis had fostered those false conceptions, leaving the people highly conformist and thus easy to manipulate by those in power. Not everything was negative, however; there were also experiences of true evangelization. The pastoral situation in the archdiocese required changes that would introduce it to the vital spirit of Vatican II, Medellín, the encyclical *Evangelii nuntiandi* (especially no. 31), as well as to the pastoral letters of Archbishop Chávez, entitled "The Responsibility of the Laity in the Temporal Order" and "Inflation in El Salvador and the Christian Conscience." It was not a question of introducing a great many changes, but only those that were considered necessary, and they would always be implemented in a planned way. The document also stated that it was important to adopt a uniform archdiocesan practice for the administration of sacraments, with the aim of promoting evangelization, fostering the community dimension, and avoiding superstition.

In its second part, "Reflections" treated the divisions in the archdiocese, arguing that the diverse conceptions of God, Christ, and the church corresponded to a deep division in society, between a privileged minority and an impoverished majority. Even more serious than the simple division between rich and poor were the growing tensions between the two poles, which were tending to degenerate into open violence. The document condemned all types of violence but also distinguished three types of violence, following the analysis of Ellacuría. The first type was the primordial violence that originated in the structure of social classes; its internal dynamism was therefore institutional. The preservation of this unjust structure required the second type of violence, repressive force, "often crude and cruel and ending in bloodshed whenever the people, long voiceless, attempt to make themselves heard and claim their rights." Such repressive violence inevitably provoked the third type of violence: the revolutionary violence that seeks to right age-old wrongs. Such violence was an understandable response to the other kinds, though at times it could become vindictive and destructive since it was giving vent to frustration that had accumulated over generations. Thus,

---

141 "First Week of Pastoral Ministry of the Archdiocese of San Salvador, January 5–10, 1976," 10.

revolutionary violence, while unwanted, had become inevitable for those who were working to build a more just society.[142]

The pastoral ministry week recognized that the church was seriously affected by the social conflict. The clergy were being classified as good or bad, democratic or communist, native-born or foreign, apolitical or subversive—depending on the stances they took regarding unjust structures. Christians were being judged "good" if they kept quiet and "bad" if they talked too much. Most dangerous, however, were the attempts to utilize the church by manipulating the pastoral agents. The church was accorded praise and respect when the government was able to get it to serve its interests, but if the church showed itself to be independent, the government accused it of abandoning its mission and being subversive. The document took note of how the government was promoting Protestant groups and likeminded Catholic movements as a way of countering an archdiocesan church that was becoming ever more independent of government influence.

In its last section, the "Reflections" document summed up the options that had been made during the pastoral ministry week. The archdiocesan assembly had made a primary option for evangelization, following the directives of *Evangelii nuntiandi*. The main aim of the evangelization was to build up base Christian communities by enlisting the collaboration of lay pastoral agents. To that end, the assembly recommended that good use be made of the diverse manifestations of popular religiosity for evangelizing the communities and for promoting both personal and communal change. The assembly urged the clergy to draw close to the people and to remain at their side so as to be able to discover and evangelize their most positive qualities. The assembly concluded its reflections by declaring that the changes would not be long in coming and would be stupendous.[143]

The success of the evangelization would depend on the clergy's willingness to allow the laity to collaborate actively in doing pastoral ministry and fomenting Christian base communities. The assembly proposed that laypeople be empowered and be given a good formation in a mature, authentic faith, and that this be done in their own communities and parishes since the best school was pastoral practice. In this regard, the assembly placed special emphasis on women and young people. It also made a strong option for Christian base communities, insisting that they were to be not so much "managed" as "accompanied" in their process of growth and solidarity. Warnings were issued about the dangers of elitism, sectarianism, and other types of "vanguard" mentality that tended to manipulate and coerce the people. Any vanguard that existed should be in function of and at the service of the majority. The assembly also

---

142 "First Week of Pastoral Ministry of the Archdiocese of San Salvador, January 5–10, 1976," 18.
143 "First Week of Pastoral Ministry of the Archdiocese of San Salvador, January 5–10, 1976," 12–13.

recommended, in passing, that the seminary be fully integrated into the pastoral ministry of the archdiocese.

Since these options required a revision of archdiocesan structures, the assembly recommended that the new pastoral guidelines be first implemented in the cathedral, some sanctuaries, and the chapels of Catholic schools. The assembly also asked that vicars be empowered to remove pastors and also to evaluate the pastoral work of religious in their jurisdictions. It was recommended that the bishops be more demanding of pastors and vicars, that they remove without delay those opposed to the pastoral line of the archdiocese, and that they create new parochial, vicarial, and archdiocesan entities for promoting these options of the pastoral ministry week. While the assembly did not reach agreement about the mechanism for selecting the members of such entities, it affirmed that, whatever the procedure, the people of God be actively involved.

The follow-up of the pastoral ministry week was left in the hands of the vicariates. The assembly recommended that the vicariates gradually but firmly implement the options agreed on; the important thing was that they be effective. The vicariate of Quezaltepeque met several times during 1976 to discuss popular organization, a burning question in the zone due to its broad reach and its conflictive nature. During one of its meetings, the vicariate received delegates from several popular organizations, listened to their presentations, and discussed with them their principles and their plans. They found the presentation of FECCAS unconvincing, while that of the FAPU was persuasive. Since the other organizations had no significant presence in the vicariate, their presentations had little relevance.

A polarized debate took place in the vicariate around FECCAS and FAPU, but instead of clarifying matters, it caused confusion, largely because of the divided sympathies of the pastors themselves. Three or four pastors were collaborating with FECCAS, two preferred FAPU, and two were indifferent. Among those favoring FECCAS was Marcelino Pérez, who had recently joined the missionary team of Aguilares and who was also meeting with pro-FECCAS priests outside the vicariate. The two pastors who worked with FAPU had concelebrated a memorial Mass for that organization to commemorate the massacre of July 30, 1975.

∼

Resuming its ordinary activities on March 16, 1976, the senate spent the following weeks, in accord with the assembly's instructions, preparing the materials to be used by the parishes during the coming Holy Week. Suddenly, though, the senate became paralyzed. To the surprise of everyone, Archbishop Chávez named by decree the members of the various commissions that would eventually spawn the archdiocesan pastoral council. Among those nominated was Rutilio, who was named to the commission on pastoral ministry and missions.[144] Some senators were perplexed by the archbishop's actions since they were quite contrary to the spirit of the pastoral ministry week, as well as to the agreement made at the first clergy meeting after the assembly. At that meeting, which Chávez had attended, it was decided that each vicariate would name its own council members, and that these would include laypeople who had taken part in the pastoral ministry week. The idea was to move upward from the bases toward the formation of the archdiocesan council.

Despite the uncertainty caused by the archbishop's actions, the senate continued to work with the vicariates and the clergy in their monthly meetings. For that purpose, the senate named a full-time executive secretary and held a series of meetings with the more problematic vicariates, that is, the ones having difficulty in forming lay pastoral agents or in finding candidates for the pastoral council.[145] In the senate's second meeting with the vicariates, the question of political involvement arose. Since in the previous meeting Archbishop Chávez had stated that priests were bad politicians and so produced bad politicians, the senate proposed to the vicars that they deliberate on the relationship between priesthood and politics.[146]

The question was a crucial one, not because the church had raised it but because the political situation of the country was forcing it onto the church's agenda. The parish of Aguilares was a good example of the consequences of political militancy. The military regime was accusing the pastors of being subversives and communists. Months before the archbishop had raised the question of priests and politics, the senate had formed a commission—Rutilio, Amaya, and Urioste—to analyze the political implications of evangelization and the role of priests in popular organizations. The senate had preferred not to raise the question at clergy meetings at that time since it is was just emerging and required further reflection.[147]

Accordingly, in the senate's second meeting with the vicariates, the vicar of La Merced, addressing Archbishop Chávez's statement about priests and politics, argued that priests, as citizens, could not abstain from politics, but that as pastors they should not take sides so as not to divide the parish community. He added that the political options of Christians should be judged in light of church teaching. The vicars of Cuscatlán stated that, while prophecy required announcing and denouncing, priests should not get involved in partisan politics. The vicar of Ilopango was of the opinion that, just like Jesus, priests should opt for the poor, and that insofar as they did so, it was necessary to take sides. Rutilio for his

---

144 ACSI. "Agreement 19: Constitution of Archdiocesan Commissions and Councils," San Salvador, May 31, 1976.
145 ACSI. "Agreement 19: Constitution of Archdiocesan Commissions and Councils."
146 ACSI. "Act No. 31: Meeting of the Priests' Senate," San Salvador, August 25, 1976.
147 ACSI. "Act No. 29: Meeting of the Priests' Senate," San Salvador, June 15, 1976.

part argued that, even though the church, in contrast to political actors, was not seeking power, there was no way that an incarnated faith could remain estranged from the political reality or refrain from making a political option. Since there was little clarity on the question, the senate decided to continue the discussion at a later meeting.[148]

---

148 ACSI. "Act No. 32: Meeting of the Priests' Senate," San Salvador, September 21, 1976.

9. The Parish and the Popular Organizations

The parish missions profoundly imprinted three ideas on people's minds: faith requires fighting injustice, love of neighbor becomes concrete in the struggle on behalf of the oppressed, and all people have the right and the duty to aspire to a decent life. However, the missionary team was unable to gauge correctly—nor could it have done so—the social and political effects of evangelization or the actual magnitude of the country's economic and political crisis.

As the ideas planted by the missions and the subsequent courses took root, the rural poor began to think and act in totally new ways, or as they themselves said, "Now we are 'de-mastered.'" For generations, they had suffered oppression and exploitation without really understanding the reasons for them, but now they were able to analyze and reflect critically on their bitter experience. As the communities became more aware that their situation was cruelly unjust and therefore not willed or desired by God, they spoke out forcefully, as they had never done before. They resolved to claim their rights, to express their aspirations, and to change their situation.

The workers gained new awareness of their rights, but the injustice and the maltreatment on the plantations did not abate. As a result, new protests and conflicts broke out during the cane harvest of 1974–75. Administrators, supervisors, and foremen exceeded what was legally permitted in assigning task work; they failed to pay the minimum wage or to pay extra for overtime hours, the seventh day, or holidays; they avoided paying year-end bonuses and severance pay through diverse tricks; they forced workers to labor through Saturday but paid them only through Friday; they paid women and youngsters only half the wages they promised them; they fired or refused employment to those who dared to protest; they evicted the tenants of several plantations and destroyed their dwellings with the help of the National Guard and the civil authorities; and in some cases they even sprayed insecticide from the air over the plantation and the people living on it. These actions proved how little legal protection rural workers had. The labor code dedicated just a handful of articles to those who were permanently employed, and none at all to seasonal workers, who were the great majority on the plantations. Whenever the workers appealed to the Ministry of Labor, the inspectors who were sent out to investigate invariably sided with the plantation owners.[1]

The workers finally decided to send a public letter to President Molina, citing phrases taken from his own discourses and asking him to protect them as he had promised. Concretely, they asked him to guarantee them stable employment in the places where they had resided for many years, to refrain from repressing

---

1   Cabarrús, *Génesis de una revolución*, 168ff.

those who denounced abuses, and to put an end to the intimidation of a colonel who was trying to force them off lands they had held for decades. The press refused to publish the letter, even as a paid advertisement. The labor conflicts during the 1974–75 harvest overwhelmed the parish, which felt itself under strong pressure since the workers were demanding that the parish make a firm commitment to their struggles.[2]

Agrarian Organization: FECCAS

FECCAS had its origin in the National Union of Catholic Workers, an organization that since 1964 had been dedicated to the education and formation of small farmers in the departments of San Salvador, La Libertad, and Cabañas. In its first congress, held in Guacotecti (Cabañas) in 1965, the organization set up an independent federation of local farmworkers' leagues. In 1968, this federation supported the steelworkers' strike at a factory in Zacatecoluca and also the national teachers' strike. Soon after that, however, the National Union of Catholic Workers dissolved as the result of corruption, and the federation of farmworkers' leagues disbanded. At that point, FECCAS brought the leagues together again and presented itself as an alternative organization whose goal was to struggle for social change and concretely for agrarian reform. In practice, the federation's main concern was the defense of workers' rights; it supported the Christian Democratic Party, and it associated itself successively with different organizations.[3]

In mid-1974, another popular front was formed to fight against the high cost of living. Called the Front for United Popular Action (FAPU), it included organizations such as the Communist Party, the teachers' union (Andes-June 21), the University Front of Revolutionary Salvadoran Students (Frente Universitario de Estudiantes Revolucionarios Salvadoreños [FUERSA]) of the University of El Salvador, and the Revolutionary University Front July 30 (FUR-July 30) of the UCA. Also affiliated with FAPU was a group of priests that had formed as a result of the May 1 demonstration in Suchitoto, convoked by FUERSA to protest the high cost of living.

FAPU never managed to become consolidated. The teachers where the first to leave because of differences with FUERSA, but they were followed by the

---

2 Cabarrús, *Génesis de una revolución*,168ff.
3 Trade Union Federation of Salvadoran Workers (Federación Sindical de Trabajadores Salvadoreños [FESTRAS]), Union of Christian Workers (Unión de Obreros Cristianos [COPSINTRANS]), Latin American Federation of Christian Trade Unions (Central Latinoamericana de Sindicatos Cristianos [CLASC]), and also apparently the Salvadoran Trade Union Council (Consejo Sindical Salvadoreño [CONSISAL]) and the Latin American Federation of Workers (Central Latinoamericana de Trabajadores [CLAT]). FECCAS, "Charter of Principles," October 18, 1975.

Communist Party and Unitary Federation of Salvadoran Labor Unions (Federación Unitaria Sindical Salvadoreña [FUSS]), which left FAPU because of its decision not to participate in the elections. In the end, there remained only FUERSA, FECCAS, FUR-30, a group of dissident teachers, and a few priests. FECCAS, for its part, engaged in a new dynamic and acquired a nationwide dimension; until then, it had been confined to the Christian communities.

But FECCAS did not remain long in FAPU either. One year after FAPU's founding, an ideological conflict between the two university groups (FUERSA and FUR-30) concluded with a rupture between them. The two groups engaged in a prolonged terminological discussion that at times became highly dramatic. The question being debated was whether the correct term to characterize the dominant political regime was "fascist" or "fascistoid." They argued over which of the two terms provided the ultimate explanation of the country's problems and therefore showed the way to overcome them. FUERSA maintained that the defeat of fascism involved the defeat of the bourgeoisie, whereas FUR-30 asserted the contrary, that is, that defeat of the bourgeoisie involved the defeat of fascism. According to this latter position, the high cost of living should be analyzed within the context of bourgeois domination. The leaders of FECCAS, who until then had sought mainly to protect workers' rights, found their political horizons broadened by participating in this ideological discussion.

FAPU reacted to the ideological controversy by proposing to break FECCAS up into small local cells of five members each, thus making it easier to control the groups and remove them from the influence of FUR-30. FECCAS rejected the proposal after consulting with its bases, but FUERSA persisted, sending representatives to the villages. The villagers rejected the representatives saying that they had resolved not to listen to anyone lacking proper authorization. The leaders of both FECCAS and FUR-30 concluded that FAPU showed no promise of being able to expand its influence, and they realized that they would not grow either if they remained part of FAPU. Accordingly, they entered into contact with the Union of Rural Workers (Unión de Trabajadores del Campo [UTC]), a farmworker organization whose main strength was in the departments of San Vicente and Chalatenango. In May 1975, the national council of FECCAS, made up of the general secretaries of the bases, decided to leave FAPU.

FECCAS adopted democratic centralism as its principle of internal organization, so that its direction and operation were highly centralized. The ideological and practical orientations came from headquarters, and the bases had to accept them. FECCAS, however, also promoted and encouraged the active participation of the bases. It wanted the bases to study important matters, to make sure agreements were observed, to choose their own leaders, and to evaluate their work. The theoretical ideal of democratic centralism was that leadership would reflect the collective experience of the bases; there was even talk of collegial leadership. The practice, however, was different. As one small farmer concisely but brilliantly expressed it: "Centralism is when there is no time; democracy is when there is time to discuss something."[4] The real power of FECCAS became evident only in its mobilizations because the bases were, for the most part, left to themselves.

The presence and the activity of FECCAS were felt particularly in the parish of Aguilares. Most of the organization's member and leaders—certainly the most capable ones—came from the Christian communities. Without abandoning their Christian identity or their pastoral responsibilities, these leaders assumed responsibilities in the organization and took part in strictly political activities. The testimony of a delegate from El Matasano is clear:

> Fifteen days after the mission there was a large mobilization. [...] Groups of delegates came together, stating that some people were exploiters and others were the exploited. We began to discover the reality of our situation, and from there we saw the need to engage in protest, even though we were not organized or anything. We saw the need for a strike; that was the reason for the one in '74 in La Cabaña. Because of the threats from the authorities and the [National] Guard, we saw that organization was not just necessary but urgent. That's when the organization of the zone began in earnest.[5]

During the cane harvest of 1975–76, FECCAS called the work crews at La Cabaña and Colima out on strike on two occasions, demanding a reduction in the size of the tasks. Some two hundred FECCAS members accompanied the tenant families who went to the Legislative Assembly to ask that they not be evicted from their homes on the Colima plantation. FECCAS members also distributed flyers in the city of Aguilares and in the surrounding villages denouncing the maltreatment of workers on various plantations. Most of those who attended the demonstration and meeting in the city of Aguilares, called by FAPU for May 1, 1975, to celebrate its first anniversary, were members of FECCAS. On the walls of many houses in the city could be read the slogans shouted during the protest. That same May 1 there were also demonstrations in Suchitoto and in a village near Aguilares.

By the end of 1975, FECCAS had not only increased its membership in Aguilares but had also developed a surprising degree of organizational capacity. Most of the ten demonstrations that were held during 1976 took place in the parish of Aguilares. By the end of 1976, FECCAS had organized, just in the parish of Aguilares, twenty-three village bases with 639 members—493 men and 146 women—260 sympathizers, forty-six cadres, fifty-eight possible cadres, five contacts, and three collaborators. Each village base was organized into nine secretariats: general, organizational, finance, educational, propaganda, conflicts, cooperative, formation, and minutes/correspondence. Each village base belonged to a regional council, which had representation on the national executive council.

---

4   See Cabarrús, *Génesis de una revolución*.
5   Cabarrús, *Génesis de una revolución*, 168ff.

9. The Parish and the Popular Organizations

Most of the FECCAS members in Aguilares were poor farmers residing in the villages of Buena Vista, Las Huertas, Natividad-Los Quebrachos, El Líbano, and El Tule. They were not the poorest farmers for they enjoyed some economic security, thanks mainly to wages they earned on the plantations and to their own farming on land they owned or leased. FECCAS attracted these small farmers because membership in the organizations gave them a measure of power and prestige and opened up some possibility of upward social mobility. The plantation tenants, in contrast, were quite vulnerable, being very dependent on the good graces of the plantation. The extremely poor farmers, for their part, found the struggle just to survive so overwhelming that they had neither the energy nor the time for organization.

Despite the influence it seemed to exert, FECCAS depended greatly on what the Christian community of each village could provide it, and that was generally not much. At first, the organization's ideological force came from the parish of Aguilares, but later it came from the organization itself. A good part of its strength lay in its ability to mobilize small farmers and workers. Such exercise of power was limited, of course, since it depended on economic and political conditions that were beyond the members' control. Moreover, FECCAS was juridically quite vulnerable.

A major fact in the development and consolidation of FECCAS was the collaboration of several Jesuit scholastics who were studying at the UCA. The initial group of three scholastics working with the missionary team was augmented in early 1975 when a community of four theology students and a superior was set up in Aguilares, independent of the parish. These students helped to establish the first two bases for FECCAS. Apolinario Serrano, known as Polín and recognized as one of the best leaders of the parish, introduced the students to the community of El Líbano. Intuitive, restless, and independent, Polín was held in great esteem by the missionary team and also by Archbishop Romero, who rendered him homage in a homily given at the time of his murder. Polín at first was in contact with Boulang; he then became a delegate but was not chosen as a preparer due to internal divisions in his community. Polín introduced three Jesuit scholastics to his community as persons who wanted to work for the good of the people and to share whatever possessions they had. El Líbano soon became the first base of FECCAS, and soon thereafter Polín and a scholastic founded the second base in Los Gramales.

The work of the Jesuit scholastics among the rural poor was not directed by FECCAS, which at the time was too caught up in the bureaucracy typical of such organizations. The next two bases arose in similar fashion in El Jicarón and Buena Vista. The communities welcomed the theology students because of their close ties with the missionary team, but they soon perceived that the students were different from the team members. They were younger, more creative, more flexible, and more able to relate to the community leaders, who, like them, were young. The students' community was always open to visitors whereas the parish rectory had strict rules and was less welcoming. The sympathy and acceptance that the students enjoyed among the communities and their leaders gave rise to a certain rivalry with the missionary team.[6]

Toward the end of 1974, during the ideological battle with FAPU, the Jesuit scholastics and several university students of FUR-July 30 offered to give a seminar on political formation for FECCAS members. When their proposal was accepted, they planned the seminar and imparted it at the UCA. Contrary to the practice of the parish, the two hundred participants in the seminar were chosen by the organizers, without any previous survey or a dialogue with the bases. The seminar organizers explained that the communities had already identified their leaders and that the aims of the seminar were very different from those of the parish. During the seminar, the participants, divided into fifteen groups, analyzed and discussed the problematic national reality at length. They subsequently made the following resolutions: to get better organized in order to struggle for the radical transformation of the capitalist system; to establish a worker–farmer alliance by incorporating day-laborers and poor subsistence farmers; and to take part in a program of political formation in order to extend the reach of the organization. These resolutions meant a radical change in the orientation of FECCAS.

In mid-1976, eighteen months after the seminar and after an intense campaign of recruitment, a base of FECCAS existed in all the villages of the parish. This success is in large part explained by the organization being presented to the communities as the perfect instrument for making Christian community a reality. FECCAS was careful not to present itself as in any way discordant with Christian community or as opposed to the parish, though it did insist on its independence of the parish. By mid-1976, there were meetings in the villages almost every night. At times, the preparers were meeting with the delegates, or the people were receiving Christian formation in preparation for the sacraments. At other times, the members and sympathizers of FECCAS were receiving political formation. Often, two meetings were being held simultaneously, one of the parish and the other of the organization.

Other important reasons for the success of FECCAS in Aguilares were the growing discontent at the miserable living conditions, the enthusiasm generated by the success of the first protests, and greater awareness of the need to seek new ways to fight for basic human rights. The organization was quite skilled in knowing how to use the particular circumstances of each village to motivate its inhabitants, but the villagers themselves helped the process, for they placed their hopes for change in the organizing project and carried it out with determination.

---

6   ACSI. "Evaluation of Communities," October 1976; and Cabarrús, *Génesis de una revolución*, 159.

The most conscientious villagers pursued their formation in numerous courses, and the organizers visited the communities within the parish and outside the parish, creating new bases and seeking out new cadres. FECCAS thus carried out the arduous labor of political organization both in Aguilares and in zones beyond the parish limits.

The dynamic presence of FECCAS in the countryside was countered by the plantations and the local security forces, giving rise to new conflicts that became ever more intense. The plantations refused to employ known members of FECCAS. La Cabaña, for example, discriminated against workers because of their political affiliation. The foremen hired only "good folk," that is, "non-strikers," a category that excluded anyone who had ever protested. One worker complained: "I am the only one they don't employ, because two years ago we went on strike. The informers denounced me, and for that reason they don't give me any work." The larger plantations circulated lists of the workers who had gone on strike. The organizers encountered difficulty not only in getting work but also in leasing land and acquiring agricultural inputs such as seeds, fertilizers, and pesticides. Wage labor, leased land, and essential inputs were all crucial for the survival of the rural poor. The plantations took advantage of their needs to impose their own conditions, knowing that they could count on the collaboration of other poor farmers who were willing to inform on those who had organized. One man explained how he felt when he could get no work:

> What has made me be this way was that at the end of last year [1974] we worked in El Matasano, and there we held the first strike; it was about the pay for Saturday, which we got, and also about raising the wage to 2.75, which we didn't get. The next day I went there, and the supervisor arrived and asked me, "You, are you working?" I said, "Yes." He said, "You are not working, striker. Get out of here." I was impressed by that, and in that instant I was filled with anger. Right there I wanted to eliminate him, and the idea took root and got ever stronger.[7]

In La Cabaña and San Rafael, they fired any workers who were not affiliated with ORDEN, the regime's paramilitary organization. It was for that reason that many small farmers then decided to infiltrate the plantations.

The plantations also took measures against workers who attended the celebrations of the Word. "They sent spies to the meetings to see who was attending and then inform the foremen so no work would be given to those people. As a result, some no longer attend the celebrations. They only attend Mass once in a while, covertly." The agents of ORDEN were also keeping a close watch on the communities in the villages:

---

7   Cabarrús, *Génesis de una revolución*, 159ff., 168ff.

ORDEN arrived here last year [1975]. There are about thirty members. [...] The only thing they do is spy on the meetings and report more or less what is said there. In the beginning they were doing it surreptitiously, but no longer. [...] What they do is discredit the meetings of the Word and the organization. They say that it is subversive doctrine and that the organization is totally communist. They use those arguments to terrorize the people. [...] The National Guard has contact with the members of ORDEN.[8]

After the demonstration in Aguilares on May 1, 1975, the workers were told: "There's no work for you! Go ask your companions who are painting the signs! Let them give you work!"[9]

Sometimes, the presence of FECCAS represented an intolerable challenge for an organization like ORDEN, which was used to having a monopoly on local power. In El Jicarón, FECCAS challenged the power of the teacher, which until then had been indisputable. The teacher, who had ties with a powerful family in the village, not only owned nearly sixty *manzanas* of land but received several incomes: as director and teacher in a school; as local doctor; as president of ORDEN, which he had introduced into the village; and as the renter of his own house for meetings of the official party. The incomes had given him access to bank loans, which in turn gave him access to seed, fertilizer, and pesticide, which he sold on credit to others at above-market prices.[10]

The Repression of Popular Organizations

FECCAS spread quickly to other departments and became more active in the political life of the nation, along with other popular organizations of a revolutionary bent. FECCAS made its appearance on the national scene during the occupation of the cathedral of San Salvador on July 31, 1975, precisely at the moment when the democratic opening that had begun in the 1960s definitively closed and the country sank into a crisis that eventually led to a twelve-year civil war.

In July 1972, a few months before the missionary team assumed responsibility for the parish of Aguilares, a new military government had come to power; it had very little legitimacy due to outrageous electoral fraud. The democratic opening of the previous decade had allowed for the emergence and consolidation of a Salvadoran middle class that was demanding a quota of political power, but the military regime, backed by the oligarchy, was unwilling to cede to the middle-class's demands. In the early 1970s, social pressures seriously threatened the durability of the regime, which survived only by increasing the repression.

---

8   Cabarrús, *Génesis de una revolución*, 168ff.
9   Cabarrús, *Génesis de una revolución*, 168ff.
10 Cabarrús, *Génesis de una revolución*, 244.

The government of Colonel Arturo A. Molina introduced a legal mechanism to suppress political discussion in the Legislative Assembly; it also stripped the municipalities of the little autonomy they had, and it made it impossible for the opposition parties— Democracia Cristiana (Christian Democracy), Unión Democrática Nacionalista (Nationalist Democratic Union), and Movimiento Nacional Revolucionario (Revolutionary National Movement)—to attain power by popular vote.

Determined to close all spaces for political dissent and social protest, the government of Colonel Molina adopted an ever more repressive stance with respect to the trade unions, the university movements, the political opposition, and rural organizations. On July 19, 1972, shortly after the Molina government took office, it sent military forces into the University of El Salvador, after obtaining the backing of a Supreme Court resolution, a legislative decree, and several executive decrees. The pretext for the invasion was to seize arms and arrest guerrillas that were presumably on the campus, but they found neither. Nevertheless, they captured eight hundred persons, closed down the university, and sent the authorities and the faculty into exile. Two months later, the government exiled twenty-one trade unionists and several political leaders of the opposition. In June 1973, it deported eighteen more citizens. The government justified the clearly unconstitutional deportations by declaring a "reason of state," while the Supreme Court and the Legislative Assembly remained silent. From that point on, the government implemented de facto measures by means of the security forces, which were directed by hardline military officials.

The deportations were followed by the first "disappearances" of labor leaders and political figures of the opposition (Nationalist Democratic Union). Surveillance of urban and rural communities was increased, as was the harassment of the national teachers union (ANDES-June 21). Foreign priests were threatened, and lay Catholics who were committed to the church's social action suffered persecution. The government set up a community development agency for the purpose of penetrating the marginalized zones of San Salvador. In 1973, the security forces assaulted the seat of the Unitary Federation of Salvadoran Trade Unions.

The military regime's brutality was laid bare in two massacres of peasant farmers. The first took place in the hamlet of La Cayetana (near the village of León de Piedra, San Vicente) on the afternoon of November 29, 1974. Arriving on government and private vehicles, a large force of national guards and police opened fire on the houses, which they then searched. After aiming a fifty-one-millimeter mortar at the houses, they parked an army ambulance in the soccer field. As the villagers returned from their labors in the field, they saw the troops and fled in terror toward the slopes of the San Vicente volcano, but they were pursued by the attackers, who caught up with them in a place known as Potrerillo. The troops captured twenty-five men and took them to a makeshift school, where they threw them on the floor and stomped on them while crying out blasphemies. One man, who dared to declare to his torturers that God would punish them, was beaten with even greater fury, and the soldiers ridiculed him, saying, "Let God come down to defend you!" Twelve were stripped naked and tied up, but then they were set free after being sprayed with teargas. The others were disappeared. Later on, other villagers arrived from the fields, and when they realized what was happening, they took refuge in nearby dwellings. The troops shot and killed seven men and hacked two more to death with machetes while their wives looked on; after loading their remains into sacks, they carried them away. The punitive operation left seven dead, thirteen disappeared, and a population that was absolutely terrified. The next day, the Ministry of Defense reported that the troops had been ambushed by common criminals; it stated that several people had been killed (fewer than the actual number) but said nothing about those who had been captured and disappeared.

The other massacre was at Tres Calles in the department of Usulután on June 21, 1975. On that day before dawn, forty soldiers and several members of ORDEN attacked a house where they claimed there were arms. They killed the father in the house and three of his sons; the fourth son, thirteen years old, they brutally beat. They also killed the father in a nearby house. Neither of these two massacres was investigated by the government.

The following months witnessed a series of attacks, disappearances, and murders committed against union and political leaders associated with the opposition. In July, the security forces attacked the leaders and members of a union in a furniture factory; they arrested six unionists and kidnapped one from a psychiatric hospital, where he had been recovering from tortures suffered in prison. In August, Carlos Carballo, leader of the April 22 community, in the northern part of San Salvador, disappeared after being captured. On September 26, Rafael Aguiñada, opposition deputy and secretary general of a trade union federation, was murdered by the paramilitary organization Armed Forces of Anti-communist Liberation (Fuerzas Armadas de Liberación Anticomunista—Guerra de Eliminación [FALANGE]). At dawn on November 2, bombs were exploded at the headquarters of Aguiñada's federation and at the offices of two opposition political parties. The mutilated corpse of labor leader Feliciano Sánchez appeared at a tourist site on the outskirts of the capital.

In December, national guards and police opened fire on unarmed workers on the Santa Barbara Hacienda in Chalatenango; the workers had declared a strike demanding better wages and improved working conditions, including better food and more reasonably sized tasks. Initially, the workers, organized by FECCAS, asked to speak with the administrator, but he left the scene. Two hours later, five police officers and national guards arrived and attacked the men who were addressing the three hundred workers with the help of a megaphone. When the workers seized their machetes to defend themselves, a brawl broke out. Two police and several workers were wounded, a policeman and a worker were

9. The Parish and the Popular Organizations

captured, several persons were beaten, and two workers were disappeared. When security reinforcements arrived, the workers dispersed amid great confusion.[11]

In the first half of 1976, the regime increased the pressure on the rural poor with the help of ORDEN. In the department of Chalatenango, members of ORDEN forced several families to abandon their homes, and they killed four villagers in El Portillo over the course of one month. The National Guard arrested and savagely tortured seventeen villagers in Arcatao, Chalatenango; among them were five women, two of whom were pregnant.

It was in this context that FECCAS made its appearance on the national scene. The first of a long series of occupations of the cathedral of San Salvador took place on July 31, 1975, just as the celebrations for the feast of the Divine Savior of the World were beginning. Several popular organizations occupied the church after a concelebrated Mass commemorating the students killed by the army the day before. The soldiers had opened fire against a peaceful demonstration of high-school and university students on Avenida Universitaria. The massacre aroused tremendous public sentiment. Many organizations and institutions repudiated the slaughter in paid notices published in the national press. The occupation of the cathedral the next day also produced great commotion.

The intense emotions that motivated the occupation dissipated quickly. The hegemonic aspirations of FAPU and other organizations made coordinated action impossible, especially during the subsequent negotiations. Two blocs formed: one consisted of FAPU and the coalition of parties called United National Opposition, and the other encompassed FECCAS, FUR, the July 19 Revolutionary University Students (UR-19),[12] the Movement of Revolutionary Secondary School Students (Movimiento Estudiantil Revolucionario de Secundaria [MERS]), the National Association of Salvadoran Educators (Asociación Nacional de Educadores Salvadoreños [ANDES]), the UTC, and the Union of Slum Dwellers (Unión de Pueblo de Tugurios [UPT]). Both blocs vied for support of forces outside the occupied cathedral, so that hegemony was exercised by those who mobilized more support. FECCAS and UTC had broad backing from their bases, and the political parties had support in the city markets. FAPU, however, had very little outside support.

After taking the cathedral, the occupiers demanded, as their conditions for leaving, that the minister of defense, the directors of the National Guard and the Finance Police, and the rector of the University of El Salvador all be dismissed; that forty thousand *colones* be given as indemnification to the families of those massacred in Chinamequita, La Cayetana, and Tres Calles; and that an unspecified amount be given to the families of the students killed on July 30.

---

11   ACSI. Rutilio Grande, notes.
12   The UR-19 was composed of students of the University of El Salvador. The students of the UCA and the national university had already held joint seminars.

The mediation between the occupiers and the government was handled by Archbishop Chávez with the support of Román Mayorga, vice-rector of the UCA. The archbishop obtained the freedom of twelve detained persons and the return of the body of one of the students murdered on July 30, but the government refused to concede anything more. President Molina refused to consider any dismissals or indemnifications, but he guaranteed the physical safety of those occupying the church and the surrounding area. He subsequently agreed to name a commission to investigate the events of July 30; it would consist of two persons nominated by the president's office and three nominated by the occupiers. On August 5, as the occupiers were preparing to leave the cathedral, the president backtracked with respect to the investigatory commission and demanded immediate acceptance of the other concessions, threatening to attack the people gathered around the cathedral otherwise. Since the negotiation process was exhausted and the organizations felt that they had achieved as much as they could, the occupiers opted to leave the cathedral, which they did that same day, after holding a meeting in front of the cathedral.

The leaders of the occupation evaluated it positively since they had succeeded in denouncing government repression during the patronal feast of San Salvador. By occupying the cathedral, which sheltered the image of the national patron, the popular organizations had been able to relate their cause to the Christian faith. Also, the families of those killed and of those disappeared had been able to give their testimony during the days of the occupation.

At that same meeting on August 5, the organizations announced the creation of the Popular Revolutionary Bloc (Bloque Popular Revolucionario [BPR]), which from the start was an organization that zealously pursued ideological purity and so was very wary of alliances and compromises. Its discrepancies with other groups that claimed to be revolutionary—and thus in sole possession of the "truth"—helped the BPR preserve its doctrinal purity but also introduced division and confusion. The adversaries of the BPR were not only the "reactionary bourgeoisie" but also the opposition parties and, of course, FAPU, for the bourgeoisie counted on the collaboration of reformist institutions like FAPU in its efforts to perpetuate capitalist exploitation.[13] The BPR criticized the political opposition as seeking merely to rescue democratic institutions, when in reality such institutions were a capitalistic façade that not only kept the class struggle contained within bourgeois legality but also narcotized and demoralized the masses. The anti-fascist struggle of FAPU was not an option for the BPR because FAPU's lack of vision had led it into the revisionist trap of the right. Similarly unacceptable was the adventurism of the Revolutionary Army of the People (Ejército Revolucionario del Pueblo [ERP]),

---

13   Unión Comunal Salvadoreña, Instituto Salvadoreño de Fomento Cooperativo, Asociación de Maestros Democráticos, etc.

which had called for the masses to rise up in arms and declare the existence of a revolutionary situation.[14]

Over against all these other forces, the BPR presented itself as the revolutionarily correct political platform, the only organization that offered an alternative to the traditional political parties and to elections as a means for obtaining power. The alternative it offered consisted in an alliance of workers and peasant farmers, led by the proletarians. The real power of the BPR lay in its revolutionary ideology and its ability to mobilize and organize the masses. When conditions were right, it was indeed capable of mobilizing many people, especially the rural poor. Without resorting to weapons, the massive mobilizations and urban strikes were effective instruments of pressure, and they had national repercussions. Rural strikes did not have the same impact as urban ones since the rural zones had so many unemployed people desperately seeking work. A retaliatory tactic was burning the cane fields, a common practice at that time, but one that could provoke increased surveillance on the plantations and cause greater repression.[15]

The division of the revolutionary left came about for two reasons: the indiscretions of some groups and the BPR's arrogant attitude toward other organizations. The BPR thought that its line would in the end prevail as the only correct one; the people themselves would prefer it since it best represented their interests. As has happened at other important junctures of history, ideology prevailed over reality, with negative consequences for the cause of the people. What was really needed—but was lacking—was constructive discussion, greater political openness, and a lot of political persuasion.[16]

Even though at first there was no direct connection between the BPR and the politico-military groups, the government and the oligarchy maliciously linked them together so as to convince the public that the suppression of both was necessary and acceptable. FECCAS was also an illegal organization, of course, but it limited its economic and social demands to those guaranteed by the Constitution. The BPR did ally itself finally with the guerrilla movement, but it did so only later, pressured by the need for better coordination. The BPR functioned mainly in the political sphere while the guerrillas waged a military campaign. For its part, the government, with the unconditional approval of the oligarchy—especially ANEP and the Agricultural Front of the Eastern Region (Frente Agropecuario de la Región Oriental [FARO])—mobilized the army, the security forces, and the paramilitary groups to combat all forms of popular organization.[17]

---

14 Cabarrús, *Génesis de una revolución*, 373ff.
15 Cabarrús, *Génesis de una revolución*, 373ff.
16 Cabarrús, *Génesis de una revolución*, 373ff.
17 Cabarrús, *Génesis de una revolución*, 390–91.

FECCAS and the Parish

Participation in the massive mobilizations in San Salvador and other cities provided the bases of FECCAS with inspiring and exciting political experience. Along with other groups of similar ideology, they denounced capitalist exploitation, urged people to join the revolutionary forces, recognized the extent of their own power, and above all realized that they were not alone in the struggle. The villages began to appear small to FECCAS activists; local problems seemed insignificant compared with the possibilities that opened up before them on the national scene. The neglect of village concerns was followed by an exodus from the Christian communities, and this had a negative impact on the work of the parish of Aguilares.

When the parishioners got involved in national politics, they took on a new political mentality, acquired a new language, drew apart from the bases and their needs, and had an ambiguous relationship with the parish. Following a line similar to that of the BPR, FECCAS identified the principal enemies of the people as the imperialist bourgeoisie and its ally, the creole bourgeoisie, while the immediate enemies were the landowner oligarchy and the "fascistoid" military regime. Among its revolutionary allies, FECCAS counted the working class, the most exploited layers of the petit-bourgeoisie (that is, small producers and merchants), and the most oppressed sectors of the middle class (that is, teachers and students).

The organizations soon began to speak glibly about hegemony, the bourgeoisie, imperialism, and socialism, but the true meaning of the terms was grasped only by the initiated:

> I have heard that there are some who think that the people don't understand what socialism is. Those who are involved in the struggle have some idea, but those who aren't have no idea. Of course, if you go to meetings, you hear things, but those who never go to meetings are lost. The people who attend FECCAS meetings already have an idea of what socialism is.[18]

The language of the organizations functioned as a syntactical ideology, that is, an ideology of phrases created without much analysis. The words took on an almost magical power so that their mere possession made it unnecessary to corroborate their relation to reality. The already initiated zealously transmitted the key terms of the language to the neophytes.

Socialism, for example, was considered something good and therefore something worth fighting for, but the meaning of the concept was not at all clear:

> There in the village, people imagine that socialism is something good, but they don't know what it is. The same with revolution: they don't know what it is. The organization sees these two things as the way to go. Yes, the people

---

18 Cabarrús, *Génesis de una revolución*, 277ff.

say that socialism is a good thing, but if there are two people who know something about socialism, that's a lot. The same goes with revolution. Most people just think about the struggle, but they don't know what the struggle is—the demonstrations, the strikes, the resistance to evictions. So the struggle moves forward, but it's hard to see where it's going. The organization encourages the people to help one another defend their rights, and that's the way the struggle is seen.[19]

The testimony of this veteran of the struggle shows that the rural poor were mobilized for the defense of their rights more than for the pursuit of utopian ideals. They had a much clearer perception of their immediate interests than their class interests, as important as these latter were for theoretical analysis.

The lack of clarity gave rise to serious deviations. The leadership of FECCAS made the dangerous assumption that all its militants understood clearly the need for linking the people's most basic (class) interests with their more immediate interests, but that assumption only revealed the problematic nature of the relationship between leadership and bases. In reality, the dynamics of national politics tended to increase the distance between the leaders and their bases in the countryside; the leaders of FECCAS neglected the immediate needs and aspirations of the villagers in order to resolve what they considered the universal contradiction, which supposedly affected everyone equally. Local problems lacked relevance and consequence compared with the enormous challenges facing the nation. Thus, in planning massive mobilizations, little thought was given by the leaders to the importance of the villages, nor was concern shown for the consequences of participation for the villagers: they might well forfeit personal security and economic welfare, as well as be subjected to stricter surveillance. The organization simply demanded a quota of participants and a definite economic contribution, requirements that admitted no discussion. Organizational development was measured by the same limited criteria, that is, by the number of meetings and mobilizations, and by the size and combativeness of these latter.[20]

As a result of the distance between leadership and bases, the great diversity of local situations tended to be homogenized by the organization. All localities were thought to have the same problems, so that the organization's manner of dealing with them was superficial and simplistic. Moreover, the distinctive behavior and language of the cadres made them appear clearly superior to the other villagers; they were perceived as now moving in different circles. Nevertheless, the organization suffered desertions and disillusionments, largely because the combination of desperate living conditions, increased surveillance, and brutal repression was leading to armed rebellion.

---

19   Cabarrús, *Génesis de una revolución*, 390–91.
20   Cabarrús, *Génesis de una revolución*, 275ff.

The relationship between FECCAS and the parish was complex and problematic. The organization not only underwent a sort of re-founding in the parish but it expanded greatly and became more consolidated thanks to the material and ideological support, as well as the protection, provided by the parish. The ideological kinship of the parish and FECCAS, which was evident from the time of the missions and the courses, was due mainly to the influence of the missionary team and its collaborators, mainly university students and Jesuit scholastics. An organization like FECCAS could not have developed and solidified as it did without the protection of the parish: the security forces and the paramilitary squads would have done away with it quickly. Despite their close bonds, neither the parish nor the organization fully grasped the real nature of their relationship, and they were hindered from understanding it better by the speed of events in which they were directly involved.[21]

Naturally, FECCAS, given its mainly political nature, soon sought to be autonomous and so distanced itself from the parish, provoking incomprehension within the missionary team and causing problems for the parish itself. Those most committed to the parish complained that the carefully developed structure of communities, delegates, and preparers was losing much of its leadership as some of the best pastoral agents became cadres of FECCAS. It was not the organization's intention to rob the parish of its leaders, but it desperately needed capable people to direct its activities at the national level, and the parish had them.

FECCAS and the parish drew closer again when harsh repression forced the organization to seek momentary refuge under the wings of the parish, but soon after that the organization distanced itself again, despite losing strength. The government was oblivious to these changes: as far as it was concerned, the parish and the organization were one and the same. And as it happened, in the villages the Christian communities and the organized members were living the same reality:

> There [in the village] we delegates are the same people who are organized. We promote the movement of the Word of God, and we promote the organization because we are not going to separate the two things. [...] The Adorers were happy with the mission, but when they saw that there was a need to make a commitment, they turned back. They thought that it was just like before, just a matter of going to nocturnal adoration. Some quit, and some are still there. They quit when they saw that they had to commit themselves to something more concrete. [...] Even some of the "Bible folk" left, people who had been reading the Bible for fourteen years. After the mission arrived, there were some who became Protestants.[22]

---

21 Cabarrús, *Génesis de una revolución*, 277ff.
22 Cabarrús, *Génesis de una revolución*, 277ff.

9. The Parish and the Popular Organizations

It was only later, after FECCAS members left the parish ambience, that they came to appreciate the pastoral labor of the missionary team. When they moved to different regions, they realized that the parish was a key factor in laying the foundation for political work. It was the missions and the courses that had helped to diminish the fatalistic and magical mindset of the rural poor:

> No Protestants have joined FECCAS. They don't belong to ORDEN either. They say that there is no need to organize, that it's enough just to pray—and we are saved! They say that all these things come from God, and only God knows why. I've talked with them, and that's what they tell me. God, they say, allows there to be good men and bad men. That's the way it has to be.[23]

The activists dedicated themselves to expanding FECCAS beyond Aguilares with an unnerving zeal that increased in intensity as they gained experience of power at the national level. They invaded other parishes and other zones with missionary zeal and with methods similar to those used by the parish. The coordinators of these proselytizing campaigns took on the role of the priest, and on several occasions they even presented themselves as envoys of the parish of Aguilares.

Joining the organization was conceived of in terms of conversion. Those who were admitted professed their acceptance of the organization's mission, with all its consequences. They were told that this second conversion brought to fulfillment their earlier, religious conversion:

> I joined the organization [...] when I woke up and saw the need for change. [...] From the moment when you make the commitment, [...] you know that it is the people's struggle. If we don't join the people's struggle and don't take seriously our love for our children and the future generations, [...] how will they remember us? This is the struggle we've begun. Even if we don't see a change, maybe our children will bring it about. That's why I joined the organization. Most of my companions are clear about the role we play in the organization, and that's the way they feel. [...] We can't say that we're the leaders in a village or that we mobilize the people; there are people who have a better understanding of revolution than we do. From the moment someone says, "I'm a member," we are already talking about revolution because we are talking about change. We are at least beginning to quit all our vices, and we are collaborating in the sense that we're setting an example for others. When others see us in this situation, they see an example.[24]

A genuine process of conversion was taking place. The rural poor were waking up from their slumber and seeing the light. They then felt a desire and a willingness to give their lives for the cause of the people. Like religious conversion, political

---

23 Cabarrús, *Génesis de una revolución*, 277ff.
24 Cabarrús, *Génesis de una revolución*, 277ff.

conversion was leading people to the light; it motivated them to abandon their vices and dedicate their lives to constant struggle for the sake of the people. At that time in El Salvador, however, the decision of a political convert to give his life was much more radical than that of a religious convert because the political repression was becoming more ruthless by the day.

In the same way that religious conversion tended to evolve toward political conversion, Christian faith was evolving, to a greater or lesser extent, toward a type of socialist faith. But as the following testimonies show, socialism was understood less in terms of ideology than of claiming one's basic rights:

> Socialism is a society where people live as brothers and sisters, where there is no more exploitation, where labor is not sold cheap, where people have more food, clothing, and footwear. That is socialism. What is going to make socialism happen is organized struggle. Taking power will be very difficult for us, and keeping that power will be a great challenge.[25]
>
> Socialism means that we are all equal, that we care for those who are suffering, that there is medicine for everyone. It's not where some people work and others don't. It means having a government made up of those same people who work, people who know what the hard work of farming means. In socialism we have to have a good knowledge of the people whom we elect from among the workers, people who can administer well the distribution of the workers' production.[26]

Political conversion and socialist faith stirred great passion in many, to the point where they were willing to risk their lives.

Accordingly, a basic Christian mystique evolved in stages, first toward a Christian mystique with revolutionary aspects, and then toward a revolutionary mystique with Christian aspects. Each stage in this process meant a crisis of growth for FECCAS and also for the parish. This progression should not be understood as a rejection of the Gospel, of the church, or of the parish; it was simply the organization's attempt to achieve ideological autonomy as a necessary concomitant of organizational autonomy.

Rutilio's "Politics"

In June 1975, a previously unknown group called the Frente Religioso Conservador (Conservative Religious Front) claimed that Rutilio and Bengoechea—along with the pastors of Nejapa, Quezaltepeque, and Suchitoto—were guilty of subversive agitation. The priests were accused of "championing hatred and class violence" and of "tossing faith, charity, and love of God into the trash bin." The accusations appeared in a set of flyers circulated by several phantasmal

---

25 Cabarrús, *Génesis de una revolución*, 390–91.
26 Cabarrús, *Génesis de una revolución*, 390–91.

9. The Parish and the Popular Organizations

organizations. After two priests were killed in Olancho, Honduras, on June 25, 1975, another flyer appeared with the title "Be Alert, Good Catholics!" and the following message:

> Don't let yourselves be deceived. Those priests want to lead you to the slaughter by getting you into a confrontation like the one in Honduras or the one that happened in El Salvador in 1932, when thousands upon thousands of innocent country folk died. Believe in God, in your holy saint, and in the true Christian priests, not in these "phonies" who are deceiving you disgracefully for their own benefit and for that of the PDC [Christian Democratic Party].[27]

The accusers warned the Salvadoran priests that their subversive activity would bring them the same consequences as those suffered by the two priests in Olancho. Around the same time, the editors of *El diario de hoy*, one of the two most widely read Salvadoran papers, added their own commentary to the account of the events in Honduras that had been sent out by the Spanish news agency EFE: "Don't let what happened in Honduras happen in El Salvador, for there are many priests whose false preaching is inciting the faithful to *Subversion*!" (edition of July 16, 1975).

On August 27, 1975, the *New York Times* mentioned the same flyer in an article about Aguilares, which was later reprinted in the Mexican daily *Excelsior*. The headline to the article, which included a photograph of President Molina, spoke for itself: "In El Salvador, Rural Workers Have Lived as Serfs for Four Hundred years."

Rutilio did not let himself be intimidated by the threats. A member of the missionary team later testified: "What was most noteworthy in him was his courage in speaking out. In his homilies he would expand and be transformed. The Spirit became powerfully manifest in his prophetic words. This was in contrast with the prudence he showed whenever the team got together for work or reflection."[28]

Rutilio was an implacable adversary when the wrath of God took hold of him. In his homily at the parish Mass the following Sunday, he spoke vibrantly, valiantly, and evangelically, clarifying several points that seemed to him important. He explained once again the work he was doing, and he boldly proclaimed

---

27 The Conservative Religious Front described the events in Olancho as follows: "On June 25, 1975, a group of subversive priests in Honduras incited the villagers of the department of Olancho to violence and subversion. In a confrontation with the national army a great many Catholics and subversive priests died. Twelve priests were captured and a like number deported. Most Catholic priests in Honduras accused the Christian Democratic Party (PDC) of that country of using for political ends those subversive priests and various movements and organizations of the Honduran church." Frente Religioso Conservador, July 17, 1975.

28 *Summarium testium*, witness 18, §345.

the fundamental principles of the one true Jesus Christ, who was a very different figure from the Christ of the "conservative Catholics." With a bit of irony, he asked the flyer's authors to take note of his real name, since they had called him "José" Rutilio Grande: "Now I learn for the first time that my name is José! I ask those who keep my name in their archives to correct it. My right name is Rutilio Grande." He also mentioned that Bengoechea had left the parish two years before.[29]

In his homily, Rutilio stated emphatically that he belonged to no political party, contrary to what the flyer asserted. Membership in a party was not permitted to him as a priest, but he did not need such membership to defend what he defended or to speak what he spoke and would continue speaking, in the name of Jesus. He then proceeded to denounce the false God that the authors of the flyer had fabricated:

> Theirs is a capricious god who allows them to continue to maltreat the poor and exploit the masses so that they can callously hoard all the things God has made for all human beings. Let them read the Bible, and do so slowly. They will find it quite subversive. They will especially find Jesus of Nazareth to be very subversive, and maybe they'll even say he belongs to one of the political parties that now exist in our poor country.[30]

In the highly polarized political context of El Salvador, the opposition parties were always accused of being antagonistic toward the military regime. Rutilio wanted to extricate himself from any such association and to make it clear that he had no need of the parties to defend the rural poor:

> There is no need to belong to any of the existing political parties to love and defend the people, who in their great majority are poor country folk, the ones who are suffering the exploitation of a foolish and reactionary minority who call themselves "Catholic" but who are not really Catholic because they are unjust, unloving, and avaricious. To proclaim these bitter truths to this minority is to show them true love, so that they will change and be converted. To disguise such nastiness is not to show love for them. It's like a doctor who doesn't want his patient to suffer and so fails to cure him by pressing the wound full of puss; loving the patient means pressing the wound so that he is cured and gets well. "Change your attitude!" was the cry of Jesus.[31]

Rutilio's denunciation became more heated and harsh as he censured the duplicity of those who declared themselves Catholic:

---

29   ACSI. Rutilio Grande, homily.
30   ACSI. Rutilio Grande, homily.
31   ACSI. Rutilio Grande, homily.

9. The Parish and the Popular Organizations

> It is now clear that theirs is a god fabricated by human hands and molded with the blood of the innocent. The main concerns of these so-called *Conservative Catholics* are the god money and their own interests. They get up in the morning thinking about the almighty name of the god money; they go to bed thinking about the almighty name of the god money. It matters not to them that thousands of rural folk suffer anemia, poverty, and squalid living conditions. Hypocrites! Stop calling yourselves conservative Catholics because it's a lie.[32]

Rutilio's reference to the false "almighty god" would appear later, in another famous homily, his very last, where he explicitly named the sources of wealth of the agro-exporting oligarchy. Their blindness and hardheartedness, he declared, were such that even the president had taken them to task. Rutilio said the president had done well in "exposing" the oligarchy as reactionary and incorrigible. "Let us hope," he commented ironically, "that they don't put me on the ballot of the official party for making these statements!"[33]

As regards the saints, the oligarchs need not worry about them since they did not really believe in them either:

> You should know that a great majority of the saints sealed their lives with martyrdom. There are some hacienda owners who take delight in parading the patron saint along the roads of their ranches, accompanied by loud bands from the capital, but they would never want the people to know the reason why the saint was killed: he was killed for speaking the truth to the powerful! Parading the saints through the streets—even Jesus himself in the Holy Burial—costs nothing at all. But explaining a little about how they died and why they died—that is unthinkable![34]

Rutilio declared how great his love was for the people: "I have absolutely no fear in defending their interests, even if it costs me my own life. Offering one's life for love of neighbor, just as Jesus did, is the greatest good fortune a person can have." He therefore thanked God for the martyrs of the Honduran church, who had incurred the same fate as Jesus and who, like Jesus, had been maligned as "vulgar politicians." Rutilio concluded by addressing his adversaries directly, assuring them that he did not hate them. To the contrary, he was ready to give his life for their conversion and their salvation, but in order to be converted and saved they would have to "recognize their injustices, for the good of the country."

The relevance of Rutilio's denunciation was demonstrated clearly in two incidents. One involved a chapel and the construction of a public school, and the other involved the celebration of the patronal feast on the most important

---

32 ACSI. Rutilio Grande, homily.
33 ACSI. Rutilio Grande, homily.
34 ACSI. Rutilio Grande, homily.

plantations in the parish. The two incidents illustrate both the gross manipulation of the Gospel message by the agro-exporting oligarchs of the region and their visceral rancor against the missionary team.

The construction of the National Institute of Aguilares provided the occasion for the owner of the La Toma Hacienda, Margot Salinas de Avilés, to express her displeasure because the parish priests were not behaving like previous pastors. What most disturbed her, apparently, was that the new pastor paid her less attention than had his predecessors. A confrontation arose when Rutilio, at the request of the school director, allowed construction materials for the new building to be kept in the Salinas chapel, if the owners of the property were agreeable and if the construction firm made itself responsible for the locale.[35] The Salinas chapel, dedicated to Saint Joseph, took its name from the settlement where it was located; it had been built by the owner of the hacienda, who had also donated two *manzanas* of land for the construction of the new school.

When an engineer met with Margot Salinas to request permission to use the chapel, she used the occasion to express her contempt for the missionary team and her bitterness about the way the parish was being run:

> My husband and I didn't believe it [the request to store materials in the chapel] was true. He told the engineer to bring the parish's authorization in writing, certain that they would not give it to him. But how wrong we were! [...] The engineer brought the letter, legally signed and sealed by a member of a *"Missionary Team." Incredible, but true!* [...] What will the archbishop think of this?[36]

She thought Archbishop Chávez would take her side because he had sent her a personal note thanking her for the donation of the "beautiful" chapel. The donation in fact was not formalized since the owner never signed the title.

In her fury, Margot Salinas made the carved image of Saint Joseph the victim of a non-existent offense while completely ignoring the working conditions of the laborers on her plantation:

> It is quite possible that, since it is this missionary team, they are ignorant even of what belongs to the curia itself. Or it is also possible that they knew quite well that an offense was being committed in letting a chapel be used as a storeroom. Even though the chapel is very small, it is consecrated to the worship of God our Lord. Nevertheless, they did not even have the valor to say that "they were authorizing the Chapel of Saint Joseph to be used as a rubbish dump." Instead they called it the *Salinas Chapel* as a way of easing the slap being given to the face of Saint Joseph. "Salinas Chapel?" Saint

---

35 ACSI. Rutilio Grande to Carlos Avilés and Mrs. Aguilares, August 13, 1974.
36 ACSI. Margot Salinas de Avilés to Miguel Ángel Portillo Artiga and other members of the Board of Directors of the Colonia Salinas, Aguilares.

Joseph has already been removed from there, and he will never return. He will remain in this house, where he is respected and venerated.[37]

Still feeling outraged, she turned the chapel over to the council that she and her husband had set up with the tenants of the Colonia Salinas in November 1974. According to Rutilio, it was a "phantasmal" council that was not representative of the tenants and had no juridical status, but Margot Salinas wrote to it to express her indignation:

> For persons of good will, there stand the ruins of what was a *Beautiful Chapel*. You can use it with all confidence and freedom, and you can enthrone there whatever saint you wish and celebrate him as you wish, and you can be certain that my husband and I will not interfere in the least and that we are not thieves or liars or villains or cowards. […] Have no fear. Be aware that my husband and I have ceased to exist. Do as you wish with what is left of the ruins of the chapel.[38]

When the director of the health clinic in Aguilares asked Margot Salinas for a locale where milk could be given to the poor children, she took advantage of the request to complain again about the missionary team:

> *The New Pastor Has Asked for the Locale that the Former Pastor Gave* [the clinic] *at the Entrance of the Parish Church*. Of course, it is this same team. […] Oh, you poor little angels of Aguilares, it is clear that the members of this team are forgetting sweet Jesus who said, *Let the Little Children Come to Me*.[39]

Contrary to what she said, Margot Salinas had not handed over the title of the chapel property, nor would she do so because "the chapel is of no importance to the missionary team; they have made it into a storeroom." If they had proceeded thus even without the title, she asked, what would they do if they had it? "I don't want to imagine." She also complained that even the tenants had failed to take good care of the chapel and that "groups of suspicious individuals" were prowling about in its vicinity.

Shortly before the new school's inauguration, Margot Salinas ordered that the house of the sacristan of the chapel be destroyed since it was a "miserable hut" and would be an "eyesore when the president came." The house, which had been built by the sacristan, was behind the chapel. When the village council,

---

37 ACSI. Margot Salinas de Avilés to Miguel Ángel Portillo Artiga and other members of the Board of Directors of the Colonia Salinas, Aguilares.
38 ACSI. Margot Salinas de Avilés to Miguel Ángel Portillo Artiga and other members of the Board of Directors of the Colonia Salinas, Aguilares.*I*
39 ACSI. Margot Salinas de Avilés to Miguel Ángel Portillo Artiga and other members of the Board of Directors of the Colonia Salinas, Aguilares.

which had appointed the sacristan, refused to obey the order of Margot Salinas, she reacted angrily, saying that she had granted permission only for the use of the chapel, not for the chapel property. She stated that "this will bring problems, and to avoid them I have decided that we will again take charge of the care and reconstruction of the chapel. Of course, you will continue to be our collaborators."[40] She proposed that the sacristan move his house to a nearby property that also belonged to her, but the council still objected. Besides pressuring the council and the sacristan, Margot Salinas also distributed flyers. In the end, the sacristan left the chapel property.

The National Institute of Aguilares was to be inaugurated by President Molina on January 20, 1975. Rutilio was invited by the school board to bless the facilities, and he prepared his homily with his customary diligence; moreover, on this occasion he paid special attention to the circumstances. At the last minute, however, the Avileses arranged for the blessing to be given by another priest, Rogelio Esquivel. Later that same day, Rutilio sent a telegram to Archbishop Chávez: "Profoundly surprised at presence of priest from outside parish blessing presidential inauguration Instituto Aguilares today. Esquivel unaware important pastoral details."[41]

Despite the conflict, Rutilio tried to dialogue with the Avileses the day after the inauguration, hoping to clear up doubts and misunderstandings: "I do not think that adult persons like us, with a certain degree of culture, should allow ourselves to be swayed by simple suppositions." He warned the couple that if they did not want to engage in a serious, responsible dialogue, he would take the controversy to the public:

> I hope that is not necessary because I am still counting on your good will. In no way should you take it as a moral threat; it is simply a sign of the frankness that comes from my true Christian love for you, which I profess in the Lord. It has never been my intention to offend you, and it is a great shame that it has been very difficult to contact you personally and for us to dialogue as Christians.[42]

Rutilio also wanted to explain the matter to President Molina, but the president did not receive him. In any case, he gave a copy of the homily he had prepared to a member of the presidential party whom he knew, a man whose son had studied at the Colegio Externado when Rutilio was prefect of discipline there.

The other revealing incident occurred on October 4, 1975, the feast of Saint Francis of Assisi. On that day each year, the owners of the San Francisco Hacienda, the Nottebohn family, had the custom of traveling to their plantation to

---

40   ACSI. Margot Salinas de Avilés to Doña María de la Paz de Artola, Aguilares, January 14, 1975.
41   ACSI. Rutilio Grande to Archbishop Luis Chávez, Aguilares, January 20, 1975.
42   ACSI. Rutilio Grande to Carlos Avilés and Doña Margot de Avilés, Aguilares, January 21, 1975.

organize a festival for the workers and their families. Ordinarily, a priest from San Salvador who was a friend of the family would celebrate Mass in the local chapel, during which the workers' children would receive their first Communion, wearing suits and dresses donated by the plantation. After the Mass, there would be two banquets, one outside for the workers and their families, another inside for the Nottebohns and their guests. This particular year the missionary team accepted the plantation's invitation to celebrate the Mass and designated Salvador Carranza to do so.

The Mass started on time, and Carranza began his homily by talking about Saint Francis. However, when he realized that this was the only time during the year when the Nottebohn family visited the plantation, a prophetic spirit took hold of him, and he denounced the hypocrisy of the event. As Carranza preached, sternly and at length, the Nottebohn family and their guests appeared increasingly distressed, but the faces of the workers and their families were glowing with delight: at long last, someone was speaking the truth to the plantation owners. They were accustomed to hearing the "contracted priest" remind them of their duty to behave well, to flee from sin and rebellion, and to cultivate resignation. On this occasion, unexpectedly, the priest was speaking clearly about their real-life situation and their daily desperation, something they had never heard from the pulpit before.

An anonymous flyer distributed later that same day in San Salvador told of the rudely frustrated expectations of the Nottebohn family and their guests: "All of us present were pleased because a Jesuit was going to be giving us what only they know how to offer: a word full of love that would lift the spirits of those whose religious devotion had become lukewarm." But their contentment was transformed into stupor when the preacher stopped talking about Saint Francis, as the flyer explained:

> But a moment came when the Jesuit priest's mask came off, and there was revealed a person full of prejudice, slander, and rancor, delivering a socio-communist [sic] political discourse and injecting into the humble minds of the workers and all present hatred for the landlords and the established authorities of the nation.[43]

"He directed disedifying words" against the plantation owners, the circular continued, claiming that they had "no awareness of the misery" of their workers, and he held them responsible for the high cost of living and the poor living conditions of the workers. He urged the workers to rebel and to change their lives, labeling those who refused to do so "loyalists," "elephant ears," "wicked tongues," and "other gross names unworthy of a member of the *Society of Jesus*."

---

43 ACSI. Anonymous account, "Mass Celebrated at the Hacienda San Francisco," Aguilares, October 4, 1975.

He condemned the government as repressive, a claim the flyer considered "injurious and calumnious" since the preacher had not personally witnessed the deeds he denounced. The author of the flyer was especially disturbed by the dramatic tone of the preacher's discourse:

> Words like that spoken to simple people stir them up, with many disastrous consequences for the society in which we live, because the people get a distorted idea of what happened to those two citizens he called martyrs. He claimed that they were maltreated by the authorities, who make sure the laws of the nation are obeyed.[44]

The flyer stated that those present at the Mass—that is, the Nottebohn family and their guests—left the chapel "verbally battered." The preacher's words seemed strange and novel to the author of the flyer, who contended that the priest's proper role was

> to encourage spirits to sing together a hymn to honest work, to infuse love of private property, and to teach the mutual respect we owe one another in our society. That is what all of us were expecting, not inflaming people with hatred. He who sins most is the one who strews thistles in clean minds, such as those of our beloved rural folk.[45]

The greatest worry of the flyer's author was that the rural folk, who were ignorant but were still good people with "clean minds," might come to think that they were suffering oppression and injustice. He feared that they would be deprived of their natural simplicity because "it is very, very dangerous to sow strange ideas in unrefined minds." The danger was very real because the preacher had great influence among rural folk, especially those who had "hearts that would absorb like sponges everything the priest told them."[46]

In concluding, the author claimed to be scandalized that the preacher failed to exalt the kindness and the Catholicism of the plantation owners: "He pronounced not a word of praise [...] for the patrons, nor did he respect the pain of the honorable lady whose brother had died just a few days before. He offered no condolences for several patrons who were absent due to poor health."[47] Most definitely, in the opinion of the author, what was supposed to have been a devout Mass became a three-and-a-half hour "political meeting" that those attending had to "put up with." In the end, he stated, "we gave thanks to God when it ended so that we could leave and think about what was awaiting us with this class of people who claim to be spiritual leaders. Another Cuba! It is hell!"[48]

---

44   Anonymous account, "Mass Celebrated at the Hacienda San Francisco."
45   Anonymous account, "Mass Celebrated at the Hacienda San Francisco."
46   Anonymous account, "Mass Celebrated at the Hacienda San Francisco."
47   Anonymous account, "Mass Celebrated at the Hacienda San Francisco."
48   Anonymous account, "Mass Celebrated at the Hacienda San Francisco."

The Difficult Relationship between the Parish and FECCAS

The tensions between the parish and FECCAS began early in 1974, as the parish was defining its internal structure and imparting courses for the pastoral agents. FECCAS was organizing its first bases during that time, and its activities attracted a lot of the best leaders from the communities. By mid-November of that year, the missionary team was expressing concern about the loss of leaders since the parish depended heavily on a good supply of delegates. Many of the best delegates had passed to the ranks of FECCAS, leaving only the less capable ones to attend to the communities. To remedy this loss of some of the parish's most valuable lay ministers, the missionary team decided to create several itinerant groups of delegates; these delegates would go, two by two, to visit the most neglected communities and encourage them to persevere. They would also collaborate with the priests in imparting courses in the villages.

No communities were in fact totally abandoned. The delegates who joined FECCAS understood that they should continue to attend the community meetings; indeed, their own base was to be found there in the community. Sometimes, the FECCAS activists even ran the meetings, reinforcing the perception that the parish and FECCAS were one and the same. The strong influence of the organization on the communities was observable also in the ways in which the political implications of the Gospel were drawn out for the people, so that the demands made of Christians were radicalized. Despite the organization's virtues, its presence and its influence in the communities did not tranquilize but rather greatly worried the missionary team.

The itinerant teams of delegates, which functioned at least until April 1975, did not succeed in reinvigorating the communities; the delegates abandoned the enterprise relatively quickly, considering it impossible. They reported that attendance at celebrations of the Word and other community gatherings had diminished, that many delegates had responsibilities incompatible with their ecclesial work, and that the most charismatic delegates tended to join FECCAS. To combat the decline in evangelical enthusiasm, the missionary team decided to impart several four-week courses in Aguilares and weekend courses in the villages; they would also conduct new missions.

The team considered good parish leadership essential to effective evangelization, but statistics showed clearly that the parish had lost some of its best leaders. The loss was due partly to the emergence of FECCAS but also to the fact that the first stage of parish growth had reached a natural limit. Then, just as the parish team was searching for a fresh creative impulse that would initiate a new stage, FECCAS emerged and drew away some of the most valuable pastoral agents. Not all of them left the parish, of course, and some of those who did returned again to lead the communities. Many delegates, though, took up regional and national posts in FECCAS and, later, in the BPR.

The exodus of the delegates had another negative consequence for parish life. Since many delegates viewed working with the communities as less important than working with FECCAS, the parish found it difficult to hold onto them. The leadership of FECCAS would sometimes assign delegates to posts within its structure without considering the effect on the communities. The devaluing of pastoral work was evident in the attitude of FECCAS members toward the Bible course for delegates, a course that even the organization's leadership considered beneficial. Every week, two delegates from each community went to Aguilares to get four texts that had been prepared by the Center for Theological Reflection of the UCA; the texts would subsequently be used for reflection and discussion in the meetings of delegates. The series of texts examined various biblical themes with the aim of deepening the delegates' understanding of them. The delegates who attended these sessions were sometimes ridiculed by those who had joined FECCAS; this attitude greatly troubled the missionary team and eventually led to the rupture of personal relations between the team members and the impertinent delegates.

Still another source of tension, apart from the exodus of delegates and the devaluing of pastoral work, was the tendency of FECCAS members to distance themselves from the evangelization process and to concentrate exclusively on political activity. Much of the success of the organization was due to the fact that it used the method and the content of the parish missions to recruit members outside the parish; the rural poor interpreted the proselytizing zeal of the FECCAS promoters as genuinely evangelical. The missionary team objected to what they considered manipulation of the Gospel and warned FECCAS that such a strategy would not get the organization very far, because while the immediate results might be positive, the confusion in people's minds would make them unsustainable. Indeed, they could end up "vaccinating" the rural poor against politics.

The missionary team also severely criticized the dogmatic views of FECCAS and its arrogance in claiming that all who support the people must also support FECCAS and that anyone who rejects FECCAS also rejects the people; even those who remained indifferent were viewed as opposing the organization. FECCAS considered all criticism, even the parish's, to be contrary to the people's interests and discounted it as revisionist. The FECCAS leadership sought the parish's unconditional support, but the missionary team did not want to become closely identified with a political organization. At the same time, the team was committed to defending the struggles of workers and the rural poor insofar as they were compatible with the parish's goals. Since the team considered an organization like FECCAS to be necessary, it was willing to collaborate with it, but it refused to recognize it as the only viable popular organization. The team especially resisted any attempts by FECCAS to identify itself with the parish and to use pastoral activities, including preaching, for its own ends.

9. The Parish and the Popular Organizations

FECCAS justified its pretensions by arguing that the church was incapable of committing itself to the true interests of the people. In the best of cases, the church could speak on behalf of the people. The organization argued that the church—and concretely the parish—should serve its interests; they did not enjoy autonomy. Using this type of logic, FECCAS tried to force the parish of Aguilares to make a political decision it did not want to make. The organization insisted that the parish should obey its dictates unconditionally; to do so, of course, it would have to pay a price, suffer a type of cross. Thus FECCAS aspired to form part of the parish's decision-making process; it wanted to be able to specify the services it required from the parish. The organization denied that it was being manipulative or lacking in neutrality.

The missionary team did not refuse to have structural links with FECCAS. In fact, the team included the organization in its pastoral planning even though it recognized the ambiguity and confusion produced by the relationship. The parish and FECCAS tended to be seen as closely identified, both within the parish and without, and too often activities carried out by the organization were attributed to the parish. During his pastoral visit in 1976, Bishop Rivera informed the missionary team that the neighboring parishes had expressed concern. Grounds certainly existed for the ambiguity and confusion: the parish was effectively in favor of FECCAS and even protected it when it was threatened by the military regime. However, the only practical aid it gave the organization was the use of parish locales for its meetings.

The missionary team engaged in long, heated discussions about the nature of its relationship with FECCAS but in the end reached no conclusions, mainly because of differences among the team members. Father Pérez, for example, had joined the advisory team of FECCAS and favored much closer ties with the organization. At the end of November 1975, the missionary team decided that a protocol should be drawn up defining the relations between the parish and the organization; the principle governing the relationship was to be mutual support but "relative autonomy." The parish would accompany, illumine, and motivate the political activity from the perspective of faith. The missionary team, in consultation with a representative pastoral council, would assume responsibility for courses, including the study of the national reality from the perspective of faith, and it would appoint the instructors. The courses would be open to those in the organization since they formed part of the parish community. The parish was also willing to organize a specialized course on the faith for the leadership of FECCAS. The idea was to promote Christian practice among the organization's members and to prevent them from being manipulated by false conceptions of the faith. The team also considered the possibility of providing Christian formation for MERS, but it had serious doubts about doing so because it saw the movement as a giddy group of youngsters playing at politics.

The parish's mission did not coincide with the objectives of FECCAS, even though the organization called itself Christian. The priority of the parish was announcing the kingdom of God and the building of a Christian community open to all those who desired to live in accord with Gospel values. The parish was opposed to the formation of closed, dogmatic elites, and it therefore took into consideration the strengths and weaknesses of all its members, without discrimination. The parish also aspired to strengthen the Christian motivation of those undertaking transformative action, and it did so by announcing God's reign and denouncing sin. Hence, the ultimate criterion for judging the actions of persons and groups was their fidelity to Gospel values.

While the parish did not seek any form of secular power, it allowed into its ranks those who legitimately sought such power in order to serve the people. At the same time, it declared itself opposed to any type of political hegemony, and it resisted attempts to identify service of the Christian community with political leadership. Invoking the relative autonomy that the team had agreed upon, Rutilio in November 1975 considered it appropriate to begin to separate the parish from FECCAS. He therefore ruled that the organization could no longer use locales of the parish for its meetings; he prohibited FECCAS members from "processing freely" through the rectory and disturbing other business being transacted there, though he allowed them to use the porch and the outside areas; he ordered all secret meetings to stop since they provoked distrust and useless rumors. Furthermore, he instructed, when large groups of members passed through the city, they should request the pastor's authorization beforehand, and the final decision about lodging for those spending the night would be made by the pastor and the missionary team. Rutilio thought that these norms were necessary in order to prevent the collective suicide of both works.

Subsequently, after appropriate consultation, Rutilio denied the request of the secretary general of FECCAS to use the locales of the parish for the celebration of its national congress:

> Let me remind you that we are moving within the narrow confines of a parish, and this event will have a national character. Although it is quite true that FECCAS is not hierarchically structured, it is difficult in reality—given the prevailing mentality, even among enlightened persons of the church, and more so among others—to separate this aspect from our ecclesial pastoral ministry properly speaking, which is linked to the [church] hierarchy.[49]

Despite the harshness of Rutilio's response and the abovementioned disciplinary measures, he assured the secretary general that he would do everything possible to help them:

---

49 ACSI. Rutilio Grande, pastor of Aguilares, to the secretary general of FECCAS, Aguilares, January 15, 1976.

I guarantee you that I will try to help you at the higher levels, here and everywhere in the republic, as long as you maintain yourselves as an organization inspired by Christian principles. For yours is a legitimate and necessary organization that deserves the moral support of the institutional church.[50]

Despite the parish's notices and norms, FECCAS held its meetings in the facilities of the rectory.

Dissatisfied with the level of "relative autonomy" agreed upon, the missionary team sounded out the opinions of the FECCAS members with a questionnaire, after first obtaining the approval and collaboration of the FECCAS leadership. Responses to the questionnaire were received from sixteen bases and from the secretaries general, who were surveyed separately. The results were unsatisfactory, however, since the intermediaries had registered only the majority opinions, making statistical analysis impossible.

In response to perhaps the most interesting question—"What do you, as an organized Christian, think that priests should do to help those who are organized?"—the bases asked for greater collaboration and support; they wanted the priests to "get fully involved" in the struggle and "not let go." The bases wanted unconditional commitment from the priests, which meant teaching people how to be just and to demand justice according to the Gospel; they wanted the priests to visit the bases and help them gain members; they wanted greater awareness from a religious perspective; they wanted a mission and courses about organizing; they wanted more publicity about organizing; they wanted the organization's messages to be read during Mass; they wanted homilies that encouraged and supported the organizing; they wanted help for parish members who moved elsewhere; they wanted the parish to make joint denunciations with the organization; they wanted a priest to be present at meetings of the regional council; they wanted the parish to allow its locales to be used, especially for the national congress; they wanted to win over other priests to their cause; they wanted to engage in dialogue and mutual correction with the pastors of Suchitoto. Those surveyed considered that the support given by the parish was strong in the areas of conscientization, lodging, courses, Masses, clarification of doubts, denunciations, and personal support: eighty-nine respondents said it was "extremely strong," sixteen said it was "very strong," thirty-eight said it was "fairly strong," and one person said it was "deficient." Despite this, 123 respondents said that they desired greater collaboration.[51]

The responses of the secretary general of the zone coincided with those of the bases; he agreed that the collaboration of the parish had been honest and sincere. He was pleased that other organizations, like FAPU and its allies, had

---

50   ACSI. Rutilio Grande, pastor of Aguilares, to the secretary general of FECCAS, Aguilares, January 15, 1976.
51   ACSI. Survey, Aguilares, 1975.

not been permitted to enter the parish. He complained, however, that the parish did not always accept the policies of the FECCAS leadership, a serious fault in the eyes of an organization with absolutist pretensions. He said that one member of the missionary team had referred to the organization in terms that were none too clear, giving rise to confusion and division. In agreement with the bases, the secretary general requested more collaboration from the parish in promoting the organization, urging more delegates to join, persuading other priests to defend its cause, and imparting courses on politics to its members. He also wanted the priests to identify FECCAS with Gospel values, to attend the regional council meetings, and to mention the organization in homilies, talks, courses, and so on. Finally, he demanded that the parish abandon its petit-bourgeois stance, characterized by lack of passion, vacillation, hegemonic pretensions, and concentration of attention on young women to the detriment of young men.[52]

The bases gave several reasons for not expressing their needs to the parish: they lacked opportunity, they did not think it proper, they received help from elsewhere, they found answers in the homilies, or they simply lacked trust. Perhaps the main reason was the perception that the parish was petit-bourgeois, so that its position with respect to FECCAS was inconsistent—sometimes favorable, sometimes disapproving. The secretaries generally responded along the same lines, but they added that they were now able to distinguish between the Gospel and the organization. Some, however, complained of the parish's indifference and lack of recognition, and one expressed discouragement and confusion.[53]

The parish responded to the survey in December 1975. The missionary team reaffirmed its support for FECCAS, saying that it was critical support, based on faith and not on politics. In the note it sent to FECCAS, the team stated that from the start it had considered it to be an organization born of the Gospel, not something separated from or contradicting the Gospel. Its principles were therefore recognized as evangelical. The team also asserted that it had never censured the organization or attempted to direct it, even though some answers to the questionnaire would seem to claim otherwise. The missionary team granted that it did have doubts about the organization, and for several reasons: the flight to it of many of the parish's best delegates, the distance between the organizational leadership and the bases, the danger of moving too fast and risking failure, the insufficient assimilation of the Gospel spirit, and the expansion of the organization outside the parish.[54]

The missionary team corroborated its support in its qualified acceptance of most of the requests of FECCAS. It agreed to allow delegates to continue to work for the organization as a valid option for practicing Christian commitment, but

---

52   Survey, Aguilares, 1975.
53   Survey, Aguilares, 1975.
54   Survey, Aguilares, 1975.

without confusing being a delegate with being a member. The team also agreed to other requests: to visit the bases, but not periodically, for lack of time; to collaborate in the training of the bases by promoting justice; to attend the regional council meetings, but with two, not one, members of the team; to make joint denunciations with the organization; and to speak of FECCAS more openly, especially with priests who were negatively disposed to the organization and to Aguilares. With regard to the courses, the team responded that those on the national reality should be taken on by the members themselves since they were the most capable in that regard; it rejected the idea of specialized courses on politics since it did not consider itself qualified.[55]

The missionary team took advantage of the petitions of FECCAS to present its own. It requested that the organization's members not introduce themselves as representatives of the parish in their proselytizing activities; the pastors of other parishes were resentful, considering such activity an intrusion into their territories by Aguilares. The team also asked FECCAS to help preserve the celebrations of the Word, which were a fertile seedbed for evangelization as well as for the organizing efforts. The team asked FECCAS not to request the use of the parish seal for its fundraising because the people did not understand, even when it was explained to them, that the funds were not for the parish but for the activities of the organized groups. The team asked FECCAS to explain what it meant by its claim that the parish had concentrated its efforts on working with young women more than with young men. Finally, the team asked for a copy of the organization's statutes.[56]

The missionary team was more concerned about clarifying the meaning of "relative autonomy" than FECCAS was. It made an effort to define precisely the terms of collaboration and independence, but FECCAS did not show the same interest, nor did it fulfill its part of the agreement.

Country Christmas, 1975

The first national demonstration of FECCAS took place in Aguilares on December 21, 1975, and the political repercussions of the event demonstrated the futility of trying to separate the parish from the organization. To those outside, the activities of both entities seemed identical, so that the parish was held responsible for whatever the organization did. Ultimately, the responsibility for everything that happened in Aguilares fell directly on Rutilio.

President Molina had by that time already made several declarations against those he called "liberationist priests," and he had reproached the bishops, claiming that their clergy were responsible for the subversion in the rural areas. In December 1974, Molina launched a furious attack against the clergy

---

55   Survey, Aguilares, 1975.
56   Survey, Aguilares, 1975.

before an audience of military officers representing several regiments. That speech was given before the occupation of the cathedral, which was to make even more evident the opposition of a fair number of priests to the regime. In August 1975, Molina made a similar criticism of the clergy in an interview with ACAN-EFE, an international news agency, whose story was reprinted in the Salvadoran press.[57] The minister of defense also warned the clergy not to "get involved in subversive matters." In May 1975, the priest Rafael Barahona had been captured and beaten, and at dawn on August 3 ten national guards had raided La Providencia, the social promotion center of the diocese of Santa Ana. On August 8, one of the first of the infamous "death squads," FALANGE, threatened to execute the "communist" priests secretly, along with assembly members and journalists, to keep the country from falling into the "claws of the communists."

Given this political context, Rutilio recommended to FECCAS that a Mass be celebrated before the demonstration on Sunday, December 21 so that the event would be illumined by the Gospel. The organization agreed, but it asked that Rutilio be the priest who presided and preached. In response, Rutilio laid down some conditions. The first was that the Mass not be used for political ends, lest other groups ask for similar favors. He said that the Mass would be at nine in the morning, the regular time for Sunday Mass, and that he would make no mention of FECCAS during it. He was insistent that the Mass should not be used to promote the demonstration: there should be no banners or shouting of slogans during the Mass. He explained that all the doors of the church would be opened, allowing FECCAS members to have access to the inner courtyard, but he did not want church properties to be used for elaborating banners and posters. If the organization needed benches or other things from the parish, they were to be taken the night before so that "people wouldn't be traipsing in and out with those things that same day."[58]

Rutilio ruled that the slogans should be shouted only in the street, after they had left church property. He did not want a repeat of what had happened on May 1, when a demonstrator shouted "death to the government" at the church entrance. Rutilio also told the FECCAS leadership not to allow slogans to be painted on the walls of houses or in public places, as had happened at the May 1 demonstration. Such activity bothered many residents, even those well disposed to the organization, and besides, more than a few people had no idea what the expressions meant. Rutilio said that after the May 1 demonstration he had had to explain, at different Masses in the city and the villages, certain phrases that seemed to be more the work of university students than of Christian folk from the countryside. On this occasion, he said,

57 *La prensa gráfica* (August 5, 1975).
58 ACSI. Rutilio Grande, "Notes for the Sermon for the Country Christmas of 1975."

I will personally abstain from defending you with explanations, simply because I myself judge it to be poor tactics to ruin what is most important by things of that nature. But you are free to do what you think proper. Just remember: weigh the pros and the cons, and take full responsibility.[59]

Finally, Rutilio expressed his desire that the organization avoid provocations "so as not to mar with violence this event which seeks to be peaceful and free of weapons."

The theme of the Mass and the preaching was to be "Country Christmas," what Rutilio later told the archbishop was a "happy idea" since "there was no way we could multiply ourselves to celebrate Christmas Day in thirty communities." The missionary team was aware of the ambiguity of celebrating Mass in those circumstances, but it could not disregard the demonstration. When the archbishop later requested an explanation, Rutilio responded that ignoring the event would have meant "incurring for myself and for the parish as such the hatred of a good number of our most capable people."[60]

Basing his homily on Luke 7:19–23, which tells how John's disciples came to question Jesus about his identity, Rutilio compared the parish and its mission with Jesus and his message. He took up the questions in the Gospel and applied them to the present, attempting once again to dispel doubts and clarify ambiguities about the parish's mission given the nation's tense political atmosphere. Speaking for the whole missionary team, Rutilio responded to the challenge made by its adversaries: "Are you followers of Jesus, or do we have to wait for someone else?" In reality, he said, it was Jesus himself who was challenging the team regarding its mission. "That is the same question many confused people are asking about us: Are you communists? Are you deceivers? Are you changing our religion? Are you guerrillas?"[61]

Rutilio recalled the public commitment the team had made on Sunday, September 24, 1972, when it took charge of the parish in the presence of the archbishop. That day, speaking in the name of all, Rutilio had promised to evangelize the parish according to the command Jesus had given his followers, that is, by giving preference to the poor, for whom his words were good news. That was why the members of the missionary team had taken the side of the poor: they wanted to "be with them and promote in their persons and their communities a genuine faith that would help them relate the whole of their lives with the Gospel and with God, who created this world for everybody and who gave us life so that we might have it in abundance."[62] So nobody should have any doubt about the

---

59   Grande, "Notes for the Sermon for the Country Christmas of 1975."
60   ACSI. Rutilio Grande to Archbishop Luis Chávez clarifying what happened. Aguilares, January 7, 1976.
61   Grande, "Notes for the Sermon for the Country Christmas of 1975."
62   Grande, "Notes for the Sermon for the Country Christmas of 1975."

mission of the missionary team: its first aim was to "*announce the Gospel* cleanly and simply to the people who want to listen to us, whose hearts are open and whose minds are free of prejudices and created idols," and its second aim was to found Christian communities committed to the words and deeds of Jesus. Rutilio repeated once again that since the Gospel encompassed all the activities of human beings, it was directly related to human life and demanded a change of conduct.

The message of Jesus was quite simple and clear, so only "the perverse are confused by it." Since Jesus plainly proclaimed that God was the Father of all, all human beings were his children and were sisters and brothers to one another, images of the living God, all equal in dignity. That God, the only "private Proprietor of this great hacienda of a world," turned the earth over to all his sons and daughters so that they could live and flourish in it in peace—everyone with the same opportunities, free of all forms of slavery or domination. So the will of God was clear.

But human beings "have destroyed the world with that special idolatry that produces slavery: desire to possess wealth/privilege/influence/power/domination/selfishness/Cain." The Cains have effectively destroyed God's image by taking control of the world as if they alone were the heirs, by enslaving the Abels who are their brothers and sisters, and by erecting their own gods. The Cains say to themselves:

> These thousands of *manzanas* are my private property. My money is *All for Me*. As for the others, let them accept it. It's the Law of the shrewdest. Those poor folk who are multitudes, let them continue that way. We will keep deceiving them; we will drain the sweat from their brows. We are not their brothers; we are producers of our wealth, which accumulates thanks to their labor. [...] They will continue in their ignorant ways, deprived of the common goods of our Father God. That God and his plan are a bother to us. What we want is for him to stay in the clouds.[63]

Since the world of the Cains was opposed to the express will of God, the children of God had to struggle against them and their selfish ways in order to build God's kingdom in the world. As followers of Jesus, all Christians were obliged to contribute to the building of that kingdom to the extent that their weaknesses allowed. Rutilio then cautioned that the death of those who undertook that task would probably resemble that of Jesus:

> The death of that child who was born in poverty at the first *Christmas* was caused by those who crushed him because he was making them uncomfortable with his Message of Salvation and his deeds. At the young age of

---

63 Grande, "Notes for the Sermon for the Country Christmas of 1975."

thirty-three he died for the greatest and noblest cause, one venerated by the people of that time and by the people of this time—a cause that will be venerated by future generations.[64]

Besides the Cains, Rutilio pointed out two other groups that had falsely arrogated to themselves the possession of the message of salvation. One group was made up of "those who profess to be *Catholics*. They lie. They are as atheistic as the communists. At least the communists are honest, but these are hypocrites who want to use religion to defend their privileges."[65] The other group was the evangelical sects:

> They preach a Christ in the clouds who has nothing to do with material reality. […] [For them] sin consists in smoking and eating chicken with the blood still in it. […] They always go about arguing in their holy way but forgetting the most important—and [they do so] with checks from the USA and the protection of the powerful.[66]

But even the poor were not free of the danger of arrogance. Rutilio asked the priests to do all they could to help prevent the oppressed of today from becoming the oppressors of tomorrow. This danger could be avoided only by the creation of new men and women for a new society. This new world would come about through legalization of peasant organizations and through a series of structural changes in land ownership and the exercise of public power, which should be at the service of the great majority of people, not just a minority. Another danger Rutilio warned against was hatred, which often appeared during the struggle for liberation. The struggle itself was inevitable because freedom would not come easily; it had to be won by the poor people themselves because the minorities would not willingly let go of their power. In the midst of the struggle, however, hatred was avoidable if the rural poor remained loyal to their faith and to Gospel values.

In keeping with his role as religious leader, Rutilio issued a call to the parish communities, reminding them that they had the right and the duty in conscience to be actively engaged in sound politics. Being politically involved meant seeking the good of the great majority of people by means of "the urgent, important transformations needed for the good and salvation of this whole people, who must have at their service the laws, the governments, the intellectuals, and the priests as illuminators and educators of an authentic and true faith."[67]

Since the arrival of the missionary team in Aguilares, its exclusive goal had been to follow Jesus and proclaim his message of salvation. Fidelity to Jesus had

---

64 Grande, "Notes for the Sermon for the Country Christmas of 1975."
65 ACSI. Rutilio Grande, handwritten addition to the original text of the sermon.
66 Grande, handwritten addition to the original text of the sermon.
67 Grande, handwritten addition to the original text of the sermon.

led the team to denounce with clarity, courage, and honesty all the Cains of the parish. The disciples of Jesus were obliged to unmask sin wherever it might be found, "coiled up like a snake," but that did not mean hatred: "*We hate nobody. We cannot have hatred for anyone.*" To the contrary, the team members loved the unjust hoarders of wealth, power, and privilege, and that is why they were telling them the truth plainly, even as they were announcing the good news of the Gospel to the poor, who were the great majority.

No one should be surprised, therefore, that the team, always seeking guidance from the Gospel, had openly and publicly taken the side of those in Aguilares and other parts of the country who were raising their voices to demand justice, which meant just wages and fair tasks, better working conditions, and rights for the plantation tenants. For that very reason, Rutilio added, "we feel profound sorrow for what happened at the Santa Barbara Hacienda."[68]

The members of the missionary team of Aguilares were priests, he asserted, not political leaders. From the start, they had declared, and they did not tire of repeating, that they were not "married" to any political party or any secular organization. "Of course," Rutilio explained, "we cannot remain indifferent to politics; it is necessary for the common good of the great majority of the people, in view of their urgent and serious problems. We cannot ignore their plight, not now, not ever."[69] Rutilio therefore asked the political parties, especially the official party and the Christian Democratic Party, not to ask priests to be advocates in their electoral campaigns. If the politicians were in fact Catholics and Christians, as they professed, they should show it by their actions, promoting the urgently needed changes that would benefit the Salvadoran people:

> Let them stop their prattle and stop traveling to towns to stage their circuses, promising everything and deceiving the people time after time. Let them stop their robbery, and let them stop seeking political posts as a way to form business factions in the city halls and at high levels of government. That is not politics. It is foulness, vileness, a degrading and horrendous crime.[70]

Thus, Rutilio said, when anyone asked about the identity and the mission of the missionary team of Aguilares, he responded the way Jesus did: telling the questioners to behold the deeds the team performed. The communities were coming together to reflect on the Gospel and apply it to their lives, the delegates were dedicated to announcing the Good News, and the organization consisted of men and women from the communities who were committed to Gospel values. They were men and women who had decided

---

68   Grande, "Notes for the Sermon for the Country Christmas of 1975."
69   Grande, handwritten addition to the original text of the sermon.
70   Grande, handwritten addition to the original text of the sermon.

not to be satisfied with mere words and reflection but to struggle together for a free and just society and for a country that lived up to the most sacred values of the Gospel, for a country in which there would no longer be unorganized multitudes suffering blindness, paralysis, deafness, evil spirits, malnutrition, hunger, endemic infirmities, and ignorance.[71]

No one, then, should be scandalized or disillusioned by the team, lest they suffer the same fate as the contemporaries of Jesus, who did not understand the message of salvation. Finally, Rutilio addressed all the pastoral agents, urging them "not to forget for a minute that the soul of our evangelizing work is the Holy Spirit, while we are only instruments, instruments that will not be used unless we remain humble and filled with hope, joy, and love."[72]

After the Mass, Rutilio avoided the demonstration, as he said he would, but during the announcements at the end of Mass he announced, "as a personal inspiration," that there would be a demonstration and that it would be "good or bad depending on people's behavior." He made it clear that the demonstration had not been organized by the parish but by FECCAS, so that it was not within his competence to encourage people to participate or prohibit them from doing so.[73] The demonstration and the subsequent meeting took place without incident; there were no provocative or violent actions. Rutilio was displeased, however, with the decision of two members of the missionary team, who were close to FECCAS, to march with the demonstrators.

The Country Christmas and the FECCAS demonstration were quickly followed by negative reactions. Within a few days, the president of the republic, in a memorandum with many inaccuracies, blamed Rutilio for the demonstration and accused him of urging people during the Mass to join in the event. The memorandum claimed that about a thousand rural folk and students from Aguilares and Suchitoto had participated in the demonstration, under the leadership of the "priests" Crescencio Alas and Ángel Bengoechea, a "Belgian." The two priests had carried signs saying "Down with the bourgeoisie! Down with the military!" and they had shouted: "If you want a real Christmas, you have to fight, because Christmas is now only for the rich." In the course of the march, said the memorandum, the demonstrators carried signs with slogans painted in red: "FECCAS and the Peasant People, United We Will Overcome!"; "FAPU, We Begin the Struggle, and We Will Overcome!"; "Long Live Viet Nam [sic]!"; "Long Live Cuba!"; and "Long Live Socialism!" The memorandum also gave the registration number of a vehicle that had provided security for the demonstration, and it named several priests whom it accused of giving instructions to the

---

71 Grande, "Notes for the Sermon for the Country Christmas of 1975."
72 Grande, handwritten addition to the original text of the sermon.
73 ACSI. Rutilio Grande to Archbishop Luis Chávez clarifying what happened, Aguilares, January 7, 1976.

demonstrators: Benigno Fernández, Guatemalan; Luis Eduardo Pellecer; Andrés Salvador Carranza, also Guatemalan; and Higinio Alas.

The memorandum suffered from many errors and inaccuracies; some were the result of the author's ignorance, but others were due to simple malevolence. It was therefore useless to try to explain the relation between the parish and FECCAS—their enemies considered them one and the same—or to clarify the identities of the members of the missionary team. Bengoechea had left the parish some time before; the last names of Bengoechea and Fernández were misspelled; and neither Fernández nor Carranza was Guatemalan. Moreover, FAPU had not even participated in the demonstration.

In early January 1976, Archbishop Chávez demanded an explanation, which Rutilio gave him in writing on January 7.[74] In his letter, Rutilio explained all the measures that had been taken to avoid ambiguity; he enclosed a copy of his homily so that the bishop could judge its orthodoxy;[75] and he suggested that the archbishop question the rest of the team about the event, to remove any doubts. Rutilio wrote that he knew risks were involved but that he had personally assumed responsibility for the risks for pastoral reasons: "I was aware that the matter was extremely delicate and could be interpreted ambivalently, but I assumed the crucial risk of ambiguity involved in the event, rather than pastorally maltreat the best and most conscious group of Christians we have in the parish."[76] He admitted to the archbishop that he had thought about consulting him about the Mass but in the end did not do so, "simply because I thought that I would be transferring to your person a perhaps disagreeable matter. I preferred to take all the responsibility on myself, with all its consequences, in order not to involve you as bishop." Rutilio expressed his regret that others had informed the archbishop before he did and that they had distorted the facts. He thanked the archbishop for having his expressed his concern "with paternal sincerity," to which he wished to respond with "filial sincerity." The demonstration had taken place with "complete order and composure," Rutilio stated, but he had no knowledge of what was painted on the posters or spoken in the meeting: "I have no knowledge of the harangues." He suggested to the archbishop that he have a frank dialogue "as soon as possible" with the Jesuit provincial about the scholastics who were involved in activities outside the parish jurisdiction, adding: "If you wish, I can be present at that meeting so that certain matters are made quite clear for the good of all."[77]

---

74 ACSI. Rutilio Grande to Archbishop Luis Chávez clarifying what happened, Aguilares, January 7, 1976.
75 Here, I have used some notes found among Rutilio's papers. It is quite likely that the homily adhered to them.
76 ACSI. Rutilio Grande to Archbishop Luis Chávez clarifying what happened, Aguilares, January 7, 1976.
77 ACSI. Rutilio Grande to Archbishop Luis Chávez clarifying what happened, Aguilares, January 7, 1976.

The discussion went beyond the archdiocese: it was taken up by the bishops' conference and also came to the attention of the nuncio, who had also received the memorandum from the president's office. Except for Rivera, the bishops were opposed to FECCAS and other popular organizations. They appealed to the Jesuit provincial to have FECCAS stop calling itself "Christian," and they prohibited priests from having any explicit or public affiliation with it. Archbishop Chávez opposed FECCAS because he considered its "Marxist" ideology antagonistic to Christianity, but he also had pastoral reasons: many of his pastors were complaining about the presence in their parishes of FECCAS organizers, who claimed to be evangelizers but whose main aim was to recruit new members. For its part, FECCAS and its collaborators viewed the archbishop as an oppressor beholden to the oligarchy, someone they wanted to unmask. While they did not confront him openly, they did so quietly and occasionally made public their criticisms.

President Molina appealed to the nuncio, Archbishop Emanuele Gerada, with his complaints against the "the 'third-worlder' priests" and particularly against Rutilio. In a meeting he had with the nuncio on March 6, 1976, the president asked the nuncio for more details about the December 21 demonstration in Aguilares. It is strange that, instead of asking Archbishop Chávez for an explanation—the complaint was about one of his pastors, after all—the president should have brought his concerns to the nuncio. The reason might have been that the nuncio had only recently arrived in the country and was a diplomat by training, whereas the ancient archbishop had, during his thirty-nine years in office, seen many presidents come and go—a fact of which he publicly boasted. While clearly favoring the positions of the president, the nuncio was willing to mediate between him and the archbishop. The nuncio responded to the president's inquiry on March 30, drawing on the letter Rutilio had sent to the archbishop on January 7. Most likely Rutilio himself gave the nuncio a copy of his letter during a conversation he had with him in the nunciature. In his letter to the president, the nuncio stated that Rutilio had asked for the opportunity to meet personally with the president to explain the events in Aguilares, but his petition had not been heeded.

The leaders of FECCAS, for their part, asked to meet with the bishops' conference to explain their identity and their activities, but they were turned down. Their respectful letter, dated December 3, 1975, explained the organization's mission as protecting the right of the rural poor to organize for the defense of their interests, a right that Archbishop Chávez himself had affirmed in his most recent pastoral letters. The letter insisted that FECCAS had preserved its "Christian" voice because it was inspired by Gospel values; most of its members were Christian, and they had enlisted in its ranks precisely out of Christian commitment. That did not mean that FECCAS was a formally Catholic organization and therefore dependent on the hierarchy. On the contrary, it was independent.⁷⁸ The reference to the archbishop's pastoral letters did little to help their cause: the other bishops disagreed not only with the archbishop's teaching but also with his performance.

At one point, Rutilio raised questions about the validity of the political organization's decision to call itself "Christian." According to the testimony of a member of the missionary team, Rutilio argued and "even fought" with the leaders of the organization about using that term: "'Drop that word "Christian,"' he'd tell them. 'We've already had our fill of "Christian Democracy."' [...] 'Father Tilo,' they'd reply, 'the Christian Democrats are neither democratic nor Christian. Encourage us, and help us to be organized Christians.' Replies like that disarmed Rutilio, but they evangelized him, he said."⁷⁹

Despite the archbishop's opposition to FECCAS, Rutilio defended the organization and sought the counsel of the juridical office of the Association of Salvadoran Universities, which viewed FECCAS as one of the so-called intermediate organizations that had an undeniable right to exist since it was neither a guild nor a political party. Rutilio reminded the archbishop that the documents of Medellín and his own pastoral letters had defended this type of intermediate organization and that the most recent documents of the magisterium urged Christians to become agents of change. Rutilio included as evidence a document with quotations from the papal magisterium, Vatican II, and Medellín.⁸⁰ In light of those documents, he argued, pastors could not oppose such organizations; on the contrary, they had the duty to shed on them the light of the Gospel. In the particular case of FECCAS, he continued, it should be remembered that its origins, its associations, and its membership were all Christian. The mission of the pastor, therefore, was to help the organization's members to remain faithful to Gospel values and to maintain their ties to the Christian communities. At least, that was how the parish of Aguilares understood its responsibility: "It is our duty and our serious obligation to accompany them on this journey with the light of faith. Otherwise we will become the prey of Marxist groups and other radicals who proliferate around the country, forming organizations that are divorced from the faith in both ideology and praxis."⁸¹ Rutilio came out in defense of the rural poor who were organized because he knew there was no way he could abandon them; they were "his people" even though they were politically active in an organization with which he had serious differences. Besides, as he told the archbishop, they were members of the Christian communities of his

---

78   ACSI. "National Executive Committee of FECCAS to the Bishops' Conference of El Salvador, by Way of Archbishop Chávez and Bishop Rivera, and to All Its Bases in the Salvadoran Countryside, December 3, 1975."
79   *Summarium testium*, witness 2, §22.
80   ACSI. "Intermediate Organizations and Structures of Subsistence Farmers."
81   ACSI. Rutilio Grande to Archbishop Luis Chávez clarifying what happened, Aguilares, January 7, 1976.

parish. Their political militancy was not a sufficient reason to abandon them to their enemies and leave them defenseless.

Few people understood Rutilio's pastoral stance and how it flowed directly from his sense of Christian duty and ministerial responsibility. The confusion about the parish's mission was to some extent inevitable given the growing ideological polarization of Salvadoran society and the effects of the evangelization and the subsequent organization of the rural poor. It was predictable that the parish and the pastor of Aguilares would be accused of promoting class struggle and class enmity. The landowners of Aguilares and their allies in San Salvador claimed to be Catholics who loved and respected the church, but they were viscerally opposed to what they viewed as a perverse dissemination of a hatred of capitalism and an atheistic diffusion of socialism. Rutilio and the missionary team, despite all their explanations and good intentions, were fated to be perceived in those terms. They had attacked the established order by undermining the traditional religiosity that was one of its strongest bulwarks and a major source of its legitimacy.

Rutilio was now no longer identified with a political party or with a faction of the opposition. His most serious crime, defending the common good and the right of the rural poor to organize, made him a revolutionary and a subversive. His charismatic leadership when confronting both local and national authorities at critical moments reinforced this false perception. Despite possible misunderstanding, Rutilio believed that as a religious leader he could not remain on the sidelines of the political struggle for the common good, a struggle founded on the eternal values of the Gospel, which coincided with the most basic human values. Though fully conscious of the risks he was taking, Rutilio did not retreat; he understood that calumny, contradiction, and persecution were an integral part of his priestly ministry.

A Real "Galilee Crisis"

The irruption of FECCAS into the parish disrupted the carefully prepared pastoral plan of Rutilio and the missionary team. Just as they seemed to be making good progress with pastoral work in the rural areas, the import of the organization's activities called into question the soundness of the evangelization project,

> not only because it meant the project might have to be reconceived, but because it was disheartening to see another force "destroying" the project that was the result of so much effort. We felt that what was being destroyed was the very process that had produced and invigorated a good group of people, and we feared that the whole project was being led toward suicide.[82]

---

82 ACSI. "Document of the Missionary Team on the Relations between the Parish and the Organization."

The real crisis, Rutilio's last, came about unexpectedly. The missionary team had always planned on promoting organization of the rural poor as part of its pastoral project, but it was viewed as a medium-term goal. The sudden emergence of FECCAS, the ensuing ambiguity, and the resulting conflict surprised the team, sinking it into another period of vacillation, anxiety, and even desolation. For Rutilio, the dream of a lifetime was coming undone. As had also happened in the seminary, he was tempted simply to leave. Despite the sense of dejection that overcame him, he revealed his anxiety to no one apart from the missionary team and his Jesuit companions.

At the end of September 1975, for example, Rutilio wrote with buoyant enthusiasm from La Antigua, Guatemala, to "his brothers, sisters, and friends" in Aguilares. At the time, he was taking part in a monthlong course on pastoral ministry (September 8 to October 4) that had been organized by CELAM for fifty priests from Central America and Panama:

> It is wonderful to see how everywhere in our five nations of Central America and in Panama people are making laudable efforts in our church to announce the Gospel faithfully. It is the Gospel of Jesus, and its dynamic (transformative) force is what is changing the face of our church. I encourage you with all my personal conviction to keep working in all our communities so that we understand and try to live the Gospel for the benefit of our peoples. That is what all the bishops of our continent want.[83]

Apparently, the camaraderie and the opportunity to share experiences with other priests of the region lifted Rutilio's spirits. His letter reveals that his stay in La Antigua helped him feel confirmed in his experience in Aguilares; he came to understand that the problems there were normal. The other priests probably expressed interest in and admiration for the Aguilares experience, and they were impressed by the presence and personality of Rutilio himself.

The crisis was in large measure inevitable because the two essentially divergent dynamics—the pastoral ministry of the missionary team and the political activities of FECCAS—coincided in the same time and space and affected the same population; moreover, they shared the same intermediate leaders, the same infrastructures, and the same methodology. The divergent dynamics led parish and organization to adopt different and even contradictory stances in confronting the same social reality. Rutilio compared the situation to that of a father at odds with his sixteen-year-old son who refuses to obey his orders, demands his independence, and rejects the father's advice—but also asks him for money so that he can live on his own and have fun with his friends. Trying to understand the contradiction involved, the father struggles so that his love for his son will

---

83 ACSI. Rutilio Grande to dear friends and relatives of Aguilares, La Antigua, September 24, 1975.

overcome his feelings of disapproval and rejection. Even then, the father is ignorant of the son's activities.[84]

Rutilio's leadership was misunderstood. His repeated efforts to dispel the confusion about the relationship between the parish and FECCAS failed for at least three reasons: he continually defended the right of the rural poor to organize, he protected the FECCAS members being persecuted by the military regime, and he objected to the bishops' reservations and condemnations of the organization. Even within the parish, his reasons for insisting on a sharp separation between parish and organization were not well understood. It seems that Rutilio was unable to discern clearly the contours of that separation himself, as was evident from the protection he gave the persecuted members, using any means he had at his disposal. As pastor and defender of the common good, he felt he could not act otherwise. Rutilio foresaw that the consequences of the ever more brutal government repression could be devastating for both the organization and the parish. "What am I going to do when they bring me a murdered catechist?" he once exclaimed, according to the testimony of a Jesuit who was living with him then.[85]

Beginning in mid-1975, Rutilio frequently sought assistance at the Christian Legal Aid Office, which had been founded earlier that year in the Colegio Externado San José. The director of the office at the time gave the following testimony:

> For more than a year and a half, from September 1975 until a week before his death, we had discussions with Father Grande and tried to solve problems related to land ownership and labor relations. He also asked us to provide him professional help in setting up educational programs for men and women in the rural areas.[86]

On countless occasions, Rutilio declared his solidarity with the small farmers and rural workers; he helped them strengthen their faith and be personally converted; and he urged them to work to transform personal, community, and social life in order to guarantee freedom to organize, reform of social structures, and respect for basic human rights. Despite the expectations of FECCAS, however, Rutilio did not believe he could help them in the specifically political realm:

> For my part, I want to tell you that such a task requires an expert in political matters (tactics, strategies, concrete actions). I am not an expert, so don't expect that of me (though I admit I must do everything possible to stay abreast of political events in order to avoid blunders). But I repeat: I am not nor do I believe I should be a political leader involved in your political

---

84 ACSI. "The Relationship between Organization and Parish: Opinion of the Group."
85 *Summarium testium*, witness 10, §141.
86 *Summarium testium*, witness 19, §368.

actions. It may be the case that, if you're lacking for a time laypeople well equipped in this area, one of us can play a supplementary role as an advisor.[87]

The FECCAS leadership accepted Rutilio's position but insisted that the team should at least "be with us in everything." In other words, the organization's leaders wanted the parish and its structures to serve them in a preferential way. Rutilio could not accept such a demand since it negated the autonomy of the parish. He told them that the organization could count on the parish's support and his own, especially in denouncing the regime's abuses and in defending the cause of the poor, but the support did not mean that the team was in agreement with the ideology and the practice of FECCAS. The support was a consequence of the parish's evangelical convictions, which in this case coincided with those of the organization.

Accordingly, from the end of 1975 until mid-1976, Rutilio was willing to exercise a pastoral ministry of accompaniment, a theme that Archbishop Romero would later take up in his homilies and above all in his *Tercera carta pastoral: Sobre la Iglesia y las organizaciones políticas populares* (Third pastoral letter: On the church and the people's political organizations), published on August 6, 1978. For Rutilio, the goal of such a ministry of accompaniment was not to weary "the most outstanding people nor to exhaust the already exhausted, but to encourage the leaders and to motivate the laggards, without dividing the flock."[88]

On March 9, 1975, the missionary team explained the situation in the parish to the national council of the Jesuits and asked for guidance. Rutilio expressed his fear that the pastoral work might suffer due to several factors: the "displacement or capture" of the best community leaders by FECCAS; the increasingly elitist attitude of the FECCAS leaders and their ever greater distance from their bases, with the danger that the bases ignore them or repudiate them; the consequent sense of abandonment felt by the Christian communities; the absolutizing tendencies of the country's politics, with a "unidimensional vision" overwhelming other dimensions of human life; a certain "puritan mentality" that was resistant to the parish's pastoral ministry; and a tendency to instrumentalize religion. The missionary team considered that at that moment the activity of the FECCAS organizers was "falling at an acute angle on the community spaces, presenting the manifest danger that the work will disintegrate":

> We believe that the pace of growth of these leaders has been excessive. They have utilized the parish's internal activities in a way that endangers the parish's work, [and they engage in] actions we judge to be precipitous. [...] We do not want to serve as a stage for a process with which we do not agree.[89]

---

87 ACSI. Rutilio Grande, "Our Work and Our Objectives."
88 "Relationship between Organization and Parish: Opinion of the Group."
89 ACSI. "The Aguilares Affair and the Society of Jesus, March 1, 1975," edited by Salvador Carranza, discussed by the missionary team, and presented to the Jesuits' national council on March 9, 1975.

The organizers' instrumentalization of the parish called into question their faith and sincerity, and it forced the team to "ask what difference exists between them and other groups we oppose because of their desire to 'instrumentalize' religion."[90] The clergy would run a similar danger whenever they allowed themselves to be used for political purposes.[91]

The team reported that "our most conscientized faithful" were meeting in the parish's facilities for endless hours on weekends, and even on workdays, but they could find no time to share their faith, their commitment, and their hope; they were not seeking reconciliation or bearing witness to the Lord's presence in their activities. For Rutilio, it was especially shocking that the great majority of believers, despite being "sprinkled" Christians with less commitment, came to church on Sundays to participate in the Eucharist, while the "great conscious ones" were meeting in a nearby facility, busy in discussions about the affairs of FECCAS:

> Even granting that life is liturgy, that action is prayer, and blah, blah, blah, […] it is possible for us to go from one sacramentalist extreme to the other: the law of the pendulum. And if the Eucharist can find a place in any group, it would certainly be in that handful of "conscious ones" who hole up in the catacomb of our little yellow house.[92]

Rutilio even came to regret the abandonment of the traditional confessional: "We hardly ever put ourselves in the wooden boxes to hear confessions." He thought that the parish had not made enough effort to celebrate periodic penitential acts with the most conscious elements, "acts of reconciliation in which the 'collective' penitential acclamation allows the opportunity for some individuals to seek to confess a hidden serious sin."[93] The abandonment of traditional confession was probably due not just to the neglect of the missionary team but to a change in people's attitude: "Most people now see sin as social sin, the domination of some by others, the taking advantage of others. Previously, people didn't think that way; now they do." Rutilio also feared that the organizers would refuse to recognize the church's hierarchical authority since the team had not stressed that essential aspect of Catholicism sufficiently. The team even wondered whether their failure in this regard had not contributed to a weakening of the organizers' faith.

A significant aspect of the crisis was the presence and activity of theology students, especially the ones who, in the team's opinion, had adopted radical stances. Even though the team valued their work and accepted some of their positions, they considered them unviable when taken as a whole. The differing visions made it difficult for the team to achieve good coordination with the

---

90 ACSI. Rutilio Grande, "Sharing Our Concerns."
91 Grande, "Our Work and Our Objectives."
92 The "little yellow house" was a dependency of the rectory. Grande, "Our Work and Our Objectives."
93 Grande, "Our Work and Our Objectives."

students and their other collaborators. On July 31, 1975, for example, there was a concelebrated Mass in the cathedral for the students who had been killed by the army the day before. As Rutilio was leaving after the Mass, a Jesuit scholastic informed him that a group would be occupying the church. During the subsequent occupation, various "processions [left] Aguilares to feed into the demonstration at the doors of the cathedral." The parish thus found itself at the center of the protest even though the members of the missionary team had no idea who was behind it. Their only thought was: "This is serious, [...] and we know nothing."[94]

Nor did the team know anything about what the collaborators were doing outside the parish. In fact, some theology students, accompanied by promotors of FECCAS, were presenting themselves in other parishes as envoys of Aguilares. Rutilio had not only not commissioned them but he knew nothing of their activities. "All this falls outside my competence," he explained.[95] Moreover, the theology students were no longer living in Aguilares: in early 1976, they were moved by superiors to San Salvador, for fear of possible repression. FECCAS took over the house where the scholastics had been living. Since Rutilio did not have access to information about the activities of FECCAS and the scholastics, he could not evaluate them and was forced in the end to take on "an uncomfortable role, one that sometimes exceeds the limits of my competency."[96]

The real possibility of repression was of increasing concern to the team, but it seemed not to worry the leaders of FECCAS or the Jesuit scholastics. The danger to the parish increased to the degree that the organization became more consolidated, and the team feared for the personal safety of the communities and the organizers. In early 1976, the security forces captured two students of the Colegio Externado who were working with the adult literacy program. When informed of their detention, Rutilio was quite distressed, and he visited several communities—El Líbano (March 3), Tres Ceibas (March 6), and Buena Vista (March 7)—to gather firsthand information. "If they kill us or put us in prison, magnificent!" he wrote to the archbishop. "But let us hope that they don't crush the villagers and our collaborators because of us!"[97] As the dangers for the parish increased, the members of the team were personally exposed to risks without fully realizing it.

The situation was complicated even more by certain personalities and temperaments that hampered the team's relations with the scholastics, with Marcelino Pérez, and with some of the leaders of FECCAS. Feeling they were in a stalemate, Rutilio complained about Pérez, objecting to his obstinacy, his aggressiveness,

---

94 "Aguilares Affair and the Society of Jesus, March 1, 1975."
95 "Aguilares Affair and the Society of Jesus, March 1, 1975."
96 ACSI. Rutilio Grande to Archbishop Luis Chávez, Aguilares, January 11, 1976.
97 ACSI. Rutilio Grande to Archbishop Luis Chávez, Aguilares, January 11, 1976.

and his "excessive confidence in his own ideas." At the same time, the leaders of FECCAS offered harsh criticism of the missionary team's "prudence":

> Within the team there are some who, after saying that we [FECCAS] were the ones that brought the Gospel down to earth, are now claiming that we are asking too much and that not everybody is going to support the mobilizations. They [the team's members] started things off, but now they don't want to follow through. Since the bishop is wealthy and quite content, he doesn't want to meet with us. That is why not all the priests want to support us. So we are the ones who have to take the reins in this struggle because we are the ones being maltreated.[98]

In the national council of Jesuits, the superior of the community of theology students, Father Rafael Moreno, disagreed with the opinion expressed by Rutilio. He thought that what was obstructing good relations with the FECCAS leaders was the lack of leadership in the missionary team: "It seems to me that they [the team] hold positions that are too rigid as regards perspectives and practice. There is certain absolutization." Moreno consequently proposed that the parish be headed by someone with the appropriate charism.

At that point, Rutilio gave a long, detailed narration of his own personal journey: his departure from the seminary, his time at the Colegio Externado, and his "landing" in the parish. In retrospect, he said, "I committed a sin of idealism in my precipitous decision to join the team [...] in such a precarious work. It was idealism, naiveté, lack of true realism and prior engagement!" He said that when he left the college he investigated the possibility of working in Nicaragua and Panama. He had not chosen the parish in Aguilares. "I was quite surprised by the choice of site, for obvious personal reasons." His decision to go to Aguilares was influenced by "certain elements" that had pressured him to accept the assignment. He did not identify those elements, but he was probably referring to Bengoechea and, through him, to Boulang and his group. Rutilio said that even then he was feeling frustrated because he considered that he would be wasting time and energy on an unviable project. The rise of FECCAS shortly afterward had only aggravated his sense of crisis.[99]

The national council attributed the disagreement between the missionary team and the scholastics to differences of method and rhythm, which were aggravated by the lack of dialogue and coordination. The council noted that, after the establishment of the community of theology students in Aguilares, both groups had committed themselves to engaging in dialogue and coordination. They felt it was important to avoid the difficulties that had arisen with the first community of scholastics, made up of philosophy students. This mutual commitment

---

98 ACSI. "Evaluation of the Communities," Aguilares, October 1976.
99 Grande, "Address to the National Council."

provided for the independence of each community and the collaboration of the scholastics with the parish, but it the end it did not work out. The missionary team thought that it should determine the extent of the parish's collaboration with FECCAS, but the scholastics felt that their pastoral activity was one thing and their political activity was another. One of the scholastics most involved in FECCAS claimed that the main difficulty was that the missionary team understood liberation in religious terms when in reality it was a political question. He explained that, while the organization was not taking on a religious role, the parish still had an important part to play in the political realm: "The parish has to take on itself the whole of the people's struggle in order to be able to give it theological meaning. [...] That is why the parish is important." Another theology student summed the matter up as follows:

> The people think well of you [the missionary team] who began the work and opened our eyes, but now we have to seek out new ways to express ourselves. You were the seed, the kernel. [...] Now we have to seek out new channels. We are thankful for what you did. Some people think that the fathers have been absent from their hardest struggles. The parish is appreciated for lending its locales to the organization; that shows that the priests still agree with us. The villagers have defended the sermon [of Salvador Carranza at the San Francisco Hacienda], and even though he said Mass at the exploiters' chapel, they recognize that he did not sell out to them and that he declared to them the truth.[100]

The national council of the Jesuits finally concluded that it was necessary to find a way to facilitate dialogue, respect the rhythm of the people, overcome dogmatism, avoid despotic leaders, and unite the Gospel with praxis. The council recommended that the Jesuit provincial explain the position of the theology students to the archbishop. The two communities met regularly from April 3 on, as the council had requested, but the relationship did not improve appreciably, due to lack of clarity and mutual resentment. They were not totally isolated from one another, however, since the informal channels of communication functioned quite effectively.[101]

Despite the misunderstandings, the misinterpretations, and the sharp remarks exchanged, Rutilio genuinely appreciated the contribution of the Jesuit scholastics, about whose good will he had no doubt. Moreover, he considered them to be excellent persons: sacrificial, hard-working, and committed. He especially admired their capacity for dedicated service to the rural poor. "In regards to the parish, I have nothing of substance against the work of these young men," he wrote to Archbishop Chávez, who had asked him to explain the controversial activities during the celebration of the Campesino Christmas in 1975:

---

100 ACSI. "Meeting between Theology Students and the Parish," Aguilares, October 29, 1975.
101 Grande, "Address to the National Council."

> Yes, I have made clear my disagreements with them on some issues before the higher authorities of the Company of Jesus here in Central America. Concretely, I have personally objected to the accelerated pace in certain areas where they have taken advantage of the parish process and the parish itself. Thanks to a little dialogue and patience, but not without understandable tensions, it was possible to moderate them somewhat starting in May [1975], and the results have been beneficial.[102]

Rutilio not only exonerated the scholastics before the archbishop but recognized that he was indebted to them despite the problems:

> It is important to keep in mind that we are dealing with young people, and some of their actions are in keeping with the characteristics of their age. It is possible that we adults sin in the opposite direction. What is certain is that they have helped me personally in my process of conversion and developing greater awareness, but that does not mean that I accept all the positions of some of them without reserve.[103]

Months later, when three of the scholastics—Alberto Henríquez, a theology student, and Fernando Ascoli and Antonio Cardenal, who were in special studies—decided to leave the Society of Jesus, Rutilio was distressed and wrote to the provincial, Father Jerez, asking him to do everything he could to get the young men to reconsider their decision. When this proved no longer possible, Rutilio interceded with the provincial to help get the young men work; he even said that he would be very happy to see them continue their work in Aguilares as laymen employed by the Society.[104]

Rutilio had a generally very positive opinion of the younger Jesuits. Expressing himself in a more serene context, he recognized that there was perhaps "more authenticity" in their spiritual formation than in that of older Jesuits. The younger men had "a greater opportunity for formation in freedom," and their studies were "appropriate" whereas "ours were lamentable." Their style of community life favored personal relationships: "They were formed to live in community and not to be just a number in the community." Their immersion in the Central American reality was "suitable and laudable"; their relations with the laity were "normal and correct"; their obedience was "more adult, more responsible, and more freely assumed, though it is hard for us older folk to acknowledge it"; "in general," their political commitment was "significant"; they made a "praiseworthy" effort as regards personal and communal poverty; their knowledge of the Society of Jesus tended to favor the early traditions, "and that is good, as with Christianity itself." Rutilio expressed his desire to live in a community

---

102 ACSI. Rutilio Grande to Archbishop Luis Chávez, Aguilares, January 11, 1976.
103 ACSI. Rutilio Grande to Archbishop Luis Chávez, Aguilares, January 11, 1976.
104 Personal communication of Father César Jerez, provincial, with the author.

that included young Jesuits because he thought it "the best way to establish generational bridges and complementarities," but he confessed: "It might be hard for me." The new patterns of formation undoubtedly involved certain risks, he granted, but "every age has its risks. It is better to run the present risks than to go back to forming the *mummies* of the past."[105]

At the end of 1975, Rutilio and the missionary team sensed that they were at an impasse, and that impression grew stronger during the first weeks of 1976. The dialogues and agreements with the FECCAS leadership had not produced the hoped-for results. The persistence of the difficult entanglement caused Rutilio to doubt the validity of the team's perspective since they had been unable to respond adequately to the challenge presented by FECCAS. "We are going through a good Galilee crisis," he wrote, a crisis he wanted to navigate with integrity, courage, and creativity. Experience had taught him that crisis was not only a time of existential anguish but also a call to conversion.

During those months, the missionary team considered three options. The first (and easiest) was to abandon the parish to its fate, but it rejected that option out of hand. The second option was to seek an internal solution along the lines of previous efforts, but that was no longer possible since the situation had changed. The third option was to foster the development of both the parish and FECCAS with the help of suitable mechanisms and to assume the ambiguity and risks involved. This option did not appear easy, but given the circumstances, there seemed to be no viable alternative. The precipitousness of events was forcing the members of the team to act swiftly. The worst option would be to do nothing and let events overwhelm them.

It was in this context, probably around the middle of 1976, that the team began to talk about doing a general evaluation of the parish: assessing its trajectory thus far and considering future possibilities. Rutilio had already expressed such a desire, which was shared by the team, in the following terms:

> I would like to see the genesis of these events; they are very strange. I would like to see an analysis of the profound causes of what is happening. I believe there are two parallel lines that correspond to two different methods: one of organization and one of pastoral action. [...] It's not just something anecdotal. I'm mystified by this qualitative leap.[106]

In his homily during the Festival of Maize in August 1976, Rutilio announced the evaluation:

> We are at the point of calling a break in our parish activities. Four years after arriving here, we have entered into a new dynamic. We call the break in order to carry out an honest evaluation in which we will be assisted by

---

105 Ministries Commission, Technical Group, survey of Rutilio Grande, San Salvador, 1976.
106 "Aguilares Affair and the Society of Jesus, 1 March 1975."

other older heads who come from outside. The break will be for reflection, for seeing what the good things are that we must continue to support, what paths we must follow, and what things we must avoid, so that we can move forward in this colossal work of yours with the help of God and with our own humble service.[107]

The provincial, Father Jerez, approved the evaluation project, and after making his canonical visit to the community from January 18 to 24, 1977, he commissioned three Jesuits to carry it out: anthropologists Ricardo Falla and Carlos R. Cabarrús and a theology student of the community in Aguilares, who by that time had been ordained a priest:

> The question that most worried Father Rutilio Grande was this: How did this phenomenon in Aguilares originate? What is the best way to explain the extremely rapid growth of the pastoral work and the decision of the rural people to organize autonomously to defend their rights and even form a political front at the national level?[108]

The two researchers spent more than a month visiting the communities, interviewing many of their members, and conducting surveys. In April 1977, they submitted to the provincial two long, dense studies that were kept confidential for security reasons. Rutilio never learned of the results of the evaluation and the subsequent recommendations. Indeed, his death on March 12 cast a new light on the whole situation.

From the time the crisis began, in early 1975, Rutilio considered the possibility of leaving the parish. Nearly a year later, on January 11, 1976, he presented his formal resignation to Archbishop Chávez and to the provincial. During the Spiritual Exercises he made from April 22 to 29, 1975, Rutilio gave much thought to the question of whether he should resign, and the events of that year only confirmed his decision to do so. His request to resign, therefore, was not the "fruit of a whimsical or immature decision,"[109] nor was it due to any desire to escape the difficulties and risks in the pastoral work. He explained his reasoning to the archbishop:

> You know well, from the many private conversations we have had, that I love the church and my priestly vocation as a religious, despite my own deficiencies and limitations. And with the help of the Lord I want to continue serving in this unique vocation of radical Christian commitment in ministry and in religious life.[110]

---

107 Grande, homily during the Festival of Maize.
108 ACSI. César Jerez to Pedro Arrupe, San Salvador, July 21, 1977.
109 ACSI. Rutilio Grande to Archbishop Luis Chávez, Aguilares, January 11, 1976.
110 ACSI. Rutilio Grande to Archbishop Luis Chávez, Aguilares, January 11, 1976.

Rutilio had no doubts about the importance of the work being done in a parish like Aguilares: "I sincerely believe that this work is a valuable experience that deserves to be continued, and that the Society must be completely responsible for it, even if only for a limited time."[111] Afterward, he believed, duly prepared diocesan priests could carry on. The team had, in fact, already thought about Father Octavio Cruz, one of its members, as the diocesan priest who might best give continuity to the work. In any case, Rutilio felt overwhelmed by the highly complex entity that the parish had become. Even though the Society of Jesus had assumed responsibility for the work and had offered its help, in the end the brunt of the responsibility fell on him.

In his letter of resignation to the archbishop, Rutilio said that his case was not exceptional since many other priests of the archdiocese also found themselves in a similar situation. More and more priests, in fact, were facing problems like the ones he was having with the popular organizations. At the same time, the situation of the country as a whole was becoming more complicated by the day, and it required concrete, faith-inspired answers. Rutilio had presented the question to the priests' senate, where the discussion was inconclusive, but he still believed that there was a pressing need to address the question rigorously since the social scene was becoming ever more volatile. It was one thing, he wrote, to sin out of naiveté and let the church be instrumentalized for lack of preparation, but it was something quite different to prepare oneself carefully by analyzing and confronting the ideologies that were eager to take advantage of the faith and the ecclesial groups. In Rutilio's opinion, the church itself was being called into question by the reality of the nation.[112]

Despite his resignation, Rutilio continued at the head of the parish, but he took a short vacation during Holy Week of 1976. He spent those days in the company of a former student of the seminary, Gregorio Landaverde, who was the pastor of Juigalpa, Chontales, Nicaragua. He helped him with the parish chores.

The increasingly turbulent situation made it necessary to discuss the nature of the relationship of the Society of Jesus with the parish of Aguilares. On November 7, 1975, the team proposed that the Society of Jesus and the archdiocese of San Salvador sign a contract that would replace the generic verbal agreement by which the Society had originally taken charge of the parish. The contract would be for two years, until September 30, 1977, and it could be renewed or rescinded by either party provided written notice was given six months before. When this proposal did not prosper, the provincial presented an alternative to the missionary team. The signatories of the contract would be the archbishop and Rutilio, who "will procure from the provincial the assignment of the Jesuit priests necessary for the collaborative work." Although no time period was defined, the

---

111 ACSI. Rutilio Grande to Archbishop Luis Chávez, Aguilares, January 11, 1976.
112 ACSI. Rutilio Grande to Archbishop Luis Chávez, Aguilares, January 11, 1976.

contract was rescindable with prior written notice of three months. This contract was never signed either because Rutilio refused to be the signatory. In a meeting he had with the archbishop and the provincial, he said that he did not want to be the only one shouldering the responsibility for the four-person team, the "gang of seven" theology students, and the popular organization that was seeking support and protection.

Rutilio not only continued on as pastor of Aguilares but he also extended his influence to the neighboring parish of Guazapa, which had no priest. Another Jesuit, José Luis Ortega, was added to the missionary team and helped him there. The pastoral plan in Guazapa was patterned after that of Aguilares: the missionary team went ahead of the sheep in search of "good pasture," but when the sheep were well on the way to the house of the Father, the team would follow behind. It would accompany those who were in the lead and would provoke and encourage those who lagged behind, always keeping one eye on the vanguard and the other on the rearguard. The challenge was twofold: not holding back those who were running ahead and not neglecting those who walked slowly. The team gave seven missions during November and December 1976. Since Rutilio took part in all of them, he was unable to accept the invitation to direct the spiritual exercises of the archdiocesan clergy.[113]

During his canonical visit from the January 18 to 24, 1977, the provincial, Father Jerez, found in Aguilares a community with a profound spiritual life and an apostolic ministry inspired by decree 2 of the Society's Thirty-Second General Congregation:

> I can say that the community has an intense spiritual life, is dedicated to service of the people—both priestly service and service of the faith in ways that are not strictly sacramental—and is very seriously committed to the promotion of justice. For the most part they have daily prayer and Mass, and all have made the annual spiritual exercises.[114]

It was also a poor community. "The house is a poor one; it has just enough so that they can live in it with great simplicity and sobriety. The economic scarcity they have experienced has not caused them problems." In fact, the provincial found that "in Aguilares there is no concern about economic matters, about where we will get money, about what we need or don't need, etc. I have also seen how they share the little they have with those in need."[115]

During his account of conscience, Rutilio spoke with the provincial at length and with confidence, as he enjoyed doing. Indeed, not only Rutilio but all the

---

113 ACSI. Salvador Carranza, "Preliminary Project for Extending the Pastoral Ministry of Aguilares: Toward an Interreligious Team of Rural Evangelization," Aguilares, July 18, 1976.
114 ACSI. César Jerez to Pedro Arrupe, San Salvador, July 21, 1977.
115 ACSI. César Jerez to Pedro Arrupe, San Salvador, July 21, 1977.

members of the team had given their accounts of conscience with great trust: "I can say that some of them gave their account of conscience with great clarity, as if they were novices. I want to make it clear now that Father Grande did so in a quite extraordinary manner; it took me the whole day to attend to him."[116] From that conversation, Father Jerez concluded that Rutilio was "an extraordinary man with great leadership qualities within the parish team, and I would say, within the whole vicariate and within the archdiocese as well." In his report on the visit, written after Rutilio's murder, Father Jerez summed up Rutilio's life with these words: "Father Rutilio Grande García has given his life for the service of faith and the promotion of justice in this zone, and we can say that he is a martyr that the Central American province can claim in this century."[117]

---

116 ACSI. César Jerez to Pedro Arrupe, San Salvador, July 21, 1977.
117 ACSI. César Jerez to Pedro Arrupe, San Salvador, July 21, 1977.

10. Persecution of the Church

For a time, the relative openness of the military regime made it possible for the agrarian movement to gain some strength in different parts of the country. FECCAS, for example, was able to develop and consolidate its bases under the aegis of the church. However, toward the end of Molina's government, as local authorities were proving incapable of containing the pressure being generated by the rural movements, the regime repressed them violently, and the church along with them. It was in the context of this brutal repression against the church that Rutilio was murdered on March 12, 1977.

Rutilio and the missionary team were apparently not fully unaware of how quickly the situation had evolved. They were working intensely during those days, with neither the time nor the energy needed to reflect calmly on the developing events. They were ill-prepared to face the impending crisis, but they remained in the parish.

The Agrarian Reform

On June 29, 1976, the government approved an agrarian reform project, which was immediately opposed by the oligarchy, especially the agro-exporting sector.[1] The resulting confrontation was not only between the regime and the oligarchy but also between the regime and the church. For three months, the forces opposed to the reform project fought ferociously against the measure. Finally, on October 30, despite the president's promise not to retreat, the government caved in to the landowners' demands. With the oligarchy obliging the government to desist from confiscating their properties, the project was condemned to failure. Capital came out of the confrontation emboldened; it now had enormous power over the regime and could impose its will.

The first "Project of Agrarian Transformation," as it was called, was actually quite modest. It proposed distributing agricultural properties larger than fifty *manzanas* in only two departments: Usulután and San Miguel, where some of the best-managed and most-productive cotton plantations were to be found. The project therefore did not affect the zone of Aguilares. The land affected by the law was to be confiscated from the owners and resold to some twelve thousand families. The government would not only compensate the landowners for the declared value of their properties but it would also offer them incentives if they invested in industry. A subsequent change in the law

---

[1] The 1976 agrarian reform was a pilot program affecting only four percent of El Salvador's agricultural land. Even though it was small scale and offered very generous terms for former owners, it was successfully resisted by landlords, with military and vigilante support.

allowed the landowners to sell their properties at market price. The project was to be financed by the Inter-American Development Agency, an organism of the US government that had made preliminary studies. According to the terms of the project, several decades would be needed before the agrarian reform could encompass the whole country.

The Project of Agrarian Transformation and its vicissitudes unleashed a virulent ideological struggle not only between oligarchic capital and the government but also between oligarchic capital and those sectors that backed the reform despite its clear limitations. When the UCA, on July 9, 1976, publicly expressed its support for the project itself but not for the regime's intentions, there were furious reactions against the university's decision, both from the private sector and from the BPR. The editorial team of the university's official journal, *Estudios Centroamericanos* (*ECA*), under the direction of Father Ellacuría, dedicated a special issue to agrarian transformation, with an editorial expressing support for the project. When Molina's government finally ended, *ECA* denounced what it called the dictatorship of the oligarchy in an editorial titled, "A sus órdenes, mi capital" (At your orders, Lord Capital).[2] Two articles in the January 1977 issue of the journal analyzed the modifications introduced into the original decree of the reform. Some of the clergy in Usulután and San Miguel found themselves in the same awkward position as the UCA since they also had lent some credibility to the regime by supporting the project. A number of them even met with functionaries of the Institute for Agrarian Transformation to assess the reach of the project and to consider the wisdom of supporting it in their respective parishes. Although the missionary team in Aguilares made no public statement, it was in agreement with the UCA's position.

ANEP, which included some thirty large companies, reacted with extreme virulence against the UCA. A well-financed press campaign accused the university, along with the regime, of being communist. FARO, which included the large landowners of the areas affected by the reform, acted as a spearhead for the big business sector as a whole. FARO claimed that its aim was to prevent "any unexpected law [from being passed] and especially to work for the derogation of the law that creates the first Project of Agrarian Transformation." Another key objective of FARO was to keep track of the activities of FECCAS and UTC, which it claimed were organizations dedicated to inciting "unrest and turmoil" among their members.[3] FARO adopted an extremely aggressive, insolent attitude and became obsessively sectarian. The reactions of groups like FARO and ANEP derived from their obdurate defense of private property and their objection to any state interference in the economy.

---

2   *ECA* 337 (1976): 637–43.
3   "Falsos líderes son denunciados por FARO" [False leaders denounced by FARO], *El diario de hoy* (November 23, 1976).

At the other extreme, the BPR considered the agrarian reform to be opportunistic and insufficiently radical; it therefore attacked the UCA and other sectors that were in favor of the project. Stating its goals in the national press, the BPR declared that its duty was to unmask imperialism's plans of domination, help rural workers in the struggle to own the land, and engage the working class in a worker–farmer alliance. In view of its goals, the BPR viewed the agrarian reform as an imperialist measure that was economically and politically counterrevolutionary. In the view of BPR, the contradiction between ANEP, an organ of the creole bourgeoisie, and the military regime, an organ of imperialism, was simply a difference of criterion regarding the best way to control and exploit the people. BPR therefore opposed the UCA for supporting the military; it opposed FAPU for explaining the conflict between the private sector and the government as a political ploy of the oligarchy aimed at concealing the real unity that existed between them; and it opposed the Communist Party for its opportunism since its support for the agrarian project would contribute to the consolidation of the capitalist system and the modernization of exploitation. In the end, BPR called on the people to fight for a true and complete project of agrarian transformation.[4] Meanwhile, in the UCA, the relations between the university authorities and the FUR-30 became tense.

On the very day that the agrarian reform project was announced, July 30, 1976, BPR organized a demonstration to commemorate the first anniversary of the massacre of university students. The organization's propaganda spoke of ten thousand demonstrators, but there were in fact fewer than five thousand, and three thousand of those were members of FECCAS and the UTC. The other organizations contributed only a few hundred.[5] All the same, the size of the crowds and the discipline of the demonstration impressed the general public. The demonstration culminated with a Mass in the cathedral of San Salvador, followed by a vigil on the campus of the University of El Salvador that lasted the whole night. The Mass was something new, and it greatly pleased the BPR members who believed that religion had a place in their struggle.

Archbishop Chávez was not happy about the Mass, however, and he sanctioned the priests who concelebrated for disobeying his express prohibition. There had in fact been two concelebrated Masses, just as there had been two demonstrations, one organized by FAPU and the other by BPR. Given the circumstances, Chávez thought it best to prohibit both Masses. The pro-FAPU priests said they would be willing to obey the order if the pro-BPR priests did the same. No agreement was reached, and confusion ensued since the archbishop,

---

4 *La prensa gráfica* (July 30, 1976) and *La prensa gráfica* (September 4, 1976).
5 Union of Slum Dwellers (Unión de Pobladores de Tugurios), two hundred; Movement of Revolutionary Secondary School Students (Movimiento de Estudiantes Revolucionarios de Secundaria), 150; ANDES-June 21, 250; FUR-30, thirty; and UR-19, an undetermined number.

not knowing their respective sympathies, had not communicated his prohibition to all the possible concelebrants. Rutilio attended the BPR Mass but did not concelebrate. When summoned to meet with the bishops, the disobedient priests[6] asked to be heard in the presence of other clergy, including Rutilio.[7] The archbishop agreed and asked Fathers Cristóbal Cortés (the chancellor), Segura, and Amílcar Torruella to attend the meeting as well. The priests explained that they had concelebrated as a sign of their commitment and their solidarity with an oppressed, suffering people. They said they wanted to be a light for them at this critical moment, as they had been bidden to do by the universal magisterium, the archbishop himself, and the archdiocesan week of pastoral ministry. They regretted that they had been condemned before being heard. In response, the archbishop asked them to make the spiritual exercises, not as a punishment but as a time for reflection. The priests agreed, but they asked that the director and the dates of the exercises be changed and that the exercises focus on the conclusions of the pastoral ministry week. The archbishop agreed to their petitions and named Rutilio as director of the exercises.

On August 3, 1976, a month before that decision was made, Rutilio had criticized the bishops' attitude during a meeting of the priests' senate. He had insisted on the importance of reflecting on the situation of the country, precisely to avoid being surprised by situations such as the demonstration of July 30. Events were developing quickly and disorienting everyone. The popular organizations needed to improve their *modus operandi*, especially their mobilizing activities. The old ways of reacting to events were no longer valid because the situation had changed; responses could no longer be partial and improvised. Rutilio reminded the senate that already in 1970 the bishops' conference had discussed the matter in a reasonable way, but now the moment had arrived to accept the consequences of those declarations:

> Archbishop López Trujillo himself stated during the pastoral ministry course in Guatemala that the church had to implement this type of pastoral ministry decisively in our countries. One would have to be blind not to see the urgency of the situation in the rural areas of the country, and not to realize that the people's awareness is increasing progressively as a result of event and the concrete circumstances. [...] The government itself is up against a wall of events, and it is enough just to read the programmatic discourses of Mr. Molina. [...] He has said some significant things, whether he wanted to or not, and it's because of the pressure of the masses.[8]

---

6   Miguel Arévalo, Rutilio Sánchez, Rafael E. Barrera, Benito Tobar, Guillermo Rodríguez, Julio César Avelar, and Trinidad Nieto.
7   The other priests were Ástor Ruiz, Alfonso Navarro, and Carlos Mejía.
8   ACSI. "Act 31: Extraordinary Joint Meeting of the Priests' Senate and the Venerable Ecclesiastical Council," San Salvador, August 3, 1976.

Rutilio defended the basic goodness of the intermediate organizations and asked the archdiocese to accept the challenge they presented. Before those who expressed reservations, especially the archbishop, he argued convincingly that labor organizations were the only way to protect the fundamental rights of Salvadorans, and that the values defended by those organizations coincided with Gospel values, as the bishops' synod of 1975 had duly recognized.

Rutilio again insisted on the need to pay more attention to the situation of the priests, and he lamented the fact that the bishops' conference had thus far done little in that regard. His long experience in the seminary and his intimate knowledge of the diocesan clergy convinced him that many priests were serving with genuine apostolic zeal, but that they were also experiencing the same anguish as he was. Since the crisis in the country was causing them tremendous stress, they needed to be given assistance so that they might fulfill their apostolic mission. Rutilio said that he knew whereof he spoke and what he was asking of the bishops since he himself was experiencing the risks of carrying out evangelization in such circumstances.[9]

Defense of the People: Liberation on the Horizon

The BPR was not satisfied with simple pronouncements but insisted on organizing several demonstrations, one of them in Aguilares. Such mobilizations were the organization's means for consolidating its position on the national political stage. The demonstration in Aguilares, called for Sunday, September 12, was organized by FECCAS. Two days before that, MERS and UTC organized another demonstration in Usulután, one of the agrarian reform zones, for the purpose of "unmasking the much-trumpeted agrarian transformation." Most of the demonstrators were students of the zone and villagers who came from other regions for the occasion. The protest ended with a clash between villagers and police, in which one elderly lady was killed and four other persons, two villagers and two police, were wounded. The tumult began when the police tried to capture two villagers, who defended themselves. The death and the woundings were caused by the gunfire of plainclothes agents.

In Aguilares, there were no violent incidents. The demonstration to "unmask national independence" began at nine in the morning, the same time as the parish Mass. Rutilio was quite vexed by this coincidence of timing and the fact the organization, in order to attract crowds, had announced to the communities that there would be a Mass before the demonstration. Generally, any such activities would begin after Mass was over. To show his irritation, Rutilio placed the church's loudspeakers outside and declared, "Those of you who are attending Mass are the real Christians." Some people who were outside the church, when

---

9 "Act 31: Extraordinary Joint Meeting of the Priests' Senate and the Venerable Ecclesiastical Council."

they heard this, entered for the service. This sharp disagreement caused a rupture of nearly three months between the parish and FECCAS.

In his homily that day, Rutilio ardently defended the Salvadoran people even as he gave a negative assessment of the heroes of independence, the army, and the power of capital. He began by saying, "I am Salvadoran, and I love my country as much any anyone. [...] Even though I spent long years outside my homeland, I have at no moment betrayed my sincere devotion to her." Despite his journeys, he said, he had not lost his Salvadoran identity, nor could his ideas or his teachings be characterized as "foreign," an accusation often heard from 1968 on. His many trips abroad had opened his mind to "a type of wisdom founded on common sense." The basic theme for his homily was that Salvadoran society found itself stuck in "sweet memories" of a half-won independence. He claimed it was consequently necessary

> to recognize a bitter historical truth: it was not our people who won political emancipation from Spain. When I say "people," I am referring to that great majority which forms the essential and basic element of a nation, together with the territory. Our people were always silent; they were absent from what was happening.[10]

Rutilio's historical reasoning revealed uncommon knowledge of Central American history.

The foundation of the republic, he asserted, was democracy, the power of the people. Nevertheless, he asserted,

> we must humbly confess that in 1821[11] the people, the great majority of whom were culturally and economically marginalized, were not the ones who benefited from emancipation. Only a culturally and economically privileged minority were able to enjoy the benefits of emancipation from the beginning. Republican democracy was merely a formal, decorative framework for the existing state of things [...]. The people remained absent.[12]

Among the national leaders were the Aguilar brothers (Nicolás, Manuel, and Vicente), after whom the city of Aguilares was named. Even though they were priests, Rutilio said, they "owned their little haciendas near here, just to speak of the closest properties." Manuel José Arce, another national hero celebrated by the fervent nationalists, was also a landlord. The majority of the people, indigenous and *mestizo*, were secluded in the villages and on the indigo plantations "while events were taking place at the top," in the cities. A revolution "at the top" could

---

10 ACSI. Rutilio Grande, "The First Independence," Aguilares, September 12, 1976.
11 Central America became independent on September 15, 1821.
12 Grande, "First Independence."

not help the people. "The revolution was over. It was a revolution with no new content. In practical terms, it was only a change of metropole."[13]

There existed, then, "a most serious danger" of commemorating a "fictitious" independence and a freedom that did not exist, and doing so

> with parades, anthems, and flags which do no more than cover the sick patient with a blanket, while he lies in painful agony in the road. Enough! The time is coming and is now here when we have to face our reality if we truly want to keep from betraying the people once again![14]

In the body of his homily, Rutilio showed how the Salvadoran people, made up primarily of indigenous peoples, the natural proprietors of the land, had been betrayed:

> They are copper-skinned people with slanted eyes, like those of the people of the East. They are our Indians, whose blood we all carry within us; they have lived humiliated, dispossessed, and disconsolate since these lands were wrenched from their hands. They are the indisputable, unquestionable foundation of our people; we cannot deny it unless we want to deny our own identity. We have indigenous blood, and we are proud of it![15]

The indigenous peoples, who were the very bedrock of Salvadoran identity, had been cruelly robbed of their lands:

> These people, the original owners of these lands, which they received from their autochthonous forebears, are now dispossessed and reduced to begging! There are too many barbed-wire fences and stone walls stretched across the broad landscape of the homeland. So our people flee to the rocky slopes, crying out in lament: "We lack even a plot of land to sow our maize and our beans. We can't even collect firewood from the lands of the boss." Is this possible? Is this tolerable? Is this just? No! Never![16]

The second constitutive element of the Salvadoran people, according to Rutilio, was the mixed blood, the *mestizaje*. It would be wrong, he agreed, to deny the Spanish component, but it had arrived as an armed invasion, so that the process of *mestizaje* was simply "an oppressive incursion in which the European race oppressed the indigenous one." The oppression was both economic, because the indigenous peoples were dispossessed of their lands, and sexual, because their women were violated. Thus, "the East and the West came together in a violent fusion, and the product of that encounter is the *People*, the great majority."[17]

---

13   Grande, "First Independence."
14   Grande, "First Independence."
15   Grande, "First Independence."
16   Grande, "First Independence."
17   Grande, "First Independence."

The third important element of Salvadoran identity was the people's religiosity: "To ignore that reality would be to ignore the people themselves." The religious dimension was as important as the economic, social, and political dimensions. To those who viewed the people's religious spirit as alienating, Rutilio responded that any alienating elements in it were due simply to lack of adequate religious formation. The task, therefore, was to purify the people's religiosity by grounding it in the Gospel and orienting it toward the transformation of social structures. Doing that would give birth to men and women who were conscious of their dignity and convinced of the need to take an active role in the construction of their own history. Those who rejected the popular religiosity would be setting themselves against the people and playing into the hands of the usual detractors, who "raise the strawman of atheism forged in their own minds, in pursuit of a false god." For Rutilio, in contrast, the alternative was to struggle in faith to be liberated from every form of slavery.[18]

In a homily he gave years earlier, in September 1971, when the country was celebrating 150 years of independence, Rutilio wondered aloud whether the situation of the people had been improved by independence. His answer was negative. "There you have the people, that great majority who live on the plains, along the banks of the rivers, on the slopes and crests of our mountains, on the great plantations and haciendas or near them." They were a marginalized, oppressed majority because "any politician, of whatever shade, can come and go, babbling nonsense among the people, spouting slogans received from the city." The people were suffering because "any teacher or any priest is tempted to become a little chieftain, pretending to be learned and wise." Every time the "common folk" humbled themselves with the words, "Since I don't know anything, but you do [...]," it should be felt as "a tremendous lash falling on our conscience." The illiterate people were at the mercy of petty tyrants and party hacks who appeared every two or five years—during local, legislative, or presidential elections—"to stage a circus of outrageous fraud against the same people." There were already too many broken promises, said Rutilio: "Let things be done for the people!"[19]

The democracy of the republic of El Salvador was merely formal because the people were excluded from the exercise of political power. Very little had been done to grant the people the power that in theory belonged to them. For that reason, they were not organized, and no legislation existed that even allowed for that possibility. Instead, any attempt to help the people become organized aroused suspicion:

> The solemn words of the Constitution ring hollow because of our disrespect for them: "The Constituent Assembly, in the name of the Salvadoran People"

---

18 Grande, "First Independence."
19 ACSI. Rutilio Grande, "Reflecting on September 15, 1971, the 150th Anniversary of Independence," San Salvador, August 11, 1971.

[preamble of the Constitution]. [...] "El Salvador is a sovereign state; the sovereignty resides in the people" (Art.1). [...] "All political power emanates from the people" (Art 6). That is how the language is throughout, but what people are being talked about? Who are they, when in fact they are ignored in national affairs when it comes to consulting and deciding?[20]

Despite all problems, Rutilio announced the dawning of a "great hope." True independence was on the horizon, rising in the Salvadoran people. "A strong wind is blowing across the whole continent! Our historical past, long hidden beneath the waters of oblivion, is in a process of fermentation, impelling a movement of true liberation, from one corner of the continent to the other."

No human or inhuman force, Rutilio added in his homily of September 1976, could prevent the hope that is abroad in Latin America from becoming a historical reality:

> Ideas cannot be imprisoned or killed; even less can they be suppressed. They fly like messenger pigeons through all regions of the earth. They are the eternal human values that crash like a roaring wave over the conscience of the peoples of the continent. We are at the dawning of a second, genuine independence, for which the first was nothing but a feeble prologue. The first cries are now being heard, in one form or another, all up and down the continent. The world is changing, and it will change even more.[21]

The foundation of the new independence, he stressed, would be an agrarian reform that would return the land to its true owners. "The land must be returned to our people as a sign of true, authentic independence, for they deserve it. A government that sides with the people and brings about an effective, decisive agrarian reform will have returned to the people the freedom and autonomy they lost centuries ago!"[22]

The process of liberation already visible on the horizon presented every Salvadoran with an inescapable dilemma: either identifying with the people or taking a stand against them. "Every ambiguous stance is a farce and a felony—it is treasonous!" During the rest of his homily, Rutilio confronted the teachers, the military, and the priests with this dilemma for they had the obligation to "wash away many sins committed against the people."[23]

The teachers had two paths before them. One was to continue with the "encyclopedic" type of education[24] that had thus far prevailed: filling the minds of the students with contents "just as one fills a clay jar with objectified deposits." The

---

20 Grande, "Reflecting on September 15, 1971, the 150th Anniversary of Independence."
21 Grande, "First Independence."
22 Grande, "First Independence."
23 Grande, "First Independence."
24 Reference to the pedagogy of Freire.

other path was education for liberation from oppression. The teachers, though "sprung from the people," not only persisted in the "banking type of education" but were even refusing to serve their own people in the "humble schools of the villages and hamlets." Rutilio did not hesitate to warn the teachers that they had a most serious responsibility to contribute, by means of education, to the liberation of a people who were culturally colonized and economically subjugated. It was the task of teachers to form new persons, that is, persons who were active, critical, and creative; their students should not be satisfied with receiving the customary "donations of sages" but should commit to search out the truth for themselves.[25]

Invited by a teachers' union (ANDES-June 21) to address them on Teachers' Day, June 22, 1974, at the National Institute of Aguilares, Rutilio urged them to follow the example he gave, as an educator in the faith, by forming young people to be free of all types of servitude. They could take on that task from a simply human perspective, apart from any confessional commitment. If they opted for a liberating education, they would find many other persons engaged in the same endeavor. They would especially find allies in priests since between priests and teachers "there is no divorce," even if the teachers belonged to a union. Rather, between them there was a "necessary and genuine integration if we are dealing with what is truly religious." Both teachers and priests were educators of the people, the former by means of culture, the latter by means of faith. Rutilio concluded by telling the teachers that he was firmly convinced that they were closer to God than they thought.[26]

Like the teachers, the soldiers came from the simple folk, and they faced the same dilemma as the teachers. In a homily he gave on the occasion of the war with Honduras,[27] Rutilio described soldiers as follows:

> When I see a couple of guards passing by on the roads of my land with rifles on their shoulders, when I see soldiers coming and going and spending their weekends with family in their own town or village, I realize that the great majority of our military are eminently men of the people; that is, they come from our families in the countryside; they emerge from the quintessentially Salvadoran marrow which is the people.[28]

The soldiers faced a great dilemma: either to take the side of the great majority of people from whom they sprang or to defend the minority who bribed them and manipulated them for their particular ends. Rutilio had recourse to article 12 of the Constitution to resolve this dilemma. The functions of the army, according

---

25   Grande, "First Independence."
26   ACSI. Homily given at the Instituto Nacional of Aguilares on June 22, 1974, Teachers' Day.
27   The conflict lasted only a few days, from July 14 to 18, 1969.
28   ACSI. Rutilio Grande, "Homily at the Memorial Mass for the Fallen," Aguilares, July 14, 1973.

to that article, were to defend the territorial integrity and the sovereignty of the nation, to enforce the law, to maintain public order, and to guarantee people's constitutional rights. Rutilio held that the army's first responsibility was to protect the foundation of the nation, namely "all the habitants, especially the great majority [...] who live in the countryside and migrate to the cities"; its second responsibility was to love the people, "to be concerned for these great disorganized masses who live on the cultural margins, excluded from the national economy and deprived of their basic rights." Rutilio summed it up by saying, "To love the homeland is to love the collectivity."[29] He was therefore grieved "to see soldiers and cadets, sons of humble Salvadoran families, too often lined up against the people, defending the greedy interests of the minorities who are assaulting the people!"[30]

Both soldiers and officers "should have as a compass for their own conscience love for the homeland, serving it to the utmost, even to death!"[31] Placing their admirable disposition of total commitment at the service of the people, they must not let themselves be "hired by a bunch of bullies to fight against the people."[32] Rutilio delivered the very same message to a colonel three days before he was murdered. The official had written to Rutilio to complain about the preaching of Father Alfonso Navarro, who was murdered two months after Rutilio, on May 11, 1977:

> We hope that the security forces will protect the poor, humble folk on certain nearby haciendas whose basic rights as human persons are being violated as regards their work, their wages, etc. They are given tasks which require more time to finish than is established by law. The situation in Bonito is bad,[33] but the situation here, all around us, is also very bad, for it is creating many Bonitos in the homes of the rural poor. [...] We know that there are posts of the Guard on the haciendas around here, but they are not there to protect the humble and the poor. [...] They are there to protect the interests of the powerful, who can do anything they want thanks to their money and their influence. And that is so despite the fact that the agents of the Guard are humble sons of the people. It's a painful paradox and a tremendous alienation.[34]

Rutilio stressed to the colonel that, if the military took the side of the great majority of the people, they would quickly vanquish the presumed communist

---

29 Grande, "Homily at the Memorial Mass for the Fallen."
30 Grande, "First Independence."
31 Grande, "Homily at the Memorial Mass for the Fallen."
32 ACSI. Rutilio Grande, "Reflection on the Day of the Soldier: Novena of the Lord of Mercies," Aguilares, n.d.
33 The Cuban prison to which the colonel had referred in his letter, the scene of many injustices.
34 ACSI. Rutilio Grande to Colonel Alberto Martínez, Aguilares, March 9, 1977.

threat that so worried the colonel. Injustice, insisted Rutilio, was the most favorable seedbed for communism: "This situation of conflict has its manifest origin in the abuse and the sin of not a few people, and you know that well."

In his homily of July 14, 1973, Rutilio declared that the military bore "much responsibility" for the failure to solve the problems that had caused the emigration of Salvadorans to Honduras. The worst casualties of the armed conflict with Honduras were the tens of thousands of Salvadorans who were expelled by the Honduran government. Deported, they returned to El Salvador with empty hands due to the incompetence of the military and other forces in society. In their struggle to survive, the people would always migrate massively, seeking the bread they needed and "a little piece of land for their maize and their beans":

> Those thousands of Salvadorans who one day crossed the border, hoping to find a better future outside El Salvador, returned to their native soil persecuted, distressed, and empty-handed. [...] Our spirit should be pierced by some painful questions. Those thousands of Salvadorans, [...] when they returned to the country, did they find conditions better than they were when they felt obliged to leave as migrants? Did they find work? Did they find a little piece of land for their maize and their beans? Did they find what [Alberto] Masferrer called a vital minimum?[35]

On the contrary, claimed Rutilio, those Salvadorans, like those who remained in the country, were submitted to diverse forms of veritable slavery. He therefore called upon the military to be true to the proclamation that José Simeón Cañas made to the constituent assembly of 1823 and that subsequently became article 151 of the Constitution: "Every person is free in the Republic. No one who enters the territory will be a slave, nor will anyone who traffics in slaves be a citizen." The military would earn the respect of the people when it took the side of the people and defended them against their true enemies.

Priests also, said Rutilio, had to turn wholeheartedly to the people to keep from betraying them. He lamented that "in the past and even in the present, the religion that was offered to the people was concerned mostly about the great beyond and very little about the here and now." That religion spoke more about souls than about bodies, as if these could be separated—"I have never seen souls floating about." Such religious teaching was

> a distortion and a grievous betrayal of the message of Jesus. The kingdom of God, according to what the Gospels say, begins to become reality in this world that God created for all human beings equally, and nobody will be able to enter into the second stage of the kingdom if they have not made an effort to implant it here on earth, in justice, in love, and in true solidarity.[36]

---

35 Grande, "Homily at the Memorial Mass for the Fallen."
36 Grande, "First Independence."

The ones responsible for this deviation were the clergy, who had silenced or muted the Gospel of Jesus, especially when it stressed values that coincided with the basic welfare of human beings.

This failure on the part of the clergy made it easy for the powerful to manipulate religion so that they could maintain fully intact the unjust structures that benefited them greatly. Meanwhile, "there has been a proliferation of the festering wounds of injustice, which for a long time now have been crying out for the pure, clean salve of the Gospel."[37] Consequently, whenever the clergy returned to the Gospel and used it to shine a bright light on reality, their preaching would take on new power, but some people would be scandalized:

> We shouldn't be surprised if some persons poorly instructed in the scriptures leave the church, rending their vestments when they hear the sincere language of the true Gospel of Jesus. They were always accustomed to hearing sweet celestial tunes that made them oblivious to the serious obligations they had toward other human beings, images of the living God.[38]

Despite scandal and even persecution, good priests would make every effort to remain faithful to the Gospel and to the people:

> Blessed those ministers who are not traitors or laggards in this decisive hour because if they are so, they will be sinning against the light, they will be sinning against justice, and they will be sinning once more against the people. And most definitely they will be sinning against the true God, whose sacrosanct name we have perversely manipulated through all our history. We have not listened to his voice as it finds expression in the great multitude of the earth's humiliated and disinherited peoples.[39]

There was a great and urgent need, then, to listen to the people and to Jesus, who was a man of that same people:

> The man Jesus is a man of the people: he was born among the people, born in a cave after the manner of the outcasts of this world. [...] The man Jesus lives full-time among the people, and he goes out into the streets to announce to those same people a Message of Salvation for everyone, for time and for eternity. He sealed his commitment to his people with his blood: he was killed in the time of Pontius Pilate.[40]

History would severely judge priests, teachers, and soldiers for having forgotten the people and the true Jesus. Everyone had to make an effort to serve the people,

---

37 Grande, "First Independence."
38 Grande, "First Independence."
39 Grande, "First Independence."
40 Grande, "First Independence."

never to take advantage of the people. Consequently, no one should enter into alliance with or be at the service of the minorities, who trample on the basic interests of the people. Rather, "all of us, within our specific vocations, must work hard for a better country, one in which a new order reigns."[41] Priests in particular could not "disdain, belittle, or simply ignore the conclusions of Medellín," which summoned Christians to collaborate in the construction of a more just and peaceful society; to do so would be "a most serious betrayal of the church, whose voice resounds full of hope."[42] The task was urgent; the hour was decisive. The moment had arrived when the word "Enough!" had to be shouted out against the many injustices committed in the name of the faith and the people.

The first step was conversion to the people. "I feel," Rutilio honestly admitted, "that I myself must be converted day after day to the people. I must show them my love, and I must make it effective in deeds and not mere words if I truly want to be what I appear to be: Minister and Servant of All!"[43] As a consequence, his only politics was that of the common good, that is, the politics of the people:

> There is no one in the world who can prohibit me, by virtue of any law or mandate, from being concerned for the common good of the people: neither the pope, nor the bishop, nor any government official or authority. A priest owes himself totally to the community in a spirit of service, and until death if necessary.[44]

Serving the people meant being identified with the people, "even in the small details of daily life," and it meant defending their culture:

> Where are you, marimba? Why can't I see you? We are quite tired of these bands around the country that do nothing but imitate and reproduce songs in a foreign tongue, devoid of native creativity. Let us drive these barbarisms from our familiar world. [...] Even our everyday language is being infected with colonialism, though we talk a lot about nationalism.[45]

In September 1971, Rutilio evoked the memory of the priests who had participated actively in the independence of 1821. They were venerated as "heroes of the homeland," he said, but in reality they were "subversives" because they had rebelled against the imperial monarchy. It was clear, then, that the birth of the nation owed much to priests who were totally committed to the Salvadoran people. No one should be surprised, therefore, that priests now wanted to continue that tradition of commitment by placing their power at the service of that same people, just as their predecessors had done:

---

41   Grande, "Homily at the Memorial Mass for the Fallen."
42   Grande, "Reflecting on September 15, 1971, the 150th Anniversary of Independence."
43   Grande, "First Independence."
44   Grande, "First Independence."
45   Grande, "First Independence."

We venerate the heroes of the independence of the homeland, a century and a half ago. Among them we highlight especially certain priests who were at the head of the movement for freedom. We hear anthems in their honor, and we pronounce their names with reverence. We even place their portraits in the great hall of the Legislative Assembly, in our schools, and in our public buildings. Poor priests! Today we consider them heroes, but in their day they were considered to be nothing but conspirators against the established order. They had to hold their meetings in secret, behind locked doors and by candlelight! They were constantly persecuted by the guardians of the throne and the empire. As they considered the concrete historical circumstances of their people, they rightly judged that they had to act as they did, making use of their natural leadership qualities and engaging them for the common good of their people.[46]

Rutilio thus provided historical justification for viewing priestly ministry in terms of service to the people of God, and he pointed out the contradictions of those who devoutly celebrated the independence of 1821 but condemned living priests who wanted to continue the struggle to liberate the people. The oligarchic minorities were using the historical past as a simple pretext, "something with which to fill our mouths so that we can be literally loquacious on the holidays, in our civic celebrations, and even in the primary and secondary laws of the republic. We are masters of beautiful laws that are ignored through the length and breadth of the republic."[47]

Priests could not remain apart from the yearnings for liberation that were shaking the Latin American continent. "Perhaps we are at the dawn of a new independence, one being born with greater pangs and vicissitudes than the first one."[48]

Rutilio also stressed the presence of the church in Salvadoran history in the scripts and commentaries he wrote for the traditional *Te Deum* on September 15, 1968, an event that took place in the metropolitan cathedral, with government officials and the diplomatic corps in attendance. According to those texts, the church "was present in the very acts of emancipation, that is, at the birth of our homeland, through the outstanding activities of its illustrious sons who were priests: Father Delgado, the Fathers Aguilar, and later Father José Simeón Cañas." There was therefore no reason at all for the government to fear a church whose sole interest was serving the Salvadoran people, apart from all political and materialist ambition. Affirming a continuous ecclesial tradition, Rutilio declared that wherever there was a true son of the church, there was also a true Salvadoran. That reality was symbolized by the special greeting given by the archbishop, at the end of the *Te Deum* event, to the president and other government officials.

---

46   Grande, "Reflecting on September 15, 1971, the 150th Anniversary of Independence."
47   Grande, "Reflecting on September 15, 1971, the 150th Anniversary of Independence."
48   Grande, "Reflecting on September 15, 1971, the 150th Anniversary of Independence."

"At this moment, no one is better able to interpret these sentiments of the church toward the Salvadoran state than the archbishop himself."[49]

For Rutilio, it was clear that the participation of priests in the liberation of the Salvadoran people formed part of the church's historical tradition. To keep from being a "religiously alienated being," a priest had to stand close to the reality of the people to whom he ministered; he should be "a man incarnated in the problems of his times and rooted in the communities he nourishes spiritually for the benefit and the salvation of concrete, whole human beings." Priests who act thus, however, are dubbed "political," "subversive," and "communist" by the minorities, "who languidly practice a cheap and superficial Christianity."[50] If Christ were to return now, claimed Rutilio, he would

> almost certainly not be allowed to travel through the villages and towns preaching some of those irritating things of his Gospel! Without any doubt, he would be labeled "political," "communist," and "subversive." He would be altogether too troublesome, and we would make him disappear—who knows, maybe some priests would help![51]

The Rupture between the Parish and FECCAS

After the demonstration of September 12, 1976, and its aftermath, the parish took its distance from FECCAS. In fact, Rutilio promptly put into effect certain measures to make it clear that there were differences between them. The measures disturbed some of the customary practices of the FECCAS members. For example, the locking of the garden gate made it difficult for them to enter parish facilities from the street, and the opening of the side doors of the church left the persons meeting there exposed to the scrutiny of spies and curious passersby. Rutilio later threatened to close down the house that FECCAS members were using for their meetings; it was located very near the church.

Rutilio's strict new rules included restrictions on Marcelino Pérez: he did not allow him to deal with the delegates; for several months he refused to let him say Mass in the parish church; he excluded him from the missions in Guazapa even though Pérez had helped prepare them and had been assigned a village—on the condition that he would not allow FECCAS to get involved; and he did not consent to Pérez's participation in the ordination of the theology students on December 5, 1976. These measures were taken because of Pérez's organizing activities: while Rutilio was striving to keep the parish autonomous and separate from FECCAS, Pérez was doing the opposite. In his preaching, Pérez was more

---

49 ACSI. Rutilio Grande, "Guides and Commentaries for the *Te Deum* of September 15, 1968."
50 Grande, "Reflecting on September 15, 1971, the 150th Anniversary of Independence."
51 Grande, "Reflecting on September 15, 1971, the 150th Anniversary of Independence."

explicit than the other team members in supporting FECCAS; he sponsored their meetings in the parish facilities; he closed the side doors of the church; he opened the house alongside the church for meetings; he met with the executive committee of ANDES-June 21; he organized, against the advice of the team, a group dynamics workshop for thirty-two young members of FECCAS and UTC; and he met periodically with a group of young priests who supported FECCAS.

During the latter half of 1976, the differences of opinion and attitude regarding the organization made for tense relations within the missionary team and especially between Rutilio and Pérez. The crisis did not fracture the team, nor did Pérez leave the parish, but his presence and activity caused extreme tension. The Jesuit provincial refused to move Pérez from Aguilares even though the archbishop had asked him to; he thought the work Pérez was doing with the FECCAS bases was very important. Pérez's presence in the parish made it difficult for the other team members to keep their distance from the organization during the most critical months. Pérez, for his part, kept the provincial informed of his activities. In his memorandum on the canonical visit he made to Aguilares in January 1972, the provincial formally asked Pérez to keep the missionary team, or at least Rutilio, well informed of his activities so as to avoid any divided loyalties, which in the long run could be dangerous.[52]

Although the missionary team tried to keep hidden from others its internal tensions and divisions, these were discussed at the regional and national meetings of FECCAS. The organization's leaders blamed the tensions on the bishops, who they said had asked Rutilio to break with FECCAS for the sake of autonomy. The archbishop was reported to have said that he had once heard Marxism being discussed behind the church even as Mass was being celebrated inside the church. The FECCAS leaders also expressed their regret that the missionary team had failed to take any security measures, and that one team member had complained about being kept awake because FECCAS members were making too much noise when they washed their hands. The same team member had also said, "If I were the pastor, I would already have closed the doors to that organization." Meanwhile, Rutilio was constantly heard repeating, "If I were not here, they would already have smashed FECCAS." To corroborate their criticism of the parish, the FECCAS leaders cited the texts used in recent Masses, which they considered to be irrelevant to the problems of the rural poor. The bases of FECCAS subsequently refused to have anything to do with the members of the team, except for Pérez. The organization's basic fear was that the pastors would turn their backs on them and "go over to the other side"; were they to do that, they would be strengthening the "enemy" and would themselves become "enemies of the people." Despite the disagreements, the regional council of FECCAS formed a commission to dialogue with the missionary team, but no meeting ever took

---

52 ACSI. César Jerez to Pedro Arrupe, San Salvador, July 21, 1977.

place; the reason, said the council, was that the Jesuits did not find it useful given the circumstances.

Throughout the crisis, Rutilio constantly referred his pastoral decisions to the archbishop, to whom he felt not only hierarchically responsible but also closely bonded by their long years of friendship and a relation of mutual confidence. Rutilio took the archbishop's opinion into account in matters relating to FECCAS, but he reserved the final decision to himself. At the same time, he assured the missionary team that he would always exercise his authority as pastor exclusively in service to the common good; that he would constantly seek their opinion and the opinion of the laypeople involved in the parish structure, including the FECCAS members; and finally, that he would consult with the other pastors and the laypeople of the vicariate.[53]

In the course of those trying months, Rutilio stopped smiling, and his expression grew somber. His serious demeanor contrasted with the joviality of Pérez, who was always lavish with his smiles and embraces. The divergent attitudes of the two priests perplexed the FECCAS members. Rutilio grumbled that he found it ridiculous to think that all the team members should be standing by the rectory door handing out smiles and embraces: "Don't they realize that we're involved in very different things, even though there's just one common work?" "Don't they understand that there are all kinds of temperaments?" Realizing he could not hide his overly serious nature, Rutilio excused himself by saying, "I have work that extends beyond the parish, and I have lots of ideas in my head, so [it's difficult] when people come by and I'm expected to smile and chat with anyone who enters."[54]

The rupture with FECCAS and the tension within the team caused Rutilio great suffering. According to some loose notes he made at the time, he was rebelling against himself and against his "primary and fundamental option," which had seemed so clear and consistent when he first formulated it but which was proving unviable, to judge from the latest events. He said that he felt he had lost his external freedom, though interiorly he still felt quite free. What made him suffer most, apparently, was his strong desire to keep his clerical status intact, free of any questioning by others, especially the bishops. "I am a hurting hybrid after all," he wrote. He confessed his disillusionment: he still felt like a foreigner in his own country and amid his own people, estranged even from those he lived with; he projected an image that did not correspond to his personal reality; and he loved solitude, perhaps more than he did activity. Aware of his inability to deal with the impossibly complex situation in the parish, he contemplated "leaving it all once and for all."[55]

---

53   ACSI. Rutilio Grande, "Various Witty Matters: I, as Pastor," n.d.
54   ACSI. Rutilio Grande, "Scattered Things," n.d.
55   ACSI. Rutilio Grande, "Notes on the Aguilares Affair," 1976.

At such moments, Rutilio felt that he did not have the strength to keep going; he regretted that he was "authoritarian and self-taught." He listened to others, but he always followed "his own paths." Even though he did not approve of the way the process had turned out, he felt responsible for having initiated it. Convinced that his own mission in Aguilares was finished. he resolved that he should leave the parish, but at the same time he felt himself a prisoner of human motivations. He feared that his image would be ruined since he would have to "take the blame" for the failure, the rumors, and the criticisms. Even so, he was ready to leave if his departure was for the greater good of the parish; he would humbly bear with the consequences.[56]

In the midst of the crisis, Rutilio visited the Jesuit community at the UCA, looking for advice and insight. After listening to Rutilio, Father Ellacuría, along with five other Jesuits and two lay collaborators, gave him a long document with some simple considerations that might help him clarify his ideas. These considerations focused with surprising precision on the very perceptions that were causing Rutilio the most distress. In the document, Ellacuría stressed first of all the pastoral achievements of the parish; in four years, the missionary team had "happily" created a new image of what a parish should be, one that aroused expectations. The parish was no longer identified with a church building or with a religious tradition that revolved around worship and the administration of sacraments. Instead, the parish was an ecclesial platform that allowed people to discover and practice a new type of faith, one committed to justice for the poor. Since most of the faithful in the parish were oppressed villagers, faith had to insist on the "here-and-now efficacy of Christian life."[57]

From a doctrinal perspective, such a vision of parish was defined more or less clearly in the new ecclesiology of Vatican II, it was given strong backing by Medellín, and it was justified theologically by liberation theology. The magisterium of the local church, as found in the archdiocesan pastoral plan that emerged from the pastoral week of 1976, officially sanctioned many of the basic pastoral practices of the parish of Aguilares, such as the formation of base communities and integral evangelization, making a clear option for service of the faith and promotion of justice. The archdiocesan document spoke of prophetic pastoral ministry only in vague terms, but in the Salvadoran context it had to mean openly denouncing social sin, as the parish of Aguilares was doing. The doctrinal principles were clear, but in most places they were hardly evident in the pastoral practice. In the archdiocese, reference was often made to the importance of intermediate organizations that promoted the basic rights and the common

---

56 Grande, "Notes on the Aguilares Affair."
57 ACSI [Ignacio Ellacuría]. "The Dynamics of a New Pastoral Action and General Principles on Rural Organizing." The document is unsigned. I have placed the name of Ignacio Ellacuría in brackets since he was the principal author, with the collaboration of other Jesuits in the community.

good of the poor majority, but there had still not been sufficient reflection on the complexity of actual practice,[58] something that Rutilio had requested of both the priests' senate and the archbishop.

Historically, people expected priests to be able to impart a clear understanding of the meaning of human existence, regardless of whether the priests were respected or disdained as persons. Anything new introduced by priests was taken in earnest and in its totality. It was for that reason that priests, because of the new message they were preaching, came to function as religious or political leaders. In novel and unforeseen situations, history often required priests to exercise leadership, but such a demand complicated their traditional role of accompaniment, even when it was made clear to the people that priests were not political leaders but simple companions and guides. Rutilio had repeatedly attempted to make just such a clarification, but his attempts had been in vain. Such ambiguity regarding the ministerial function was inevitable given the dynamics of the historical process. Indeed, the ministerial function had always been ambiguous, and it would continue to be so.[59]

The people, including the rural poor, had the right to form organizations that defended their interests and at the same time worked for the general good of society. The need for organizing among the rural poor was especially evident, and it was only proper that the church, in fidelity to the Gospel and its own magisterial teaching, should encourage the establishment of rural organizations. The role of the church was to inspire such organizations on the basis of the Gospel and ethical demands, but determining the procedures and activities of an organization was the responsibility of its leaders, not of the church. The criterion for judging the value of an organization was, in Ellacuría's opinion, the contribution it made to social justice. While it encouraged organizations, the church did not condone recourse to violence or collaboration with the armed groups that were beginning to form in El Salvador at that time, but neither could the church discount *a priori* the possibility of a just war.[60]

In El Salvador, where the government itself had recognized the existence of "tremendous social injustices," the emergence of autonomous rural organizations was inevitable. From a Christian social perspective, such organizations were necessary to prevent an exacerbation of the injustices that could eventually lead the country to complete chaos. Since the injustice was fundamentally structural, it was evident to Ellacuría that the organizations would seek structural solutions. The situation required unconventional actions and methods since the goal was historical efficacy of a particular type.[61]

---

58   "Dynamics of a New Pastoral Action and General Principles on Rural Organizing."
59   "Dynamics of a New Pastoral Action and General Principles on Rural Organizing."
60   "Dynamics of a New Pastoral Action and General Principles on Rural Organizing."
61   "Dynamics of a New Pastoral Action and General Principles on Rural Organizing."

The situation also required a new type of pastoral action, and this would create understandable tensions, as was the case in Aguilares. When Ellacuría reached this point, he became aware of the futility of remaining on the theoretical level and began to speak of the concrete tensions the parish faced. The first type of tension was produced by a series of coincidences and differences. Historically, FECCAS was born thanks to the direct support of the church, but then it sought to be autonomous while maintaining its Christian inspiration. Though the parish as such did not seek political power, FECCAS sought such power directly but, again, still recognizing its Christian inspiration. Since FECCAS pursued political power as part of its faith commitment, it would necessarily stay related to the parish. Both the parish and FECCAS coincided to some extent in regard to the ends they pursued, but they had different structures and so were two different organizations. Tension arose when FECCAS expected the parish's resources to be used for its own purposes, or vice versa, when the parish expected the organization's resources to be used for its purposes.[62]

The second type of tension derived from the ethical and political realms. The parish as such was obliged to emit ethical judgments about the situation. In practice, such judgments were also political, but pronouncing political judgments was not a proper function of the parish since it lacked suitable instruments. In contrast, organizations like FECCAS could properly emit political judgments, supposedly founding them on an ethics of Christian inspiration, and such judgments about political viability implied that they would be implemented. Furthermore, while the church could and should pronounce a Christian ethical judgment about the organization, it could not prevent some of the organization's members from acting occasionally in ways it found offensive. In this regard, Ellacuría thought it very important that taking a social ethical position based on faith not be confused with adopting a partisan posture. The church as such should not enter into the arena of partisan politics; its role was simply to promote ethical awareness and the actions such awareness required, independently of particular political affiliations. Nonetheless, if actions of a social ethical nature had concrete political implications, the church could not abstain from making a social ethical judgment regarding them, even though it risked being accused of meddling in partisan politics.[63]

The third type of tension arose from the exclusivist/totalizing dynamic of both faith and politics. Since both realms were capable of completely absorbing an individual, it was normal for the political realm to tend to pervade all levels of life, including that of faith. On the negative side, the absolutizing of politics led to dogmatic rejection of whatever failed to serve its ends—that was the path to a sectarian spirit. The resulting feeling of ethical superiority made dialogue

---

62 "Dynamics of a New Pastoral Action and General Principles on Rural Organizing."
63 "Dynamics of a New Pastoral Action and General Principles on Rural Organizing."

with others difficult or impossible. Generally, only small groups were capable of sacrificing everything for the sake of a totalizing option. Ellacuría recommended to Rutilio that he analyze whether in practice, apart from explicit statements, the totalizing factor in the parish was Christian faith, with its political implications, or rather the political option. Moreover, Rutilio should not be surprised to learn that Christian faith and inspiration were being shrewdly manipulated for political ends.[64]

Ellacuría considered still another similar tension, arising from the relation between Christianity and Marxism. This point was especially important since at that time that relation was the source of widespread tension throughout the Latin American continent. The question was complicated because, in Ellacuría's judgment, Marxism was a possible, and even a necessary, mediation of faith; it could serve as an operative ideology. Ellacuría recommended to Rutilio that he analyze carefully whether the organization, apart from its declarations, presented itself specifically as Marxist or as Christian.[65]

The final type of tension that Ellacuría considered was that between the masses and the minorities, a particular concern of Rutilio. In principle, the parish was open to the majority, but its pastoral practice had been oriented toward the formation of base communities, and from these had arisen the delegates, the preparers, and the leaders of FECCAS—that is, an elite. Even though both the parish and the organization sought to reach the greatest number of people possible, their rhythms were different. The rhythm of the parish was slower than that of FECCAS, and that difference created tension. The difference of rhythms was also observable in the appreciation that was shown for traditional Christian elements and manifestations of popular religiosity.[66]

All these tensions seemed to Ellacuría historically unavoidable because both the parish and FECCAS had the same origin, professed the same ethics, and shared the same desire to help the rural poor be liberated. However, to the degree that the two institutions developed ever more complex structures, their concrete mechanisms gave rise to a diversity of rhythms, alliances, and tactics so that conflict became inevitable.[67]

Ellacuría offered Rutilio several practical recommendations. The solution was not retreat, for that would resolve none of the problems presented. What would help most was clarifying the precise aims of both the parish and FECCAS. The parish should make "very clear" its ecclesial nature and its commitment to promoting the integral development of Christians, and it should take pains to spell out all the implications of that commitment. There was no doubt about the

---

64 "Dynamics of a New Pastoral Action and General Principles on Rural Organizing."
65 "Dynamics of a New Pastoral Action and General Principles on Rural Organizing."
66 "Dynamics of a New Pastoral Action and General Principles on Rural Organizing."
67 "Dynamics of a New Pastoral Action and General Principles on Rural Organizing."

need for the parish to opt resolutely for justice, and in practice that meant providing clear support for FECCAS, but it should do so indirectly, through evangelization, gradual conscientization of the masses, animation of communities, and emphasis on the ethical import of the Christian message. The parish might also offer direct support at certain critical moments, especially if the parish's inaction were to place it on the side of the oppressor.

Another of Ellacuría's recommendation was to clarify the respective autonomies in light of the criteria indicated. The need to define the proper spheres of each entity was becoming more necessary since FECCAS had moved beyond the limits of the parish. Moreover, both entities would benefit if they had their respective autonomies. Collaboration would be undertaken with the understanding that they were two distinct institutions, each self-sufficient enough to have mechanisms that were autonomous and therefore not interchangeable. Even though FECCAS had originated within the parish, it had sunk its own roots, over which the parish had no control and which were not the parish's business. It would be just as absurd for the parish to instrumentalize FECCAS for purely ecclesial ends as it would be for the organization to instrumentalize the parish for its purely political ends. Autonomy was important for the parish since it helped to safeguard its identity and protect itself from being manipulated by other political groups lacking Christian inspiration.[68]

The relations among the team members began to improve on December 5, when Rutilio sent Pérez to celebrate Mass in a village. Rutilio's change of heart was apparently due to his learning that three Jesuits scholastics who were working with FECCAS had left the Society; they were Alberto Henríquez, Fernando Ascoli, and Antonio Cardenal. The departures caused great commotion, coming at the same time as the ordination of Carlos R. Cabarrús and Luis E. Pellecer to the priesthood and Jorge Sarsanedas to the diaconate. Rutilio himself, as previously mentioned, had interceded on behalf of the scholastics with the provincial. The departure of the three young men helped clarify the ambiguity of the parish's relationship with FECCAS. Around Christmas time, Rutilio said to Pérez, "You're so ungrateful! Come here, and forgive me everything!"[69]

In mid-1977, after Rutilio had been killed, the Society of Jesus publicly defended the parish of Aguilares and the right of the rural poor to organize to protect their rights and to work for the common good. A series of articles called "The Jesuits Address the Salvadoran People," published first in the national press and then as booklet, responded to the attacks of the agro-exporting oligarchy against the presence and the work of the Society of Jesus in El Salvador. This response was directed by Ellacuría, who also wrote most of the texts. The article "Jesuits and Organizations" stated that the Jesuits in the parish of Aguilares, because of their

---

68   "Dynamics of a New Pastoral Action and General Principles on Rural Organizing."
69   Personal communication of Marcelino Pérez with the author.

commitment to Christian principles, could not oppose the growth of FECCAS, an organization that the rural poor had developed into an effective instrument for justly promoting their rights. The aim of the organization, the construction of the common good, coincided with the social dimension of the Gospel.[70]

From a constitutional perspective, the rural villagers, as Salvadoran citizens, had the right to associate freely and to form organizations. Secondary laws and regulations could not contradict what was expressly established by the Constitution. Peasant associations were legitimate organizations formed by the people for the sake of gaining their just rights. That was the understanding of both the Jesuits in Aguilares and those in the rest of the country. Naturally, the Jesuits' respect and support for autonomous peasant organizations did not mean that they renounced the right to criticize them from a Christian perspective.[71]

The real question of the oligarchy was not whether the Jesuits were directing the popular organizations. What concerned the oligarchs was the simple existence of autonomous peasant organizations that were free of government tutelage and the pressures of landowners. They were extremely disturbed that these organizations were defending the justice of interests that were very different from their own; they believed that the common good could be reached only by striving for the particular good of the privileged few, even if that meant keeping millions of Salvadorans in misery. Frustrated by their inability to maintain the rural poor as an amorphous, subservient mass, the oligarchs called them "murderous hordes" and demanded that the government repress them, "forcing them down on their knees again, not before God but before injustice and oppression."[72]

Persecution against the Church

Open and systematic oppression against the church began toward the end of the government of Colonel Molina, when local security forces showed themselves incapable of containing the surge of agrarian mobilization throughout the country, in collaboration with progressive social and political organizations. Apparently Rutilio and the missionary team were not fully aware of the speed with which these forces were evolving. The team was already experiencing a very intense existence, having neither time nor energy for reflection. Even as the crisis spread far beyond them, they remained in the parish.

Pronouncements and Deportations
Two important sociopolitical events, a demonstration and the unexplained murder of a plantation owner in the zone of Aguilares, goaded the agro-exporting

---

70 "Los jesuitas ante el pueblo salvadoreño" [The Jesuits address the Salvadoran people], San Salvador, June 1977. See *ECA* 344 (1977): 434–50.
71 *Los jesuitas ante el pueblo salvadoreño.*
72 *Los jesuitas ante el pueblo salvadoreño.*

oligarchy into issuing a series of pronouncements that insulted the church and the hierarchy in ways that would have previously been unthinkable in a mainly Catholic country.

The demonstration took place on November 14, 1976, in Quezaltepeque, and it was one of four that took place the same day: the others were in Zacatecoluca (La Paz), Cancasque (Chalatenango), and Ilobasco (Cabañas). The demonstration in Quezaltepeque provided FARO with an opportunity to attack the church and especially the parish of Aguilares.[73] The four demonstrations were organized by FECCAS and the UTC in support of a request the BPR had presented to the National Assembly on October 28, asking that the wages of plantation workers be increased. The BPR wanted workers in export crops to be paid a daily wage of nine *colones* (a little more than three dollars at that time), plus a daily allowance of three *colones* (a little more than a dollar) for food.[74] The demonstrators also protested the arrest of eight villagers and demanded the freedom of two others.

Some 2,500 persons took part in the demonstration in Quezaltepeque, according to a bulletin of the Federation of Rural Workers. In the course of the demonstration, which took place in front of the city hall, two municipal police officers captured a worker who had become separated from the group. When the master of ceremonies denounced the capture, a commission of six workers went to the police inspector and asked for the release of their companion. While the commission was insisting with the police inspector, the demonstrators were being inflamed by the master of ceremonies, who was shouting through the loudspeakers that they would not leave until their companion was freed. At one point, the police opened fire against the workers' commission inside the municipal building and wounded several of them. In reaction, some of the demonstrators who had arms started firing into the building and wounded several police. Other demonstrators, armed with clubs and stones, assaulted the building, broke windows, and rescued their captured companion and seven others who had been detained. The police and the others inside the building fled from the mob. At the end of the melee, one person was dead and several were wounded.[75]

The demonstration was excessively belligerent and exposed many people to danger. Had the police, instead of fleeing, opened fire against the assailants, most of whom were from Aguilares, there would have been a massacre. In any case, the turmoil made the government and the oligarchy very aware of the power of the people when organized: the masses had not only protested but had demonstrated their ability to use force effectively. The national press blamed the clergy

---

73   Frente Agropecuario Nacional [National Ranchers Front], "¡Alerta salvadoreños! Bajo el terror del machete y la sotana" [Watch out, Salvadorans! Beware the terror of the machete and the cassock], *El diario de hoy* (November 30, 1976).
74   ACSI. "Dossier on the Persecution of the Church in El Salvador," San Salvador, 1977.
75   "Dossier on the Persecution of the Church in El Salvador."

for the ruckus.[76] "Several priests were accused by the authorities and by residents of this city of taking part in the peasants' demonstration that yesterday attacked the city hall."[77]

The murder of Eduardo Orellana, one of the owners of the Colima Hacienda, happened a few days later, on December 5, during a protest to support the many tenants being evicted from the villages of Colima and El Tule, which were to be flooded as part of the construction process for a dam known as the Cerrón Grande. For three months, the villagers affected had been requesting a just evaluation of their losses, satisfactory compensation, and help with relocation. The Lempa River Hydroelectric Commission, which was responsible for the project, and the owners of the Colima Hacienda did not respond to the villagers' pleas. Finally, the commission accepted some of them, but the question of relocation remained unsettled. The Orellana brothers, for their part, ignored the problem, arguing that the future of those affected was no concern of theirs since they were simply tenants of the hacienda. At that point, FECCAS and UTC joined in solidarity with the people and asked to speak with the brothers on Sunday, December 5.[78]

Around two in the afternoon on that day, according to FECCAS, about 250 members of the organization approached the Orellana residence on the hacienda. The leaders ordered the crowd to remain peaceful and not let themselves be provoked. The leaders spoke first with the administrator, an army captain, who refused them access to the Orellana brothers. When they insisted and the administrator continued to refuse, they reported to the crowd the failure of their attempt and gave the order to withdraw. Suddenly, the two brothers came out of the house and opened fire, causing panic among the people, some of whom threw themselves to the ground while others sheltered behind the walls of the hacienda. When Eduardo Orellana, who was walking ahead of his brother Francisco, found himself without bullets, he turned toward his brother, who shot him in the stomach, evidently by accident. Eduardo cried out to him, "Aye, now you've screwed me." The events were witnessed by four hacienda police, who shot in the air to disperse the crowd. It was clear that, if the workers had actually been attacking the Orellana brothers, those officers would have shot not into the air but into the crowd, causing a massacre. In his rage, Francisco Orellana grabbed a pregnant woman, threw her on the ground, put his knee on her belly, and aimed his pistol at her. Only the intervention of the administrator and one of the workers prevented another murder.[79]

The death of Orellana infuriated the oligarchy, and their organizations subsequently blamed FECCAS for the murder. Spokespersons for FARO and ANEP

---

76   "Falsos líderes son denunciados por FARO."
77   "Dossier on the Persecution of the Church in El Salvador."
78   ACSI. FECCAS to Archbishop Luis Chávez, "En el campo salvadoreño" [In the Salvadoran countryside], December 8, 1976.
79   ACSI. FECCAS to Archbishop Luis Chávez, "En el campo salvadoreño."

claimed that the group that killed Orellana had planned the assault during the ordination of the three young Jesuits that took place the morning of that same Sunday. FARO and ANEP accused the workers of being the material authors of the murder and the missionary team of Aguilares of being the intellectual authors, even though many eyewitnesses declared that Eduardo had been killed by his own brother. No judicial authority investigated the case.[80]

In a public pronouncement, the Association of Cattle Ranchers of El Salvador (Asociación de Ganaderos de El Salvador [AGES]) appealed to President Molina and the army on December 7. AGES attributed the crime to FECCAS and named the UTC as an accomplice. It criticized the passivity of the government, which, "not wanting to let itself be provoked," had allowed "murderous hordes" to attack the city hall of Quezaltepeque, kill a watchman at the La Paz Hacienda (in Tecoluca, San Vicente) on November 29, and murder "our beloved and unforgettable companion, Guayito Orellana Valdez." According to the pronouncement, the "murderous hordes" had been spurred on at the morning Mass by the "third-worlder priests" of the parish of Aguilares, who were also training the villagers at night with wooden rifles.[81]

A pronouncement published on December 8 by ANEP "*demanded* of the Supreme Authorities the merited punishment for the crime committed" against Eduardo Orellana. It attributed the deed to "the hordes" of FECCAS and UTC and to "the instigators who cravenly shield themselves in their religious condition, both the third-worlder creole priests and the foreigners."[82] A third pronouncement, issued the same day by the Salvadoran Feminist Front (Frente Feminista Salvadoreño [FFS]), was similar to ANEP's; in fact, the similarity of vocabulary and semantic twists made it appear to come from the same pen.[83]

A fourth pronouncement, from FARO, was harsher, repeating the previous accusations and adding some new ones. It called the popular organizations "subversive" and stated erroneously that FECCAS and UTC were the shock troops of the Communist Party. It also named certain "third-worlder" priests—Juan Roberto Trejos, pastor of Quezaltepeque; David Rodríguez, pastor of Tecoluca; and Rutilio Grande—and demanded that the "leadership of the Catholic Church" make the clergy obey the Constitution.[84]

These accusations did not go unanswered. On December 11, Archbishop Chávez made a courageous and thoughtful statement. He said that he condemned the murder of Orellana, just as he would condemn the violent and unjust death

---

80 "Dossier on the Persecution of the Church in El Salvador."
81 Ranchers' Association of El Salvador, *El diario de hoy* (December 7, 1976).
82 *El diario de hoy* (December 8, 1976). "Dossier on the Persecution of the Church in El Salvador."
83 The Salvadoran Feminist Front, "Demands Respect for Life and Observance of the Law," *El diario de hoy* (December 8, 1976). "Dossier on the Persecution of the Church in El Salvador."
84 "Dossier on the Persecution of the Church in El Salvador."

of any person, but then he added that the church "cannot do less than denounce any situation of injustice and sinfulness, especially when it affects the weakest persons, which in our case means the majority of the nation." He said he therefore wanted everyone to become "keenly aware of the degraded conditions of life to which our society oppressively submits our people":

> It is false and calumnious to call this [statement of facts] a "poisoning" of the people and to see in it an incitement of the rural poor to contradict the basic principles of Christianity or to fill our country with grief and violence by sowing class hatred and class struggle. The situation is unjust, and the church must fight against the injustice. The persons responsible for this unjust situation are the ones who are really responsible for whatever may happen. Announcing the requirements of the Gospel and following the example of Jesus—that is not communism. It is faithful commitment to the Christian faith.[85]

The archbishop reaffirmed the church's independence of the political parties and the popular organizations, but he stated that they were legitimate and necessary. Finally, he flatly denied that "the fathers of Aguilares" had made any reference to the problems at the Colima Hacienda during the two Masses on Sunday, December 5. Hundreds of trustworthy witnesses could verify that. Consequently, the archbishop stated, the organizations of the powerful were making "false and calumnious declarations" and should instead have "taken a position in light of the Christian faith." The most exceptional aspect of the archbishop's statement was his expression of solidarity with the accused priests, especially the missionary team of Aguilares.

Rutilio received the message with delight because it contained the hierarchical backing he needed. "Look," he told a friend,

> this document is great. The church is committing itself to guarding against any rigged judgment of the Cains. It's telling us that the rural poor have the right and the duty to organize. [...] This is very prophetic. I'm already thinking that soon the villagers will be coming to confession, and they'll tell me: "I confess that I have sinned against love because I've been afraid to join the organization, and the bishop says that it is my duty, [...] but today I have decided to take that risk."[86]

That same day, Rutilio gave the archbishop the letter in which FECCAS explained exactly what had happened at the Colima Hacienda on December 5; the account was accompanied by sketch.

---

85   *El diario de hoy* (December 11, 1976). "Dossier on the Persecution of the Church in El Salvador."
86   "Portico for Rutilio," *Abra* 4 (1977): 21–24.

10. Persecution of the Church

The government made a brash display of military force in Aguilares, perhaps in response to the demands the organizations were making of the oligarchy. On December 9, army troops occupied El Paisnal "pacifically" for twenty-four hours. A column of heavily armed vehicles, ambulances, and trucks filled with soldiers invaded the town during the night. In the morning, they were deployed along two kilometers of the road leading to Aguilares. When Rutilio, accompanied by Fernández, arrived in El Paisnal in the parish's VW Safari, he found the town overrun with national guardsmen, police officers, and soldiers. When they attempted to drive to El Conacaste, a village beyond El Paisnal, they were blocked by a military vehicle. Several soldiers got out of the vehicle and made Rutilio and Fernández raise their hands; they handcuffed them, searched their car, and interrogated them. Rutilio responded to their questions ironically and evasively, as was his manner. In the afternoon, he walked on foot along the highway to El Paisnal "so that they would see him." Meanwhile, in the town square a lieutenant explained to Fernández that the mobilization of troops was in response to what had happened at Colima. Observing the lieutenant's manner, Rutilio said, "This guy seems quite decent, not like the other one," referring to the soldier who had detained and interrogated them earlier. He then added sarcastically that he hoped it was "not just today" that they would enjoy a visit from the army. Later in the day, the soldiers passed through the neighboring villages, firing into the air to intimidate the people. They searched a couple of houses and finally withdrew.

Three oligarchic organizations—AGES, FFS, and FARO—responded publicly to the archbishop's statement. In an incoherent pronouncement, AGES claimed to be "distressed" and "disturbed" at the archbishop's solidarity with the "third-worlder priests" who were preaching "revolutionary justice," which according to them was any justice obtained by means other than the tribunals.[87] The FFS for its part announced in the press that it was canceling an interview it was scheduled to have with the archbishop "since his position is completely defined."[88] The third group, FARO, ordinarily more aggressive than the others, rejected the archbishop's statement in a sardonic declaration.[89]

This new series of pronouncements did not go unanswered. On December 18, the archdiocese stated that "misery, hunger, and injustice do not come from God but from human beings—from malevolence that contradicts God's plan."[90] A group of priests, organized as a clergy coordinating committee, publicly

---

87 *El diario de hoy* (December 16, 1976). "Dossier on the Persecution of the Church in El Salvador."
88 *El diario de hoy* (December 16, 1976). "Dossier on the Persecution of the Church in El Salvador."
89 *El diario de hoy* (December 17, 1976). "Dossier on the Persecution of the Church in El Salvador."
90 "Dossier on the Persecution of the Church in El Salvador."

supported the archbishop's position. They denounced the actions of the associations as selfish and mean-spirited and accused them of trying to cause division in the church.[91] FARO stated that priests were "the greatest exploiters of the people" and told them not to get involved in politics. If there were Salvadoran priests who wanted to engage in politics, they should first "hang up their cassocks." Foreign priests, of course, could not get involved in politics even if they ceased to function as priests.[92] On December 23, the Archdiocesan Secretariat of Cursillos also backed the archbishop's position.

Around Christmastime, two other bishops contributed to the polemic, but their position was quite different from that of the archdiocese, thus making evident the differences among the bishops themselves. On December 22, the bishop of San Vicente, Pedro Arnaldo Aparicio, issued his Christmas message, entitled "Christmas in Turmoil," in which he asserted that the church found itself besieged by both the right and the left. He claimed that certain "elements" lodged in the University of El Salvador and directed by Moscow, Beijing, and Havana had taken control of the secondary schools and were "poisoning" the nation's teachers. He also accused FECCAS and UTC of being Marxist-inspired and insisted that they were in no way organizations of the church. He added that any priest who supported such organizations or urged people to join them was acting outside the law and contrary to his priestly calling.[93]

The bishop of Santa Ana, Benjamín Barrera, in "Christmas and New Year's Greetings," dated December 27, made it clear that the Salvadoran church did not have just one system of governance; each of the five presiding bishops was the head of his own diocese. He further stated that there was no "coordinating commission of the clergy," that neither FECCAS nor UTC had been recognized by the church, and that the teachings of radicalized priests and religious who were fomenting class struggle were in no way Christian. On December 23, the archdiocese of San Salvador published its own Christmas greeting, but it made no reference to the recent conflicts.[94]

FARO took advantage of these statements to deepen the division in the episcopacy. It praised the two bishops for censuring "the third-worlder priests' campaign of agitation and hatred," and it asserted that, while rejecting the archbishop's statement, it had never attacked the church or the clergy as such, but only a few particular priests. In addition, FARO claimed that the archbishop's staff had been infiltrated by "international agents of subversion," it attributed the archdiocesan statement of December 9 to "some Jesuits in complicity with high ecclesiastical dignitaries of the country," and it denounced the existence of

---

91   *El diario de hoy* (December 18, 1976).
92   FARO, "Responds to the Communiqué of the Priests," *El diario de hoy* (December 21, 1976). "Dossier on the Persecution of the Church in El Salvador."
93   "Dossier on the Persecution of the Church in El Salvador."
94   "Dossier on the Persecution of the Church in El Salvador."

an internal struggle for the "ecclesiastical leadership" of San Salvador. Finally, the FARO statement pointed out that there were many Jesuits "entrenched" in the UCA and the Externado San José, as well as in the parishes of Quezaltepeque and Aguilares, and it accused Father Rodríguez of committing many crimes in the central region and of disobeying his bishop, who had ordered him to leave the parish of Tecoluca.[95]

On December 30, several persons published a "respectful petition" they had sent to the nuncio. Citing the conflicts in the bosom of the Salvadoran church, they said they were happy that some of the church's members were resisting the "professional revolutionaries" and their "subversive movement," but they wanted to know whether the "political directives" followed by "our priests" were approved by the Vatican and whether the "Marxist–Leninist" theology of liberation had biblical foundations.

The persecution did not remain at the level of pronouncements in the national press; it soon developed into concrete actions. On December 3, a bomb exploded near the building that housed the office of the UCA's rector; it was the sixth and most powerful bomb set off until then, and the White Warriors' Union (Unión de Guerreros Blancos [UGB]) took credit for it. Systematic persecution against the clergy started early in 1977. The first targeted were the foreign clergy: some priests were deported while others traveling outside the country were denied re-entry. The first priest to be deported was the pastor of Apopa, the Colombian Mario Bernal.

Before the deportation of Bernal on January 5, 1977, the government expelled two Jesuit scholastics from the country: the Nicaraguan Antonio Cardenal and the Guatemalan Fernando Ascoli, both of whom were working closely with the leadership of FECCAS. Both men had already asked to leave the Society and were no longer living in Jesuit houses; the government was aware of the change in their status. On January 6, FECCAS and UTC protested in the national press against the deportation of the two "seminarians [who were our] collaborators." The organizations protested again two days later, but this time they included details of the deportation, adding that that "two seminarians" were Jesuits. On January 10, the BPR joined in the protest and convoked a "grand demonstration" on December 29 to demand the return of the two young men and the release of political prisoners. On January 15, the BPR repeated the invitation to the demonstration, putting the principal stress on the release of the political prisoners, whose names it included in the pronouncements, while also mentioning the names of those who had been disappeared, exiled, or deported.[96]

---

95 FARO, "Congratulates the Pastors of the Catholic Church Who Disapprove of the Campaign of Agitation and Hatred Being Promoted by the 'Third-Worlder' Priests," *El diario de hoy* (December 30, 1976).
96 *El diario de hoy* (January 6, 8, 10, and 15, 1977).

Although all three pronouncements emphasized the expulsion of church workers in order to provoke widespread repudiation of the military regime, their effectiveness was dubious since most of the rural poor did not read the newspapers; moreover, the two seminarians had already asked to leave the Jesuits. Consequently, not only was there no large-scale reaction against the regime, but the church's enemies were supplied with new arguments thanks to the details revealed about the deportations. The enemies' main target was not the popular organizations but the Society of Jesus. In a public statement, FARO denounced the Jesuits, insisting that it was not opposing the church but only "the priests who were preaching hatred," specifically the Jesuits. FARO claimed that the Jesuits constituted a "most serious national problem" because they were violating the Constitution by their constant meddling in national politics. The organization stated that the government had correctly applied article 21 of the Constitution in deporting foreigners who had become involved in national politics. All foreigners, FARO concluded, should "accept the laws and respect our government, or they should leave the country."[97]

The Society of Jesus remained silent for several reasons. The popular organizations had already made statements that were somewhat ambiguous, and clarifications did not seem opportune given the circumstances. The Jesuits could not effectively defend the two young men since they had already asked to leave the Society and were living outside its houses. Moreover, the Jesuits who had been key figures in the press campaign against the oligarchs during the failed attempt at agrarian reform were at that moment outside the country. Finally, and more basically, the argument of FARO was valid: the Jesuits had in fact been collaborating with the leadership of FECCAS.

The deportation process of Bernal on January 29 was similar to that of the two ex-Jesuits. Arriving in El Salvador in 1971, Bernal had spent a few years teaching in the minor seminary and working as an associate pastor in Santa Tecla. When he became pastor of the parish of Apopa in 1974, he was very effective, bringing together the traditional religious associations that had been at odds with the previous pastor, doing evangelization work in the villages and the city, and paying special attention to young people. His pastoral vision was in harmony with that of the vicariate of Quezaltepeque, to which Aguilares also belonged. Bernal also had a weekly program on Radio Vanguardia, and some statements he made on the program displeased the government. Bernal's deportation made it clear that the government was attacking the church directly, not just the popular organizations. The regime clearly wanted to debilitate the church. The deportation was used by the national press as proof that class hatred was being propagated from the pulpits and in classrooms, unions, and mass meetings. Class hatred was the cause of crimes like the one committed against Roberto Poma, a wealthy

---

97   *El diario de hoy* (January 15, 1977).

businessman who was director of the Salvadoran Institute of Tourism; on January 28, he was kidnapped and murdered, along with three companions, by ERP, a politico-military organization.

On February 3, a few days after Bernal's deportation, the regime captured another ex-Jesuit, Juan José Ramírez, in Santa Rosa de Lima, a town in the east of the country. Ramírez was captured, along with two university students and four secondary school students, during a strike at the San Sebastián mines. At that time, Ramírez had already left the Society of Jesus, but the regime still treated him as a Jesuit priest. The national guardsman denied arresting him and torturing him brutally for ten days, at the end of which they gave his body to the security forces of Guatemala. The BPR issued a public protest on February 7 but refrained from identify Ramírez as a priest or a collaborator; it identified him simply as a psychology student of the UCA and a native of Spain.[98] On February 13 in Apopa, the vicariate of Quezaltepeque held a demonstration of religious faith, which concluded with a Mass at which Rutilio preached his last major homily.

The tactic used by the leaders of the popular organizations, of having frequent recourse to the national press to make their protests and present their demands, turned out to be mistaken. It did not achieve the results desired or influence the course of events; it simply meant wasting funds to buy space in the papers. The ineffectiveness of the tactic was shown by the fact that not one of the eight pronouncements published in early 1977 aroused any reaction from the agro-exporting oligarchy or the government. Of course, the oligarchy and the government read the pronouncements attentively, extracting from them valuable information about the church and the Jesuits, with a view to attacking them.

The Sermon in Apopa: "In El Salvador Being a Christian Is a Crime"
The demonstration of religious faith organized by the vicariate of Quezaltepeque took place on February 13 in Apopa; its purpose was to protest the deportation of Mario Bernal. People came from the valleys, the villages, and the hamlets to demand the return of their pastor. The demonstration began on the outskirts of Apopa and made its way toward the parish church, stopping at four places along the way. At each stop, a delegate of the Word preached.

In his homily during the Mass, Rutilio commented on the emphasis that the delegates placed on the prophetic dimension of the ecclesial mission:

> The brothers who preached in the course of the procession [reminded us that] we are prophets. As an ecclesial body, we continue the mission of Jesus Christ. This body that is the church includes entire communities, and it has the mission of announcing the kingdom of God here in this world and preparing the way for it. We must incarnate the values of the kingdom in our

---

98 *El diario de hoy* (February 7, 1977).

national reality in order to transform the country effectively, just as yeast transforms the dough.[99]

The characteristics of that mission, Rutilio continued,

> were already spelled out for us by a brother right at the beginning of the procession. The mission is a demanding one: "I send you forth!" That is what the church says, and it says it to each one of us: "Go and speak to the people!" [...] The prophet has to go forth with the Word of God in his hand! [...] [The Gospel] is a lightning rod; it is divine reality. It is crystal clear and clean like the stream flowing from the mountain. Only the blind are unable to understand that! [...] It is a thermometer and a scale for measuring our human realities, and it makes demands of the realities around us. [...] All of us, then, have a prophetic mission.[100]

"This is an emergency meeting for us priests," explained Rutilio. "We resolved—along with the faithful, conscientious Christians of our parish—to have this *demonstration of faith*." He warned the people that, since FECCAS was taking part in the demonstration and distributing leaflets, the church was "not responsible for all the flyers that have been handed out." The statement of the Christian communities, which contained the vicariate's reflections on the country's situation, would be handed out at the end of Mass. Therefore, he insisted, "each flyer will be good or bad according to its content. They are not the responsibility of our vicariate."[101]

In his homily, Rutilio recalled the reason for their coming together in Apopa that morning:

> But what event has brought us together this day? Why are we here under the hot sun in Apopa? (At least you are, brother and sisters! We're quite comfortable here in the shade!) What brings us together today in Apopa, from every corner of the vicariate and even from some other communities, [...] is the case of Father Mario.

The demonstration was about the church, not about politics. It had an ecclesial character not unlike that of the Eucharist:

> It is an ecclesial event. The church cannot remain silent. It cannot remain indifferent to what has happened. We feel deeply affected. We have heard the people asking, "What are you going to do?" There in the villages, the simple, humble folk were asking us, [...] "What are you going to do?" Well, here we

---

99 *El diario de hoy* (February 7, 1977).
100 *El diario de hoy* (February 7, 1977).
101 ACSI. Rutilio Grande, homily on the expulsion of Father Mario Bernal, Apopa, February 13, 1977.

are! At the very least, we can make this an official symbol of protest of the church and our communities.[102]

They had not gathered together as a "detached sect of the church," Rutilio stated; "we feel we are a part of this church we love." All those assembled in Apopa were an integral part of the church:

> We form part of a church made up of lay folk: you are the majority of the People of God. And even if we [priests] are perched here on this platform, our ministry has no reason to exist except for all of you. "Ministry" comes from the verb "to minister," which means to serve the people of God.[103]

The central theme of Rutilio's last and most important homily was one of his favorites—God, the common Father of all humankind:

> All of us human beings have a common Father. It follows that we are all children of that Father, even though we have been born from the wombs of different mothers here on earth. It also follows obviously that all of us human beings are brothers and sisters. All of us equal with one another![104]

God the Father created the "material world for all, without borders," and he gave it to humankind. Rutilio emphasized the materiality of creation and even of the Mass, "with the material bread and the material cup that we will hold up in memory of Christ the Lord." The created world belonged to God the Father of all, and no human being could take control of it:

> It's not a question of me saying: "I bought half of El Salvador with my money, so I have the right to own it, and nobody can dispute that! It is a right which I bought because I have the right to purchase half of El Salvador." That is a denial of God! There is no such right over against the majority![105]

The Cains have imposed that idea of a "right to purchase" on El Salvador, "but Cain is an abortion of God's plan, [...] and there exist groups of Cains! [That idea] is also an abominable denial of the Kingdom of God." The Cains have robbed the majority of the population—"the martyred Abels, the people who have been enslaved"—of the goods that belonged to them according to the plan of God:

> In certain places [...] they are not owners either of the land or of life. They have to hike up as far as the conacaste trees, but not even the trees are theirs, not even the conacastes! The yellow birds can fly up there and make their

---

102 Grande, homily on the expulsion of Father Mario Bernal.
103 Grande, homily on the expulsion of Father Mario Bernal.
104 Grande, homily on the expulsion of Father Mario Bernal.
105 Grande, homily on the expulsion of Father Mario Bernal.

nests in the branches, but the poor Salvadorans are still slaves on this land that belongs to the Lord, according to the Bible.[106]

The statistics on poverty were "frightful," Rutilio claimed, and the political situation was no better: the country was a democracy in name only. "There is a lot of talk. Mouths are full of talk of 'democracy.' The power of the people is the power of a minority, not of the people! Let's not fool ourselves!" And the worst thing, according to Rutilio, was that those Cains professed to be Catholics:

> We cloak everything with false hypocrisy and splendid works. Woe to you hypocrites who pay lip service to Catholicism but inside are disgustingly evil. You are Cains, and you crucify the Lord as he walks by—bearing the name Manuel, or the name Luis, or the name Chabela, the name of the lowly rural worker![107]

From a Christian perspective, said Rutilio, there was no reason for minorities to exist, not even religious minorities. Everything had to be done "in function of the great majority who make up the Salvadoran people."

The common good, understood as the well-being of the majority, came before private property. The life of the people as a whole had priority over ownership of property that God had made for all humankind. Rutilio expressed this idea eloquently, using words that a popular singer-composer later included in his "Misa Salvadoreña":

> The material world is for everybody, without borders. It is a common table, with long tablecloths, for one and all, each with his own little stool. May this table and tablecloth and the "wherewithal" be there for everybody. With good reason did Christ want a supper to signify the kingdom, [...] [it is] a table shared in solidarity, where all have their proper place.[108]

On another occasion, Rutilio developed this same metaphor of the Eucharist as a common table with long tablecloths for one and all. The life and the work of Jesus had been condensed, by his express wish, into a meal of friendship, fraternity, and equality. At that table, all those who shared one single heart and desire were welcome. "The bread is shared among all equally, with nobody looking down on anybody, and no one feeling superior to others." Jesus's mission consisted in bringing a reconciled humanity together at a common table "as children of the same Father, so that we can share our common inheritance here on earth both now and in the kingdom to come. [...] For that very reason, his body was crushed as the grains of maize are crushed to form the bread of the tortilla." Accordingly, those who would sit at this table to share in the meal of solidarity

---

106 Grande, homily on the expulsion of Father Mario Bernal.
107 Grande, homily on the expulsion of Father Mario Bernal.
108 Grande, homily on the expulsion of Father Mario Bernal.

should be ready to "die to themselves in order to live with others and for others," and they should do so fearlessly since that table of solidarity would be extended into daily life:[109]

> That is, the Supper of the Lord cannot be separated from our family lives or our lives in community. If it could, then we could not sit here at this table; we would be false Christians, hypocrites, liars, and J.C. [*sic*] would not really be for us the *Bread of Life*.[110]

Rutilio made it clear that his talk about the Cains was motivated not by hatred but by love, "a key word that sums up all the ethical codes of humankind, sublimates them, and surpasses them in Jesus":

> It is shared fraternal love that breaches and breaks down every type of barrier and prejudice, and it overcomes hatred itself. We are not here because of hatred! We love even those Cains. They are not our enemies—obviously they have not understood! Christians do not have enemies. The Cains are our brothers.[111]

Of course, Rutilio asserted, such love "causes conflict" and "demands of believers […] *moral violence*," but he immediately explained: "I did not say physical violence, but moral violence! I say this for the recorders because on my way here I saw some recorders that did not belong to the faithful. […] They are traitors to the Word of God." The congregation at that point applauded enthusiastically, but Rutilio advised them: "Better not to applaud. […] Otherwise we will never finish!" Having made his point, he returned to the question of moral violence:

> I said we have not come here with machetes. That is not our kind of violence. Our violence is in the Word of God, which confronts us and confronts our society, but which also unites us and brings us together even as it thrashes us. Therefore, our code is summed up in the one word *Love* against anti-love, against sin, against injustice, against the domination of human beings, against the destruction of solidarity.[112]

The second part of the homily was a defense of Bernal, who Rutilio said had been kidnapped and deported "without a formal accusation in court and without an opportunity to defend himself." Such an action was therefore a clear violation of "human rights as understood by all civilized nations on earth. I regret that this happened in my land." Even Jesus Christ had been submitted to a public trial—"rigged" to be sure—but "poor Mario" had been denied any hearing at all:

---

109 ACSI. Rutilio Grande, commentary for a Mass, Aguilares, n.d.
110 Grande, commentary for a Mass.
111 Grande, homily on the expulsion of Father Mario Bernal.
112 Grande, homily on the expulsion of Father Mario Bernal.

> They tell me he was a foreigner! Was Father Mario was a foreigner? Certainly, but one from Latin America. I wonder whether we can ever be foreigners in this Latin America discovered by Columbus, where we're are all mixed together as *café con leche* and share the same kind of blood! Are there really foreigners among us? [...] We talk much about being Hispanic, and we celebrate the Day of the Race, the Day of Latin America, when countless children and their teachers clap their hands and raise little flags. [...] What does that mean? [...] Mario a foreigner? [...] But that is not the problem![113]

The fundamental question was what it meant "to be a Christian today" and "to be a priest today in our country and on this continent that is passing through a time of martyrdom":

> To be or not to be faithful to the mission of Jesus Christ in the concrete reality that is our lot in this country. In this country, if you are a poor priest or a poor catechist in our community, you will be maligned, you will be threatened, you will be taken away at night in secret, and possibly you'll even be bombed. It has happened already! And if you are a foreigner, they will deport you. They have already deported many foreigners![114]

But those misfortunes were no more than symptoms. The basic question was something else:

> It is dangerous to be Christian in our society! It is dangerous to be truly Catholic! It is practically illegal to be authentically Christian in our society, in our country. For the world around us is essentially founded on an established *disorder*, which will inevitably be subverted by the mere proclamation of the Gospel. And that is the way it must be! It cannot be any other way! We are shackled *not by order but by disorder*.[115]

The disorder prevailing in the country could never tolerate the presence and preaching of Jesus of Nazareth. If he were to return, he would be arrested and crucified again:

> I very much fear [...] that if Jesus of Nazareth were to return and do today as he did then, traveling from Galilee to Judea, that is, from Chalatenango to San Salvador—I dare say that with his preaching and actions he would not, in our days, reach as far as Apopa. I believe they would arrest him right there around Guazapa. They would make him a prisoner and throw him in jail.[116] Don't worry! [...] Here I have a little thing that makes my voice reach as

---

113 Grande, homily on the expulsion of Father Mario Bernal.
114 Grande, homily on the expulsion of Father Mario Bernal.
115 Grande, homily on the expulsion of Father Mario Bernal.
116 At that moment, there was a power outage and the microphone went dead.

> far as the mountains.[117] [...] They would carry Jesus before many Supreme Juntas and accuse him of being unconstitutional and subversive.
>
> They would accuse the man-God, the prototype of humanity, of being rebellious. They would say he was a foreign Jew confusing people with strange, exotic ideas contrary to "democracy," that is, contrary to the minority whose ideas are opposed to God because they belong to the clan of the Cains. No doubt about it, sisters and brothers, they would crucify him again.
>
> May God deliver even me, who perhaps would also be there in that gang of crucifiers![118]

The tribe of the Cains might even prohibit the Bible from entering and circulating in the country. "I very much fear [...] that quite soon the Bible and the Gospel won't be able to cross our borders. Only the covers will reach us because all their pages will be torn out as subversive. [...] And of course they are subversive—of sin!" As it turned out, after Rutilio was killed, many of the rural poor experienced repression simply for having a Bible in their home.

The Cains, said Rutilio, rejected Jesus of Nazareth, the man who was a "stumbling-block for the Jews and folly for the pagans," and for the same reason they also persecuted his followers. The Cains wanted

> a God who does not interrogate them, who leaves them at peace in their establishment, and who does not declare to them these fateful words: "Cain, what have you done with your brother Abel?" No one has the right to take away another person's life. No one has the right to stomp on the neck of another person, dominating him and humiliating him.[119]

By contrast, "in Christianity we must be ready to give our own lives to create a just order and to save others, for the values of the Gospel." The god of the Cains was a dead god, not a God of life. He was therefore a god of "gravediggers" and "undertakers":

> Without any doubt, brothers and sisters, we would crucify him again today, because we prefer a Christ of gravediggers and undertakers. Many prefer [...] a mute, mouthless Christ suitable for parading around the streets. A Christ with a muzzle over his mouth. A Christ fashioned after our own notions and according to our paltry interests. *That is not the Christ of the Gospel!* [...] Some want a god in the clouds.[120]

---

117 The audience broke into loud applause when Rutilio continued, using a megaphone they provided him.
118 Grande, homily on the expulsion of Father Mario Bernal.
119 Grande, homily on the expulsion of Father Mario Bernal.
120 Grande, homily on the expulsion of Father Mario Bernal.

Father Mario, said Rutilio, shared the same fate as Jesus of Nazareth; like Jesus, he had been the victim of persecution for preaching the living God. There had really been no other reason to deport him, claimed Rutilio, for he was "a good and simple man, forthright and plain like the message of Jesus." That was why people paid keen attention to him at vicariate meetings. He was very diligent in fulfilling his responsibilities as a priest, and he never "exceeded" them; that is, "he was not a guerrilla, nor did he lead any organized political group":

> What he *did* do was spread the Word of the Lord, clearly and plainly, with his customary cordiality and without the least bit of arrogance. In his parish, he tried to energize the various groups with Gospel values. He wanted the folks in his parish not to be simply followers of dead traditions, not just gravediggers year after year, not worshipers of images carved out of wood, but true adorers of the living God and followers of the Lord who is present in each of the brothers and sisters passing by in the street.[121]

Proof of Mario's evangelical witness, asserted Rutilio, was his opposition during the recent patronal feast of Saint Catherine to allowing booths to be set up around the church for "poor, enslaved women, brought bound from other places." Saint Catherine, he had declared, could "in no way be honored by such hypocrisy and stupidity." On that occasion, he had acted as a prophet "but gently and firmly." "Were Jesus of Nazareth to see such a thing, he would say: 'That is what I did too!'"

Father Mario's power was the power of the Gospel. "Likewise with us: our power does not reside in weapons or in armies or in the G-3 [a German military rifle], and not even in legions of angels, as Jesus told Pilate." The power of Jesus was in his weakness, and that was how he triumphed:

> Your enemies, who are the enemies of the Gospel, have been overcome. They are irrational, and in their irrationality they want to block out the sun of truth, which cannot be blocked out by a finger or by brute force. Your voice, Mario, will resound in the dales and the mountains of our villages and hamlets. Your exile will be united to the martyrdom of the church in the different nations of Latin America.[122]

At this point, Rutilio recalled the history of martyrdom in the Latin American church: the murder of the priests Iván Betancourt and Casimiro Cypher and a large number of poor villagers at Los Horcones in Olancho, Honduras; the disappearance of the priest Héctor Gallego in Santa Fe de Veraguas, Panama; the murders of a Salesian priest and a Jesuit priest in Brazil; and the deportation of several priests from Paraguay. "And here among us as well, the list grows longer as people are being expelled from our country."

---

121 Grande, homily on the expulsion of Father Mario Bernal.
122 Grande, homily on the expulsion of Father Mario Bernal.

After citing at length the words Paul VI addressed to the rural poor during his visit to Colombia in 1968, as the Medellín conference was beginning, Rutilio introduced the theme of the Eucharist, "the ideal we sustain":

> Long tablecloths, a common table for all, stools for all—and with Christ in the middle, the one who took nobody's life but rather offered his own life for the noblest cause. This is what he said: "Lift the cup in a toast of love for me, remembering me and devoting yourselves to building up the kingdom, [...] which is the solidarity of a table shared among all, the Eucharist."[123]

After the Mass, a priest who was working closely with the popular organizations sought Rutilio out; he later gave this testimony:

> He tugged at my shirt and told me, "Remember the Gospel: he who kills by the sword dies by the sword." I think he was saying that the struggle should be peaceful, not violent, but and at that time [...] the situation had become violent. [...] He pulled at my shirt again and said, "Listen to what I'm telling you: there's no need for violence."[124]

The mobilization in Apopa was not only a "demonstration of religious faith," which was what the vicariate had proposed. The popular organizations were also present, carrying banners, shouting slogans, and distributing flyers, all with political content. The mix of motivations and interests was such that Father Carranza gave the demonstration a negative assessment. In his view, what happened in Apopa made it clear that there was,

> if not conflict, then at least tension between the religious and pastoral leadership, on the one hand, and the political—or better, sectarian—leadership, on the other. Once again an effort was made to confuse the lard with the butter, and the tripe that resulted is sure to be indigestible. [...] All these conditions produced an ambiguous, explosive, hybrid cocktail that is intoxicating for a moment but then brings on a hangover. Few conscientious folk will now be satisfied.[125]

Carranza thought that the "demonstration of religious faith" contained a large dose of sham because FECCAS had used it for its own purposes, under the aegis of the vicariate. At the same time, it had also served as an escape valve for "the boiler in which we find ourselves, under many atmospheres of pressure." Carranza concluded that the demonstration had directly benefited the regime and the oligarchy but that it had hurt "the most overwrought folk, [...] the weakest, the rural poor."

---

123 Grande, homily on the expulsion of Father Mario Bernal.
124 *Summarium testium*, §15.
125 ACSI. Salvador Carranza, "Pseudo-religious Mascarade or Mascaraded Pseudo-Politics?," Aguilares, n.d.

On the other hand, FECCAS was unhappy with Rutilio's homily, which it judged negatively because he had spent too much time explaining what the demonstration was *not*. Taking Rutilio's clarification to be a criticism of its activities, the organization was resentful because it had lent him its sound equipment and had helped organize the demonstration.

El mundo, in its issue of February 14, called attention to the demonstration with a large headline and a photograph. It portrayed the event as a political act since one of the flyers distributed by the popular organization contained an incitement to class struggle.

Óscar Arnulfo Romero: Archbishop of a Persecuted Church

On February 8, the nunciature announced that the pope had accepted the resignation of Archbishop Luis Chávez and had named Bishop Óscar Romero as the new archbishop of San Salvador. Archbishop Chávez would remain at the head of the archdiocese while the appropriate pontifical bulls were being prepared.

Romero's nomination caused discouragement and dismay among the archdiocesan clergy, who inclined more toward Bishop Rivera, thinking that he would give continuity to the pastoral line that Chávez followed in his later years. The naming of Romero was interpreted as a triumph of the more conservative and traditionalist sector of church and society, the sector most resistant to the teachings of Vatican II and Medellín. The great jubilation of the oligarchy showed that Romero's appointment was thus interpreted. The national press celebrated his nomination with huge headlines that were accompanied by full-color photographs and followed up with warm greetings for the new archbishop.

The joy of the more conservative sector was due to what they saw as the Holy See's preference for Romero over Rivera. Rivera was the target of FARO when it claimed on December 30, 1976, that the archdiocese had been infiltrated by international agents of subversion "in complicity with high ecclesiastical dignitaries of the country." The national press assumed that the new archbishop would quickly dispense of the services of Rivera as auxiliary bishop and request in his place Marco R. Revelo, who at that moment was auxiliary bishop of Santa Ana. On February 10, Romero encouraged such speculation when he stated that he would like to have Revelo as his auxiliary. He also announced that his installation as archbishop would take place on February 26, several days earlier than planned.

On February 7, the day before the nunciature officially announced Romero's nomination, Archbishop Chávez paid a courtesy visit to *El mundo*, which was celebrating the tenth anniversary of its founding. The archbishop took advantage of the visit to declare that he had never supported Marxism, that the leftist image projected onto the archdiocese was due to its promotion of the cooperative movement, and that he was in favor of harmonious social change, carried out by peaceful means, never by violent ones. He added that he recognized the

10. Persecution of the Church

valuable contribution the private sector made to resolving the country's social problems by supporting just laws and appropriate measures.

Archbishop Chávez also paid a courtesy visit to President Molina on February 8. Before entering the president's office, he told the press that he condemned communism as atheistic and materialist, and he denied that the church was infiltrated by communism. He further clarified that his clergy were not preaching socialism "in a political sense" but only as a "socializing" ideal. During the meeting, the president sought to flatter the archbishop by asking him to bless the first stage of the Cerrón Grande dam on February 15. He said he regretted that he could not bestow on him the supreme national honor, the order of José M. Delgado, since the archbishop had already received it a decade earlier.

The archbishop's clarifications did little good. FARO launched a vicious personal attack against him on February 12. The interrogatory title of the pronouncement, "The Innocence of Archbishop Chávez y González?," spoke for itself:

> The priests named by FARO—the ones in Opico, Aguilares, Tecoluca, Suchitoto, etc.—*have in their Sunday and daily preaching taught (and still teach) that it is not a sin to take from the rich in order to give to the poor. They preach that it is not a sin to use violence; in a word, they are inciting to crime. Those same priests, along with the Jesuits, have organized FECCAS and UTC, both of which in their public demonstrations provoke hatred for the rich and call for violence and death.*[126]

The responsibility for this situation, claimed the pronouncement, lay with the head of the archdiocese, Archbishop Chávez, who must be "living in limbo or saturated with *galactic innocence*," since he claimed to "know nothing of this reality" and was "unaware of the true ideological nature of those priests who are preaching a bloody revolution of hatred and violence." Pitying his benightedness, FARO declared sarcastically that "Archbishop Chávez deserves rather to be decorated with the Great Medal of the Order of 'Turning the Blind Eye.' Those priests are little angels with red wings, carrying machine guns under their habits."[127]

In Apopa, Rutilio boldly defended Chávez, Paul VI, and the universal magisterium, while at the same time reaffirming the practical dimension of the Gospel:

> Our humble archbishop, who will soon leave office, has, like us priests, his weaknesses and faults. [...] Just yesterday he was harshly attacked by a group of Cains who call themselves Catholics, and he has been publicly branded a "communist" by a recalcitrant minority, simply because his pastoral letters are based on the Gospel.
>
> He has been publicly attacked with incredible impudence [...] in the newspapers of the nation, and so have church documents, such as those

---

126 *El diario de hoy* (February 11, 1977).
127 *El diario de hoy* (February 11, 1977).

of Vatican II. Even Paul VI—who is internationally famous up there, in the empire's circles of high finance on Wall Street—has been condemned by some, who call his acclaimed encyclical on the *Progress of the Peoples* "warmed-over Marxism." That is the scandal that always comes with the preaching of the Gospel and above all with its practice.[128]

On February 15, the national press was brimming with pronouncements related to the elections programmed for February 20. Quite remarkable was that of FARO, which claimed that the principal enemies of the nation were the members of FECCAS, UTC, BPR, ANDES-June 21, the Unitary Federation of Salvadoran Unionists, the General Association of Salvadoran University Students, and other, virtually unknown organizations, which "with the false epithet of 'revolutionaries' had reaped lives and bloodied the soil of the homeland." In view of this threat, FARO asked the public to vote for General Carlos H. Romero who, unlike the existing government, would not tolerate the "communist hordes."[129] FECCAS and UTC, for their part, urged the "Salvadoran people" to join "the struggle." This exhortation, their ninth and final one, appeared strangely enough in the written press, which did not even reach the rural poor to whom it was addressed; moreover, the stated objectives were vague.

In the zone of Aguilares, flyers were circulated depicting Bishop Rivera as a communist infiltrator, surrounded by the priests whom FARO had accused of subversion. Around this time, Rutilio received an insulting and menacing letter. Addressed to "Don Rutilio or Tiloso," the crudely written document pretended to thank him for his collaboration during the patronal feast in Aguilares and during Holy Week:

> The church has had its changes. For a while it was the market of those vilifications, insults, and rumors that never fail. Then it turned into "La Praviana" Restaurant[130] with its giddy *zafacaites*.[131] It seems the situation is driving you crazy. Religion has declined, Grande, Grande! You're not cultured. It's unfortunate that you're using the studies the government financed for you to offend your friends and the people who relieved your hunger in grueling situations. We sign here: The Drunks, The Womanizers, [...] The Thieves, The Loan Sharks, The Bachelors minus the faggots and the shaggy lads.

The deepening of the country's sociopolitical crisis and the intensification of the persecution against the church forced Archbishop Chávez to ask that he be relieved of his post as soon as possible. The installation of Romero was therefore

---

128 Grande, homily on the expulsion of Father Mario Bernal.
129 "FARO Alerts the Citizenry: The Republic Threatened by Blackmail," *El diario de hoy* (February 15, 1977).
130 A restaurant then famous for its Mexican-style mariachi bands.
131 *Zafacaite* is a traditional dance of the department of Chalatenango.

moved up again, to February 22. The new archbishop began his ministry just as the persecution was growing fierce.

Two foreign priests—Guillermo Denaux, a Belgian from the diocese of Bruges, and Bernardo Survil, an American—were kidnapped and tortured by the security forces on February 17 and 18, respectively. Denaux had arrived in El Salvador in 1972 and was serving as pastor of San Antonio Abad, a suburban district of San Salvador, where he formed Christian communities, supported a credit union and a consumer cooperative, and opened a mechanics workshop and a medical clinic. Survil had arrived in the country in 1975 and was assisting the pastor of Lourdes, another suburban district of the capital; there he evangelized through groups of friends and systematic visitation of homes. Neither priest had any relationship with the so-called "communist hordes" denounced by FARO, nor had they appeared on the earlier lists of "subversive" priests. In a letter addressed to the bishops of the archdiocese, Denaux gave an account of his kidnapping and torture. In poor handwriting, he explained that he was still bedridden, with one eye damaged, because of the torture inflicted on him by the National Guard. The bishops read the letter at the March meeting of the clergy.[132]

Sufficient evidence exists to show that these repressive acts and others mentioned below were a concession the Molina government made to the oligarchs, who accused him of being weak and demanded stronger action against the church. The regime attacked the foreign clergy first because they were the most vulnerable. Each attack on the church was followed by a defamation campaign in the mass media, in which the clergy were blamed for the country's sociopolitical crisis. The director general of migration, Colonel Roberto E. Santibáñez, confirmed to the Jesuit provincial on February 19 that the prior actions had been meant to test the church's reaction; the intention was to level a strong blow against the church at an opportune moment, as FARO was demanding. The official made it clear, though, that the government understood that the principal threat was coming not from the clergy but from the armed groups, which they had not been able to infiltrate. The regime would therefore have absolutely no pity with anyone linked to the guerrillas, even if he were the son of a military officer. Santibáñez also indicated that after the election on February 20 the regime would "sweep away" the pastors in Aguilares, Nejapa, Opico, Suchitoto, and other parishes; he therefore recommended the removal from Aguilares of the missionary team, all of whom he knew by name, except one.[133]

---

132 "Dossier on the Persecution of the Church in El Salvador."
133 Personal communication of Father César Jerez, provincial, with the author, San Salvador, January 1980.

A Parish under Siege

The day after the elections, the provincial, Jerez, met with the three Jesuits of the missionary team to decide what to do in light of Santibáñez's statement. After some discussion, it was decided that the two foreigners, Carranza and Pérez, should leave Aguilares, though they would return on the weekends to help with the Masses. (Fernández had traveled to Spain ten days earlier to attend to his mother, who was seriously ill.) One of the team members later testified, "We were all aware of the dangers involved, and [Rutilio] was always willing to stay in the parish despite the risk he was running."[134] Rutilio was determined to stand fast, claiming that he could not abandon his people at that most difficult moment. His companions were concerned for him, but they thought that his Salvadoran nationality would keep him safe from repressive action. Rutilio was too important as a symbol.

According to the testimony of another team member, Rutilio "was very aware that a hit man hired by a local boss could easily eliminate him or, more likely, one of us foreigners while we were traveling in the countryside. This worried him greatly, and so he went overboard in caring for us."[135] After the meeting with the provincial, Rutilio thought it best to remove from the rectory in Aguilares several persons who wanted to stay there with him. The only person he allowed to remain was seventy-two-year-old Manuel Solórzano, one of the two companions who would die with him. Writing to Fernández on March 8 to offer condolences on the death of his mother, Rutilio described the situation: "As you can see, conditions are turbulent and shifting. I'm all alone. At night the bookseller [Solórzano] comes to take care of things as usual. The patronal feast of El Paisnal and Holy Week are approaching."[136]

State versus Church

The Salvadoran clergy became the direct targets of persecution on February 21, the day before the installation of Romero as archbishop. Some were threatened, others were tortured, and still others were besieged in their parishes or driven out of them. The first was Barahona, pastor of Tecoluca in the diocese of San Vicente; Tecoluca was one of the parishes named by FARO. Barahona was kidnapped near Olocuilta and tortured at the headquarters of the National Guard. Through the intervention of his bishop, the priest was freed, but in very poor physical and psychological shape.[137]

Romero took possession of the archdiocese in a private ceremony in the chapel of the San José de la Montaña Seminary on February 22, before the

---

134 *Summarium testium*, witness 7, §98.
135 *Summarium testium*, witness 2, §25.
136 ACSI. Rutilio Grande to Benigno Fernández, Aguilares, March 8, 1977.
137 "Dossier on the Persecution of the Church in El Salvador."

pontifical bulls were received. The public installation of the new archbishop in the cathedral was postponed until March 5. The archdiocesan clergy received Romero with great reserve; some of the finest and most influential priests even showed hostility toward him. Though Rutilio himself was surprised by Romero's appointment, he reacted quickly and positively, urging his fellow priests to give the new archbishop a chance to prove himself and making it clear that he was personally ready to collaborate with him.

Rutilio was impressed and pleased by the letter Romero sent out to the clergy of San Salvador the day before his installation.[138] Even though its tone was impersonal, Rutilio found in it a message for every priest of the archdiocese. He especially appreciated Romero's readiness to collaborate closely with the archdiocesan clergy in building up the church and his emphasis on shared responsibility. Rutilio also valued the new archbishop's willingness to offer his "modest services" to the clergy and his promise always to remain open to dialogue, with "the simplicity of a friend." As proof of his availability, Romero said that priests who were visiting San Salvador would be allowed to stay overnight at the seminary.[139] Rutilio was also deeply moved by Romero's avowal of his admiration and affection for Archbishop Chávez, and he wrote to Romero expressing his gratitude: "It sums up a long history of filial love and affection. [...] It touches a very deep fiber of my being."[140]

Evidence exists that Rutilio made an effort to pacify the irate members of the clergy and to encourage the disappointed. He was aware, however, that Romero distrusted him because of his views on the national reality and on ecclesial matters: "You no doubt have heard many things about poor me in one sense or another. I'm not ignorant of the concrete history of the local church of San Salvador." But Rutilio was not worried: "God has his designs, and we encounter him again as we live out the concrete history of our local church." He therefore insisted that the two of them should trust in God's plan and accept the challenge it presented, keeping in mind their long friendship and their days together in the seminary, when they conversed frequently about what was happening in the country. "Accordingly, count on my cooperation within my human limits, in a framework of ecclesial co-responsibility and dialogue." Rutilio ended his letter promising to inform Romero about "the pastoral adventure" of Aguilares: "I am well aware that you are concerned about the pastoral coordination of our local church."[141]

---

138 ACSI. Bishop Óscar A. Romero of Santiago de María, "Circular to Clergy of the Archdiocese," Santiago de María, February 21, 1977.
139 Bishop Óscar A. Romero of Santiago de María, "Circular to Clergy of the Archdiocese."
140 The final phrase is crossed out in the original letter. ACSI. Rutilio Grande to Archbishop Óscar A. Romero, draft letter, Aguilares, March 9, 1977.
141 Rutilio Grande to Archbishop Óscar A. Romero, draft letter, Aguilares, March 9, 1977.

On the same day that Archbishop Romero took possession of the archdiocese, February 22, the bishops were received by President Molina[142] in his official residence. According to the press report, one item of discussion was the "subversive priests." The president in fact gave the bishops a list of the priests who he claimed were subversive, and he was unyielding when the bishops protested about the expulsion of the foreign priests without consulting first with them, the bishops, as was the custom. His only concession was to free Barahona, but not without requiring Bishop Delgado, as representative of the diocese of San Vicente, to sign a document certifying that he had received the prisoner in a good physical state, even though the national press had reported that he had been tortured. The office of the president later informed the press that "a cordial exchange of impressions" had taken place between the president and the bishops.

The situation in the country became even more fraught when the political opposition protested against electoral fraud. When the opposition parties held a demonstration in the Plaza Libertad on February 27, it was broken up by the security forces in a melee in which many were killed and wounded. At the request of the Red Cross, Archbishop Chávez and Bishop Rivera attempted to mediate between the demonstrators and the government; Archbishop Romero was away from the capital at the time for unknown reasons. In San Salvador, the elections were orderly, but in the other cities and in the towns there were many incidents, some of them violent. In Aguilares, there was gunfire, a ballot box was stolen, and members of the official party were shut up in the city hall.

Despite the resistance of the bishops, the regime continued to expel priests. On February 25, John Murphy, a Benedictine from the United States, left the country after being pressured by the nuncio, who told him that the choice before him was leaving on his own or being tortured and then deported. Murphy had arrived in El Salvador in 1969 and served first as assistant priest in the parish of Ayutuxtepeque; in 1974, he was made pastor of the parish of San Sebastián Ayutuxtepeque; in both parishes, he promoted the base Christian communities. When Archbishop Chávez learned of the order of deportation, he made President Molina promise not to maltreat the priest. Murphy had already made strong statements to the *New York Times* about the persecution of the church in El Salvador, so the nuncio persuaded him to leave quickly.[143]

Meanwhile, seven other priests were prevented from returning to the country: (1) Pedro Declercq, Belgian, pastor of the church in Zacamil, San Salvador, and professor at the seminary (Molina had promised him, before his trip, that

---

142 Present at the meeting, besides the president, were the heads of the legislature and the judiciary, the minister and sub-secretary of defense, the minister of the interior, the private secretary of the president, and the secretary of information.
143 "Dossier on the Persecution of the Church in El Salvador."

he could return); (2) Jean Deplancke, also Belgian, advisor to the Catholic Student Youth Movement and collaborator with Belgian pastors in the country; (3) Lorenzo McCulloch, American, assistant pastor in San Juan Opico; (4) Juan Ramón Vega, Nicaraguan, executive secretary since 1961 of the Interdiocesan Social Secretariat, which helped finance the social works of the archdiocese, and regional secretary since 1972 of Justice and Peace for Central America, Panama, and the Antilles; (5) Ignacio Ellacuría, Spanish Jesuit naturalized as a Salvadoran; (6) Luis de Sebastián, also a Spanish Jesuit naturalized as a Salvadoran, academic vice-rector and economics professor in the UCA (the government claimed his life would be in danger if he returned); and (7) Benigno Fernández.[144]

In this context, Rutilio was surprised when a three-day clergy conference was called (February 28 to March 2) and the main topic of discussion was "Protestantism." He was all the more perplexed when Bishop Rivera asked him to present the theme. Given the gravity of the persecution, Rutilio asked Rivera to suspend the conference or at least to relieve him of making the presentation. He said that he felt incapable of preparing the topic well since he was alone in the parish and under great pressure. Carranza's residency permit was about to expire on March 4, and it is uncertain whether the immigration office would renew it. Besides, the patronal feast of El Paisnal was imminent.[145]

Bishop Rivera insisted on holding the conference, and Rutilio had no choice but to make the presentation. He asked the Jesuits at the UCA for suggestions, as was his custom in such cases. Father Jon Sobrino suggested that he analyze the phenomenon of Protestantism from three perspectives: sociopolitical, Christian, and ecclesial.[146] Rutilio told those attending the conference that meeting the challenge of Protestantism would require creativity and boldness because of the aggressive and belligerent proselytism of various groups. He proposed to the clergy that they reflect on the real reasons for the success of the "providentialist" vision of the Protestants. He urged them not to yield to the temptation of engaging in "sectarian word battles" and "lamentations": in doing so, they would be responding to one type of sectarianism with another. He warned them also not to resort to the church's traditional response, taking refuge in dogmatism and clericalism instead of facing the real crisis. It was necessary, he stated, to accept the Protestant challenge and to respond to its arguments directly. As a practical matter, he urged the participants to think seriously about the promotion of lay pastoral agents and their full integration into church ministry. These same ideas are found also in the presentation Rutilio gave at the monthly meeting of clergy on October 1, 1974.

---

144 "Dossier on the Persecution of the Church in El Salvador."
145 ACSI. Rutilio Grande to Bishop Arturo Rivera, Aguilares, February 22, 1977.
146 ACSI. Jon Sobrino, "The Protestant Phenomenon in El Salvador: A Handbook of Ideas," San Salvador, February 1977.

The assembled clergy also discussed the ongoing persecution during that three-day meeting, and they suggested possible measures to be taken. They recommended that the archdiocese broadcast press bulletins over the archdiocesan radio station, YSAX, to counter the campaign of disinformation being waged by the regime and the national press, which was controlled by the oligarchy. They recommended that an emergency committee, consisting of three priests, be set up; it would hold open meetings every day in the archbishop's office for the purpose of analyzing the course of events; any priest could have recourse to the committee to provide information or seek assistance. They asked that the official installation of the archbishop, programmed for March 5, be postponed. Finally, they asked that the public be made aware that any attack against the physical integrity of a priest would mean excommunication for those responsible. They hoped that the archdiocese would make it clear that

> if such excommunication were to fall on persons of authority, no matter what their rank—even if they were to take part, for example, in a Te Deum, Masses of Thanksgiving, or other official acts of the Catholic Church—they would be doing so merely as an external act, not in the Communion of the church.[147]

The persecution did not lessen. In the pre-dawn hours of March 4, a contingent of about forty national guards and paramilitary agents, armed with machine guns, besieged the church and the rectory of San Martín, with the intention of arresting the pastor, Rutilio Sánchez. However, the people in the town, aroused by the constant peeling of the church bells, turned out en masse and prevented the arrest. The armed agents then broke into the house of four seminarians and ransacked it. In other incidents, Fathers David Rodríguez of Tecoluca and Inocencio Alas of Suchitoto, after receiving death threats, had to stay away from their respective parishes.

On March 10, Archbishop Romero held a meeting to analyze the situation, especially the plight of the foreign clergy. This was the first and last meeting convoked and presided over by Archbishop Romero that Rutilio was able to attend. The 154 priests and religious sisters in attendance were pleasantly surprised when the archbishop began the meeting by saying that nobody should feel like a foreigner, that all church workers should feel that they belonged in El Salvador. Assuring all those assembled of his support and esteem, he invited them to unite around him as pastor. Romero then asked the assembly to consider recent events and invited suggestions about how to proceed. Those attending met by vicariates and later shared their discussion in a plenary session. At the end of the meeting, the archbishop was left with two pages of suggestions. A notable spirit of ecclesial

---

147 Archdiocesan bulletin no 1, San Salvador, March 1, 1977. See "Dossier on the Persecution of the Church in El Salvador."

unity pervaded the meeting, and both clergy and religious were surprised to find that unity with their bishop, which until then had seemed impossible, was becoming reality.[148]

During the plenary, Rutilio asked whether "those hiding in the caves could now come down into the valley," that is, whether there were sufficient guarantees of safety for the priests in hiding so that they could resume their ordinary pastoral activities. Among them were Carranza and Pérez. Romero responded that it would be advisable to act with caution.

During the recess, Rutilio sought out the rector of the seminary, Father Gregorio Rosa, to talk with him about the parish. Rosa later testified: "He told me that he saw much danger and that he was worried about some things that were happening in the parish. He spoke to me specifically about some young priests that were with him, and he told me, 'These guys are moving too quickly.'"[149] Rosa interpreted the visit as the result of

> a premonition Rutilio had, that he could not run away from that place. He was conscious of the danger because the attacks were constant and the persecution was increasing. He was in the eye of the hurricane, but he remained calm and serene, always smiling. Even though he was interiorly suffering anguish, he did not show it.[150]

The Bishops Speak Up

The persecution also united the bishops' conference, although only momentarily. In fact, all the bishops of the ecclesiastical province signed a message dated March 5, saying that they were moved by "the events of recent days and months, […] which require us to pronounce a clear, serene, and firm word. […] We cannot elude this responsibility." The message was important not only because it made manifest an episcopal unity that was rare for the Salvadoran church but also because it ratified the pastoral option of the archdiocese and of the parishes and pastors accused of heterodoxy by the oligarchy and the military regime. The bishops particularly endorsed the pastoral activity of Rutilio and the missionary team of Aguilares. Not only that, but the bishops stated that they were committed to continuing pastoral work along the same lines.[151]

The bishops spoke of the events "that have plunged us into perplexity and sadness." They expressed their distress first and foremost at the repression of the rural poor who were "coming to awareness" and at the tortures, the killings,

---

148 ACSI. "Report on the Meeting of the Clergy of the Archdiocese of San Salvador," San Salvador, March 10, 1977.
149 *Summarium testium*, witness 5, §66.
150 *Summarium testium*, witness 5, §66.
151 "Message of the Bishops' Conference of El Salvador," San Salvador, March 5, 1977. See "Dossier on the Persecution of the Church in El Salvador."

and the disappearances, all in unexplained circumstances. Second, they were disturbed by the persecution directed against the church, which took various forms: "The campaign, through the press and other media, to threaten and intimidate priests, laypeople, institutions, and publications with a Christian orientation"; the expulsion of "distinguished" foreign priests "without due explanation and without the prior dialogue between military and ecclesiastical authorities that always took place previously in similar situations"; the refusal to allow returning priests to enter the country; the threats against native-born priests; and the disrespect shown to the "distinguished" figure of Archbishop Chávez in the publicity campaign being waged by the organizations of the oligarchy.[152] At the center of the bishops' message were the people of El Salvador, their aspirations, their struggles, and their sufferings: "In enumerating all these facts, we realize that at stake are the human rights of Salvadorans and also of those priests who were born elsewhere but who have identified with our people for the sake of contributing to the betterment of our homeland."[153] The bishops left the church and the clergy in the background in order to show that the persecution against them was understood as part of the larger repression of the people themselves, especially the rural poor. The bishops said they were speaking in order to "arouse and channel" the hopes of those who "have no voice" and "to provide them assistance as they become fully aware of their dignity as Christians and citizens."

These painful events reflected "a much greater and more radical evil," asserted the bishops. "Our country is living through dramatic social conditions," as shown by statistics and confirmed by "the daily experience of most of our people":

> It has already been frequently cited, but we still have to repeat that statement of Medellín [...] so applicable to our country: "The most noteworthy fact of our time is the generalized misery of vast groups of humans." Such a situation has been denominated "collective injustice" and "institutionalized violence." [...] All of us want these things to be otherwise, but they are not otherwise, and they will not be as long as the majority of our people are left out of the picture, as long as solutions are not sought for their problems, and as long as solutions are sought exclusively for the problems of a minority that seeks to maintain and increase its social, economic, and political power.[154]

Contrary to the opinion of the regime and especially the oligarchy, said the bishops, "this analysis is simple, and it is independent of ideologies" leftist or communist. It is "a moral judgment rising up from the heart of Christian faith: this

---

152 "Message of the Bishops' Conference of El Salvador," San Salvador, March 5, 1977. See "Dossier on the Persecution of the Church in El Salvador."
153 "Message of the Bishops' Conference of El Salvador," San Salvador, March 5, 1977. See "Dossier on the Persecution of the Church in El Salvador."
154 "Message of the Bishops' Conference of El Salvador," San Salvador, March 5, 1977. See "Dossier on the Persecution of the Church in El Salvador."

cannot be so. We cannot continue answering as Cain did, if not in words then in deeds: 'Am I my brother's keeper?'"

The bishops then took up the question of the church's mission that "some want to discredit." The mission was none other than that of Jesus himself: "The church must promote the kingdom with all the energy it can muster, [...] even though it knows that its realization [...] on earth will always be partial and incomplete." In El Salvador, promoting the kingdom of God involved specific responsibilities:

> Struggling for and promoting justice, knowing the truth, achieving a political, social, and economic order in accord with God's plan. All this means unmasking those who have pursued a false humanization through wealth, power, privilege, and social position. It also means restoring human dignity and material means to those who live forgotten on the margins of society. In sum, the church must work to make our society more human and more just.[155]

Since "the injustice is quite concrete, the promotion of justice must also be concrete." No one, therefore, especially not the military regime or the oligarchy, "should be surprised that the church encourages, guides, and promotes concrete mechanisms for doing justice." To be sure, the means had to be rigorously assessed and the most effective ones adopted, and in that sense "the church has to keep learning what concrete mechanisms are best for bringing about the kingdom of God." The bishops had no doubt, however, that as long as "there is no decisive attempt [...] to resolve the problems such as the just distribution of wealth and land, participation in politics, and the organization of rural and city folk, then the people's status as citizens and children of God will continue to be discounted."[156]

Consequently, the struggle "for justice, peace, human development, and the defense of basic human rights is not a matter of politics; it is simply laying the foundation of the common good." In fidelity to its mission, "the church cannot do less than raise its voice when injustice takes hold of a society, even if it risks being misunderstood or persecuted for doing so. The church cannot remain silent when human rights are violated."[157] The bishops explained the radicality of their position, which no doubt surprised the more traditional sectors, in terms of conversion. The church and its members, they wrote, were going through a "painful but real" process by which "they are becoming conscious of the radical 'No' that God pronounces on our sins of omission." Consequently, "we also

---

155 "Message of the Bishops' Conference of El Salvador," San Salvador, March 5, 1977. See "Dossier on the Persecution of the Church in El Salvador."
156 "Message of the Bishops' Conference of El Salvador," San Salvador, March 5, 1977. See "Dossier on the Persecution of the Church in El Salvador."
157 "Message of the Bishops' Conference of El Salvador," San Salvador, March 5, 1977. See "Dossier on the Persecution of the Church in El Salvador."

are determined to collaborate in creating a more humane society, which for us Christians is the coming of God's kingdom."[158]

The bishops' message did not forget "the rich": nobody was excluded from the kingdom of God. Everyone, "rich and poor, powerful and dispossessed," was called to conversion and salvation, "but they are called by God in different ways." For that reason, the church

> cannot remain unmoved when there are some who possess great extensions of land while others possess not even the minimum necessary to subsist; or when some have access to culture, entertainment, and luxury while others struggle day by day to survive, lacking regular work and suffering hunger that results in tragic cases of malnutrition.

This reality obliged the church to take the side of "the dispossessed, those about whom nobody cares, those who matter to nobody." And it had to do so even if such an option "brings upon it, as it did on Jesus, persecution and the incomprehension of the powerful, who are perhaps surprised that the church is involving itself in things of this world and disturbed because they view this mission as a threat." The bishops lamented that whenever there has been a struggle to create

> a more just society which truly takes account of the dispossessed and the marginalized—whether these be small farmers, workers, indigenous peoples, or slum dwellers—the reaction has always been very similar: power has turned against these Christians, and they have been killed, disappeared, expelled, and threatened.[159]

The bishops' conference, in fidelity to its "pastoral duty" and "without any other interest than that of collaborating in the creation of a just and fraternal society," called for the cessation of every type of violence, the guarantee of security for the population, the liberation of political prisoners, the freedom of all to take part in politics, and respect for human rights. Finally, it asked the government to put an end to torture, persecution, abuse of power, and the arbitrary deportation of Salvadoran citizens and foreign clergy.[160]

The bishops' conference ordered that their message be read at all Masses on Sunday, March 13. The evening before, Archbishop Romero informed Bishop Rivera that he would read the message at the eight o'clock Mass in the cathedral but not at the twelve noon Mass in the church of San José de la Montaña, whose members came from the wealthiest neighborhoods of the capital. Bishop Rivera

---

158 "Message of the Bishops' Conference of El Salvador," San Salvador, March 5, 1977. See "Dossier on the Persecution of the Church in El Salvador."
159 "Message of the Bishops' Conference of El Salvador," San Salvador, March 5, 1977. See "Dossier on the Persecution of the Church in El Salvador."
160 "Message of the Bishops' Conference of El Salvador," San Salvador, March 5, 1977. See "Dossier on the Persecution of the Church in El Salvador."

thought that that was a good idea since the eight o'clock Mass was broadcast directly by the archdiocesan radio station YSAX. The next day, however, Archbishop Romero read the message at both Masses and made a "precious commentary" on it, so much so, Bishop Rivera said later, that "we sat down to hear it on the radio at supper time, and we were amazed at how the wisdom of God was with him."[161]

---

161 Personal communication of Bishop Arturo Rivera with Father César Jerez, provincial.

11. The Martyrdom

The first day of the novena of Saint Joseph, March 11, was charged with foreboding because of insistent stories of death threats against Rutilio. All day long, people were reporting to the rectory in Aguilares the rumors they had heard in the market or on the streets. On several occasions, they warned Rutilio to beware of his relative by marriage, Venancio Grande,[1] of whom they suspected the worst. Some children recounted how at a party in Venancio's house the authorities of El Paisnal had complained Rutilio was a "troublemaker" and boasted that "they would see what end he came to." For decades, control of the mayoralty of El Paisnal had been alternating between Venancio and Santos Murillo. Both men, according to the testimony of a relative of Venancio and Rutilio, took advantage of the office to make themselves "owners of many ill-gotten lands and moneys."[2] The two alternating mayors were known for their "misuse of the public domain." It was to be expected, then, that they would find the presence and the preaching of Rutilio intolerable. According to the same testimony, "there was continual familial and social friction, and it kept getting worse."[3]

Rutilio did not take the rumors seriously, and the informants were often bothered by his indifference to them. He felt that he had always been received quite cordially in the house of Venancio Grande, even though some persons claimed that Venancio's wife had burned some belongings that Rutilio had left stored in the house. These claims were corroborated by the witness cited above, who said that the same woman "went so far as to express her hatred for the priest and her desire to see him dead."[4] The persons most alarmed by the rumors were the "old ladies" of El Paisnal: they had seen Rutilio grow up and took care of him whenever he visited the town, but even they were unable to persuade him to be more careful.

In the end, Rutilio did take some precautions. Instead of spending the night in the homes of friends in El Paisnal, he stayed in the rectory; he even asked that his meals be brought there. When the townsfolk expressed surprise, he explained to them that he only wanted to protect them in case there was an attack.

A week before Rutilio was murdered, a teacher who was a faithful member of the parish received an anonymous letter stating that "they would first do away with the priests and then with her, just as one got rid of rats." She was

---

1　Venancio Grande's wife was the sister of the wife of Flavio Grande, Rutilio's older brother.
2　*Summarium testium*, witness 16, §263.
3　*Summarium testium*, witness 16, §263.
4　*Summarium testium*, witness 16, §263.

convinced that the threat was real, and she was in fact kidnapped on March 18, less than a week after the murder of Rutilio and his companions.[5] A woman who was a close friend of Solórzano was also given a warning two days before the murder. According to her testimony, "a young employee of the mayor's office [in Aguilares] told me to leave the room I was renting 'because something is going to happen.'" She did not believe what he said and did not move.[6] After the murders, she was arrested for being a friend of Rutilio and Solórzano and spent twenty-two days in prison.

Though he appeared serene and even nonchalant about the threats, Rutilio knew that he could easily be killed. On several occasions, he confided as much to Father Jaime Vera-Fajardo, with whom he had lived in the community of the Colegio Externado. Vera-Fajardo said that he and Rutilio conversed often:

> He has confided in me often, and we have spoken about his apostolic work and his fears and his hopes. He repeatedly told me that he could end up being gunned down, that they could kill him at any moment in those godforsaken places. [...] We almost always spoke about his work. This was the main topic, given the conflictive nature of the parish, even at the level of Jesuits. [...] He gave evidence of this fear, of this possibility, but I thought he was exaggerating a little. I knew the father well and considered him to be a gentle, likable, simple, kind man.[7]

Knowing Rutilio as well as he did, Vera-Fajardo left the following testimony about the causes of his death:

> As far as I can see, Grande died for preaching the true Gospel valiantly. He did not get mixed up in politics. He had no enemies except those one has whenever one preaches the Gospel. He was balanced, an enemy of violence, dedicated to others, excellent in his religious observance, and concerned about evangelization. *Evangelii nuntiandi* had a powerful effect on him, and he often told me about the riches contained in that letter of the pope.[8]

Strangers in Town

During lunch "at the rectory dinner table" on March 11, 1977, the three priests—Rutilio, Pérez, and Carranza—talked about "the repression" and "the threats" being made against the catechists, the delegates of the Word, and anyone carrying a Bible. "We were talking about how they could bomb us or shoot us. [...] We

---

5   Personal communication of the teacher with the author. San Salvador, March 1980.
6   *Summarium testium*, witness20, §379.
7   ARSI. Jaime Vera-Fajardo to Father Pedro Arrupe, San Salvador, March 16, 1977. C. América, 1011. Individuals. 1977.
8   ARSI. Jaime Vera-Fajardo to Father Pedro Arrupe, San Salvador, March 16, 1977. C. América, 1011. Individuals. 1977.

were all aware of the danger of staying there, but [Rutilio] was always ready to remain in the parish despite the risks involved."⁹

Rutilio assigned the Masses for the next day, March 12. Carranza would celebrate in Aguilares. Rutilio would go to El Paisnal, taking Pérez with him in the parish vehicle as far as Conacaste, about six kilometers from El Paisnal.¹⁰ Pérez would celebrate in the hamlet of El Tablón, where there was also a wedding, and he would stay there overnight.

Rutilio had earlier decided that he would personally attend to the services in El Paisnal, instead of Carranza, who was in charge of the zone. "He told me," declared Carranza, "that he was going to celebrate the novena of Saint Joseph in El Paisnal and that I should not leave the rectory in Aguilares for any reason."¹¹ But Rutilio, he continued, "asked me […] to accompany him on the first day of the novena so that I could introduce him to the local communities and also install a sound system for him that could be 'heard in the mountains.'" Rutilio's decision to take Carranza's place was unusual because, almost from the start of the Aguilares experience in May 1973, Carranza testified, he had been "by order and mission of Rutilio the priest responsible for the rural areas, and from 1975 on, the quasi-pastor of the town of El Paisnal, which I was told never for any reason to leave without a Mass on Sundays." He said that Rutilio contended with him earnestly "whenever he saw or thought he saw me giving more time or priority to the communities in the Guazapa hills." "The fact is," Carranza concluded, "he risked his own life in order to protect me. […] But Father Rutilio never thought that they were going to kill him, and least of all on that trip. I don't think that either he or I was thinking that one day they could kill us."¹²

The first Mass of the novena of Saint Joseph, on March 11, was the last one Rutilio celebrated in El Paisnal. In his homily, he encouraged the congregation to have faith and not lose heart. He reminded them that the Bible was not something to be kept "in a cupboard" but was to be read and studied. And he urged them to take good care of themselves and of Saint Joseph. According to a person present in the church, his words gave the impression of being a farewell speech. Some parishioners were surprised that he had talked about going away but had not said where he was going. The older women were left with the impression that he was going someplace far away and that he would not return for a long time. When Mass was over, however, Rutilio asked one of the collaborators to draw up a list of the children who would be taking part in the traditional excursion to the river and to bring it to him without fail the next day in Aguilares.

---

9   *Summarium testium*, witness 7, §97, ad. 23.
10 *Summarium testium*, witness 7, §93.
11 *Summarium testium*, witness 2, §22.
12 *Summarium testium*, witness 2, §26.

Some of those present at the Mass said that they had been surprised to see Marciano Estrada in the church since he rarely attended services and would hardly have been expected at a novena in honor of Saint Joseph. Marciano was the brother of Benito Estrada, the only person named in the legal proceedings after the murder. He was a customs officer, ordinarily stationed at border posts, but he was spending those days in El Paisnal, recovering from a wound he had received in a quarrel with some companions at work.

Standing at the left side of the main door during the Mass, Estrada had laughed derisively during the homily. A parishioner recalled this in her testimony and added: "When the father raised the host, [Marciano] laughed and said to him, 'Enjoy your time talking, wretch, for your days are numbered.' Since I was just a child, I didn't notice many things, but I do remember that Mass."[13] Other witnesses testified that Estrada had traced a cross with a razor blade on the plastic rear window of Rutilio's VW Safari, at the level of the driver's head. Upon returning to Aguilares, Rutilio repaired the hole with adhesive tape.

Around midday on Saturday, March 12, several strange persons appeared in El Paisnal, accompanied by Benito Estrada. They were seen in several places around town: near the municipal building; in the public bath, where they stopped to converse with acquaintances; and in front of the military command post, where they ate watermelon. They circled many times through the dusty streets of El Paisnal in a vehicle with California license plates. Several times they took the street leading toward Tacachico and drove near the train line and the rectory of Aguilares. After the murder, they disappeared. Nelson's sister also mentioned this vehicle in her testimony.[14]

Around five in the afternoon, Rutilio sent a telegram to Fernández in the name of Solórzano and his wife; the telegram read, "We profoundly lament death of your mother. Greetings prayers." Then, accompanied by Solórzano, Rutilio set out for El Paisnal to continue the novena, but Pérez did not go with them as planned; he later explained: "I got out of the car and went instead in the bus, which was waiting in the plaza of Aguilares and would pass through Conacaste, where I was going." He did this so that Rutilio could spend more time conversing with a visitor from San Salvador, who had arrived at the rectory just as they were leaving. "I was not prepared for martyrdom," added Pérez in his testimony.[15]

When he was finally able to leave Aguilares, Rutilio took Solórzano with him and picked up a young lad who helped out around the parish and lived in El Paisnal. The three of them sat in the front seat of the Safari, Rutilio driving, Solórzano beside him, and the lad on the right.

---

13 *Summarium testium*, witness 24, §401.
14 *Summarium testium*, witness 24, §402.
15 *Summarium testium*, witness 7, §94.

A Faithful Companion

Given the bonds that existed between Rutilio and Solórzano, it was understandable that he would accept the old man's companionship in those difficult and uncertain times. A woman who knew both men testified that Solórzano "always traveled with the father"; "he was a great friend" of Rutilio and "always helped him out." The woman said that she loved Solórzano "as my father; he gave me good advice." The relation was mutual, she said, for "[Solórzano] loved me as if I were his daughter. [...] He read to me from the Bible; he scolded me for working too much. [...] He always told me what they [he and Rutilio] were doing."[16] The witness was renting a room in the same house where Solórzano was living. The house had been left to Rutilio by Matilde Barrera, and he rented the rooms out.

Solórzano, according to this witness, "was very poor; he worked long hours and came home tired. He earned almost nothing, [but] he never complained about his economic situation. He was very happy."[17] A daughter of Solórzano testified also to his poverty: "We were always quite humble. [...] We were always very poor." But she was grateful all the same: "I thank my father, who left me no inheritance except the greater inheritance of loving God above all things and the Catholic Church."[18]

Both witnesses agreed that Solórzano was a man of faith. His daughter stated that "he always had a Bible with him" and that "he greatly enjoyed reading the Bible" even before he met Rutilio. "When we were small, we would go to the church at five in the morning. He used to say that the best breakfast was going to the church early. We didn't go to bed until we prayed the rosary, and we didn't eat without praying." When the daughter was twelve years old, she said, "They stole everything he had, and he just said, 'God be with me.' Many people in the church helped him. He used to say that God takes things away from him but that God also gives him things and that God was not going to abandon him. He was a man of prayer."[19]

The daughter remembered that her father used to collaborate in the activities of the parish. During Holy Week, he was one of those who

> took part in the processions and prepared adornments for them. I remember that once he was the Nazarene. He was carrying the cross in the procession at the moment when my brother was about to be born. They went to call him, but he said he needed to finish. My father despised everything else for God.[20]

---

16 *Summarium testium*, witness 20, §369.
17 *Summarium testium*, witness 20, §373.
18 *Summarium testium*, witness 21, §382.
19 *Summarium testium*, witness 21, §382.
20 *Summarium testium*, witness 21, §382.

The testimony given by a neighbor added that "he respected the things of God. He was very prudent and had the fear of God in him. He always wore dress pants and a long-sleeved shirt to Mass."[21]

Solórzano was born in San Luis, Chalatenango. According to his daughter,

> he lived many years on a banana plantation. Then he married my mother, and they went to live in Suchitoto, in the La Cruz neighborhood. […] As a father, he was wonderful. I imagine he wanted to give us more, but we were poor and he did what he could. When I was a child, he was especially fatherly and took good care of me.

When the daughter set up her own home, she said, "he always visited me. He liked to have lunch with us, but first there was always the prayer." She remembered that he had congratulated her for the way she educated her children. She said that her father always stayed in touch: "Wherever I was, he would come looking for me. […] I was forty years old when he paid me his last visit."[22] In sum, she could find no defect in her father: "He was a good father, a good son, a good brother, and even a good neighbor. […] He was magnificent. He was friendly with everybody and very affectionate with people. Everyone got along with him."[23]

This assessment was confirmed by the woman who was a neighbor of Solórzano and very close to him. She stated that he was "friendly with many people" and that "he would do a favor for anybody." One time, for example, "when I washed his clothes, he asked me how much I was going to charge. I told him five *colones*, but he told me he would give me eight since I needed them." The same witness added that Solórzano was "humble, modest, and courteous […] a little serious, but good […] peaceful, honest, without vices […] a man of the people […] merciful."[24]

Solórzano first met Rutilio in the church of Aguilares. That same day, said the neighbor, "he told me with great emotion that he had befriended the father and that he was going to help him. From that time on, he didn't want the father to go anywhere alone; he always went with him." The witness said that after the situation in Aguilares had become tense and threatening, she had asked Solórzano whether he was afraid when traveling with Rutilio. He answered that "he wasn't going to leave the father" even though "he knew that something could happen to him. He told me that he was never going to leave the father because […] if someone was with him, nothing bad would happen to him. His fear was always that something would happen to the father, not to himself." Solórzano had also told the witness "that people sometimes were telling him to leave the

---

21 *Summarium testium*, witness 20, §374.
22 *Summarium testium*, witness 21, §384.
23 *Summarium testium*, witness 21, §384.
24 *Summarium testium*, witness 20, §373.

things of the church. But he told me he would not do so. He was always quite serene." She remembered March 12 especially: "He told me he was heading home because the father was going to give some children a ride. I had just given him the clothes I had washed for him."[25]

A Helpful Boy

On that same day, March 12, according to the testimony of his aunt, a young boy named Lemus Rutilio Nelson had gone to Aguilares to leave a load of firewood for his godmother and "to buy himself a few things." She added that sometimes "the father would give him a ride so that he could sell the firewood" around town.[26]

The oldest of five siblings, Lemus had just turned fifteen. He was in the seventh grade, but like many youngsters, he worked in his spare time to help out his parents. His sixty-five-year-old father was the postman of El Paisnal. His mother made various products for sale. A sister of Lemus confirmed that "we were quite poor economically,"[27] and the aunt stated that "they were poorly off, very poorly off; everything was quite scarce."[28] A cousin added that "they were very honest and respectable. [...] They went to church and were married in the church."[29] Lemus's mother had very reluctantly left the movement of the delegates of the Word because of threats made against her husband: he had been told that he would be fired if she continued "learning about communism." Nevertheless, she remained close to the delegates and secretly collaborated with them whenever she could.

Various persons testified that Lemus was a very active boy, attentive, affectionate, and generous. His sister recalled that their father had "always said that he was special, that he'd been very lively since he was a baby."[30] She remembered especially that "with us he was very tender; he was loving with his parents and all his brothers and sisters." He was kind to others as well: "He liked to dedicate his time to being with people. [...] He was always well mannered. [...] He enjoyed carrying little children."[31] The aunt added that "he was generous and always ready to help people. [...] What I liked most about Nelson was that when I spoke he always paid me heed. He was very obedient and helpful."[32]

Indeed, as Lemus's sister testified, "if anyone needed a favor, he would do it without even being asked and without receiving anything in return. He had many

---

25 *Summarium testium*, witness 20, §373.
26 *Summarium testium*, witness 22, §386.
27 *Summarium testium*, witness 24, §ad. 5.
28 *Summarium testium*, witness 22, §ad. 5.
29 *Summarium testium*, witness 23, §389.
30 *Summarium testium*, witness 24, §395.
31 *Summarium testium*, witness 24, §395.
32 *Summarium testium*, witness 22, §390.

virtues." At home, "he was always helpful. [...] He used to get firewood, and he always helped my father with all his work. [...] He always protected us, especially me, since I was the sister nearest to him in age."[33] His cousin added that "he used to help cleaning pots and washing clothes. He helped his mother in various little things. He was the one who helped most [...] since the others were smaller."[34]

Lemus was a normal young man and very spirited. According to his aunt, "he did not stand on formality. [...] He would play with his siblings as any child would. [...] Our games were marbles, snatching the onion, and hide-and-seek. Sometimes we'd compete with all the other kids and their mothers." She added that Lemus "was not stingy. He was a child of faith. He liked to share."[35] Both sister and cousin agreed that Lemus was obedient, though the sister added, "he was not perfect."[36] And the cousin noted that "he had quarrels with his siblings, but that was normal."[37]

Despite his good qualities, Lemus had been burdened since infancy with the cross of epilepsy. Though medical treatment produced some improvement, he was frequently in a bad mood and at times even reacted violently. His cousin testified that generally "he behaved well with his parents and siblings. It was only when they exasperated him that he would leave the house until the anger passed." He had a better relationship with his father than with his mother: "He was obedient with his father," but "he would get angry with [his mother] Evelia when she got on his nerves. He would get angry because she didn't give him food." The cousin suggested that Lemus's mother "used to drive him a little crazy" because "she maltreated him." His father was calmer: "he was a very kind man," but Evelia "was a little more difficult; she was irritable."[38]

According to Lemus's aunt, "he suffered a lot because of his mental disorder." For that reason, she said, "we always pampered him":

> The quality I saw in him was that he wanted to feel loved. He needed affection, and he reached out with his kindness. The problem was with my sister [Evelia]. She was very strict with him since he was the oldest. Since the other children were younger, they robbed all the mother's affection. Perhaps he took refuge in the father [Rutilio] because he felt there the affection he needed.[39]

At school, the other youngsters made life difficult for Lemus. Unaware of his illness, they were cruel to him and called him names, causing him to respond in kind. As a result, he was often involved in street fights with other boys. In

---

33 *Summarium testium*, witness 24, §400.
34 *Summarium testium*, witness 23, §392.
35 *Summarium testium*, witness 22, §397.
36 *Summarium testium*, witness 24, §399.
37 *Summarium testium*, witness 23, §392.
38 *Summarium testium*, witness 23, §389.
39 *Summarium testium*, witness 22, §387.

contrast, his relationship with smaller children was quite good; he could adapt to them with great ease. If people treated him in a friendly way, he responded with great affection. One of his teachers had great difficulty with him because of his temper, but after he calmed down, she would make peace with him. His mother wanted him to leave school because of his illness and the family's poverty, but a teacher intervened and persuaded her to leave him in school because he was capable and intelligent, despite his limitations. In catechism class, he was always the first to answer questions; he made his first Communion in El Paisnal with fourteen other children.

According to Lemus's sister, "our parents always taught us to know about God and to respect other people." She recalled that Lemus used to tell her, "Look, pay attention to God," and that "he delighted in the things of God. He would read me bits of the Bible, the story of the prodigal son. He would sing to me." Also, "he would correct my sisters and brothers. He would tell us not to do bad things because he would tell my mother. [...] When he was sick, he would always ask God to heal him. He trusted in God at all times and in all circumstances."[40] His aunt summed up her testimony: "As far as I can see, he feared God and was busy with the things of God whenever he could be."[41]

Lemus was thoroughly familiar with the parish activities in El Paisnal and was often found near the church, always ready to help. One of his tasks was ringing the church bells to let people know that the priest had arrived in the town. According to his sister, whenever Lemus heard that the priest was about to arrive, "he would run to toll the bells, even if he was wearing just undershorts."[42] The cousin said that Lemus had been taught to ring the bells by Rutilio himself.[43]

The families of Lemus and Rutilio were related by marriage: a cousin of Lemus married Rutilio's brother Flavio. "That gave rise to [Rutilio's] affection" for the family, affirmed the sister: "The father drew close to us." Flavio was godfather to both Lemus and his sister.[44] The familial relationship was strengthened, according to the aunt, by Rutilio's kindness "toward everybody" and by Lemus's generous attitude.[45] "We enjoyed going about with the father," stated the sister. "Nelson was always happy there. He always gave me candy the father had given him, because [the father] would ask us questions about the Bible." The Bible quiz was a little game Rutilio played with the youngsters when he took them on a trip to the river. "I always say," testified the sister, "that if the father had been a bad man, the people would not have followed him as they did. The people loved the father."[46]

---

40 *Summarium testium*, witness 24, §398.
41 *Summarium testium*, witness 22, §388.
42 *Summarium testium*, witness 24, §392.
43 *Summarium testium*, witness 23, §400.
44 *Summarium testium*, witness 24, §400.
45 *Summarium testium*, witness 22, §388.
46 *Summarium testium*, witness 24, §402.

The Murder

As the Safari approached the train line, Rutilio stopped to pick up three small children, who were also on their way to El Paisnal; they sat in the back seat of the vehicle. A member of the missionary team later testified that if Rutilio had known what was about to happen, he would never have allowed the children to board the vehicle; nor would he have taken Solórzano and Lemus with him."[47] Lemus's sister corroborated this testimony: "If the father had known what was going to happen, he would never have picked up the children." She added, regarding her own brother: "He was not afraid. [...] He had great love and affection for the father."[48] Lemus's cousin also confirmed that "he was not afraid. Who would ever have imagined such a thing was going to happen! Nobody knew."[49]

Meanwhile, in El Paisnal people were already beginning to gather in the church since Rutilio liked to find them assembled when he arrived. The children riding in the back seat of the Safari later testified that they had seen several men at the edge of a cane field, a little beyond the hamlet of Los Mangos. Two or three men had been standing on either side of the road, holding objects like clubs or machetes; one of them, the children said, was Benito Estrada. Another person who had passed along the road shortly before the murder confirmed the testimony of the children; he also reported that he had seen five men in the blue vehicle with California plates, one of them a redhead and one a man he knew personally. He said another man was standing outside the vehicle near a cane field, as if urinating; he held an object that looked like a weapon.

The children further testified that, immediately after seeing the men at the edge of the cane field, they noticed a pickup truck approaching the Safari from behind; it had apparently been following them from Aguilares. In the back of the pickup were two men who had their gaze fixed forward. The children said that at that point Solórzano and Lemus were looking anxiously toward Rutilio. Lemus was pressing his back hard against the seat and gripping the door with his right hand, as if the vehicle were about to collide with something. At that moment, Estrada gave the signal, and a hail of bullets struck the Safari and its occupants.

Without looking back, Rutilio said in a low voice, "Let it be what God wants," according to one of the children in the car.[50] As the bullets struck, Rutilio lost control of the vehicle. It rolled over on its left side, with the motor still running and the wheels spinning. Inside were three bleeding corpses. Solórzano's body was positioned as if to shield Rutilio, in an effort to protect him from the bullets. The pickup truck pulled up beside the overturned Safari, and its occupants

---

47   *Summarium testium*, witness 2, §25.
48   *Summarium testium*, witness 24, §401.
49   *Summarium testium*, witness 23, §393.
50   *Summarium testium*, witness 2, §25.

approached the scene. Rutilio and Solórzano were both dead, leaning toward the left. Lemus was still in his seat, with a bullet in his forehead.

The three children in the back of the Safari were crying out in terror. Estrada ordered them to get out. They climbed over the corpses without looking at them. They survived, according to the same witness, thanks to "our small stature. The bullets entered from behind but did not hit us. The killers let us escape into the cane fields that bordered the road."[51] As they were racing away, the children heard one more shot. After running through the fields and crossing some gullies, they finally reached El Paisnal, covered with dirt and blood. One of them, when he reached his home, was completely out of breath, but he shouted: "Mama, Mama, Uncle Benito has killed Father Tilo!" His mother gave him a push and ordered him, "Keep quiet, stupid. Why are you saying that?" But the boy kept crying out: "Mama, he was the one who pointed him out and also shot him! They would have killed us too because we wanted to get Nelson out, but Nelson had an attack, and he couldn't get out. And we ran away because Benito knew us and wanted to kill us."[52]

The news reached El Paisnal with the arrival of the first public transport vehicle, which passed by the site of the assassination soon after its occurrence. The first report was that Rutilio had had an accident and rolled over on the road. When the people gathered in the church heard the report, they were shocked and rushed outside. They stopped the first vehicle they found and demanded that the driver take them directly to the scene of the supposed accident. A passerby suggested to the driver that he charge each passenger fifty cents, an inflated fare, to prevent them from being "newsmongers, nosing about in things that don't concern them." One villager cried out that he was not getting paid for spying; he said the little money he had he earned honestly.

When the parishioners arrived at the site of the murder, the Safari was surrounded by national guardsmen who would not let them get near. Lemus's cousin, who was able to get close to the scene, testified: "I saw the little car turned over. I saw Nelson there with his arm sticking out."[53] Thinking that the occupants of the vehicle were still alive, the parishioners wanted to take them to the hospital. A national guard struck the face of a young woman who tried to get too close to the Safari; it was Cristina, Rutilio's sister. The parishioners remained there until the bodies were taken away. Then they remembered Rutilio's homily of the day before.

Some of the parishioners traveled immediately to Aguilares to inform the parish and the judiciary. Carranza was alone in the rectory at the time, and he

---

51 *Summarium testium*, witness 2, §25.
52 Personal communication of a resident of El Paisnal with the author, San Salvador, March 1980.
53 *Summarium testium*, witness 23, §394.

immediately drove to the scene of the murder. Meanwhile, in El Tablón, where Pérez was celebrating a Mass and a wedding, some guests who had traveled from San Salvador for the festivities told him that "the parish vehicle just had an accident." Around seven o'clock that night, Pérez walked to El Paisnal, accompanied by four villagers, where he found the plaza full of people who were grieving and weeping. He later testified: "I was there in that crowd when someone tapped me on the back and said, 'You escaped, scoundrel!' One of the killers was right there in the crowd."[54]

Someone called the cathedral rectory in San Salvador, and the pastor there informed the Jesuit provincial, Jerez. Meanwhile, the justice of the peace in Aguilares, José Cruz Rodríguez, examined the bodies and determined that they had died "as the result of lesions produced by firearms," according to his succinct statement in the official record. The bodies were then turned over to the parish and transported to Aguilares, where they were placed on a table in the rectory. The Safari, which was registered in Rutilio's name, was taken to the city hall.

Upon learning of the killings, the residents of Aguilares and nearby villages gathered in consternation around the rectory. When Jerez arrived, he ordered the bodies to be taken to the church just as they were, so that the people could see for themselves that Rutilio and his companions had been murdered. He also wanted to celebrate Mass for them immediately. The three bodies were placed on tables before the main altar. Someone had put a clean shirt on Rutilio, but soon it also became stained with blood. The church was filled to overflowing, and a large crowd gathered in the plaza. Radio station YSAX broadcast information and commentary all during the night so that people in the villages soon learned what had happened and began flooding toward town. Thousands descended from the hills, and thousands more came from the valley and the four municipalities encompassed by the parish: Aguilares, El Paisnal, Suchitoto, and Quezaltepeque. The tremendous rage of the people was especially evident in the plaza, and many feared that a riot would break out. Perceiving the danger of violence, Father Jerez urged that the liturgy place great stress on Christian hope in order not to fuel hatred or a desire for vengeance.[55]

By ten o'clock that night, more than a dozen priests were vested and ready to begin Mass. When Archbishop Romero arrived, he agreed to preside at the Eucharist, along with Bishop Rivera. Father Jerez gave the homily, emphasizing that the mission of the Jesuits, as defined by the recent general congregation, was the service of the faith and the promotion of justice. Rutilio had been faithful to that mission, and that was why they had killed him. He had fallen alongside two companions: an elderly man who had been born and had lived under a regime of oppression and injustice, and a youth who had hoped for a better life. The three

---

54 *Summarium testium*, witness 7, §96.
55 "Dossier on the Persecution of the Church in El Salvador."

of them had died because of their faith, murdered when they were on their way to celebrate Mass. Archbishop Romero then spoke. The long, emotional Mass began at ten-thirty and finished around midnight. The congregation expressed both pain and hope. Meanwhile, an unending parade of dismayed and distressed parishioners passed through the church, viewing the three bodies. A large crowd remained in and around the church all night.

During the homily, the army and other security forces took up positions around Aguilares and closed the approaching roadways, perhaps fearing an uprising. For some unknown reason, the city's telephone service was suspended. At seven o'clock that Saturday evening, when very few persons even knew what had happened, President Molina called Archbishop Romero to offer his condolences, and he promised that there would be an exhaustive investigation. The national press later reported, incorrectly, that it was the archbishop who had called the president.[56]

The Jesuits and the bishops wanted an autopsy to be performed on the bodies, to supplement the finding of the justice of the peace. Bishop Rivera, a canon law expert, and several other priests presented themselves before the justice to request a forensic ruling. The justice and other local authorities cited difficulties, saying that it was too late for an autopsy, no personnel were trained for it, and the proper instruments were lacking. Nevertheless, a doctor with forensic experience appeared and agreed to examine the bodies, though he could not perform a genuine autopsy for lack of instruments. For the same reason, he could not extract the bullets. His past experience, however, made up quite well for the lack of suitable equipment. According to the doctor, expert sharpshooters had used nine-millimeter armored bullets, which they had shot with a Mauser rifle, a weapon used by the national police. The shots had been fired from both sides of the road, from a distance of about fifteen or eighteen meters, that is, from near the green fences separating the edge of the road from the cane field. Most of the shots were fired from the sides and from behind the vehicle, though photographs showed bullet holes in the front of the vehicle as well. Rutilio was hit by twelve bullets, and all would have killed him except one in his left foot. Some bullets hit the right side of his jaw and neck, while others broke his pelvis and his hipbone.[57]

Once the forensic examination was completed, Lemus's father asked for the body of his son, saying that his mother was awaiting him at home. Father Jerez told the boy's father that he had the right to claim his son's body, but that the archbishop wanted to have a solemn funeral Mass on Monday in the cathedral so that no one would ever forget the cruel deaths. The boy's father agreed as he

---

56 Bulletin no. 5, "Clarification of the Archbishop regarding the Death of Father Rutilio Grande, S.J., and His Companions," San Salvador, March 15, 1977. See "Dossier on the Persecution of the Church in El Salvador."
57 Bulletin no. 4, "On the Murder of Rutilio Grande and His Two Companions." San Salvador, March 13, 1977. See "Dossier on the Persecution of the Church in El Salvador."

broke down in tears. Venancio Grande also arrived, wanting to claim the body of Rutilio, but Jerez refused to give it to him. Jerez arranged for three simple caskets, all alike. When Bishop Romero offered to help with some money, Jerez refused, but when the archbishop insisted, he accepted it.[58]

The bodies were then washed and clothed. They vested Rutilio in white priestly robes and put a wooden cross in his hands. Solórzano and Lemus were clothed in white shirts and dark trousers. Once the three caskets were placed in the center aisle of the church at dawn on Sunday, thousands of the grieving faithful passed reverently before them during the morning.[59]

The Funeral

A priest who supported FECCAS presided at the early Mass in El Paisnal on that Sunday, March 13. Before Mass began, Father Jerez advised him privately to be prudent, saying, "I don't want another Rutilio killed." The ten o'clock Mass was concelebrated by about ten priests, both Jesuits and diocesan clergy. As the Mass was about to start, the nuncio's secretary, Monsignor Lorenzo Baldisseri, arrived—the nuncio was in Guatemala—and asked to preside, but Father Jerez said that he as provincial should preside and preach. And he did.[60]

Later that Sunday, the caskets were taken to the parish church in Aguilares, which overflowed with barefoot, poorly dressed country folk; there were women holding babies in their arms, visibly distressed youngsters, and many others. The crowds wept bitterly and also sang of the hope for liberation that Rutilio had represented for them. At first, it was difficult to impose order, but eventually, with the help of religious sisters and delegates, a long line formed, and the faithful passed slowly by the caskets throughout the day. Many priests also paid their respects, voicing their sorrow before the body of Rutilio, their teacher, their prefect, and their spiritual father. At night, reflection groups were organized to dialogue about the significance of the deaths. Meanwhile, the messages being broadcast by YSAX were being heard in homes throughout the country. That night, some Jesuits arrived from Guatemala to attend the funeral, which was to be held the next day in the cathedral.[61]

At dawn on Monday, huge crowds set out from the countryside toward San Salvador. The three hearses left Aguilares around eight in the morning. The Mass began at nine-thirty with the nuncio, Archbishop Romero, Bishop Rivera, and Archbishop Chávez presiding. Some 150 priests concelebrated in a packed cathedral. The clergy stretched from the main altar down the central aisle, while the

---

58 Bulletin no. 4, "On the Murder of Rutilio Grande and His Two Companions." See "Dossier on the Persecution of the Church in El Salvador."
59 "Dossier on the Persecution of the Church in El Salvador."
60 "Dossier on the Persecution of the Church in El Salvador."
61 "Dossier on the Persecution of the Church in El Salvador."

faithful crowded into every available space along the sides. Those who could not make it into the church stood in the plaza in front of the main façade. The archbishop's office distributed copies of the homily Rutilio had given in Apopa. Political groups also handed out flyers to the crowd. Even though it was a workday, the center of the capital was paralyzed.[62]

Archbishop Romero, visibly moved by the immense multitude in the church and the even greater audience he was reaching through YSAX, declared that the cathedral was at that moment a sign of the universal church:

> It is here that the whole rich pastoral ministry of a local church is gathered together and joined to the pastoral ministry of all the dioceses of our country and the whole world. We feel that the presence not only of the living but of these three deceased persons gives this image of the church a dimension of openness to the Absolute, to the Infinite, to the One Beyond: the universal church, the church beyond history, the church beyond human life.[63]

In that ecclesial setting, Romero thanked "these collaborators of Christian liberation, Father Grande and his two companions, now on their journey to eternity," for having made possible the unity of the church manifest there in the cathedral, where the clergy were "joined with their bishop," along with priests from the other dioceses and "in union with the Holy Father who is present here through the nuncio."[64]

If it were an ordinary funeral, Romero continued, he would have spoken "about the human and personal relationship I shared with Father Rutilio Grande, whom I consider a brother. At very critical moments in my life he was very close to me, and I will never forget his gestures of friendship."[65] But that tragic moment was not a suitable one for thinking in personal terms; rather, it was a time for delving deeper into the message of the martyrs. This homily was the first of a series of five homilies that Romero dedicated to Rutilio and his two companions. The other four were given on March 20, 1977, also in the cathedral of San Salvador; on June 19, 1977, in Aguilares; on November 1, 1977, in El Paisnal; and on March 5, 1978, also in El Paisnal.

The key to the life and death of Rutilio Grande, according to Archbishop Romero, was to be found in *Evangelii nuntiandi*, especially section 38, and in the 1974 synod of bishops. Paul VI had declared that "the church cannot be absent in this struggle for liberation" from "such great human misery," and that was precisely the struggle in which Rutilio was engaged:

---

62 "Dossier on the Persecution of the Church in El Salvador."
63 Homily of March 14, 1977, "The Motivation of Love: Funeral Mass of Father Rutilio Grande," in Óscar A. Romero, *A Prophetic Bishop Speaks to His People* (Miami: Convivium Press, 2015), 1:59.
64 Homily of March 14, 1977, "Motivation of Love," 63.
65 Homily of March 14, 1977, "Motivation of Love," 59.

> The liberation that Father Grande preached is inspired by faith, a faith that speaks to us about eternal life, a faith that he, with his face raised toward heaven and accompanied by two *campesinos*, offered up in its totality and perfection. It is liberation which culminates in happiness with God, liberation which begins from repentance for sin, liberation based on Christ, the only saving power. This is the liberation that Father Rutilio Grande preached, and he has therefore lived the church's message.[66]

Rutilio's struggle "to lift up and dignify human beings" was "a very original mission" because he carried it out with the "illumination of faith that distinguishes Christians from any liberation of a purely political, economic, or worldly sort, and from any liberation that does not move beyond this world's ideologies, interests, and realities." For that reason, as "the pope states: the church's liberation cannot be confused with other liberation movements that lack supernatural and spiritual horizons and especially the inspiration of faith"—that was why "the world will be unable to understand."[67]

Rutilio's preaching, said the archbishop, was characterized by a religious sense that "beholds God and, from the perspective of God, sees the neighbor as brother or sister and becomes aware that 'what you did for one of these least brothers or sisters of mine, you did for me.'" Rutilio invited people to "harmonize their hearts with the heart of God" and to be concretely committed and motivated by "fraternal love" because Christians could never forget "the misery that surrounds them":[68]

> This is what Father Rutilio Grande preached. And because this doctrine is often misunderstood, even murderously, that is why Father Rutilio Grande died. He died because the social doctrine of the church is confused with the political doctrines that disturb the world. The church's social doctrine is often slandered as subversive, like other things far removed from the prudence which the church's doctrine posits at the basis of existence.[69]

Later that year, on November 1, 1977, Archbishop Romero declared in El Paisnal that he had found in Rutilio the three essential characteristics of the type of liberation preached by the church: the inspiration of faith, the inspiration of love, and a praxis founded on the church's social doctrine. "These three things are what make Christians today the true liberators of their people."[70]

The "motivation of love" was the ultimate explanation of Rutilio's life and death:

---

[66] Homily of March 14, 1977, "Motivation of Love," 60.
[67] Homily of March 14, 1977, "Motivation of Love," 60.
[68] Homily of March 14, 1977, "Motivation of Love," 61.
[69] Homily of March 14, 1977, "Motivation of Love," 61.
[70] Homily of November 1, 1977, in Romero, *Prophetic Bishop Speaks to His People*, 1:405.

True love is what moved Father Rutilio Grande as he died with the two *campesinos* at his side. That is how the church loves. She dies with them, and with them she presents herself to heaven's transcendence, for she loves them. And it is significant that Father Grande was gunned down precisely when he was traveling to impart to his people the message of the Mass and salvation. A priest was with his *campesinos*, on his way to meet his people, to identify himself with them, to live with them—this was an inspiration of love and not revolution.[71]

In Rutilio, therefore, there was no hatred and no violence, despite what his detractors claimed:

> Those of us who heard Father Rutilio and shared his ideals know that he was incapable of preaching hatred; he was incapable of stirring up violence. Perhaps that is why God chose him for this martyrdom: because all those who knew him are well aware that he never uttered any call to violence, vengeance, or hatred. He died loving, and without a doubt, when he felt those first impacts that brought him death, he was able to say as Christ did, "Father, forgive them for they know not what they do."[72]

Declaring that that message of love could not be lost but had to be carried forward, Romero invited the clergy to embrace "this precious legacy" and unite around the church's mission. One of the fruits of Rutilio's death, said Romero, was the visible unity of the church in the cathedral:

> My brother priests, this message of Father Rutilio Grande is extremely important for us. Let us embrace it, and in the light of this doctrine and this faith let us work together. Let us not be separated by wildly dangerous ideologies, by ideologies that are not inspired in the faith of the Gospel. […] I am happy, dear priests, for the fruits of this death we lament and of the other difficult circumstances at this moment: the clergy are united with their bishop, and the faithful understand that the light of faith leads us along paths that are quite distinct from other ideologies that are not of the church, for the church offers a third way—a motivation of love.[73]

Therefore, said the archbishop, "there should be no feeling of vengeance among us. […] We should not call for revenge." Romero expressed his certainty that such sentiments had no place in the heart of Rutilio; to the contrary, his love would have moved him to forgive his murderers and pray for their conversion:

---

71 Homily of March 14, 1977, in Romero, *Prophetic Bishop Speaks to His People*, 1:62.
72 Homily of March 14, 1977, 61.
73 Homily of March 14, 1977, 62.

> I can imagine Father Grande and the other martyrs of this persecution in heaven,[74] earnestly praying to the Lord for their executioners, asking that they be converted so that they will one day share the joy that comes from being faithful to the Lord. [...] We cannot imagine Father Grande hating, asking for vengeance, or inciting violence, as they falsely accused him of doing. Those who knew him know that it was impossible for him to harbor in his priestly, apostolic heart those feelings of hatred that his crude assassins imagined.[75]

At the funeral Mass on March 14, the archbishop asserted that the church, inspired by love, also forgave the murderers:

> It is precisely because it is love that inspires us, sisters and brothers, that we want to tell those responsible that we love them. Who knows if those who are responsible for this criminal act (and are therefore excommunicated) are hearing these words on a radio there in their hideout and in their conscience? We want to tell them, "Brother criminals, we love you, and we ask God to pour forth repentance into your hearts because the church is incapable of hatred; the church has no enemies." Her only enemies are those who declare themselves as such. But even these she loves, and like the dying Jesus she says, "Father, forgive them for they know not what they do."[76]

Accordingly, "no one here present should ever think that this gathering around Father Grande's body is some political act." Rather, it was "a gathering in faith, a faith that through Father Grande's body, dead in hope, is opened to eternal horizons."[77]

Love and forgiveness are not incompatible with demanding justice. "It is true that we have asked the authorities to investigate this criminal act, for they have in their hands the instruments of this nation's justice, and they must clarify this situation. We are not accusing anyone, nor are we making judgments beforehand." The church would await the findings of impartial justice; it could not do otherwise because "even with the motivation of love, justice cannot be absent. There can be no true peace and no true love based on injustice or violence or intrigue."[78]

Finally, Archbishop Romero made a call for hope. In the course of his three years as archbishop, he never lost hope. Even in the darkest moments for society and the church, he always pointed forward, toward the God that he could glimpse on the horizon:

---

74 By that time, the Salvadoran church already had other martyrs in addition to Rutilio.
75 Homily of November 1, 1977, 1:403.
76 Homily of March 14, 1977, 1:62.
77 Homily of March 14, 1977, 1:60.
78 Homily of March 14, 1977, 1:62.

We are a pilgrim church, exposed to misunderstanding and persecution, but we are a church that walks calmly because we carry within us this power of love. Dear people of El Salvador, at this crossroad in our history there may seem to be no peaceful solution, and some feel they must resort to violent means. But I tell you, my sisters and brothers, blessed be God who through the death of Father Grande is telling the church: Yes, there is a solution. The solution is love. The solution is faith. The solution is experiencing the church, not as an enemy, but as the circle in which God wants to encounter all people. Let us understand this church; let us be inspired with this love; let us live this faith, and I assure you that there will be a solution to all of our great social problems.[79]

Father Jerez also said a few words during the Mass. He stressed the great love Rutilio had for the church, for the Salvadoran people, and for the Society of Jesus, and he insisted that his pastoral work was always guided by the church's teaching. He had pioneered for the Society a new style of apostolate, and he had sealed it forever with his blood.

When the Mass was over, the three caskets were carried out of the cathedral by the clergy. The funeral procession, led by the bishops, headed to the church of San Francisco. The procession was disorderly but dramatic, with the crowds extending along four city blocks. For a short stretch, political slogans mixed in with the religious hymns: while some were asking God's forgiveness, others demanded justice and even promised vengeance. Thousands of flyers with political propaganda were distributed among the mourners. Apart from this political intrusion, nothing unfortunate occurred. According to some, though, a military helicopter was observing this manifestation of grief from a distance, and armored trucks were stationed at nearby street corners.

At the church of San Francisco, the caskets were again placed in the hearses, and the funeral cortege headed out, joined by hundreds of vehicles. Upon reaching Aguilares, the villagers took the caskets on their shoulders and carried them to the train line; from there, they marched the final five kilometers to El Paisnal. When they reached the town, they returned the caskets to the hearses, and the cortege moved forward slowly, accompanied by a great crowd of people protecting themselves from the scorching sun with colorful parasols and by a lengthy motorcade of cars, pickups, and minibuses carrying people from the capital and the towns around. A group of delegates, animating the procession with a small loudspeaker from the parish, told the people that they were accompanying Rutilio on his way to El Paisnal just as they accompanied Christ on his way to the cross.

When the cortege reached El Paisnal, Rutilio and his two companions were buried in front of the main altar of the church. The interment took place

---

79 Homily of March 14, 1977, 1:63.

without the authorization of the Legislative Assembly, as required by law. Around three in the afternoon, as the people began leaving, a small band of guitarists played several times, to vigorous applause, a folk song composed in memory of Rutilio and his companions.

During the musical performance, angry activists could be heard calling for Rutilio's death to be "avenged." Some priests interpreted these exclamations as expressions of hatred while others understood them simply as the inevitable voicing of the people's profoundly felt need to continue the struggle on the political terrain.

A novena was held in the days that followed; it was a time for sharing memories, tears, and profound reflection. Each day in Aguilares there were Masses in the morning and the evening, during which the people testified movingly about what the life and death of Rutilio meant to them.

Early in the morning on March 19, the feast of Saint Joseph, two pilgrimages set out, one from Aguilares and the other from El Paisnal, both of them heading toward the site where the murder had occurred. The pilgrimage from Aguilares, led by Fathers Carranza and Pérez, carried a large wooden cross; the one from El Paisnal carried a statue of Saint Joseph and two smaller crosses. Under a blazing sun and before hundreds of villagers, the pilgrims planted the three crosses at the spot where Rutilio and his companions had fallen, and they poured out their feelings and thoughts in songs, poems, and simple but profound homilies. Finally, the two pilgrimages joined forces and made their way to El Paisnal to celebrate the town's patron saint.

It was during that celebration, according to the testimony of a member of the missionary team, that an elegiac tribute by a young songwriter from Cerro de Guazapa became popular: "March 12 is an unforgettable date. They killed our brother, Father Rutilio Grande. The man who preached the truth of the Gospel came to teach love, and hatred ordered him killed." The same witness also stated that "Rutilio's communities spontaneously changed the words of a refrain they used to sing at the beginning of major Masses. With Rutilio, they had once learned to sing the words, 'Together we walk with you [*contigo*], O Lord!' but now they sang, 'Together we walk with Tilo [*con Tilo*], Lord!'"[80]

Archbishop Romero, accompanied by fifteen priests, arrived at ten in the morning to commemorate the patronal feast that Rutilio had always celebrated with great emotion and simplicity. The concelebrated Mass took place outside, in front of the church, and when it was over, a steady flow of the faithful entered the church to pray before the tombs and to adorn them with candles and bouquets of flowers. In San Salvador, Archbishop Chávez presided at a Eucharist in the chapel of the Colegio Externado to commemorate the nine days.

---

80 *Summarium testium*, witness 2, §18.

Meanwhile, a tremendous number of telegrams and letters of condolence arrived in San Salvador, coming from all parts of the world, many bearing eloquent testimony about Rutilio. Among the letters was one addressed to Father Jerez and written by the provincial of the Jesuits in Argentina, Father Jorge Mario Bergoglio:

> For some days I have wanted to write you these lines to convey my fraternal greetings and my condolences for the moments you are experiencing there. We are all moved by what has happened to Rutilio. It is true that the Lord has his ways, [...] but at times they are hard. In this province, we have held a celebration, and all the brothers, through me, send you their sincerest condolences. I leave you. A strong embrace. Do not forget me in your prayer.[81]

A year later, Father Jerez received another letter from the provincial of Argentina, acknowledging receipt of the first biography of Rutilio:

> I have received the book on Father Rutilio Grande, which you graciously sent me. I am reading it now but don't want more time to pass before sending you these words of gratitude. I thank you not only for sending it to me but also for wishing to share with all of us who are your brothers the "times" the Lord has wanted you to experience there.
>
> We are praying earnestly here, asking the Lord to strengthen you in these difficult hours. And do not forget to pray for us, for our faithfulness to what Jesus wants.
>
> An embrace, and united in the same vocation.[82]

Unity around the Bishop: The One Mass

The death of Rutilio and his companions brought the clergy of the archdiocese together around their pastor. What had been considered unthinkable only a few weeks before came to pass. Despite the reservations and resentments first expressed when Romero was named archbishop, the clergy now were "flocking together" around their pastor.

In the days following the funeral, Romero met with the clergy several times to discuss the best ways to conduct pastoral ministry in view of the murders and in the midst of continued persecution against the church. Communication between the clergy and the archbishop was especially intense between March 15 and 23. The collective desire to keep alive the message of the martyrdom of Rutilio and his companions gave rise to a completely new experience of ecclesial unity for the archdiocese, a unity that continued during the three years of Romero's episcopal ministry, which ended in March 1980.

---

81 ACSI. Jorge Mario Bergoglio to Father César Jerez, San Miguel, April 26, 1977.
82 ACSI. Jorge Mario Bergoglio to Father César Jerez, San Miguel, May 3, 1978.

The archbishop convoked the clergy on Tuesday, March 15 to discuss the archdiocese's reaction to the persecution and the murder of Rutilio and his companions. The response was massive: the great majority of the diocesan clergy attended, as well as many religious sisters, several priests from the diocese of Santa Ana, and a number of laypeople. Drawing on Gospel texts, Father Jerez invited the assembly to take coordinated action, to put aside fear, to banish any desire for vengeance, and to be open to forgiveness.

Archbishop Romero kept the government informed of what the church was doing. On March 14, he wrote a letter to President Molina to inform him that various commentaries were circulating, "many of them unfavorable to your government" because of its failure to investigate the crime. Romero reminded Molina of his promise to carry out an investigation and complained that nothing had so far been done: "I judge it to be of great urgency that you order an exhaustive investigation of the deeds since the supreme government has in its hand the necessary instruments for investigating crimes and exercising justice in the country." He also informed the president that "the archdiocese has already published the decree of excommunication," and that "it will refuse to participate in any official government function as long as the government fails to make every effort to bring about justice for this unspeakable sacrilege." He closed the letter by expressing his confidence that the president would not defraud him, given the personal friendship that united them: "Knowing well your ability and your noble personal sentiments, thanks to the friendship you have afforded me, I have no doubt that you will feel obliged to satisfy these just demands of an eminently Catholic people, thereby rescuing your good name from every shadow of complicity."[83] These lines show that Romero demanded justice not so much in the name of the church but in the name of "an eminently Catholic people."

Romero reported to the clergy that the president had replied promptly, saying that he had already ordered an "exhaustive investigation." He wrote:

> As head of the government and responsible for national security, I am deeply concerned about this deed. [...] My government does not discount—and you will surely understand given your excellent judgment—that deeds like this one may form part of a series of anti-social actions that, for eminently political ends, attempt to disrupt the peace and order of the nation. Such actions are aimed directly at justifying the [perpetrators'] objectives nationally and internationally and indirectly at blaming the government.[84]

---

83   ACSI. Óscar A. Romero to Colonel Arturo Armando Molina, San Salvador, March 14, 1977. See "Dossier on the Persecution of the Church in El Salvador."
84   ACSI. Arturo A. Molina to Archbishop Óscar A. Romero, San Salvador, March 14, 1977. See "Dossier on the Persecution of the Church in El Salvador."

In this way, the president blamed the murders on persons not connected with the government, insinuating instead that they were "subversives." Molina referred to the meeting he had had with the bishops on February 22, when he gave them a list of the "subversive priests": "You will recall the views I submitted to the consideration of the bishops who accompanied you in the meeting we recently held at the presidential offices."[85] In the president's opinion, the murders were committed by "subversives" for the purpose of harming the government; he therefore not only exempted the government of responsibility for the crime but presented it as a victim of subversion.

Finally, Archbishop Romero informed the clergy about the telegram he had sent to the attorney general, asking him to begin an immediate investigation of the murders. No evidence exists that any investigation was ever carried out. After hearing the archbishop's report, those attending the meeting divided into small groups, one for each vicariate and additional groups for the priests from Santa Ana, the seminarians, and the religious sisters working in education. A plenary session subsequently received reports from the groups. The assembly unanimously agreed that the church and other organizations fighting for social justice were being persecuted by those who held political and economic power. The assembly also agreed that the reason for the persecution was the church's fidelity to the teaching of Vatican II and Medellín, especially the condemnation of social injustice and the proclamation of the kingdom of God. Since the persecution was a consequence of the church's option for the poor, the assembly reaffirmed its desire for unity: both inwardly—between clergy and bishop and between the People of God and their pastors—and outwardly—in pursuing the mission, in promoting justice, and in denouncing unjust situations. The means proposed for building such unity were constant two-way communication and consultation about key decisions. Since there were still some priests who disagreed with the pastoral approach of the archdiocese, the assembly recommended that they apply themselves to study and reflection.

The assembly also presented to Archbishop Romero a long list of suggestions, such as: strengthening ecclesial unity and strongly supporting the archbishop himself; giving not "the least expression" of collaboration with the government or the oligarchy; seeking the resignation of all the military chaplains since their work could be seen as collaboration; reading the archdiocesan bulletins in the churches every Sunday; and drawing up a manifesto of protest by the clergy, which appeared on March 15. Other recommendations stressed the importance of the church's communications media and recommended various measures: broadcasting regular and reliable accounts of events, accompanied by judgments based on Christian values; revitalizing *Orientación*, the official publication of

---

85 ACSI. Arturo A. Molina to Archbishop Óscar A. Romero, San Salvador, March 14, 1977. See "Dossier on the Persecution of the Church in El Salvador."

the archdiocese; reinforcing the work begun the evening of March 12 by YSAX; drawing up homily guides for the coming Sundays; and distributing widely publications such as Romero's letter to the president, pertinent declarations of the archdiocese, and the *Justicia y pax* bulletins put out by the archdiocesan vicariate for social justice.

Other proposals were these: publishing a strong pastoral letter that viewed recent events from the perspective of the church's social doctrine, not neglecting to denounce injustice when speaking of forgiveness, encouraging the study of both the national and the ecclesial reality, suspending ordinary academic activity in Catholic schools as a sign of protest and as a means for making students aware of the situation, warning laity and clergy of possible dangers, offering refuge in churches and rectories to those being persecuted, and having just one single Mass in the archdiocese on Sunday, March 20. Finally, the assembly requested the publication and distribution of Rutilio's most eloquent homilies, the production and broadcasting of radio programs about his life and work, the elaboration of a biography, and the creation of a fitting memorial to him.

Before closing, the assembly expressed its gratitude to the bishops of the archdiocese, especially Romero, for their enlightened guidance and firm action. It affirmed its support for the priests being persecuted and encouraged them to stay strong in their mission. It expressed its appreciation of the archbishop's letter to the president, his refusal to attend the credentialing of the president-elect, the decision not to make the archbishop's installation a public event, the calling of the assembly itself, the openness to dialogue, the magnificent performance of YSAX, the information bulletins published by the archdiocese, and the message sent by the bishops' conference.

At the same time, the assembly criticized the actions of the nuncio, who had not attended the earlier meeting of the clergy but had been present the next day at the credentialing of the president-elect. Some claimed that his presence at the funeral Mass had inhibited many of those from taking part. The assembly also lamented the lack of solidarity on the part of the bishops of the other dioceses, and especially their absence from the funeral Mass for Rutilio. It regretted the disobedience of a small number of priests of the archdiocese who had refused to read the message of the bishops' conference at the Sunday Masses and who had also refused to attend the meetings called by the archbishop.

Archbishop Romero immediately considered two suggestions made by the assembly: the One Mass and the suspension of academic activity in Catholic schools. He asked the assembly to express itself freely in order to guide him in taking a course of action. On March 14, the day before the assembly met, the board of the Association of Catholic Schools had discussed the suspension of academic activity with Archbishop Romero and with Bishop Aparicio, head of the San Vicente diocese and the bishops' delegate for Catholic education. When the board voted, thirty-one were in favor of the suspension and twenty-three were opposed, including the two bishops. When a new vote was called for, twenty-nine were in favor and twenty-four were opposed. Despite the favorable balance, the decision was made not to suspend academic activity.[86]

In the assembly the next day, when Romero was asked whether his decision not to suspend was definitive, he responded that he would like to hear people's opinions. Those who argued in favor emphasized the positive social impact of suspending the ordinary activity of the schools and the opportunity it would provide for making both students and parents better informed about the situation. The few who argued against the suspension pointed to the risks involved. The subsequent vote was almost unanimous in favor of the suspension; only six voted against, and seven abstained. It was then decided that the measure should include elementary as well as secondary schools. Romero ratified the assembly's decision.[87]

Discussion of the proposal to have the One Mass on Sunday, March 20 passed through three phases. First, the theological and pastoral arguments were put forward; then, the clergy expressed their opinions; finally, Archbishop Romero made the decision. Those opposing the proposal on theological grounds argued that the Mass, as an act of worship, could not be suppressed and that, to the contrary, there should be many Masses. They contended that such a measure could have negative pastoral effects: it might be misunderstood by the faithful, and some would be unhappy about not being able to receive Communion. Moreover, some people might consider it a manifestation of power with political connotations. The theological arguments in favor the proposal recalled that worship of God should be closely related to the lived reality of the people and that, given the critical situation of the country, it was pastorally appropriate to express the sense of general crisis by celebrating the One Mass. Such an event would also be an excellent opportunity for imparting good catechesis about the Eucharist. When a first sounding was taken, the result was quite balanced: eighty-four in favor and eighty-two opposed. When a second vote was taken in the afternoon, after lengthy discussion, a clear majority was in favor of the One Mass.[88]

That night, Romero met with representatives of the Catholic schools and with the commission named to draw up a press statement. The commission consisted of Fathers Jesús Delgado, Amaya, and Sobrino, and had the collaboration of Fathers Cabarrús and José Óscar Barahona, a professor at the seminary. The discussion continued until Romero felt that he was sufficiently informed about the various issues. He then communicated his decision: there would be only One Mass in the archdiocese on Sunday, March 20, and it would be celebrated in the cathedral at ten o'clock. The commission then proceeded to draw up a document announcing the celebration of the One Mass and the suspension of ordinary

---

86 "Dossier on the Persecution of the Church in El Salvador."
87 "Dossier on the Persecution of the Church in El Salvador."
88 "Dossier on the Persecution of the Church in El Salvador."

activities in Catholic schools for three days; it also included a protest statement from the clergy and the archbishop. Once the document was edited and approved by Romero, it was given to the communications media.[89]

The decision to have the One Mass brought diverse complications. On Friday, March 18, Archbishop Romero convoked the clergy in San Salvador to reflect on the theological and pastoral import of the measure; the aim of the meeting was not to debate the decision itself but to unify the clergy around the bishop. Most of the pastors attended the meeting, and there were some religious sisters as well. After beginning the meeting by calling for a spirit of prayer and ecclesial unity, Romero named Father Jesús Delgado as moderator and Fathers Rosa and Sobrino as secretaries. Delgado said that the communiqué issued on March 15 had been well received though some persons had criticized the suspension of school activities and the celebration of the One Mass. Romero then read a document of the Holy See that spoke of persecution of the church and violation of human rights.[90]

Most of the pastors supported the archbishop's decision; they were convinced that, given the circumstances, it was theologically and pastorally fitting to celebrate only a single Mass on that Sunday. Some disagreed, however. Three pastors expressed reservations, though two of them could also see the advantages. One pastor stated that the pastoral council in his parish considered the One Mass to be a mistake since it would deprive many parishioners of Mass and Communion; another pastor claimed that the One Mass was unnecessary since there had already been a big funeral Mass on March 14; still another feared that the One Mass could easily degenerate into a political show. Several alternative proposals were made: the morning Masses could be suppressed but not the evening ones; the One Mass could be celebrated in the cathedral, as Romero had decided, but later Communion could be distributed in the parishes.[91]

The reasons offered against the One Mass did not convince the great majority of the pastors, who voted in favor of it. Their interventions stressed the advantages of demonstrating ecclesial unity; the Mass would be a highly effective means for manifesting and strengthening that unity. Reversing course would seriously blunt the hopes of the people of God who, according the pastors of both urban and rural zones, had received the decision—and also the message of March 15—with great joy. They considered the bold action to be a clear sign of the church's salvific presence in their lives. Moreover, backtracking at this point would give evidence of weakness in the face of the powerful forces that were trying to prevent the celebration of the One Mass. The decision in favor of the One Mass could be explained to the pusillanimous, but explaining it to the Pharisees

---

89 "Dossier on the Persecution of the Church in El Salvador."
90 "Dossier on the Persecution of the Church in El Salvador."
91 "Dossier on the Persecution of the Church in El Salvador."

11. The Martyrdom

was impossible because they refused to understand. Such opposition, however, was not a valid objection to celebrating the One Mass; indeed, it confirmed that the decision was correct.[92]

Speaking theologically, the pastors stressed that the church was a singular sacrament of the presence of Christ in the midst of his people. Sacramental unity was manifest at the local level in the Communion of the clergy with their bishop and in the Communion of the people of God with their pastors and their bishop. The unity was manifested at the regional level since persecution was uniting the Salvadoran church with the Latin American church, which was also being persecuted in several countries. At the universal level, sacramental unity was manifest in the martyrdom of Rutilio and his two companions, who had given their lives out of fidelity to the Gospel and the social doctrine of the church. The other theological conception taken up by the pastors was the traditional idea of the Mass as the "sacrament of the real presence of Christ," present through love. The aim of the One Mass, "the eternal and unrepeatable sacrifice of Christ," was to highlight the Mass's sacrificial character by relating it to the sacrifices of the martyrs, especially Rutilio and his companions. The sacrifice of Christ, commemorated in the Mass, was thus united to the sacrifice of his historical body:

> Given the situation of the country, this sacramental presence of Christ takes on great meaning when it is seen to have empowered Christians who out of love have given their lives. This Mass is therefore a privileged occasion for showing the unity of Christ's presence both in the Mass and in real life; it is an occasion for relating the liturgical expression of the Christian faith with the real life of Christians, and for relating the love and commitment of Christ in the Mass with the love and commitment of Christians, who are his body, as they dedicate themselves to propagating love and justice in the world.[93]

The Mass would thus have a prophetic, not political, dimension because it would be denouncing injustice, the sin of the world that had long ago murdered Christ and that continued to deal out death to the children of God. The Mass would also announce Christian hope in the midst of the dark depths of persecution. Since the people's hope had not died but was "more alive than ever," the Mass would be a public manifestation of that hope, "uniting the people in prayer and thanksgiving, precisely because there are martyrs who keep our hope strong."[94]

After hearing these explanations, Archbishop Romero asked the clergy to express their opinion by voting. There was near unanimity, with seventy-one in favor of the One Mass; there was one opposing vote and one abstention. Among those in favor were all sixty-three of the pastors and chaplains who worked in the

---

92 "Dossier on the Persecution of the Church in El Salvador."
93 "Dossier on the Persecution of the Church in El Salvador."
94 "Dossier on the Persecution of the Church in El Salvador."

capital. The clergy then asked Romero to inform the nuncio about the decision, and they named a delegation to accompany him: Delgado, Arturo García Véliz, Rosa, Urioste, and Sobrino.[95]

The nuncio had in fact asked to see Romero on March 17, that is, two days after the general assembly of the clergy on March 15 and the day before Romero's meeting with the pastors on March 18. Other unavoidable commitments prevented Romero from arriving at the nunciature for his ten-thirty appointment on the morning of the seventeenth, but when the nuncio insisted that Romero come quickly since he had plans to go to the beach, the archbishop arrived at eleven-fifteen. There, Romero was surprised to see his own personal secretary, who evidently had arrived beforehand to give the nuncio his version of the facts. According to the secretary, Romero was being manipulated by a group of communist priests who had obliged him to change his views radically. As proof, he adduced that Romero had always been a self-sacrificing man of prayer, too good a priest to fall into the pastoral errors he was now committing. The nuncio then told the secretary, in the presence of Romero, that he could take as much time as he needed to speak with the archbishop; it thus became clear to Romero that the nuncio and the secretary had already come to an agreement.[96]

After talking with Romero, the secretary took him back to the nuncio, who was waiting for him in the company of Father Delgado, who had arrived in the meantime. Romero listened patiently for more than fifteen minutes while the nuncio reproached him loudly and offensively, calling him irresponsible and ineffective in his role as pastor. Delgado took advantage of a pause in the nuncio's harangue to make it clear that the archbishop had made his decisions in close consultation with the clergy on the fifteenth, during a meeting that the nuncio had promised to attend but did not. The nuncio explained that he had been invited to a meeting of diplomats and that, besides, he was having problems with his vehicle.[97]

Archbishop Romero then explained to the nuncio the theological and pastoral significance of the One Mass, emphasizing the importance of manifesting the unity of the clergy with their bishop. The nuncio replied that such unity could be made equally manifest without the One Mass. Romero responded that the intention was to have an extraordinary celebration that would achieve very effectively, and in quite extraordinary circumstances, the union of the presbyterate and the people around their pastor. The archbishop concluded by saying that the decision seemed to him providential because it had not been planned in advance. Romero's reasoning made little impact on the nuncio, who refused to grant it any validity. To all the archbishop's arguments, he responded, "No, that's not right,"

---

95   "Dossier on the Persecution of the Church in El Salvador."
96   "Dossier on the Persecution of the Church in El Salvador."
97   "Dossier on the Persecution of the Church in El Salvador."

while shaking his head to indicate his disagreement. However, he was unable to offer any contrary argument to convince the archbishop. Finally, Romero told the nuncio gently but firmly that the matter had already been discussed at length with the clergy and that the decision had been made.[98]

Father Delgado intervened to propose an alternative solution: celebrate the One Mass at ten in the morning, as Romero had decided, but leave pastors free to celebrate other Masses if they wished. The suggestion did not appeal to either the nuncio or Romero. The nuncio made a final attempt to dissuade Romero by commenting that the Mass could degenerate into disorder, with grave consequences for the church. The archbishop replied that they had taken organizational measures to avoid that type of disturbance. The nuncio then mentioned the existence of a state of siege, but Romero objected that the government was nevertheless allowing huge crowds to gather in the stadium for soccer games. Little by little, the nuncio calmed down.[99]

The nuncio's attitude during this initial encounter bothered Romero, who felt unjustly accused and unfairly judged in a matter that was strictly his responsibility as archbishop and pastor. Curiously, some of the arguments put forward by the nuncio were the same ones used by the president and vice-presidents of ANEP when they spoke with Romero in his office on March 16. From the start, they had attempted to impose their will on Romero, citing the power they had in society. Their arrogant attitude made dialogue difficult and mutual trust impossible.

Taking the initiative, the president of ANEP had asked the archbishop whether it would be appropriate for the organization to express in the national press its condolences to the church for the death of Rutilio, who he said was "shamefully murdered." The board of ANEP had proposed such an action, but the general assembly had thought it imprudent since it could be misinterpreted by the people. The matter was felt to be urgent since the church seemed to be blaming ANEP and FARO for the crime. Romero and the priests who were with him—Urioste, Amaya, and Delgado—remained silent. One of the vice-presidents then stressed the danger of linking the two organizations together, as the bishops' conference had done in their message of March 5. Urioste asked the vice-president whether he had read the message, and he replied that he had not. Romero then showed them the text of the message, making it clear that no such linkage had been made.[100]

The true motive of the ANEP leaders became clear later in the conversation. One of the vice-presidents, blaming the church for the social unrest and accusing YSAX of provoking rebellion, made several recommendations: that the radio station broadcast only classical music and what he called "instructive" programs,

---

98 "Dossier on the Persecution of the Church in El Salvador."
99 "Dossier on the Persecution of the Church in El Salvador."
100 "Dossier on the Persecution of the Church in El Salvador."

that academic activity be renewed immediately in the Catholic schools, and that the One Mass be canceled since it could bring dreadful consequences in its wake. Amaya replied that the true cause of unrest among the people was injustice, but there was no further discussion on that point.[101]

The priests with Romero responded to the demands made by the business leaders by asking them what they would do to pacify the situation. They replied that they had not even thought about that question. Delgado warned them that if they were not willing to cooperate, the church could not cooperate either. When the ANEP leaders were asked to restrain FARO, they responded that they had no relations with that organization. Urioste then demonstrated to them not only that they did have relations with FARO but that ANEP exercised power over FARO. At that point, the meeting arrived at a dead-end. Before leaving, the business leaders proposed that a joint communiqué be drawn up, but the archbishop refused, saying that there was really nothing to communicate.[102]

After the meeting with the pastors of San Salvador on March 18, Romero returned to the nunciature with Fathers Delgado, Rosa, García Véliz, and Sobrino to inform the nuncio that the great majority of the pastors were in favor of the One Mass. The delegation stressed this point since the nuncio had been saying that the pastors had many doubts about the One Mass. As it turned out, the nuncio had left the country, and the delegation was received by Monsignor Baldisseri, the secretary of the nunciature, who immediately brought up the theological, pastoral, and canonical difficulties. While he believed that the nuncio had already treated the theological and pastoral difficulties satisfactorily with Romero, he thought that the most important difficulty, the canonical one, had not yet been sufficiently treated. It had to do with paragraph 8 of the conciliar decree *Christus Dominus*, according to which the archbishop had dispensed from attendance at Sunday Mass all those who could not attend the Mass at the cathedral. The dispensation had been announced when Romero was interviewed by Father Rosa, the director of YSAX. After playing a recording of the interview to corroborate his statement, the secretary asserted that the archbishop did not have the authority to grant such a general dispensation since the decree referred only to particular cases. He stated bluntly that Romero had exceeded himself in his exercise of episcopal authority.[103]

The priests accompanying Romero responded that Bishop Rivera, the vicar general and an excellent canonist, had participated in all the deliberations but had never posed any objections. They also reminded the secretary that the bishop had ample power in his diocese, according to paragraph 27 of *Lumen gentium*. In any case, they said, the archbishop had not signed any document regarding the

---

101 "Dossier on the Persecution of the Church in El Salvador."
102 "Dossier on the Persecution of the Church in El Salvador."
103 "Dossier on the Persecution of the Church in El Salvador."

dispensation; he had limited himself to speaking about it in a radio interview, with the aim of tranquilizing the consciences of the people. What he had told the people who were worried was that they should consider themselves dispensed if they were unable, for good reason, to go to the cathedral. The secretary repeated that the archbishop lacked the authority to make such a decision and that he considered it pastorally mistaken since it deprived the faithful of a right that was theirs.[104]

Archbishop Romero, who until that point had remained silent, then humbly and respectfully began to express his opinion, but the secretary rudely interrupted him. From the start of the conversation, the secretary had adopted a disrespectful and even arrogant attitude toward Romero. At times, he seemed to pass judgment on the archbishop even while insisting that his own opinion was irrelevant. When finally allowed to speak, Romero, conscious of his pastoral responsibility and confident of his clergy's support, repeated that he had not violated any norm of canon law or ecclesiastical legislation. He insisted again on the theological and pastoral reasons for the One Mass and reaffirmed his decision, pointing out that it was the fruit of lengthy deliberation with the clergy and several good theologians. The process used to reach the decision had been in accord with the church's hierarchical structure. He had himself made the decision but had then consulted further with his clergy, who had ratified it. He concluded, therefore, that he as archbishop would take responsibility for the One Mass, and he would do so with perfect tranquility since he knew that he was acting correctly. He added that the only persons opposed to the One Mass were wealthy Catholics who generally did not share the mind of the church generally, much less the church of Vatican II and Medellín.[105]

After the archbishop's intervention, the conversation with Baldisseri returned to the same topics, but there was no further progress and the meeting soon concluded. Archbishop Romero decided then that, given his many other concerns and the negative attitude of the nunciature, the matter had been sufficiently discussed and that further debate was useless.

One more meeting was held, however, to clear up any canonical doubts. Bishop Rivera, Delgado, and Segura, a canonist and former seminary rector, reviewed the latest norms of the church on this matter and concluded that the situation of the country was an exceptional case, one that authorized the archbishop to adopt a measure such as the One Mass and to dispense anyone who could not attend from the Sunday obligation.[106]

Beginning at dawn, then, on Sunday, March 20, great crowds of people began gathering in front of the cathedral, filling the plaza and the adjacent streets. Before Mass began, a large number of priests circulated in the crowd,

---

104 "Dossier on the Persecution of the Church in El Salvador."
105 "Dossier on the Persecution of the Church in El Salvador."
106 "Dossier on the Persecution of the Church in El Salvador."

offering the faithful the sacrament of reconciliation. That morning, some people confessed for the first time in thirty years, stating that the figure of Rutilio had moved them to return to the church. Later on, several confessors gave testimonies about authentic conversions that had taken place at that time.

The Eucharist began at ten o'clock, as programmed, with Archbishop Romero presiding and some 150 priests concelebrating. In his homily, Romero gave a catechesis on the Eucharist; he emphasized ecclesial unity, confirmed the clergy in their pastoral mission, and explained the significance of the One Mass. He began by stating that "this concelebration is a beautiful gesture"; it was evidence that "the priests consider the bishop to be the center of the liturgy and the center of sacramental life." He added: "What a precious sign we have here, as the priests gather around the altar where the hosts have been prepared to be consecrated into the Body of the Lord and then distributed to the people as nourishment for their life."[107]

Romero not only welcomed the faithful but also greeted "those who have no faith in the Mass but are still present here." He said that these had come "seeking something that the church is offering." He was therefore delighted to be able to offer them what they were seeking in the One Mass: "You who do not believe in the Mass, hear this once and for all: what you have found today is Christ."[108]

Welcoming one and all to "this ancestral home of the diocese," the archbishop invoked unity around the bishop: "As the lowliest member of the whole church family, but chosen by God to be the sign of unity, this bishop thanks you warmly for joining him in giving the awaiting world the church's word." This word was not limited to speech but was being "proclaimed by our presence here at the only Mass that is celebrated in the archdiocese today":

> Through this celebration we want to give great value to the Masses that are celebrated in all our parishes, in all our chapels—the value that the Mass has when a family in mourning asks that it be celebrated for a relative who is about to be buried or when a family gathers to give thanks to God on the fifteenth birthday of a daughter or to bless the marriage of two people who promise to love one another until death. At this time the Mass is recovering all its value. Perhaps because it is celebrated so frequently, it is often seen as an adornment and does not possess the greatness it is attaining at this moment.[109]

Alluding to the liturgical readings for the Fourth Sunday of Advent, Cycle C, Romero declared that the Mass was

> an encounter with the Promised Land, a breath of hope, or better still, the prodigal son. [...] The prodigal son is each one of us; he is the people; he is the one who often goes astray in search of false freedoms. He is the one

---

107 Homily of March 20, 1977, in Romero, *Prophetic Bishop Speaks to His People*, 1:67.
108 Homily of March 20, 1977, 65.
109 Homily of March 20, 1977, 64.

searching for happiness, [...] [but] in the end finds only emptiness. What a great image of someone seeking happiness apart from God![110]

True happiness could be found only in "Christ who evangelizes. The Mass is Christ offering his Body and Blood for the life of the world." In the liturgy of the Word, Christ was inviting the people to seek "the solution to all [their] problems: political, economic, and social. These problems cannot be solved with human ideologies or worldly utopias or narrow Marxisms or atheisms that exclude the one force that can save: Jesus, who speaks to us of true liberation."[111]

Archbishop Romero then cited Paul VI to reaffirm the pastoral approach adopted by the archdiocese. He recalled the homily the pope gave at the CELAM meeting on November 3, 1977, when he had encouraged the bishops of the continent to find and use an intelligible language for transmitting the message of Jesus to the Latin American people. When the language of preaching became more comprehensible to the people, the pope said, the Gospel would take on new dimensions and become a "radiation that illuminates human activity on earth." And that, Romero insisted, was precisely what Rutilio was doing in Aguilares. Despite his death, that "desire to evangelize the men and women of today around their actual concerns" should not be obstructed by "those who are insensitive to the world's real problems." At the same time, people should not resort to "the tactics of those who want to introduce into the Gospel of Christ solutions that are not Christian":[112] "Let no one hold us back in this language that the church speaks; let no one tell people that there is no hope in the church. But also, let no one abuse our language and attempt to use the Gospel to justify doctrines that are not those of Christ."[113]

The church of the archdiocese had sought and found a "healthy balance in its evangelization." The judgments and the accusations of the oligarchy and the military regime were therefore unjust and wrong-headed. Romero assured the clergy and the people that the options made by the archdiocese were orthodox:

> Be assured, my sisters and brothers, that the evangelical line that the archdiocese follows is authentic. All those religious and laypeople who collaborate with our beloved priests are secure in their positions as long as they remain in communion with their bishop. Indeed, this is the meaning of today's celebration. It is an authorization of the bishop as authentic teacher of the faith, who assures all those who are in communion with him that they are preaching a doctrine that is in communion with the pope and is therefore also the true doctrine of our Lord Jesus Christ.[114]

---

110 Homily of March 20, 1977, 65.
111 Homily of March 20, 1977, 65.
112 Homily of March 20, 1977, 66.
113 Homily of March 20, 1977, 66.
114 Homily of March 20, 1977, 67.

The archbishop then thanked the clergy for their efforts to announce God's kingdom and their willingness to strengthen the unity of the church: "I want to thank all of these beloved priests publicly, before the whole archdiocese, as we gather here in unity around the one and only Gospel. Many of them risk danger and even the greatest sacrifice, the one that Father Grande made. Thank you."[115] The loud applause that followed, said Romero,

> ratifies the profound joy I feel in my heart as I take possession of this archdiocese. I feel that my own weaknesses and my own inabilities find their complement, their power, and their courage in this united priesthood. Beloved priests, let us remain united in the authentic truth of the Gospel. This is another way for me to say, as Christ's humble successor and representative here in the archdiocese, that anyone who attacks one of my priests, attacks me.[116]

Toward the end of his homily, Archbishop Romero reflected further on the meaning of the One Mass:

> We also want to bear witness to the people who are left without Mass today so that they understand what the persecution of a priest means. What would it be like if one day this small group of priests were taken from the people? How would people be without Mass? How would the parishes be without baptisms? My sisters and brothers, I believe everyone has understood the meaning of our celebrating just one Mass today. There is nothing of demagogy in this action. The church is not being manipulated by some political party. She is not raising a protest in a merely human manner. She is simply stating what the Mass means, whether it is celebrated by the pope in the Vatican, by the bishop in his cathedral, or by the humble pastor in the humblest village of the diocese. And we want to urge you all to value the Mass.[117]

Archbishop Romero had begun his homily by welcoming the people, and now as he concluded, he expressed his satisfaction: "I am happy to have had the opportunity to explain to you, with simple words, the meaning of the Mass":

> I hope that those who did not previously believe in the Mass will now become followers of that Christ who becomes present in the Mass of every Sunday and in the Mass of every human circumstance. Thank you very much for helping us give this sign of what the church wants to give you.[118]

---

115 Homily of March 20, 1977, 66.
116 Homily of March 20, 1977, 66.
117 Homily of March 20, 1977, 68.
118 Homily of March 20, 1977, 68.

The Indifference of the Military Regime

The government did not investigate the murder of Rutilio and his companions. Despite the promises he had made, President Molina showed no interest in knowing the facts. On the morning of March 23, he met in his office with Archbishop Romero, Urioste, and Delgado. The president, who was accompanied by his private secretary, Colonel López Abarca, allowed the archbishop to preside.[119]

Romero set out an agenda for the meeting, which included: investigation of the murder of Rutilio and his companions, guarantee of the safety of the priests and lay ministers doing evangelization, clarification of the situation of the deported priests, the hostility of FARO and ANEP toward the church, agreement on a common policy regarding abortion, a forum that would allow accused priests to defend themselves, and teaching religion classes in the public schools as a guarantee of religious freedom.[120]

The agenda was not followed because Molina remained focused on the first item. He spent about a half-hour rambling about other points of the agenda, but his main concern was to dissociate the government from the assassination. He offered what he said was a strictly personal conjecture: Rutilio and his companions were "a sacrificial quota" offered up by international communism as a way of provoking unrest among the people and causing conflict between the government and the church. The president also took for granted that Eduardo Orellana had been killed by members of FECCAS and UTC even though evidence was completely lacking and several witnesses had stated the contrary; no police investigation had been done of the case. Molina maintained that the murder of Rutilio and his companions had already been exhaustively investigated, as he had promised, but he added that the judicial system was corrupt so that he could not guarantee the result of the investigation. He refused to accept the collaboration of the team of lawyers and experts that the archdiocese had established to investigate the case. He said that the government would take care of its own affairs and that that archbishop should take care of what corresponded to him, namely purifying the church's pastoral work of all vestiges of communism.[121]

Regarding the deported priests and those prohibited from returning to the country, the president responded categorically, saying that the government would not change its position. He did promise, however, that he would instruct ORDEN, an organization authorized by the president, to act prudently with respect to persons and organizations related to the church. The archbishop responded that he would wait and see what actually happened.[122]

---

119 "Dossier on the Persecution of the Church in El Salvador."
120 "Dossier on the Persecution of the Church in El Salvador."
121 "Dossier on the Persecution of the Church in El Salvador."
122 "Dossier on the Persecution of the Church in El Salvador."

The archbishop and his companions left the presidential office with the impression that Molina was not interested in discussing the questions they had presented even though he had wanted to have the meeting. The president had spent most of the session in digressions, and whenever Romero brought up a specific point of the agenda, he evaded it. The archbishop left the meeting convinced that the president had no intention of keeping his promises.

Nevertheless, the two men met again at the presidential office on April 20; also present were the nuncio and the other bishops. The president was accompanied by the president-elect, the vice-president elect, and members of his cabinet. He had called the meeting, he explained, in view of the deteriorating relations between the church and the government. He assured the bishops that the government was incapable of considering, much less executing, anything like the murder of Rutilio, a man for whom he said he felt affection. He blamed international communism for the assassination, and also for the murder of Roberto Poma and the kidnapping of Foreign Minister Mauricio Borgonovo, which had happened just the day before.

Without pausing, the president complained of some priests who during Holy Week had blamed the government for murdering Rutilio and had further claimed that the government was planning to use ORDEN to destroy Christian communities. He therefore asked the bishops to require those priests, especially the foreigners, to observe the law in order to avoid further deterioration in church–state relations.

Archbishop Romero responded by saying that he had prohibited church personnel from publicly accusing persons or institutions for deeds where responsibility was not clearly established, such as the murder of Rutilio. When he also asked for evidence that priests had made such accusations during Holy Week, the president displayed a photograph taken in a parish of the archdiocese, claiming that it proved that accusations had been made against the government. Romero took advantage of the occasion to point out that it was erroneous to confuse Marxism–Leninism with evangelization that adhered to the teachings of Vatican II and Medellín. Romero also reminded the president that he had been seeking to engage in dialogue with the government since he was made archbishop.[123] When the president's information and press office issued an incomplete account of the meeting, Romero sent out a more detailed report.[124]

Despite President Molina's repeated promises, there was never an exhaustive police investigation of the murder of Rutilio and his companions. A judicial case

---

123 ACSI. Information and Press Office, Presidency of the Republic, San Salvador, April 20, 1977; and the Archdiocese of San Salvador, *Boletín informativo* 9, San Salvador, April 21, 1977.
124 ACSI. Information and Press Office, Presidency of the Republic, San Salvador, April 20, 1977; and the Archdiocese of San Salvador, *Boletín informativo* 9, San Salvador, April 21, 1977.

was opened as a matter of course, but no one was ever charged. The military regime's manner of dealing with such crimes soon became regular practice: there was never any investigation of murders, forced disappearances, tortures, or other violations of human rights. Their perpetrators acted with the certainty that they enjoyed impunity. Such was the conclusion of the final report of the Truth Commission that was established as a result of the peace agreements of 1992.[125]

The justice of the peace of Aguilares initiated proceedings for what he called a "common" crime. He interrogated several witnesses, ordered a ballistics report, took photographs, and made a topographical map of the site of killings. Judicial evidence showed that Benito Estrada—thirty-five years old, unmarried, employed—had been at the scene of the murder and had pointed the victim out to the gunmen. The justice therefore ordered Estrada's detention, a disposition that was later confirmed by the judge in Quezaltepeque, who called several witnesses to testify.[126] However, the judicial order was never executed, and Estrada remained living undisturbed in El Paisnal. The government prosecutor, José Marenco Rivas Valdez, showing some willingness to collaborate with the archdiocese, made an effort to collect testimonial evidence, but in April he abandoned the case in order to prepare for his final career exam. After that, the case was at the mercy of judicial inertia.[127]

Apart from these facts, the only other information came from a short document of the National Guard, which reported the death of three persons near the Los Mangos Hacienda; their bodies had been found in a Volkswagen with license plate 97-449. The ballistics experts concluded that the killers had shot twelve-calibre pellets into the vehicle from the front, from the back, and from both sides, but they could not determine the caliber of the bullets found in the seat and the fender since they were deformed. The judicial record did not mention possible reasons for the crime, but the fanciful pen of a journalist mentioned an amorous entanglement as a possible motive. None of these details had any foundation; they were simply designed to confuse public opinion. The morning newspapers, *El diario de hoy* and *La prensa gráfica*, also helped to distort the motives for the crime. In their March 14 editions, both papers stated that the reasons were similar to those of any other common crime, a statement that was later echoed in the document issued by the justice of the peace of Aguilares. The newspapers also asserted that the shots had been fired from shotguns, and that the archbishop had called the president the night of the murder, not the reverse,

---

125 El Salvador Truth Commission, *From Madness to Hope: the 12-Year War in El Salvador* (New York: United Nations, 1993).
126 María Chávez de Lemus, Alirio Grande Paredes, Tomás García, María Luisa Gálvez, Joaquín Antonio Cáceres, Fernando Tejada, Antonia Guillén de Solórzano, and Isabel Solórzano.
127 ACSI. Fernando Augusto Méndez, "Report of the Archdiocesan Lawyer," San Salvador, April 11, 1977. *Boletín de información y prensa* 14.

as was actually the case. This falsified information obliged the archdiocesan press office to issue a clarification in one of its bulletins.

The final judicial formality was a resolution that ordered the exhumation of the bodies in order to make a definitive determination of the caliber of the bullets and the type of arms used. However, the provincial, Father Jerez, refused to allow it, saying it was evident that the judge was not interested in clarifying the crime. No exhumation took place.

Diverse sources indicated that the murder of Rutilio and his companions had been ordered by the directors of the Customs Police and the National Guard. The information coming from these sources was consistent, even though it was provided at different moments. It is hard to believe that the directors of those military units could have ordered the murder without advising the president's office, if not the president himself. It is interesting to note that when Molina left the presidency, the same director of the Customs Police became the head of the ex-president's personal security force. This close relationship could explain the very quick phone call that Molina made to the archbishop on the night of March 12, when very few persons knew anything about the murder.

On March 11, 1978, one year after the crime, a former soldier identified as Salvador Rosales gave Archbishop Romero the following information:

> Ex-president Molina was involved in the case of Father Grande, and the intellectual author of the crime was Lieutenant Bautista Garay, who according to news I've received is the ex-president's chief of security; at that time he was director of the Customs Police. An inspector under Garay's command was involved in the killing.[128]

This assertion was later confirmed by Santibáñez, who had been an army colonel and general director of migration when the murder occurred. In a press conference he gave in Washington, DC on March 21, 1985, Santibáñez said that the main person responsible for the murder of Rutilio was Juan Garay Flores, also a former officer of the Salvadoran army. Garay Flores had been trained at the International Police Academy in Georgetown, Washington, DC, at the same time as Santibáñez and Roberto D'Aubuisson, who had been an army major and was accused of being the intellectual author of the murder of Archbishop Romero in 1980.[129]

Lieutenant Garay Flores had in fact been the general director of customs at that time, and it was out of his headquarters that the political police operated. Political prisoners were incarcerated there without formal accusation, and some were tortured. Garay Flores was quite likely close to Molina and enjoyed his confidence; otherwise he would not have been put in charge of Molina's personal

---

128 Archive of the Archdiocese of San Salvador. Salvador Rosales to Óscar A. Romero, San Pedro Nonualco, March 11, 1978. Section 30, no. 002465, March 15, 1978.
129 El día (April 14, 1985).

security after he left the presidency. The inspector mentioned by Salvador Rosales was Marciano Estrada, brother of Benito and a customs agent. According to witnesses, he had been present in the church in El Paisnal on March 11; he was the man who had marked the cross on the back window of the VW Safari. He was murdered himself on October 31, 1980. Rosales decided to tell the archbishop what he knew about Rutilio's murder because "some people believe that those who kill the fathers are different people who are made to take the blame" and because "I feel moved by the blood that has been shed."[130]

Julio Sánchez, a former agent of the National Guard at the time of the murder who also belonged to a death squad, according to residents of his hometown (Oratorio de Concepción, Cuscatlán), has since provided further details about the murder of Rutilio and his companions to a Salvadoran journalist in Los Angeles, where he was living. Sánchez told the journalist that the actual perpetrators of the crime were six or eight members of the National Guard and that the director general of the guard from 1975 to 1978, General Ramón Alfredo Alvarenga, had personally ordered the murder of Rutilio for being a communist, for speaking ill of the government, and for inciting the rural poor. The agents chosen for the assassination inspected the site and shadowed Rutilio several times, always dressed in civilian clothes. According to Sánchez, the murder was to have been committed several days before, but for some reason Rutilio had not arrived at the place prepared for the ambush. On the day of the crime, a unit of the National Guard stationed in Aguilares had reported that Rutilio was headed in the direction of El Paisnal. After they had shot at the vehicle and it had rolled over on its side, the agents approached it and kept firing; the general's order had been that no one was to be left alive. The agents then went to the National Guard headquarters, where they were given three days' leave, after which they were assigned to different military units.[131]

Sánchez wept while he spoke to the journalist, partly because he was inebriated and partly because he wanted to be heard with compassion and make it clear that he was not the only guilty party: "We were always considered the bad guys, but we were only receiving orders. […] I have often repented, but I was only obeying orders. Besides, now it is too late for repentance." He was near the end of his life when he made this confession. He had had both legs and an arm amputated as a result of diabetes; he had had a stroke and also suffered from Parkinson's. After four difficult months in a hospital, he died of a heart attack.[132]

---

130 Archive of the Archdiocese of San Salvador. Salvador Rosales to Óscar A. Romero, San Pedro Nonualco, March 11, 1978. Section 30, no. 002465, March 15, 1978.
131 Carlos Santos, "Testimony of One of the Killers of Father Rutilio Grande," ContraPunto, March 15, 2015. Available at http://www.contrapunto.com.sv/archivo2016/reportajes/testimonio-de-uno-de-los-asesinos-del-padre-rutilio-grande (accessed December 19, 2019).
132 Santos, "Testimony of One of the Killers."

Aguilares: A Light for the Church

The threat of repression made by Colonel Santibáñez, director general of migration, was carried out at dawn on May 19, 1977. The region around Aguilares was militarized under the pretext of evicting the small farmers who had occupied lands that they had traditionally leased but that had been denied them that year. The national guardsmen searched the houses of the city and arrested many residents indiscriminately. In the homes where they found pictures of Rutilio or copies of the New Testament, they beat the men brutally and treated the women savagely. One of those arrested and beaten that morning was the pastor of Chalatenango, Víctor Guevara, who had spent the night in the house of a friend in Aguilares. The next day, the National Guard turned him over to the archbishop at its headquarters in San Salvador. The government reported that one guardsman and six civilians had been killed in an exchange of fire, but the residents of Aguilares reported that around fifty persons had been killed and many more arrested.

The three Jesuits who stayed in Aguilares after Rutilio's murder—Carranza, Pérez, and Ortega—decided to sleep in the sacristy since it seemed to be the safest place, but it was there that the national guardsmen found them. The sacristan was killed by the guardsmen while he was climbing up the tower to ring the bells to alert the people. The Jesuits were handcuffed, blindfolded, and transferred to the National Guard's headquarters. Around two in the afternoon, they were taken to the border and handed over to the police in Guatemala. They were kept incommunicado in Guatemala City for a week and then deported: Carranza and Ortega to Spain, Pérez to Panama.

That same day, the nineteenth, Archbishop Romero visited the minister of the interior, who informed him that the Jesuits had been deported. At five in the afternoon, Romero went to the president's office, where he found Bishops Aparicio, Barrera, and Álvarez meeting with Molina and the president-elect. Romero reminded the president of his promise not to expel more priests without prior discussion with the bishops. Not only had the government deported three priests, but it had accused them of subversive activities. Romero's protest went unheeded, and the results of this meeting were similar to the previous ones: neither president nor president-elect bothered to offer any explanations to the bishops. Later Santibáñez confided to a Jesuit he knew that he had been present in Aguilares during the arrest of the Jesuits to make sure that they were not maltreated.

Before talking any further with functionaries of the regime, Archbishop Romero wanted to go to Aguilares to remove the Blessed Sacrament from the church, which had been turned into a barracks for the national guardsmen. When military roadblocks kept him from proceeding, he sent one of the National Guard chaplains to the church, but he also was prevented from going. Several days passed before Romero could finally reach Aguilares. In the church there, he found the tabernacle destroyed by bullets, with the consecrated hosts strewn on the floor. The rectory had been sacked.

On Sunday, June 19, one month after the military occupation, Archbishop Romero returned to Aguilares to re-open the church for worship and to install Father Octavio Cruz[133] as the new pastor. Collaborating with him would be Jesuit Father Jon de Cortina and three Oblate Sisters of the Sacred Heart of Jesus. From early in the morning, the people packed the church and all the surrounding area, and they received Romero with fervent applause when he arrived. During a very emotional Mass, the archbishop began his homily with these words:

> It is my job to gather up the assaults, the bodies, and all that the persecution of the church leaves in its wake. Today I have come to gather up in this church and in this profaned convent a destroyed tabernacle and above all else a people that has been disgracefully humiliated and sacrificed.[134]

During the military occupation, the city residents had been able to been able to move about only with a safe-conduct pass. Without the pass, they could easily be arrested or summarily executed. For the first few days, the people were obliged to remain in their houses, but when food became scarce, the occupying forces allowed businesses to open and permitted people to circulate a few hours each day to buy what they needed. Even the archbishop was prevented from visiting:

> Therefore as I come here finally—I wanted to be with you from the beginning, but I was not permitted to enter—I bring you, sisters and brothers, the word that Jesus commands me to share with you: a word of solidarity, a word of encouragement and orientation, and finally a word of conversion.[135]

In this memorable homily, Romero stressed most especially the solidarity he felt with the people of the zone:

> We are with you now, and we have been with you at every moment. Indeed, if the church can ever say, "We have been with you in a very special way," it is in these circumstances of Aguilares, because chief among the victims are three beloved priests who have been shackled and exiled.[136]

After expressing his solidarity with the three deported Jesuits, Romero commemorated "our many beloved dead and our murdered friends. In this Mass we ask eternal rest for them, certain that the Lord will grant them this blessing and that from their place in heaven they will continue to work for

---

133 Octavio Cruz moved to San José, Costa Rica, in early 1976 to do postgraduate studies in the Central American sociology program of the Superior Council of Universities of Central America.
134 Homily of June 19, 1977, in Romero, *Prophetic Bishop Speaks to His People*, 1:161.
135 Homily of June 19, 1977.
136 Homily of June 19, 1977.

this holy liberation that Aguilares has set in motion." And he remembered the many other victims of the persecution: "We also suffer with those who are lost, with those whose whereabouts is unknown, and with those who are fleeing and don't know what's happening with their families. We are witnesses of this suffering and this separation":[137]

> We experience it close at hand because as pastors we experience the aching trust of those who through the church hope to reunite again with those whom cruelty has dispersed. But be assured, dear sisters and brothers, that in the eyes of God they are not lost; rather, they are very close to the heart of the Lord even though their families who cannot find them are in pain. For God there is no one lost. For God there is only the mystery of suffering, which, if accepted as sanctification and redemption, will also be redemptive suffering like that of Christ our Lord.[138]

Humiliation and suffering were not to be met with hatred and desire for revenge. The faithful of Aguilares, faced with this very real temptation, were reminded by Romero of "that startling saying of the Lord, 'All who take up the sword will perish by the sword,'" and they were warned that there would be "terrible consequences if sincere conversion does not first overtake the sinner."[139] Reminding the people that the true Christian response was forgiveness, Romero asked that the Lord give the people "courage so that they know how to forgive." He quoted Father Carranza, one of the deported priests, who from his exile had written that "the harsh voice of rifles will be silenced, and the prophetic voice of God will continue to resound." He assured the people: "The word of God is once again here, to tell you that God always rejects violence. God has no dealings with those who kill, with those who persecute, with those who assault." There could be no doubt about God's judgment: "Be aware, sisters and brothers, that God condemns violence, wherever it comes from, and especially when it comes from the armed forces, who instead of defending the people commit outrageous acts. God our Lord can never bless this violence."[140]

Archbishop Romero reminded the faithful that their suffering had a redemptive value. Using the readings of that Sunday, the twelfth Sunday in Ordinary Time of Cycle C,[141] he pointed out that the same prophet who had sung of the desolation of Jerusalem had also promised that "the Lord's mercy and goodness would rain down upon the suffering people." In the same vein, Romero promised that the humiliation and suffering of the people of Aguilares, if undergone with faith, would become a "new source of blessings." The archbishop then spoke

---

137 Homily of June 19, 1977, 162.
138 Homily of June 19, 1977, 162.
139 Homily of June 19, 1977, 162.
140 Homily of June 19, 1977, 162–63.
141 Zech. 12:10–11; Gal. 3:26–29; Lk. 9:18–24.

11. The Martyrdom

sublimely of the suffering people—or the crucified people, as he called them on other occasions:

> You are the image of the Divine One who has been pierced, the one of whom the first reading speaks in prophetic, mysterious language. That figure representing Christ nailed on the cross and pierced by the lance is the image of all those people who, like Aguilares, have been pierced and violated. But if you suffer with faith and give your suffering redemptive meaning, then Aguilares will sing a joyful hymn of liberation because when they look on the one they have pierced they will repent, and they will see the heroism and the joy of those whom the Lord blesses in their suffering.[142]

The second message of Archbishop Romero that morning was one of encouragement and orientation. Persecution, with its quota of death and pain, was a sign of the Lord's predilection:

> Take courage! Don't let your spirit flag! In the Archdiocese of San Salvador, Aguilares already has a very special place, for it is here that Father Grande and his two beloved companions fell victim to the assassins' bullets. After that, the blatant persecution of priests and catechists has been without a doubt a sign of the Lord's favor.[143]

The Lord was undoubtedly pleased by the parishioners' fidelity to the Gospel despite the infidelity in other places: "We have mutilated the Gospel greatly. We have tried to live a Gospel that is very comfortable without handing over our lives. We accept only a Gospel of piety which makes us feel comfortable." But

> here in Aguilares you have started a bold movement with a more steadfast Gospel. [...] You have understood that we are making a very serious commitment with Christ crucified, and this commitment demands the renunciation of many pleasant things that we cannot have when we embrace the cross of our Lord.[144]

"Right here," Romero continued, "priests and laypeople have handed their lives over to the Lord without worrying about martyrdom and suffering. [...] All these heroes, the priests and catechists of Aguilares who have died for the name of the Lord, are without doubt participating already in the unfading glory of the resurrection." Their testimony "is marvelous; it is the frontline of the church; it is the commitment of the church's members to proclaim what is most dangerous in the church's doctrine but also most necessary. [...] We take this testimony

---

142 Homily of June 19, 1977, 1:162.
143 Homily of June 19, 1977, 1:163.
144 Homily of June 19, 1977, 1:163–64.

away from Aguilares in order to present it to all the parishes."¹⁴⁵ The testimony offered in Aguilares was "a torch raised on high." Indeed, that image of the torch, which summed up his message to the people, became the title Romero gave to this homily: "We want to congratulate you in spite of the pain you feel because you are raising this torch on high."¹⁴⁶

He also thanked the Society of Jesus for having made such a bold commitment to preaching the Gospel. His expression of gratitude made it clear that he ratified the labor of the missionary team in Aguilares and the other Jesuit works in the country, thus discrediting the accusations made by their adversaries:

> I want here to thank in a very special way the Society of Jesus, which illuminated these paths in Aguilares. Many perhaps did not understand them. Certainly those who persecuted them and struck repressively against the "Gospel of subversion" did not understand anything. The Gospel of the Jesuits is the Gospel of Jesus Christ and the Gospel of the church, and there is no reason to confuse it with anything else. I want to thank the Jesuit fathers for having enlightened so many *campesinos* and for having organized so many communities with a Christian spirit and goodness of heart. With affection we remember Father Grande and his collaborators who knew how to instill into many hearts the light of the Gospel, which should never be extinguished.¹⁴⁷

Worried by the possibility that both the Gospel and the work of Rutilio could be distorted, Romero expressed his hope that the light that had shone brightly in Aguilares would not be dimmed: "May you never let it be confused with other fatuous flames; rather, let it be the authentic light of Christ that shines in the midst of confusion and darkness."¹⁴⁸ Since the danger of distortion came not only from the military regime but also from the peasant organizations, Romero begged the people "not to confuse the liberation of Christ with the false liberations that are merely temporal." Workers and small farmers had the right to organize and decide what was best for them in the light of the Gospel, for they had been inspired and motivated by the Gospel, but he warned them:

> Be careful not to betray those evangelical, Christian, supernatural convictions, replacing them with liberations of a merely economic, political, or temporal sort. Even though Christians collaborate in the work of liberation with other ideologies, they must preserve the original liberation that Saint Paul announces to us today, the liberation based on Christ and inseparable from Christ.¹⁴⁹

---

145 Homily of June 19, 1977, 1:163.
146 Homily of June 19, 1977, 1:165.
147 Homily of June 19, 1977, 1:165.
148 Homily of June 19, 1977, 1:165.
149 Homily of June 19, 1977, 1:164.

Union with Christ was fundamental because without Christ that "future kingdom" so desired by workers and small farmers "will never arrive"; "There will be nothing but tears, nothing but violence. No sound will be heard except that of machine guns and the anguished screams of those being massacred." "Authentic liberation" would come only by "working in the light of Christ" and by "dying with faith in Christ." Only in this way was it possible for Salvadorans to become new men and new women:

> We become new persons who purify their hearts of all sin, new persons who do not speak with resentful hearts, new persons who never foment violence, hatred, or rancor. We love with the heart of Jesus even as we defend our rights with love, which is the power of our church. We never promote hatred or class struggle, which are the false powers of other kinds of liberation that really lead to no liberation.[150]

Archbishop Romero concluded his homily with a call to conversion. The Eucharist, he said, was "a call to be reconciled with God and with our sisters and brothers," but he granted that reconciliation was not easy: "I understand that it is very difficult to pardon after so many offenses. Still, this is the word of the Gospel: 'Love your enemies, do good to those who hate you and persecute you.'"[151] But even while forgiving, he insisted, the people should not desist from demanding and fighting for their rights. He exhorted them rather: "Let us be firm in defending our rights, but let us do so with great love in our hearts, because by defending in this way, with love, we are also seeking the conversion of sinners. That is the revenge of Christians!"

> Let us pray for pardon and also for the needed repentance of those who have made this place a prison and a torture chamber. May the Lord touch their hearts before the dreadful sentence is carried out: "All who take up the sword will perish by the sword." May they truly repent and have the satisfaction of beholding the One whom they have pierced so that from his side a torrent of mercy and goodness may rain down and we may all see ourselves as sisters and brothers.[152]

Romero repeated the call for the people to practice solidarity among themselves and thus bring the kingdom of God ever closer: "How blessed will be that moment when this terrible tragedy disappears from El Salvador, this epoch when we live in fear of one another and when there are so many places where our sisters and brothers are suffering." This profoundly felt desire of Romero then turned into a prayer for peace and solidarity:

---

150 Homily of June 19, 1977, 1:164.
151 Homily of June 19, 1977, 1:166.
152 Homily of June 19, 1977, 1:166.

> May the Lord make these realities disappear from our midst with an outpouring of his mercy and goodness, with a torrent of graces to convert all our hearts. Indeed, the Creator has gifted us with a paradise, a truly beautiful nation which the Divine Savior has blessed with his own name. May it become truly a land where we all feel redeemed as sisters and brothers, just as Saint Paul has told us today, "There are no longer any differences, because we are all one in Christ our Lord."[153]

He assured the people that, despite the uncertainties and difficulties, there were always powerful reasons to keep hoping, "because the light of the Lord will always illuminate these paths."[154] He then transitioned into the Eucharistic celebration:

> We are going to change the bread and wine into the Body and Blood of the Lord. We are going to place it again in the tabernacle from which it was taken by sacrilegious hands, and we are going to restore it to the hearts of the people of Aguilares and all those who have come here to express their solidarity. Out of love for this sacred host, we want to love. We know that our hearts are small, but Jesus lends us his heart so that his one heart on the altar represents the hearts of all of us. Thus united we give glory to God, we give thanks because we are alive, we offer pardon to our enemies, and we ask forgiveness for our sins and the sins of our people.[155]

The congregation received the homily with long, emotional applause. During the offertory, Romero introduced the new pastoral team that would be in charge of the parish, assuring the faithful that they would have new pastors "but always the same Gospel." He exhorted the new pastors to "continue this work with the same light and courage [...] and to guide the people along the true path of Christian liberation, as the church today desires."[156] The congregation applauded again in a sign of approval and welcome.

After Mass, the people accompanied the archbishop and the concelebrants in a procession of the Blessed Sacrament around the plaza, singing heartily. When they arrived at the city hall, the national guardsmen deployed themselves in a menacing formation and aimed their rifles at the procession. The tension was strong, and the people, fearful and uncertain, turned to Archbishop Romero, who with amazing tranquility said simply, "Forward!" The procession kept going, the guardsmen stepped aside, and the people passed through them.

---

153 Homily of June 19, 1977, 1:166.
154 Homily of June 19, 1977, 1:165.
155 Homily of June 19, 1977, 1:167.
156 Homily of June 19, 1977, 1:165.

The Sign of Martyrdom

On March 5, 1978, a week before the first anniversary of the murder, Archbishop Romero visited El Paisnal to celebrate the Eucharist beside the tomb of the martyrs. He moved the commemoration up one week in order to avoid misunderstandings since elections for the National Assembly and for mayors were to be held on the following Sunday, March 12.[157] "We have come to the tomb of Father Grande, which is also his birthplace," Romero explained, because "we know that the Spirit of the Lord is throbbing in him, and the memory of him brings hope for our people."[158] The Eucharistic celebration was intended to highlight

> the example of their courage and commitment so that the voice their enemies tried to silence through violence may never die. May it continue to cry out like Jesus Christ, "Do not fear those who can kill only the body but leave fully alive the word and the message of the eternal Gospel."[159]

This homily, which closed the cycle that Romero dedicated specifically to Rutilio, penetrated deeply into the reality of Rutilio's life and death. The archbishop reflected first on Rutilio's human character and then focused on his Christian dimension, highlighting his priestly vocation as marked by martyrdom. He stressed that Rutilio and his two companions had died "under the sign of martyrdom."[160] As was his custom, Romero organized this homily around three points: the human, the Christian, and the priestly dimensions of Rutilio. These dimensions revealed "his full greatness, of which the Church is proud."[161]

The first reading of the day, the Fourth Sunday of Lent of Cycle A,[162] made Romero exclaim, "How wonderful it is to hear today's first reading here in El Paisnal." He marveled at the likeness he found between David and Rutilio: like David, Rutilio had also been born under "the sign of one chosen by God in the midst of his people. God came and anointed him as he did David." Despite this anointing, Rutilio always remained a man of the people:

> This man carried from this place the gift of love for his people. This man saw the same landscape that we see at this moment, and like the children who live in El Paisnal today, he passed through the dust of these streets, the sadness of the poverty, and the difficulties of living in a remote village. But he also experienced the moral richness of our people, the wealth of a home where he learned to pray, where he learned to see God and love his neighbor.[163]

---

157 On Saturday, March 11, there was another Eucharistic commemoration in the cathedral of San Salvador.
158 Homily of March 5, 1978, in Romero, *Prophetic Bishop Speaks to His People*, 2:296.
159 Homily of February 26, 1978, in Romero, *Prophetic Bishop Speaks to His People*, 2:268.
160 Homily of March 5, 1978, 2:303.
161 Homily of March 5, 1978, 2:290.
162 1 Sam. 16:1b.6–7,10–13a; Eph. 5:8–14; Jn. 9:1–41.
163 Homily of March 5, 1978, 2:291.

Despite his humble origins, Rutilio was *grande* because he never forgot his people. That was why, after his long years of study, he returned to them more human, more committed, and more fraternal:

> To see true human greatness, sisters and brothers, you don't have to go to a big city; it's not a matter of having titles or wealth or money. Human greatness resides in becoming more human. That is why, when Rutilio reached the fullness of his humanity, we find him returning here to El Paisnal. Last year on the eve of the patronal feast of this little town, he returned here with all the affection of one whose heart grew steadily during the time of his university studies. This man had come to understand that true greatness did not consist in leaving El Paisnal and becoming rich in some other place. Rather, his intelligence and his vocation led him to return to this town out of love for his people and in order to help them to grow in their humanity. Yes, this is true greatness![164]

But Romero observed something more: Rutilio possessed a special dimension that revealed the depths of his inner spirit. He had not only learned about Christ "in his catechism, in the seminary, in his religious life," but he had also "met Christ":

> Like the man born blind, he prostrated himself every day before Christ and said, "Yes Lord, I believe in you. I will follow you. My doctrine is Christian, and my liberation is that of the Gospel. I do not want this liberation to be confused with other doctrines that are merely temporal. I want to be a Christian who inspires hope for the true progress of this society. While paradise will never be found here on earth, yet this earth should reflect the paradise toward which we journey. This is the kingdom of God that we human beings are working for, a kingdom that is necessary even if people do not accept it. Even if we must die as martyrs, this kingdom must be preached and announced."[165]

Drawing inspiration from the second reading that Sunday (Ephesians 5:8–14), Romero declared that Rutilio had walked as a child of the light, always seeking goodness, justice, and truth and always doing what pleased the Lord. There could be no doubt that "great Christian ideals were what made this man great and enhanced his humanity. His was a human Christianity that expands toward God and motivates us to live in hope." For that reason, Rutilio was "the example that must be followed [...] by everyone who is concerned about the liberation of our people."[166] Archbishop Romero used the occasion to urge the faithful not to pursue

---

164 Homily of March 5, 1978, 2:291.
165 Homily of March 5, 1978, 2:292.
166 Homily of March 5, 1978, 2:293.

other forms of liberation that are content with merely earthly horizons. No, let us open ourselves to the horizons of faith. Let us believe as Father Grande believed. Let us proclaim the church's doctrine of liberation, with the confidence that one does not die when one is killed; rather, one rises above death and continues to be incarnated in the lives of those who follow.[167]

Besides being human and Christian, Rutilio was also a Jesuit priest whose very life was "the best answer" to the questions posed by Saint Ignatius to those standing before Christ crucified: "What have I done for Christ? What am I doing for Christ? What should I do for Christ?"[168] The answers Rutilio gave to these questions revealed much about him:

> He was inspired to live a life consecrated to God and to travel tirelessly along these dusty roads, carrying a backpack like a needy pilgrim, visiting humble homes, and feeling himself to be a brother to the poor. Among the rural poor he felt totally at home because, like a good Jesuit, he carried Christ in his heart.[169]

Living and working among the impoverished folk of the parish of Aguilares, Rutilio and the other members of the missionary team had a vivid experience of following Christ:

> Here in El Paisnal the Jesuits also learned how to be true Christians because you, the people, showed them the true image of Christ, the image that Saint Ignatius taught. That image is not discovered only during a spiritual retreat; it is discovered by living here where Christ is flesh that suffers, where Christ is carrying his cross. Christ is here, not as a meditation in the chapel on the Way of the Cross, but as alive in the midst of the people. This is Christ with his cross on the way to Calvary. This is the Christ who was incarnated in this religious priest, in this Jesuit follower of Jesus.[170]

Archbishop Romero then united his own gratitude to that the people felt toward the Jesuits: "I want to thank you for all that you as a team brought here: you taught the people to love Jesus, and you helped them see in their poverty and suffering the source of salvation, liberation, and redemption."[171]

Rutilio's priesthood, Romero explained, was marked by a twofold anointing—with chrism on the day he was ordained and with blood on the day he was martyred:

---

167 Homily of March 5, 1978, 2:293.
168 Ignatius of Loyola, *Spiritual Exercises*, 53.
169 Homily of March 5, 1978, 2:293.
170 Homily of March 5, 1978, 2:293–94.
171 Homily of March 5, 1978, 2:294.

Rutilio embraced his priestly vocation here. Not only was he anointed with the holy oil with which all ministers of the altar are anointed, but we venerate him now because he was anointed with the oil of martyrdom, with his own blood. That is how he appeared to me that night when I saw him in the church of Aguilares: prostrate, dead, as when the priests prostrate themselves to be anointed. He was prostrate there, immortally a priest, and as a martyr his Mass was already being celebrated in heaven. But he had lived here, and we feel that he is very much ours.[172]

Therefore, declared the archbishop, "we have in El Paisnal a Jesuit martyr. His tomb gives glory to the Society of Jesus and the church."[173]

Rutilio had been snatched away before his time: "We feel that he should still be walking with us [...]. He should still be walking with us and doing so much good. He was strong; he was young; he could do so much!" But "something killed him that should not have done so. It was a crime"[174] committed because he was denouncing the evil deeds of "the children of darkness": "And how difficult it is to reveal and bring this evil into the light, to denounce it as injustice, to preach against the disorder, cruelty, and abuse! Yet because Father Grande had the courage to unmask so many things, they marked him for death and killed him."[175] Romero observed that on the day of the murder someone had joked, "Now we've proved that even the skin of priests can be pierced by bullets," but that was not the end: "As a man Rutilio died one year ago, but as a Christian he can never die. The immortal light of Christ has shone on him." His preaching had not been silenced:

> What they did not expect was that the death of a priest would cause storms and bring about the springtime that Christian El Salvador has experienced over the past year. They did not know that they had planted a seed that would burst into a great harvest, as Christ said: "The grain of wheat dies but it does not remain buried." They have not triumphed over Father Grande, sisters and brothers. How abundant the harvest of persecution has been![176]

That abundant harvest in the archdiocese moved Archbishop Romero to give thanks for the lives of Rutilio and his companions and for the work of all those who were preaching the Gospel of the kingdom in the parish of Aguilares:

At this time I want to thank this Christian man and the Christians who died with him, along with the Christians who worked with him to plant the seeds of

---

172 Homily of March 5, 1978, 2:294.
173 Homily of March 5, 1978, 2:294.
174 Homily of March 5, 1978, 2:294.
175 Homily of March 5, 1978, 2:292.
176 Homily of March 5, 1978, 2:292.

spring that we are now harvesting. It is said that there has never been so much joy and hope in our archdiocese and in the church as there is in these days.[177]

The persecution had not ended with the assassination of Rutilio and his companions but still continued. Now it was targeting "those who follow his teaching" since "they cannot kill him" again. "This is the commitment we have taken on, not with him, but with the one whom [he] preached: the immortal Jesus Christ." Romero accordingly encouraged those who were carrying on Rutilio's work not to lose heart but to "honor him by embracing his true message in Christ Jesus. Otherwise, we will never understand the depths of hope that filled his heart—a hope that makes him rejoice in heaven because he knows that better times will come for these lands":[178]

Let us hope, my sisters and brothers, that this anniversary will remind us of the great commitment that all of us who are baptized—not just Father Grande—have with Christ. May his absence motivate us to continue to be faithful to the teachings of Christ, in whom we believe and whom we carry within us through baptism.[179]

---

177   Homily of March 5, 1978, 2:292.
178   Homily of March 5, 1978, 2:295, 294.
179   Homily of March 5, 1978, 2:295.

Afterword: The Martyrs and Their Legacy

This volume by Father Rodolfo Cardenal, S.J. recounts in detail the "life, passion, and death" of one of the first martyrs of the contemporary Salvadoran church, Jesuit Rutilio Grande. I have been asked to write an essay to provide a more general context for Father Cardenal's excellent work and to emphasize the importance of these martyrs for the church and the Society of Jesus.[1]

I have gladly accepted the request because I am convinced that the martyrs, especially when they are close to us in space and time, can help us cure a world that is gravely ill. The martyrs are the women and men who most make it possible for us to be true followers of Jesus. They are the ones who place us face to face with the unfathomable God, though as I will try to explain at the end, they do so mysteriously.

As a title for this essay, I have chosen "The Martyrs and Their Legacy."[2] In due course, I will speak of that legacy, but I begin writing now, by chance, on March 24, the very day when, forty years ago, Archbishop Romero was martyred. Rodolfo writes in his prologue, "Archbishop Óscar Arnulfo Romero cannot be fully understood without understanding Rutilio Grande." He briefly describes the relationship and the likenesses between the two men, and he concludes his prologue with some words of Pope Francis that made a profound impression on him. While attending a meeting in Rome at the end of October 2015, Rodolfo happened to meet the pope, and he relates the encounter thus:

> When I found myself before Francis, I told him I was the author of the two earlier biographies of Rutilio and was also a member of the commission of experts working on his cause. He told me he was familiar with the first biography. He then looked at me and asked whether we already had a miracle. I told him no. With a big smile, he told me that we *did* have a miracle: "The great miracle of Rutilio Grande was Archbishop Romero!" The serene certainty with which he said this made a deep impact on me. In sharing with me his thoughts about Rutilio, he provided me the key for understanding and interpreting his life.

---

1 We owe an enormous debt of gratitude to Rodolfo Cardenal, S.J. for all the research and work he has put into writing this biography. Our thanks are also due to Casey Beaumier, S.J. for publishing it through the Institute of Jesuit Sources at Boston College, and to Chepe Owens, S.J. for rendering it into English.

2 I spoke at length on this theme at the Universidad Centroamericana (UCA) on November 15, 2019, as part of the commemoration of the thirtieth anniversary of the martyrs of the UCA.

Like Rodolfo, I want to begin with Archbishop Romero, and I will then offer some reflections on other martyrs, on the crucified people, and on the diversity of martyrdom. As I write, we find ourselves caught in the middle of the coronavirus pandemic, so I will end with a short reflection that asks: Where is God now? And where are the new martyrs today?

Words of Archbishop Romero about the Martyrs

The priest Rafael Palacios was murdered in June 1979. In the homily he gave the following Sunday, Romero stated: "Several priests have already been killed. Why are they killing priests and Christians who are trying to be faithful to their vocation?" And he answered his own question:

> I am convinced, and I'm proud to say this, that the archdiocese of San Salvador cannot be indifferent to or complicit with the situation of sin and the structural violence that exists in our country. For years now the archdiocese has felt obliged, by virtue of its evangelical mission, to denounce injustices from a strictly Christian perspective. Doing this has cost the church the lives of some of her most beloved members.[3]

Romero returned constantly to the theme of martyrdom. Witnessing the ruthless slaughter of *campesinos*, he asked why so many people were being killed, and he had the courage and honesty to answer: "They are killed because they are a 'brother.'"[4] Before Romero himself was killed in 1980, Rutilio and five other priests had been murdered. "They were truly men who dared to go to the dangerous limits," he preached, "to the places where the UGB[5] threatens people with death and ends up killing them, as they killed Christ."[6]

Romero was often carried away in rhetorical raptures that came out of a heart that was pained and indignant. I had never heard anything like it before, nor have I since:

- "It is my job to gather up the horrors, the bodies, and all that the persecution of the church leaves in its wake."[7]
- "In a country where so many people are being murdered so horribly, it would be sad if we found no priests also among the victims. They are the testimony of a church incarnated in the problems of her people."[8]

---

3   Homily of June 24, 1979. The complete homilies of Archbishop Romero are available in English in six volumes: *A Prophetic Bishop Speaks to His People* (Miami: Convivium, 2015).
4   Homily of September 23, 1979.
5   The UGB was a network of death squads known as the Unión Guerrera Blanca, the "White Warrior Union."
6   Homily of September 23, 1979.
7   Homily in Aguilares on June 19, 1977.
8   Homily of July 15, 1979.

• "In the name of God, then, and in the name of this suffering people, whose laments rise up each day more tumultuously toward heaven, I beg you, I beseech you, I order you in the name of God: stop the repression!"[9]

Words of a *Campesino* about Archbishop Romero as Martyr

Shortly after the assassination, someone asked a *campesino*, "Who was Archbishop Romero?" and without hesitation the man answered: "Archbishop Romero spoke the truth. He defended us as poor folk. And that is why they killed him." A more lucid and beautiful statement could hardly have been uttered. I would like to comment briefly on each of his phrases.

"Archbishop Romero Spoke the Truth"

Romero spoke the truth *unequivocally*: "There is nothing as important as human life and human persons, above all the poor and the oppressed."[10] At the Puebla conference, he made a request of Leonardo Boff: "You theologians must help us to defend the humblest trace of what is the greatest gift of God: life!" Romero spoke the truth *expansively* so as to speak the "whole" truth, and that is why his homilies could last an hour or longer. Using the cathedral pulpit and the radio station YSAX, he spoke the truth *openly*, "from the rooftops," as Jesus instructed. He also spoke the truth *colloquially*, drawing from the many things he learned from the people. He assured the poor that they were the co-authors of his homilies and pastoral letters. "You and I together create this homily."[11] "You and I together," he told them, "have written this fourth pastoral letter."[12] He made amazing statements about how his relations with ordinary folk enabled him to speak the truth. "I feel that the people are my prophet."[13] "So deep was the reflection we had that I realized that the bishop always has a lot to learn from his people."[14]

Romero was a man "of the people" in a very special way. He respected the "reasoning" and the "argument" of the people, and he valued their ability to understand complex realities. He avoided anything that might lead to infantilized forms of religion, an all too common danger. Once, when speaking of the scapular in the church of Our Lady of Mount Carmel in Santa Tecla, he told the people that wearing the scapular was "a sign of the hope for salvation" and protection against "the flames of hell,"[15] but he carefully explained to the people that

---

9   Homily of March 23, 1980, the day before he was killed.
10 Homily of March 16, 1980.
11 Homily of September 16, 1979.
12 Homily of August 6, 1979.
13 Homily of July 8, 1979.
14 Homily of September 9, 1979.
15 His precise words were these: "First of all I say that the scapular of the Virgin of Mount Carmel is a sign of the hope for salvation that all persons have in their souls, in their hearts, in their lives. Those who die wearing this scapular will not see the flames of hell. This is a

"salvation demands work here in history, among temporal realities." If some are condemned, he insisted, it would be only because they could have done good but did not do it. "They had wealth in their hands and could have made their sisters and brothers happy, but because of selfishness they did not do so."[16]

"He Defended Us as Poor Folk"

At their conference in Puebla, the Latin American bishops spoke with conviction and eloquence about the church's option for the poor. In a daunting litany, they described the faces of the poor (nos. 32–39), their multitudinous reality (no. 29), the structural causes of their poverty, and their just demands (no. 30). But most importantly, the Puebla conference provided *theological* grounding for the church's option for the poor; that is, it explored the question of *why and how God makes his option for the poor*, a question that is rarely given the consideration it deserves. Any attempt to answer it may seem audacious, or even arrogant, but Puebla had that audacity, and it was free of arrogance. It stated boldly: "The poor deserve preferential attention, whatever the moral or personal situation in which they find themselves. They are made in the image and likeness of God to be his children, but this image has been derided and defaced. For that reason God comes to their defense and loves them" (no. 1142).

That Salvadoran *campesino* probably did not know much about Puebla, but he understood well that Romero had made a preferential option for the poor: "He defended us as poor folk." Romero *made an option* for the poor, and he actively *defended* them. He *encouraged people to organize* and *provided legal aid* to protect the poor from those who were oppressing and repressing them. When the repression was at its worst, *he opened the doors of the seminary*—much to the displeasure of other bishops—to receive and defend the *campesinos* who were fleeing from the hills of Chalatenango. And most certainly he defended the crucified people with the truth he proclaimed in his homilies, week after week, fearlessly naming the institutions and even the individuals who were erecting the crosses.

Romero Defended the Poor with All that He Was and with All That He Had

Five days before he was killed, he was asked by a foreign reporter how it was possible to be in solidarity with the Salvadoran people in such a difficult situation. He responded: "If you can't do anything else, then pray!" Do what you can, he insisted, but *do all that you can*. To be human, we must do something. "Do not forget that we are human beings," he told the reporter, "and that people here are suffering, dying, fleeing, taking refuge in the mountains." At the University of Louvain, six weeks before his assassination, Romero proclaimed that "the glory of God is the poor person fully alive." He made that statement less to increase

---

promise of salvation. But I want to tell many people frankly that it is not a false promise; it is not a promise that is unrelated to the reality of each one of us" (Homily of July 16, 1977).
16 Homily of July 16, 1977.

God's glory—a concern of some!—than to defend lives that were threatened and to do so in the most radical way possible. And what he preached to others he applied to himself first of all.

"And That Is Why They Killed Him"
It is important to understand what it means *to defend*. Defending the poor means *confronting and*, when necessary, *battling against those who attack, impoverish, persecute, oppress, and repress the poor*. In his efforts to defend the poor, Romero fearlessly confronted those who lied and killed, whether they were persons, institutions, or structures, and he accepted the *price that always has to be paid* when defending the oppressed. That was the price that all of us Jesuits accepted in 1975 at our Thirty-Second General Congregation, which was for me the congregation of Father Pedro Arrupe.

Romero defended the poor in the most radical way possible. He went far beyond what is conventionally understood by *defending a case*, where there is the natural desire to *win the case*, the plot of many films and novels. Romero clearly never thought about *personally winning a case*. Rather, he worked and fought for the victory of justice, truth, and maltreated reality. He had the wild hope that the poor would at least once in a while win. *That is why they killed him*. Just as they killed Jesus of Nazareth.

Romero impressed me from the very start. Immediately after his assassination, I was called on to write and speak about him. The first thing I said was that *Archbishop Romero believed in God*, and immediately after that I insisted that *Romero was a true prophet*. Toward the end of the 1970s, renowned scripture scholar José Luis Sicre came to our university to teach some Old Testament courses. I remember quite well that one day he told us, "Archbishop Romero is numbered among the seven or eight prophets of the Christian biblical tradition."

The Legacy of the Jesuit Martyrs of the Universidad Centroamericana (UCA)

On November 16, 1989, Salvadoran soldiers invaded the Jesuit residence at the Universidad Centroamericana and killed six priests and two women, a mother and her daughter. The first are *Jesuan martyrs*. The two women are an expression of *the crucified people*.

They Were Followers of Jesus
The six Jesuits reproduced the life of Jesus *authentically*, not just intentionally or devotionally. "They looked with love" on the truly poor; on those who lived and died subjected to the tyranny of injustice, poverty, hunger, and contempt; on those who suffered the repression of murders, tortures, and disappearances. *They stood by* those who did not take for granted either life or health or education, those whose poverty was so often compounded by pointless cruelty.

"They were moved to compassion, and they performed miracles," that is, deeds that seemed impossible. They dedicated their knowledge and talent, their time and labor, to continuing the work of Jesus. That is why I call them "Jesuan" and not just "Christian."

They also "drove out demons," or at least they fought against them. Certainly they battled the external demons: the oppressors, the oligarchs, the regimes, the armed forces. From those demons, "they protected the poor." They also struggled against the demons that attacked from within: religious and ecclesiastical hierarchies, even in the Society of Jesus.

They were not lacking models: they could look to Rutilio Grande, Archbishop Romero, María Julia Hernández, and many, many others.

They Were the Companions of Jesus That Saint Ignatius Wanted

Rutilio Grande, the protagonist of this book, was a Jesuit. So am I, and so are Rodolfo Cardenal and all those responsible for this book. It is fitting, then, to analyze the Ignatian legacy of the martyrdom of Jesuits.

In the Spirit of Saint Ignatius

Not all will agree with me, but I fear that there exists today too strong a stress on what is "Ignatian." While this stress can be valuable, it can also lose sight of the most profound legacy of Saint Ignatius. The adjective "Ignatian" is used quite freely: there is talk of Ignatian spirituality, Ignatian psychology, Ignatian sociology, Ignatian discernment, Ignatian education, Ignatian retreats, Ignatian administration, and so on. And the tendency seems to be on the upswing. Sometimes the adjective is used in all simplicity, but other times it carries with it an air of superiority, which is no help at all. Excessive use of the adjective may end up reducing the vigor and heft of matters that were really important to Saint Ignatius, such as *the path of poverty*. Something similar tends to happen, perhaps even more crudely, when the adjective "Jesuit" is applied to things.[17]

The six Jesuit martyrs took Saint Ignatius very seriously but without falling into the excesses I criticize. Perhaps the very situation in which they were living helped them in this regard. Ignacio Ellacuría, then rector of the university, reinterpreted the Spiritual Exercises of Saint Ignatius to reflect the reality of the Third World, and we have just published a stupendous 285-page book of the Ignatian Exercises that Juan Ramón Moreno gave to some religious sisters in Panama.

---

17 Certainly there are many important principles in the Ignatian tradition that should be kept mind—the *magis*, the "greater glory of God," "in all things, to love and to serve," "the more universal the good, the more divine"—and these are proclaimed far and wide in our day. All these phrases drawn from Ignatius offer ideals that need to be made reality, but I also see some danger in the current expansion of "Ignatianism": those ideals are reeled off without sufficient modesty, as if we Jesuits lived up to them faithfully, or at least made a serious effort to do so.

The UCA martyrs were steeped in the spirit of Saint Ignatius. They kept three principles of Saint Ignatius always in mind, and these principles continue to function today as *effective* Ignatian values, especially regarding the option for the poor and the struggle for justice.

- Closely observing the reality of our world and grasping it in terms of the "crucified people." The basic response when faced with them must be "working redemption." For this, no discernment is needed.
- Being honest with ourselves as Jesuits and asking ourselves: What have we done for the crucified people, and what are we doing now to take them down from their crosses?
- Taking seriously the decision to walk "in poverty rather than riches," perhaps the most difficult path and the one that is least often taken.

According to Saint Ignatius, there are two ways of living our lives or building our church and civic institutions, and the two ways are in conflict with one another. One way is the *path of poverty*, which initially leads to censure and contempt, slander and defamation, but then can produce humility, authenticity, true life. The other way is the *path of riches*, which first wins prestige and vain honors from the grandees of this world, but eventually engenders arrogance and inauthenticity, both personal and institutional. In the end, the first path leads to salvation (humanization) while the second leads to perdition (dehumanization).

What is ultimately at stake is saving one's life or losing it, as Jesus told us. It is a question of being ready to pay the price or refusing to pay it. This is what Saint Ignatius says in the Meditation on Two Standards, which was a meditation of the utmost importance for Ellacuría. He insisted that we have to choose between *a civilization of poverty*—akin to a civilization of labor—and *a civilization of wealth*—akin to a civilization of capital. The civilization of wealth, which prevails now in the world, has produced a society that is mortally infirm. The civilization of poverty, which still must be built, is the only way to reverse the course of history and bring healing to the world.

These essential elements—*crucified people, practicing liberation, walking in poverty, being honest with ourselves*—are in my view what constitute the truly Ignatian character of the UCA martyrs. These elements explain why they ended as they did.

In Community

These Jesuits "lived and died in community." It could have been otherwise. Their "living in community" was the result of their working together in the university. Their "dying in community" was a consequence of the aberrant behavior of the criminals. Theoretically, it would have been enough for them to have killed only Ellacuría, but their dying together was fitting: the life and the work of these

Jesuits had always been "in community," with its joys and tensions, its virtues and defects. The community included "all of them"; it was a "body," not a collection of individuals, some of them brilliant, others more normal, all of them valuable.

In this context of community, it is important to realize that the martyrs of the UCA never, as far as I know, discussed together or publicly whether it was God's will for them to stay in the country despite all the risks, threats, and persecution that came with staying there. At least, it never occurred to them to think seriously about leaving, and I was living there with them. Shortly before that fateful November 16, Father Peter-Hans Kolvenbach, superior general of the Jesuits, visited the community and asked the men: "Have you thought about whether it might not be better to leave the country and work for El Salvador from outside?" Their answer left no room for doubt: "Father Kolvenbach, you lived in Lebanon in times of great violence and persecution, and you didn't leave."

To understand the *Ignatian* character of their way of proceeding, it is necessary to consider what Saint Ignatius says in the *Spiritual Exercises* about "the first time for making a decision." In such a case, "God our Lord so moves and attracts the will" that the person acts "without doubting or being able to doubt" (no. 175). I cannot say exactly how it was that the UCA martyrs decided to remain in the country, whether it was through personal experience of God, such as the *Exercises* describe, or through some simple human experience, but I can say that they stayed "without doubting or being able to doubt."

I can draw on my own experience to state the reasons they did not hesitate to remain: the stirring memory of Romero and the eleven priests and four women religious who had already been killed; the binding force of their community; and the shame they would inevitably have felt at abandoning a people who were suffering so grievously. They may even have become inured to persecution. Personally, my Christology courses and my meditation on the path of Jesus toward Jerusalem kept me focused. As I beheld him murdered on the cross and heard his urgent call to follow him, there was no doubt in my mind.

These were the factors that moved our wills, influenced our decisions, and showed us the path to follow. In the language of the *Exercises*, it was in and through such realities that God was leaving us "without doubt and without the ability to doubt." But God was not acting through just any reality; he was acting through the harsh historical realities just mentioned.

Until the end

And the martyrs were faithful to the end, in the midst of bombs and death threats, with mercy ensuing. Dying as Jesus died, they have joined the ranks of the many witnesses—Christians, believers, and agnostics as well—who have given their lives for justice. They show us how to live decently in this world.

By their martyrdom, this community of six Jesuits became part of a much larger community in the body of the universal Society. Since the Thirty-Second

General Congregation in 1975, there are certainly more than sixty Jesuits—some say over a hundred—who have been killed in the Third World.

Often mentioned among the glories of the Society are the Paraguay reductions, the work of Matteo Ricci in China, and other extraordinary endeavors. Today it is these many martyrs—some more famous, others less so—who are the true glory of the Society. We say this not to make vain boasts but because they are the ones who inject new life and vigor into the Society. Just one week after the murder of Rutilio Grande, the superior general of the Jesuits, Pedro Arrupe, wrote a letter to the universal Society in which he stated:

> These are the Jesuits of the mold that the world and the church need today: men driven by the love of God to serve their brothers and sisters without distinction of race or class; men who are able to identify themselves with those who suffer, who live with them and even give up their own lives on their behalf; strong men who know how to defend human rights in the Gospel spirit and even to the sacrifice of life itself, if that be necessary.[18]

The Jesuit martyrs of the UCA were not perfect Christians nor were they perfect Jesuits, but they allowed themselves to be completely caught up in the reality of a crucified people, and they did so *in a way that was human, Christian, and theologal*. They were followers of Jesus and companions of Jesus. This is an important way of describing their legacy: *living and dying like Jesus*.

The Legacy of Julia Elba and Celina

Supreme Iniquity and Sublime Tenderness

Two women were murdered along with the Jesuits: Julia Elba and Celina. Julia Elba Ramos, forty-two, was the cook for a community of young Jesuits; she was poor, joyful, intuitive, and a hard worker all her life. Her daughter Celina, fifteen, was a vibrant young woman who worked as a catechist. She and her boyfriend were thinking about getting engaged in December. The two women had decided to spend the night in the residence of the Jesuits since there they felt more secure: traveling the streets was dangerous. But the order that had been given to the soldiers was criminal: "Leave no witnesses." A photo taken after the murders shows clearly that Julia Elba was trying to defend her daughter with her own body when the assassins burst into their room. It is a mother's tenderness to the very end.

Crucified people

Like Julia Elba and Celina, hundreds of millions of women and men in our world are perpetuating a history that never seems to end. It is the history of the New

---

18 The complete letter, issued on March 19, 1977, can be found in *Acta Romana Societatis Iesu* 17 (1978): 21–23.

World, plundered by the Spanish in the sixteenth century; it is the history of Africa, enslaved by Europeans in the sixteenth and despoiled by them in the nineteenth; it the history of our planet, suffering today an oppressive globalization under the aegis of the United States. Countless multitudes are still being slain, either swiftly by violence and repression or slowly by poverty and oppression.[19]

The high ideals that the world's powers formulated to celebrate the new millennium have turned out to be another fraudulent offense against the poor, who are the "suffering servant of Yahweh" in our time. In the words of Ellacuría, they are "the crucified people." They are also unknown and invisible. Who cares about the five million men and women who were killed in a senseless war in the Congo, a war devised and waged to provide minerals like coltan for mega-corporations that produce missiles, computers, and cell phones? Who even knows about them? Who is willing to risk anything important to take them down from their crosses? They died with no one to defend them.

The question may appear absurd, but many times I have asked myself: Who is more a martyr, Ellacuría or Julia Elba? Who reproduces more truly the *cross of Jesus*? The Jesuan martyrs express more clearly the *freely taken decision* to risk one's life, but they reflect only faintly the darkness experienced by the crucified people: the unrelenting injustice, the cruelty of impotence, the awful struggle just to survive.

While the deaths of the crucified people do not usually reveal the same will to resist as those of the Jesuan martyrs, they manifest more clearly the reality of historical innocence, for they have done nothing to deserve to die. They are totally defenseless, unable even to flee from their fate. It is they who best portray the enormous suffering there is in the world. It is they who have borne the heavy weight of the sin that has been exterminating them steadily, bit by bit in life, and once and for all in death. Unintentionally and unwittingly, they "are completing in their flesh what is lacking in the afflictions of Christ."[20]

The Jesuits of the UCA were not murdered for their commitment to abstract ideals of truth and justice; they were murdered for defending a crucified people. We cannot understand the martyrs unless we recognize also the reality of those millions of crucified victims. It would be like trying to understand the cross

---

19 In 2006, Bishop Pedro Casaldáliga of Brazil spoke these words: "There is more wealth on Earth, but also more injustice. Africa has been called the 'dungeon' of the world, a continental 'Shoah.' Some 2.5 billion people survive on Earth on less than two dollars a day, and 25,000 persons die every day of hunger, according to the FAO. Desertification threatens the lives of 1.2 billion people in a hundred countries. Migrants are denied fraternity, the soil under their feet." Neither the G-7 nor the G-8 nor, to my knowledge, any of the subsequent G's has done anything significant to reverse this history.

20 And we should keep in mind the comment of an eminent exegete: "completing" here does not mean "adding" something to the passion of Jesus of Nazareth; it means "re-enacting" that passion.

of Jesus without envisaging the poor wretches that he spent his life defending against the intrigues of lawyers and Pharisees, against the assaults of high priests and Herodians.

The Diversity of Martyrdom

February 2, 2020, marked the seventy-fifth anniversary of the execution of the German Jesuit Alfred Delp. As I studied his case, what most impressed me is that he died at the hands of the Nazis.[21] Delp was clearly a martyr, but there was something quite new in the way he was killed. That realization made me think about the various types of martyrdom and the importance of considering each case concretely.

We are justified in seeking common elements that are essential to every martyrdom, but I think we have to be careful in doing so. From a historical point of view, what is common to every martyrdom is that the martyrs do not simply *die*; they *are killed*. In today's world, they are killed, either slowly or swiftly, just for belonging to the crucified people and/or for trying to defend those people. From a Christian point of view, what is common to every martyrdom is that the martyrs remind us of Jesus. Since they resemble Jesus of Nazareth in their lives and their deaths, I call them *Jesuan martyrs*. There are also those multitudes who live in penury and oppression. We call them the *crucified people* because *their lives are stretched out on a cross*.

The question of the diverse types of martyrdom is important. It was discussed some years ago, especially in the Third World, when theologians were considering *the reasons* for the killing of Christians. After much debate, it was agreed that there was true martyrdom when the death was inflicted *in odium fidei* ("out of hatred of the faith," as the traditional formula has it) but that there was also true martyrdom when the death was inflicted *in odium justitiae* ("out of hatred of justice," according to more recent formulations). In 1983, theologian Karl Rahner posed the question: "Why would Archbishop Romero not be a martyr, since he fell in a struggle for social justice, a struggle he waged from his most profound Christian convictions?" For the people of Latin America, the question of who was a martyr—or who was a saint—did not need much discussion. Only hours after Romero was killed, a woman cried out in a loud voice as she wept: "They have killed the saint!" And a few days later, Bishop Pedro Casaldáliga wrote a beautiful poem called "Saint Romero of America, Our Pastor and Martyr."[22]

As I delve more deeply into the reality of martyrdom, I am ever more amazed at the different ways in which the martyrs were killed. The apostle Peter

---

21   See Jon Sobrino, "Our World Cruelty and Compassion," in *Rethinking Martyrdom*, ed. Teresa Okure, Jon Sobrino, and Felix Wilfred (London: SCM-Canterbury Press, 2003), 15–23.
22   Find the poem at http://www.servicioskoinonia.org/romero/poesia.htm (accessed April 29, 2020).

was executed in the horrendous, prolonged torture of crucifixion. A form of execution the Romans borrowed from the Persians, crucifixion was the punishment for non-citizens judged guilty of very serious crimes, such as instigating riots against the state or attempting to liberate slaves. The savage cruelty of the cross was designed to discourage the perpetration of such crimes.[23]

The apostle Paul, for his part, was beheaded, supposedly with dispatch. Perhaps he died feeling anguish, but he died with dignity. According to Plato, Socrates died quite tranquilly, drinking the hemlock. And then there were the "red martyrs" of Ernst Bloch, those who died heroically.

The diversity of *places* and *times* in which the martyrs were killed also impresses me. My brother Jesuits were slain quickly in a small, grass-covered yard within a university. Others, like Delp, were killed in an execution chamber at the end of a long corridor of death, where he had been waiting a very long while. Many Christians were devoured by beasts in the Roman Colosseum.

Here in El Salvador, martyrdom has taken strikingly diverse forms, especially when it comes to the crucified people. At the Sumpul River, which flows between El Salvador and Honduras, the Salvadorans who were trying to flee from the army plunged into the stream. Some drowned because they could not swim. Others were killed by the Honduran soldiers who awaited them on the far shore. In El Mozote, the soldiers of the Atlacatl battalion, who were trained in the United States, divided a thousand *campesinos* into three groups and placed them in different buildings: the men in the church, the children in a large house, and the women in an adjoining house. Most horrifying was the situation of the women, who were separated from their children but could still hear the screams of their little ones being slaughtered. Such was the testimony I heard from the survivor Rufina Amaya, who was there when the soldiers arrived. She escaped death only because she quickly hid behind the branches of a tree; there she spent hours, until the soldiers left.

Whatever elements may be common to every martyrdom, and however the hierarchy may define it, *the concrete reality of the martyrs' suffering* must never be minimized, neglected, or forgotten. Every martyrdom is concrete and *sui generis*; that is why I have insisted on the particulars. Theologian Johann Baptist Metz constantly insisted that we cannot do theology unless we "take Auschwitz with the utmost seriousness." Auschwitz was not just another site of martyrdom.

Pandemic, God, and Martyrs

I want to end this essay differently from the way that I thought I would. The reason is the current onslaught of the coronavirus pandemic, which has hit especially hard in these days of Holy Week, when we remember the crucifixion of

---

23 So shameful was death by crucifixion that Spartacus, the liberator of slaves, was never honored by any preacher, nor were the hundreds of slaves who were crucified in the city of Rome in the time of Nero.

Jesus. It was a frightfully cruel death that demands of us something more than routine piety. In view of this, I would like to treat five complex themes that I feel we should not ignore.

1. The Seriousness and the Horror of the Pandemic

The secretary general of the United Nations has stated that the pandemic "is the most challenging crisis we have confronted since the Second World War." And he has focused on *the victims*: "The ones paying the highest price are those who are most vulnerable: women and children, migrants and displaced persons, the disabled. And doubly vulnerable are the refugees and all those displaced by violent conflicts." He has made two demands: "Put an end to the sickness of war, and fight against this plague that is devastating our world."

To grasp the "sickness of war," we should remember that between fifty-five and sixty million persons were killed during the Second World War. To understand the devastation that a plague can cause, we should remember that at least fifty million persons died in the "Spanish flu" pandemic of 1918–19 and that some five hundred million people, a third of the world's population, were infected with the virus. No one yet knows what levels the current pandemic will reach.

The pandemic is a specific evil. It is a horror. At first, it can inspire a paralyzing fear, but more than anything, it produces an indignation that drives us to work relentlessly to find a solution that will make it disappear.

2. How God Is Spoken of in the Pandemic

The reality of evil has often led people *to think and talk about God*, and certainly catastrophes like Auschwitz have done just that. When people ponder such calamities, they often talk about *the problem of God* or *the issue of God*. Even if only indirectly, God comes to light; he is revealed. The matter is complex and challenging, but it is important to be aware of what becomes of God in this long history of debating about God. In what follows, I will simply mention the different ideas people have in this regard, without making a judgment about them.

Where God Is, What He Does, What He Does Not Do

The Effects of an Earthquake

In 1755, Lisbon was shaken by a powerful earthquake that caused massive destruction. Someone recently wrote—and I believe correctly—that what happened in Lisbon "would have been just one more terrible earthquake […] if it had not been for the fact that it had a greater impact on minds than it did on bodies." The earthquake created a situation in which the old dogmatic beliefs were gradually replaced by a more rational type of thought, but this did not happen automatically. Catholic thinkers of that time generally adhered to the ideas of the famous thinker Leibniz, who argued that human beings who did God's will would always live "in the best of all possible worlds." This being the case, anything tragic that happened in this world was willed by God as punishment for the evil deeds of human beings. Of course, many thinkers, Voltaire among them, opposed this way of "justifying" God.

The Dilemma of Epicurus
The most important effect of the Lisbon earthquake was to provoke questions about God. People began to doubt that God could be both powerful and good, thus returning to the old dilemma posed by philosopher Epicurus: Is there a good God who does not want evil to exist, and if so, does he have the power to prevent evil? Considering the calamitous state of the world, he concluded: "If God is good, he is not all-powerful. And if God is all-powerful, he is not good." The logic of Epicurus did not prove the non-existence of God, but it did raise radical doubts about attributes of God that for centuries were considered to be evident: his omnipotence, his goodness, his love for human beings. In the centuries since then, great thinkers like Thomas Aquinas have tried to prove the existence of God despite the many evils that exist in the world. Reason may be soothed, but not necessarily.

Earthquake, Terrorism, and Barbarity in Recent Times
In 2002, I was asked to write some reflections on the catastrophes that were occurring in those days. They appeared in a little book entitled *Earthquake, Terrorism, Barbarity, and Utopia*.[24] Just as the book was being published, in January 2003, a strong earthquake devastated El Salvador. Not long before that, on September 11, 2001, the twin towers were destroyed in New York City. In the years that followed, Afghanistan suffered constant terrorist attacks. To show the need for hope as we experienced "earthquake, terrorism, and barbarity," I added a reflection on "utopia."

Prayer of Petition and Thanksgiving, and Excess of Credulity
In countries like El Salvador, the poor and the priests constantly call upon God, whether in the ordinary trials of life or in catastrophes like an earthquake or a pandemic. They ask God to help, to heal, to strengthen, and to console all the afflicted and all the distressed. They also ask God to care especially for those attending to the needs of those who are suffering—and to give them their reward. And they thank God when something good happens to them.

With or without a pandemic, faith in God is not usually treated as a matter of great moment in a world of abundance. Many people can live peacefully without even thinking about whether God exists or not. And if God matters little to them, then they are hardly concerned about proving his non-existence. At one time, there were atheists and agnostics who asked whether God was responsible

---

24   Jon Sobrino, *Terremoto, terrorismo, barbarie y utopia* (Madrid, Trotta, 2002). It was published in English as *Where Is God? Earthquake, Terrorism, Barbarity, and Hope* (Maryknoll, NY: Orbis, 2004).

for the evils of this world, and one of them concluded: "What justifies God is that he does not exist." No longer do we hear this type of irony.

With or without catastrophes, *theodicy*, which literally means "justification of God," is not, in my view, very important today. There is barely a mention of it any time in the churches, in the seminaries, or in the countless meetings held by church movements of all kinds.

3. The Abandonment of God on the Cross of Jesus

As I said, I am finishing this reflection during Holy Week. For years now, I have been averse to liturgies that stress the power of God and that repeatedly insist on God's goodness and mercy. In these days, we have heard constantly, "God is always with us. We can always place our hope in him. He never lets us down."

In the Old Testament, God possesses great power. He uses it to defend his chosen people but also at times to punish them for their infidelity. Most often, he uses his power against the enemies of Israel, even destroying them. But God acts also in other ways in the Old Testament. The Suffering Servant Songs of Isaiah present a God whose power does not consist in exterminating foes, a God whose servant brings salvation not by crushing his adversaries but in being crushed by them.

The Abandonment of God

When Pope Francis celebrated the Eucharist a few days ago in the chapel of his Santa Marta residence, we heard the agonizing cry from Psalm 22 as recorded by the Gospel of Mark: "My God, my God, why have you forsaken me?" In reflecting on this cry, Pope Francis asked what God is doing now in the face of so much suffering.

For many years now, I have had the impression that, when speaking of the passion of Jesus in theology, in liturgy, and perhaps also in pastoral ministry, we skip too quickly over this narrative of Mark—and of Matthew after him—in which Jesus dies with the complaint of Psalm 22 on his lips. We have an easier time with the narrative of Luke, in which Jesus dies praying a psalm of trust, "Into your hands I commend my spirit." We have even fewer problems with the Gospel of John, where Jesus dies with a certain mastery and even majesty, saying, "It has been completed."

I also think that people state too glibly that the horror of Jesus's crucifixion is an expression of God's infinite love. We hear: "The Father handed over his son Jesus; he did not spare him. Then he exalted him and made him Lord because he handed himself over to death on a cross. And that is why we are saved."

Before the horror of the cross, such statements do not sit well with me. Nor am I content to appeal to the resurrection of Jesus as a kind of happy ending. Many years ago, feeling uncomfortable with the general tendency to avoid the problem of God and the cross, I wrote a short article called "The Risen One is the Crucified One."²⁵ The Risen One has more to do with the transcendent, while the Crucified One has to do more with the historical. I tend to believe that we can understand the transcendent only by keeping the historical very explicitly in view, rather than the reverse.

My reflections may now seem out of date, and frankly, I do not feel comfortable returning to them, but I cannot avoid raising these troubling questions again. Readers may find the reflections strange or at least surprising—some may even find them offensive—but I present them again with the hope that any uneasiness they cause will eventually produce a different, but far greater serenity.

The Crucified God of Moltmann
After the Jesuits were murdered in the UCA in 1989, the body of Juan Ramón Moreno was carried to my room, which was empty at the time since I was in Thailand. In the process, someone jostled my bookcase, causing Jürgen Moltmann's book, *The Crucified God*, to fall to the floor, where it absorbed the blood of Juan Ramón. I sent Moltmann a photo of the blood-stained volume. Some years later, he came to visit us, and in the Museum of the Martyrs he could behold directly the blood that corroborated the thesis of his work. He ended his visit in the nearby Garden of Roses,²⁶ where he meditated a long while.

The great contribution of Moltmann is his affirmation that *God is affected by suffering*. He has demonstrated this boldly and, in my opinion, brilliantly. Omnipotent or not, God is affected by the cross. The enigma of the cross of Jesus is not clarified, nor is it made into a mystery, by appealing to the resurrection.

Moltmann first became famous for writing another book, *The Theology of Hope*. He later wrote the *Crucified God* because he felt the need to include the cross more directly in his theology. "Not every life produces hope," he explained, "but the lives of those who lovingly bore the cross do produce hope." This way of expressing the hope that comes from Jesus I personally find very illuminating.

The Crucified God of Dietrich Bonhoeffer
A pastor of the Lutheran Church, Bonhoeffer was a great theologian and one of the first to speak about secularization. He is well known for his statement, "We have to live *etsi Deus non daretur*—as if God were not a given." After taking part in a failed plot to eliminate Hitler, he was arrested, and at the express order of Hitler, he was hanged. April 9 was the seventy-fifth anniversary of his death in a Berlin prison. He is now honored as a martyr, and he stands side by side with Archbishop Romero over the Great West doorway of Westminster Abbey. From prison, he wrote the following verses on July 18, 1944.

---

25   Jon Sobrino, "El resucitado es el crucificado," *Sal terrae* 826 (1982): 181–94.
26   The Garden of Roses marks the site where the bodies of the dead Jesuits were found. What had been the backyard of the house was planted in roses by the gardener, Obdulio, husband of Julia Elba and father of Celina.

> All go to God in their distress,
> Seeking help, praying for bread and gladness,
> For salvation from sickness, shame, and death.
> All go to God, Christians and pagans alike.
>
> Some go to God when God is in grief,
> Find him poor, reviled, without shelter or bread,
> Watch him tortured by sin, weakness, and death.
> Christians stand by their God in agony.

Years ago, when I read those verses to a class, there was a silence like no other silence I can remember—not even when I mentioned that God had raised up his Son. To speak in Christian terms of the relation between victims and God, we must keep in mind that they express two ultimate realities that can be related to one another only through a type of *perichoresis*, that is, the intertwining of divinity and humanity. That means that *we must place God in the victims*, thus *making the victims divine*, and *we must place the victims in God*, thus *making God a victim*.

4. The Newness of the Martyrs of the Pandemic

This newness of these martyrs is clearest in *the crucified people* produced by the pandemic. Diseases, like earthquakes, are caused by nature, not by human will. Those who die from disease may even exceed in number those who die in the catastrophes caused by human malevolence.

The Jesuan martyrs of the pandemic are the persons who, as a result of caring for those infected by the coronavirus, suffer distress, exhaustion, sickness, and death. They are usually family members, medical personnel, and pastoral ministers.

On March 15, 2020, the coronavirus began to overwhelm the clergy in Italy. Many priests tried to help the sick as best they could, and in the space of two or three weeks some sixty priests died. I was reminded of Saint Aloysius Gonzaga. When I was a young seminarian, he was proposed to us as a model since he was a virtuous young Jesuit known especially for his modesty and his chastity. Only years later did I learn how he died: working in Rome with the victims of the bubonic plague, he contracted the disease from the patients for whom he was caring. He was twenty-three years old.

5. The Legacy of the Martyrs of the Pandemic

Love and Suffering

These martyrs leave the same legacy as do all those who have lost their lives attending to the needy and defending the vulnerable. Some of them, the Jesuit martyrs, were killed for taking care of the needy and for defending the oppressed. All martyrs make perfectly clear the truth of Jesus's saying: "There is no greater love than to lay down one's life for one's friends" (John 15:13).

Martyrdom is primordially related with love and with its inseparable qualities, justice and dignity. And it is also primordially related to the sacrifice of the martyrs. It sublimely unites loving and giving one's life. That happens also, in a different way, with the crucified people who, as I have written elsewhere, are possessed of a primordial holiness.

God Passes through Our World
In these days of coronavirus, the religious sphere is filled to overflowing with discourses and writings about strange happenings, about apparitions that have been conceded to women and especially to children, about witnessing and working wonders impossible for the rest of mortals. Some have even seen a light in the clouds taking the shape of a cross. They seem to be dreaming and hoping that God will pass through this world of pandemic, in ways that he failed to do when he passed through this world with Jesus of Nazareth.

But the passing of God has not always been seen in this way; it has been seen quite differently. Forty years ago, at the funeral Mass at the UCA a few days after the assassination of Romero, Ignacio Ellacuría proclaimed: "With Archbishop Romero God passed through El Salvador." Later he explained what he meant by that powerful statement:

> Romero was an envoy, not simply a product of our hands. He became—though not equally for all—the great gift of God, and a very special gift. He was accused of engaging in politics by the wise and the prudent of this world; by the ecclesiastical, civil, and military authorities; by the rich and powerful of this world. But the people of God, those who hunger and thirst for justice, the pure of heart, the poor *with* spirit—they all knew that that claim was false. They had never felt God so close or the Spirit so present. They had never felt Christianity to be so genuine, so full of grace and truth.[27]

That we may feel God so close to us, the Spirit so real, Christianity so true—*that* is the legacy of the martyrs. It is the legacy of those who lived and died as Jesus did. It is the legacy of the crucified people.

With Rutilio Grande, God passed through Aguilares and El Paisnal. The *campesinos* never felt God so close to them. And his legacy is not diminishing: it is ever increasing.

—Jon Sobrino
April 16, 2020
San Salvador

---

27 Ellacuría wrote these words in an article published by the Spanish journal *Razón y Fe* a few months after the assassination of Archbishop Romero.

Index

Abarca, López, 425
Achaerandio, Luis, 32
active passivity, 155
the Adorers
  overview of, 60
  Corpus Christi feast (1970), 61
  generational changes, 168–69
  importance of, 153
  leadership of, 155
  membership declines, 168
  and the missionary team, 167
  Rutilio and, 60–62, 168–69
  vigils, 60, 168
  women in, 60, 168
Adveniat, 218
AGES (Association of Cattle Ranchers), 361, 363
agrarian reform projects, 335–37, 339, 343
Agricultural Front of the Eastern Region. *See* FARO
Aguilares, city of. *See also* El Paisnal
  overview of, 140
  businesses, 143
  demonstrations in, 339–40
  history of, 142
  military occupations of, 430–31
  pastoral practices, 263–64
  peripheral settlements, 144–45
  prostitution in, 215–16
  schools, 143
  social organizations, 143
  taverns, 143–44
  violence in, 216
  women in, 143–44
  youth mission, 227
Aguilares parish. *See also* FECCAS and Aguilares parish
  activity declines, 152
  activity statistics, 208–9
  baptisms
    administration criteria, 233–34
    catechesis, 197, 231–33
    cost of, 155
    decline in, 217–18
    desire for, 221
    Holy Week, 167
    Rutilio on, 110, 112, 221, 232
    statistics on, 208–9
  Bible study promotion, 255–56
  catechesis, 154, 231–34
  celebrations of the Word, 192, 195, 222
  Chávez and, 11, 208–9, 212
  Christian Democrats, 182
  communities of
    consolidation of, 222
    Corpus Christi feast posters, 245–47
    delegate involvement in, 222–24
    desertions, 223–24
    difficulties facing, 223
    division, causes of, 225
    faith experiences, 224–25
    and FECCAS, 222–23, 225, 283–84
    growth of, 222
    instability in, 223
    and the military regime, 226
    and ORDEN, 222, 225–26
    peasant organizing, 226
    youth groups in, 227–28
  community councils, 167
  community meetings, 222
  creation of, 142
  as ecclesial platform, 353
  evangelized population, 221–22
  feasts
    overview of, 236
    celebration principles, 236
    Corpus Christi, 61, 243–47
    Festival of Maize, 206–7, 249–57
    Holy Week, 242–43
    Lord of Mercies, 238–40
    of Pentecost (1973), 191
    Rutilio and, 236–41, 244
    Sacred Heart of Jesus, 248–49
    Saint Joseph, 241–42
  First Communions, 247–48
  historical situation, passivity toward, 154–55
  Holy Week, 242–43
  hymnbook, 237
  individualism, 153
  Jerez's visit, 331, 333–34
  justice, sense of, 170–71

mayoral elections, 215
and the military regime, 276
millenarianism in, 186, 205–6
morality, senses of, 155–56
novenas, 153–55, 238–39, 241
and pastoral ministry week, second, 271
pastoral visit, Rivera's
  baptism discussions, 231–33
  benefits of, 236
  catechist dialogues, 234
  Chávez's absence, 229
  city pastoral committee dialogues, 234–35
  community representative dialogues, 230–32
  confirmations, 229–30
  delegate complaints about, 229–30
  and FECCAS, 235–36
  missionary team meeting, 235–36
  preparer dialogues, 234
  Rutilio's announcement of, 228–29
  sacrament administration discussions, 232–33
  versus traditional visits, 229
pastors, pre-Rutilio, 152–54
popular religiosity, 153–54, 221–22
population sectors, 221
rectory, sacking of, 430–31
regions of, 142–43
repression of, 230–1
rezadora women, 153–54
Romero and
  and the Blessed Sacrament, 430–31
  Eucharist at the martyrs' tomb, 437–41
  homily at church re-opening, 431–36
  homily on Rutilio's life and death, 437–41
  Octavio Cruz, installation of, 431
rural villages, 144–46
sacrifice and suffering, 154–55
and the Society of Jesus, 332–33
socio-economic conditions
  acceptance of, 154–55
  family groups, 149–50
  illnesses, 145
  labor conditions, 148–50, 185
  land scarcity, 144–45, 148–51
  plantations, 147–50, 156, 185
  Protestant evangelicals, 147
  and rebellion, 151–52
  security forces, 146

  services, lack of, 145
  small farmers, 148–51
  sugarcane production, 147, 150
  traditionalism, 153–56
  village patrols, 180–81, 210
  worship, emphasis on, 152
Aguilares parish, missionary team. *See also* Bengoechea, Jesús; Carranza, Salvador; Jesuit scholastics; Pérez, Marcelino
  and agrarian reform, 336
  bishops' endorsement of, 385
  and Boulang, 187–88
  Christian identity concerns, 254
  collaborators, 161, 189–90, 192, 197
  communism, accusations of, 187
  communities, relationship with, 217
  community assessment, 221–28
  community visits, 238
  complaints about, 300–1
  cooperatives, interest in, 199–200
  crisis within
    and Bernardo Boulang, 187–88
    common project lack, 189
    community organizing, 186–87
    decline in, 217
    evangelization methods, 187–88, 216
    FECCAS's knowledge of, 351–52
    improvements, 357
    and internal relations changes, 216
    parish activity reorganization, 189–90, 216
    Pérez causing, 351–52
    revolutionary theory and analysis, 188–89
    and Rutilio's pastoral decisions, 352
    Rutilio-Bengoechea disagreements, 188–90, 216
    team reorganizations, 217
    urban-rural divide, 190
  Cruz, 142, 189, 209, 217, 332, 431
  and FECCAS
    bases survey response, 310–11
    courses, 311
    pastoral planning inclusion, 306
    support of, 310–11
    tensions between, 305–7, 310
    work of, 295
  Fernández, Benigno and, 142, 189, 216–17
  government spying on, 187
  hardships endured, 166
  Holy Week activities, 242–43

homily preparations, 158
ideas impressed on the people, 279
leadership losses, 305
members of (1976), 222
national council of Jesuits meeting, 324–27
and Orellana's death, 361
removal recommendation, government's, 379–80
and Rivera's pastoral visit, 235–36
rural poor organization, support for, 322
threats against, 296–97
vicariate meeting attendance, 264
youth organization attempts, 226–28
Aguilares parish, pastoral program. *See also* delegates of the Word
community councils, 167
confession, abandonment of, 325
courses and cursillos phase
  overview of, 192
  analytical and theoretical tools, 203–4
  benefits of, 203
  Bible study, 203–5
  catechists, urban, 196
  community development, 192
  the cursillos, 196–200
  delegates of the Word meetings, 195–96
  delegates of the Word training, 193–96, 216, 300–3
  evangelization of popular religiosity, 192–93
  and Festival of Maize, 206–7
  Jesus Christ, 203–6
  liturgical celebrations, 206–9
  Luis Chávez celebration, 208
  millenarianism, failure of, 205–6
  Moses, 203–6
  parish courses, 193–96
  political vaccination course, 200–3
  reorganization of the parish, 216
  salvation history, 193, 204–5
  social consciousness, impact on, 206
  sociological and political formation, 216
  transition to, 191
  violence, discussions on, 204–5
crises in
  evaluation project, 330–31
  and FECCAS, 321–25, 327–28, 330
  inevitability of, 322
  liberation disagreements, 328
  and national council of Jesuits, 324–28

Pérez and, 326–27
repression dangers, 326
Rutilio's resignation, 331–32
Rutilio's views on, 322–28, 330
solution options, 330
dimensions of, 166
economic repercussions, 217–19
evaluation of, 330–31
evangelization
  to adults, 163–65
  approaches to, 157, 187, 228
  Holy Week, 242
  and labor conflicts, 179
  parish leadership importance, 305
  and politics, 158, 181, 183, 187
  and popular religiosity, 192–93, 228
fatalism, confronting, 159
goals of, 160
Gospel, approach to, 181
guiding principles, 191
Ignacio Ellacuría's support for, 353–54
income sources, 217–18
injustice, denouncements of, 181
integration proposal, 140–41
Jesus Christ as model, 158
military authority conflicts, 210–16
missions phase
  overview of, 161
  adult evangelization, 163–65
  celebrations, 165–67
  in the city, 161–62
  community activities, 167
  community emphasis, 166
  complaints about, 165
  delegate selection and training, 165–66
  difficulty of, 166
  evangelization approach, 157, 187
  goal of, 161
  herder priests, 167
  local information collection, 163
  New Testament distribution, 163, 166, 169, 196
  novelty of, 165
  plenary sessions, 164–65
  preparation of, 162–63
  readings, 164
  religious consciousness, impact on, 167–71
  in the villages, 162
mobile church vision, 160

and ORDEN, 210–16
parish council, 190
and the people's organizing, 186–87
polarizing effects of, 186
political consequences as byproduct, 157
political contexts, 181, 321
politics
 and evangelization, 158, 181, 183, 187
 and faith, 158–59
 neutrality, 181–86, 191
the poor, support for, 160
and popular religiosity, 157–60, 221, 228
population sectors identified, 221
as poverty experience, 219
and priestly identity crisis, 159
project proposal, 127–30, 140
purposes of, 183
sacraments, 159–60, 217–18
site selection reasons, 140–41
social consciousness, impact on, 206
sociological methods, promotion of, 206
socio-political contexts, 142
successes of, 186
success of, 221
task organization, 189–90
temporary nature of, 160
theological support for, 353–54
Aguilares parish, Rutilio's pastorship. *See also* homilies, Rutilio's
absences, 258, 322
acceptance of position, 141–42
and the Adorers, 60–62, 168–69
La Antigua stay, 322
assignment to, 140
on baptismal practices, 232
Bengoechea, conflict with, 188–89
bishops' endorsement of, 385
and the Christian Legal Aid Office, 323
clergy retreats, 258
community, approach to, 181
community visits, 238
concerns and fears
 community relations, 217
 FECCAS causing, 321–23, 352–53
 holy impatience, 206, 217
 rapidity of changes, 186–87, 217
 relatives, behavior of, 141
on constitutional *versus* gospel values, 214
and the crisis, missionary team, 188–90, 216, 352

death threats against, 391–92
decision to go, 327
and delegates of the Word, 192, 208
denunciations made
 of alcoholism, 186
 of conservative Catholics, 298–99
 of the mayor, 181–83
 of the oligarchy, 299
 of ORDEN commander, 211–15
 of plantations, 185
 of prostitution, 186
departure from, 190
disillusionment experienced, 352–53
facility regulation, 237–38
family visits, 8
fear for his life, 392
feast days, 191, 236–41, 244
and FECCAS
 Country Christmas demonstration, 311–17, 319
 criticisms of, 320
 defenses of, 320, 323, 351
 demonstrations, 339–40
 expectations from, 324
 fears caused by, 321–23, 352–53
 the rural poor, 323–24
 separations from the parish, 308, 323, 352
 support for, 308–9, 324
First Communions, 247
and Guazapa parish, 333
Holy Week activities, 243
impact of, 134
indecisiveness, 40
and the Jesuit scholastics, 188, 209, 328–30, 357
on land ownership, 249
leadership, strength of, 216
and literacy courses, 199
location of, 140
Luis Chávez's visit, 208–9
and the mayor
 denunciations of, 181–83
 esteem for, 183
 letters to, 183–85
 President Molina's visit, 183–85
ministry of accompaniment, 324
and the Ministry of the Interior, 215
and the missionary team's safety, 380
and mission team tensions, 186–90
and Molina, 183–86, 214–15

Index 465

national council of Jesuits meeting, 324–27
and National Institute of Aguilares, 300, 302
and nationalism, 213–14
and ORDEN, 210–11
and Orellana's death, 362
and El Paisnal military occupation, 363
partisan politics, homily on, 202–3
the people, defenses of, 181–82, 185, 187
persecution fears, 385
political neutrality, 181–86
popular religiosity, 153–54
post-election, 380
and the president's secretary, 215
on priests *versus* soldiers, 213–14
public nature of, 4
resignation, 331–32
as revolutionary, perceptions of, 321
and the rural poor, 156
Sacred Heart of Jesus celebrations, 248–49
and Salinas chapel, 300–1
speed of changes, concerns with, 217
threatening letter received, 378
threats against, 297
UCA visit, 353
on village life, 144–46
young people, defenses of, 227–28
Aguiñada, Rafael, 288
Alas, Higinio, 125, 318
Alas, Inocencio, 384
alienation, Rutilio's, 129
Alvarado, Napoleón, 161
Alvarenga, Ramón Alfredo, 429
Álvarez, José Eduardo, 83, 261
Amaya, Fabián, 270–71, 276
Amaya, Rufina, 454
Amayo, 245*tab*
ANEP
  overview of, 254n90
  agrarian reform opposition, 336
  and Eduardo Orellana's death, 360–61
  and FARO, 420
  popular organization suppression, 291
  Romero, meetings with, 419–20
Aparicio, Pedro Arnaldo, 364
Apopa parish
  Bernal as pastor of, 366
  demonstration of faith, 367, 375–76
  Rutilio's homily on Bernal's expulsion, 367–78
Araditas, 222–23, 246*tab*
archbishops. *See* the bishops

archdiocesan pastoral council, 275–76
Arrupe, Pedro, 451
Ascoli, Fernando, 329, 357, 365
Aserradera, 234, 246*tab*
Asparicio, Pedro, 83
Azcue, Segundo, 42, 115

Barahona, 380
Barahona, Rafael, 312, 380, 382
Fr. Bariain, 28
Barrera, Benjamín, 83, 85, 121–22, 364
Barrera, Facundo, 7, 11–13
Belloso, José Alfonso, 46
Beltrán, Edgard, 82, 84
benediction, Rutilio's writings on, 103
Bengoechea, Jesús
  and Bernardo Boulang, 140–41, 187, 189–90
  and the consumer cooperative, 200
  courses given by, 216
  defamation of, 210
  departure from Aguilares, 190, 216
  evangelization approach, 157–58
  government attacks on, 317
  and Jesuit scholastics, 141
  missionary team organization, 140–41
  pastoral project proposal, 127–30, 140
  political approach, 188–89
  rural community control, 190
  Rutilio, conflicts with, 188–90, 216
  as Rutilio's assistant, 142
  Rutilio's defenses of, 212
Bergoglio, Jorge Mario, 411
Bernal, Mario
  deportation of, 365–67
  Rutilio's defense of, 371–72, 374
the bishops. *See also* Chávez, Luis; Rivera Damas, Arturo; Romero, Óscar Arnulfo
  Álvarez, José Eduardo, 83
  Asparicio, Pedro, 83, 364
  and attacks on the church, 364
  Belloso, José Alfonso, 46
  Benjamín Barrera, 83, 85, 121–22, 364
  Casariego, Mario, 53
  Castro Ramírez, Francisco José, 67
  criticisms of clergy, 88–89
  FECCAS, views on, 236, 319
  and the homily of August 6, 1970, 115
  Mansilla, Demetrio, 20
  Medellín, reaction to, 81
  and the mission camps, 67

Molina, meetings with, 382
and pastoral ministry week, first, 81–83
Prigione, Girolamo, 85
Ramírez, Castro, 83
Rutilio, suspicion towards, 119
Rutilio's views of, 73, 119, 338–39
and San Salvador seminary
  baccalaureate program, 49, 51
  dissatisfaction with, 73
  formation practices, 56–57
  mission camps, Rutilio's, 64, 67
  reform proposal indifference, 81
  UCA collaboration, 53
  Vatican II, reaction to, 81
the bishops' conference. *See also* the Medellín
  conference
  Country Christmas 1975 discussion, 319
  FECCAS's meeting request, 319–20
  option for the poor, 446
  pastoral ministry commitment, 385
  and pastoral ministry week, first
    and Medellín, 94–95
    response document, 85–89, 92–95
    Rutilio's response to, 92–99
    and Vatican II, 94
  persecution responses, 385–89
  and the priests' senate, 268
  Romero as secretary, 120
  and San Salvador seminary
    apostolic visitation to, 53–54
    regulation approval, 73
    Rutilio's rectorship candidacy, 115, 118–19, 122
    staff discussions, 76–78
    UCA collaboration, 53
Bonhoeffer, Dietrich, 458
Borgonovo, Mauricio, 426
Boulang, Bernardo
  and the Aguilares missionary team, 187
  and Jesús Bengoechea, 140–41, 187, 189–90
  organizing, popular, 175
  pastoral ministry of, 140
  and Polín, 283
  and Rutilio, 187–88
BPR (Popular Revolutionary Bloc)
  agrarian transformation goals, 337
  creation of, 290
  delegates of the Word and, 305
  demonstrations organized by, 337–39, 367
  and the guerrilla movement, 291
  ideological purity demands, 290
  and other revolutionary groups, 290–91
  plantation wage increase request, 359
  power of, 291
  pronouncements, reaction to, 365
Buena Vista, 223, 234, 283

La Cabaña plantation, 174–77, 231, 285
Cabarrús, Carlos R., 331, 357
El Calvario, 243, 245*tab*
Cañas, Simeón, 213n46
Carballo, Carlos, 288
Cardenal, Antonio, 329, 357, 365
Carranza, Salvador
  Aguilares, departure from, 380
  attacks on, 210, 318
  capture and deportation, 430
  on demonstration of faith, Apopa, 375
  education, 212
  Feast of Saint Francis homily, 303–4
  on the missionary team, 142, 189, 216–17
  Nottebohm family denunciation, 303–4
  on Rutilio, 39–40
  Rutilio's murder, news of, 401–2
  Rutilio's protection of, 392–93
  writings of, 432
the Carranza Herrera family, 126–27
Casaldáliga, Pedro, 452n19, 453
Casariego, Mario, 53
Castro Ramírez, Francisco José, 67
catastrophes and God, 455–56
La Cayetana massacre, 287–88
Central American vice-province
  liberation of the poor, 131–32
  pastoral ministry difficulties, 130–32
  personnel shortages, 139
  Rutilio as vice-provincial assistant for pastoral
    ministry, 131–32, 139–40
  Rutilio's recommendations for, 132, 134
  Rutilio's travels through, 123–24, 126
  schools, 133–34, 139–40
  Spanish Jesuits in, 135–36
  Spanish province dependency, 16
  and traditionalism, 132
  vice-provincial congregation, Rutilio address, 134–39
Cerrón Grande dam protests, 360–62. *See also*
  Orellana, Eduardo, death of

Chalatenango vicariate, 258, 262–63, 267, 289
Chávez, Luis
  and Aguilares parish, 11, 208–9, 212, 229
  archdiocesan pastoral council creation, 275–76
  and Barrera, Facundo, 11
  and the BPR Mass, 337–38
  celebrations of, 207–8
  communism, condemnations of, 377
  FARO attacks on, 377
  FECCAS opposition, 318–21
  golden anniversary of priesthood, 13
  government-protester mediation attempts, 290, 382
  and Molina, 207–8, 377
  El Mundo visit, 376–77
  Orellana's death, statement on, 361–64
  El Paisnal visit, 11
  pastoral letters of, 273
  and pastoral ministry weeks, 83, 85, 269
  resignation as archbishop, 376, 378
  and Rutilio
    Aguilares pastorship, 141–42, 208–9
    correspondence between, 11–14, 64, 302
    Country Christmas 1975 explanation, 328–29
    encouragement and support, 11–13, 16, 20
    FECCAS discussions, 318, 320–21
    first Mass attendance, 25
    the funeral, 404
    impact on, 11
    the mission camps, 65
    ordination invitation, 20
    rectorship consideration, 115
    relationship between, 13–14, 208
    Romero's episcopal consecration, 119
    seminary proposal, 11
  and San Salvador seminary, 57
Christian Federation of Salvadoran Farmworkers. *See* FECCAS
Christian Legal Aid Office, 323
the church. *See also* persecution of the church
  clergy, bishops' critiques of, 88–89
  conciliar definition debate, 101–2
  crises of, 93–94, 97–98, 132
  divides in, 81
  and the dominant classes, 81, 84
  feast of the transfiguration of the Lord, 105
  and the Medellín conference, 81–82
  and national independence, 348–49
  pastoral ministry week, first, 81–85
  in popular religiosity, 273
  and Vatican II, 81–82, 84, 94
Ciudad Barrios, 64–65
Colima, 223–24, 246*tab*, 360
collaborative pastoral ministry week. *See* pastoral ministry week, first
Comasagua vicariate, 262, 267
the Conservative religious front, 296–97
Constitution, the Salvadoran
  church and state separation, 184
  clergy, political limits on, 213n42
  FECCAS's emphasis on, 291
  government disregard for, 287
  organizing, the right to, 358
  in political vaccination courses, 202
  Rutilio and
    autographed copy of, 115, 182
    familiarity with, 74, 182
    invocations of, 74, 113, 182, 213–14, 342–43, 344–46
    respect, calls for, 215
the coronavirus pandemic, 454–55, 457–60
Cortés, Cristóbal, 338
crucifixion, 453–54
Cruz, Octavio, 142, 189, 209, 217, 332, 431
Cuscatlán vicariate, 262–63, 267

Dada, Héctor, 83–84
Declercq, Pedro, 382–83
Decluve, George, 24
delegates of the Word
  and baptisms, 232
  Bible courses, 306
  and BPR, 305
  commitment, professions of, 165–66
  community involvement, 222–24
  as community-parish links, 166–67
  and community relations, 217
  and the cursillos, 197
  and FECCAS, 194, 223, 305–6
  itinerant, 305
  justice, emphasis on, 201
  and Luis Chávez, 208–9
  meetings of, zonal, 166–67, 195–96
  missionary team conflicts, 186, 306
  and ORDEN, 222, 226
  pastoral visit, Rivera's, 229–30

political vaccination course, 200–3
preparers, 193–96, 217, 222, 234
responsibilities of, 166
and Rutilio, 192, 208–9
selection of, 165
training of
for celebrations of the Word, 194–95
impact of, 195
introductory course, 166
parish courses, 193–96
political vaccination course, 200–3
for preparers, 193–96
problems with, 193
reasons for, 192
responsibility for, 216
women, 223
Delgado, Freddy, 82
Delgado, Jesús, 415–16, 418–21, 425–26
Las Delicias, 223–24
Delp, Alfred, 453–54
demonstrations. *See also* FECCAS and Aguilares parish; labor conflicts
BPR-organized, 337–39, 367
Country Christmas, 311–17, 319
electoral fraud protests, 382
eviction protests, 360
of faith, 367–69, 375–76
of November 14, 1976, 359–60
plantations, against the, 359–60
and Rutilio's pastorship, 311–17, 319, 339–40
violence, church blame for, 359–62
Denaux, Guillermo, 379
dependency theory, 84
Deplancke, Jean, 383

Elba Ramos, Celina, 451–52
Elba Ramos, Julia, 451–52
electoral fraud protests, 382
Ellacuría, Ignacio
on Aguilares parish and FECCAS, 355–57
Aguilares pastoral program support, 353–55
on Christianity-Marxism tensions, 356
the crucified people concept, 452
expulsion from El Salvador, 383
on faith-politics tensions, 355–56
martyrdom of, 447–51
and the Meditation on Two Standards, 449
and pastoral ministry week, first, 84
on Romero, 459
Spiritual Exercises reinterpretation, 448

Epicurus's dilemma, 456
ERP (Revolutionary Army of the People), 290–91, 367
Escondido, 246*tab*
Esquivel, Rogelio, 302
Estrada, Benito, 394, 400–1, 427
Estrada, Marciano, 394, 429
Estrada, Miguel Francisco, 117, 130
Estudios Centroamericanos (ECA), 336
Evangelii nuntiandi, 405–6
evangelization
to adults, 163–65
approaches to, 157, 187, 228
goals of, 274
Holy Week, 242
and labor conflicts, 179
the Medellín conference on, 158, 271
methods, missionary team, 187–88, 216
parish leadership importance, 305
and politics, 158, 181, 183, 187
and popular religiosity, 192–93, 228
sociopolitical *versus* popular religiosity, 157
Ezcurdia, José Antonio, 38

faith
experiences of, 224–25
and Marxism, 356
and politics, 158–59, 355–56
Rutilio's, 2–3, 105–6
FALANGE (Armed Forces of Anti-communist Liberation), 288, 312
Falla, Ricardo, 331
FAPU (Front for United Popular Unity), 251, 275, 280–81, 289–90
FARO (Agricultural Front of the Eastern Region)
agrarian reform opposition, 336
Chávez, attacks on, 377
the church, attacks on, 363–65
and FECCAS, 336
the Jesuits, attacks on, 366
and Orellana's death, 360–61, 363–64
popular organization suppression, 291, 336, 378
Rivera, attacks on, 376, 378
the feast of the transfiguration of the Lord, 105–6, 108. *See also* homilies, Rutilio's
FECCAS (Christian Federation of Salvadoran Farmworkers). *See also* Aguilares parish, Rutilio's pastorship

allies of, 292
bishops' conference meeting request, 319–20
the bishops' views of, 236, 319
Cerrón Grande dam protests, 360
Chávez, view of, 319
Christian identity of, 319–20
and Christian mystique, 296
the church, views of, 307
communities, dependence on, 283
the Constitution, focus on, 291
criticism, view of, 306
and demonstration of faith, Apopa, 375–76
demonstrations organized by, 339, 359
deportation protests, 365
elitism of, 324
enemies of, 292
and evangelization, 306
expansion of, 295
and FAPU, 251, 281, 289
and FARO, 336
and the Festival of Maize, 250
goals of, 280
the Gospel inspiring, 225
impact of, 222
and Jesuit scholastics, 283–84
joining as conversion process, 295–96
and labor strikes, 175, 180
leadership of, 293
and literacy courses, 197
ORDEN conflicts, 286
and Orellana's death, 360–61
organization of, 281–82
origins of, 280, 289
Pérez's work for, 350–51
plantation discrimination against, 285
and political critique, 295–96
political power pursuit, 355
and the press, 378
and Quezaltepeque vicariate, 275
and Rivera's pastoral visit, 235–36
Rivera's support for, 231, 235
San Salvador cathedral occupations, 286, 289–90
spread of, 286
strength of, 283
and student massacre commemorations, 337
success metrics, 293
villages, neglect of, 292–93
FECCAS and Aguilares parish
agreements between, 310–11

autonomy, relative, 307–9, 311, 357
bases, 282, 309–10
Christian identity concerns, 254–55
and Christian mystique, 296
community meetings, 305
community presence, 222–23, 225, 283–84, 305
connections between, strength of, 307, 311, 318
crisis caused by, 321–25, 351
and delegates of the Word, 194, 223, 305–6
demonstration, first national
 aftermath of, 317–20
 bishops' discussions of, 318–19
 government memorandum on, 317–18
 missionary team involvement, 317
 Molina's appeal to the nuncio, 319
 Rutilio and, 312–17, 319
demonstrations, 282, 339–40
emergence into, 283
government perception of, 294
Jesuit scholastics, 283–84, 294
membership in, 282–83
the missionary team
 bases survey response, 310–11
 courses, 311
 pastoral planning inclusion, 306
 support of, 310–11
 tensions between, 305–7, 310
 work of, 295
missionary team tensions, 351
organizational expansion, 295
parish leaders, 294
and pastoral labor, 295
Pérez, Marcelino, 350–52
political formation seminar, 284
political judgments, differences between, 355
roles distinctions, 307
Rutilio's interventions, 308–9, 323, 350–52
Rutilio's position, 351–52
secretary general's views of, 309–10
separation of, 308, 323, 350–52
success in, 284–85
tensions between
 and delegates of the Word, 305–6
 demonstration timing, 339–40
 Ellacuría's assessment of, 355–57
 ideological differences, 306–7
 leadership positions, 282, 305, 324
 objectives, differing, 308

origins of, 305, 355–56
pastoral ministry disruptions, 321–22, 324–25
policies, 310
Fernández, Benigno
  addition to, 142
  attacks on, 210, 318
  education of, 212
  expulsion from El Salvador, 383
  on the missionary team, 142, 189, 216–17
  mother, death of, 380
  and El Paisnal military occupation, 363
  and Rutilio, 380
Festival of Maize. *See also* homilies, Rutilio's
  overview of, 206
  1974, 206–7
  1976, 250–57
  and FECCAS, 250
  goals of, 249–50
  missionary team concerns, 251
  offertory of the Mass, 250, 257
  origins of, 249
  patronesses, 206–7, 251, 253, 257
  socio-political aspects, 250–51
  songs of, 250
FFS (Salvadoran Feminist Front), 361, 363
La Florida, 246*tab*
formation, priestly, 56–57
Francis (Pope), 5, 443, 457
Freire, Paulo, 163n23, 197
Front for United Popular Unity, 251, 275, 280–81, 289–90
FUERSA (University Front of Revolutionary Salvadoran Students), 280–81
the funeral of Rutilio Grande
  absences, 414
  attendees, 404–5
  Chávez and, 404
  internment, 409–10
  Mass, 404–9
  military presence, 409
  processions, 404, 409
  Romero's homily, 120, 405–9
  vengeance, calls for, 410
FUR-30 (Revolutionary University Front), 280–81

Garay, Bautista, 428
Garay Flores, Juan, 428
García, Jesús, 269
Garrido, Santiago, 14–16, 27–28

General Congregation 32, 131
Gerada, Emanuele, 319
God
  abandonment of, 457
  and catastrophe, 455–56
  and the cross, problem of, 457–58
  Old Testament power, 457
  in popular religiosity, 272, 456
  in Rutilio's homilies, 369
  suffering, as affected by, 458
Gonzaga, Aloysius, 459
Grande, Rutilio
  biographies of, 4–5
  and the BPR Mass, 337–38
  and the *campesinos*, 3–4, 25–26
  character of
    overview, 4, 39
    anxiety, 39
    decision-making, 41
    irritability, 40
    judgment, 42
    leadership, 43
    novelty, difficulties with, 40
    patience, 40
    perfectionism, 40, 42
    and personal crises, 39–40
    quick temper, 237
    reports on, 116–17, 128
    shyness, 9–10
    sympathy, 43
    traditionalism, 40–41
    uncertainty, 39–40
    work ethic, 43
  documentation left behind, 4
  faith of, 2–3
  Jesus Christ, surrender to, 44
  ministry of, 1–3
  minor orders, doubts about, 30–34
  miracle of, 1–2, 5
  missionary work, 124, 126–27
  the people, identification with, 25–26, 70
  preaching style, 41
  priesthood, doubts about, 34–39
  priests, view of, 97–98
  on priests *versus* soldiers, 213
  primary and fundamental option, 127–34
  reputation of, 257–58
  responsibility, positions of, 43
  Romero, similarities to, 1
  Salvadoran clergy, influence on, 2, 55

self-acceptance, 43–44
social justice, calls for, 2–3
and the Society of Jesus, 2–4
and Solórzano, Manuel, 380, 394–95
spiritual exercises 1966, 43
Grande, Rutilio, biography of
  overview, 1
  birth and baptism, 7
  childhood, 7–12
  in minor seminary, 11–15, 17
  novitiate, Loss Chorros, 14–16
  in Quito, 17, 140
  post-college assignments, 17
  in Panama, as counselor of students, 17–18, 27–28
  at San José de la Montaña Seminary, 1950s, 18
  at Colegio Máximo San Francisco Javier, Oña
    apostolic work, 18–19, 23
    Chavez, invitation to, 20
    doubts and uncertainties, 30–32
    first mass, 21
    and the Guerricagoitia family, 20–23
    health concerns, 19, 22, 29–30
    letters received, 22
    major orders, reception of, 19–20, 30–31
    and Marcelino Zalba, 19
    ordination, 19–22, 30–32
    papal benediction, 20
    philosophy studies, 18
    prayer, benefits of, 29
    and the Salvadoran consul, 21
    Spiritual Exercises, giving of, 23
    theology studies, 19, 30
    thesis, 18
    the United States, interest in, 19, 23
  at San Salvador seminary (*See* San Salvador seminary, Rutilio at)
  tertianship, Córdoba, 23, 33
  at Lumen Vitae International Institute, Brussels, 24–25, 33–39
  El Paisnal return, 25
  at Colegio Externado San José (1971), 42–43
  Central American travels, 123–24
  murder of (*See* the martyrdom of Rutilio Grande)
Grande, Rutilio, family of
  brother, Alberto, 8–9, 124
  brother, Flavio
    closeness to, 8–9
    as household head, 8, 10–11
  and Lemus Nelson, 399
  letters to, 22–23, 64
  and Rutilio's return, 25
  Rutilio's vocation, support for, 11–12
  brother, Joaquín, 9
  brother, Luis, 7
  crises, 7–8, 11
  farm, 8
  father, Salvador Grande, 7, 11–12
  godfather, Vincente Tejada, 7, 22
  grandmother, Francisca, 9
  half-sister, Cristina, 8–9
  home of, 7
  mother, Cristina García, 7–8
    in El Paisnal, 7
    and Rutilio's reputation, 141
  siblings, closeness to, 8
  sister, Matilde, 12–13
  store owned by, 7
Grande, Venancio, 391, 404
Guadalupe, 244, 246*tab*
Guazapa parish, 264, 268, 333
Guevara, Víctor, 430

health issues, Rutilio's
  overview of, 27
  anxiety, 28, 39
  and character, 40
  confidence, as diminishing, 19
  diabetes, 26–27, 190
  and diet, 28
  exercise mitigating, 29
  fevers, 22
  impact of, 3, 29–30
  isolation exacerbating, 33, 39
  as limiting, 39
  nervous crises, 18, 27
  in Oña, Spain, 19, 22, 29–30
  in Panama, 18, 27–28
  post-formation rest, 23, 32
  rest, need for, 29
  schizoid traits, 27, 39
  and state of soul, 40
Henríquez, Alberto, 329, 357
homilies, Romero's
  homily at church re-opening, 431–36
  homily on Rutilio's life and death, 437–41
  at the One Mass, 422–24
  Rutilio's funeral, 120, 405–9
  unity, emphasis on, 2

homilies, Rutilio's
　the Adorers in, 62, 168–69
　of August 6, 1970
　　overview of, 105
　　and the archbishop, 107–8
　　audience, questioning of, 107
　　the bishop's reaction to, 115
　　on Christians, true, 107–8, 111–12
　　Church-government collaboration, 112–13
　　faith-homeland connections, 105–6
　　and Fidel Sánchez, 114–15
　　inspirations for, 133
　　on Jesus Christ, 108–10, 114
　　liberation theology inspiring, 133
　　patriotic aspects, 106, 108, 113
　　on the people, 60
　　populism of, 112–13
　　and *Populorum progressio*, 111–12
　　priests, roles of, 113–14
　　revolutionary aspects, 109, 112–14
　　and Rutilio's rectorship candidacy, 115
　　salvation, 112
　　social realities, 110–11
　　transfiguration theme, 105–6, 109–10, 112–14
　on Bernal's expulsion, Apopa parish
　　Bernal, defense of, 371–72, 374
　　the Cains, 369–71, 373
　　Cains and the people, 369–71
　　Chávez, defense of, 377–78
　　Christianity, danger of, 372–73
　　the church, 369
　　the common good, 370
　　the ecclesial mission, 367–68
　　Eucharist theme, 370, 375
　　and FECCAS, 368, 376
　　God as common Father, 369
　　love, 371
　　martyrs, Latin American, 374
　　minorities, 370
　　moral violence, 371
　　Paul IV, defense of, 377–78
　　the people, 369–71
　　purpose of the demonstration, 368–69
　on Chávez, 208
　on conservative Catholics, 297–99
　Country Christmas (1975), 313–17
　on countryside visits, 60
　cousin's mayoral inauguration, 184
　on the delegates, 208–9

　on the election, 184
　on family, 22
　feast of Pentecost (1973), 191
　Festival of Maize (1976)
　　the Adorers, 62, 168–69
　　bible study, 255–56
　　Christian identity, 254–55
　　communities, praise of, 250–51, 255
　　delegates, 256
　　dialogue, importance of, 256
　　the Eucharist, 256–57
　　Magnificats, 252–53
　　Mary, 252–53
　　parish evaluation announcement, 330–31
　　the patronesses, 251–53
　　political contexts of, 251, 254
　on independence, national, 341–43, 348–49
　Jesus and the people, 347
　the last, 299
　on liberation, 343–44, 349–50
　on the Lord of Mercies, 239–40
　in the market, 248–49
　mayor, denunciation of, 181–83
　on the military, 344–47
　Mother's Day, 253
　ORDEN commander, denunciation of, 211
　on partisan politics, 202–3
　on the people, serving, 347–48
　on priests, 346–50
　print copies of, 302
　publication requests, 414
　Sacred Heart of Jesus celebrations, 248–49
　on Salvadoran identity and peoples, 340–43
　at Santelices, 22
　structure of, 41
　on teachers, 343–44, 347
　writing-out of, 183, 211
Honduras, 127, 297, 346
Las Huertas, 223, 246*tab*, 283
Huitiupa, 223–24

identity, Rutilio's
　Latin American, 128
　Salvadoran, 25–26, 55, 70, 135, 340
Ignatian values, 449
Ignatius of Loyola, Saint, 449–50
Ilopango vicariate, 262–63, 267
individualism, 133–34
Iriarte, Isidro, 28

Jerez, César
  Aguilares visit, 331, 333–34
  condolence letters to, 411
  missionary team removal, 380
  and Rutilio, 329, 333–34
  on Rutilio, 43
  and Rutilio's biographies, 4
  and Rutilio's murder, 402–4, 409, 412, 428
Jesuit scholastics
  Alberto Henríquez, 357
  Cardenal, Antonio, 357
  community involvement, 283–84
  courses given by, 216
  and the cursillos, 197
  departures from the Society, 357
  deportations of, 365–66
  and FECCAS, 283–84, 294, 357
  Fernando Ascoli, 357, 365
  Holy Week activities, 242
  and Jesús Bengoechea, 141
  and missionary team tensions, 188
  and parish crises, 325–28
  and Rutilio, 188, 209, 328–30, 357
Jesus Christ
  Aguilares pastoral program and, 158, 203–6
  appeal to the people, 203–6, 272
  and martyrs, 453
  the passion of, 457
  as revolutionary, 106–7
  in Rutilio's homilies, 108–10, 114, 435
  Rutilio's surrender to, 44
El Jicarón, 227, 246*tab*, 283, 286

Kolvenbach, Peter-Hans, 450

labor conflicts, harvest
  denunciations, 172–74*tab*
  and evangelization, 179
  and the Gospel, 177–78
  labor code violations, 172, 178
  and the ministry of labor, 176
  and the missionary team, 176–77
  national guard presence, 176–80
  origins of, 279
  parish support for laborers, 172
  plantation anti-activism, 179–80
  protests, 179
  public letters to Molina, workers', 279–80
  Rutilio and, 177–78, 180

  sources of, 174–75, 177–78
  strike at La Cabaña, 174–77
  strike at Hacienda El Matasano, 178–79
  village patrols, 180–81
  workers, abuses of, 279
Landaverde, Gregorio, 332
Landaverde, Santana, 161
Larraín, Manuel, 125
Latin American Pastoral Institute (IPLA), 125–26
Latin American Pastoral Institute (IPLA),
  Rutilio at, 123, 125–27, 130–31
El Líbano, 222, 225, 245*tab*, 283
liberation
  missionary team disagreements over, 328
  and pastoral ministry week, first, 81, 84, 86–87
  and pastoral ministry week, second, 270
  of the poor, 131–32
  priests' role in, 348–50
  Romero on, 406
  Rutilio on
    homilies, 343–44, 349–50
    pastoral ministry week, first, 93, 95–97, 102–3
  the Society of Jesus and, 132
liberation theology, 132–33, 353, 365
La Libertad, 262
López, Amando, 117–18, 190
La Luz vicariate, 263

Magnificats, 252–53
Mansilla, Demetrio, 20
Manzanares, Rosendo, 84
the martyrdom of Rutilio Grande. *See also* the funeral of Rutilio Grande
  aftermath of
    academic suspension, 414–16
    the clergy assembly, 413–14
    confessions and information, 427–29
    government response, 425–27
    investigations, local, 427–28
    memorial proposals, 414
    nuncio, criticism of, 414
    One Mass, 414–24
    Rivera and, 420–21
  aftermath of, Romero and
    academic suspension proposal, 414–15
    in Aguilares, 431–36
    ANEP meetings, 419–20

clergy meetings, 411–12, 416–18
the funeral, 120, 405–9
information given to, 428–29
investigation demands, 412–13
and Molina, 412–13, 425–26
the nuncio, meetings with, 418–20
the nuncio's secretary, meeting with, 420–21
and the One Mass, 416–22
press statement, 415–16
recommendations made to, 413–14
Carranza and, 401–2, 410
condolence letters, 411
danger, Rutilio's awareness of, 392–93
death threats against Rutilio, 391–92
events preceding, 391–94, 397
the funeral, 120, 404–10, 414
historical contexts, 335
Jaime Vera-Fajardo on, 392
Jerez and, 402–4, 409, 412, 428
last words, Rutilio's, 3
Molina's views on, 412–13
the murder
 Benito Estrada and, 394, 400–1, 427
 bodies, display of, 402–3
 forensic examination, 403
 Julio Sánchez's confession, 429
 Marciano Estrada and, 394
 Mass following, 402–3
 Molina's call to Romero, 403, 427–28
 Molina's investigation promise, 403, 412
 news of, 401–2
 ordering of, government, 428
 passengers in the car, 394, 400
 peoples' rage over, 402
 responsibility for, 428–29
 scene of, 401–2
 sequence of events, 400–4
 testimonies, 394, 400–1
musical tributes, 410
National Guard report, 427
newspaper distortions, 427–28
novena following, 410
Pérez and, 402, 410
pilgrimages to the murder site, 410
reasons for, 3
Rivera and, 402–3, 405
Romero and
 conversion, 1
 the funeral, 404–9

the murder, 402–4
the sign of martyrdom, 437–41
martyrs
 Bonhoeffer, Dietrich, 458
 common elements, 453–54
 the coronavirus pandemic, 454–55, 458–60
 crucified people, 452–53, 459
 Delp, Alfred, 453–54
 diverse types of, 453–54
 Jesuan, 447–48, 452–53, 459
 Jesuits of UCA, 447–52
 and Jesus Christ, 453
 and love, 459
 Paul, 454
 Peter, 453
 power of, 443
 Romero as, 453
Marxism
 accusations of, 137, 364
 Boulang's group and, 189
 Chávez and, 376
 and faith, 356
 FECCAS and, 319, 351
 and liberation theology, 365
 Rivera on, 235–36
 Romero on, 423
 and the rural poor, 205
 Vatican II, confusion with, 426
Mary, Rutilio's homily on, 252–53
El Matasano, 223
Mayorga, Román, 269, 290
McCulloch, Lorenzo, 383
the Medellín conference
 the church and, 81–82
 on evangelization, 158, 271
 identity crisis arising from, 159
 and the IPLA, 125
 Marxism, confusion with, 426
 parishes as ecclesial platforms, 353
 Rutilio and, 1, 3, 81, 97
 and seminary training, 97–98
 traditionalist rejections of, 101
Mejicanos vicariate, 262
La Merced vicariate, 267
MERS (Movement of Revolutionary Secondary
 School Students), 289, 307, 339
Metz, Johann Baptist, 454
the military regime. *See also* Molina, Arturo A.;
 ORDEN; persecution of the church

Aguilares, occupations of, 430–31
and Aguilares parish, 210–16, 226, 276
and the cathedral occupation, 289–90
church, repression of, 335
electoral fraud, 185, 187, 286
oligarchy support, 151, 286
opposition blocs, 289–91
oppressive tactics of, 286–89, 427
El Paisnal occupation, 363
and pastoral ministry week, second, 260–61
political police, 429
power, assumption of, 286
revolutionary group suppression, 291
rural movements, repression of, 335
Rutilio's death, role in, 428–29
University of El Salvador invasion, 287
millenarianism, 186, 205–6
Molina, Arturo A.
  Aguilares town meeting, 183
  Aguilares visit, 183–85
  and the bishops, 382
  cathedral occupation negotiations, 290
  and Chávez, 207–8, 377
  clergy, attacks on, 311–12
  and Delgado, Jesús, 425–26
  and Garay Flores, Juan, 428–29
  and Gerada, Emanuele, 319
  letters to
    public, 279–80
    Rutilio's, 185–86, 214–15
  and National Institute of Aguilares, 302
  and the nuncio, 319
  Orellana's death, views on, 425
  and Rutilio, 183–86, 214–15
  and Rutilio's martyrdom
    call to Romero, 403, 427–28
    investigation promise, 403, 412
    Romero, exchanges with, 412–13, 425–26
    views on, 412–13
  and Urioste, Ricardo, 425–26
Moltmann, Jürgen, 457–58
Montserrat vicariate, 267
Moreno, Juan Ramón, 448, 457–58
Moreno, Rafael, 327
Moses, appeal to the people, 203–6
El Mundo, 376–77
Murillo, Venancio, 391
Murphy, John, 382

National Association of Private Enterprise. *See* ANEP
National Institute of Aguilares, 300, 302
Nationalist Democratic Organization. *See* ORDEN
Natividad, 223, 283
Navarro, Alfonso, 345
Nelson, Lemus Rutilio
  character of, 397–99
  church involvement, 399
  epilepsy, 398
  faith of, 399
  family life, 397–98
  internment, 409–10
  murder of, 400–4
  Rutilio, relation to, 399
  school life, 398–99
Nicaragua, Rutilio's experiences in, 123–24
the Nottebohm family, 302–4

the oligarchy, Salvadoran. *See also* ANEP; FARO
  and agrarian reform, 335–36
  agrarian reform resistance, 151
  the church, pronouncements against, 359
  and Eduardo Orellana's death, 360–61
  as FECCAS's enemy, 292
  the Gospel, manipulation of, 300
  military regime backing, 151, 286
  and the missionary team, 300
  peasant organizations, views of, 358
  revolutionary group suppression, 291
  Rutilio on, 99, 299
  and the traditionalist church, 81
  the One Mass, after Rutilio's death
    clergy approval of, 417–18
    clergy meetings on, 416–18
    conversions at, 422
    crowds attending, 421–22
    decision to hold, 415–16
    the Eucharist, 422
    the nuncio, debates with, 418–20
    the nuncio's secretary, debates with, 420–21
    proposal for, 414–15
    review and approval of, 421
    Rivera and, 420–21
    Romero and the planning of, 416–21
    Romero's homily, 422–24
    theological debates, 417
    theological significance, 418

option for the poor
  the bishops' conference, 446
  the church's, 82, 134, 413, 446
  as Ignatian value, 449
  Romero's, 446
  Rutilio and, 127, 138–39
ORDEN
  overview of, 210
  and Aguileras communities, 222, 225–26
  Aguileras mission, conflicts with, 210–16
  and celebrations of the Word, 285–86
  Chalatenango, abuses in, 289
  Chalatenango oppression, 289
  and delegates of the Word, 222, 226
  FECCAS conflicts, 286
  and plantations, 285
  and the rural population, 210
  and Rutilio, 210–15
Orellana, Eduardo, death of, 360–63, 425
Orellana, Francisco, 360
organizations, peasant. *See also individual organizations*
  Christian social perspectives on, 354
  Jesuit support for, 357–58
  need for, 354
  press tactics, 367
  rapidity of action, 338
  the right to, 358
  Rutilio's support for, 308–9, 324, 338–39
  the Society's defense of, 357–58
Ortega, José Luis, 333, 430

El Paisnal
  the Adorers, 60–62, 153
  Corpus Christi feast, 245–46*tab*, 247
  feasts of Saint Joseph, 241, 410
  mayor, Vincente Tejada, 7
  mayoralty, control of, 391
  military occupation, 363
  resident views of Rutilio, 25
  rumors of threats against Rutilio, 391
  Rutilio and, 9, 25–26, 64, 184
  Rutilio's family in, 7
  Rutilio's ministry in
    biblical reading promotion, 61
    community organizing, 62–64
    cooperative, plans for, 61–62
    effects of, 129, 153
    importance of, 60, 64

  last Mass in, 393–94
  ministries performed, 60–61
  neighborhood association, 63–64
  resident recollections of, 10
  seminarians accompanying, 60
  schools, 143
Palacios, Rafael, 444
Las Pampas, 246*tab*
Panama, Rutilio's travels in, 124, 127
parishes as ecclesial platforms, 353
partisan politics, 202–3, 355
pastoral agents, 260, 263–66, 269–70
pastoral councils, 259n110, 260
pastoral ministry. *See also* Aguilares parish, pastoral program; Aguilares parish, Rutilio's pastorship; Latin American Pastoral Institute
  Bernardo Boulang's, 140
  requirements for, 130
  Rutilio's generally, 64–67, 131–32, 321
pastoral ministry week, first bishops' conference on
  document produced, 85–89, 92–95
  and Medellín, 94–95
  Rutilio's response, 92–99
  and Vatican II, 94
Chávez and, 83, 85
conclusions of, 84–88
diocese participation, 82
internal conflicts, 82–83
Jesuit attendance, 82
and liberation, 81, 84, 86–87
national situation presentations, 83–84
origins of, 81
Rivera and, 82–83, 85
Romero and, 83, 85
Rutilio and
  attendance at, 82–83, 85
  bishops, letter to, 90–92
  bishops' conference, response to, 92–99
  conflict, desire to avoid, 99
  criticisms of, 92
  on liberation, 93, 95–97, 102–3
  priests, view of, 97–98
  proposals made, 94, 99
  social problems, emphasis on, 96–97
  support for, 99, 101–5
  and The Sacred Congregation for the Clergy, 89–90

Index 477

traditionalist responses to, 100–2
pastoral ministry week, second
  Aguilares parish attendees, 269
  archdiocese divisions identified, 273
  Arturo Rivera and, 271
  commission of synthesis, 269
  conclusions drawn, 270–75
  evangelization discussions, 270, 274
  liberation signs identified, 270
  Luis Chávez and, 269
  national reality study, 269
  organizing commission, 269
  participation in, 269
  pastoral council recommendations, 271
  planning of
    Beltrán, 260
    goals of, 260
    information gathering, 260, 263–66
    and pastoral practices, existing, 263
    proposal for, 259
    Rutilio and, 260–61, 263
    themes identified, 266–67
    Urioste and, 260n111, 261, 267
    vicariate involvement, 260–63, 267
  popular religiosity study, 269, 272–73
  Quezaltepeque vicariate attendees, 269
  recommendations arising from, 271–75
  "Reflections of the Archdiocesan Pastoral Ministry Week," 271–74
  results of, 271
  Rutilio's participation in, 269, 271
  social conflict, 274
  temptations identified, 270
  theological reflection, 269–70
  violence, types identified, 273–74
pastoral project, Rutilio and Bengoechea's proposal, 127–30, 140
the path of poverty *versus* of riches, 449
Paul VI, 259n110, 405–6
peasant organizations. *See* organizations, peasant
Pellecer, Luis E., 197, 199, 318, 357
Pérez, Marcelino
  Aguilares, departure from, 380
  capture and deportation, 430
  demeanor of, 352
  and FECCAS, 275, 350–52
  and missionary team crisis, 351–52
  organizing activities, 350–51

  and pastoral program crises, 326–27
  and Rutilio's martyrdom, 394, 402
  and UTC, 351
persecution of the church
  beginning of, 358
  and bishop-president meetings, 381–82
  bishops' conference responses, 385–89
  blame for demonstration violence, 359–62
  capture and torture of priests, 367, 379–80, 382
  death threats, 384
  defamation campaigns, 379
  deportations, 365–67, 430
  expulsion of priests, 382–83
  foreigners, emphasis on, 379
  internal discussions of, 384
  oligarchs' role in, 379
  and Orellana's death, 361–64
  pronouncements, 358–59, 361–66, 377
  reasons for, 413
  Romero's meeting on, 384–85
  San Martín attack, 384
  subversive priest lists, 382
  systematic persecution, 365
  terror attacks, 365
  as tests, 379
Pius XII, 105
plantations
  anti-labor activism, 179–80
  La Cabaña, 174–77, 231, 285
  and celebrations of the Word, 285
  demonstrations against, 359–60
  and FECCAS, 285, 359
  and ORDEN, 285
  rural poor, oppression of, 147–50, 156, 185, 285
  strikes, 174–77
  wage increase requests to, 359
  worker blacklists, 285
Polín, 283
Pólit, Aurelio Espinosa, 17
political conversion, 295–96
political neutrality, 181–86
political vaccination courses, 200–3
politics *versus* faith, 158, 355–56
Poma, Roberto, 366–67, 426
Popol Vuh, 257
popular religiosity
  in Aguileras, 153–54, 221–22
  the church in, 273

and evangelization, 157, 192–93, 228
God in, 272, 456
Jesus Christ in, 272
in Quezaltepeque vicariate, 264–65
"Reflections of the Archdiocesan Pastoral Ministry Week" on, 271–73
Rutilio and, 153–54
study of, 269, 272–73
Popular Revolutionary Bloc. *See* BPR
populism, Rutilio's
in addresses, 134–36
and Aguilares parish, 144–46
in homily of August 6, 112–13
organizations, support for, 308–9, 324, 338–39
Portero Grande, 223, 234, 246*tab*
poverty
missionary experiences of, 219
option for the poor, Rutilio on, 138–39
the people's acceptance of, 104
Rutilio's emphasis on, 113, 129–30, 185
Salvadoran, 151
the press, Rutilio's articles in, 102–4
priests
expectations of, 354
identity crises, 98
Rutilio on, 346–47
and Salvadoran church crisis, 97–98
the priests' senate. *See also* pastoral ministry week, second
and archdiocesan pastoral council, 275–76
and the bishops, 258, 268
and clergy welfare, 267
closing of, 268
evangelization study commission, 276
functions of, 258
meetings of, 259
and national problems, 268
objectives of, 259
officer elections, 258
and pastors, naming of, 267–68
priesthood and politics debates, 276–77
problems with, 261–62
procedural improvements, 262
responsibilities of, 267
and Rivera, 258–59
vicariate involvement, 260–63, 276–77
the priests' senate, Rutilio and
clergy retreats, 258
countryside conflict warnings, 268

election to, 257–58
evaluation of, 262
evangelization study commission, 276
meeting attendance, 258
pastor naming recommendations, 267–68
priesthood and politics debates, 276–77
as secretary, 258–59, 268–69
Prigione, Girolamo, 85
primary and fundamental option, Rutilio's, 127–34
Proaño, Leónidas, 125–26, 216
Project of Agrarian Transformation, 335–37, 339, 343
Protestantism conference, 383–84

Quezaltepeque vicariate
and Aguileras parish, 144, 221
and Boulang's group, 140
demonstrations in, 359–60
evangelization approach, 265
and FAPU, 275
and FECCAS, 275
lay activity, 262
mission camps, 64–66
pastoral agents in, 263–66
pastoral ministry plan, 263–66
pastoral ministry week, second, 262, 267, 269
political consciousness in, 265
popular organization discussions, 275
and popular religiosity, 264–65
Rutilio and, 60, 119, 267–68
women in, 266
Quito, Rutilio's visits to, 124

Rahner, Karl, 453
Ramírez, Castro, 83
Ramírez, Juan José, 367
regency, Rutilio's, 20, 28, 33, 47–48, 128
renewal projects, 130–31, 139
Revelo, Marco R., 125, 376
revolutionary consciousness, Rutilio's
and benediction, 103
and the homily of August 6, 1970, 109, 112–14
and Jesus Christ, 106–7
and religion, 104–5
theological basis, 102–5
and unjust social structures, 103–4
vice-provincial congregation address, 134–35, 137, 139

the revolutionary left, 251, 289, 291–93. *See also* organizations, peasant
Rivera Damas, Arturo
  Aguileras pastoral visit, 228–36
  and bishops' statement on persecution, 388–89
  clergy's views of, 376
  FARO attacks on, 376, 378
  and FECCAS, 231, 235–36
  government-protester mediation attempts, 382
  and the One Mass, 420–21
  and pastoral ministry week, first, 82–83, 85
  and pastoral ministry week, second, 271
  and the priests' senate, 258–59
  Protestantism conference, 383
  and Rutilio
    correspondence, 122
    IPLA program, 127
    the murder of, 402–3
    rectorship candidacy, 122
    Romero's episcopal consecration, 119
Rodríguez, David, 361, 365, 384
Romero, Óscar Arnulfo. *See also* homilies, Romero's; the martyrdom of Rutilio Grande
  at Aguilares parish, 430–41
  archbishop appointment
    assumption of, 380–81
    date of, accelerated, 376–38
    public installation, 381
    reactions to, 376, 381
    Revelo as auxiliary, 376
  biographical overview, 1
  as bishop conference secretary, 120
  and bishops' statement on persecution, 388–89
  clergy meetings, 411
  and Emilio Simán, 100–1
  feast of Saint Joseph, El Paisnal, 410
  on liberation, 406
  on martyrs, 444
  and Molina
    correspondence, 412
    deportation meetings, 430
    phone call from, 403, 427–28
    Rutilio's martyrdom, 412–13, 425–26
  murder of, 444–45, 447
  the nuncio, meetings with, 418–20
  pastoral letters, 324
  and pastoral ministry week, first, 83, 85
  and the people, 445–46
  persecution, meeting on, 384–85
  and Polín, 283
  and the poor, 446–47
  as prophet, 447
  on Rafael Palacios's murder, 444
  rhetorical abilities of, 444–45
  and Rutilio
    correspondence, 381
    death and conversion experience, 1
    episcopal consecration, 119–21
    friendship between, 90, 119–20, 381
    the murder of, 402–3
    persecution, meeting, 385
    similarities to, 1
    support from, 381
  in San Miguel, 119
  in San Salvador, 119
  truth, dedication to, 445–46
  unity, emphasis on, 2
Rosa, Gregorio, 385
Rosales, Salvador, 428–29
Rosero, Sofía, 126
the rural poor. *See also* organizations, peasant
  liberation of, 131–32
  missionary team support for, 322
  national politics involvement, 292
  political conversion of, 295–96
  and revolutionary concepts, 292–93
  rights, awareness of, 279
  as Rutilio's people, 320–21
  socio-economic conditions of
    acceptance of, 154–55
    family groups, 149–50
    illnesses, 145
    labor conditions, 148–50, 185
    land scarcity, 144–45, 148–51
    plantations, 147–50, 156, 185
    Protestant evangelicals, 147
    and rebellion, 151–52
    security forces, 146
    services, lack of, 145
    small farmers, 148–51
    sugarcane production, 147, 150

Salinas, 243, 300–2
Salinas de Avilés, Margot, 300–2

El Salvador
  agrarian crisis, 148, 151
  economic crisis of 1929, 3
  God, calls on, 456
  national symbols, reverence for, 106
  rebellion, origins of, 151–52
  repression of the church, 4
  structural crises of, 3
  sugarcane production, 147–48
San Antonio El Grande, 246*tab*
Sánchez, Feliciano, 288
Sánchez, Fidel, 114–15
Sánchez, Julio, 429
Sánchez, Rutilio, 384
San Francisco Hacienda, 302–4
San Francisco vicariate, 267
San José de la Montaña vicariate, 267
San Martín, attack on, 384
San Rafael plantation, 285
San Salvador
  cathedral occupation, 286, 289–90
  pastoral approach, 2, 263–64
  pastoral ministry week promotion, 262
San Salvador seminary. *See also* Azcue, Segundo
  apostolic visitation and report, 53–54, 57
  baccalaureate program establishment, 49–51
  Barrera's concerns about, 121–22
  bishop dissatisfaction with, 73
  and the bishops
    apostolic visitation, 53–54
    baccalaureate program, 49, 51
    dissatisfaction with, 73
    formation practices, 56–57
    mission camps, Rutilio's, 64, 67
    reform proposal indifference, 81
    regulation approval, 73
    Rutilio's rectorship candidacy, 115, 118–19, 122
    staff discussions, 76–78
    UCA collaboration, 53
  capacity problems, 52
  and educational institutions, local, 68–69
  impressions of, public, 72–73
  major-minor seminary separation, 52
  minor seminary difficulties, 51–52
  pastoral ministry, 56–57
  personnel problems, 54, 68
  philosophy students at UCA, 53
  prefects, challenges facing, 42

  rector Scheifler, 78–79, 115, 117
  rectorship change, 115, 117–19, 122
  seminarians, neglect of, 75
  Spanish mentality of, 69–70
  students, isolation of, 56
San Salvador seminary, Rutilio at
  as community consultor, 43
  departure from, 118, 121, 123
  failure, sense of, 75–78
  health concerns, 32–33, 78
  pastoral formation provided by
    Jesuit involvement, 59
    mission camps, 64–67
    El Paisnal visits, 60–64
    reasons for, 55–58
    risks of, 58
    role of, 57–58
  as prefect
    administrative council, 59
    and the baccalaureate program, 50
    changes made, 58
    delegation, 47–48
    difficulty of the position, 42
    disciplinary approaches, 42, 45–47, 51, 76
    evaluations of, 42, 49, 78
    formation approach, 57
    formation team, 58–59, 75–76
    habit-wearing, 46
    on Jesuit overwork, 54
    and Jesuit-seminarian relations, 69–70
    liturgical and choral training, 47
    master of ceremonies, 46
    moderation, 46
    pastoral ministry, 59–64
    period of, 45
    reassignment requests, 68, 78–79, 118
    review of life groups, 59, 75
    Salvadorian realities, emphasis on, 69–71
    seminarians, relationship with, 55, 70, 118
    spirituality, 48, 57, 70–71
    successes, 42, 48–49
    of theology, 45
    theology proposals, 70
  problems identified by
    and administrative work, 77
    admissions, 72–73
    bishops, non-communication with, 73
    community coherence, 76–77
    community meetings, lack of, 77

disconnect from local contexts, 69–70
living conditions, 76
major seminarians, 71–72
minor seminarians, 72–73
neglect of seminarians, 75
personnel shortages, 68
rector, conflicts with, 68, 72, 76–77
spirituality taught, 70–72
support, lack of, 68–69
reasons for going to, 23, 32–33
rector Segura, conflicts with, 50–51, 68, 72
rectorship candidacy, 79, 81, 115–18, 122
reform proposals, 81
return to (1965), 77
teaching at, 45, 49, 74
Santa Cruz vicariate, 267
Santibáñez, Roberto E., 379–80, 428, 430
Sarsanedas, Jorge, 357
Scheifler, José Ignacio, 78–79, 102n58, 115, 117
scholastics, Jesuit. *See* Jesuit scholastics
Sebastián, Luis de, 383
Second Episcopal Conference of Latin America. *See* the Medellín conference
Segura, Ladislao
  and the BPR Mass, 338
  One Mass review, 421
  on Rutilio as seminary prefect, 42, 45, 48
  on Rutilio at vice-provincial congregation, 134
  Rutilio's rectorship, support for, 117
  as San Salvador rector
    and the apostolic visit, 53–54
    baccalaureate program establishment, 49–51
  on minor seminary recruiting, 52
  removal, 118
  Rutilio, support for, 32–33
  and Rutilio's health, 32
  Rutilio's views of, 50–51, 68
  and seminary course accreditation, 52
  and UCA, 53
Serrano, Apolinario (Polín), 283
Sesma, Ramón, 28
Simán, Emilio, 100–1
Sobrino, Jon, 383
social ethics, 355
socialism, 188, 292–93, 296, 321, 377
social sciences, Rutilio's interest in, 45
the Society of Jesus
  and Aguilares parish, 332–33

attacks on, 366
and deportations, 366
FECCAS collaboration, 366
financial support for Aguilares mission, 219
"Ignatian" adjective use, 448
Ignatian values, 449
incarnation requirement, 69
and liberation, 132
martyrs, 447–53
organizations, defense of, 357–58
and pastoral ministry weeks, 82
Solórzano, Manuel
  character of, 395–96
  faith of, 395–97
  family life, 396
  friends, arrests of, 392
  internment, 409–10
  murder of, 400–4
  poverty of, 395
  rectory, permission to stay in, 380
  and Rutilio, 394–96
Soriano, Juan Ramón, 161
student massacre commemorations, 337–38
Suchitoto parish, 140, 282
Survil, Bernardo, 379

El Tablón, 223–24, 246*tab*
teachers, kidnapping of, 391–92
Tecoluca, 380
Te Deum, Rutilio's writings for, 349–50
the crucified people, 451–52
the Lisbon earthquake (1755), 455–56
theodicy, 456
theology, Latin American, 125
La Toma Hacienda, 300
Torres, Rosendo, 15
Torruella, Amílcar, 338
El Trapiche, 222, 224
Trejos, Juan Roberto, 361
Tres Calles massacre, 288
Tres Ceibas, 222, 227, 247*tab*
El Tule, 223–24, 246*tab*, 283, 360
Las Tunas, 246*tab*

UGB (White Warriors' Union), 365
Universidad Centroamericana José Simeón Cañas (UCA)
  and agrarian reform, 336–37
  the bishops and, 53

founding of, 53
Jesuit martyrs of, 447–52
pastoral program proposal, 130
Rutilio's visits to, 353
seminary students at, 53
University of El Salvador, military invasion of, 287
Urioste, Ricardo
  ANEP, meetings with, 419–20
  evangelization and politics commission, 276
  at Molina meetings, 425–26
  and the One Mass, 418
  and pastoral ministry week, first, 82
  and pastoral ministry week, second, 260n111, 261, 267
  on the priests' senate, 257n102
UTC (Union of Rural Workers)
  overview of, 281
  and agrarian reform, 339
  attacks on, 365
  Cerrón Grande dam protests, 360
  condemnations of, 365
  deportation protests, 365
  and FARO, 336
  Marcelino Pérez's work for, 351
  and Orellana's death, 360–61
  partner organizations, 281, 289
  plantation wage increase demands, 359
  and the press, 378
  and student massacre commemorations, 337

Vatican II
  aggiornamento, 270n135
  on evangelization, 158
  Marxism, confusion with, 426
  parishes as ecclesial platforms, 353
  pastoral councils recommendation, 259n110
  Rutilio, influence on, 1, 3, 45, 81, 97
  Salvadoran church, 81–82, 84, 94
  seminary training, 97–98
  specialist rejections of, 101

Vega, Juan R., 82, 270, 383
Vera, Carlos, 126
Vera-Fajardo, Jaime, 392
the vicariates
  joint meetings of, 262
  and pastoral ministry week, second, 260–63, 267, 275
  pastoral practices survey, 263–64
  violence as historical necessity, 204

White Warriors' Union. *See* UGB
women
  in the Adorers, 60, 168
  in Aguilares, 143–44
  delegates of the Word, 223
  patronesses, Festival of Maize, 206–7, 251, 253, 257
  in Quezaltepeque vicariate, 266
  rezadoras, 153–54
  Rutilio's exaltations of, 252–54

YSAX radio station
  ANEP attacks on, 419–20
  and the church, defense of, 384
  as commercial station, 231n28
  morning prayers, 270
  Romero's broadcasts on, 445
  Rutilio's funeral broadcast, 405
  Rutilio's homilies, 107
  Rutilio's murder, broadcasts on, 402, 404
  Rutilio's views on, 145–46

Zacamil vicariate, 263, 267
Zalba, Marcelino, 19, 30–32, 34–39